NEW MERMAIDS

General editors:
William C. Carroll, Boston University
Brian Gibbons, University of Münster
Tiffany Stern, University of Oxford

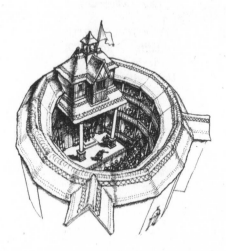

Reconstruction of an Elizabethan theatre
by C. Walter Hodges

NEW MERMAIDS

CHRISTOPHER MARLOWE
FOUR PLAYS

TAMBURLAINE PARTS I & II
Edited by Anthony B. Dawson
University of British Columbia

THE JEW OF MALTA
Edited by James R. Siemon
Boston University

EDWARD II
Edited by Martin Wiggins
The Shakespeare Institute, University of Birmingham
and Robert Lindsey
Oriel College Oxford

DOCTOR FAUSTUS
Edited by Roma Gill
Revised by Ros King
University of Southampton

NEW MERMAIDS

CHRISTOPHER MARLOWE

FOUR PLAYS

TAMBURLAINE PARTS I & II
THE JEW OF MALTA
EDWARD II
DOCTOR FAUSTUS

Introduction by Brian Gibbons

methuen | drama

LONDON • NEW YORK • OXFORD • NEW DELHI • SYDNEY

METHUEN DRAMA
Bloomsbury Publishing Plc
50 Bedford Square, London, WC1B 3DP, UK
1385 Broadway, New York, NY 10018, USA
29 Earlsfort Terrace, Dublin 2, Ireland

BLOOMSBURY, METHUEN DRAMA and the Methuen Drama logo are
trademarks of Bloomsbury Publishing Plc

This New Mermaid edition first published in Great Britain 2011
Reprinted by Bloomsbury Methuen Drama 2018 (twice), 2019, 2020, 2021, 2022

Doctor Faustus
First New Mermaid edition 1968 © 1968 Ernest Benn Ltd
Second edition 1989 © 1989 A & C Black Publishers Ltd
Thir d edition with new introduction published 2008 © A & C Black Publishers Ltd

Edward II
First New Mermaid edition 1967 © 1967 Ernest Benn Ltd
Second edition 1997 © 1997 A & C Black Publishers Ltd

The Jew of Malta
First New Mermaid edition 1996 © 1996 Ernest Benn Ltd
Second Edition 1994 © 1994 A & C Black Publishers Ltd
Thir d edition with new introduction published 2009 © 2009 A & C Black Publishers Ltd

Tamburlaine, Parts One and Two
First New Mermaid edition 1971 © 1971 Ernest Benn Ltd
Second Edition 1997 © 1997 A & C Black Publishers Ltd

Bloomsbury Publishing Plc does not have any control over, or responsibility for, any third-party websites
referred to or in this book. All internet addresses given in this book were correct at the time of going to press.
Th e author and publisher regret any inconvenience caused if addresses have changed or sites have ceased
to exist, but can accept no responsibility for any such changes.

All rights whatsoever in this play are strictly reserved and application for performance etc. should be
made before rehearsals by professionals and by amateurs to the publisher. Mail to:
Performance.permissions@bloomsbury.com. No performance may be given unless a licence has been obtained.

No rights in incidental music or songs contained in the work are hereby granted and performance rights for any
performance/presentation whatsoever must be obtained from the respective copyright owners.

No responsibility for loss caused to any individual or organization acting on or refraining from action as a
result of the material in this publication can be accepted by Bloomsbury or the author.

A catalogue record for this book is available from the British Library.

A catalog record for this book is available from the Library of Congress.

ISBN: PB: 978-1-4081-4949-2
ePDF: 978-1-4725-7386-5
ePub: 978-1-4725-7387-2

Series: New Mermaids

Printed and bound in Great Britain

To find out more about our authors and books visit www.bloomsbury.com and sign up for our newsletters.

CONTENTS

ACKNOWLEDGEMENTS

This new anthology, *Christopher Marlowe, Four Plays*, brings together the texts and commentaries from the individual Marlowe plays in the current New Mermaid series and edited by Anthony B. Dawson, James L. Siemon, Martin Wiggins and Robert Lindsey, Roma Gill and Ros King. A full critical and scholarly Introduction is a valuable feature of each New Mermaid; the present Anthology's Introduction, in more concentrated form, discusses the astonishing variety of the four plays but also their essential Marlovian character.

In the original Mermaid Series the very first volume to be published, in 1887, was devoted to Christopher Marlowe, and contained these four plays. Its editor was Havelock Ellis, with a general introduction by J.A. Symonds; both were strong-minded Victorian Men of Letters. The original publisher of Mermaids was Henry Vizetelly, who had previously published French and Russian novels, many, such as Zola's *Nana*, advertised as 'realistic' – that is, sexually outspoken. For Vizetelly the Mermaid Series was a new venture aimed at the educated gentleman reader: and so, facing the title-page, provided a full-page etching, protected by fine tissue-paper, of the portrait of the great actor Edward Alleyn in Dulwich College. Opposite this a sub-title declared THE BEST PLAYS OF THE OLD DRAMATISTS; but old habits die hard, and Vizetelly added an ornament depicting a naked mermaid brushing her hair, with a caption from Beaumont: 'I lie and dream of your full Mermaid wine'. Finally, below, in bold type, stood the sensational proclamation UNEXPURGATED EDITION.

In his Introduction Havelock Ellis praised Marlowe especially as poet, and the 'vivid and passionate blood' with which he clothed the 'dry bones of his story'. Marlowe's 'licentiousness' was touched on, but lightly. Only at the very end, and quoted for its very lack of 'moral edification', is the spurious claim that Marlowe was 'killed by a serving-man, a rival in a quarrel over bought kisses'.

As the first half of the twentieth century unfolded, cultural change, advances in textual scholarship, in theatre history and archaeology, in literary criticism, as well as unexpurgated, intelligent, professional stage interpretation, brought new serious attention to Elizabethan drama. By the late 1950's Marlowe the playwright was once more coming into his own; then in the early 1960's the publishers Ernest Benn Ltd. inaugurated the New Mermaid Series, scrupulous modern textual editing and fresh critical interpretation making Elizabethan drama popularly available in paperback form. Today, half a century on, the success of the New Mermaids is seen in the Series list comprising some sixty titles.

And now for something different: *Christopher Marlowe, Four Plays* is the inaugural volume of a new series, *New Mermaid Anthologies*, offering themed selections from the full list. Forthcoming anthologies will include *City Comedy*, *Revenge Tragedy*, *Thomas Middleton*, and *Plays of Sex and Death* – recalling the enterprise of Havelock Ellis, while beginning anew.

Brian Gibbons
Fulford, 2011

INTRODUCTION

Marlowe was a ground-breaking playwright. The dramatic structure of each one of his plays is strikingly different from any other: each is an exploration of a different form of theatre. He was an innovator in black comedy and a master in the use of theatrical spectacle, ranging from the sublime to the grotesque. He was imaginatively drawn to the depiction of violence and his plays and poetry vividly explore personal instability, and states of extreme disordered passion and consciousness. The submerged threat of violence, too, is often implied through his use of irony, as in the half-hidden form of Classical allusion – that fashionably Elizabethan manner.

The sheer scale of Marlowe's ambition is apparent in his choice of classical models. His earliest completed literary work was probably his 'Englishing' of the highly erotic elegies of Ovid (in 1599 the Bishop of London was to order the book to be burned) while for what was probably his first play, *The Tragedy of Dido Queen of Carthage*, he took the story from epic, Virgil's *Aeneid*, in places closely following the original, with the *Metamorphoses* of Ovid also strongly present as imaginative inspiration. Probably while still at Cambridge Marlowe also drafted his translation of the first book of Lucan's *Pharsalia*. For the outline story of his poetic masterpiece *Hero and Leander* Marlowe went to Musaeus, but the poem is composed, indeed saturated, in the best Renaissance spirit of Ovid.

In Marlowe sexual desire, whether rough, tender, or comic, is expressed with uninhibited clarity; and this goes equally for same-sex desire, notwithstanding the official phobic hostility of Elizabethan religion and law. When Marlowe places homosexual love in a human context and specific historical situation, that of the English royal Court of Edward II, it is not so much the king's sexuality but rather his whole self-indulgent attitude to rule which provokes rebellion. After all, say his political opponents,

> The mightiest kings have had their minions:
> Great Alexander loved Hephaestion;   (*Edward II*, 4.392–3)

The impulse to break bounds and taboos energises the action in all Marlowe's works. Take for example Marlowe's brilliant work in the mock-heroic, *Hero and Leander*: 'amorous and young' Leander inspires the poem's ironic narrator to adapt the conventional poetic 'blazon', (which is usually reserved for the idealised female) so that he can linger pleasurably over each part of Leander's perfect, naked, male body:

> Even as delicious meat is to the taste
> So was his neck in touching, and surpass'd
> The white of Pelops' shoulder.   (*Hero and Leander*, I. 63–5)[1]

This passing allusion to Pelops' white shoulder is actually a perfect instance of Marlowe's black humour, which casts an ominous shadow on his young innocent hero.[2] There is no simple pattern in the career of the Marlovian hero, however aspiring he may be: rather, Marlowe's drama is essentially dialectical, he always gives an audience a wider perspective on the action than that available to his characters: he makes apparent to us the whole panorama within which his characters perform. This is particularly obvious when, as in *Dido Queen of Carthage* and in *Hero and Leander*, the gods shape the fate of the humans and intervene directly in the action. Yet although the inherited tragic scheme of *Hero and Leander* is summarised in a fatalistic couplet:

> It lies not in our power to love, or hate,
> For will in us is overrul'd by fate.
>
> (*Hero and Leander*, I. 167–8)

Marlowe's poem actually breaks off just at the point where the lovers achieve ecstatic union. This may or may not be accidental, but it seems consonant with the poem's comic spirit – and its author's reputation for iconoclasm.[3] Marlowe's Classical gods are as reckless as they are imperious: his poetry, correspondingly, has a brilliantly unstable texture, and paradoxically insists on the gods' carnality while at the same time magnifying to superhuman scale their passions and their power: as when (*Hero and Leander* I. 523) Venus is flippantly described in terms of a wench at her domestic tasks – 'kindling fire, to burn such towns as Troy' – whereas behind that humble verb 'kindling' and the lowly noun 'towns'

---

1   Millar Maclure, ed., *Christopher Marlowe, The Poems*, 1968.

2   In Ovid, *Metamorphoses* VI, Pelops bares his left shoulder to show it is made of white ivory, and tells how his father Tantalus had killed him by cutting his body up in pieces; although the gods restored Pelops to life by reuniting the severed parts, the shoulder was missing: one made of ivory replaced it. (Greek mythology tells how Tantalus boiled the parts of the body and served them as a feast for the gods. The gods would not eat, but Demeter, distracted by the abduction of her daughter, did eat the shoulder. Afterwards Pelops was restored to life, the parts of his body were first boiled in a sacred cauldron and a shoulder was fashioned from ivory.)

3   A point well made by Brian Morris, 'Comic Method in Marlowe's *Hero and Leander*', in Brian Morris, ed., *Christopher Marlowe: Mermaid Critical Commentaries*, 1968, p. 115. More generally see Chapter 15 of *The Cambridge Companion to Christopher Marlowe*, 2004, pp. 245–61.

stands a graver subject, nothing less than the epic tradition itself, stemming from Homer's immortal beauty Helen,

> ... the face that launched a thousand ships,
> And burnt the topless towers of Ilium?[4]
>
> (*Doctor Faustus*, 12.89–90)

Marlowe's first great theatrical success was *Tamburlaine Part I*. In this play there are no scenes featuring supernatural beings, although the action has epic scale and the constant allusions in the text to the Bible, and to Classical mythology, exalt the status of his hero:

> Ye petty kings of Turkey, I am come,
> As Hector did into the Grecian camp
> To overdare the pride of Graecia
> And set his warlike person to the view
> Of fierce Achilles, rival of his fame.
> I do you honour in the simile,
>
> (*Tamburlaine Part II*, III.v.64 ff)

Tamburlaine himself is not Classical, not Christian, not European – indeed he is basically not fiction. Neil Asherson describes a present-day visit to some ruins on the Black Sea: 'I looked down into a huge, untidy pit. Its sides were made of fire-blackened earth, wood-ash and calcined plaster. Out of them spilled human skulls and thigh-bones, white debris against the black soil. Nearby ... fragments of amphoras imported from Trebizond for shipping caviar, broken bottles of fluted Venetian glass, shards of caramel-coloured Byzantine pottery and of exquisite green-glazed bowls made by Tatar craftsmen of the Golden Horde at Saray. Lumps of black rust turned out to be the shoulder-plates of a Venetian cuirass, lying among iron cross-bow quarrels'. This, Asherson explains,[5] is the actual wreckage left by the armies of Timur from their sack of Tana in 1395.

For *Tamburlaine* Marlowe used the map of the world by Ortelius, and recent accounts by Perondinus and Mexia of the historical Scythian Timur the Lame, the last great nomad Mongol Khan, who defeated the two Muslim states which menaced the Christian Byzantium, winning a final battle, against Bayazid I at Angora in 1402. Though in the short term this brought relief to the Christians, in the long run it led to their defeat. Marlowe exploits the mixture of admiration and anxiety aroused in the

---

4 See also *Tamburlaine Part II*, II.iv.87–8.
5 In his *Black Sea: The Birthplace of Civilisation and Barbarism*, 1996, pp. 93–4.

Western world by Asia, given the proximity of the fault-line running north from Byzantium that separated (and still separates) the two continents. Timur's thirteenth-century predecessor Chingis (Genghis) Khan had used his swift and devastating cavalry to win an empire embracing China and nearly all Asia.[6] Ottoman Turks themselves had been horsemen from the steppes before converting to Islam and mounting a holy war against Christianity. In Tamburlaine's time America had yet to be discovered. Elizabethan spectators, however, could have recognized the applicability of Tamburlaine's career to the activities of sixteenth-century European conquerors (conquistadors) in the Americas, that new fourth region across the Atlantic. Near at hand there were also current colonial crises in Ireland and the Spanish Netherlands.

Marlowe focuses key questions of statehood and empire in *Tamburlaine*. To do so his poetic imagination multiplies associations, mythical and religious as well as historical. As a source for the treatment of the central ideas and for the scale of the conception, the special importance of the Bible must be stressed: this is from the Geneva version of *Revelation* (19.12–15):

> And his eyes were as a flame of fire and on his head were many crowns: and he had a name written, that no man knew but himself.
> And he was clothed with a garment dipped in blood, and his name is called, THE WORD OF GOD.
> And the warriors which were in heaven followed him upon white horses, clothed with fine linen white and pure.
> And out of his mouth went out a sharp sword, that with it he should smite the heathen: and he shall rule them with a rod of iron: for he it is that treadeth the wine press of the fierceness and wrath of the almighty God.

Tamburlaine displays superb eloquence and a supremely commanding personality. His use of shows, of visual display, is a key feature of his political strategy: he devises ever-more ambitious shows to keep pace

---

6   J.H. Parry, *The Age of Reconnaisance*, new ed. 1981, pp. 22–4. Niall Ferguson, *The War of the World*, 2007, pp. 651–2, observes that Chingis Khan's violent campaigns are said to have resulted in a population decline of more than thirty-seven million in Central Asia and China – this figure, if correct, is equivalent to nearly 10% of the entire world population at that time. The campaigns of Timur the Lame are said to have had a death toll of more than ten million. The Mongols habitually and systematically slaughtered the entire populations of cities in the path of their advance, but the majority of the victims almost certainly died from famines and epidemics resulting from the Mongol incursions.

with his astonishing triumphs, and their ever-greater cruelty. Marlowe uses Zenocrate to provide a perspective on these developments. In *Part I* IV.ii. Tamburlaine is at his most vaunting. It is only right at the end of the scene that Zenocrate finds she must speak out: her style is absolutely different from his, it is plain, measured, the tone is grave:

ZENOCRATE

    Yet would you have some pity for my sake

    Because it is my country's, and my father's.

TAMBURLAINE

    Not for the world, Zenocrate, if I have sworn.

                   (*Tamburlaine Part I*, IV.ii.123–5)

Her use of the plain style is poignant: only the key words 'pity', 'because', 'country's' and 'father's' are not monosyllabic: and Tamburlaine's reply is also monosyllabic, except for the central, and crucially isolated, name 'Zenocrate'.

There is intellectual drive in the design and articulation of scenes – anticipating a film-editor's technique in using 'cuts' to sharpen narrative meaning as well as speed up action – as in *Part II* when Callapine is taken by surprise (*Part II*, III.v.57) or the cut from the end of IV.iv, which shows Tamburlaine's army marching towards Babylon, to V.i, where the city is already falling. The great themes are treated in magnificent arias – 'I hold the fates bound fast in iron chains' (*Part I*, I.ii.174 ff) – 'Nature that framed us of four elements' (*Part I*, II.vii.18 ff) – but Marlowe is no less a master of tightly handled, direct and plainly worded dialogue: here are some examples:

TAMBURLAINE

    Behold my sword, what see you at the point?

FIRST VIRGIN

    Nothing but fear and fatal steel, my lord.

TAMBURLAINE

    Your fearful minds are thick and misty then,

    For there sits Death, there sits imperious Death,

    Keeping his circuit by the slicing edge

                 (*Tamburlaine Part I*, V.ii.45–9)

ORCANES

    If there be Christ, we shall have victory.

                 (*Tamburlaine Part II*, II.ii.64)

GOVERNOR
    My heart did never quake, or courage faint.
TAMBURLAINE
    Well now I'll make it quake: go draw him up,
    Hang him in chains upon the city walls
                      (*Tamburlaine Part II*, V.i.106–8)

Marlowe's stage images are in themselves clear but frequently contain covert allusions – some spectators probably recognised in Bajazeth's humiliation an allusion to the 1580 frontispiece of Foxes' *Book of Martyrs* with its engraving showing King Henry VIII using the Pope as a footstool to the English throne.[7] Or they might have recalled Psalm 110:1: 'The Lord said unto my Lord, sit thou at my right hand vntil I make thine enemies thy footstole'. As to the cage for Bajazeth and Zabina, some spectators might have known the fate of defeated Anabaptists in Münster in 1535, after torture and execution their bodies were left to rot in iron cages hung from the tower of the city's Lambertikirche.[8] Even a Christian audience in that superstitious age could have been disconcerted by Tamburlaine burning a copy of the Koran (*Part II*, V.i.184). There is no reaction from heaven – except that a moment later Tamburlaine does sense the first symptom – 'Something, Techelles, but I know not what' – of sickness. He makes one last effort but in vain:

    Come let us march against the powers of heaven
    And set black streamers in the firmament
    To signify the slaughter of the gods.
    Ah friends, what shall I do? I cannot stand –
                     (*Tamburlaine Part II*, V.iii.48 ff)

An audience is then confronted by the physician's detailed medical diagnosis: Tamburlaine's death has natural causes. Marlowe puts an audience on the spot: are they to accept that Tamburlaine's death is merely natural, thus putting away superstition as childish? Or is his death divine revenge for defying god? Or, should Tamburlaine be seen as divinely chosen to scourge god's enemies, then to be himself scourged? Whichever choice a spectator makes, a deep question about Tamburlaine remains: as William Blake asked of the tiger, 'did he who made the lamb make thee'?

---

7   Park Honan, *Christopher Marlowe, Poet and Spy*, 2005, p. 386, notes that in Marlowe's time two copies of Foxe were set up in Canterbury Cathedral, in the choir and north aisle.
8   Today three iron cages commemorating the victory over the Anabaptists hang from the (rebuilt) steeple of the chief Roman Catholic church in Münster.

Writing *Tamburlaine*, Marlowe needed a map of the world; in contrast, when he wrote *The Jew of Malta* he restricted the location to a small Mediterranean island, and within its confines he focused on an isolated individual, Barabas – isolated by his race, by his religion, and by the wealth he derives from off-shore trading. Malta may indeed be small, but its appeal for Marlowe was its representative significance, in having a strategic position since the Crusades, lying right on the Europe–Asia fault-line, and also on major world trade-routes. It was also newly famous as the site of a great Christian victory against the Turkish siege of 1565 – and rumour had it that Suleiman the Magnificent had financed that Turkish siege with loans from Jewish bankers.

There was also an important literary precedent for choosing an island setting, Thomas More's *Utopia* (English translation 1551), a political and cultural fable located in a fictional island-state ('utopia' being Greek for 'no place' or 'pleasant place'). Marlowe's play inclines to the dystopian side of this lively literary kind, as would Shakespeare's *The Tempest* twenty years later: for Shakspeare in *The Tempest* was to subject utopian ideals to pressure when dramatising problems of current colonial expansion and cultural conflict, making his play's island location ambiguously suggestive of the Americas as well as the Mediterranean.[9]

Marlowe's play is from the outset provocative, starting with the name of his hero: for 'Barabas' was the name of the thief whom the crowd at the Crucifixion chose to be released and replaced by Jesus. It is all one to Marlowe's Barabas that his account-books list a kaleidoscope of client races and nations, Persian, Samnite, men of Uz, Spanish, Greek, Arabian, Indian, Moorish, Egyptian; the thing that matters is the bottom line, to win a maximum profit in its most concentrated form, precious stones or gold:

> Whereof a man may easily in a day
> Tell that which may maintain him all his life.
>
> *(Jew of Malta*, I.i.10–11)

Indeed, so Barabas muses, the value of just one precious stone 'may serve in peril of calamity'. He does not yet know that the same idea has just occurred to the Christian governor Fernese. This Knight of Malta has by mismanagement made Malta bankrupt. The Turk Calymath has just arrived with a fleet demanding repayment of the large Turkish loan.

---

9 When Gonzalo in *The Tempest*, 3.3. attempts to make a distinction between the 'monstrous' islanders and 'Our human generation', this was one of the central debates at the time concerning the nature of the peoples of the Americas. See David Lindley, ed., *The Tempest*, *The New Cambridge Shakespeare*, 2002, Introduction p. 32.

Fernese needs cash and he needs it right away. The Jew Barabas is in the frame. If Barabas were as clever as he seems to think he is, surely he would find this no surprise at all: yet it shocks him to be forced to pay. Thus straight away Marlowe begins to expose limitations in his hero. Barabas is not a true follower of Machiavelli despite the insistent repetitions of the buzz-word 'policy'.

The play has a Prologue in the shape of Machevill, but he is a crude enough caricature, owing much to hostile propagandists against the real Machiavelli, such as Gentillet.[10] Marlowe's play was first performed in 1592 and was frequently revived, but it was not published until 1633, and the general quality of the text may have suffered as a result – leading possibly to the coarsening of the serious content, if not of the humour and irony of its presentation. The play is composed of intrigue-plots rendered in a satiric mode, melodrama mingles with clowning, and Marlowe makes fresh comic use of Asides:

LODOWICK

Barabas, thou know'st I am the Governor's son.

BARABAS

I would you were his father too, sir, that's all the harm
I wish you. (The slave looks like a hog's cheek new singed).

(*Jew of Malta*, II.iii.40 ff)

PILIA-BORZA

There's two crowns for thee, play.

BARABAS

(How liberally the villain gives me mine own gold.)

(*Jew of Malta*, IV.iv.45–6)

Barabas is a victim of injustice sharpened by the anti-semitism of the Knights of Malta, but his conduct sinks precipitately to the base moral level of his enemies. The centre of the play's action presents a grand emblem of what makes the world go around: buying and selling: it features a sale of slaves in a market-place. Barabas the Jew (having earlier had to pay the Christian debt to the Turkish power) now buys from a Spanish Admiral one of the newly landed Turkish slaves. This is Ithamore, who is to serve the Jew in his vengeances and his trapping of the Christian governor Fernese. Ithamore duly betrays the Jew, who in turn poisons

10 Innocent Gentillet published his *Discours contre Machievel* in 1576. James R. Siemon in his edition of *The Jew of Malta*, The New Mermaids, 2009, pp. xxviii–xxvix, and Appendix, pp. 133–6, discusses the marginal group of merchant 'Strangers' in Elizabethan London (there were no openly practicing Jews) whose capitalist practices were denounced in terms linked to the popular notion that Machiavellianism legitimated immoral self-interest.

him. As Judith Weil says, 'religious distinctions disappear when the Turk Ithamore plays the 'morality' role of the prodigal son, when a Jew, Barabas, rises from the dead and tempts a Turk, Calymath, with a pearl of great price, (V.iii.27) and when Calymath's followers are dined and destroyed in a Catholic monastery'.[11]

The Jew's explicit materialist beliefs, his ironic performance of the stereotype role of cunning Jew citing Scripture, his chilling ruthlessness towards his daughter, his cruel murders, all make it progressively difficult for an audience to see him as a tragic figure, especially given the play's relentlessly satiric and comic dramaturgy. The plot mechanism of the Jew's end is violent but farcical, produced as it is by an actual mechanism of ropes, platform and trapdoor above a cauldron. This makes immediate and atrociously incarnate – and secular – what in Christian tradition was a metaphysical image signifying divine punishment.[12] In one sense the punishment obviously fits the crime, but when Barabas, being boiled to death, screams in agony while Fernese laughs, who would say the justice of it pleases? In any case, however atrocious, the death of the Jew is not the end of Marlowe's play, since the Jew's fall and the destruction of the Turkish force are simultaneous. The *Teufelskreis*, the vicious circle, has no end, for now it is Fernese who is back on top, and looking forward to the huge ransom the Turks must pay for Calymath. The Christian's final words are exquisitely cynical:

> . . . and let due praise be given
> Neither to fate nor fortune, but to heaven.
>
> (Jew of Malta, V.v.122–3)

Like *The Jew of Malta*, Marlowe's *Edward II* begins with a solitary figure on the bare stage, Gaveston: his first speech is somewhat Prologue-like, and he is to prove more than somewhat Machiavellian. He makes the theatre resound with an echo of *Tamburlaine*:

> What greater bliss can hap to Gaveston,
> Than live and be the favourite of a king?   (*Edward II*, 1.4–5)

---

11 Weil, p. 43.

12 Park Honan, op.cit., pp. 265–6, notes that Marlowe, having grown up in Canterbury, may also have heard of a memorable event there in the 1530's concerning a Friar named Stone who refused to acknowledge the supremacy of Henry VIII and was executed by hanging and parboiling: the city of Canterbury accounts for 1539–40 record payments for the gallows, firewood, executioners, and for the woman 'that scowred the Ketyll' afterwards. For Marlowe's interest in cauldrons see also note 2 above.

and alludes to *Hero and Leander*:

> Sweet prince, I come; these, these thy amorous lines
> Might have enforced me to have swum from France,
> And, like Leander, gasped upon the sand,
>
> (*Edward II*, 1.6–8)

Moments later he is showing off his taste for Ovidian erotic fantasy in Marlowe's best over-decorated-adjectival style:

> Sometime a lovely boy in Dian's shape,
> With hair that gilds the water as it glides,
> Crownets of pearl about his naked arms,
>
> (*Edward II*, 1.60–62)

But, as a guide to the play to come this is entirely misleading. *Edward II* itself presents a grim phase of English history selected from the chronicles of Holinshed and Stow and stripped down to delineate the fiercest and bleakest power-play. To a significant degree Marlowe's aim is a serious study of politics, but at the play's centre he places once again an isolated figure: this time young, English, married, already a king; but whereas to Tamburlaine wealth was a means to power, 'The sweet fruition of an earthly crown', and to Barabas power was a means to wealth, 'Infinite riches in a little room', to Edward, just to be separated from his lover Gaveston induces an extremity of despair:

> ... could my crown's revènue bring him back,
> I would freely give it to his enemies
> And think I gained, having bought so dear a friend.
>
> (*Edward II*, 4.309–11)

In another play (say *Dido*) such an outburst would be heard as sheer hyperbole, in the heat of the moment, but here, given Edward's temperament, what Edward means by 'it' is (at least subconsciously) the crown itself, not merely its revenue: Edward brokenly admits utter submission to Gaveston's hold over him.

In performance the play has extraordinary pace – a major modern stage production was admired for its 'athletic forcefulness'.[13] In place of Ovidian ornament, direct meaning is driven plainly home,[14] vigorous active verbs generate the energy for terse exchanges to sharpen the clash of will against will. Take for example the end of Scene 1 and the start of

Scene 2. Towards the end of Scene 1 Edward, depressed by failure to get his will, suddenly notices an opponent, the Bishop of Coventry, passing in full ceremonial robes: Edward vents his frustration on the Bishop in a violent physical (and blasphemous) assault: his brother Kent pulls him back, Gaveston makes a move, Edward restrains him:

EDWARD

    Throw off his golden mitre, rend his stole,
    And in the channel christen him anew.

KENT

    Ah brother, lay not violent hands on him,
    For he'll complain unto the See of Rome.

GAVESTON

    Let him complain unto the See of Hell;
    I'll be revenged on him for my exile.

EDWARD

    No, spare his life, but seize upon his goods.

                            (*Edward II*, 1.186–92)

The Bishop is led away. Directly Marlowe cuts to the next phase of the action. The barons enter, are surprised by news that the Bishop is already in prison and that Gaveston has been given two great offices of state – and an earldom. Before they can absorb this shock they are interrupted by the Archbishop, who enters hurriedly dictating an urgent message for the Pope. Lancaster bluntly confronts him:

    My lord, will you take arms against the King?

                              (*Edward II*, 2.39)

Such forcefully direct speech is superbly effective in this exciting fast-paced kind of theatre. There is no supernatural agency and no call for it. The action is human, all too human.

---

13 This is John Russell Brown's description: see Toby Robertson, 'Directing *Edward II*', in *Tulane Drama Review,* vol. 8 no. 4 (1964), 174.

14 Writing a lament for Isabella in *Edward II*, 8.17–20, Marlowe remembers a speech he gave Dido, but in place of Dido's elaborated metaphors – 'O that I had a charme to keepe the windes / Within the closure of a golden ball, / Or that the Tyrrhen sea were in mine armes, / That he might suffer shipwracke on my breast, / As oft as he attempts to hoyst vp saile' (ed. Tucker Brooke, 1305–9). In *Edward II* Marlowe gives force to Isabella's speech without the use of colour: 'O that mine arms could close this isle about / That I might pull him to me where I would, / Or that these tears that drizzle from mine eyes / Had power to mollify his stony heart'.

Toby Robertson in 1958 came fresh to directing Marlowe after two years as an actor in Shakespeare productions encumbered by scenery. He chose a bare stage for *Edward II*, 'to push the focus completely and totally on to the actors'. To begin with, his Edward was very young, then gradually 'the iron enters into his being and he grows from the cockerel into the lion . . . the shape and structure of the play is brought out mainly through the development of Edward'.[15] Robertson made two breaks in the action. The first break was at Scene 6, line 217, after the barons go away finally to raise their troops. Edward was alone when Gaveston appeared out of the darkness and Edward said 'Poor Gaveston, that hast no friend but me' and they both turned and went. The next scene began as if several years had passed, on the line 'And, so I walk with him about the walls'. A second break was at Scene 16. It marked another time gap. Therefore Robertson's Edward was able to start the play as a young man of about eighteen or twenty and finish as a broken man of about fifty: Robertson remarked 'There is tragedy even in the physical alteration from the young god to the filthy, degraded, disgusting old man who's suffered every form of physical degradation'.[16]

Marlowe ensures that the stages in Edward's career are reflected in the carefully patterned reactions of Kent, his brother, and Isabella, his queen: the play's design stresses that the moments each of them makes a final break with Edward mark successive turns in the plot. A crucial step in Edward's decline is marked (19.45) by the anonymous figure of a mower (who may carry a scythe, hence suggesting the allegorical figure Death), a 'gloomy fellow', who looks silently on when Edward surrenders in a field somewhere in Wales. In the great scene when Edward at last abdicates, (Scene 20) he finds it almost unbearably difficult to give up his crown: his reluctance at that point is in bitter ironic contrast to his impatient youth, when the golden crown was to him an iron shackle on his desire.

Repetition is a structural principle in the play: it reinforces and clarifies a complex narrative, as well as adding ironic twists to it. In verbal form repetition can have the force of epigram in condensing dramatic conflict:

EDWARD
    Lay hands on that traitor Mortimer!
MORTIMER SENIOR
    Lay hands on that traitor Gaveston!   (*Edward II*, 4.20–21)

---

15 Op.cit., p. 176.
16 Ibid., p. 182.

ISABELLA
Villain, 'tis thou that robb'st me of my lord.
GAVESTON
Madam, 'tis you that rob me of my lord.   (4.160–61)

EDWARD
Yet, shall the crowing of these cockerels
Affright a lion? Edward, unfold thy paws   (6.200–201)

EDWARD
But when the imperial lion's flesh is gored,
He rends and tears it with his wrathful paw,   (20.11–12)

Repetition is also powerfully effective in terms of stage spectacle: the king's blasphemous attack on the ceremonially robed Bishop, early in the action (1.186 ff.) is ironically recalled in the assault on the king himself when finally reduced to rags, new-christened in 'puddle-water' (see 22.27–36 and s.d.); and Gaveston, the seductive, gallantly dressed tempter (see 4.408–20) is ironically linked to his grim counterpart Lightborne, who repeats on Edward's body – in the form of horrifying murder[17] – Gaveston's act of love.

Marlowe begins *Dr. Faustus* with a solitary figure, a gowned scholar, in his study among his books; but in contrast to Barabas enjoying his riches in his counting-house, Faustus no longer finds satisfaction in his books, whether of philosophy, medicine, law, or divinity. Faustus is in the grip of an irresistible ambition, an 'aspiring mind' – apparently a truly Marlovian hero,

Still climbing after knowledge infinite
And always moving as the restless spheres,
        (*Tamburlaine Part I*, II.vii.24–5)

He bids divinity farewell and decides to replace it with magic:

These metaphysics of magicians
And necromantic books are heavenly!
        (*Doctor Faustus*, 1.49–50)

17 At 24.30 Lightborne tells his accomplices to get him a spit made red-hot: he also says he will need a table and feather bed. The 1594 text lacks a s.d. for the murder itself, which evidently takes place after 24.110. Marlowe's source, Holinshed, *Chronicles*, 2nd ed. 1587, vol. 3, p. 341, gives an explicitly detailed account of how a red hot spit was used for anal penetration: it is quoted in Martin Wiggins and Robert Lindsey, ed., *Edward II*, The New Mermaids, 1997, pp. xxxi–xxxii.

A would-be Prometheus, ravished by the idea of stealing fire from heaven, by the thought of a dominion that 'Stretcheth as far as doth the mind of man'? (1.61) From the outset Marlowe makes warning voices heard, and also lays a trail of implied questions about his hero's state of 'ravishment': his nobler philosophical ambitions are strangely muddled up with materialist greed, he wants wealth and power, to 'ransack the ocean for orient pearl' and 'wall all Germany with brass', let alone 'fill the public schools with silk' (1.82 ff.) – and airily dismisses 'these vain trifles of men's souls' (3.60). Already, without his being aware of it, has the iron entered his soul? Should what he calls ravishment have a darker name? Marlowe presents an extreme case for debate.

The term 'atheist' in Marlowe's time was used in various senses including what today would be called scepticism. Marlowe was certainly very aware that he was not writing in a vacuum. Cambridge, where he held an Archbishop Parker scholarship at Corpus Christi to read divinity, was a centre of radical Calvinism. A Cambridge divine, William Perkins, was trying to reconcile the Calvinist doctrine of pre-destination (that God chose in advance his 'elect', those who were to be saved) with Luther's doctrine of salvation by faith (salvation for all who believed in the efficacy of Christ's sacrifice). Perkins taught that God prepared the heart to be capable of faith, but some hearts were not faithful, would therefore become hardened, and so fall into despair.[18] Remarkably, and very obviously, Faustus misinterprets Christian scriptures, citing the beginning of *Romans* vi. 23: 'The reward of sin is death' and commenting 'That's hard': (1.40) but he does not read out the rest of the verse: ' but the gift of God is eternal life through Jesus Christ our Lord'. A learned doctor, educated at Luther's Wittenberg, apparently refuses to acknowledge these doctrinally crucial words. Although one could suppose Marlowe is ironically pointing to that besetting sin in doctrinal disputes, distortion by selective quotation, a more straightforward interpretation is that Marlowe means to show that Faustus already has a hard heart.

To an audience in a Christian culture the statement 'That's hard' is shocking. Marlowe then shows Faustus using his necromantic books to conjure. He is joined on stage by Mephastophilis who invites him to sign a bond in his own blood. He is visited by angels, one good, one evil, and an anonymous Old Man, who urges him not to sign, but to recover his faith. Yet to describe the bare bones of the action in this way – as a tragedy of damnation – is to leave out of account not only a substantial amount

---

18   See Roma Gill and Ros King, ed., *Doctor Faustus*, The New Mermaids, 2008, pp. xiii–xiv, and G.M. Pinciss, 'Marlowe's Cambridge years and the writing of *Dr. Faustus*', *Studies in English Literature*, vol. 33, no. 2 (1993), 249–64.

of the text, the farce scenes, but the salient fact that the play's original theatrical popularity was owed to its spectacle and comedy.[19] In any case, the farce scenes repeat, though to Bahktinian ironic effect, the content of serious scenes. They have a destabilising effect, they are not just empty distraction. Marlowe's farce, as T.S. Eliot pointed out when writing about *The Jew of Malta*, was not the 'enfeebled humour of our times', but 'the old English humour', 'terribly serious, even savage'.[20]

Dr. Faustus may have been in existence as early as 1589 though the first edition of the play was not published until 1604: this is now referred to as the 'A' Text. A second, longer edition, the 'B' Text, published in 1616, contains additions, presumably those referred to by the impresario of the Rose Theatre, Philip Henslowe, who recorded payment of £4 on 22 November 1602 to William Byrde and Samuel Rowley for 'adicyones in docter fostes'.[21] Most modern critics optimistically assume that both printed texts are close to what was originally performed. On that basis it has recently been further speculated that these additions in 'B' were designed to clarify rather than alter or censor the 'A' text play,[22] and that the 'A' Text's presentation of the ending, where devils enter to carry Faustus off, was taken – by the companies who first acted it – to indicate the imminent dismemberment of Faustus. Hence, supposedly, the 'B' text's macabre addition, where scholars enter: 'O help us heaven! See, here are Faustus' limbs / All torn asunder' (13b.6–7) served only to clarify how the 'A' text was previously performed – rather than restraining a more dangerous 'Marlowe' play by making it more conventional.

Perhaps. And yet – and yet – as to that more dangerous 'Marlowe' play: in his 'A' Text final speech, Faustus suffers agonizing surreal visions, expresses intense longing for grace, alternating with, and mingled with, terror: the pace accelerates, tension is gripping to the very last moment:

> See, see where Christ's blood streams in the firmament! . . .
> Where is it now? 'Tis gone: and see where God

19 On the relation of serious to farcical scenes in *Dr. Faustus*, see Lois Potter, 'Marlowe in Theatre and Film', in Patrick Cheney, ed., *The Cambridge Companion to Christopher Marlowe*, 2004. A production in 2010 at Manchester's Royal Exchange Theatre impressed reviewers with its spectacular farce scenes: see Lynne Walker's review in *The Independent*, 16 September 2010 and Clare Brennan's in *The Observer*, 19 September 2010

20 T.S. Eliot, 'Christopher Marlowe', in *Selected Essays*, 1951, p. 123. Among modern examples of black humoured farce is Stanley Kubrick's movie *Dr Strangelove* and its witty treatment of apocalypse: the image of a hydrogen bomb exploding accompanied on the sound-track by Vera Lynn singing 'We'll meet again'.

21 These additions are presented as an Appendix to *Dr. Faustus* in the present volume.

22 Thomas Healy, '*Doctor Faustus*', in Patrick Cheney, ed., *The Cambridge Companion to Marlowe*, pp. 184–5.

Stretcheth out his arm, and bends his ireful brows!
Mountains and hills, come, come and fall on me,
And hide me from the heavy wrath of God.
No, no?   (*Dr Faustus*, 13.68, 72–6)

Faustus appeals to the earth to hide him, then to the stars to draw him up into 'yon labouring cloud' and vomit forth into the air his dismembered limbs in a bolt of lightning, if his soul 'may but ascend to heaven' (85). The clock strikes – he has half an hour to live – eighteen more lines – he pleads for a limit to the pains of hell, then curses his parents, himself, Lucifer – *The clock striketh twelve*' – time's up – he pleads simply for extinction, to 'turn to air' – he sees God again: 'My God, my God, look not so fierce on me!' – he offers to renounce magic – then 'ah, Mephastophilis!' It is an exclamation, not an explanation.

CHRONOLOGY

In 1564 Christopher Marlowe was born the son of a shoemaker and baptised in Canterbury. He lived in the city, attending petty school and grammar school. In 1579 he won a scholarship to King's School Canterbury. From there he won a scholarship to Cambridge, going up in 1580 to Corpus Christi College, where he was an Archbishop Parker scholar. His education would have given him a thorough grounding in Latin rhetoric, grammar and logic, and he may have enjoyed, as recreation, acting in plays in Latin as well as English. He proceeded to BA in 1584.

From 1581 to 1586 he was intermittently away from Cambridge, in London or abroad on government service. Also probably in this period he translated Ovid's *Elegies* and the first book of Lucan, *Pharsalia*, and, probably in 1585–6, he wrote *The Tragedy of Dido* . The title-page of its first edition, published much later in 1594, gives (dubiously) Thomas Nashe as co-author. In 1587 he was granted his MA degree at Cambridge University but (because of absences) only after the Privy Council wrote attesting to his 'good service', some of which is thought to have been in espionage.

In 1587–8 *Tamburlaine* was performed by the Admiral's Men to great acclaim. Evidence from contemporary allusions in 1588–9 indicates that he may also have written *Dr. Faustus* then, though some scholars believe he wrote it later, in 1592–3. The first record of a performance of *Dr. Faustus* was in 1594.

On 18 September 1589 Marlowe was put in Newgate prison with the poet Thomas Watson on suspicion of murder, after a sword fight in which William Bradley, a gentleman, was killed. Marlowe was released on bail on 1 October and on 3 December he was discharged.

In 1590 *Tamburlaine* was published without Marlowe's name on the title-page. Also perhaps in this year he wrote *The Jew of Malta*.

In 1591 he was sharing a room with Thomas Kyd, the author of *The Spanish Tragedy*.

In 1592 he was arrested in the Dutch town Vlissingen (Flushing) on suspicion of counterfeiting, he was sent to London, then released. On 9 May after an affray in Hackney, London, he was bound over to keep the peace. The composition of *Edward II* and of *The Massacre at Paris* is likely to have taken place at this time.

1593 was the last year of Marlowe's life, some of it spent at Sir Thomas Walsingham's house at Scadbury. Marlowe may have been serving Walsingham on secret business, and Marlowe was caught up in a flurry of trouble with the authorities in the weeks preceding his death.

On 30 January *The Massacre at Paris* was staged at the Rose Theatre.

On 5 May a libel attacking immigrants and signed 'per Tamerlaine' was posted on the wall of the Dutch church in London.

On 12 May Thomas Kyd was arrested for libel, and found to possess heretical papers, but he claimed they were Marlowe's.

On 18 May the Privy Council issued a warrant for Marlowe's arrest. On 20 May Marlowe answered the warrant.

On 30 May Marlowe spent the day in a Deptford tavern with three companions, Frizer, Skeres, and Poley. All had form as secret agents, but what they discussed is uncertain. After an altercation Marlowe was stabbed to death by Frizer. The coroner's report says that Marlowe attacked Frizer after a dispute about paying 'the reckoning'.

On 1 June Marlowe was buried in St Nicholas' Church, Deptford. An (undated) letter was sent by Kyd to Sir John Puckering, the Lord Keeper, about Marlowe's dangerous opinions. A 'Note' about Marlowe's dangerous opinions was written by Richard Baines shortly after Marlowe's death and sent to the Privy Council. On 15 June Frizer's case was summoned to the Court of Chancery, and on 28 June Frizer was pardoned.

Marlowe's Published Works

1590   *Tamburlaine* published without Marlowe's name on the title-page.

1593   30 January, *The Massacre at Paris* staged at the Rose Theatre; an undated edition appeared, probably later that year.

1594   Publication of *The Tragedy of Dido* and *The Tragedy of Edward II*: Marlowe's name appearing for the first time on title-pages.

1597   28 September, *Hero and Leander* and the First Book of Lucan, *Pharsalia*, were entered in the Stationer's Register.

1598   *Hero and Leander* by Christopher Marlowe published, as an 818-line poem.

1599   Marlowe's undated translation of Ovid's *Elegies* (bound with Davies's *Epigrams*) burned in public by order of the Bishop of London.

1600   Publication of *Lucans First Booke Translated Line for Line, by chr.Marlow*.

1602   Henslowe paid £4 to Birde and Rowley for 'adicyons in docter fostes'.

1604   Publication of *Dr. Faustus* first edition (the 'A' text) with Marlowe's name.

1616   Publication of *Dr. Faustus* second edition (the 'B' text) with Marlowe's name.

1633   *The Jew of Malta* was published, with an epistle by the playwright Thomas Heywood.

FURTHER READING

Annotated Bibliographies
Jonathan F.S. Post, 'Recent Studies in Marlowe (1968–76)', in *English Literary Renaissance*, vol. 7 (1977)

Ronald Levao, 'Recent Studies in Marlowe (1977–86)', in *English Literary Renaissance*, vol. 18 (1988)

Patrick Cheney, 'Recent Studies in Marlowe (1987–1998)', in *English Literary Renaissance*, vol. 31 (2001)

Kenneth Friedenreich, *Christopher Marlowe, an Annotated Bibliography since 1950*, 1979

Bruce E. Brandt, *Christopher Marlowe in the Eighties*, 1992

Christopher Marlowe: Complete Works
ed. C.F. Tucker Brooke, 1910

ed. R.H. Case, repr. 1966

ed. Fredson Bowers, rev. ed., 1981

ed. Roma Gill, 1987–8

Sources
Vivien Thomas and William Tydeman, *Christopher Marlowe: The Plays and their Sources*, 1994

Biography
John Bakeless, *The Tragicall History of Christopher Marlowe*, 1942

Constance Kuriyama, *Christopher Marlowe: A Renaissance Life*, 2002

David Riggs, *The World of Christopher Marlowe*, 2004

Park Honan, *Christopher Marlowe Poet and Spy*, 2005

Criticism
Harry Levin, *Christopher Marlowe: The Overreacher*, 1952

David Bevington, *From Mankind to Marlowe*, 1962

Eugene Waith, *The Herculean Hero in Marlowe, Chapman, Shakespeare and Dryden*, 1962

J.B. Steane, *Marlowe: A Critical Study*, 1964

Nicholas Brooke, 'Marlowe the Dramatist', in John Russell Brown and Bernard Harris, ed., *Elizabethan Theatre*, 1966

Wilbur Sanders, *The Dramatist and the Received Idea*, 1968

David Hard Zucker, *Stage and Image in the Plays of Christopher Marlowe*, 1972

Judith Weil, *Christopher Marlowe: Merlin's Prophet*, 1977

Constance Kuriyama, *Hammer or Anvil: Psychological Patterns in Christopher Marlowe's Plays*, 1980

Simon Shepherd, *Marlowe and the Politics of Elizabethan Theatre*, 1986

Thomas Cartelli, *Marlowe, Shakespeare, and the Economy of Theatrical Experience*, 1991

Emily C. Bartels, *Spectacles of Strangeness: Imperialism, Alienation and Marlowe*, 1993

Patrick Cheney, *Marlowe's Counterfeit Profession*, 1997

Scott McMillin and Sally-Beth MacLean, *The Queens Men and Their Plays*, 1998

Ruth Lunney, *Marlowe and the Popular Tradition*, 2002

John Parker, *The Aesthetics of Antichrist: from Christian Drama to Christopher Marlowe*, 2007

A.D. Nuttall, *The Alternative Trinity: Gnostic Heresy in Marlowe, Milton and Blake*, 2007

Collections of Criticism

OFFERING ESSAYS ALREADY PUBLISHED

Clifford Leech, ed., *Marlowe: A Collection of Critical Essays: Twentieth Century Views*, 1964

Millar Maclure, ed., *Marlowe, The Critical Heritage 1588–1896*, 1979

John Russell Brown, ed., *Marlowe: a Casebook*, 1982

Emily Bartels, ed., *Critical Essays on Christopher Marlowe*, 1996

OFFERING NEW ESSSAYS

Tulane Drama Review, Marlowe Issue, vol.8, no. 4 (1964)

Brian Morris, ed., *Christopher Marlowe: Mermaid Critical Commentaries*, 1968

Alvin B. Kernan, ed., *Two Renaissance Mythmakers*, 1977

Kenneth Friedenreich, Roma Gill and Constance Kuriyama, ed., *'A Poet and a Filthy Play-maker': New Essays on Christopher Marlowe*, 1988

Darryl Grantley and Peter Roberts, ed., *Christopher Marlowe and English Renaissance Culture*, 1996

Paul Whitfield White, ed., *Marlowe, History and Sexuality*, 1998

J.A. Downie and J.T. Parnell, ed., *Constructing Christopher Marlowe*, 2000

Patrick Cheney, ed., *The Cambridge Companion to Christopher Marlowe*, Cambridge 2004

Sara Deats and Robert A. Logan, ed., *Placing the Plays of Christopher Marlowe*, 2008

Important criticism is also found in editors' introductions to separate Marlowe plays in The New Mermaids and in The Revels Plays.

Criticism on Separate Plays

TAMBURLAINE

Anthony B. Dawson, ed., *Tamburlaine Parts I and II*, The New Mermaids, 1997

J.S. Cunningham, ed., *Tamburlaine Parts I and II*, The Revels Plays, 1989

Ethel Seaton, 'Marlowe's Map' in *Essays and Studies*, vol. 10 (1924)
——— , 'Marlowe's Light Reading', in H. Davis and Helen Gardner, ed., *Elizabethan and Jacobean Studies Presented to F.P. Wilson*, 1959

J.S. Cunningham and Roger Warren, '*Tamburlaine the Great* Rediscovered', *Shakespeare Survey*, vol. 31 (1978)

Peter Berek, '*Tamburlaine's* Weak Sons', *Renaissance Drama*, vol. 13 (1982)

Richard Levin, 'The Contemporary Perception of Marlowe's *Tamburlaine*', *Medieval and Renaissance Drama in England*, vol. 1 (1984)

Alexander Leggatt, 'Killing the Hero: Tamburlaine and Falstaff', in Paul Budra and Betty Schellenberg, ed., *Part II: Reflections on the Sequel*, 1998

Jonathan Burton, 'Anglo-Ottoman Relations and the Image of the Turk in *Tamburlaine*', *Journal of Medieval and Early Modern Studies*, vol. 30 (2000)

THE JEW OF MALTA

James R. Siemon, ed., *The Jew of Malta*, The New Mermaids, 2009

N.W. Bawcutt, ed., *The Jew of Malta*, The Revels Plays, 1978

T.S. Eliot, 'Christopher Marlowe', in *Elizabethan Dramatists*, 1963

G.K. Hunter, 'The Theology of Marlowe's *The Jew of Malta*', *Journal of the Warburg and Courtauld Institutes*, vol. 27 (1964)

Eric Rothstein, 'Structure as Meaning in *The Jew of Malta*', *Journal of English and Germanic Philology*, vol. 65 (1966)

James L. Smith, '*The Jew of Malta* in the Theatre', in Brian Morris, op.cit.

N.W. Bawcutt, 'Machiavelli and Marlowe's *The Jew of Malta*', *Renaissance Drama*, n.s. (1970)

Catherine Minshull, 'Marlowe's "Sound Machevill"', *Renaissance Drama*, vol. 13 (1982)

David H. Thurn, 'Economic and Ideological Exchange in Marlowe's *Jew of Malta*', *Theatre Journal*, vol. 46 (1994)

James Shapiro, *Shakespeare and the Jews*, 1996

N.W. Bawcutt, 'The "Myth of Gentillet" Reconsidered', *Modern Language Review*, vol. 99 (2004)

EDWARD II

Martin Wiggins and Robert Lindsey, ed., *Edward II*, The New Mermaids, 1997

Charles R. Forker, ed., *Edward II*, The Revels Plays, 1994

Nicholas Brooke, 'Marlowe as Provocative Agent in Shakespeare's Early Plays', *Shakespeare Survey*, vol. 14 (1961)

Toby Robertson, 'Directing *Edward II*', *Tulane Drama Review*, vol. 8 no. 4 (1964)

George L. Geckle, *'Tamburlaine' and 'Edward II': Text and Performance*, 1988

Bruce R. Smith, *Homosexual Desire in Shakespeare's England*, 1991

Valerie Traub 'Studies in Homoeroticism', *English Literary Renaissance*, vol. 30 (2000)

There is a DVD of the Derek Jarman film

DOCTOR FAUSTUS

Roma Gill and Ros King, ed., *Doctor Faustus*, The New Mermaids, 2008

H.J. Oliver, ed., *Doctor Faustus*, The Revels Plays, 1968

M.C. Bradbrook 'Marlowe's *Doctor Faustus* and the Eldritch Tradition', in Richard Hosley, ed., *Essays on Shakespeare and Elizabethan Drama* 1962

John D. Jump, ed., *Marlowe, Doctor Faustus: A Casebook*, 1969

William Tydeman, *Dr. Faustus: Text and Performance*, 1984

J.H. Jones, ed., *The English Faust Book*, 1994

John Parker, *The Aesthetics of Antichrist: from Christian Drama to Christopher Marlowe*, 2007

Tamburlaine

the Great.

Who, from a Scythian Shephearde,
by his rare and woonderfull Conquests,
became a most puissant and migh-
tye Monarque.

And (for his tyranny, and terrour in
Warre)was tearmed,

The Scourge of God.

Deuided into two Tragicall Dis-
courses, as they were sundrie times
shewed vpon Stages in the Citie
of London.

By the right honorable the Lord
Admyrall, his seruantes.

Now first, and newlie published.

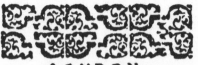

LONDON.

Printed by Richard Ihones: at the signe
of the Rose and Crowne neere Hol-
borne Bridge. 1590,

TO THE GENTLEMEN READERS

and others that take pleasure in reading histories

Gentlemen, and courteous readers whosoever: I have here published in print for your sakes, the two tragical discourses of the Scythian shepherd, Tamburlaine, that became so great a conqueror, and so mighty a monarch. My hope is that they will be now no less acceptable unto you to read after your serious affairs and studies, 5 than they have been (lately) delightful for many of you to see, when the same were showed in London upon stages. I have (purposely) omitted and left out some fond and frivolous gestures, digressing (and in my poor opinion) far unmeet for the matter, which I thought, might seem more tedious unto the wise, than any way else to be 10 regarded, though (haply) they have been of some vain conceited fondlings greatly gaped at, what times they were showed upon the stage in their graced deformities: nevertheless, now, to be mixtured in print with such matter of worth, it would prove a great disgrace to so honourable and stately a history. Great folly were it in me to 15 commend unto your wisdoms either the eloquence of the author that writ them, or the worthiness of the matter itself; I therefore leave unto your learned censures, both the one and the other, and myself the poor printer of them unto your most courteous and favourable protection: which if you vouchsafe to accept, you shall 20 evermore bind me to employ what travail and service I can, to the advancing and pleasuring of your excellent degree.

Yours, most humble at commandment,
R. J., Printer

8   *fond* foolish
12   *fondlings* fools
18   *censures* judgements
24   *R.J.* Richard Jones, a printer and bookseller, for whom the two parts of
     Tamburlaine were entered in the Stationers' Register on 14 August 1590

3

[DRAMATIS PERSONAE

PROLOGUE
MYCETES, *King of Persia*
COSROE, *his brother*
CENEUS
ORTYGIUS   5
MEANDER   } *Persian lords*
MENAPHON
THERIDAMAS
TAMBURLAINE, *a Scythian shepherd*
TECHELLES   } *his followers*   10
USUMCASANE
AGYDAS   } *Median lords*
MAGNETES
BAJAZETH, *Emperor of the Turks*
KING OF ARGIER   15
KING OF FEZ   } *tributary kings to Bajazeth*
KING OF MOROCCO
ALCIDAMUS, *King of Arabia*
SOLDAN OF EGYPT
CAPOLIN, *an Egyptian*   20
GOVERNOR OF DAMASCUS
A SPY
MESSENGERS, *including* PHILEMUS
BASSOES, LORDS, CITIZENS, MOORS, SOLDIERS, *and* ATTENDANTS

ZENOCRATE, *daughter of the Soldan of Egypt*   25
ANIPPE, *her maid*
ZABINA, *wife of Bajazeth*
EBEA, *her maid*
VIRGINS OF DAMASCUS]

---

13 *MAGNETES* The name appears nowhere in the text but has been adopted by editors from the speech prefix 'Mag.' in O1.
15 *ARGIER* Algeria
19 *SOLDAN* Sultan
24 *BASSOES* pashas

THE PROLOGUE

From jigging veins of rhyming mother wits
And such conceits as clownage keeps in pay,
We'll lead you to the stately tent of war,
Where you shall hear the Scythian Tamburlaine
Threat'ning the world with high astounding terms   5
And scourging kingdoms with his conquering sword.
View but his picture in this tragic glass,
And then applaud his fortunes as you please.

1–3 These lines are Marlowe's challenge to the stage conventions of the time, proclaim-
     ing a new kind of verse, unrhymed and heroic, to replace the doggerel rhymes and
     jog-trot rhythms of the popular drama of the previous years. He rejects the whims
     and tricks ('conceits') of clowns and jesters, preferring a more elevated and 'stately'
     theme.
   1 *mother wits* those who possess 'mother wit', i.e. native or natural wit *(O.E.D.;* here
     used contemptuously)

ACT I, SCENE i

[*Enter*] MYCETES, COSROE, MEANDER, THERIDAMAS,
ORTYGIUS, [MENAPHON], *with others*

MYCETES

Brother Cosroe, I find myself aggrieved
Yet insufficient to express the same,
For it requires a great and thund'ring speech.
Good brother, tell the cause unto my lords,
I know you have a better wit than I.   5

COSROE

Unhappy Persia, that in former age
Hast been the seat of mighty conquerors
That in their prowess and their policies
Have triumphed over Afric and the bounds
Of Europe, where the sun dares scarce appear   10
For freezing meteors and congealèd cold,
Now to be ruled and governed by a man
At whose birthday Cynthia with Saturn joined,
And Jove, the Sun, and Mercury denied
To shed their influence in his fickle brain!   15
Now Turks and Tartars shake their swords at thee,
Meaning to mangle all thy provinces.

MYCETES

Brother, I see your meaning well enough,
And through your planets I perceive you think
I am not wise enough to be a king.   20
But I refer me to my noblemen,
That know my wit and can be witnesses.
I might command you to be slain for this –
Meander, might I not?

MEANDER

Not for so small a fault, my sovereign lord.   25

---

8   *policies* diplomacy
11 *meteors* any atmospheric phenomena
13–15 *At . . . brain* The unfavourable influence of Cynthia (the moon – a symbol of
change and fickleness) and Saturn (stupidity) presided over Mycetes' birth,
whereas Jove (Jupiter – magnanimity), Apollo (the sun – kingliness), and Mercury
(wit) were absent.

MYCETES

    I mean it not, but yet I know I might.
    Yet live, yea live, Mycetes wills it so.
    Meander, thou my faithful counsellor,
    Declare the cause of my conceivèd grief,
    Which is, God knows, about that Tamburlaine   30
    That like a fox in midst of harvest time
    Doth play upon my flocks of passengers,
    And, as I hear, doth mean to pull my plumes.
    Therefore 'tis good and meet for to be wise.

MEANDER

    Oft have I heard your majesty complain   35
    Of Tamburlaine, that sturdy Scythian thief
    That robs your merchants of Persepolis,
    Treading by land unto the Western Isles,
    And in your confines with his lawless train
    Daily commits incivil outrages,   40
    Hoping (misled by dreaming prophecies)
    To reign in Asia, and with barbarous arms
    To make himself the monarch of the East.
    But ere he march in Asia or display
    His vagrant ensign in the Persian fields,   45
    Your grace hath taken order by Theridamas,
    Charged with a thousand horse, to apprehend
    And bring him captive to your highness' throne.

MYCETES

    Full true thou speak'st, and like thyself, my lord,
    Whom I may term a Damon for thy love.   50
    Therefore 'tis best, if so it like you all,
    To send my thousand horse incontinent

---

32   *passengers* travellers, traders
36   *Scythian* Marlowe's atlas, Ortelius' *Theatrum Orbis Terrarum,* located Scythia on
     the north shore of the Black Sea, west of Crimea, but the name was often used to
     refer generally to a large area in central Asia. Marlowe seems to have used the terms
     Scythian and Tartar interchangeably, the Scythians being a branch of the Tartar
     race.
37   *Persepolis* the ancient capital of Persia, situated on the river Araxes
38   *the Western Isles* Britain
45   *vagrant ensign* nomadic banner
47   *Charged with* placed in command of
50   *Damon* Damon and Pythias provided the classic example of friendship.
52   *incontinent* immediately

To apprehend that paltry Scythian.
How like you this, my honourable lords?
Is it not a kingly resolution?   55

COSROE

It cannot choose, because it comes from you.

MYCETES

Then hear thy charge, valiant Theridamas,
The chiefest captain of Mycetes' host,
The hope of Persia, and the very legs
Whereon our state doth lean, as on a staff   60
That holds us up and foils our neighbour foes.
Thou shalt be leader of this thousand horse,
Whose foaming gall with rage and high disdain
Have sworn the death of wicked Tamburlaine.
Go frowning forth, but come thou smiling home,   65
As did Sir Paris with the Grecian dame.
Return with speed, time passeth swift away,
Our life is frail and we may die today.

THERIDAMAS

Before the moon renew her borrowed light,
Doubt not, my lord and gracious sovereign,   70
But Tamburlaine and that Tartarian rout
Shall either perish by our warlike hands
Or plead for mercy at your highness' feet.

MYCETES

Go, stout Theridamas, thy words are swords,
And with thy looks thou conquerest all thy foes.   75
I long to see thee back return from thence
That I may view these milk-white steeds of mine
All loaden with the heads of killèd men,
And from their knees, even to their hoofs below,
Besmeared with blood; that makes a dainty show.   80

THERIDAMAS

Then now, my lord, I humbly take my leave.   *Exit*

MYCETES

Theridamas farewell ten thousand times.
Ah Menaphon, why stay'st thou thus behind,
When other men press forward for renown?

56   *choose* be otherwise
66   *Grecian dame* Helen of Troy
74   *stout* powerful

Go Menaphon, go into Scythia   85
And foot by foot follow Theridamas.

COSROE

Nay, pray you let him stay, a greater task
Fits Menaphon than warring with a thief:
Create him prorex of Assyria
That he may win the Babylonians' hearts,   90
Which will revolt from Persian government
Unless they have a wiser king than you.

MYCETES

Unless they have a wiser king than you?
These are his words Meander, set them down.

COSROE

And add this to them, that all Asia   95
Lament to see the folly of their king.

MYCETES

Well here I swear by this my royal seat –

COSROE

[*Aside*] You may do well to kiss it then.

MYCETES

– Embossed with silk as best beseems my state,
To be revenged for these contemptuous words.   100
O where is duty and allegiance now?
Fled to the Caspian or the ocean main?
What, shall I call thee brother? No, a foe.
Monster of nature, shame unto thy stock
That dar'st presume thy sovereign for to mock.   105
Meander come, I am abused Meander.

> *Exit* [MYCETES *with his train*].
> COSROE *and* MENAPHON *remain*

MENAPHON

How now, my lord, what, mated and amazed
To hear the king thus threaten like himself?

COSROE

Ah Menaphon, I pass not for his threats –

---

87   *greater task* ed. (greater O1)
89   *prorex* viceroy
     Assyria ed. (Africa O1), an emendation suggested by B. A. van Dam on the grounds
     that 'Africa' does not fit the context, and supported by Bowers and Cunningham in
     their editions
107 *mated* rendered helpless
109 *pass* care

The plot is laid by Persian noblemen 110
And captains of the Median garrisons
To crown me emperor of Asia.
But this it is that doth excruciate
The very substance of my vexèd soul:
To see our neighbours that were wont to quake 115
And tremble at the Persian monarch's name
Now sits and laughs our regiment to scorn;
And that which might resolve me into tears,
Men from the farthest equinoctial line
Have swarmed in troops into the Eastern India, 120
Lading their ships with gold and precious stones,
And made their spoils from all our provinces.

MENAPHON

This should entreat your highness to rejoice.
Since fortune gives you opportunity
To gain the title of a conqueror 125
By curing of this maimèd empery.
Afric and Europe bordering on your land
And continent to your dominions,
How easily may you with a mighty host
Pass into Graecia, as did Cyrus once, 130
And cause them to withdraw their forces home,
Lest you subdue the pride of Christendom.

COSROE

But Menaphon, what means this trumpet's sound?

MENAPHON

Behold, my lord, Ortygius and the rest,
Bringing the crown to make you emperor. 135

---

111   *Median* from Media, the north-eastern part of the Persian empire, south of the
      Caspian Sea
113   *excruciate* torment
117   *sits and laughs* a common plural form in the play and in Elizabethan English
      generally
      regiment rule, authority
118   *resolve* dissolve
126   *empery* empire
128   *continent to* touching, bordering upon
130   *Cyrus* the son of Cambises and founder of the Persian empire. He conquered the
      Greek settlements of Asia Minor ('Graecia').
132   *pride of Christendom* probably Byzantium (Constantinople)

Enter ORTYGIUS *and* CENEUS *bearing a crown,*
with others

ORTYGIUS
    Magnificent and mighty Prince Cosroe,
    We in the name of other Persian states
    And commons of this mighty monarchy,
    Present thee with th'imperial diadem.
CENEUS
    The warlike soldiers and the gentlemen   140
    That heretofore have filled Persepolis
    With Afric captains taken in the field,
    Whose ransom made them march in coats of gold
    With costly jewels hanging at their ears
    And shining stones upon their lofty crests,   145
    Now living idle in the wallèd towns,
    Wanting both pay and martial discipline,
    Begin in troops to threaten civil war
    And openly exclaim against the king.
    Therefore, to stay all sudden mutinies,   150
    We will invest your highness emperor,
    Whereat the soldiers will conceive more joy
    Than did the Macedonians at the spoil
    Of great Darius and his wealthy host.
COSROE
    Well, since I see the state of Persia droop   155
    And languish in my brother's government,
    I willingly receive th'imperial crown
    And vow to wear it for my country's good
    In spite of them shall malice my estate.
ORTYGIUS
    And in assurance of desired success,   160
    We here do crown thee monarch of the East,
    Emperor of Asia and of Persia,
    Great lord of Media and Armenia,

---

  135   s.d. CENEUS ed. (Conerus O1)
  137   *states* noblemen
  140   s.p. ed. (Conerus O1)
153–4   Alexander the Great defeated the Emperor Darius of Persia at the battle of Issus in
        333 B.C.
  159   *malice* show ill will to

Duke of Assyria and Albania,
Mesopotamia and of Parthia,   165
East India and the late-discovered isles,
Chief lord of all the wide vast Euxine Sea,
And of the ever-raging Caspian lake.
Long live Cosroe, mighty emperor!

COSROE

And Jove may never let me longer live   170
Than I may seek to gratify your love,
And cause the soldiers that thus honour me
To triumph over many provinces,
By whose desires of discipline in arms
I doubt not shortly but to reign sole king,   175
And with the army of Theridamas,
Whither we presently will fly, my lords,
To rest secure against my brother's force.

ORTYGIUS

We knew, my lord, before we brought the crown,
Intending your investion so near   180
The residence of your despisèd brother,
The lords would not be too exasperate
To injure or suppress your worthy title.
Or, if they would, there are in readiness
Ten thousand horse to carry you from hence   185
In spite of all suspected enemies.

COSROE

I know it well, my lord, and thank you all.

ORTYGIUS

Sound up the trumpets then, God save the king!

Exeunt

---

164   *Assyria* ed. (Africa O1)
166   *late-discovered isles* perhaps the West Indies
167   *Euxine Sea* Black Sea
170   *Jove may never* may Jove never
177   *presently* immediately
180   *investion* investiture
182   *lords* ed. (Lord Ol)
       exasperate exasperated
188   lineation ed.

[Enter] TAMBURLAINE *leading* ZENOCRATE, *[with]*
TECHELLES, USUMCASANE, *[*MAGNETES, AGYDAS
and] other Lords and Soldiers loaden with treasure

TAMBURLAINE

Come, lady, let not this appal your thoughts;
The jewels and the treasure we have ta'en
Shall be reserved, and you in better state
Than if you were arrived in Syria,
Even in the circle of your father's arms,   5
The mighty Soldan of Egyptia.

ZENOCRATE

Ah shepherd, pity my distressèd plight,
If, as thou seem'st, thou art so mean a man,
And seek not to enrich thy followers
By lawless rapine from a silly maid   10
Who, travelling with these Median lords
To Memphis from my uncle's country of Media,
Where all my youth I have been governèd,
Have passed the army of the mighty Turk,
Bearing his privy signet and his hand   15
To safe conduct us thorough Africa.

MAGNETES

And since we have arrived in Scythia,
Besides rich presents from the puissant Cham,
We have his highness' letters to command
Aid and assistance if we stand in need.   20

TAMBURLAINE

But now you see these letters and commands
Are countermanded by a greater man,
And through my provinces you must expect

---

8 *mean* lowly (i.e. a shepherd)
10 *silly* helpless
15 *hand* signature (guaranteeing safe passage)
16 *thorough* 'Through' was often thus spelled and pronounced in Elizabethan verse
   when the metre demanded a disyllable. There are several examples in *Tamburlaine*.
18 *puissant* mighty
   Cham Tartar emperor

Letters of conduct from my mightiness
If you intend to keep your treasure safe.   25
But since I love to live at liberty,
As easily may you get the Soldan's crown
As any prizes out of my precinct,
For they are friends that help to wean my state
Till men and kingdoms help to strengthen it,   30
And must maintain my life exempt from servitude.
But tell me, madam, is your grace betrothed?

ZENOCRATE

I am, my lord, for so you do import.

TAMBURLAINE

I am a lord, for so my deeds shall prove,
And yet a shepherd by my parentage.   35
But, lady, this fair face and heavenly hue
Must grace his bed that conquers Asia
And means to be a terror to the world,
Measuring the limits of his empery
By east and west as Phoebus doth his course.   40
Lie here ye weeds that I disdain to wear!

> [*He removes his shepherd's clothing to reveal
> his armour beneath*]

This complete armour and this curtle-axe
Are adjuncts more beseeming Tamburlaine,
And, madam, whatsoever you esteem
Of this success and loss unvaluèd,   45
Both may invest you empress of the East.
And these that seem but silly country swains
May have the leading of so great an host

28   *precinct* province
29   *wean my state* nurture my power
33   *for . . . import* i.e. for you do appear to be a lord
40   *Phoebus* Apollo, the sun
41   *weeds* garments
41   s.d. Such has been the practice of modern productions. The text itself does not pre-
       clude the possibility that after removing his shepherd's cloak Tamburlaine gestures
       to his men to bring him his armour, which he then dons with a theatrical flourish.
42   *curtle-axe* heavy slashing sword
45   *success* result
       loss unvalued the inestimable loss you have incurred
47   *these* Tamburlaine's followers
       silly . . . swains simple shepherds

As with their weight shall make the mountains quake,
Even as when windy exhalations   50
Fighting for passage tilt within the earth.

TECHELLES

As princely lions when they rouse themselves,
Stretching their paws and threat'ning herds of beasts,
So in his armour looketh Tamburlaine.
Methinks I see kings kneeling at his feet   55
And he, with frowning brows and fiery looks,
Spurning their crowns from off their captive heads.

USUMCASANE

And making thee and me, Techelles, kings,
That even to death will follow Tamburlaine.

TAMBURLAINE

Nobly resolved, sweet friends and followers.   60
These lords perhaps do scorn our estimates
And think we prattle with distempered spirits.
But since they measure our deserts so mean,
That in conceit bear empires on our spears,
Affecting thoughts co-equal with the clouds,   65
They shall be kept our forcèd followers
Till with their eyes they view us emperors.

ZENOCRATE

The gods, defenders of the innocent,
Will never prosper your intended drifts
That thus oppress poor friendless passengers.   70
Therefore at least admit us liberty,
Even as thou hop'st to be eternized
By living Asia's mighty emperor.

AGYDAS

I hope our lady's treasure and our own
May serve for ransom to our liberties.   75
Return our mules and empty camels back
That we may travel into Syria
Where her betrothèd lord Alcidamus

---

51   *tilt* joust
63   *deserts* worth
64   *conceit* imagination
65   *Affecting* aspiring to
67   *they* O2–3, Q (thee O1)
69   *drifts* purposes

Expects th'arrival of her highness' person.

MAGNETES

And wheresoever we repose ourselves,   80
We will report but well of Tamburlaine.

TAMBURLAINE

Disdains Zenocrate to live with me?
Or you, my lords, to be my followers?
Think you I weigh this treasure more than you?
Not all the gold in India's wealthy arms   85
Shall buy the meanest soldier in my train.
Zenocrate, lovelier than the love of Jove,
Brighter than is the silver Rhodope,
Fairer than whitest snow on Scythian hills,
Thy person is more worth to Tamburlaine   90
Than the possession of the Persian crown,
Which gracious stars have promised at my birth.
A hundred Tartars shall attend on thee
Mounted on steeds swifter than Pegasus;
Thy garments shall be made of Median silk,   95
Enchased with precious jewels of mine own
More rich and valurous than Zenocrate's;
With milk-white harts upon an ivory sled
Thou shalt be drawn amidst the frozen pools
And scale the icy mountains' lofty tops,   100
Which with thy beauty will be soon resolved;
My martial prizes with five hundred men
Won on the fifty-headed Volga's waves
Shall all we offer to Zenocrate,
And then myself to fair Zenocrate.   105

TECHELLES

What now? In love?

TAMBURLAINE

Techelles, women must be flatterèd,
But this is she with whom I am in love.

---

88   *Rhodope* a snow-capped mountain range in Thrace, famous for silver mines
94   *Pegasus* the mythical winged horse
96   *Enchased* adorned
97   *valurous* valuable
101 *resolved* melted
103 *fifty-headed . . . waves* i.e. the numerous tributaries of the Volga river

Enter a SOLDIER

SOLDIER
　News, news!
TAMBURLAINE
　How now, what's the matter?　　　　　　　　　　　　110
SOLDIER
　A thousand Persian horsemen are at hand,
　Sent from the king to overcome us all.
TAMBURLAINE
　How now, my lords of Egypt and Zenocrate?
　Now must your jewels be restored again,
　And I that triumphed so be overcome?　　　　　　　115
　How say you, lordings, is not this your hope?
AGYDAS
　We hope yourself will willingly restore them.
TAMBURLAINE
　Such hope, such fortune, have the thousand horse.
　Soft ye, my lords and sweet Zenocrate,
　You must be forcèd from me ere you go.　　　　　　120
　A thousand horsemen! We five hundred foot!
　An odds too great for us to stand against.
　But are they rich? And is their armour good?
SOLDIER
　Their plumèd helms are wrought with beaten gold,
　Their swords enamelled, and about their necks　　125
　Hangs massy chains of gold down to the waist,
　In every part exceeding brave and rich.
TAMBURLAINE
　Then shall we fight courageously with them,
　Or look you I should play the orator?
TECHELLES
　No: cowards and faint-hearted runaways　　　　　130
　Look for orations when the foe is near.
　Our swords shall play the orators for us.
USUMCASANE
　Come let us meet them at the mountain foot
　And with a sudden and an hot alarm
　Drive all their horses headlong down the hill.　　135

127　*brave* splendid

TECHELLES

Come let us march.

TAMBURLAINE

Stay Techelles, ask a parley first.

The Soldiers [of TAMBURLAINE*] enter*

Open the mails, yet guard the treasure sure.
Lay out our golden wedges to the view
That their reflections may amaze the Persians,   140
And look we friendly on them when they come.
But if they offer word or violence
We'll fight five hundred men-at-arms to one
Before we part with our possession,
And 'gainst the general we will lift our swords   145
And either lanch his greedy thirsting throat
Or take him prisoner, and his chains shall serve
For manacles till he be ransomed home.

TECHELLES

I hear them come, shall we encounter them?

TAMBURLAINE

Keep all your standings and not stir a foot;   150
Myself will bide the danger of the brunt.

Enter THERIDAMAS *with others*

THERIDAMAS

Where is this Scythian Tamburlaine?

TAMBURLAINE

Whom seek'st thou Persian? I am Tamburlaine.

THERIDAMAS

[*Aside*] Tamburlaine?
A Scythian shepherd, so embellishèd   155
With nature's pride and richest furniture?
His looks do menace heaven and dare the gods,
His fiery eyes are fixed upon the earth
As if he now devised some stratagem,

138   *mails* packs, baggage
139   *wedges* ingots
146   *lanch* cut
151   *brunt* attack
154   lineation ed.
156   *furniture* equipment

19

Or meant to pierce Avernus' darksome vaults 160
And pull the triple-headed dog from hell.

TAMBURLAINE

[*To* TECHELLES] Noble and mild this Persian seems to be,
If outward habit judge the inward man.

TECHELLES

His deep affections make him passionate.

TAMBURLAINE

With what a majesty he rears his looks! 165
[*To* THERIDAMAS] In thee, thou valiant man of Persia,
I see the folly of thy emperor.
Art thou but captain of a thousand horse,
That by characters graven in thy brows
And by thy martial face and stout aspect, 170
Deservest to have the leading of an host?
Forsake thy king and do but join with me
And we will triumph over all the world.
I hold the Fates bound fast in iron chains
And with my hand turn Fortune's wheel about, 175
And sooner shall the sun fall from his sphere
Than Tamburlaine be slain or overcome.
Draw forth thy sword, thou mighty man-at-arms,
Intending but to raze my charmèd skin,
And Jove himself will stretch his hand from heaven 180
To ward the blow and shield me safe from harm.
See how he rains down heaps of gold in showers
As if he meant to give my soldiers pay,
And as a sure and grounded argument
That I shall be the monarch of the East, 185
He sends this Soldan's daughter rich and brave
To be my queen and portly emperess.
If thou wilt stay with me, renownèd man,

---

160   *Avernus* a lake anciently regarded as the entrance to the underworld
161   *And* O1 catchword (To O1 text).
      triple-headed dog Cerberus, who guarded the entrance to the underworld
164   *affections* emotions
174   *Fates* the three goddesses, Clotho, Lachesis, and Atropos, who governed human destiny
176   According to Ptolemaic astronomy, the sun moved in an orbit around the earth.
179   *raze* graze
187   *portly* stately
      emperess original spelling here and elsewhere retained for the sake of the metre

And lead thy thousand horse with my conduct,
Besides thy share of this Egyptian prize   190
Those thousand horse shall sweat with martial spoil
Of conquered kingdoms and of cities sacked.
Both we will walk upon the lofty cliffs,
And Christian merchants, that with Russian stems
Plow up huge furrows in the Caspian Sea,   195
Shall vail to us as lords of all the lake.
Both we will reign as consuls of the earth,
And mighty kings shall be our senators.
Jove sometime maskèd in a shepherd's weed,
And, by those steps that he hath scaled the heavens,   200
May we become immortal like the gods.
Join with me now in this my mean estate
(I call it mean, because being yet obscure
The nations far removed admire me not)
And when my name and honour shall be spread   205
As far as Boreas claps his brazen wings
Or fair Boötes sends his cheerful light,
Then shalt thou be competitor with me,
And sit with Tamburlaine in all his majesty.

THERIDAMAS

Not Hermes, prolocutor to the gods,   210
Could use persuasions more pathetical.

TECHELLES

Nor are Apollo's oracles more true
Than thou shalt find my vaunts substantial.

TAMBURLAINE

We are his friends, and if the Persian king

189   *conduct* direction
194   *merchants* merchant ships
       stems prows and hence, by synecdoche, ships
196   *vail* lower the topsail in homage
199   *maskèd ... weed* disguised himself as a shepherd
200   *that* by which
206–7 *As ... light* as far as Boreas (the north wind) blows or Boötes (a northern constel-
       lation) shines; i.e. the northern limit of the empire
208   *competitor* partner
210   *Hermes* the god of eloquence
       prolocutor spokesman
211   *pathetical* moving
213   *vaunts* boasts

21

Should offer present dukedoms to our state,   215
We think it loss to make exchange for that
We are assured of by our friend's success.

USUMCASANE
And kingdoms at the least we all expect,
Besides the honour in assured conquests,
Where kings shall crouch unto our conquering swords   220
And hosts of soldiers stand amazed at us,
When with their fearful tongues they shall confess
These are the men that all the world admires.

THERIDAMAS
What strong enchantments 'tice my yielding soul?
Ah, these resolvèd noble Scythians!   225
But shall I prove a traitor to my king?

TAMBURLAINE
No, but the trusty friend of Tamburlaine.

THERIDAMAS
Won with thy words and conquered with thy looks,
I yield myself, my men and horse to thee
To be partaker of thy good or ill,   230
As long as life maintains Theridamas.

TAMBURLAINE
Theridamas my friend, take here my hand,
Which is as much as if I swore by heaven
And called the gods to witness of my vow –
Thus shall my heart be still combined with thine   235
Until our bodies turn to elements
And both our souls aspire celestial thrones.
Techelles and Casane, welcome him.

TECHELLES
Welcome, renownèd Persian, to us all.

USUMCASANE
Long may Theridamas remain with us.   240

TAMBURLAINE
These are my friends in whom I more rejoice
Than doth the King of Persia in his crown,

---

215   *offer . . . state* offer to make us dukes immediately
224   *tice* entice
225   *Ah* ed. (Are O1)
235   *still* forever

And by the love of Pylades and Orestes,
Whose statues we adore in Scythia,
Thyself and them shall never part from me   245
Before I crown you kings in Asia.
Make much of them, gentle Theridamas,
And they will never leave thee till the death.

THERIDAMAS

Nor thee nor them, thrice noble Tamburlaine,
Shall want my heart to be with gladness pierced   250
To do you honour and security.

TAMBURLAINE

A thousand thanks, worthy Theridamas.
And now, fair madam, and my noble lords,
If you will willingly remain with me,
You shall have honours as your merits be,   255
Or else you shall be forced with slavery.

AGYDAS

We yield unto thee, happy Tamburlaine.

TAMBURLAINE

For you then, madam, I am out of doubt.

ZENOCRATE

I must be pleased perforce, wretched Zenocrate!

Exeunt

---

243   *Pylades and Orestes* Pylades was the faithful friend of Orestes, helping him in the
      murder of his mother and sharing his exile and suffering.
249–50 *Nor . . . heart* Neither to thee nor to them . . . shall my heart fail
251   *security* protection

ACT II, SCENE i

[*Enter*] COSROE, MENAPHON, ORTYGIUS,
CENEUS, *with other Soldiers*

COSROE

Thus far are we towards Theridamas
And valiant Tamburlaine, the man of fame.
The man that in the forehead of his fortune
Bears figures of renown and miracle.
But tell me that hast seen him, Menaphon,   5
What stature wields he, and what personage?

MENAPHON

Of stature tall and straightly fashionèd,
Like his desire, lift upwards and divine;
So large of limbs, his joints so strongly knit,
Such breadth of shoulders as might mainly bear   10
Old Atlas' burden; 'twixt his manly pitch,
A pearl more worth than all the world is placed,
Wherein by curious sovereignty of art
Are fixed his piercing instruments of sight,
Whose fiery circles bear encompassèd   15
A heaven of heavenly bodies in their spheres
That guides his steps and actions to the throne
Where honour sits invested royally;
Pale of complexion, wrought in him with passion,
Thirsting with sovereignty, with love of arms,   20
His lofty brows in folds do figure death,
And in their smoothness, amity and life;
About them hangs a knot of amber hair,

 3–4 An allusion to the supposed Muslim belief that Allah wrote every man's fate in signs
       upon his forehead.
   8 *lift* lifted
  10 *mainly* entirely
  11 *Atlas' burden* Atlas the Titan bore the heavens upon his shoulders.
       pitch shoulders
  12 *pearl* i.e. his head
15–17 *Whose . . . throne* The glowing spheres of his eyes contain a constellation of stars
       and planets favourable to his gaining the throne.
  21 *in folds* when furrowed

Wrapped in curls as fierce Achilles' was,
On which the breath of heaven delights to play,   25
Making it dance with wanton majesty;
His arms and fingers long and sinewy,
Betokening valour and excess of strength –
In every part proportioned like the man
Should make the world subdued to Tamburlaine.   30

COSROE

Well hast thou portrayed in thy terms of life
The face and personage of a wondrous man.
Nature doth strive with Fortune and his stars
To make him famous in accomplished worth,
And well his merits show him to be made   35
His fortune's master and the king of men
That could persuade at such a sudden pinch,
With reasons of his valour and his life,
A thousand sworn and overmatching foes.
Then, when our powers in points of swords are joined   40
And closed in compass of the killing bullet,
Though strait the passage and the port be made
That leads to palace of my brother's life,
Proud is his fortune if we pierce it not.
And when the princely Persian diadem   45
Shall overweigh his weary witless head
And fall like mellowed fruit, with shakes of death,
In fair Persia noble Tamburlaine
Shall be my regent and remain as king.

ORTYGIUS

In happy hour we have set the crown   50
Upon your kingly head, that seeks our honour

---

24   *Achilles* the greatest Greek warrior in the Trojan war
26   *wanton* unrestrained
27   *sinewy* ed. (snowy O1)
29–30   *In . . . Tamburlame* Each separate part of him is perfectly proportioned, as he himself is, to subdue the world.
31   *terms of life* vivid terms
37   *pinch* critical situation
41   *compass* range
42   *port* entrance
42–4   Cosroe compares his brother's body to a besieged town, his heart, the seat of his life, to the palace.

In joining with the man ordained by heaven
To further every action to the best.

CENEUS

He that with shepherds and a little spoil
Durst in disdain of wrong and tyranny   55
Defend his freedom 'gainst a monarchy,
What will he do supported by a king,
Leading a troop of gentlemen and lords,
And stuffed with treasure for his highest thoughts?

COSROE

And such shall wait on worthy Tamburlaine.   60
Our army will be forty thousand strong
When Tamburlaine and brave Theridamas
Have met us by the river Araris,
And all conjoined to meet the witless king
That now is marching near to Parthia,   65
And with unwilling soldiers faintly armed,
To seek revenge on me and Tamburlaine –
To whom, sweet Menaphon, direct me straight.

MENAPHON

I will my lord.

Exeunt

55   *Durst* dared
63   *river Araris* probably the Araxes, which flows into the Caspian Sea
65   *Parthia* a kingdom south-east of the Caspian

ACT II, SCENE ii

[Enter] MYCETES, MEANDER, *with other*
Lords and Soldiers

MYCETES

Come, my Meander, let us to this gear.
I tell you true my heart is swoll'n with wrath
On this same thievish villain Tamburlaine,
And of that false Cosroe, my traitorous brother.
Would it not grieve a king to be so abused,   5
And have a thousand horsemen ta'en away?
And, which is worst, to have his diadem
Sought for by such scald knaves as love him not?
I think it would. Well then, by heavens I swear,
Aurora shall not peep out of her doors,   10
But I will have Cosroe by the head
And kill proud Tamburlaine with point of sword.
Tell you the rest, Meander, I have said.

MEANDER

Then having passed Armenian deserts now,
And pitched our tents under the Georgian hills,   15
Whose tops are covered with Tartarian thieves
That lie in ambush, waiting for a prey,
What should we do but bid them battle straight
And rid the world of those detested troops,
Lest if we let them linger here a while   20
They gather strength by power of fresh supplies?
This country swarms with vile outrageous men
That live by rapine and by lawless spoil,
Fit soldiers for the wicked Tamburlaine,
And he that could with gifts and promises   25
Inveigle him that led a thousand horse

1   *gear* business
3–4 *On, of* here used interchangeably to mean 'because of
5   *abused* deceived
8   *scald* scurvy, low
10   *Aurora* goddess of the dawn
15   *pitched* O2–3, Q (pitch O1)
18   *straight* immediately

And make him false his faith unto his king,
Will quickly win such as are like himself.
Therefore cheer up your minds, prepare to fight.
He that can take or slaughter Tamburlaine   30
Shall rule the province of Albania.
Who brings that traitor's head Theridamas
Shall have a government in Media,
Beside the spoil of him and all his train.
But if Cosroe (as our spials say,   35
And as we know) remains with Tamburlaine,
His highness' pleasure is that he should live
And be reclaimed with princely lenity.

[*Enter a* SPY]

SPY

An hundred horsemen of my company
Scouting abroad upon these champion plains   40
Have viewed the army of the Scythians,
Which make reports it far exceeds the king's.

MEANDER

Suppose they be in number infinite,
Yet being void of martial discipline,
All running headlong after greedy spoils   45
And more regarding gain than victory,
Like to the cruel brothers of the earth
Sprung of the teeth of dragons venomous,
Their careless swords shall lanch their fellows' throats
And make us triumph in their overthrow.   50

MYCETES

Was there such brethren, sweet Meander, say,
That sprung of teeth of dragons venomous?

MEANDER

So poets say, my lord.

MYCETES

And 'tis a pretty toy to be a poet.

27   *false* betray
31   *Albania* in Ortelius' atlas, the district lying along the west coast of the Caspian
35   *spials* spies
40   *champion plains* stretches of level grassland
47–8 Cadmus sowed the earth with dragons' teeth from which sprang armed men who
      began to fight one another.
54   *toy* trifling pastime

28

Well, well, Meander thou art deeply read   55
And, having thee, I have a jewel sure.
Go on, my lord, and give your charge I say.
Thy wit will make us conquerors today.

MEANDER

Then noble soldiers, to entrap these thieves
That live confounded in disordered troops,   60
If wealth or riches may prevail with them
We have our camels laden all with gold,
Which you that be but common soldiers
Shall fling in every corner of the field,
And while the base-born Tartars take it up,   65
You, fighting more for honour than for gold,
Shall massacre those greedy-minded slaves;
And when their scattered army is subdued
And you march on their slaughtered carcasses,
Share equally the gold that bought their lives   70
And live like gentlemen in Persia.
Strike up the drum and march courageously,
Fortune herself doth sit upon our crests.

MYCETES

He tells you true, my masters, so he does.
Drums, why sound ye not when Meander speaks?   75

Exeunt

ACT II, SCENE iii

[*Enter*] COSROE, TAMBURLAINE, THERIDAMAS,
TECHELLES, USUMCASANE, ORTYGIUS, *with others*

COSROE

    Now, worthy Tamburlaine, have I reposed
    In thy approvèd fortunes all my hope –
    What think'st thou, man, shall come of our attempts?
    For even as from assured oracle,
    I take thy doom for satisfaction.   5

TAMBURLAINE

    And so mistake you not a whit, my lord,
    For fates and oracles of heaven have sworn
    To royalize the deeds of Tamburlaine
    And make them blest that share in his attempts.
    And doubt you not but, if you favour me   10
    And let my fortunes and my valour sway
    To some direction in your martial deeds,
    The world will strive with hosts of men-at-arms
    To swarm unto the ensign I support.
    The host of Xerxes, which by fame is said   15
    To drink the mighty Parthian Araris,
    Was but a handful to that we will have.
    Our quivering lances shaking in the air
    And bullets like Jove's dreadful thunderbolts,
    Enrolled in flames and fiery smouldering mists,   20
    Shall threat the gods more than Cyclopian wars;
    And with our sun-bright armour as we march

    1   *reposed* placed
    2   *approvèd* successfully tried
    5   *doom* judgement, opinion
        satisfaction certainty
    7   *of* ed. (O1 omits)
    8   *royalize* celebrate, make famous
 11–12   *sway . . . in* have some authority over
 15–16   The vast army assembled by Xerxes for the invasion of Greece was said to have drunk
        rivers dry.
   19   *bullets* projectiles
   20   *Enrolled* enfolded
   21   *Cyclopian wars* Marlowe apparently identifies the Cyclopes with the Titans who
        warred against Jove.

We'll chase the stars from heaven and dim their eyes
That stand and muse at our admirèd arms.

THERIDAMAS

You see, my lord, what working words he hath,   25
But when you see his actions top his speech,
Your speech will stay or so extol his worth
As I shall be commended and excused
For turning my poor charge to his direction.
And these his two renownèd friends, my lord,   30
Would make one thrust and strive to be retained
In such a great degree of amity.

TAMBURLAINE

With duty and with amity we yield
Our utmost service to the fair Cosroe.

COSROE

Which I esteem as portion of my crown.   35
Usumcasane and Techelles both,
When she that rules in Rhamnis' golden gates
And makes a passage for all prosperous arms
Shall make me solely emperor of Asia,
Then shall your meeds and valours be advanced   40
To rooms of honour and nobility.

TAMBURLAINE

Then haste, Cosroe, to be king alone,
That I with these my friends and all my men
May triumph in our long-expected fate.
The king your brother is now hard at hand: 45
Meet with the fool, and rid your royal shoulders
Of such a burden as outweighs the sands
And all the craggy rocks of Caspea.

[*Enter a* MESSENGER]

MESSENGER

My lord, we have discovered the enemy

25   *working* effective, moving
26   *top* ed. (stop O1) exceed
27   *Your . . . stay* you will be at a loss for words
33   *and* Q (O1 omits)
37   *Rhamnis' golden gates* the temple of Nemesis (Vengeance) at Rhamnus in Attica
40   *meeds* merits
41   *rooms* places
48   *Caspea* the Caspian Sea

Ready to charge you with a mighty army.   50

COSROE

Come, Tamburlaine, now whet thy wingèd sword
And lift thy lofty arm into the clouds
That it may reach the king of Persia's crown
And set it safe on my victorious head.

TAMBURLAINE

See where it is, the keenest curtle-axe   55
That e'er made passage thorough Persian arms.
These are the wings shall make it fly as swift
As doth the lightning or the breath of heaven,
And kill as sure as it swiftly flies.

COSROE

Thy words assure me of kind success.   60
Go, valiant soldier, go before and charge
The fainting army of that foolish king.

TAMBURLAINE

Usumcasane and Techelles come,
We are enough to scare the enemy,
And more than needs to make an emperor.   65

[*Exeunt*]

60   *kind* favourable

ACT II, SCENE iv

To the battle, and MYCETES *comes out alone with
his crown in his hand, offering to hide it*

MYCETES

    Accursed be he that first invented war!
    They knew not, ah, they knew not, simple men,
    How those were hit by pelting cannon shot
    Stand staggering like a quivering aspen leaf
    Fearing the force of Boreas' boisterous blasts.   5
    In what a lamentable case were I
    If nature had not given me wisdom's lore?
    For kings are clouts that every man shoots at.
    Our crown the pin that thousands seek to cleave.
    Therefore in policy I think it good   10
    To hide it close, a goodly stratagem,
    And far from any man that is a fool.
    So shall I not be known, or if I be,
    They cannot take away my crown from me.
    Here will I hide it in this simple hole.   15

Enter TAMBURLAINE

TAMBURLAINE

    What, fearful coward, straggling from the camp
    When kings themselves are present in the field?

MYCETES

    Thou liest.

TAMBURLAINE

    Base villain, dar'st thou give the lie?

MYCETES

    Away, I am the king! Go, touch me not!   20

       Scene iv ed. (O1 omits)
  0.2 s.d. *offering* endeavouring
    3 *those were* those who were
    5 *Boreas* the north wind
    8 *clouts* The clout is the central mark of the target in archery.
    9 *pin* nail holding the clout in place
  11 *close* secretly
  19 *give the lie* accuse a person of lying

Thou break'st the law of arms unless thou kneel
And cry me 'Mercy, noble king!'

TAMBURLAINE

Are you the witty king of Persia?

MYCETES

Ay, marry, am I; have you any suit to me?

TAMBURLAINE

I would entreat you to speak but three wise words.   25

MYCETES

So I can when I see my time.

TAMBURLAINE

Is this your crown?

MYCETES

Ay, didst thou ever see a fairer?

TAMBURLAINE

You will not sell it, will ye?

MYCETES

Such another word, and I will have thee executed.   30
Come give it me.

TAMBURLAINE

No, I took it prisoner.

MYCETES

You lie, I gave it you.

TAMBURLAINE

Then 'tis mine.

MYCETES

No, I mean, I let you keep it.   35

TAMBURLAINE

Well, I mean you shall have it again.
Here, take it for a while, I lend it thee
Till I may see thee hemmed with armed men:
Then shalt thou see me pull it from thy head.
Thou art no match for mighty Tamburlaine.   [*Exit*]   40

MYCETES

O gods, is this Tamburlaine the thief?
I marvel much he stole it not away.

     Sound trumpets to the battle, and he runs in

23 *witty* wise

34

ACT II, SCENE v

[Enter] COSROE, TAMBURLAINE, THERIDAMAS,
MENAPHON, MEANDER, ORTYGIUS, TECHELLES,
USUMCASANE, *with others*

TAMBURLAINE

    Hold thee, Cosroe, wear two imperial crowns.
    Think thee invested now as royally,
    Even by the mighty hand of Tamburlaine,
    And if as many kings as could encompass thee
    With greatest pomp had crowned thee emperor.   5

COSROE

    So do I, thrice renownèd man-at-arms,
    And none shall keep the crown but Tamburlaine:
    Thee do I make my regent of Persia
    And general lieutenant of my armies.
    Meander, you that were our brother's guide   10
    And chiefest counsellor in all his acts,
    Since he is yielded to the stroke of war,
    On your submission we with thanks excuse
    And give you equal place in our affairs.

MEANDER

    Most happy emperor, in humblest terms   15
    I vow my service to your majesty
    With utmost virtue of my faith and duty.

COSROE

    Thanks, good Meander. Then Cosroe reign
    And govern Persia in her former pomp.
    Now send embassage to thy neighbour kings   20
    And let them know the Persian king is changed
    From one that knew not what a king should do
    To one that can command what 'longs thereto.
    And now we will to fair Persepolis
    With twenty thousand expert soldiers.   25
    The lords and captains of my brother's camp

Scene v ed. (O1 omits)
17   *virtue* commitment
23   *'longs* belongs

With little slaughter take Meander's course
And gladly yield them to my gracious rule.
Ortygius and Menaphon, my trusty friends,
Now will I gratify your former good   30
And grace your calling with a greater sway.

ORTYGIUS

And as we ever aimed at your behoof
And sought your state all honour it deserved,
So will we with our powers and our lives
Endeavour to preserve and prosper it.   35

COSROE

I will not thank thee, sweet Ortygius –
Better replies shall prove my purposes.
And now, Lord Tamburlaine, my brother's camp
I leave to thee and to Theridamas
To follow me to fair Persepolis.   40
Then will we march to all those Indian mines
My witless brother to the Christians lost
And ransom them with fame and usury.
And till thou overtake me, Tamburlaine,
Staying to order all the scattered troops,   45
Farewell lord regent and his happy friends –
I long to sit upon my brother's throne.

MENAPHON

Your majesty shall shortly have your wish
And ride in triumph through Persepolis.

Exeunt [all except] TAMBURLAINE, TECHELLES,
THERIDAMAS, [*and*] USUMCASANE

TAMBURLAINE

And ride in triumph through Persepolis?   50
Is it not brave to be a king, Techelles?
Usumcasane and Theridamas,

27   *course* example
30   *gratify . . . good* repay your service
31   *grace . . . sway* give you a more authoritative position
32   *aimed* O3, Q (and O1)
      behoof profit
33   *sought your state* sought for your position
37   *Better replies* i.e. actions
38   *camp* troops
43   *with . . . usury* to our glory and advantage
51   *brave* wonderful

Is it not passing brave to be a king
And ride in triumph through Persepolis?

TECHELLES

O, my lord, 'tis sweet and full of pomp.   55

USUMCASANE

To be a king is half to be a god.

THERIDAMAS

A god is not so glorious as a king.
I think the pleasure they enjoy in heaven
Cannot compare with kingly joys in earth.
To wear a crown enchased with pearl and gold,   60
Whose virtues carry with it life and death,
To ask and have, command and be obeyed,
When looks breed love, with looks to gain the prize –
Such power attractive shines in princes' eyes.

TAMBURLAINE

Why, say, Theridamas, wilt thou be a king?   65

THERIDAMAS

Nay, though I praise it, I can live without it.

TAMBURLAINE

What says my other friends, will you be kings?

TECHELLES

Ay, if I could, with all my heart my lord.

TAMBURLAINE

Why that's well said, Techelles, so would I,
And so would you, my masters, would you not?   70

USUMCASANE

What then, my lord?

TAMBURLAINE

Why then, Casane, shall we wish for ought
The world affords in greatest novelty
And rest attemptless, faint and destitute?
Methinks we should not. I am strongly moved   75
That if I should desire the Persian crown
I could attain it with a wondrous ease,
And would not all our soldiers soon consent
If we should aim at such a dignity?

53 *passing* exceedingly
61 *virtues* powers
73 *in . . . novelty* no matter how new and rare
75 *moved* inwardly convinced

THERIDAMAS

    I know they would, with our persuasions.   80

TAMBURLAINE

    Why then, Theridamas, I'll first assay

    To get the Persian kingdom to myself,

    Then thou for Parthia, they for Scythia and Media.

    And if I prosper, all shall be as sure

    As if the Turk, the Pope, Afric and Greece   85

    Came creeping to us with their crowns apace.

TECHELLES

    Then shall we send to this triumphing king

    And bid him battle for his novel crown?

USUMCASANE

    Nay quickly then, before his room be hot.

TAMBURLAINE

    'Twill prove a pretty jest, in faith, my friends.   90

THERIDAMAS

    A jest to charge on twenty thousand men?

    I judge the purchase more important far.

TAMBURLAINE

    Judge by thyself, Theridamas, not me,

    For presently Techelles here shall haste

    And bid him battle ere he pass too far   95

    And lose more labour than the gain will quite.

    Then shalt thou see the Scythian Tamburlaine

    Make but a jest to win the Persian crown.

    Techelles, take a thousand horse with thee

    And bid him turn his back to war with us   100

    That only made him king to make us sport.

    We will not steal upon him cowardly,

    But give him warning and more warriors.

    Haste thee, Techelles, we will follow thee.

    What saith Theridamas?

THERIDAMAS   Go on, for me.   105

                                  [*Exeunt*]

---

81   *assay* attempt

86   *apace* immediately

88   *novel* newly gained

89   *before . . . hot* before he is well established in his new position

92   *purchase* undertaking   94   *presently* immediately

96   *than . . . quite* than the benefit of defeating Cosroe would requite

105   *for me* as far as I am concerned

[Enter] COSROE, MEANDER, ORTYGIUS, MENAPHON,
with other Soldiers

COSROE

    What means this devilish shepherd to aspire
    With such a giantly presumption
    To cast up hills against the face of heaven
    And dare the force of angry Jupiter?
    But as he thrust them underneath the hills   5
    And pressed out fire from their burning jaws.
    So will I send this monstrous slave to hell
    Where flames shall ever feed upon his soul.

MEANDER

    Some powers divine, or else infernal, mixed
    Their angry seeds at his conception: 10
    For he was never sprung of human race
    Since with the spirit of his fearful pride
    He dares so doubtlessly resolve of rule
    And by profession be ambitious.

ORTYGIUS

    What god or fiend or spirit of the earth,   15
    Or monster turned into a manly shape,
    Or of what mould or mettle he be made,
    What star or state soever govern him,
    Let us put on our meet encountering minds
    And, in detesting such a devilish thief,   20
    In love of honour and defence of right
    Be armed against the hate of such a foe,
    Whether from earth or hell or heaven he grow.

---

3   *cast . . . heaven* i.e. as did the Titans who warred against Jupiter
5   *them* i.e. the Titans. Recalling Enceladus' imprisonment beneath Mount Aetna,
     Marlowe imagines all the defeated Titans as imprisoned under mountains.
13 *doubtlessly* without hesitation
     resolve of determine to
14 *by profession* openly
19 *Let . . . minds* let us put ourselves in a proper frame of mind to meet the challenge

COSROE

 Nobly resolved, my good Ortygius.
 And since we all have sucked one wholesome air   25
 And with the same proportion of elements
 Resolve, I hope we are resembled
 Vowing our loves to equal death and life.
 Let's cheer our soldiers to encounter him,
 That grievous image of ingratitude,   30
 That fiery thirster after sovereignty,
 And burn him in the fury of that flame
 That none can quench but blood and empery.
 Resolve, my lords and loving soldiers, now
 To save your king and country from decay.   35
 Then strike up drum, and all the stars that make
 The loathsome circle of my dated life
 Direct my weapon to his barbarous heart,
 That thus opposeth him against the gods
 And scorns the powers that govern Persia.   40

           [*Exeunt*]

26–7 *And . . . Resolve* and will decompose into the same elements
 27 *resembled* alike in
 34 *Resolve* Be resolute
 37 *dated* limited, transitory

ACT II, SCENE vii

Enter to the battle, and after the battle enter COSROE
wounded, THERIDAMAS, TAMBURLAINE, TECHELLES,
USUMCASANE, *with others*

COSROE

Barbarous and bloody Tamburlaine,
Thus to deprive me of my crown and life!
Treacherous and false Theridamas,
Even at the morning of my happy state,
Scarce being seated in my royal throne,   5
To work my downfall and untimely end!
An uncouth pain torments my grievèd soul
And death arrests the organ of my voice,
Who, entering at the breach thy sword hath made,
Sacks every vein and artier of my heart.   10
Bloody and insatiate Tamburlaine!

TAMBURLAINE

The thirst of reign and sweetness of a crown,
That caused the eldest son of heavenly Ops
To thrust his doting father from his chair
And place himself in the empyreal heaven,   15
Moved me to manage arms against thy state.
What better precedent than mighty Jove?
Nature that framed us of four elements
Warring within our breasts for regiment,
Doth teach us all to have aspiring minds: 20
Our souls, whose faculties can comprehend
The wondrous architecture of the world

---

0   s.d. The stage direction here suggests that the battle begins onstage, moves offstage,
    and culminates in the re-entry of the wounded Cosroe and Tamburlaine victorious.
    In O1 there is no new scene here, nor any indication that Cosroe and his followers
    leave the stage at the end of II.vi, prior to the onset of the battle.

7   *uncouth* strange, novel

10 *artier* artery

13 *eldest . . . Ops* Jupiter, the yougest (not the eldest) son of Saturn and Ops

15 *empyreal heaven* empyrean, i.e. the outermost sphere of the universe, with a sar-
    donic pun on 'imperial'

18 *four elements* i.e. the earth, water, air, and fire of ancient physiology

19 *regiment* rule

41

And measure every wand'ring planet's course,
Still climbing after knowledge infinite
And always moving as the restless spheres,   25
Wills us to wear ourselves and never rest
Until we reach the ripest fruit of all.
That perfect bliss and sole felicity,
The sweet fruition of an earthly crown.

THERIDAMAS

And that made me to join with Tamburlaine,   30
For he is gross and like the massy earth
That moves not upwards nor by princely deeds
Doth mean to soar above the highest sort.

TAMBURLAINE

And that made us, the friends of Tamburlaine,
To lift our swords against the Persian king.   35

USUMCASANE

For as when Jove did thrust old Saturn down,
Neptune and Dis gained each of them a crown,
So do we hope to reign in Asia,
If Tamburlaine be placed in Persia.

COSROE

The strangest men that ever nature made!   40
I know not how to take their tyrannies.
My bloodless body waxeth chill and cold
And with my blood my life slides through my wound.
My soul begins to take her flight to hell
And summons all my senses to depart.   45
The heat and moisture, which did feed each other
For want of nourishment to feed them both
Is dry and cold, and now doth ghastly death
With greedy talents gripe my bleeding heart

---

25   *restless spheres* the eternally revolving hollow globes that were believed to carry the
      planets and the stars around the earth.
31–3 *For . . . sort* anyone who does not aspire to soar upwards is gross and earth-bound
37   Neptune, the god of the sea, and Dis, the god of the underworld, were the brothers
      of Jove (i.e., Jupiter).
46–8 *The heat . . . cold* 'Blood, the element which combines the properties of moisture
      and heat, being removed, the balance of the "temperament" or constitution is
      destroyed and only the properties of cold and dryness, those of the melancholy
      humour in the constitution of man, and of the earth in the material universe,
      remain' (Ellis-Fermor).
49   *talents* talons

And like a harpy tires on my life.   50
Theridamas and Tamburlaine, I die,
And fearful vengeance light upon you both.
     [*Dies.* TAMBURLAINE] *takes the crown and puts it on*

TAMBURLAINE
Not all the curses which the Furies breathe
Shall make me leave so rich a prize as this.
Theridamas, Techelles, and the rest,   55
Who think you now is king of Persia?

ALL
Tamburlaine! Tamburlaine!

TAMBURLAINE
Though Mars himself, the angry god of arms,
And all the earthly potentates conspire
To dispossess me of this diadem,   60
Yet will I wear it in despite of them
As great commander of this eastern world,
If you but say that Tamburlaine shall reign.

ALL
Long live Tamburlaine and reign in Asia!

TAMBURLAINE
So now it is more surer on my head   65
Than if the gods had held a parliament
And all pronounced me king of Persia.

                          [*Exeunt*]

50   *harpy* O2 (Harpyr O1), monstrous bird of prey with a woman's face
      tires tears flesh in feeding (a term from falconry)
53   *Furies* the avenging deities of classical mythology
59   *potentates* monarchs

ACT III, SCENE i

[*Enter*] BAJAZETH, *the* KINGS OF FEZ, MOROCCO *and*
ARGIER, [BASSOES], *with others, in great pomp*

BAJAZETH

    Great kings of Barbary and my portly bassoes,
    We hear the Tartars and the eastern thieves
    Under the conduct of one Tamburlaine
    Presume a bickering with your emperor,
    And thinks to rouse us from our dreadful siege   5
    Of the famous Grecian Constantinople.
    You know our army is invincible:
    As many circumcised Turks we have
    And warlike bands of Christians renied
    As hath the ocean or the Terrene sea   10
    Small drops of water when the moon begins
    To join in one her semi-circled horns.
    Yet would we not be braved with foreign power,
    Nor raise our siege before the Grecians yield
    Or breathless lie before the city walls.   15

KING OF FEZ

    Renowned emperor and mighty general,
    What if you sent the bassoes of your guard
    To charge him to remain in Asia,
    Or else to threaten death and deadly arms
    As from the mouth of mighty Bajazeth?   20

BAJAZETH

    Hie thee, my basso, fast to Persia,
    Tell him thy lord the Turkish emperor.
    Dread lord of Afric, Europe and Asia,
    Great king and conqueror of Graecia,
    The ocean, Terrene, and the coal-black sea,   25
    The high and highest monarch of the world.

    1   *Barbary* the north coast of Africa
        bassoes pashas
    9   *renied* apostate
    10   *Terrene sea* the Mediterranean
  11–12   *moon . . . horns* i.e. when the moon is full and the tides are high
    13   *braved with* harassed by

Wills and commands (for say not I entreat)
Not once to set his foot in Africa,
Or spread his colours in Graecia,
Lest he incur the fury of my wrath.   30
Tell him I am content to take a truce
Because I hear he bears a valiant mind.
But if presuming on his silly power
He be so mad to manage arms with me,
Then stay thou with him, say I bid thee so,   35
And if before the sun have measured heaven
With triple circuit thou regreet us not,
We mean to take his morning's next arise
For messenger he will not be reclaimed,
And mean to fetch thee in despite of him.   40

BASSO

Most great and puissant monarch of the earth,
Your basso will accomplish your behest
And show your pleasure to the Persian
As fits the legate of the stately Turk.

KING OF ARGIER

They say he is the king of Persia,   45
But if he dare attempt to stir your siege
'Twere requisite he should be ten times more,
For all flesh quakes at your magnificence.

BAJAZETH

True, Argier, and tremble at my looks.

KING OF MOROCCO

The spring is hindered by your smothering host,   50
For neither rain can fall upon the earth
Nor sun reflex his virtuous beams thereon,
The ground is mantled with such multitudes.

BAJAZETH

All this is true as holy Mahomet,
And all the trees are blasted with our breaths.   55

---

33 *silly* weak, unskilled
38 *his* the sun's
39 *For . . . reclaimed* as a sign that Tamburlaine will not relent
41 *puissant* mighty
52 *reflex* cast

KING OF FEZ

> What thinks your greatness best to be achieved
> In pursuit of the city's overthrow?

BAJAZETH

> I will the captive pioners of Argier
> Cut off the water that by leaden pipes
> Runs to the city from the mountain Carnon;   60
> Two thousand horse shall forage up and down
> That no relief or succour come by land;
> And all the sea my galleys countermand.
> Then shall our footmen lie within the trench,
> And with their cannons mouthed like Orcus' gulf   65
> Batter the walls, and we will enter in:
> And thus the Grecians shall be conquered.

> > > > > > > > *[Exeunt]*

---

58   *pioners* advance guard of trench-diggers
63   *countermand* control
65   *Orcus' gulf* hell. Orcus was one of several names for Hades.

ACT III, SCENE ii

[*Enter*] AGYDAS, ZENOCRATE, ANIPPE, *with others*

[AGYDAS]
    Madam Zenocrate, may I presume
    To know the cause of these unquiet fits
    That work such trouble to your wonted rest?
    'Tis more than pity such a heavenly face
    Should by heart's sorrow wax so wan and pale,   5
    When your offensive rape by Tamburlaine,
    Which of your whole displeasures should be most.
    Hath seemed to be digested long ago.

ZENOCRATE
    Although it be digested long ago,
    As his exceeding favours have deserved,   10
    And might content the Queen of Heaven as well
    As it hath changed my first conceived disdain,
    Yet, since, a farther passion feeds my thoughts
    With ceaseless and disconsolate conceits,
    Which dyes my looks so lifeless as they are,   15
    And might, if my extremes had full events,
    Make me the ghastly counterfeit of death.

AGYDAS
    Eternal heaven sooner be dissolved,
    And all that pierceth Phoebe's silver eye,
    Before such hap fall to Zenocrate.   20

ZENOCRATE
    Ah, life and soul, still hover in his breast,
    And leave my body senseless as the earth,
    Or else unite you to his life and soul,
    That I may live and die with Tamburlaine.

---

  6   *rape* seizure
 11   *Queen of Heaven* Juno
 14   *conceits* fancies
 16   *extremes* violent passions
       events expression in action
 17   *counterfeit* likeness
 19   *all . . . eye* all that the moon beholds

Enter [behind], TAMBURLAINE *with* TECHELLES
and others

AGYDAS

With Tamburlaine? Ah, fair Zenocrate,   25
Let not a man so vile and barbarous,
That holds you from your father in despite
And keeps you from the honours of a queen,
Being supposed his worthless concubine,
Be honoured with your love but for necessity.   30
So now the mighty Soldan hears of you,
Your highness needs not doubt but in short time
He will with Tamburlaine's destruction
Redeem you from this deadly servitude.

ZENOCRATE

Leave to wound me with these words,   35
And speak of Tamburlaine as he deserves.
The entertainment we have had of him
Is far from villainy or servitude,
And might in noble minds be counted princely.

AGYDAS

How can you fancy one that looks so fierce,   40
Only disposed to martial stratagems?
Who when he shall embrace you in his arms
Will tell how many thousand men he slew,
And when you look for amorous discourse
Will rattle forth his facts of war and blood,   45
Too harsh a subject for your dainty ears.

ZENOCRATE

As looks the sun through Nilus' flowing stream,
Or when the morning holds him in her arms,
So looks my lordly love, fair Tamburlaine;
His talk much sweeter than the Muses' song   50
They sung for honour 'gainst Pierides,

---

31   *So* Provided that
35   *Leave* Cease
37   *entertainment* treatment
40   *fancy* love
50–1   The nine daughters of King Fierus were defeated by the Muses in a singing contest
       and transformed into birds.

Or when Minerva did with Neptune strive,
And higher would I rear my estimate
Than Juno, sister to the highest god,
If I were matched with mighty Tamburlaine.   55

AGYDAS

Yet be not so inconstant in your love,
But let the young Arabian live in hope
After your rescue to enjoy his choice.
You see though first the King of Persia,
Being a shepherd, seemed to love you much,   60
Now in his majesty he leaves those looks,
Those words of favour and those comfortings,
And gives no more than common courtesies.

ZENOCRATE

Thence rise the tears that so distain my cheeks,
Fearing his love through my unworthiness.   65

TAMBURLAINE *goes to her, and takes her away lovingly*
by the hand, looking wrathfully on AGYDAS,
and says nothing.

[*Exeunt all except* AGYDAS]

AGYDAS

Betrayed by fortune and suspicious love,
Threatened with frowning wrath and jealousy,
Surprised with fear of hideous revenge,
I stand aghast; but most astonièd
To see his choler shut in secret thoughts   70
And wrapped in silence of his angry soul.
Upon his brows was portrayed ugly death,
And in his eyes the fury of his heart,
That shine as comets, menacing revenge,
And casts a pale complexion on his cheeks.   75
As when the seaman sees the Hyades
Gather an army of Cimmerian clouds

. 52 Minerva (Athene, goddess of wisdom) and Neptune (Poseidon, god of the sea) strove
for control of Athens.
65 *Fearing his love* fearing to lose his love
69 *astonièd* astonished
74 *comets* signs of disaster
76 *Hyades* a constellation of seven stars which were supposed to bring rain if they rose
at the same time as the sun
77 *Cimmerian* dark. The Cimmerii were said to live in perpetual darkness.

49

(Auster and Aquilon with wingèd steeds
All sweating tilt about the watery heavens
With shivering spears enforcing thunderclaps,   80
And from their shields strike flames of lightning),
All fearful folds his sails and sounds the main,
Lifting his prayers to the heavens for aid
Against the terror of the winds and waves:
So fares Agydas for the late-felt frowns   85
That sent a tempest to my daunted thoughts,
And makes my soul divine her overthrow.

        Enter TECHELLES *with a naked dagger*
          [*and* USUMCASANE]

TECHELLES

See you, Agydas, how the king salutes you.
He bids you prophesy what it imports.

AGYDAS

I prophesied before and now I prove   90
The killing frowns of jealousy and love.
He needed not with words confirm my fear,
For words are vain where working tools present
The naked action of my threatened end.
It says, Agydas, thou shalt surely die,   95
And of extremities elect the least.
More honour and less pain it may procure
To die by this resolvèd hand of thine
Than stay the torments he and heaven have sworn.
Then haste, Agydas, and prevent the plagues   100
Which thy prolongèd fates may draw on thee;

---

78   *Auster and Aquilon* the south and north winds
79   *tilt* fight
82   *sounds the main* measures the depth of the waves
87   *divine* foretell
89   *imports.* O3, Q (imports. *Exit* O1–2)
89ff.   The precise stage movement is uncertain here. Perhaps Techelles enters alone at l. 87, menaces Agydas and exits two lines later (as O1 seems to indicate). But O3 has no stage direction indicating re-entry at l. 106. It seems simpler to imagine both of Tamburlaine's men entering at l. 87 and threatening Agydas, who might even take the proffered dagger. Techelles and Usumcasane then step back to observe Agydas's soliloquy and suicide and come forward at l. 106 to comment and bear away the body.
90   *prove* find by experience
99   *stay* await

Go wander free from fear of tyrant's rage,
Removed from the torments and the hell
Wherewith he may excruciate thy soul.
And let Agydas by Agydas die,   105
And with this stab slumber eternally.

                              [Stabs himself]

TECHELLES

Usumcasane, see how right the man
Hath hit the meaning of my lord the king.

USUMCASANE

Faith, and Techelles, it was manly done,
And since he was so wise and honourable,   110
Let us afford him now the bearing hence
And crave his triple-worthy burial.

TECHELLES

Agreed Casane, we will honour him.

                     [Exeunt, bearing out the body]

ACT III, SCENE iii

[*Enter*] TAMBURLAINE, TECHELLES, USUMCASANE,
THERIDAMAS, BASSO, ZENOCRATE, *with others*

TAMBURLAINE

    Basso, by this thy lord and master knows
    I mean to meet him in Bithynia.
    See how he comes! Tush, Turks are full of brags
    And menace more than they can well perform.
    He meet me in the field and fetch thee hence!   5
    Alas, poor Turk, his fortune is too weak
    T'encounter with the strength of Tamburlaine.
    View well my camp, and speak indifferently,
    Do not my captains and my soldiers look
    As if they meant to conquer Africa?   10

BASSO

    Your men are valiant but their number few,
    And cannot terrify his mighty host.
    My lord, the great commander of the world,
    Besides fifteen contributory kings
    Hath now in arms ten thousand janissaries   15
    Mounted on lusty Mauritanian steeds
    Brought to the war by men of Tripoli,
    Two hundred thousand footmen that have served
    In two set battles fought in Graecia,
    And for the expedition of this war,   20
    If he think good, can from his garrisons
    Withdraw as many more to follow him.

TECHELLES

    The more he brings, the greater is the spoil,
    For when they perish by our warlike hands
    We mean to seat our footmen on their steeds   25

---

  2   *Bithynia* a district in Asia Minor south of the Black Sea
  3   *See . . . comes* i.e. Bajazeth has not yet arrived
  8   *indifferently* without prejudice
 15   *janissaries* Turkish soldiers
 16   *Mauritanian steeds* Mauritania in north-west Africa on the Barbary coast was
      famous for its horses.

And rifle all those stately janissars.
TAMBURLAINE
But will those kings accompany your lord?
BASSO
Such as his highness please, but some must stay
To rule the provinces he late subdued.
TAMBURLAINE
[*To his men*] Then fight courageously, their crowns are yours.   30
This hand shall set them on your conquering heads
That made me emperor of Asia.
USUMCASANE
Let him bring millions infinite of men,
Unpeopling western Africa and Greece,
Yet we assure us of the victory.   35
THERIDAMAS
Even he, that in a trice vanquished two kings
More mighty than the Turkish emperor,
Shall rouse him out of Europe and pursue
His scattered army till they yield or die.
TAMBURLAINE
Well said, Theridamas, speak in that mood,   40
For 'will' and 'shall' best fitteth Tamburlaine,
Whose smiling stars gives him assurèd hope
Of martial triumph, ere he meet his foes.
I, that am termed the scourge and wrath of God,
The only fear and terror of the world,   45
Will first subdue the Turk, and then enlarge
Those Christian captives which you keep as slaves,
Burdening their bodies with your heavy chains
And feeding them with thin and slender fare
That naked row about the Terrene sea,   50
And, when they chance to breathe and rest a space,
Are punished with bastones so grievously
That they lie panting on the galley's side
And strive for life at every stroke they give.
These are the cruel pirates of Argier,   55

26   *rifle* pillage
29   *late* lately
38   *rouse* cause to rise from cover
46   *enlarge* set free
52   *bastones* cudgels

That damnèd train, the scum of Africa,
Inhabited with straggling runagates,
That make quick havoc of the Christian blood.
But, as I live, that town shall curse the time
That Tamburlaine set foot in Africa.   60

Enter BAJAZETH *with his Bassoes and contributory* KINGS
[OF FEZ, MOROCCO, *and* ARGIER, ZABINA *and* EBEA]

BAJAZETH
Bassoes and janissaries of my guard,
Attend upon the person of your lord,
The greatest potentate of Africa.

TAMBURLAINE
Techelles and the rest, prepare your swords,
I mean t'encounter with that Bajazeth.   65

BAJAZETH
Kings of Fez, Morocco and Argier,
He calls me Bajazeth, whom you call lord!
Note the presumption of this Scythian slave!
I tell thee, villain, those that lead my horse
Have to their names titles of dignity,   70
And dar'st thou bluntly call me Bajazeth?

TAMBURLAINE
And know thou, Turk, that those which lead my horse
Shall lead thee captive thorough Africa.
And dar'st thou bluntly call me Tamburlaine?

BAJAZETH
By Mahomet my kinsman's sepulchre   75
And by the holy Alcoran, I swear
He shall be made a chaste and lustless eunuch,
And in my sarell tend my concubines,
And all his captains that thus stoutly stand
Shall draw the chariot of my emperess,   80
Whom I have brought to see their overthrow.

TAMBURLAINE
By this my sword that conquered Persia,

56   *train* troop
57   *runagates* apostates, deserters
70   *to* in addition to
76   *Alcoran* Koran
78   *sarell* seraglio, harem

Thy fall shall make me famous through the world.
I will not tell thee how I'll handle thee,
But every common soldier of my camp   85
Shall smile to see thy miserable state.

KING OF FEZ

What means the mighty Turkish emperor
To talk with one so base as Tamburlaine?

KING OF MOROCCO

Ye Moors and valiant men of Barbary,
How can ye suffer these indignities?   90

KING OF ARGIER

Leave words and let them feel your lances' points,
Which glided through the bowels of the Greeks.

BAJAZETH

Well said, my stout contributory kings,
Your threefold army and my hugy host
Shall swallow up these base-born Persians.   95

TECHELLES

Puissant, renowned and mighty Tamburlaine,
Why stay we thus prolonging all their lives?

THERIDAMAS

I long to see those crowns won by our swords
That we may reign as kings of Africa.

USUMCASANE

What coward would not fight for such a prize?   100

TAMBURLAINE

Fight all courageously and be you kings.
I speak it, and my words are oracles.

BAJAZETH

Zabina, mother of three braver boys
Than Hercules, that in his infancy
Did pash the jaws of serpents venomous,   105
Whose hands are made to grip a warlike lance,
Their shoulders broad for complete armour fit,
Their limbs more large and of a bigger size
Than all the brats ysprung from Typhon's loins,
Who, when they come unto their father's age,   110

94   *hugy* huge
105   *pash* smash, crush
109   *ysprung* sprung
      Typhon's Typhon was a hundred-headed giant, the father of various monsters,
      including Hydra (see l. 140 below).

Will batter turrets with their manly fists,
Sit here upon this royal chair of state,
And on thy head wear my imperial crown
Until I bring this sturdy Tamburlaine
And all his captains bound in captive chains.   115

ZABINA

Such good success happen to Bajazeth.

TAMBURLAINE

Zenocrate, the loveliest maid alive,
Fairer than rocks of pearl and precious stone,
The only paragon of Tamburlaine,
Whose eyes are brighter than the lamps of heaven   120
And speech more pleasant than sweet harmony,
That with thy looks canst clear the darkened sky
And calm the rage of thund'ring Jupiter,
Sit down by her, adornèd with my crown
As if thou wert the empress of the world.   125
Stir not, Zenocrate, until thou see
Me march victoriously with all my men,
Triumphing over him and these his kings
Which I will bring as vassals to thy feet.
Till then take thou my crown, vaunt of my worth,   130
And manage words with her as we will arms.

ZENOCRATE

And may my love, the King of Persia,
Return with victory and free from wound.

BAJAZETH

Now shalt thou feel the force of Turkish arms,
Which lately made all Europe quake for fear.   135
I have of Turks, Arabians, Moors and Jews
Enough to cover all Bithynia.
Let thousands die, their slaughtered carcasses
Shall serve for walls and bulwarks to the rest;
And as the heads of Hydra, so my power,   140
Subdued, shall stand as mighty as before:

---

119 *paragon* match, consort
130 *vaunt of* extol
131 *manage . . . arms* fight her with words as we shall fight with weapons
139 *bulwarks* ramparts, defences
140 *Hydra* a many-headed monster, whose heads grew back as quickly as they were cut off

If they should yield their necks unto the sword,
Thy soldiers' arms could not endure to strike
So many blows as I have heads for thee.
Thou knowest not, foolish-hardy Tamburlaine,   145
What 'tis to meet me in the open field,
That leave no ground for thee to march upon.

TAMBURLAINE

Our conquering swords shall marshal us the way
We use to march upon the slaughtered foe,
Trampling their bowels with our horses' hoofs –   150
Brave horses, bred on the white Tartarian hills.
My camp is like to Julius Caesar's host
That never fought but had the victory,
Nor in Pharsalia was there such hot war
As these my followers willingly would have.   155
Legions of spirits fleeting in the air
Direct our bullets and our weapons' points,
And make your strokes to wound the senseless air.
And when she sees our bloody colours spread,
Then Victory begins to take her flight,   160
Resting herself upon my milk-white tent.
But come, my lords, to weapons let us fall.
The field is ours, the Turk, his wife and all.

Exit, with his followers

BAJAZETH

Come, kings and bassoes, let us glut our swords
That thirst to drink the feeble Persians' blood.   165

Exit, with his followers

ZABINA

Base concubine, must thou be placed by me
That am the empress of the mighty Turk?

ZENOCRATE

Disdainful Turkess and unreverend boss,
Call'st thou me concubine that am betrothed
Unto the great and mighty Tamburlaine?   170

ZABINA

To Tamburlaine the great Tartarian thief?

148   *marshal* point out, lead
154   *Pharsalia* Julius Caesar defeated Pompey in 48 B.C. at the battle of Pharsalus.
158   *your . . . air* ed. (our . . . lure O1)
168   *boss* fat woman

57

ZENOCRATE

    Thou wilt repent these lavish words of thine

    When thy great basso-master and thyself

    Must plead for mercy at his kingly feet

    And sue to me to be your advocates.   175

ZABINA

    And sue to thee? I tell thee, shameless girl,

    Thou shalt be laundress to my waiting-maid.

    How lik'st thou her, Ebea, will she serve?

EBEA

    Madam, she thinks perhaps she is too fine,

    But I shall turn her into other weeds,   180

    And make her dainty fingers fall to work.

ZENOCRATE

    Hear'st thou, Anippe, how thy drudge doth talk,

    And how my slave, her mistress, menaceth?

    Both for their sauciness shall be employed

    To dress the common soldiers' meat and drink,   185

    For we will scorn they should come near ourselves.

ANIPPE

    Yet sometimes let your highness send for them

    To do the work my chambermaid disdains.

               They sound [to] the battle within, and stay

ZENOCRATE

    Ye gods and powers that govern Persia

    And made my lordly love her worthy king,   190

    Now strengthen him against the Turkish Bajazeth,

    And let his foes like flocks of fearful roes

    Pursued by hunters fly his angry looks,

    That I may see him issue conqueror.

ZABINA

    Now Mahomet, solicit God himself   195

    And make him rain down murdering shot from heaven

    To dash the Scythians' brains, and strike them dead

    That dare to manage arms with him

    That offered jewels to thy sacred shrine

    When first he warred against the Christians.   200

               [Trumpets sound] to the battle again

180   *weeds* clothing

188   s.d. Trumpets announce the battle and then cease.

192   *roes* small deer

ZENOCRATE

By this the Turks lie weltering in their blood
And Tamburlaine is lord of Africa.

ZABINA

Thou art deceived, I heard the trumpets sound
As when my emperor overthrew the Greeks
And led them captive into Africa.   205
Straight will I use thee as thy pride deserves;
Prepare thyself to live and die my slave.

ZENOCRATE

If Mahomet should come from heaven and swear
My royal lord is slain or conquerèd,
Yet should he not persuade me otherwise   210
But that he lives and will be conqueror.

BAJAZETH *flies* [*across the stage*] *and* [TAMBURLAINE]
pursues him [*off*]. *The battle* [*is*] *short, and they* [*re-*]*enter.*
BAJAZETH *is overcome*

TAMBURLAINE

Now, king of bassoes, who is conqueror?

BAJAZETH

Thou, by the fortune of this damnèd foil.

TAMBURLAINE

Where are your stout contributory kings?

Enter TECHELLES, THERIDAMAS, USUMCASANE

TECHELLES

We have their crowns, their bodies strew the field.   215

TAMBURLAINE

Each man a crown? Why kingly fought i'faith.
Deliver them into my treasury.

ZENOCRATE

Now let me offer to my gracious lord
His royal crown again, so highly won.

TAMBURLAINE

Nay, take the Turkish crown from her, Zenocrate,   220
And crown me emperor of Africa.

ZABINA

No Tamburlaine, though now thou gat the best,

213   *foil* ed. (soile O1) defeat
222   *gat the best* got the upper hand

Thou shalt not yet be lord of Africa.
THERIDAMAS
Give her the crown, Turkess, you were best.
He takes it from her and gives it [to] ZENOCRATE
ZABINA
Injurious villains, thieves, runagates,   225
How dare you thus abuse my majesty?
THERIDAMAS
Here madam, you are empress, she is none.
TAMBURLAINE
Not now, Theridamas, her time is past:
The pillars that have bolstered up those terms
Are fallen in clusters at my conquering feet.   230
ZABINA
Though he be prisoner, he may be ransomed.
TAMBURLAINE
Not all the world shall ransom Bajazeth.
BAJAZETH
Ah, fair Zabina, we have lost the field,
And never had the Turkish emperor
So great a foil by any foreign foe.   235
Now will the Christian miscreants be glad,
Ringing with joy their superstitious bells
And making bonfires for my overthrow.
But ere I die those foul idolators
Shall make me bonfires with their filthy bones,   240
For though the glory of this day be lost,
Afric and Greece have garrisons enough
To make me sovereign of the earth again.
TAMBURLAINE
Those wallèd garrisons will I subdue
And write myself great lord of Africa.   245
So from the East unto the furthest West
Shall Tamburlaine extend his puissant arm.
The galleys and those pilling brigandines
That yearly sail to the Venetian gulf
And hover in the straits for Christians' wrack,   250

225   *runagates* vagabonds
229   *terms* statuary busts set on pillars
247   *puissant* powerful
248   *pilling brigandines* pillaging pirate ships
250   *wrack* destruction

Shall lie at anchor in the Isle Asant
Until the Persian fleet and men-of-war,
Sailing along the oriental sea,
Have fetched about the Indian continent
Even from Persepolis to Mexico,   255
And thence unto the Straits of Jubaltar,
Where they shall meet and join their force in one,
Keeping in awe the Bay of Portingale
And all the ocean by the British shore.
And by this means I'll win the world at last.   260

BAJAZETH

Yet set a ransom on me, Tamburlaine.

TAMBURLAINE

What, think'st thou Tamburlaine esteems thy gold?
I'll make the kings of India ere I die
Offer their mines to sue for peace to me,
And dig for treasure to appease my wrath.   265
Come bind them both and one lead in the Turk.
The Turkess let my love's maid lead away.

They bind them

BAJAZETH

Ah villains, dare ye touch my sacred arms?
O Mahomet, O sleepy Mahomet!

ZABINA

O cursèd Mahomet that mak'st us thus   270
The slaves to Scythians rude and barbarous!

TAMBURLAINE

Come bring them in, and for this happy conquest
Triumph, and solemnize a martial feast.

Exeunt

251   *Isle Asant* Zante, off the west coast of Greece
252–9 Tamburlaine imagines his fleet circumnavigating the globe, going east across the
       Indian Ocean ('oriental sea') and the Pacific to Mexico and thence to Gibraltar
       ('Jubaltar') and the Bay of Biscay ('Portingale').

ACT IV, SCENE i

[Enter] SOLDAN OF EGYPT, *with three or four Lords,*
CAPOLIN, [MESSENGER]

SOLDAN

    Awake, ye men of Memphis, hear the clang
    Of Scythian trumpets! Hear the basilisks
    That, roaring, shake Damascus' turrets down!
    The rogue of Volga holds Zenocrate,
    The Soldan's daughter, for his concubine,   5
    And with a troop of thieves and vagabonds
    Hath spread his colours to our high disgrace
    While you faint-hearted base Egyptians
    Lie slumb'ring on the flowery banks of Nile,
    As crocodiles that unaffrighted rest   10
    While thund'ring cannons rattle on their skins.

[MESSENGER]

    Nay, mighty Soldan, did your greatness see
    The frowning looks of fiery Tamburlaine,
    That with his terror and imperious eyes
    Commands the hearts of his associates,   15
    It might amaze your royal majesty.

SOLDAN

    Villain, I tell thee, were that Tamburlaine
    As monstrous as Gorgon, prince of hell,
    The Soldan would not start a foot from him.
    But speak, what power hath he?

MESSENGER   Mighty lord,   20
    Three hundred thousand men in armour clad,
    Upon their prancing steeds, disdainfully
    With wanton paces trampling on the ground;
    Five hundred thousand footmen threat'ning shot,
    Shaking their swords, their spears and iron bills,   25
    Environing their standard round, that stood

---

  2   *basilisks* large cannons
  18 *Gorgon* Demogorgon, a devil
  23 *wanton* insolent in triumph, merciless
  25 *bills* long-handled axes, halberds

As bristle-pointed as a thorny wood;
Their warlike engines and munition
Exceed the forces of their martial men.

SOLDAN

Nay, could their numbers countervail the stars,   30
Or ever-drizzling drops of April showers,
Or withered leaves that autumn shaketh down,
Yet would the Soldan by his conquering power
So scatter and consume them in his rage,
That not a man should live to rue their fall.   35

CAPOLIN

So might your highness, had you time to sort
Your fighting men and raise your royal host.
But Tamburlaine by expedition
Advantage takes of your unreadiness.

SOLDAN

Let him take all th'advantages he can;   40
Were all the world conspired to fight for him,
Nay, were he devil, as he is no man,
Yet in revenge of fair Zenocrate,
Whom he detaineth in despite of us,
This arm should send him down to Erebus   45
To shroud his shame in darkness of the night.

MESSENGER

Pleaseth your mightiness to understand,
His resolution far exceedeth all:
The first day when he pitcheth down his tents,
White is their hue, and on his silver crest   50
A snowy feather spangled white he bears,
To signify the mildness of his mind
That satiate with spoil refuseth blood;
But when Aurora mounts the second time,
As red as scarlet is his furniture –   55
Then must his kindled wrath be quenched with blood,
Not sparing any that can manage arms;

28   *engines* instruments of assault
30   *countervail* equal in number
38   *expedition* speed
45   *Erebus* the son of Chaos and the brother of Night, whose name came to signify the
      dark region beneath the earth
54   *Aurora* goddess of the dawn
55   *furniture* military equipment

But if these threats move not submission,
Black are his colours, black pavilion,
His spear, his shield, his horse, his armour, plumes,   60
And jetty feathers menace death and hell;
Without respect of sex, degree or age,
He razeth all his foes with fire and sword.

SOLDAN

Merciless villain, peasant ignorant
Of lawful arms or martial discipline: 65
Pillage and murder are his usual trades.
The slave usurps the glorious name of war.
See, Capolin, the fair Arabian king
That hath been disappointed by this slave
Of my fair daughter and his princely love,   70
May have fresh warning to go to war with us,
And be revenged for her disparagement.

[Exeunt]

ACT IV, SCENE ii

[Enter] TAMBURLAINE *[all in white]*, TECHELLES,
THERIDAMAS, USUMCASANE, ZENOCRATE, ANIPPE,
two Moors drawing BAJAZETH *in his cage,
and his wife* [ZABINA] *following him*

TAMBURLAINE

Bring out my footstool.

They take [BAJAZETH] *out of the cage*

BAJAZETH

Ye holy priests of heavenly Mahomet,
That, sacrificing, slice and cut your flesh,
Staining his altars with your purple blood,
Make heaven to frown and every fixèd star   5
To suck up poison from the moorish fens,
And pour it in this glorious tyrant's throat!

TAMBURLAINE

The chiefest god, first mover of that sphere
Enchased with thousands ever-shining lamps,
Will sooner burn the glorious frame of heaven   10
Than it should so conspire my overthrow.
But, villain, thou that wishest this to me,
Fall prostrate on the low disdainful earth
And be the footstool of great Tamburlaine,
That I may rise into my royal throne.   15

BAJAZETH

First shalt thou rip my bowels with thy sword
And sacrifice my heart to death and hell,
Before I yield to such a slavery.

TAMBURLAINE

Base villain, vassal, slave to Tamburlaine,
Unworthy to embrace or touch the ground   20
That bears the honour of my royal weight,
Stoop, villain, stoop! Stoop, for so he bids

---

7   *glorious* boastful
8–9   Tamburlaine invokes the Aristotelian conception of God as the 'prime mover', who
      initiates the movement of the outermost sphere whose motion causes that of the other
      heavenly spheres.

That may command thee piecemeal to be torn,
Or scattered like the lofty cedar trees
Struck with the voice of thund'ring Jupiter. 25

BAJAZETH

Then as I look down to the damnèd fiends,
Fiends, look on me, and thou, dread god of hell,
With ebon sceptre strike this hateful earth
And make it swallow both of us at once!

            [TAMBURLAINE] *gets up upon him to his chair*

TAMBURLAINE

Now clear the triple region of the air, 30
And let the majesty of heaven behold
Their scourge and terror tread on emperors.
Smile, stars that reigned at my nativity
And dim the brightness of their neighbour lamps,
Disdain to borrow light of Cynthia, 35
For I, the chiefest lamp of all the earth,
First rising in the east with mild aspect,
But fixèd now in the meridian line,
Will send up fire to your turning spheres
And cause the sun to borrow light of you. 40
My sword struck fire from his coat of steel,
Even in Bithynia, when I took this Turk,
As when a fiery exhalation,
Wrapped in the bowels of a freezing cloud,
Fighting for passage, makes the welkin crack, 45
And casts a flash of lightning to the earth.
But ere I march to wealthy Persia,
Or leave Damascus and the Egyptian fields,
As was the fame of Clymen's brain-sick son

28   *ebon* black
30   An allusion to the contemporary belief that the air, between the earth and the
       sphere of fire, was divided into three 'regions' according to distance from the earth
       and temperature.
35   *Cynthia* the moon
38   *the meridian line* an imaginary arc through the sky, running from north to south
       directly above the observer's head so that the sun passed through it at noon
43   *exhalation* a vapour drawn from the earth's atmosphere
45   *makes* ed. (make O1)
       welkin sky
49   *Clymen's* O2 (Clymenes; Clymeus O1)
       Phaëton, son of Clymen and the sun god Apollo, met disaster when he tried to drive
       his father's horses across the sky.

That almost brent the axle-tree of heaven,   50
So shall our swords, our lances and our shot
Fill all the air with fiery meteors.
Then, when the sky shall wax as red as blood,
It shall be said I made it red myself,
To make me think of naught but blood and war.   55

ZABINA

Unworthy king, that by thy cruelty
Unlawfully usurp'st the Persian seat,
Dar'st thou that never saw an emperor
Before thou met my husband in the field,
Being thy captive, thus abuse his state,   60
Keeping his kingly body in a cage,
That roofs of gold and sun-bright palaces
Should have prepared to entertain his grace,
And treading him beneath thy loathsome feet,
Whose feet the kings of Africa have kissed?   65

TECHELLES

You must devise some torment worse, my lord,
To make these captives rein their lavish tongues.

TAMBURLAINE

Zenocrate, look better to your slave.

ZENOCRATE

She is my handmaid's slave, and she shall look
That these abuses flow not from her tongue.   70
Chide her Anippe.

ANIPPE

Let these be warnings for you then, my slave,
How you abuse the person of the king,
Or else I swear to have you whipped stark naked.

BAJAZETH

Great Tamburlaine, great in my overthrow,   75
Ambitious pride shall make thee fall as low
For treading on the back of Bajazeth,
That should be horsèd on four mighty kings.

50   *brent* burnt
     axle-tree of heaven the axis of the universe on which all of the heavenly spheres were
     believed to turn
60   *state* high rank
67   *lavish* free-speaking

TAMBURLAINE

    Thy names and titles and thy dignities
    Are fled from Bajazeth, and remain with me,   80
    That will maintain it against a world of kings.
    Put him in again.

                        [They put BAJAZETH *into the cage]*

BAJAZETH

    Is this a place for mighty Bajazeth?
    Confusion light on him that helps thee thus.

TAMBURLAINE

    There, whiles he lives, shall Bajazeth be kept   85
    And where I go be thus in triumph drawn,
    And thou his wife shall feed him with the scraps
    My servitors shall bring thee from my board.
    For he that gives him other food than this
    Shall sit by him and starve to death himself.   90
    This is my mind, and I will have it so.
    Not all the kings and emperors of the earth,
    If they would lay their crowns before my feet,
    Shall ransom him or take him from his cage.
    The ages that shall talk of Tamburlaine,   95
    Even from this day to Plato's wondrous year,
    Shall talk how I have handled Bajazeth.
    These Moors that drew him from Bithynia
    To fair Damascus, where we now remain,
    Shall lead him with us wheresoe'er we go.   100
    Techelles, and my loving followers,
    Now may we see Damascus' lofty towers,
    Like to the shadows of Pyramides
    That with their beauties graced the Memphian fields.
    The golden statue of their feathered bird   105
    That spreads her wings upon the city walls
    Shall not defend it from our battering shot.
    The townsmen mask in silk and cloth of gold,

---

  84   *helps* treats
  96   *Plato's wondrous year* In *Timaeus* (39 D) Plato writes of the future year when all of
       the planets will have returned to their original positions.
102–4   Tamburlaine compares the towers of Damascus to the Egyptian ('Memphian')
       pyramids.
 105   *statue* O3, Q (stature O1)
       bird the ibis, a bird sacred to the Egyptians
 108   *mask* dress

And every house is as a treasury –
The men, the treasure, and the town is ours.   110
THERIDAMAS
Your tents of white now pitched before the gates
And gentle flags of amity displayed,
I doubt not but the governor will yield,
Offering Damascus to your majesty.
TAMBURLAINE
So shall he have his life, and all the rest.   115
But if he stay until the bloody flag
Be once advanced on my vermilion tent,
He dies, and those that kept us out so long.
And when they see me march in black array,
With mournful streamers hanging down their heads,   120
Were in that city all the world contained,
Not one should 'scape, but perish by our swords.
ZENOCRATE
Yet would you have some pity for my sake,
Because it is my country's and my father's.
TAMBURLAINE
Not for the world, Zenocrate, if I have sworn.   125
Come, bring in the Turk.

                                                Exeunt

---

120   *streamers* long and narrow pointed flags, pennons

[Enter] SOLDAN, [KING OF] ARABIA, CAPOLIN, *with*
streaming colours; and Soldiers

SOLDAN

Methinks we march as Meleager did,
Environèd with brave Argolian knights,
To chase the savage Calydonian boar,
Or Cephalus with lusty Theban youths
Against the wolf that angry Themis sent   5
To waste and spoil the sweet Aonian fields.
A monster of five hundred thousand heads,
Compact of rapine, piracy and spoil,
The scum of men, the hate and scourge of God,
Raves in Egyptia and annoyeth us.   10
My lord, it is the bloody Tamburlaine,
A sturdy felon and a base-bred thief
By murder raisèd to the Persian crown,
That dares control us in our territories.
To tame the pride of this presumptuous beast,   15
Join your Arabians with the Soldan's power;
Let us unite our royal bands in one
And hasten to remove Damascus' siege.
It is a blemish to the majesty
And high estate of mighty emperors   20
That such a base usurping vagabond
Should brave a king or wear a princely crown.

KING OF ARABIA

Renownèd Soldan, have ye lately heard
The overthrow of mighty Bajazeth

---

  0   s.d. 1 *streaming* O3, Q (steaming O1)
1–3   Meleager was a warrior who, along with other Greek ('Argolian') knights, hunted a
       wild boar sent by Artemis. Although he killed the boar, the incident led to his own
       death. See Ovid, *Metamorphoses* viii, 270ff.
  3   *Calydonian* O2 (Caldonian O1)
  4   *Cephalus* a hunter who destroyed a wild beast that was ravaging the Theban terri-
       tories. See Ovid, *Metamorphoses* vii, 759ff.
  5   *Themis* a Greek deity, the symbol of order and justice
  6   *Aonian* Theban

About the confines of Bithynia?   25
The slavery wherewith he persecutes
The noble Turk and his great emperess?

SOLDAN

I have, and sorrow for his bad success.
But, noble lord of great Arabia,
Be so persuaded that the Soldan is   30
No more dismayed with tidings of his fall,
Than in the haven when the pilot stands
And views a stranger's ship rent in the winds
And shiverèd against a craggy rock.
Yet in compassion of his wretched state,   35
A sacred vow to heaven and him I make,
Confirming it with Ibis' holy name,
That Tamburlaine shall rue the day, the hour,
Wherein he wrought such ignominious wrong
Unto the hallowed person of a prince,   40
Or kept the fair Zenocrate so long,
As concubine, I fear, to feed his lust.

KING OF ARABIA

Let grief and fury hasten on revenge.
Let Tamburlaine for his offences feel
Such plagues as heaven and we can pour on him.   45
I long to break my spear upon his crest
And prove the weight of his victorious arm;
For fame I fear hath been too prodigal
In sounding through the world his partial praise.

SOLDAN

Capolin, hast thou surveyed our powers?   50

CAPOLIN

Great emperors of Egypt and Arabia,
The number of your hosts united is
A hundred and fifty thousand horse,
Two hundred thousand foot, brave men-at-arms,
Courageous and full of hardiness,   55
As frolic as the hunters in the chase

25   *confines* borders
28   *bad success* ill fortune
37   *Ibis* See note to IV.ii.105 above.
47   *prove* test
49   *partial* biased
56   *frolic* merry

Of savage beasts amid the desert woods.

KING OF ARABIA

My mind presageth fortunate success,
And, Tamburlaine, my spirit doth foresee
The utter ruin of thy men and thee.   60

SOLDAN

Then rear your standards, let your sounding drums
Direct our soldiers to Damascus' walls.
Now, Tamburlaine, the mighty Soldan comes
And leads with him the great Arabian king
To dim thy baseness and obscurity,   65
Famous for nothing but for theft and spoil,
To raze and scatter thy inglorious crew
Of Scythians and slavish Persians.

Exeunt

65   *thy baseness and obscurity* i.e. Tamburlaine's low birth

ACT IV, SCENE iv

The banquet, and to it cometh TAMBURLAINE *all in scarlet,*
[ZENOCRATE], THERIDAMAS, TECHELLES, USUMCASANE,
the Turk [BAJAZETH *in his cage,* ZABINA], *with others*

TAMBURLAINE

Now hang our bloody colours by Damascus,
Reflexing hues of blood upon their heads
While they walk quivering on their city walls,
Half dead for fear before they feel my wrath.
Then let us freely banquet and carouse 5
Full bowls of wine unto the god of war,
That means to fill your helmets full of gold
And make Damascus' spoils as rich to you
As was to Jason Colchos' golden fleece.
And now, Bajazeth, hast thou any stomach? 10

BAJAZETH

Ay, such a stomach, cruel Tamburlaine, as I could willingly feed
upon thy blood-raw heart.

TAMBURLAINE

Nay, thine own is easier to come by, pluck out that and 'twill
serve thee and thy wife. Well Zenocrate, Techelles, and the rest,
fall to your victuals. 15

BAJAZETH

Fall to, and never may your meat digest!
Ye Furies that can mask invisible,
Dive to the bottom of Avernus' pool
And in your hands bring hellish poison up
And squeeze it in the cup of Tamburlaine! 20
Or, wingèd snakes of Lerna, cast your stings
And leave your venoms in this tyrant's dish!

ZABINA

And may this banquet prove as ominous

---

2   *Reflexing* casting
9   *Jason* a Greek hero who led his Argonauts to Colchis in quest of the golden fleece
10–11   *stomach* (1) hunger, (2) anger
15   *victuals* food
18   *Avernus'pool* See note to I.ii.160 above.
21   *Lerna* a region near Argos where Hercules killed the Hydra

As Progne's to th'adulterous Thracian king
That fed upon the substance of his child.   25

ZENOCRATE

My lord, how can you suffer these
Outrageous curses by these slaves of yours?

TAMBURLAINE

To let them see, divine Zenocrate,
I glory in the curses of my foes,
Having the power from the empyreal heaven   30
To turn them all upon their proper heads.

TECHELLES

I pray you give them leave, madam, this speech is a goodly
refreshing to them.

THERIDAMAS

But if his highness would let them be fed, it would do them
more good.   35

TAMBURLAINE

Sirrah, why fall you not to? Are you so daintily brought up
you cannot eat your own flesh?

BAJAZETH

First legions of devils shall tear thee in pieces.

USUMCASANE

Villain, knowest thou to whom thou speakest?

TAMBURLAINE

O let him alone. Here, eat sir, take it from my sword's point, or   40
I'll thrust it to thy heart.

                              [BAJAZETH] *takes it and stamps upon it*

THERIDAMAS

He stamps it under his feet, my lord.

TAMBURLAINE

Take it up, villain, and eat it, or I will make thee slice the brawns
of thy arms into carbonadoes and eat them.

USUMCASANE

Nay, 'twere better he killed his wife, and then she shall be sure   45

24–5   After Tereus, King of Thrace, had raped his sister-in-law Philomela, his wife Progne
         revenged herself by tricking him into eating the body of Itys, their son. See *Meta-*
         morphoses vi, 433ff.

26–7   lineation ed.

  30   *empyreal heaven* See note to II.vii.15 above.

  31   *proper* own

  43   *brawns* muscles

  44   *carbonadoes* thin strips of meat

not to be starved, and he be provided for a month's victual
beforehand.

TAMBURLAINE

Here is my dagger, dispatch her while she is fat, for if she live
but a while longer, she will fall into a consumption with fret-
ting, and then she will not be worth the eating.   50

THERIDAMAS

Dost thou think that Mahomet will suffer this?

TECHELLES

'Tis like he will, when he cannot let it.

TAMBURLAINE

Go to, fall to your meat. What, not a bit? Belike he hath not
been watered today, give him some drink.

They give him water to drink, and he flings it on the ground

Fast and welcome, sir, while hunger make you eat. How now,   55
Zenocrate, doth not the Turk and his wife make a goodly show
at a banquet?

ZENOCRATE

Yes, my lord.

THERIDAMAS

Methinks 'tis a great deal better than a consort of music.

TAMBURLAINE

Yet music would do well to cheer up Zenocrate. Pray thee tell,   60
why art thou so sad? If thou wilt have a song, the Turk shall
strain his voice. But why is it?

ZENOCRATE

My lord, to see my father's town besieged,
The country wasted where myself was born,
How can it but affect my very soul?   65
If any love remain in you, my lord,
Or if my love unto your majesty
May merit favour at your highness' hands,
Then raise your siege from fair Damascus' walls,
And with my father take a friendly truce.   70

---

51 *suffer* allow
52 *let* prevent
55 *while* until
59 *consort of music* company of musicians
62 *strain his voice* i.e. sing

TAMBURLAINE

    Zenocrate, were Egypt Jove's own land,
    Yet would I with my sword make Jove to stoop.
    I will confute those blind geographers
    That make a triple region in the world,
    Excluding regions which I mean to trace,   75
    And with this pen reduce them to a map,
    Calling the provinces, cities and towns
    After my name and thine, Zenocrate.
    Here at Damascus will I make the point
    That shall begin the perpendicular –   80
    And wouldst thou have me buy thy father's love
    With such a loss? Tell me Zenocrate.

ZENOCRATE

    Honour still wait on happy Tamburlaine:
    Yet give me leave to plead for him, my lord.

TAMBURLAINE

    Content thyself, his person shall be safe,   85
    And all the friends of fair Zenocrate,
    If with their lives they will be pleased to yield,
    Or may be forced to make me emperor –
    For Egypt and Arabia must be mine.
    [*To* BAJAZETH] Feed, you slave, thou may'st think thyself   90
    happy to be fed from my trencher.

BAJAZETH

    My empty stomach, full of idle heat,
    Draws bloody humours from my feeble parts,

---

74   *triple region* Asia, Africa, and Europe

76   *this pen* i.e. his sword

79–80   Although Ellis-Fermor suggests that 'perpendicular' here should be read as meri-
        dian, the more likely explanation is provided by D. K. Anderson, who argues that
        Marlowe is referring to the archaic 'T-in-O' maps of the medieval known world,
        which featured a 'T' circumscribed by an 'O'. The upper half of the circle, above the
        cross-bar, is the east, representing Asia, the lower left quadrant represents Europe
        (north and west) and the lower right quadrant Africa (south and west), with the lines
        of the 'T' standing for bodies of water. Tamburlaine imagines such maps being re-
        drawn to place Damascus, rather than the traditional Jerusalem, at the 'point' where
        vertical and horizontal lines meet, i.e. the spiritual centre of the world. See *N & Q*
        N.S. 21.8 (1974), 284–6.

83   *still* forever

91   *trencher* wooden platter

92–6   Bajazeth's hunger draws blood, one of the four chief fluids of the body
        ('humours'), into his stomach, and away from his limbs and sinews, thus drying

Preserving life by hasting cruel death.
My veins are pale, my sinews hard and dry,   95
My joints benumbed – unless I eat, I die.

ZABINA

Eat, Bajazeth. Let us live in spite of them, looking some happy
power will pity and enlarge us.

TAMBURLAINE

Here, Turk, wilt thou have a clean trencher?

BAJAZETH

Ay, tyrant, and more meat.   100

TAMBURLAINE

Soft, sir, you must be dieted, too much eating will make you
surfeit.

THERIDAMAS

So it would, my lord, 'specially having so small a walk, and so
little exercise.

Enter a second course of crowns

TAMBURLAINE

Theridamas, Techelles, and Casane, here are the cates you   105
desire to finger, are they not?

THERIDAMAS

Ay, my lord, but none save kings must feed with these.

TECHELLES

'Tis enough for us to see them, and for Tamburlaine only to
enjoy them.

TAMBURLAINE

Well, here is now to the Soldan of Egypt, the King of Arabia,   110
and the Governor of Damascus. Now take these three crowns,
and pledge me, my contributory kings. I crown you here,
Theridamas, King of Argier; Techelles, King of Fez; and
Usumcasane, King of Morocco. How say you to this, Turk?
These are not your contributory kings.   115

BAJAZETH

Nor shall they long be thine, I warrant them.

and weakening them. Hence his body, in working to preserve life, works against
itself to hasten his death.

97–98   *looking . . . us* hoping that some favourable power will pity and free us
   104   s.d. At this point, kingly crowns and perhaps also delicacies in the shape of crowns
         are brought in.
   105   *cates* delicacies

TAMBURLAINE

   Kings of Argier, Morocco, and of Fez,
   You that have marched with happy Tamburlaine
   As far as from the frozen place of heaven
   Unto the watery morning's ruddy bower,   120
   And thence by land unto the torrid zone,
   Deserve these titles I endow you with
   By valour and by magnanimity.
   Your births shall be no blemish to your fame,
   For virtue is the fount whence honour springs,   125
   And they are worthy she investeth kings.

THERIDAMAS

   And since your highness hath so well vouchsafed,
   If we deserve them not with higher meeds
   Than erst our states and actions have retained,
   Take them away again and make us slaves.   130

TAMBURLAINE

   Well said, Theridamas. When holy fates
   Shall 'stablish me in strong Egyptia,
   We mean to travel to th'antarctic pole,
   Conquering the people underneath our feet,
   And be renowned as never emperors were.   135
   Zenocrate, I will not crown thee yet.
   Until with greater honours I be graced.

                                 [*Exeunt*]

---

120   *bower* O3, Q (hour O1)
123   *valour* ed. (value O1)
124   *births* humble origins
125   *virtue* power and ability
127   *vouchsafed* granted (the crowns)
128   *meeds* merits
129   *erst* formerly
            retained warranted
134   *underneath our feet* i.e. who live in the southern hemisphere

ACT V, SCENE i

[Enter] the GOVERNOR OF DAMASCUS, *with three or four
Citizens, and four* VIRGINS *with branches of laurel
in their hands*

GOVERNOR

Still doth this man or rather god of war
Batter our walls and beat our turrets down,
And to resist with longer stubbornness
Or hope of rescue from the Soldan's power,
Were but to bring our wilful overthrow   5
And make us desperate of our threatened lives.
We see his tents have now been alterèd
With terrors to the last and cruellest hue.
His coal-black colours everywhere advanced
Threaten our city with a general spoil,   10
And if we should with common rites of arms
Offer our safeties to his clemency,
I fear the custom proper to his sword,
Which he observes as parcel of his fame
Intending so to terrify the world,   15
By any innovation or remorse
Will never be dispensed with till our deaths.
Therefore for these our harmless virgins' sakes,
Whose honours and whose lives rely on him,
Let us have hope that their unspotted prayers,   20
Their blubbered cheeks and hearty humble moans,
Will melt his fury into some remorse,
And use us like a loving conqueror.

FIRST VIRGIN

If humble suits or imprecations –
Uttered with tears of wretchedness and blood   25

13   *proper . . . sword* which is a part of his code of war
14   *parcel* an essential part
16   *innovation* change of mind
      remorse pity
21   *blubbered* tear-stained
      hearty heart-felt
24   *imprecations* prayers

79

Shed from the heads and hearts of all our sex,
Some made your wives, and some your children –
Might have entreated your obdurate breasts
To entertain some care of our securities
Whiles only danger beat upon our walls,   30
These more than dangerous warrants of our death
Had never been erected as they be,
Nor you depend on such weak helps as we.

GOVERNOR

Well, lovely virgins, think our country's care,
Our love of honour, loath to be enthralled   35
To foreign powers and rough imperious yokes,
Would not with too much cowardice or fear
Before all hope of rescue were denied
Submit yourselves and us to servitude.
Therefore in that your safeties and our own,   40
Your honours, liberties and lives were weighed
In equal care and balance with our own,
Endure as we the malice of our stars,
The wrath of Tamburlaine and power of wars,
Or be the means the overweighing heavens   45
Have kept to qualify these hot extremes,
And bring us pardon in your cheerful looks.

SECOND VIRGIN

Then here before the majesty of heaven
And holy patrons of Egyptia,
With knees and hearts submissive we entreat   50
Grace to our words and pity to our looks,
That this device may prove propitious,
And through the eyes and ears of Tamburlaine
Convey events of mercy to his heart.
Grant that these signs of victory we yield   55
May bind the temples of his conquering head
To hide the folded furrows of his brows
And shadow his displeasèd countenance

27   *made* being
31   *warrants* signs (i.e. Tamburlaine's black colours)
45   *overweighing* overruling
54   *events* results

With happy looks of ruth and lenity.
Leave us, my lord and loving countrymen,   60
What simple virgins may persuade, we will.

GOVERNOR

Farewell, sweet virgins, on whose safe return
Depends our city, liberty, and lives.

Exeunt [all except the VIRGINS]

59   *ruth* pity
      lenity mercy

ACT V, SCENE ii

[Enter] TAMBURLAINE, TECHELLES, THERIDAMAS,
USUMCASANE, *with others:* TAMBURLAINE *all in black,
and very melancholy*

TAMBURLAINE

What, are the turtles frayed out of their nests?
Alas poor fools, must you be first shall feel
The sworn destruction of Damascus?
They know my custom. Could they not as well
Have sent ye out when first my milk-white flags   5
Through which sweet mercy threw her gentle beams,
Reflexing them on your disdainful eyes,
As now, when fury and incensed hate
Flings slaughtering terror from my coal-black tents
And tells for truth submissions comes too late?   10

FIRST VIRGIN

Most happy king and emperor of the earth,
Image of honour and nobility
For whom the powers divine have made the world,
And on whose throne the holy Graces sit,
In whose sweet person is comprised the sum   15
Of nature's skill and heavenly majesty,
Pity our plights! O pity poor Damascus!
Pity old age, within whose silver hairs
Honour and reverence evermore have reigned.
Pity the marriage bed, where many a lord   20
In prime and glory of his loving joy
Embraceth now with tears of ruth and blood
The jealous body of his fearful wife,

V, ii Though this is not strictly a new scene, most editors retain O1's scene division here.

1 *turtles frayed* turtle-doves frightened
2 *fools* helpless ones
7 *Reflexing* reflecting
10 *submissions* the act of yielding
14 *Graces* three daughters of Jupiter, bestowers of beauty and charm
23 *jealous* apprehensive

Whose cheeks and hearts, so punished with conceit
To think thy puissant never-stayèd arm   25
Will part their bodies and prevent their souls
From heavens of comfort yet their age might bear,
Now wax all pale and withered to the death;
As well for grief our ruthless governor
Have thus refused the mercy of thy hand,   30
Whose sceptre angels kiss and Furies dread,
As for their liberties, their loves or lives.
O then for these and such as we ourselves,
For us, for infants, and for all our bloods
That never nourished thought against thy rule,   35
Pity, O pity, sacred emperor,
The prostrate service of this wretched town –
And take in sign thereof this gilded wreath,
Whereto each man of rule hath given his hand
And wished as worthy subjects happy means   40
To be investers of thy royal brows,
Even with the true Egyptian diadem.

TAMBURLAINE

Virgins, in vain ye labour to prevent
That which mine honour swears shall be performed.
Behold my sword, what see you at the point?   45

[FIRST] VIRGIN

Nothing but fear and fatal steel, my lord.

TAMBURLAINE

Your fearful minds are thick and misty then,
For there sits Death, there sits imperious Death,
Keeping his circuit by the slicing edge.
But I am pleased you shall not see him there.   50
He now is seated on my horsemen's spears,
And on their points his fleshless body feeds.

---

24   *punished with conceit* tormented by the thought
26–7   *prevent . . . From* deprive . . . of
29–32 *As well . . . lives* i.e. the people of Damascus are as pained by their Governor's
       refusal as they are by their personal losses.
34   *bloods* i.e. spirits
40   *happy means* fortunate opportunity
41–2 i.e. to crown Tamburlaine
49   *circuit* Death is likened to a judge whose circuit, or journey in a particular district
       to hold court sessions, is equal to the distance reached by Tamburlaine's sword.
52   *fleshless body* the medieval image of Death as a skeleton

Techelles, straight go charge a few of them
To charge these dames, and show my servant Death
Sitting in scarlet on their armed spears.   55
[VIRGINS]
O pity us!
TAMBURLAINE
Away with them I say and show them Death.
                    [TECHELLES *and others*] *take them away*
I will not spare these proud Egyptians
Nor change my martial observations
For all the wealth of Gihon's golden waves,   60
Or for the love of Venus, would she leave
The angry god of arms and lie with me.
They have refused the offer of their lives
And know my customs are as peremptory
As wrathful planets, death, or destiny.   65

Enter TECHELLES

What, have your horsemen shown the virgins Death?
TECHELLES
They have, my lord, and on Damascus' walls
Have hoisted up their slaughtered carcasses.
TAMBURLAINE
A sight as baneful to their souls I think
As are Thessalian drugs or mithridate.   70
But go, my lords, put the rest to the sword.
                    Exeunt [*all except* TAMBURLAINE]
Ah fair Zenocrate, divine Zenocrate,
Fair is too foul an epithet for thee,
That in thy passion for thy country's love
And fear to see thy kingly father's harm   75

---

55   *scarlet* (1) judge's robe, (2) blood
59   *observations* customary practices
60   *Gihon* the second river of Eden (*Genesis* 2:13)
62   *god of arms* Mars, the lover of Venus
64   *peremptory* absolute
69   *baneful* deadly
70   *Thessalian* Thessaly was traditionally regarded as the land of witchcraft and strange drugs.
     mithridate Here, apparently, poison. But generally mithridate was regarded as an antidote to poison.

84

With hair dishevelled wip'st thy watery cheeks;
And like to Flora in her morning's pride,
Shaking her silver tresses in the air,
Rain'st on the earth resolvèd pearl in showers
And sprinklest sapphires on thy shining face,   80
Where Beauty, mother to the Muses, sits
And comments volumes with her ivory pen,
Taking instructions from thy flowing eyes –
Eyes when that Ebena steps to heaven
In silence of thy solemn evening's walk,   85
Making the mantle of the richest night,
The moon, the planets, and the meteors, light.
There angels in their crystal armours fight
A doubtful battle with my tempted thoughts
For Egypt's freedom and the Soldan's life,   90
His life that so consumes Zenocrate,
Whose sorrows lay more siege unto my soul
Than all my army to Damascus' walls;
And neither Persians' sovereign nor the Turk
Troubled my senses with conceit of foil   95
So much by much as doth Zenocrate.
What is beauty saith my sufferings then?
If all the pens that ever poets held
Had fed the feeling of their masters' thoughts,
And every sweetness that inspired their hearts,   100
Their minds, and muses on admired themes,
If all the heavenly quintessence they still
From their immortal flowers of poesy,
Wherein as in a mirror we perceive
The highest reaches of a human wit,   105

77ff.   The looseness of the syntax here may indicate Tamburlaine's uncharacteristically
       rapt and uncertain state.
  77   *Flora* the Roman goddess of springtime and flowers
  79   *resolvèd pearl* i.e. tears
  84   *Ebena* No such deity is known. The sense here is Zenocrate's eyes at night light up
       the various heavenly bodies.
  91   *consumes* wastes with anxiety
  95   *conceit of foil* the thought of defeat
101   *muses* meditations
103   *quintessence* most essential part
       still distil
105   *wit* imagination

If these had made one poem's period
And all combined in beauty's worthiness,
Yet should there hover in their restless heads
One thought, one grace, one wonder at the least,
Which into words no virtue can digest.   110
But how unseemly is it for my sex,
My discipline of arms and chivalry,
My nature and the terror of my name,
To harbour thoughts effeminate and faint!
Save only that in beauty's just applause,   115
With whose instinct the soul of man is touched –
And every warrior that is rapt with love
Of fame, of valour, and of victory,
Must needs have beauty beat on his conceits –
I thus conceiving and subduing both   120
That which hath stooped the topmost of the gods,
Even from the fiery-spangled veil of heaven,
To feel the lovely warmth of shepherds' flames
And march in cottages of strewèd weeds,
Shall give the world to note, for all my birth,   125
That virtue solely is the sum of glory

106–7   *made . . . worthiness* been combined to form a single poem in beauty's praise

110   *Which . . . digest* which no power can express in words

114   *faint* weak

115–27   A notoriously difficult passage, coming just at a crucial point in Tamburlaine's development as a character. He suggests (somewhat paradoxically) that, though it may be 'unseemly' (l. 111) for great warriors like himself to be affected by love, it is also inevitable, since the soul of man is properly stirred by the prompting ('instinct') of beauty (ll. 115–16). The long concessive clause beginning at l. 115 ('Save' = except) is incomplete, leading to a break at l. 120; at that point, Tamburlaine turns to his own power over the incursions of beauty: he is able both to conceive of it in his soul *and* subdue it (l. 120). He thereby outdoes even the highest ('topmost') of the gods, who have typically 'stooped' to the power of Beauty by coming down to earth disguised as shepherds and the like, and hence shown themselves unable to master temptation. Thus Tamburlaine is able to show the world that, despite his low birth (l. 125), his 'virtue' (i.e. his power and self-command as a warrior) is the noblest attribute of men.

119   *beat on his conceits* impinge on his thoughts

121   *stooped the topmost* ed. (stopt the tempest O1). An emendation suggested by G. I. Duthie.

122   *fiery-spangled veil* stars

124   *cottages of strewèd weeds* simple dwellings with rushes strewn on the floor

126   *sum* the highest attainable point

And fashions men with true nobility.
Who's within there?

        Enter two or three [ATTENDANTS]

Hath Bajazeth been fed today?
ATTENDANT
   Ay, my lord.   130
TAMBURLAINE
   Bring him forth, and let us know if the town be ransacked.
                    [*Exeunt* ATTENDANTS]

      Enter TECHELLES, THERIDAMAS, USUMCASANE,
                  and others

TECHELLES
   The town is ours, my lord, and fresh supply
   Of conquest and of spoil is offered us.
TAMBURLAINE
   That's well, Techelles. What's the news?
TECHELLES
   The Soldan and the Arabian king together   135
   March on us with such eager violence
   As if there were no way but one with us.
TAMBURLAINE
   No more there is not, I warrant thee, Techelles.

      They bring in [BAJAZETH,] *the Turk* [*in his cage,*
             followed by ZABINA]

THERIDAMAS
   We know the victory is ours, my lord,
   But let us save the reverend Soldan's life   140
   For fair Zenocrate that so laments his state.
TAMBURLAINE
   That will we chiefly see unto, Theridamas,
   For sweet Zenocrate, whose worthiness
   Deserves a conquest over every heart.
   And now, my footstool, if I lose the field,   145
   You hope of liberty and restitution.
   Here let him stay, my masters, from the tents,
   Till we have made us ready for the field.

130   s.p. ed (An. O1)

Pray for us, Bajazeth, we are going.

Exeunt [all except BAJAZETH *and* ZABINA]

BAJAZETH

Go, never to return with victory! 150
Millions of men encompass thee about
And gore thy body with as many wounds!
Sharp forkèd arrows light upon thy horse!
Furies from the black Cocytus lake
Break up the earth and with their firebrands 155
Enforce thee run upon the baneful pikes!
Volleys of shot pierce through thy charmed skin
And every bullet dipped in poisoned drugs,
Or roaring cannons sever all thy joints,
Making thee mount as high as eagles soar! 160

ZABINA

Let all the swords and lances in the field
Stick in his breast, as in their proper rooms!
At every pore let blood come dropping forth,
That ling'ring pains may massacre his heart
And madness send his damned soul to hell! 165

BAJAZETH

Ah fair Zabina, we may curse his power,
The heavens may frown, the earth for anger quake,
But such a star hath influence in his sword
As rules the skies and countermands the gods
More than Cimmerian Styx or destiny. 170
And then shall we in this detested guise,
With shame, with hunger, and with horror aye
Griping our bowels with retorquèd thoughts,
And have no hope to end our ecstasies.

ZABINA

Then is there left no Mahomet, no God, 175
No fiend, no fortune, nor no hope of end

154 *Cocytus* a river in the underworld, though here Marlowe refers to it as a lake
156 *Enforce thee* force thee to
162 *as in . . . rooms* as if that were their proper home
170 *Styx* the chief river of Hades, here described as black (Cimmerian)
171 *we in* 'Live' or 'continue' is understood after 'we' – its omission may be a sign of
Bajazeth's anguish.
172 *aye* forever
173 *retorquèd* twisted back upon themselves
174 *ecstasies* frenzies

To our infamous monstrous slaveries?
Gape earth, and let the fiends infernal view
A hell as hopeless and as full of fear
As are the blasted banks of Erebus,   180
Where shaking ghosts with ever-howling groans
Hover about the ugly ferryman
To get a passage to Elysium.
Why should we live O wretches, beggars, slaves,
Why live we, Bajazeth, and build up nests   185
So high within the region of the air
By living long in this oppression,
That all the world will see and laugh to scorn
The former triumphs of our mightiness
In this obscure infernal servitude?   190

BAJAZETH

O life more loathsome to my vexèd thoughts
Than noisome parbreak of the Stygian snakes,
Which fills the nooks of hell with standing air,
Infecting all the ghosts with cureless griefs!
O dreary engines of my loathèd sight   195
That sees my crown, my honour and my name
Thrust under yoke and thraldom of a thief,
Why feed ye still on day's accursèd beams
And sink not quite into my tortured soul?
You see my wife, my queen and emperess,   200
Brought up and proppèd by the hand of fame,
Queen of fifteen contributory queens,
Now thrown to rooms of black abjection,
Smeared with blots of basest drudgery,
And villainess to shame, disdain and misery.   205
Accursèd Bajazeth, whose words of ruth

180   *Erebus* hell. See note to IV.i.45 above.
182–3 lineation ed.
182   *ferryman* Charon, who conveyed the souls of the dead across the river Styx to the
       underworld ('Elysium').
184   The 'O' in mid-line is probably a cry, not an apostrophe.
185–6 *build . . . air* subsist on false hopes. Cf. the expression 'to build castles in the air'.
192   *parbreak* vomit
193   *standing* stagnant
195   *engines* instruments (i.e. his eyes)
203   *abjection* degradation
205   *villainess* servant

That would with pity cheer Zabina's heart
And make our souls resolve in ceaseless tears,
Sharp hunger bites upon and gripes the root
From whence the issues of my thoughts do break.   210
O poor Zabina, O my queen, my queen,
Fetch me some water for my burning breast
To cool and comfort me with longer date,
That in the shortened sequel of my life
I may pour forth my soul into thine arms   215
With words of love, whose moaning intercourse
Hath hitherto been stayed with wrath and hate
Of our expressless banned inflictions.

ZABINA
Sweet Bajazeth, I will prolong thy life
As long as any blood or spark of breath   220
Can quench or cool the torments of my grief.

She goes out

BAJAZETH
Now Bajazeth, abridge thy baneful days
And beat thy brains out of thy conquered head,
Since other means are all forbidden me
That may be ministers of my decay.   225
O highest lamp of ever-living Jove,
Accursèd day infected with my griefs,
Hide now thy stainèd face in endless night
And shut the windows of the lightsome heavens.
Let ugly Darkness with her rusty coach   230
Engirt with tempests wrapped in pitchy clouds
Smother the earth with never-fading mists,
And let her horses from their nostrils breathe
Rebellious winds and dreadful thunderclaps,
That in this terror Tamburlaine may live,   235
And my pined soul, resolved in liquid air,

208   *resolve* dissolve
213   *date* term of life
218   *expressless* inexpressible
          banned cursed
225   *ministers . . . decay* instruments of death
236   *pined* tormented
          resolved dissolved
          air O3, Q (ay O1)

May still excruciate his tormented thoughts.
Then let the stony dart of senseless cold
Pierce through the centre of my withered heart
And make a passage for my loathèd life.   240

He brains himself against the cage

Enter ZABINA

ZABINA

What do mine eyes behold, my husband dead?
His skull all riven in twain, his brains dashed out?
The brains of Bajazeth, my lord and sovereign!
O Bajazeth, my husband and my lord,
O Bajazeth, O Turk, O emperor, give him his liquor?   245
Not I. Bring milk and fire, and my blood I bring him
again, tear me in pieces, give me the sword with a ball
of wildfire upon it! Down with him, down with him! Go
to, my child, away, away, away! Ah, save that infant, save
him, save him! I, even I, speak to her – the sun was   250
down. Streamers white, red, black, here, here, here!
Fling the meat in his face! Tamburlaine, Tamburlaine,
let the soldiers be buried. Hell, death, Tamburlaine, hell,
make ready my coach, my chair, my jewels, I come, I come,
I come!   255

She runs against the cage and brains herself

[*Enter*] ZENOCRATE *and* ANIPPE

ZENOCRATE

Wretched Zenocrate, that livest to see
Damascus' walls dyed with Egyptian blood,
Thy father's subjects and thy countrymen,
The streets strowed with dissevered joints of men,
And wounded bodies gasping yet for life.   260
But most accursed, to see the sun-bright troop
Of heavenly virgins and unspotted maids,
Whose looks might make the angry god of arms
To break his sword and mildly treat of love,
On horsemen's lances to be hoisted up   265
And guiltlessly endure a cruel death;

237 *excruciate* torment

For every fell and stout Tartarian steed
That stamped on others with their thund'ring hooves,
When all their riders charged their quivering spears
Began to check the ground and rein themselves,   270
Gazing upon the beauty of their looks.
Ah Tamburlaine, wert thou the cause of this,
That term'st Zenocrate thy dearest love.
Whose lives were dearer to Zenocrate
Than her own life or aught save thine own love?   275
But see another bloody spectacle!
Ah wretched eyes, the enemies of my heart,
How are ye glutted with these grievous objects
And tell my soul more tales of bleeding ruth!
See, see, Anippe if they breathe or no.   280

ANIPPE

No breath nor sense nor motion in them both.
Ah madam, this their slavery hath enforced,
And ruthless cruelty of Tamburlaine.

ZENOCRATE

Earth, cast up fountains from thy entrails,
And wet thy cheeks for their untimely deaths: 285
Shake with their weight in sign of fear and grief.
Blush, heaven, that gave them honour at their birth
And let them die a death so barbarous.
Those that are proud of fickle empery
And place their chiefest good in earthly pomp,   290
Behold the Turk and his great emperess!
Ah Tamburlaine, my love, sweet Tamburlaine,
That fights for sceptres and for slippery crowns,
Behold the Turk and his great emperess!
Thou, that in conduct of thy happy stars   295
Sleep'st every night with conquest on thy brows
And yet wouldst shun the wavering turns of war,
In fear and feeling of the like distress
Behold the Turk and his great emperess!

267   *fell and stout* fierce and proud
269   *charged* levelled for the charge
270   *check the ground* paw the ground, hesitate
275   *aught* anything
279   *bleeding ruth* pitiable suffering
289   *empery* imperial rule
295   *in conduct* under the guidance

Ah mighty Jove and holy Mahomet,   300
Pardon my love! O pardon his contempt
Of earthly fortune and respect of pity,
And let not conquest ruthlessly pursued
Be equally against his life incensed,
In this great Turk and hapless emperess.   305
And pardon me that was not moved with ruth
To see them live so long in misery.
Ah what may chance to thee, Zenocrate?

ANIPPE

Madam, content yourself and be resolved,
Your love hath Fortune so at his command   310
That she shall stay and turn her wheel no more
As long as life maintains his mighty arm
That fights for honour to adorn your head.

Enter [PHILEMUS,] *a Messenger*

ZENOCRATE

What other heavy news now brings Philemus?

PHILEMUS

Madam, your father and th'Arabian king,   315
The first affecter of your excellence,
Comes now as Turnus 'gainst Aeneas did,
Armèd with lance into th'Egyptian fields,
Ready for battle 'gainst my lord the king.

ZENOCRATE

Now shame and duty, love and fear, presents   320
A thousand sorrows to my martyred soul.
Whom should I wish the fatal victory
When my poor pleasures are divided thus,
And racked by duty from my cursèd heart?
My father and my first-betrothed love   325
Must fight against my life and present love,
Wherein the change I use condemns my faith
And makes my deeds infamous through the world.

302   *respect of* regard for. Zenocrate prays that Tamburlaine's 'contempt' for sympathetic
      feeling may be pardoned.
305   *In* as in
316   *affecter* lover
      Turnus leader of the Italian forces against the encroaching Trojans, and rival of Aeneas
      for Lavinia's hand, defeated by Aeneas at the end of the *Aeneid*
327   *change I use* shift of allegiance I have made

But as the gods to end the Trojans' toil
Prevented Turnus of Lavinia   330
And fatally enriched Aeneas' love,
So for a final issue to my griefs,
To pacify my country and my love,
Must Tamburlaine by their resistless powers,
With virtue of a gentle victory,   335
Conclude a league of honour to my hope;
Then as the powers divine have preordained,
With happy safety of my father's life
Send like defence of fair Arabia.

They sound to the battle. And TAMBURLAINE *enjoys the*
victory, after [which the KING OF] ARABIA *enters wounded*

KING OF ARABIA
What cursèd power guides the murdering hands   340
Of this infamous tyrant's soldiers
That no escape may save their enemies,
Nor fortune keep themselves from victory?
Lie down, Arabia, wounded to the death,
And let Zenocrate's fair eyes behold   345
That as for her thou bear'st these wretched arms
Even so for her thou diest in these arms,
Leaving thy blood for witness of thy love.
ZENOCRATE
Too dear a witness for such love, my lord.
Behold Zenocrate, the cursèd object   350
Whose fortunes never masterèd her griefs –
Behold her wounded in conceit for thee
As much as thy fair body is for me.
KING OF ARABIA
Then shall I die with full contented heart
Having beheld divine Zenocrate   355
Whose sight with joy would take away my life,
As now it bringeth sweetness to my wound,

330   *Prevented* deprived
332   *issue* conclusion
334   *their* the gods'
335   *With virtue* as a consequence
336   *league* treaty
      to in accordance with
352   *conceit* imagination

If I had not been wounded as I am.
Ah that the deadly pangs I suffer now
Would lend an hour's licence to my tongue,   360
To make discourse of some sweet accidents
Have chanced thy merits in this worthless bondage,
And that I might be privy to the state
Of thy deserved contentment and thy love.
But making now a virtue of thy sight   365
To drive all sorrow from my fainting soul.
Since death denies me further cause of joy,
Deprived of care, my heart with comfort dies
Since thy desirèd hand shall close mine eyes.   [*Dies*]

Enter TAMBURLAINE *leading in the* SOLDAN, TECHELLES,
THERIDAMAS, USUMCASANE *with others*

TAMBURLAINE
Come, happy father of Zenocrate,   370
A title higher than thy Soldan's name;
Though my right hand have thus enthrallèd thee,
Thy princely daughter here shall set thee free –
She that hath calmed the fury of my sword,
Which had ere this been bathed in streams of blood   375
As vast and deep as Euphrates or Nile.

ZENOCRATE
O sight thrice welcome to my joyful soul,
To see the king my father issue safe
From dangerous battle of my conquering love!

SOLDAN
Well met, my only dear Zenocrate,   380
Though with the loss of Egypt and my crown.

TAMBURLAINE
'Twas I, my lord, that gat the victory,
And therefore grieve not at your overthrow,
Since I shall render all into your hands
And add more strength to your dominions   385
Than ever yet confirmed th'Egyptian crown.

361 *sweet accidents* favourable occurrences
362 *Have . . . merits* that have taken place as a result of your merits
365 *thy sight* i.e. my sight of you
379 *of* with
386 *confirmed* established

The god of war resigns his room to me,
Meaning to make me general of the world;
Jove viewing me in arms looks pale and wan,
Fearing my power should pull him from his throne;   390
Where'er I come the Fatal Sisters sweat,
And grisly Death, by running to and fro
To do their ceaseless homage to my sword;
And here in Afric, where it seldom rains,
Since I arrived with my triumphant host,   395
Have swelling clouds drawn from wide gasping wounds
Been oft resolved in bloody purple showers,
A meteor that might terrify the earth
And make it quake at every drop it drinks.
Millions of souls sit on the banks of Styx,   400
Waiting the back return of Charon's boat;
Hell and Elysium swarm with ghosts of men
That I have sent from sundry foughten fields
To spread my fame through hell and up to heaven.
And see, my lord, a sight of strange import,   405
Emperors and kings lie breathless at my feet:
The Turk and his great empress, as it seems,
Left to themselves while we were at the fight,
Have desperately dispatched their slavish lives;
With them Arabia too hath left his life –   410
All sights of power to grace my victory.
And such are objects fit for Tamburlaine,
Wherein as in a mirror may be seen
His honour that consists in shedding blood
When men presume to manage arms with him.   415

SOLDAN

Mighty hath God and Mahomet made thy hand,
Renownèd Tamburlaine, to whom all kings
Of force must yield their crowns and emperies;
And I am pleased with this my overthrow
If, as beseems a person of thy state,   420
Thou hast with honour used Zenocrate.

---

391   *Fatal Sisters* the three Fates
396–9   According to Renaissance meteorology, the sun could draw up blood from where
        great quantities had been spilt and transform it to a bloody rain.
398   *meteor* meteorological phenomenon
418   *Of force* perforce, by necessity

TAMBURLAINE

    Her state and person wants no pomp you see,
    And for all blot of foul inchastity,
    I record heaven, her heavenly self is clear.
    Then let me find no further time to grace   425
    Her princely temples with the Persian crown.
    But here these kings that on my fortunes wait,
    And have been crowned for provèd worthiness
    Even by this hand that shall establish them,
    Shall now, adjoining all their hands with mine,   430
    Invest her here my Queen of Persia.
    What saith the noble Soldan and Zenocrate?

SOLDAN

    I yield with thanks and protestations
    Of endless honour to thee for her love.

TAMBURLAINE

    Then doubt I not but fair Zenocrate   435
    Will soon consent to satisfy us both.

ZENOCRATE

    Else should I much forget myself, my lord.

THERIDAMAS

    Then let us set the crown upon her head
    That hath long lingered for so high a seat.

TECHELLES

    My hand is ready to perform the deed,   440
    For now her marriage time shall work us rest.

USUMCASANE

    And here's the crown, my lord; help set it on.

TAMBURLAINE

    Then sit thou down, divine Zenocrate,
    And here we crown thee Queen of Persia
    And all the kingdoms and dominions   445
    That late the power of Tamburlaine subdued.
    As Juno, when the giants were suppressed
    That darted mountains at her brother Jove,
    So looks my love, shadowing in her brows

422   *wants* lack
424   *record* call to witness
434   *for her love* for your love of her
441   *work us* bring about for us
447   *giants* Titans
449   *shadowing* portraying

Triumphs and trophies for my victories;   450
Or as Latona's daughter bent to arms,
Adding more courage to my conquering mind.
To gratify thee, sweet Zenocrate,
Egyptians, Moors, and men of Asia,
From Barbary unto the Western Indie,   455
Shall pay a yearly tribute to thy sire;
And from the bounds of Afric to the banks
Of Ganges shall his mighty arm extend.
And now, my lords and loving followers,
That purchased kingdoms by your martial deeds,   460
Cast off your armour, put on scarlet robes,
Mount up your royal places of estate,
Environèd with troops of noblemen,
And there make laws to rule your provinces;
Hang up your weapons on Alcides' post,   465
For Tamburlaine takes truce with all the world.
Thy first betrothèd love, Arabia,
Shall we with honour, as beseems, entomb
With this great Turk and his fair emperess.
Then after all these solemn exequies   470
We will our celebrated rites of marriage solemnize.

                                                    [*Exeunt*]

451   *Latona's daughter* Artemis the huntress
453   *thee* ed. (the O1)
455   *From . . . Indie* from north Africa to the Ganges
465   *Alcides' post* the doorpost of the temple of Hercules (Alcides)
468   *as beseems* as is fitting
471   *celebrated* performed with customary observances (*O.E.D.*). Most editors cut this
       extra-metrical word, despite its presence in all the early texts, but the sonorous ring
       it gives to the final line is eminently suitable to the occasion

Tamburlaine the Greate.

VVith his impaſsionate furie , for the
death of his Lady and Loue faire Zenocra-
te : his forme of exhortation and diſcipline
to his three Sonnes ,and the manner of
his owne death.

The ſecond part.

LONDON
Printed by E. A, *for* Ed. White, *and are to be ſolde*
at his Shop neere the little North doore of Saint Paules
Church at the Signe of the Gun.
1 6 0 6,

[DRAMATIS PERSONAE

PROLOGUE
TAMBURLAINE, *King of Persia*
CALYPHA
AMYRAS } *his sons*
CELEBINUS   5
THERIDAMAS, *King of Argier*
TECHELLES, *King of Fez*
USUMCASANE, *King of Morocco*
ORCANES, *King of Natolia*
KING OF JERUSALEM   10
KING OF SORIA
KING OF TREBIZON
GAZELLUS, *Viceroy of Byron*
URIBASSA
SIGISMUND, *King of Hungary*   15
FREDERICK } *Peers of Hungary*
BALDWIN
MAGNETES
CALLAPINE, *son of Bajazeth and prisoner of Tamburlaine*
ALMEDA, *his keeper*   20
KING OF AMASIA
GOVERNOR OF BABYLON
CAPTAIN OF BALSERA
His SON
Another CAPTAIN   25
MAXIMUS
PERDICAS
LORDS, CITIZENS, SOLDIERS, PIONERS, PHYSICIANS,
MESSENGERS, *and* ATTENDANTS

ZENOCRATE, *wife of Tamburlaine*   30
OLYMPIA, *wife of the Captain of Balsera*
Turkish CONCUBINES]

THE PROLOGUE

The general welcomes Tamburlaine received
When he arrivèd last upon our stage,
Hath made our poet pen his second part,
Where death cuts off the progress of his pomp
And murd'rous Fates throws all his triumphs down.   5
But what became of fair Zenocrate,
And with how many cities' sacrifice
He celebrated her sad funeral,
Himself in presence shall unfold at large.

8   *sad* ed. (said O1)

ACT I, SCENE i

[Enter] ORCANES, *King of Natolia;* GAZELLUS,
Viceroy of Byron; URIBASSA, *and their train,*
with drums and trumpets

ORCANES

Egregious viceroys of these eastern parts,
Placed by the issue of great Bajazeth
And sacred lord, the mighty Callapine,
Who lives in Egypt prisoner to that slave
Which kept his father in an iron cage: 5
Now have we marched from fair Natolia
Two hundred leagues, and on Danubius' banks
Our warlike host in complete armour rest,
Where Sigismund the King of Hungary
Should meet our person to conclude a truce.   10
What, shall we parley with the Christian,
Or cross the stream and meet him in the field?

GAZELLUS

King of Natolia, let us treat of peace,
We all are glutted with the Christians' blood
And have a greater foe to fight against –   15
Proud Tamburlaine, that now in Asia

0.2   s.d. URIBASSA ed. (Upibassa O1)

> *train* The train, or group of followers, consisted of whatever extras could be
> recruited for various large and impressive scenes (see, for example, the opening
> stage directions for Part Two, I.v; II.i; II.ii; III.iii; etc.). A quick change of costume
> could transform a journeyman actor from Turk to Christian, or from Egyptian sol-
> dier to Tamburlaine loyalist. The numbers were small, but strategic placement
> onstage could give the impression of a large army just off. In the opening chorus of
> *Henry V,* Shakespeare appeals to his audience to compensate for the inadequacies
> of stage representation: 'Piece out our imperfections with your thoughts – / Into a
> thousand parts divide one man.' Since the Rose stage, where *Tamburlaine* was
> performed during the 1590s, was considerably smaller than that at the Globe, the
> discrepancy might have seemed less glaring there, since the crowded Rose stage
> could more easily have given the impression of large numbers pressing at the sides.

1   *Egregious* Distinguished
2   *issue* offspring
6   *Natolia* a more extensive area of Asia Minor than the present-day Anatolia
11   *parley* ed. (parle O1)

Near Guyron's head doth set his conquering feet,
And means to fire Turkey as he goes.
'Gainst him my lord must you address your power.

URIBASSA

Besides, King Sigismund hath brought from Christendom   20
More than his camp of stout Hungarians,
Slavonians, Almains, Rutters, Muffs, and Danes,
That with the halberd, lance, and murdering axe,
Will hazard that we might with surety hold.

[ORCANES]

Though from the shortest northern parallel,   25
Vast Gruntland, compassed with the frozen sea,
Inhabited with tall and sturdy men,
Giants as big as hugy Polypheme,
Millions of soldiers cut the arctic line,
Bringing the strength of Europe to these arms,   30
Our Turkey blades shall glide through all their throats,
And make this champion mead a bloody fen.
Danubius' stream that runs to Trebizon,
Shall carry wrapped within his scarlet waves,
As martial presents to our friends at home,   35
The slaughtered bodies of these Christians.
The Terrene main wherein Danubius falls
Shall by this battle be the bloody sea.
The wand'ring sailors of proud Italy

17 *Guyron* Guiron, a town on the upper Euphrates, north-east of Aleppo
22 *Almains* Germans *Rutters* horsemen
  Muffs a derogatory term for Swiss or Germans
23 *halberd* a long-handled spear with an axe-edge
25 *shortest . . . parallel* the smallest circle of latitude described on the globe toward the
  north
26 *Gruntland* Greenland
  frozen sea Arctic Ocean
27–8 *Inhabited . . . Giants* a popular belief in Marlowe's day
28 *Polypheme* the Cyclops in Homer's *Odyssey*
29 *cut . . . line* cross the Arctic Circle from the north
32 *champion mead* level grassland
33–41 'Marlowe sees the waters of the Danube sweeping from the river-mouths in two
  strong currents, the one racing across the Black Sea to Trebizond, the other swirling
  southward to the Bosphorus, and so onward to the Hellespont and the Aegean;
  both currents bear the slaughtered bodies of Christian soldiers, the one to bring
  proof of victory to the great Turkish town, the other to strike terror to the Italian
  merchants cruising round the Isles of Greece.' (E. Seaton, 'Marlowe's Map', p. 33.)
37 *Terrene main* the Mediterranean

Shall meet those Christians fleeting with the tide,   40
Beating in heaps against their argosies,
And make fair Europe mounted on her bull,
Trapped with the wealth and riches of the world.
Alight and wear a woeful mourning weed.

GAZELLUS

Yet, stout Orcanes, prorex of the world,   45
Since Tamburlaine hath mustered all his men,
Marching from Cairo northward with his camp
To Alexandria and the frontier towns,
Meaning to make a conquest of our land,
'Tis requisite to parley for a peace   50
With Sigismund the King of Hungary,
And save our forces for the hot assaults
Proud Tamburlaine intends Natolia.

ORCANES

Viceroy of Byron, wisely hast thou said:
My realm, the centre of our empery,   55
Once lost, all Turkey would be overthrown.
And for that cause the Christians shall have peace.
Slavonians, Almains, Rutters, Muffs, and Danes,
Fear not Orcanes, but great Tamburlaine –
Nor he, but Fortune that hath made him great.   60
We have revolted Grecians, Albanese,
Sicilians, Jews, Arabians, Turks, and Moors,
Natolians, Sorians, black Egyptians,
Illyrians, Thracians, and Bithynians,
Enough to swallow forceless Sigismund,   65
Yet scarce enough t'encounter Tamburlaine.

40   *fleeting* floating
41   *argosies* merchant ships
42   Zeus, in the form of a bull, carried Europa, the daughter of Agenor, King of Phoenicia, across the sea to Crete.
43   *Trapped* adorned
44   *weed* garment
45   *prorex* viceroy
47   *Cairo* ed. (Cairon O1)
50   *parley* ed. (parle O1)   54 *Byron* a town near Babylon
55   *empery* empire
59   *Fear* frighten
61   *Albanese* Albanians
63   *Sorians* Syrians
64   *Illyrians* O3, Q (Illicians O1)

He brings a world of people to the field:
From Scythia to the oriental plage
Of India, where raging Lantchidol
Beats on the regions with his boisterous blows   70
That never seaman yet discoverèd,
All Asia is in arms with Tamburlaine;
Even from the midst of fiery Cancer's tropic
To Amazonia under Capricorn
And thence as far as Archipelago,   75
All Afric is in arms with Tamburlaine.
Therefore, viceroys, the Christians must have peace.

68   *oriental plage* eastern shore
69   *Lantchidol* an arm of the Indian Ocean
73–4 *from . . . Capricorn* from the Canaries, the centre of the Tropic of Cancer, to the
     region known as Amazonia, near the supposed sources of the Nile
75   *thence . . . Archipelago* northward to the Aegean islands

ACT I, SCENE ii

[Enter] SIGISMUND, FREDERICK, BALDWIN,
and their train, with drums and trumpets

SIGISMUND

    Orcanes, as our legates promised thee,
    We with our peers have crossed Danubius' stream
    To treat of friendly peace or deadly war:
    Take which thou wilt, for as the Romans used,
    I here present thee with a naked sword.   5
    Wilt thou have war, then shake this blade at me,
    If peace, restore it to my hands again
    And I will sheathe it to confirm the same.

ORCANES

    Stay, Sigismund, forgett'st thou I am he
    That with the cannon shook Vienna walls,   10
    And made it dance upon the continent,
    As when the massy substance of the earth
    Quiver about the axle-tree of heaven?
    Forgett'st thou that I sent a shower of darts,
    Mingled with powdered shot and feathered steel,   15
    So thick upon the blink-eyed burghers' heads,
    That thou thyself, then County Palatine,
    The King of Boheme, and the Austric Duke,
    Sent heralds out, which basely on their knees
    In all your names desired a truce of me?   20
    Forgett'st thou that to have me raise my siege
    Wagons of gold were set before my tent,
    Stamped with the princely fowl that in her wings
    Carries the fearful thunderbolts of Jove?
    How canst thou think of this and offer war?   25

I. ii   Though this is not really a different scene, most editors follow O1 in beginning a new
         scene here.
13   *axle-tree of heaven* See note to Part One, IV.ii.50 above.
16   *blink-eyed* unable to look steadily upon the missiles
17   *County* Count
18   *Austric* Austrian
23   *princely fowl* the eagle

SIGISMUND

    Vienna was besieged, and I was there,
    Then County Palatine, but now a king;
    And what we did was in extremity.
    But now, Orcanes, view my royal host,
    That hides these plains and seems as vast and wide   30
    As doth the desert of Arabia
    To those that stand on Badgeth's lofty tower,
    Or as the ocean to the traveller
    That rests upon the snowy Appenines:
    And tell me whether I should stoop so low,   35
    Or treat of peace with the Natolian king?

GAZELLUS

    Kings of Natolia and of Hungary,
    We came from Turkey to confirm a league,
    And not to dare each other to the field;
    A friendly parley might become ye both.   40

FREDERICK

    And we from Europe to the same intent,
    Which if your general refuse or scorn,
    Our tents are pitched, our men stand in array,
    Ready to charge you ere you stir your feet.

ORCANES

    So prest are we, but yet if Sigismund   45
    Speak as a friend and stand not upon terms,
    Here is his sword, let peace be ratified
    On these conditions specified before,
    Drawn with advice of our ambassadors.

SIGISMUND

    Then here I sheathe it, and give thee my hand,   50
    Never to draw it out or manage arms
    Against thyself or thy confederates,
    But whilst I live will be at truce with thee.

ORCANES

    But, Sigismund, confirm it with an oath,
    And swear in sight of heaven and by thy Christ.   55

SIGISMUND

    By him that made the world and saved my soul,

32   *Badgeth* Baghdad
40   *parley* ed. (parle O1)
45   *prest* ready

The son of God and issue of a maid,
Sweet Jesus Christ, I solemnly protest
And vow to keep this peace inviolable.

ORCANES

By sacred Mahomet, the friend of God, 60
Whose holy Alcoran remains with us,
Whose glorious body when he left the world
Closed in a coffin mounted up the air
And hung on stately Mecca's temple roof,
I swear to keep this truce inviolable, 65
Of whose conditions and our solemn oaths
Signed with our hands, each shall retain a scroll
As memorable witness of our league.
Now, Sigismund, if any Christian king
Encroach upon the confines of thy realm, 70
Send word Orcanes of Natolia
Confirmed this league beyond Danubius' stream,
And they will, trembling, sound a quick retreat,
So am I feared among all nations.

SIGISMUND

If any heathen potentate or king 75
Invade Natolia, Sigismund will send
A hundred thousand horse trained to the war
And backed by stout lancers of Germany
The strength and sinews of th'imperial seat.

ORCANES

I thank thee, Sigismund, but when I war 80
All Asia Minor, Africa, and Greece
Follow my standard and my thund'ring drums.
Come let us go and banquet in our tents –
I will dispatch chief of my army hence
To fair Natolia and to Trebizon, 85
To stay my coming 'gainst proud Tamburlaine.
Friend Sigismund, and peers of Hungary,
Come banquet and carouse with us a while,
And then depart we to our territories.

Exeunt

58   *protest* swear
70   *confines* borders
84   *chief* most
86   *stay* await

ACT I, SCENE iii

[Enter] CALLAPINE *with* ALMEDA, *his keeper*

CALLAPINE

Sweet Almeda, pity the ruthful plight
Of Callapine, the son of Bajazeth,
Born to be monarch of the western world,
Yet here detained by cruel Tamburlaine.

ALMEDA

My lord I pity it, and with my heart   5
Wish your release, but he whose wrath is death,
My sovereign lord, renownèd Tamburlaine,
Forbids you further liberty than this.

CALLAPINE

Ah, were I now but half so eloquent
To paint in words what I'll perform in deeds,   10
I know thou wouldst depart from hence with me.

ALMEDA

Not for all Afric, therefore move me not.

CALLAPINE

Yet hear me speak, my gentle Almeda.

ALMEDA

No speech to that end, by your favour sir.

CALLAPINE

By Cairo runs –   15

ALMEDA

No talk of running, I tell you sir.

CALLAPINE

A little further, gentle Almeda.

ALMEDA

Well sir, what of this?

CALLAPINE

By Cairo runs to Alexandria bay
Darote's streams, wherein at anchor lies   20
A Turkish galley of my royal fleet,

3   *western world* Turkish empire
12 *move* urge
15 *Cairo* ed. and so throughout (Cario O1)
20 *Darote's streams* the Nile from Cairo to Alexandria, which runs by the town of Darote

Waiting my coming to the river side,
Hoping by some means I shall be released:
Which when I come aboard will hoist up sail,
And soon put forth into the Terrene sea,   25
Where 'twixt the isles of Cyprus and of Crete,
We quickly may in Turkish seas arrive.
Then shalt thou see a hundred kings and more
Upon their knees all bid me welcome home.
Amongst so many crowns of burnished gold,   30
Choose which thou wilt, all are at thy command;
A thousand galleys manned with Christian slaves
I freely give thee, which shall cut the straits
And bring armadoes from the coast of Spain,
Fraughted with gold of rich America;   35
The Grecian virgins shall attend on thee,
Skilful in music and in amorous lays,
As fair as was Pygmalion's ivory girl,
Or lovely Iö metamorphosèd.
With naked negroes shall thy coach be drawn,   40
And as thou rid'st in triumph through the streets,
The pavement underneath thy chariot wheels
With Turkey carpets shall be coverèd.
And cloth of Arras hung about the walls,
Fit objects for thy princely eye to pierce.   45
A hundred bassoes clothed in crimson silk
Shall ride before thee on Barbarian steeds,
And when thou goest, a golden canopy
Enchased with precious stones, which shine as bright
As that fair veil that covers all the world   50
When Phoebus leaping from his hemisphere
Descendeth downward to th'antipodes.
And more than this, for all I cannot tell.

34   *armadoes* warships
35   *Fraughted* laden
37   *lays* songs
38   *Pygmalion's ivory girl* Galatea, the statue created by the sculptor Pygmalion and brought to life by Aphrodite
39   *Iö* daughter of Inachus, King of Argos. She was loved by Zeus and transformed into a milk-white heifer.
44   *cloth of Arras* rich tapestry   46   *bassoes* pashas
48   *goest* walk   49   *Enchased* adorned
50   *fair veil* i.e. the stars   51   *Phoebus* the sun
52   *antipodes* the opposite side of the earth

ALMEDA

How far hence lies the galley, say you?

CALLAPINE

Sweet Almeda, scarce half a league from hence. 55

ALMEDA

But need we not be spied going aboard?

CALLAPINE

Betwixt the hollow hanging of a hill
And crooked bending of a craggy rock,
The sails wrapped up, the mast and tacklings down,
She lies so close that none can find her out. 60

ALMEDA

I like that well; but tell me, my lord, if I should let you go, would
you be as good as your word? Shall I be made a king for my
labour?

CALLAPINE

As I am Callapine the emperor,
And by the hand of Mahomet I swear, 65
Thou shalt be crowned a king and be my mate.

ALMEDA

Then here I swear, as I am Almeda,
Your keeper under Tamburlaine the Great
(For that's the style and title I have yet),
Although he sent a thousand armèd men 70
To intercept this haughty enterprise,
Yet would I venture to conduct your grace
And die before I brought you back again.

CALLAPINE

Thanks, gentle Almeda, then let us haste,
Lest time be past and ling'ring let us both. 75

ALMEDA

When you will my lord, I am ready.

CALLAPINE

Even straight; and farewell cursèd Tamburlaine.
Now go I to revenge my father's death.

Exeunt

56 *need we not* shall we not inevitably
60 *close* concealed   66 *mate* equal
69 *style* designation
71 *haughty* grand
75 *let* hinder
77 *straight* immediately

ACT I, SCENE iv

[Enter] TAMBURLAINE *with* ZENOCRATE,
and his three sons, CALYPHAS, AMYRAS,
and CELEBINUS, *with drums and trumpets*

TAMBURLAINE

Now, bright Zenocrate, the world's fair eye,
Whose beams illuminate the lamps of heaven,
Whose cheerful looks do clear the cloudy air
And clothe it in a crystal livery,
Now rest thee here on fair Larissa plains,   5
Where Egypt and the Turkish empire parts,
Between thy sons that shall be emperors,
And every one commander of a world.

ZENOCRATE

Sweet Tamburlaine, when wilt thou leave these arms
And save thy sacred person free from scathe   10
And dangerous chances of the wrathful war?

TAMBURLAINE

When heaven shall cease to move on both the poles
And when the ground whereon my soldiers march
Shall rise aloft and touch the hornèd moon,
And not before, my sweet Zenocrate;   15
Sit up and rest thee like a lovely queen.
So, now she sits in pomp and majesty,
When these my sons, more precious in mine eyes
Than all the wealthy kingdoms I subdued,
Placed by her side, look on their mother's face.   20
But yet methinks their looks are amorous,
Not martial as the sons of Tamburlaine.
Water and air being symbolized in one
Argue their want of courage and of wit;
Their hair as white as milk and soft as down,   25
Which should be like the quills of porcupines,

5   *Larissa* a sea-coast town south of Gaza
10   *scathe* harm
21   *amorous* loving, gentle
23–4   Being overbalanced in the phlegmatic and sanguine humours (water and blood),
the boys lack the bile and choler which might give them courage and wit.

As black as jet, and hard as iron or steel,
Bewrays they are too dainty for the wars.
Their fingers made to quaver on a lute,
Their arms to hang about a lady's neck,   30
Their legs to dance and caper in the air,
Would make me think them bastards, not my sons,
But that I know they issued from thy womb,
That never looked on man but Tamburlaine.

ZENOCRATE

My gracious lord, they have their mother's looks,   35
But when they list, their conquering father's heart:
This lovely boy, the youngest of the three,
Not long ago bestrid a Scythian steed,
Trotting the ring and tilting at a glove,
Which when he tainted with his slender rod,   40
He reined him straight and made him so curvet,
As I cried out for fear he should have fall'n.

TAMBURLAINE

Well done, my boy, thou shalt have shield and lance,
Armour of proof, horse, helm, and curtle-axe,
And I will teach thee how to charge thy foe   45
And harmless run among the deadly pikes.
If thou wilt love the wars and follow me,
Thou shalt be made a king and reign with me,
Keeping in iron cages emperors.
If thou exceed thy elder brothers' worth   50
And shine in complete virtue more than they,
Thou shalt be king before them, and thy seed
Shall issue crownèd from their mother's womb.

CELEBINUS

Yes father, you shall see me if I live
Have under me as many kings as you,   55
And march with such a multitude of men
As all the world shall tremble at their view.

28   *Bewrays* betrays, reveals
36   *list* wish, choose
39   *Trotting . . . glove* jousting exercises
40   *tainted* struck (a technical term in tilting)
41   *curvet* leap, spring
44   *proof* tested strength
       curtle-axe heavy slashing sword
51   *virtue* manly qualities

TAMBURLAINE

    These words assure me, boy, thou art my son.

    When I am old and cannot manage arms,

    Be thou the scourge and terror of the world.   60

AMYRAS

    Why may not I, my lord, as well as he,

    Be termed the scourge and terror of the world?

TAMBURLAINE

    Be all a scourge and terror to the world,

    Or else you are not sons of Tamburlaine.

CALYPHAS

    But while my brothers follow arms, my lord,   65

    Let me accompany my gracious mother,

    They are enough to conquer all the world

    And you have won enough for me to keep.

TAMBURLAINE

    Bastardly boy, sprung from some coward's loins,

    And not the issue of great Tamburlaine,   70

    Of all the provinces I have subdued

    Thou shalt not have a foot, unless thou bear

    A mind courageous and invincible:

    For he shall wear the crown of Persia

    Whose head hath deepest scars, whose breast most wounds,   75

    Which being wroth, sends lightning from his eyes,

    And in the furrows of his frowning brows

    Harbours revenge, war, death and cruelty.

    For in a field whose superficies

    Is covered with a liquid purple veil   80

    And sprinkled with the brains of slaughtered men,

    My royal chair of state shall be advanced,

    And he that means to place himself therein

    Must armèd wade up to the chin in blood.

ZENOCRATE

    My lord, such speeches to our princely sons   85

    Dismays their minds before they come to prove

    The wounding troubles angry war affords.

CELEBINUS

    No madam, these are speeches fit for us,

---

76   *wroth* enraged

79   *superficies* ed. (superfluities O1) surface

86   *prove* find out by experience

For if his chair were in a sea of blood
I would prepare a ship and sail to it,   90
Ere I would lose the title of a king.

AMYRAS

And I would strive to swim through pools of blood
Or make a bridge of murdered carcasses
Whose arches should be framed with bones of Turks,
Ere I would lose the title of a king.   95

TAMBURLAINE

Well, lovely boys, you shall be emperors both,
Stretching your conquering arms from east to west;
And, sirrah, if you mean to wear a crown,
When we shall meet the Turkish deputy
And all his viceroys, snatch it from his head,   100
And cleave his pericranion with thy sword.

CALYPHAS

If any man will hold him, I will strike,
And cleave him to the channel with my sword.

TAMBURLAINE

Hold him and cleave him too, or I'll cleave thee,
For we will march against them presently.   105
Theridamas, Techelles, and Casane
Promised to meet me on Larissa plains
With hosts apiece against this Turkish crew,
For I have sworn by sacred Mahomet
To make it parcel of my empery.   110
The trumpets sound, Zenocrate, they come.

---

101   *pericranion* skull
103   *channel* throat
110   *parcel . . . empery* part of my empire

ACT I, SCENE v

Enter THERIDAMAS *and his train*
with drums and trumpets

TAMBURLAINE

Welcome Theridamas, King of Argier.

THERIDAMAS

My lord the great and mighty Tamburlaine,
Arch-monarch of the world, I offer here
My crown, myself, and all the power I have,
In all affection at thy kingly feet.   5

TAMBURLAINE

Thanks, good Theridamas.

THERIDAMAS

Under my colours march ten thousand Greeks,
And of Argier and Afric's frontier towns
Twice twenty thousand valiant men-at-arms,
All which have sworn to sack Natolia;   10
Five hundred brigandines are under sail,
Meet for your service on the sea, my lord.
That launching from Argier to Tripoli
Will quickly ride before Natolia
And batter down the castles on the shore.   15

TAMBURLAINE

Well said, Argier, receive thy crown again.

I.v   As at I.ii, this is not really a new scene.
  8   *Argier* Algiers
 11   *brigandines* brigantines, small vessels which could be either sailed or rowed

Enter TECHELLES *and* USUMCASANE *together*

TAMBURLAINE

Kings of Morocco and of Fez, welcome.

USUMCASANE

Magnificent and peerless Tamburlaine,
I and my neighbour King of Fez have brought
To aid thee in this Turkish expedition
A hundred thousand expert soldiers: 5
From Azamor to Tunis near the sea
Is Barbary unpeopled for thy sake,
And all the men in armour under me,
Which with my crown I gladly offer thee.

TAMBURLAINE

Thanks, King of Morocco, take your crown again.   10

TECHELLES

And mighty Tamburlaine, our earthly god,
Whose looks make this inferior world to quake,
I here present thee with the crown of Fez,
And with an host of Moors trained to the war,
Whose coal-black faces make their foes retire   15
And quake for fear, as if infernal Jove,
Meaning to aid thee in these Turkish arms,
Should pierce the black circumference of hell
With ugly Furies bearing fiery flags,
And millions of his strong tormenting spirits.   20
From strong Tesella unto Biledull,
All Barbary is unpeopled for thy sake.

TAMBURLAINE

Thanks, King of Fez, take here thy crown again.
Your presence, loving friends and fellow kings,

I.vi Again, not really a new scene.
  1 *Morocco* ed., and so throughout (Moroccus O1)
     Fez ed., and so throughout (Fesse O1)
  6 *Azamor* a town in North Africa
 16 *infernal Jove* Pluto. The Furies were in his service.
 17 *thee* ed. (them O1)   *these* O3, Q (this O1)
 21 *Tesella, Biledull* a town and a province in North Africa

Makes me to surfeit in conceiving joy;   25
If all the crystal gates of Jove's high court
Were opened wide, and I might enter in
To see the state and majesty of heaven,
It could not more delight me than your sight.
Now will we banquet on these plains a while,   30
And after march to Turkey with our camp,
In numbers more than are the drops that fall
When Boreas rents a thousand swelling clouds.
And proud Orcanes of Natolia
With all his viceroys shall be so afraid,   35
That though the stones as at Deucalion's flood
Were turned to men, he should be overcome.
Such lavish will I make of Turkish blood
That Jove shall send his wingèd messenger
To bid me sheathe my sword and leave the field;   40
The sun, unable to sustain the sight,
Shall hide his head in Thetis' watery lap
And leave his steeds to fair Boötes' charge –
For half the world shall perish in this fight.
But now, my friends, let me examine ye,   45
How have ye spent your absent time from me?

USUMCASANE

My lord, our men of Barbary have marched
Four hundred miles with armour on their backs
And lain in leaguer fifteen months and more,
For since we left you at the Soldan's court,   50
We have subdued the southern Guallatia,
And all the land unto the coast of Spain.
We kept the narrow Strait of Gibraltar,
And made Canaria call us kings and lords,

31   *camp* army
33   *Boreas* the north wind
36–7   Deucalion and his wife Pyrrha were the sole survivors of a flood sent by Zeus to
         exterminate the human race. They repopulated the earth by casting stones to the
         ground, from which sprang men and women.
38   *lavish* spilling, squandering
39   *winged messenger* Mercury
42   *Thetis* a sea goddess
43   *Boötes* a northern constellation
49   *lain in leaguer* been on campaign
51   *Guallatia* Gualata, a province in North Africa, south-west of the Sahara
54   *Canaria* the Canary Islands

Yet never did they recreate themselves   55
Or cease one day from war and hot alarms,
And therefore let them rest a while my lord.

TAMBURLAINE

They shall, Casane, and 'tis time i'faith.

TECHELLES

And I have marched along the river Nile
To Machda, where the mighty Christian priest   60
Called John the Great sits in a milk-white robe,
Whose triple mitre I did take by force
And made him swear obedience to my crown.
From thence unto Cazates did I march,
Where Amazonians met me in the field,   65
With whom (being women) I vouchsafed a league,
And with my power did march to Zanzibar,
The western part of Afric, where I viewed
The Ethiopian sea, rivers and lakes,
But neither man nor child in all the land.   70
Therefore I took my course to Manico,
Where unresisted I removed my camp,
And by the coast of Byather at last
I came to Cubar, where the negroes dwell,
And conquering that, made haste to Nubia;   75
There, having sacked Borno the kingly seat,
I took the king, and led him bound in chains
Unto Damascus, where I stayed before.

TAMBURLAINE

Well done Techelles. What saith Theridamas?

THERIDAMAS

I left the confines and the bounds of Afric   80

59–75   Marlowe constructs Techelles's route on the map of Ortelius from northern Africa southward to Zanzibar and northward again to Nubia. Techelles's journey takes him down the Nile to Machda, an Abyssinian town, where he defeats Prester John ('John the Great'), a legendary priest-king supposed to rule a vast empire; he then continues down to Cazates, a town near where the Nile rises out of Lake Victoria; he then invades the province of Zanzibar (not the island but an area on the west coast of Africa), and makes his way northward from there through central and west Africa ('Manico', 'Byather', and 'Cubar') across to Nubia.

65   *Amazonians* Amazons
66   *league* alliance
69   *Ethiopian sea* the South Atlantic
76   *Borno* the chief town of Nubia
78   *Damascus* ed., and so throughout (Damasco O1)

And made a voyage into Europe,
Where by the river Tyros I subdued
Stoka, Padalia, and Codemia.
Then crossed the sea and came to Oblia,
And Nigra Silva, where the devils dance,   85
Which in despite of them I set on fire.
From thence I crossed the gulf called by the name
Mare Majore of th'inhabitants:
Yet shall my soldiers make no period
Until Natolia kneel before your feet.   90

TAMBURLAINE

Then will we triumph, banquet and carouse,
Cooks shall have pensions to provide us cates
And glut us with the dainties of the world,
Lachryma Christi and Calabrian wines
Shall common soldiers drink in quaffing bowls,   95
Ay, liquid gold when we have conquered him,
Mingled with coral and with orient pearl.
Come let us banquet and carouse the whiles.

Exeunt

82–6   Theridamas's journey takes him across the Dneister river (the 'Tyros'), the southern
boundary of the province of Podalia, north-west of the Black Sea. There he sub-
dues the towns of Stoka and Codemia, and passing through the Black Forest, or
Nigra Silva, he destroys the town of Oblia. On Ortelius's map the *Nigra Silva*
resembles a body of water (hence the confusion of l. 84).

88   *Mare Majore* the Black Sea
89   *period* pause
92   *cates* delicacies
94   *Lachryma Christi* a sweet wine of southern Italy
97   *orient* ed. (orientall O1) lustrous

[Enter] SIGISMUND, FREDERICK, BALDWIN, *with their train*

SIGISMUND

    Now say, my lords of Buda and Bohemia,
    What motion is it that inflames your thoughts
    And stirs your valours to such sudden arms?

FREDERICK

    Your majesty remembers, I am sure,
    What cruel slaughter of our Christian bloods   5
    These heathenish Turks and pagans lately made
    Betwixt the city Zula and Danubius,
    How through the midst of Varna and Bulgaria
    And almost to the very walls of Rome,
    They have not long since massacred our camp.   10
    It resteth now then that your majesty
    Take all advantages of time and power
    And work revenge upon these infidels.
    Your highness knows, for Tamburlaine's repair,
    That strikes a terror to all Turkish hearts,   15
    Natolia hath dismissed the greatest part
    Of all his army pitched against our power
    Betwixt Cutheia and Orminius' mount,
    And sent them marching up to Belgasar,
    Acantha, Antioch, and Caesarea,   20
    To aid the kings of Soria and Jerusalem.
    Now then, my lord, advantage take hereof
    And issue suddenly upon the rest,
    That in the fortune of their overthrow
    We may discourage all the pagan troop   25
    That dare attempt to war with Christians.

    1   *Buda* a city on the Danube, now part of Budapest
    2   *motion* emotion
    7   *Zula* a town which Ortelius locates north of the Danube
    8   *Varna* a city in north-east Bulgaria
    9   *Rome* possibly Constantinople
   11   *resteth* remains
   14   *repair* arrival
   18   *Orminius' mount* Mt Horminius in Bithynia
 18–20   *Cutheia, Belgasar, Acantha* towns in Anatolia

SIGISMUND

    But calls not then your grace to memory
    The league we lately made with King Orcanes,
    Confirmed by oaths and articles of peace,
    And calling Christ for record of our truths?   30
    This should be treachery and violence
    Against the grace of our profession.

BALDWIN

    No whit my lord: for with such infidels,
    In whom no faith nor true religion rests,
    We are not bound to those accomplishments   35
    The holy laws of Christendom enjoin;
    But as the faith which they profanely plight
    Is not by necessary policy
    To be esteemed assurance for ourselves,
    So what we vow to them should not infringe   40
    Our liberty of arms and victory.

SIGISMUND

    Though I confess the oaths they undertake
    Breed little strength to our security,
    Yet those infirmities that thus defame
    Their faiths, their honours, and their religion,   45
    Should not give us presumption to the like.
    Our faiths are sound and must be consummate,
    Religious, righteous, and inviolate.

FREDERICK

    Assure your grace 'tis superstition
    To stand so strictly on dispensive faith,   50
    And should we lose the opportunity
    That God hath given to venge our Christians' death
    And scourge their foul blasphemous paganism,

---

32   *profession* oath
33   *No whit* Not in the least
35   *accomplishments* performances of obligation
37   *plight* pledge themselves to
38   *policy* statecraft
47   *consummate* ed. (consinuate O1) perfect
50   *dispensive faith* oath which may be set aside by special dispensation on the part of
     the church

As fell to Saul, to Balaam, and the rest,
That would not kill and curse at God's command,   55
So surely will the vengeance of the Highest
And jealous anger of his fearful arm
Be poured with rigour on our sinful heads,
If we neglect this offered victory.

SIGISMUND

Then arm, my lords, and issue suddenly,   60
Giving commandment to our general host
With expedition to assail the pagan,
And take the victory our God hath given.

Exeunt

54   Saul failed to kill King Agag and his flocks (I *Samuel* 15), but Balaam obeyed
     God in refusing to curse the children of Israel (*Numbers* 22–4); so Frederick's
     appeal to scriptural authority is confused.
62   *expedition* speed

ACT II, SCENE ii

[*Enter*] ORCANES, GAZELLUS, URIBASSA, *with their train*

ORCANES

    Gazellus, Uribassa, and the rest,
    Now will we march from proud Orminius' mount
    To fair Natolia, where our neighbour kings
    Expect our power and our royal presence
    T'encounter with the cruel Tamburlaine,   5
    That nigh Larissa sways a mighty host
    And with the thunder of his martial tools
    Makes earthquakes in the hearts of men and heaven.

GAZELLUS

    And now come we to make his sinews shake
    With greater power than erst his pride hath felt –   10
    An hundred kings by scores will bid him arms,
    And hundred thousands subjects to each score:
    Which if a shower of wounding thunderbolts
    Should break out of the bowels of the clouds
    And fall as thick as hail upon our heads   15
    In partial aid of that proud Scythian,
    Yet should our courages and steelèd crests
    And numbers more than infinite of men
    Be able to withstand and conquer him.

URIBASSA

    Methinks I see how glad the Christian king   20
    Is made for joy of your admitted truce,
    That could not but before be terrified
    With unacquainted power of our host.

              Enter a MESSENGER

MESSENGER

    Arm, dread sovereign and my noble lords!
    The treacherous army of the Christians,   25
    Taking advantage of your slender power,

  10   *erst* hitherto
  11   *bid him arms* challenge him to fight
  16   *partial* biased

Comes marching on us and determines straight
To bid us battle for our dearest lives.

ORCANES

Traitors, villains, damnèd Christians!
Have I not here the articles of peace   30
And solemn covenants we have both confirmed,
He by his Christ, and I by Mahomet?

GAZELLUS

Hell and confusion light upon their heads
That with such treason seek our overthrow,
And cares so little for their prophet Christ!   35

ORCANES

Can there be such deceit in Christians,
Or treason in the fleshly heart of man,
Whose shape is figure of the highest God?
Then if there be a Christ, as Christians say,
But in their deeds deny him for their Christ,   40
If he be son to everliving Jove
And hath the power of his outstretched arm,
If he be jealous of his name and honour
As is our holy prophet Mahomet,
Take here these papers as our sacrifice   45
And witness of thy servant's perjury.

                    [*He tears up the articles of peace*]

Open, thou shining veil of Cynthia,
And make a passage from th'empyreal heaven,
That he that sits on high and never sleeps,
Nor in one place is circumscriptible,   50
But everywhere fills every continent
With strange infusion of his sacred vigour,
May in his endless power and purity
Behold and venge this traitor's perjury.
Thou Christ that art esteemed omnipotent,   55
If thou wilt prove thyself a perfect God
Worthy the worship of all faithful hearts,
Be now revenged upon this traitor's soul
And make the power I have left behind
(Too little to defend our guiltless lives)   60
Sufficient to discomfort and confound

38 *figure* image
47 *Cynthia* the moon

128

The trustless force of those false Christians.
To arms, my lords, on Christ still let us cry –
If there be Christ, we shall have victory.

[*Exeunt*]

ACT II, SCENE iii

Sound to the battle, and SIGISMUND *comes out wounded*

SIGISMUND

Discomfited is all the Christian host
And God hath thundered vengeance from on high
For my accursed and hateful perjury.
O just and dreadful punisher of sin,
Let the dishonour of the pains I feel   5
In this my mortal well-deservèd wound
End all my penance in my sudden death,
And let this death wherein to sin I die
Conceive a second life in endless mercy!

[*Dies*]

Enter ORCANES, GAZELLUS, URIBASSA, *with others*

ORCANES

Now lie the Christians bathing in their bloods,   10
And Christ or Mahomet hath been my friend.

GAZELLUS

See here the perjured traitor Hungary,
Bloody and breathless for his villainy.

ORCANES

Now shall his barbarous body be a prey
To beasts and fowls, and all the winds shall breathe   15
Through shady leaves of every senseless tree
Murmurs and hisses for his heinous sin.
Now scalds his soul in the Tartarian streams
And feeds upon the baneful tree of hell,
That Zoacum, that fruit of bitterness   20
That in the midst of fire is ingraft,
Yet flourisheth as Flora in her pride,
With apples like the heads of damnèd fiends.

Scene iii ed. (O1 omits)
1   *Discomfited* Routed
8   *wherein . . . die* which absolves me from my sin
18   *Tartarian* of Tartarus, the region of hell where the worst sinners were punished
20   *Zoacum* (or Ezecum) a tree of hell described in the Koran, XXXVII, 60–4
22   *Flora* the Roman goddess of springtime and flowers

The devils there in chains of quenchless flame
Shall lead his soul through Orcus' burning gulf   25
From pain to pain, whose change shall never end.
What sayest thou yet, Gazellus, to his foil,
Which we referred to justice of his Christ
And to his power, which here appears as full
As rays of Cynthia to the clearest sight?   30

GAZELLUS

'Tis but the fortune of the wars, my lord,
Whose power is often proved a miracle.

ORCANES

Yet in my thoughts shall Christ be honourèd,
Not doing Mahomet an injury
Whose power had share in this our victory.   35
And since this miscreant hath disgraced his faith
And died a traitor both to heaven and earth,
We will both watch and ward shall keep his trunk
Amidst these plains for fowls to prey upon.
Go Uribassa, give it straight in charge.   40

URIBASSA

I will my lord.

      Exit URIBASSA [*and others, with* SIGISMUND'*s body*]

ORCANES

And now, Gazellus, let us haste and meet
Our army and our brother of Jerusalem,
Of Soria, Trebizon, and Amasia,
And happily with full Natolian bowls   45
Of Greekish wine now let us celebrate
Our happy conquest and his angry fate.

                                            Exeunt

---

25   *Orcus* Hades. Marlowe here fuses Muslim, Christian, and Greek notions of hell.
27   *foil* defeat
29   *his* Christ's
30   *rays of Cynthia* moonlight
32   *proved* asserted to be
36   *miscreant* vile wretch
38   *will . . . ward* decree that continuous guard
40   *give . . . charge* command it immediately
43   *Our army* i.e. the main body of our army
44   *Amasia* a district of Anatolia in northern Asia Minor
47   *angry* grievous

ACT II, SCENE iv

The arras is drawn, and ZENOCRATE *lies in her bed of state,*
TAMBURLAINE *sitting by her, three* PHYSICIANS *about her bed,*
tempering potions, THERIDAMAS, TECHELLES, USUMCASANE,
and the three sons [CALYPHAS, AMYRAS, CELEBINUS]

TAMBURLAINE

 Black is the beauty of the brightest day –
 The golden ball of heaven's eternal fire
 That danced with glory on the silver waves
 Now wants the fuel that inflamed his beams,
 And all with faintness and for foul disgrace   5
 He binds his temples with a frowning cloud,
 Ready to darken earth with endless night.
 Zenocrate that gave him light and life,
 Whose eyes shot fire from their ivory bowers
 And tempered every soul with lively heat,   10
 Now by the malice of the angry skies,
 Whose jealousy admits no second mate,
 Draws in the comfort of her latest breath
 All dazzled with the hellish mists of death.
 Now walk the angels on the walls of heaven   15
 As sentinels to warn th'immortal souls
 To entertain divine Zenocrate.
 Apollo, Cynthia, and the ceaseless lamps
 That gently looked upon this loathsome earth
 Shine downwards now no more, but deck the heavens 20
 To entertain divine Zenocrate.
 The crystal springs whose taste illuminates
 Refinèd eyes with an eternal sight,
 Like trièd silver runs through Paradise

---

s.d. 1 *arras* A curtain across the 'discovery space' or inner stage is here opened, revealing
   Zenocrate in her bed. It is then closed at the end of the scene.
  9 *bowers* i.e. the places where they were set
 17 *entertain* welcome
 18 *Apollo, Cynthia* the sun, the moon
 23 *Refinèd* given clearer sight
 24 *trièd* purified

To entertain divine Zenocrate.   25
The cherubins and holy seraphins
That sing and play before the King of Kings
Use all their voices and their instruments
To entertain divine Zenocrate.
And in this sweet and curious harmony,   30
The god that tunes this music to our souls
Holds out his hand in highest majesty
To entertain divine Zenocrate.
Then let some holy trance convey my thoughts
Up to the palace of th'empyreal heaven   35
That this my life may be as short to me
As are the days of sweet Zenocrate.
Physicians, will no physic do her good?

PHYSICIAN

My lord, your majesty shall soon perceive –
And if she pass this fit, the worst is past.   40

TAMBURLAINE

Tell me, how fares my fair Zenocrate?

ZENOCRATE

I fare, my lord, as other empresses,
That when this frail and transitory flesh
Hath sucked the measure of that vital air
That feeds the body with his dated health,   45
Wanes with enforced and necessary change.

TAMBURLAINE

May never such a change transform my love,
In whose sweet being I repose my life,
Whose heavenly presence beautified with health
Gives light to Phoebus and the fixed stars,   50
Whose absence makes the sun and moon as dark
As when opposed in one diameter
Their spheres are mounted on the serpent's head,
Or else descended to his winding train.

30   *curious* exquisite
35   *th'empyreal heaven* See note to Part One, II.vii.15.
45   *dated* having its preordained end
50   *Phoebus* the sun   51 *makes* O3, Q (make O1)
52   *opposed . . . diameter* i.e. when the earth is directly between the sun and the moon,
      or when the moon is directly between the sun and the earth
53–4 The 'serpent' is the constellation Draco (the Dragon). The moon's path intersects the
      ecliptic (thus causing an eclipse) at two points, the Dragon's head and tail ('train').

Live still my love and so conserve my life,   55
Or dying be the author of my death.
ZENOCRATE
Live still my lord, O let my sovereign live,
And sooner let the fiery element
Dissolve, and make your kingdom in the sky,
Than this base earth should shroud your majesty: 60
For should I but suspect your death by mine,
The comfort of my future happiness
And hope to meet your highness in the heavens,
Turned to despair, would break my wretched breast
And fury would confound my present rest.   65
But let me die, my love, yet let me die,
With love and patience let your true love die:
Your grief and fury hurts my second life.
Yet let me kiss my lord before I die
And let me die with kissing of my lord.   70
But since my life is lengthened yet a while,
Let me take leave of these my loving sons,
And of my lords whose true nobility
Have merited my latest memory.
Sweet sons farewell, in death resemble me,   75
And in your lives your father's excellency.
Some music, and my fit will cease, my lord.

They call music

TAMBURLAINE
Proud fury and intolerable fit,
That dares torment the body of my love
And scourge the Scourge of the immortal God!   80
Now are those spheres where Cupid used to sit,
Wounding the world with wonder and with love,
Sadly supplied with pale and ghastly death,
Whose darts do pierce the centre of my soul.
Her sacred beauty hath enchanted heaven   85
And, had she lived before the siege of Troy,
Helen, whose beauty summoned Greece to arms

56   *author* Q (anchor O1)
58   *the fiery element* the sphere of fire, separating the earth from the planetary bodies
68   *my second life* my life after death
81   *those spheres* her eyes

134

And drew a thousand ships to Tenedos,
Had not been named in Homer's Iliads –
Her name had been in every line he wrote.   90
Or had those wanton poets for whose birth
Old Rome was proud but gazed a while on her,
Nor Lesbia, nor Corinna had been named –
Zenocrate had been the argument
Of every epigram or elegy.   95

The music sounds, and she dies

What, is she dead? Techelles, draw thy sword
And wound the earth that it may cleave in twain,
And we descend into th'infernal vaults
To hale the Fatal Sisters by the hair
And throw them in the triple moat of hell   100
For taking hence my fair Zenocrate.
Casane and Theridamas, to arms!
Raise cavalieros higher than the clouds
And with the cannon break the frame of heaven,
Batter the shining palace of the sun   105
And shiver all the starry firmament,
For amorous Jove hath snatched my love from hence,
Meaning to make her stately queen of heaven.
What god soever holds thee in his arms,
Giving thee nectar and ambrosia,   110
Behold me here, divine Zenocrate,
Raving, impatient, desperate and mad,
Breaking my steelèd lance with which I burst
The rusty beams of Janus' temple doors,
Letting out death and tyrannizing war   115
To march with me under this bloody flag,
And if thou pitiest Tamburlaine the Great,
Come down from heaven and live with me again!

88   *Tenedos* a small island near Troy
90   *Her* Zenocrate's
93   *Lesbia . . . Corinna* women celebrated in the love poetry of Catullus and Ovid
94   *argument* subject, theme
99   *hale* drag
      Fatal Sisters the three goddesses who govern human destiny
103 *cavalieros* mounds on which cannon were placed
114 *Janus' temple doors* The doors of the temple of Janus in Rome were open in time of
      war, closed in time of peace.

THERIDAMAS

    Ah, good my lord, be patient, she is dead,
    And all this raging cannot make her live.   120
    If words might serve, our voice hath rent the air,
    If tears, our eyes have watered all the earth,
    If grief, our murdered hearts have strained forth blood.
    Nothing prevails, for she is dead, my lord.

TAMBURLAINE

    For she is dead? Thy words do pierce my soul.   125
    Ah sweet Theridamas, say so no more –
    Though she be dead, yet let me think she lives,
    And feed my mind that dies for want of her.
    Where'er her soul be, thou shalt stay with me
    Embalmed with cassia, ambergris, and myrrh,   130
    Not lapped in lead but in a sheet of gold,
    And till I die thou shalt not be interred.
    Then in as rich a tomb as Mausolus'
    We both will rest and have one epitaph,
    Writ in as many several languages   135
    As I have conquered kingdoms with my sword.
    This cursèd town will I consume with fire
    Because this place bereft me of my love:
    The houses burnt will look as if they mourned,
    And here will I set up her statue   140
    And march about it with my mourning camp,
    Drooping and pining for Zenocrate.

                      The arras is drawn
                            [*Exeunt*]

---

129   *thou* i.e. Zenocrate's body
130   *cassia* a fragrant shrub
       ambergris an odiferous substance used in perfumery
131   *lapped in lead* placed in a leaden coffin
133   *Mausolus* King of Caria, whose widow (also his sister) built for him a costly monument, called Mausoleum, at Halicarnassus
140   *statue* O3, Q (stature O1). Some editors emend to 'statua' for metrical reasons (see note in *O.E.D.*)

ACT III, SCENE i

[*Enter*] *the* KINGS OF TREBIZON *and* SORIA,
one bringing a sword, and another a sceptre. Next [ORCANES,
King of] *Natolia and* [KING OF] JERUSALEM *with the imperial
crown. After,* CALLAPINE, *and after him* [ALMEDA *and*] *other
Lords.* ORCANES *and* JERUSALEM *crown* [CALLAPINE]
and the other[*s*] *give him the sceptre*

ORCANES

Callapinus Cyricelibes, otherwise Cybelius, son and successive heir to the late mighty emperor Bajazeth, by the
aid of God and his friend Mahomet, Emperor of Natolia,
erusalem, Trebizon, Soria, Amasia, Thracia, Illyria, Carmonia, and all the hundred and thirty kingdoms late con-   5
tributory to his mighty father. Long live Callapinus, Emperor
of Turkey!

CALLAPINE

Thrice worthy kings of Natolia, and the rest,
I will requite your royal gratitudes
With all the benefits my empire yields;   10
And were the sinews of th'imperial seat
So knit and strengthened as when Bajazeth,
My royal lord and father, filled the throne,
Whose cursèd fate hath so dismembered it,
Then should you see this thief of Scythia,   15
This proud usurping King of Persia,
Do us such honour and supremacy,
Bearing the vengeance of our father's wrongs,
As all the world should blot our dignities
Out of the book of base-born infamies.   20
And now I doubt not but your royal cares
Hath so provided for this cursèd foe
That, since the heir of mighty Bajazeth
(An emperor so honoured for his virtues)
Revives the spirits of true Turkish hearts   25
In grievous memory of his father's shame,

4–5   *Carmonia* Carmania, south-east of Natolia and north of Syria
19   *blot our dignities* delete our noble names

We shall not need to nourish any doubt
But that proud Fortune, who hath followed long
The martial sword of mighty Tamburlaine,
Will now retain her old inconstancy,   30
And raise our honours to as high a pitch
In this our strong and fortunate encounter.
For so hath heaven provided my escape
From all the cruelty my soul sustained,
By this my friendly keeper's happy means,   35
That Jove, surcharged with pity of our wrongs,
Will pour it down in showers on our heads,
Scourging the pride of cursèd Tamburlaine.

ORCANES

I have a hundred thousand men in arms;
Some, that in conquest of the perjured Christian,   40
Being a handful to a mighty host,
Think them in number yet sufficient
To drink the river Nile or Euphrates,
And, for their power, enow to win the world.

KING OF JERUSALEM

And I as many from Jerusalem,   45
Judea, Gaza, and Scalonia's bounds,
That on Mount Sinai with their ensigns spread
Look like the parti-coloured clouds of heaven
That show fair weather to the neighbour morn.

KING OF TREBIZON

And I as many bring from Trebizon,   50
Chio, Famastro, and Amasia,
All bord'ring on the Mare Major sea,
Riso, Sancina, and the bord'ring towns
That touch the end of famous Euphrates,
Whose courages are kindled with the flames   55
The cursèd Scythian sets on all their towns,
And vow to burn the villain's cruel heart.

KING OF SORIA

From Soria with seventy thousand strong,
Ta'en from Aleppo, Soldino, Tripoli,

---

44   *enow* enough
46   *Scalonia's* ed. (Scalonians O1–3). Ascalon, a town near Jerusalem
47   *ensigns* banners
52   *Mare Major sea* the Black Sea

And so unto my city of Damascus, 60
I march to meet and aid my neighbour kings,
All which will join against this Tamburlaine,
And bring him captive to your highness' feet.

ORCANES

Our battle then in martial manner pitched
According to our ancient use shall bear 65
The figure of the semi-circled moon,
Whose horns shall sprinkle through the tainted air
The poisoned brains of this proud Scythian.

CALLAPINE

Well then, my noble lords, for this my friend
That freed me from the bondage of my foe, 70
I think it requisite and honourable
To keep my promise and to make him king,
That is a gentleman, I know, at least.

ALMEDA

That's no matter, sir, for being a king, for Tamburlaine
came up of nothing. 75

KING OF JERUSALEM

Your majesty may choose some 'pointed time,
Performing all your promise to the full:
'Tis naught for your majesty to give a kingdom.

CALLAPINE

Then will I shortly keep my promise, Almeda.

ALMEDA

Why, I thank your majesty. 80

Exeunt

65   *use* custom

ACT III, SCENE ii

[Enter] TAMBURLAINE *with* USUMCASANE, *and his three sons*
*[*CALYPHAS, AMYRAS, *and* CELEBINUS*]; four [Attendants]*
bearing the hearse of ZENOCRATE, *and the drums sounding a*
doleful march; [the town burning]

TAMBURLAINE

So, burn the turrets of this cursèd town,
Flame to the highest region of the air
And kindle heaps of exhalations
That, being fiery meteors, may presage
Death and destruction to th'inhabitants.   5
Over my zenith hang a blazing star,
That may endure till heaven be dissolved,
Fed with the fresh supply of earthly dregs,
Threat'ning a death and famine to this land.
Flying dragons, lightning, fearful thunderclaps, 10
Singe these fair plains and make them seem as black
As is the island where the Furies mask,
Compassed with Lethe, Styx, and Phlegethon,
Because my dear Zenocrate is dead.

CALYPHAS

This pillar placed in memory of her,   15
Where in Arabian, Hebrew, Greek, is writ,

---

s.d.4 Exactly how the burning of the town might have been handled on the open
   Elizabethan stage is uncertain. Perhaps fireworks were used to simulate flames or
   to produce realistic smoke (as they had been in medieval drama), perhaps a sym-
   bolic backdrop was hoisted up or fiery streamers hung from the tiring-house wall,
   or perhaps, if it could be managed, an emblematic structure of some kind, rep-
   resenting a city with 'turrets' (line 1), was actually burned. Such spectacular
   effects were not unknown in civic and courtly pageants during the 16th and 17th
   centuries.

 2 *highest . . . air* the uppermost limit of the atmosphere, next to the sphere of the
   moon

3–4 *kindle . . . meteors* may the rising flames create meteors, traditionally portents of
   disaster

 6 *zenith* the highest point of the sun's course, which Tamburlaine compares to the
   high point of his own fortunes

 12 *island . . . mask* The underworld is thought of as an island, presumably because it is
   ringed with rivers. The Furies hide ('mask') there until called into the upper world.

 13 *Lethe . . . Phlegethon* rivers of the underworld

140

'This town being burnt by Tamburlaine the Great,
Forbids the world to build it up again.'

AMYRAS

And here this mournful streamer shall be placed,
Wrought with the Persian and Egyptian arms   20
To signify she was a princess born
And wife unto the monarch of the East.

CELEBINUS

And here this table as a register
Of all her virtues and perfections.

TAMBURLAINE

And here the picture of Zenocrate   25
To show her beauty which the world admired,
Sweet picture of divine Zenocrate,
That hanging here will draw the gods from heaven
And cause the stars fixed in the southern arc,
Whose lovely faces never any viewed   30
That have not passed the centre's latitude,
As pilgrims travel to our hemisphere,
Only to gaze upon Zenocrate.
Thou shalt not beautify Larissa plains
But keep within the circle of mine arms.   35
At every town and castle I besiege,
Thou shalt be set upon my royal tent,
And when I meet an army in the field
Those looks will shed such influence in my camp
As if Bellona, goddess of the war,   40
Threw naked swords and sulphur balls of fire
Upon the heads of all our enemies.
And now, my lords, advance your spears again,
Sorrow no more, my sweet Casane, now;
Boys, leave to mourn – this town shall ever mourn,   45
Being burnt to cinders for your mother's death.

---

20   *Wrought* Embroidered
23   *table* tablet
29   *arc* hemisphere
31   *centre's latitude* equator
34   *Thou* i.e. Zenocrate's picture
39   *Those* ed. (Whose O1)
40   *Bellona* the Roman goddess of war
41   *sulphur . . . fire* primitive incendiary bombs

CALYPHAS

    If I had wept a sea of tears for her,
    It would not ease the sorrow I sustain.

AMYRAS

    As is that town, so is my heart consumed
    With grief and sorrow for my mother's death.   50

CELEBINUS

    My mother's death hath mortified my mind
    And sorrow stops the passage of my speech.

TAMBURLAINE

    But now my boys, leave off, and list to me,
    That mean to teach you rudiments of war:
    I'll have you learn to sleep upon the ground,   55
    March in your armour thorough watery fens,
    Sustain the scorching heat and freezing cold,
    Hunger and thirst, right adjuncts of the war.
    And after this, to scale a castle wall,
    Besiege a fort, to undermine a town,   60
    And make whole cities caper in the air.
    Then next, the way to fortify your men:
    In champion grounds what figure serves you best,
    For which the quinque-angle form is meet,
    Because the corners there may fall more flat   65
    Whereas the fort may fittest be assailed,
    And sharpest where th'assault is desperate.
    The ditches must be deep, the counterscarps
    Narrow and steep, the walls made high and broad,
    The bulwarks and the rampires large and strong,   70

---

56   *thorough* O2–3, Q (throwe O1)

58   *thirst* Q (cold O1)

62–90   A close paraphrase of Paul Ive's *Practice of Fortification* (1589). See Paul Kocher, 'Marlowe's Art of War', *Studies in Philology*, xxxix (1942), 207–25.

63   *champion* level and open

64–7   *For . . . desperate* and for which types of ground (i.e. rough and uneven, as distinct from 'champion') the pentagonal formation ('quinque-angle') will be most suitable, since its 'flat' and 'sharp' angles can be placed where most appropriate for either attack or defence

64   *which* ed. (with O1)

66   *Whereas* where

68   *counterscarps* the outer walls of the ditch surrounding a fort

70   *bulwarks* projecting earthworks built round the angles of a fort
        rampires ramparts supporting the walls from within

With cavalieros and thick counterforts,
And room within to lodge six thousand men.
It must have privy ditches, countermines,
And secret issuings to defend the ditch.
It must have high argins and covered ways   75
To keep the bulwark fronts from battery,
And parapets to hide the musketeers,
Casemates to place the great artillery,
And store of ordnance that from every flank
May scour the outward curtains of the fort,   80
Dismount the cannon of the adverse part,
Murder the foe and save the walls from breach.
When this is learned for service on the land,
By plain and easy demonstration
I'll teach you how to make the water mount   85
That you may dry-foot march through lakes and pools,
Deep rivers, havens, creeks and little seas,
And make a fortress in the raging waves,
Fenced with the concave of a monstrous rock,
Invincible by nature of the place.   90
When this is done, then are ye soldiers,
And worthy sons of Tamburlaine the Great.

CALYPHAS

My lord, but this is dangerous to be done –
We may be slain or wounded ere we learn.

TAMBURLAINE

Villain, art thou the son of Tamburlaine   95
And fear'st to die, or with a curtle-axe
To hew thy flesh and make a gaping wound?
Hast thou beheld a peal of ordnance strike

71 *cavalieros* mounds for heavy guns
73 *countermines* underground tunnels
75 *argins* earthworks
    covered ways protected passages
78 *Casemates* chambers within the ramparts of a fort
79 *ordnance* ammunition
80 *scour* rake with gun-shot
    curtains walls connecting the towers
81 *Dismount* Knock out
    adverse part adversary
82 *the walls* ed. (their walles O1)
85 *mount* rise
98 *peal of ordnance* discharge of cannon

143

A ring of pikes, mingled with shot and horse,
Whose shattered limbs, being tossed as high as heaven,   100
Hang in the air as thick as sunny motes,
And canst thou, coward, stand in fear of death?
Hast thou not seen my horsemen charge the foe,
Shot through the arms, cut overthwart the hands,
Dyeing their lances with their streaming blood,   105
And yet at night carouse within my tent
Filling their empty veins with airy wine
That, being concocted, turns to crimson blood,
And wilt thou shun the field for fear of wounds?
View me thy father that hath conquered kings   110
And with his host marched round about the earth
Quite void of scars and clear from any wound,
That by the wars lost not a dram of blood,
And see him lance his flesh to teach you all.

He cuts his arm

A wound is nothing be it ne'er so deep,   115
Blood is the god of war's rich livery.
Now look I like a soldier, and this wound
As great a grace and majesty to me,
As if a chair of gold enamellèd,
Enchased with diamonds, sapphires, rubies,   120
And fairest pearl of wealthy India,
Were mounted here under a canopy,
And I sat down clothed with the massy robe
That late adorned the Afric potentate
Whom I brought bound unto Damascus' walls.   125
Come, boys, and with your fingers search my wound
And in my blood wash all your hands at once,
While I sit smiling to behold the sight.
Now, my boys, what think you of a wound?

---

99   *A ring . . . horse* a ring of pike-men closely flanked by infantry and cavalry
101   *sunny motes* particles of dust in the sunlight
107-8   Wine, when digested ('concocted'), was thought to replenish a dwindling blood
        supply.
111   *marched* O3, Q (martch O1)
120   *Enchased* adorned
123   *massy* weighty
124   *Afric potentate* i.e. Bajazeth, so called from his African conquests

CALYPHAS

I know not what I should think of it. Methinks 'tis a pitiful   130
sight.

CELEBINUS

'Tis nothing: give me a wound, father.

AMYRAS

And me another, my lord.

TAMBURLAINE

Come, sirrah, give me your arm.

CELEBINUS

Here, father, cut it bravely as you did your own.   135

TAMBURLAINE

It shall suffice thou dar'st abide a wound.
My boy, thou shalt not lose a drop of blood
Before we meet the army of the Turk.
But then run desperate through the thickest throngs,
Dreadless of blows, of bloody wounds and death,   140
And let the burning of Larissa walls,
My speech of war, and this my wound you see
Teach you, my boys, to bear courageous minds,
Fit for the followers of great Tamburlaine.
Usumcasane, now come let us march   145
Towards Techelles and Theridamas,
That we have sent before to fire the towns,
The towers and cities of these hateful Turks,
And hunt that coward, faint-heart runaway,
With that accursèd traitor Almeda,   150
Till fire and sword have found them at a bay.

USUMCASANE

I long to pierce his bowels with my sword
That hath betrayed my gracious sovereign,
That cursed and damnèd traitor Almeda.

TAMBURLAINE

Then let us see if coward Callapine   155
Dare levy arms against our puissance,
That we may tread upon his captive neck
And treble all his father's slaveries.

Exeunt

135   *bravely* well
151   *at a bay* at bay

ACT III, SCENE iii

[*Enter*] TECHELLES, THERIDAMAS, *and their train*
[SOLDIERS *and* PIONERS]

THERIDAMAS

Thus have we marched northward from Tamburlaine
Unto the frontier point of Soria:
And this is Balsera, their chiefest hold,
Wherein is all the treasure of the land.

TECHELLES

Then let us bring our light artillery, 5
Minions, falc'nets, and sakers, to the trench,
Filling the ditches with the walls' wide breach,
And enter in, to seize upon the gold –
How say ye soldiers, shall we not?

SOLDIERS

Yes, my lord, yes, come let's about it. 10

THERIDAMAS

But stay a while; summon a parley, drum,
It may be they will yield it quietly,
Knowing two kings, the friends to Tamburlaine,
Stand at the walls with such a mighty power.

Summon the battle. [*Enter above*] CAPTAIN
with his wife [OLYMPIA] *and* SON

CAPTAIN

What require you my masters? 15

THERIDAMAS

Captain, that thou yield up thy hold to us.

CAPTAIN

To you? Why, do you think me weary of it?

---

s.d.   PIONERS advance guard of trench-diggers
   3   *Balsera* probably Passera, a town near the Natolian frontier
       hold stronghold
   6   *Minions . . . sakers* small cannons
  11   *parley* ed. (parle O1)
  12   *friends* O3, Q (friend O1)
  14   s.d.1 *Summon the battle* Drums call the troops (*battle*) to a parley

TECHELLES

    Nay Captain, thou art weary of thy life

    If thou withstand the friends of Tamburlaine.

THERIDAMAS

    These pioners of Argier in Africa, 20

    Even in the cannon's face shall raise a hill

    Of earth and faggots higher than thy fort

    And over thy argins and covered ways

    Shall play upon the bulwarks of thy hold

    Volleys of ordnance till the breach be made, 25

    That with his ruin fills up all the trench.

    And when we enter in, not heaven itself

    Shall ransom thee, thy wife, and family.

TECHELLES

    Captain, these Moors shall cut the leaden pipes

    That bring fresh water to thy men and thee, 30

    And lie in trench before thy castle walls

    That no supply of victual shall come in,

    Nor any issue forth but they shall die:

    And therefore Captain, yield it quietly.

CAPTAIN

    Were you that are the friends of Tamburlaine 35

    Brothers to holy Mahomet himself,

    I would not yield it: therefore do your worst.

    Raise mounts, batter, intrench, and undermine,

    Cut off the water, all convoys that can,

    Yet I am resolute, and so farewell. 40

                                 [Exeunt above]

THERIDAMAS

    Pioners away, and where I stuck the stake

    Intrench with those dimensions I prescribed;

    Cast up the earth towards the castle wall,

    Which till it may defend you, labour low,

    And few or none shall perish by their shot. 45

PIONERS

    We will my lord.   *Exeunt* [PIONERS]

TECHELLES

    A hundred horse shall scout about the plains

---

26   *trench* defensive ditch around the outer walls

38   *intrench* surround with trenches

39   *that can* that you can

To spy what force comes to relieve the hold.
Both we, Theridamas, will intrench our men,
And with the Jacob's staff measure the height   50
And distance of the castle from the trench,
That we may know if our artillery
Will carry full point blank unto their walls.

THERIDAMAS

Then see the bringing of our ordinance
Along the trench into the battery,   55
Where we will have gabions of six foot broad
To save our cannoneers from musket shot,
Betwixt which shall our ordnance thunder forth
And with the breach's fall, smoke, fire, and dust,
The crack, the echo, and the soldier's cry   60
Make deaf the air and dim the crystal sky.

TECHELLES

Trumpets and drums, alarum presently!
And, soldiers, play the men, the hold is yours.

[*Exeunt*]

---

50 *Jacob's staff* a gunner's quadrant
54 *ordinance* Marlowe's usual spelling of 'ordnance' here retained for the sake of the metre
56 *gabions* ed. (Gallons O1) great baskets filled with earth, used in defence and to steady cannons
62 *alarum* call to arms
    presently at once
63 *hold* O3 (holds O1)

[*Enter*] *the* CAPTAIN *with his wife* [OLYMPIA] *and* SON

OLYMPIA

Come, good my lord, and let us haste from hence
Along the cave that leads beyond the foe –
No hope is left to save this conquered hold.

CAPTAIN

A deadly bullet gliding through my side
Lies heavy on my heart, I cannot live.   5
I feel my liver pierced and all my veins,
That there begin and nourish every part,
Mangled and torn, and all my entrails bathed
In blood that straineth from their orifex.
Farewell sweet wife! Sweet son farewell! I die.   10

[*Dies*]

OLYMPIA

Death, whither art thou gone that both we live?
Come back again, sweet Death, and strike us both!
One minute end our days and one sepulchre
Contain our bodies! Death, why com'st thou not?
Well, this must be the messenger for thee.   15

[*Drawing a knife*]

Now, ugly Death, stretch out thy sable wings
And carry both our souls where his remains.
Tell me, sweet boy, art thou content to die?
These barbarous Scythians full of cruelty,
And Moors in whom was never pity found,   20
Will hew us piecemeal, put us to the wheel,
Or else invent some torture worse than that.
Therefore die by thy loving mother's hand,
Who gently now will lance thy ivory throat
And quickly rid thee both of pain and life.   25

SON

Mother dispatch me or I'll kill myself,

Scene iv ed. (O1 omits)
2   *cave* underground passage
9   *orifex* orifice, breach
21   *the wheel* an instrument of torture

For think ye I can live and see him dead?
Give me your knife, good mother, or strike home –
The Scythians shall not tyrannize on me.
Sweet mother, strike, that I may meet my father.   30

She stabs him

OLYMPIA
Ah sacred Mahomet, if this be sin,
Entreat a pardon of the God of heaven
And purge my soul before it come to thee.

[*She burns the bodies of her husband and son*]

Enter THERIDAMAS, TECHELLES *and all their train*

THERIDAMAS
How now madam, what are you doing?
OLYMPIA
Killing myself, as I have done my son,   35
Whose body with his father's I have burnt,
Lest cruel Scythians should dismember him.
TECHELLES
'Twas bravely done, and like a soldier's wife.
Thou shalt with us to Tamburlaine the Great,
Who when he hears how resolute thou wert   40
Will match thee with a viceroy or a king.
OLYMPIA
My lord deceased was dearer unto me
Than any viceroy, king, or emperor,
And for his sake here will I end my days.
THERIDAMAS
But lady go with us to Tamburlaine   45
And thou shalt see a man greater than Mahomet,
In whose high looks is much more majesty
Than from the concave superficies

---

33   s.d. Although it has been argued that the Rose and other early theatres did not have
      a stage trap, the staging here seems to require one to simulate a pit in which
      Olympia can place the bodies of her dead husband and son. Fireworks and smoke
      under the stage could then furnish the desired effect. Actually burning the bodies
      onstage would seem to surpass the ingenuity and technical resources even of modern
      producers.
47–51 'In Tamburlaine's looks there dwells more majesty than is to be found throughout
      the heavens, from the hollow roof ["concave superficies"] of Jove's palace to the
      shining bower where the moon sits veiled in a crystal robe like Thetis the ocean
      goddess' (Ellis-Fermor).

Of Jove's vast palace the empyreal orb,
Unto the shining bower where Cynthia sits   50
Like lovely Thetis in a crystal robe;
That treadeth fortune underneath his feet
And makes the mighty god of arms his slave;
On whom Death and the Fatal Sisters wait
With naked swords and scarlet liveries;   55
Before whom, mounted on a lion's back,
Rhamnusia bears a helmet full of blood
And strews the way with brains of slaughtered men;
By whose proud side the ugly Furies run,
Harkening when he shall bid them plague the world; 60
Over whose zenith clothed in windy air,
And eagle's wings joined to her feathered breast,
Fame hovereth, sounding of her golden trump,
That to the adverse poles of that straight line
Which measureth the glorious frame of heaven,   65
The name of mighty Tamburlaine is spread.
And him, fair lady, shall thy eyes behold.
Come.

OLYMPIA

Take pity of a lady's ruthful tears,
That humbly craves upon her knees to stay   70
And cast her body in the burning flame
That feeds upon her son's and husband's flesh.

TECHELLES

Madam, sooner shall fire consume us both
Than scorch a face so beautiful as this,
In frame of which nature hath showed more skill   75
Than when she gave eternal chaos form,
Drawing from it the shining lamps of heaven.

THERIDAMAS

Madam, I am so far in love with you
That you must go with us, no remedy.

OLYMPIA

Then carry me I care not where you will,   80

49   *empyreal orb* heavenly sphere
57   *Rhamnusia* Nemesis
61   *zenith* crest; the highest point in his career
64–5   *adverse . . . heaven* the diameter of the sphere of heaven
67–8   lineation ed.
75   *frame* forming, fashioning

And let the end of this my fatal journey
Be likewise end to my accursèd life.

TECHELLES

No madam, but the beginning of your joy –
Come willingly therefore.

THERIDAMAS

Soldiers, now let us meet the general   85
Who by this time is at Natolia,
Ready to charge the army of the Turk.
The gold, the silver, and the pearl ye got
Rifling this fort, divide in equal shares.
This lady shall have twice so much again   90
Out of the coffers of our treasury.

Exeunt

[*Enter*] CALLAPINE, ORCANES, JERUSALEM, TREBIZON,
SORIA, ALMEDA, *with their train* [*and* MESSENGER *to them*]

MESSENGER

Renownèd emperor, mighty Callapine,
God's great lieutenant over all the world:
Here at Aleppo with an host of men
Lies Tamburlaine, this King of Persia,
In number more than are the quivering leaves   5
Of Ida's forest, where your highness' hounds
With open cry pursues the wounded stag,
Who means to girt Natolia's walls with siege,
Fire the town and overrun the land.

CALLAPINE

My royal army is as great as his,   10
That from the bounds of Phrygia to the sea
Which washeth Cyprus with his brinish waves,
Covers the hills, the valleys, and the plains.
Viceroys and peers of Turkey, play the men,
Whet all your swords to mangle Tamburlaine,   15
His sons, his captains, and his followers –
By Mahomet, not one of them shall live.
The field wherein this battle shall be fought
Forever term the Persians' sepulchre,
In memory of this our victory.   20

ORCANES

Now he that calls himself the Scourge of Jove,
The emperor of the world and earthly god,
Shall end the warlike progress he intends
And travel headlong to the lake of hell,
Where legions of devils (knowing he must die   25
Here in Natolia by your highness' hands)
All brandishing their brands of quenchless fire,
Stretching their monstrous paws, grin with their teeth,
And guard the gates to entertain his soul.

6   *Ida's forest* probably Mt. Ida near Troy
8   *Natolia* Asia Minor, but here apparently a city
11   *Phrygia* an inland district of Natolia

CALLAPINE

    Tell me, viceroys, the number of your men   30

    And what our army royal is esteemed.

KING OF JERUSALEM

    From Palestina and Jerusalem,

    Of Hebrews three score thousand fighting men

    Are come since last we showed your majesty.

ORCANES

    So from Arabia Desert and the bounds   35

    Of that sweet land whose brave metropolis

    Re-edified the fair Semiramis,

    Came forty thousand warlike foot and horse,

    Since last we numbered to your majesty.

KING OF TREBIZON

    From Trebizon in Asia the Less,   40

    Naturalized Turks and stout Bithynians

    Came to my bands full fifty thousand more

    That, fighting, knows not what retreat doth mean,

    Nor e'er return but with the victory,

    Since last we numbered to your majesty.   45

KING OF SORIA

    Of Sorians from Halla is repaired,

    And neighbour cities of your highness' land,

    Ten thousand horse and thirty thousand foot,

    Since last we numbered to your majesty.

    So that the army royal is esteemed   50

    Six hundred thousand valiant fighting men.

CALLAPINE

    Then welcome, Tamburlaine, unto thy death.

    Come puissant viceroys, let us to the field,

    The Persians' sepulchre, and sacrifice

    Mountains of breathless men to Mahomet,   55

    Who now with Jove opens the firmament

    To see the slaughter of our enemies.

36   *metropolis* Babylon, whose walls were supposedly built by Semiramis
40   *Asia the Less* Asia Minor
41   *stout* bold
      Bithynians Bithynia was the north-western region of Asia Minor.
46   *Halla* a town to the south-east of Aleppo
      is repaired have travelled

[*Enter*] TAMBURLAINE *with his three sons* [CALYPHAS,
AMYRAS, *and* CELEBINUS], USUMCASANE, *with other*[*s*]

TAMBURLAINE

How now Casane! See a knot of kings,
Sitting as if they were a-telling riddles.

USUMCASANE

My lord, your presence makes them pale and wan –   60
Poor souls they look as if their deaths were near.

TAMBURLAINE

Why so he is, Casane, I am here,
But yet I'll save their lives and make them slaves.
Ye petty kings of Turkey, I am come,
As Hector did into the Grecian camp   65
To overdare the pride of Graecia
And set his warlike person to the view
Of fierce Achilles, rival of his fame.
I do you honour in the simile,
For if I should as Hector did Achilles   70
(The worthiest knight that ever brandished sword)
Challenge in combat any of you all,
I see how fearfully ye would refuse,
And fly my glove as from a scorpion.

ORCANES

Now thou art fearful of thy army's strength   75
Thou wouldst with overmatch of person fight;
But, shepherd's issue, base-born Tamburlaine,
Think of thy end, this sword shall lance thy throat.

TAMBURLAINE

Villain, the shepherd's issue, at whose birth
Heaven did afford a gracious aspect   80
And joined those stars that shall be opposite
Even till the dissolution of the world,
And never meant to make a conqueror
So famous as is mighty Tamburlaine,
Shall so torment thee and that Callapine   85

65–8   There is no such episode in the *Iliad,* but Marlowe could have found it in the post-
       Homeric Troy tales, such as Lydgate's *Troy Book.*
  74   *glove* challenge. To throw down a glove was to issue a chivalric challenge.
  76   *with . . . fight* fight personally, out of confidence in your superior strength
  80   *gracious aspect* favourable conjunction of the heavenly bodies
81–2   *And joined . . . world* which conjunction will never again be seen

155

That like a roguish runaway suborned
That villain there, that slave, that Turkish dog,
To false his service to his sovereign,
As ye shall curse the birth of Tamburlaine.

CALLAPINE

Rail not, proud Scythian, I shall now revenge   90
My father's vile abuses and mine own.

KING OF JERUSALEM

By Mahomet, he shall be tied in chains,
Rowing with Christians in a brigandine
About the Grecian isles to rob and spoil,
And turn him to his ancient trade again.   95
Methinks the slave should make a lusty thief.

CALLAPINE

Nay, when the battle ends, all we will meet
And sit in council to invent some pain
That most may vex his body and his soul.

TAMBURLAINE

Sirrah, Callapine, I'll hang a clog about your neck for running   100
away again, you shall not trouble me thus to come and fetch
you.
But as for you, viceroy, you shall have bits
And harnessed like my horses draw my coach,
And when ye stay be lashed with whips of wire;   105
I'll have you learn to feed on provender
And in a stable lie upon the planks.

ORCANES

But Tamburlaine, first thou shalt kneel to us
And humbly crave a pardon for thy life.

KING OF TREBIZON

The common soldiers of our mighty host   110
Shall bring thee bound unto the general's tent.

KING OF SORIA

And all have jointly sworn thy cruel death,

---

86   *suborned* bribed
88   *false* betray
93   *brigandine* small ship
96   *lusty* vigorous
100   *for* to prevent
106   *provender* fodder

Or bind thee in eternal torments' wrath.

TAMBURLAINE

Well sirs, diet yourselves, you know I shall have occasion shortly
to journey you. 115

CELEBINUS

See father, how Almeda the jailor looks upon us.

TAMBURLAINE

Villain, traitor, damnèd fugitive,
I'll make thee wish the earth had swallowed thee:
Seest thou not death within my wrathful looks?
Go villain, cast thee headlong from a rock, 120
Or rip thy bowels and rend out thy heart
T'appease my wrath, or else I'll torture thee,
Searing thy hateful flesh with burning irons
And drops of scalding lead, while all thy joints
Be racked and beat asunder with the wheel. 125
For if thou livest, not any element
Shall shroud thee from the wrath of Tamburlaine.

CALLAPINE

Well, in despite of thee he shall be king:
Come, Almeda, receive this crown of me.
I here invest thee King of Ariadan, 130
Bordering on Mare Roso near to Mecca.

ORCANES

What, take it man!

ALMEDA

[to TAMBURLAINE] Good my lord, let me take it.

CALLAPINE

Dost thou ask him leave? Here, take it.

TAMBURLAINE

Go to, sirrah, take your crown, and make up the half dozen. So 135
sirrah, now you are a king you must give arms.

ORCANES

So he shall, and wear thy head in his scutcheon.

---

113   Perhaps 'thee' should read 'them', and the line would then refer to the terms of the
      soldiers' oath (see Cunningham).
114   *diet yourselves* feed yourselves well
115   *journey* drive (as horses)
130   *Ariadan* a town on the Red Sea coast of Arabia, south of Mecca
131   *Mare Roso* the Red Sea
137   *scutcheon* heraldic shield

157

TAMBURLAINE

No, let him hang a bunch of keys on his standard to put him
in remembrance he was a jailor, that when I take him, I may
knock out his brains with them, and lock you in the stable when   140
you shall come sweating from my chariot.

KING OF TREBIZON

Away, let us to the field, that the villain may be slain.

TAMBURLAINE

[*To an attendant*] Sirrah, prepare whips, and bring my chariot
to my tent: for as soon as the battle is done, I'll ride in triumph
through the camp.   145

Enter THERIDAMAS, TECHELLES, *and their train*

How now, ye petty kings, lo, here are bugs
Will make the hair stand upright on your heads
And cast your crowns in slavery at their feet.
Welcome, Theridamas and Techelles both,
See ye this rout and know ye this same king?   150

THERIDAMAS

Ay, my lord, he was Callapine's keeper.

TAMBURLAINE

Well, now you see he is a king; look to him Theridamas, when
we are fighting, lest he hide his crown as the foolish King of
Persia did.

KING OF SORIA

No, Tamburlaine, he shall not be put to that exigent, I warrant   155
thee.

TAMBURLAINE

You know not, sir.
But now, my followers and my loving friends,
Fight as you ever did, like conquerors,
The glory of this happy day is yours: 160
My stern aspect shall make fair Victory,
Hovering betwixt our armies, light on me,
Loaden with laurel wreaths to crown us all.

TECHELLES

I smile to think how, when this field is fought

138   *standard* the distinctive flag of a nobleman
146   *bugs* bugbears, objects of terror to children
150   *rout* rabble
153   See Part One, II.iv.10–15.
163   *Loaden* laden

And rich Natolia ours, our men shall sweat   165
    With carrying pearl and treasure on their backs.
TAMBURLAINE
    You shall be princes all immediately:
    Come fight, ye Turks, or yield us victory.
ORCANES
    No, we will meet thee, slavish Tamburlaine.

                                        Exeunt

Alarm, AMYRAS *and* CELEBINUS *issue from the tent
where* CALYPHAS *sits asleep*

[AMYRAS]

    Now in their glories shine the golden crowns
    Of these proud Turks, much like so many suns
    That half dismay the majesty of heaven;
    Now brother, follow we our father's sword
    That flies with fury swifter than our thoughts   5
    And cuts down armies with his conquering wings.

CELEBINUS

    Call forth our lazy brother from the tent,
    For if my father miss him in the field,
    Wrath kindled in the furnace of his breast
    Will send a deadly lightning to his heart.   10

AMYRAS

    Brother ho! What, given so much to sleep
    You cannot leave it when our enemies' drums
    And rattling cannons thunder in our ears
    Our proper ruin and our father's foil?

CALYPHAS

    Away, ye fools, my father needs not me,   15
    Nor you, in faith, but that you will be thought
    More childish valorous than manly wise.
    If half our camp should sit and sleep with me,
    My father were enough to scar the foe:
    You do dishonour to his majesty   20
    To think our helps will do him any good.

AMYRAS

    What, dar'st thou then be absent from the fight,
    Knowing my father hates thy cowardice
    And oft hath warned thee to be still in field,

---

    s.d.   *issue* ed. (issues O1)
      6   *conquering* ed. (conquerings O1)
    14   *proper* own
          foil defeat
    19   *were* ed. (ware O1)
    24   *still* constantly

When he himself amidst the thickest troops   25
Beats down our foes, to flesh our taintless swords?

CALYPHAS

I know, sir, what it is to kill a man –
It works remorse of conscience in me;
I take no pleasure to be murderous
Nor care for blood when wine will quench my thirst.   30

CELEBINUS

O cowardly boy! Fie, for shame, come forth!
Thou dost dishonour manhood and thy house.

CALYPHAS

Go, go tall stripling, fight you for us both,
And take my other toward brother here,
For person like to prove a second Mars.   35
'Twill please my mind as well to hear both you
Have won a heap of honour in the field,
And left your slender carcasses behind,
As if I lay with you for company.

AMYRAS

You will not go then?   40

CALYPHAS

You say true.

AMYRAS

Were all the lofty mounts of Zona Mundi
That fill the midst of farthest Tartary
Turned into pearl and proffered for my stay,
I would not bide the fury of my father   45
When made a victor in these haughty arms
He comes and finds his sons have had no shares
In all the honours he proposed for us.

CALYPHAS

Take you the honour, I will take my ease,
My wisdom shall excuse my cowardice: 50
I go into the field before I need?
                Alarm, and AMYRAS *and* CELEBINUS *run in*
The bullets fly at random where they list.

---

26   *to flesh . . . swords* to fight our first battle
33   *tall* brave
34   *toward* forward, promising
42   *Zona Mundi* a mountain range in Tartary, an area of central Asia east of the Caspian
52   *list* like

And should I go and kill a thousand men,
I were as soon rewarded with a shot
And sooner far than he that never fights.   55
And should I go and do nor harm nor good,
I might have harm, which all the good I have
Joined with my father's crown would never cure.
I'll to cards. Perdicas!

[*Enter* PERDICAS]

PERDICAS   Here my lord.
CALYPHAS
    Come, thou and I will go to cards to drive away the   60
    time.
PERDICAS
    Content, my lord, but what shall we play for?
CALYPHAS
    Who shall kiss the fairest of the Turks' concubines first, when
    my father hath conquered them.
PERDICAS
    Agreed i'faith.   65

                                        They play [*in the tent*]

CALYPHAS
    They say I am a coward, Perdicas, and I fear as little their
    taratantaras, their swords or their cannons, as I do a naked lady
    in a net of gold, and for fear I should be afraid, would put it off
    and come to bed with me.
PERDICAS
    Such a fear, my lord, would never make ye retire.   70
CALYPHAS
    I would my father would let me be put in the front of such a
    battle once, to try my valour.

                                                          Alarm

    What a coil they keep, I believe there will be some hurt done
    anon amongst them.

---

65 s.d. The staging here, as at the beginning of the scene, requires an inner area to serve
    as the tent, visible to the audience but removed from the main playing area
67 *taratantaras* bugle calls
68 *and* i.e. who
73 *coil* commotion

Enter TAMBURLAINE, THERIDAMAS, TECHELLES,
USUMCASANE, AMYRAS, CELEBINUS, *leading the*
Turkish KINGS [OF NATOLIA, JERUSALEM,
TREBIZON, *and* SORIA; *and* SOLDIERS]

TAMBURLAINE

  See now, ye slaves, my children stoops your pride 75
  And leads your glories sheep-like to the sword.
  Bring them, my boys, and tell me if the wars
  Be not a life that may illustrate gods,
  And tickle not your spirits with desire
  Still to be trained in arms and chivalry? 80

AMYRAS

  Shall we let go these kings again, my lord,
  To gather greater numbers 'gainst our power,
  That they may say it is not chance doth this,
  But matchless strength and magnanimity?

TAMBURLAINE

  No, no Amyras, tempt not fortune so, 85
  Cherish thy valour still with fresh supplies
  And glut it not with stale and daunted foes.
  But where's this coward, villain, not my son,
  But traitor to my name and majesty?

             He goes in [*the tent*] *and brings* [CALYPHAS] *out*
  Image of sloth and picture of a slave, 90
  The obloquy and scorn of my renown,
  How may my heart, thus fired with mine eyes,
  Wounded with shame and killed with discontent,
  Shroud any thought may hold my striving hands
  From martial justice on thy wretched soul? 95

THERIDAMAS

  Yet pardon him I pray your majesty.

TECHELLES, USUMCASANE

  Let all of us entreat your highness' pardon.

                      [*They kneel*]

TAMBURLAINE

  Stand up, ye base unworthy soldiers,

---

75   *stoops* humble
78   *illustrate* adorn, shed lustre upon
94   *Shroud* shelter, harbour
      may which may

Know ye not yet the argument of arms?

AMYRAS

Good my lord, let him be forgiven for once   100
And we will force him to the field hereafter.

TAMBURLAINE

Stand up, my boys, and I will teach ye arms,
And what the jealousy of wars must do.
O Samarcanda, where I breathèd first
And joyed the fire of this martial flesh,   105
Blush, blush fair city at thine honour's foil
And shame of nature which Jaertis' stream,
Embracing thee with deepest of his love,
Can never wash from thy distainèd brows.
Here Jove, receive his fainting soul again,   110
A form not meet to give that subject essence
Whose matter is the flesh of Tamburlaine,
Wherein an incorporeal spirit moves
Made of the mould whereof thyself consists
Which makes me valiant, proud, ambitious,   115
Ready to levy power against thy throne,
That I might move the turning spheres of heaven –
For earth and all this airy region
Cannot contain the state of Tamburlaine.

[*Stabs* CALYPHAS]

By Mahomet, thy mighty friend, I swear,   120
In sending to my issue such a soul,
Created of the massy dregs of earth,

---

99   *argument of arms* necessity of military life
103   *jealousy* zeal
104   *Samarcanda* Samarkand, Tamburlaine's birthplace
105   *joyed* took delight in
106   *foil* disgrace
107   *which* ed. (with O1)
         Jaertis' stream the river Jaxartes, which flows west from Tartary to the Caspian Sea
109   *distainèd* stained, dishonoured
110–14 *Here Jove . . . consists* Ellis-Fermor paraphrases: 'Here Jove receive again the soul of
         Calyphas, a spirit (i.e. "form" almost in the sense of "idea") not worthy to be the
         immortal part (essence) of that subject whose mortal part (matter) is derived from
         the flesh of Tamburlaine – in whom moves an immortal spirit of the same mould
         as thine own.' She observes that 'form', 'subject', 'essence', and 'matter' are used in
         strict accordance with the tradition of sixteenth-century Aristotelian logic.
120   *thy* i.e. Jove's
121   *In . . . soul* by sending such a soul as Calyphas to be my child

The scum and tartar of the elements,
Wherein was neither courage, strength, or wit,
But folly, sloth, and damnèd idleness: 125
Thou hast procured a greater enemy
Than he that darted mountains at thy head,
Shaking the burden mighty Atlas bears,
Whereat thou trembling hidd'st thee in the air,
Clothed with a pitchy cloud for being seen.   130
And now ye cankered curs of Asia,
That will not see the strength of Tamburlaine
Although it shine as brightly as the sun,
Now you shall feel the strength of Tamburlaine
And by the state of his supremacy   135
Approve the difference 'twixt himself and you.

ORCANES

Thou showest the difference 'twixt ourselves and thee
In this thy barbarous damned tyranny.

KING OF JERUSALEM

Thy victories are grown so violent
That shortly heaven, filled with the meteors   140
Of blood and fire thy tyrannies have made,
Will pour down blood and fire on thy head,
Whose scalding drops will pierce thy seething brains,
And with our bloods revenge our bloods on thee.

TAMBURLAINE

Villains, these terrors and these tyrannies   145
(If tyrannies war's justice ye repute)
I execute, enjoined me from above,
To scourge the pride of such as heaven abhors;
Nor am I made arch-monarch of the world,
Crowned and invested by the hand of Jove,   150
For deeds of bounty or nobility.
But since I exercise a greater name,
The scourge of God and terror of the world,
I must apply myself to fit those terms

123   *tartar* dregs (as of a wine cask)
127   *he . . . head* the Titans who warred against Jove
128   *Atlas* the Titan who was condemned to bear the heavens on his shoulders
130   *for being seen* to avoid being seen
136   *Approve* find out by experience
140–44   See Part One, V.ii.396–9 and note.
146   *repute* regard as

In war, in blood, in death, in cruelty,   155
And plague such peasants as resist in me
The power of heaven's eternal majesty.
Theridamas, Techelles, and Casane,
Ransack the tents and the pavilions
Of these proud Turks and take their concubines,   160
Making them bury this effeminate brat,
For not a common soldier shall defile
His manly fingers with so faint a boy.
Then bring those Turkish harlots to my tent
And I'll dispose them as it likes me best.   165
Meanwhile take him in.

SOLDIERS   We will my lord.
        [*Exeunt* SOLDIERS *with the body of* CALYPHAS]

KING OF JERUSALEM
O damnèd monster, nay a fiend of hell,
Whose cruelties are not so harsh as thine,
Nor yet imposed with such a bitter hate!

ORCANES
Revenge it, Rhadamanth and Aeacus,   170
And let your hates extended in his pains
Expel the hate wherewith he pains our souls!

KING OF TREBIZON
May never day give virtue to his eyes,
Whose sight composed of fury and of fire
Doth send such stern affections to his heart!   175

KING OF SORIA
May never spirit, vein, or artier feed
The cursèd substance of that cruel heart,
But, wanting moisture and remorseful blood,
Dry up with anger and consume with heat!

TAMBURLAINE
Well, bark ye dogs. I'll bridle all your tongues   180

156   *resist in* ed. (resisting O1)
163   *faint* faint-hearted
165   *likes* pleases
170   *Rhadamanth and Aeacus* with Minos, the judges of the Greek underworld
173   *virtue* power
175   *affections* emotions
176   *artier* artery
178   *remorseful* compassionate

And bind them close with bits of burnished steel
Down to the channels of your hateful throats,
And with the pains my rigour shall inflict
I'll make ye roar, that earth may echo forth
The far resounding torments ye sustain,   185
As when an herd of lusty Cimbrian bulls
Run mourning round about the females' miss,
And stung with fury of their following,
Fill all the air with troublous bellowing.
I will with engines never exercised   190
Conquer, sack, and utterly consume
Your cities and your golden palaces,
And with the flames that beat against the clouds
Incense the heavens and make the stars to melt,
As if they were the tears of Mahomet   195
For hot consumption of his country's pride.
And till by vision or by speech I hear
Immortal Jove say 'Cease, my Tamburlaine,'
I will persist a terror to the world,
Making the meteors, that like armèd men   200
Are seen to march upon the towers of heaven,
Run tilting round about the firmament
And break their burning lances in the air
For honour of my wondrous victories.
Come, bring them in to our pavilion.   205

                                                    Exeunt

186 *Cimbrian* The Cimbri were a Celtic people who defeated several Roman armies in
     the second century BC. Marlowe's association of the Cimbri with bulls apparently
     derives from Spenser's *Faerie Queene,* I, viii, 11.
187 *females' miss* i.e. the loss of their mates
188 *their following* following them
194 *Incense* set on fire
202 *tilting* jousting

ACT IV, SCENE ii

[Enter] OLYMPIA *alone*

[OLYMPIA]

    Distressed Olympia, whose weeping eyes
    Since thy arrival here beheld no sun,
    But closed within the compass of a tent
    Hath stained thy cheeks and made thee look like death,
    Devise some means to rid thee of thy life,   5
    Rather than yield to his detested suit
    Whose drift is only to dishonour thee.
    And since this earth, dewed with thy brinish tears,
    Affords no herbs whose taste may poison thee,
    Nor yet this air, beat often with thy sighs,   10
    Contagious smells and vapours to infect thee,
    Nor thy close cave a sword to murder thee,
    Let this invention be the instrument.

                               [Taking out a vial]

Enter THERIDAMAS

THERIDAMAS

    Well met, Olympia, I sought thee in thy tent
    But when I saw the place obscure and dark,   15
    Which with thy beauty thou wast wont to light,
    Enraged I ran about the fields for thee,
    Supposing amorous Jove had sent his son,
    The wingèd Hermes, to convey thee hence.
    But now I find thee and that fear is past.   20
    Tell me Olympia, wilt thou grant my suit?

OLYMPIA

    My lord and husband's death, with my sweet son's,
    With whom I buried all affections
    Save grief and sorrow which torment my heart,
    Forbids my mind to entertain a thought   25
    That tends to love, but meditate on death,
    A fitter subject for a pensive soul.

    7   *drift* intention
   12   *close cave* place of confinement
   19   *Hermes* Zeus's herald and messenger

THERIDAMAS

    Olympia, pity him in whom thy looks
    Have greater operation and more force
    Than Cynthia's in the watery wilderness,   30
    For with thy view my joys are at the full,
    And ebb again as thou depart'st from me.

OLYMPIA

    Ah pity me, my lord, and draw your sword,
    Making a passage for my troubled soul,
    Which beats against this prison to get out   35
    And meet my husband and my loving son.

THERIDAMAS

    Nothing but still thy husband and thy son?
    Leave this, my love, and listen more to me,
    Thou shalt be stately queen of fair Argier
    And, clothed in costly cloth of massy gold,   40
    Upon the marble turrets of my court
    Sit like to Venus in her chair of state,
    Commanding all thy princely eye desires;
    And I will cast off arms and sit with thee
    Spending my life in sweet discourse of love.   45

OLYMPIA

    No such discourse is pleasant in mine ears
    But that where every period ends with death
    And every line begins with death again –
    I cannot love, to be an emperess.

THERIDAMAS

    Nay lady, then if nothing will prevail   50
    I'll use some other means to make you yield –
    Such is the sudden fury of my love,
    I must and will be pleased and you shall yield.
    Come to the tent again.

OLYMPIA

    Stay, good my lord, and will you save my honour,   55
    I'll give your grace a present of such price
    As all the world cannot afford the like.

---

30   *Cynthia's . . . wilderness* i.e. the power of the moon to govern the tides
47   *period* sentence
49   *emperess* Original spelling here and elsewhere retained for the sake of the metre.
55   *and will you* and if you will

THERIDAMAS

What is it?

OLYMPIA

An ointment which a cunning alchemist
Distillèd from the purest balsamum 60
And simplest extracts of all minerals,
In which th'essential form of marble stone,
Tempered by science metaphysical
And spells of magic from the mouths of spirits,
With which if you but 'noint your tender skin, 65
Nor pistol, sword, nor lance can pierce your flesh.

THERIDAMAS

Why madam, think ye to mock me thus palpably?

OLYMPIA

To prove it, I will 'noint my naked throat
Which, when you stab, look on your weapon's point
And you shall see't rebated with the blow. 70

THERIDAMAS

Why gave you not your husband some of it,
If you loved him, and it so precious?

OLYMPIA

My purpose was, my lord, to spend it so,
But was prevented by his sudden end,
And for a present easy proof hereof 75
That I dissemble not, try it on me.

THERIDAMAS

I will, Olympia, and will keep it for
The richest present of this eastern world.

She [a]noints her throat

OLYMPIA

Now stab, my lord, and mark your weapon's point
That will be blunted if the blow be great. 80

THERIDAMAS

Here then, Olympia.

[He stabs her and she dies]

What, have I slain her? Villain, stab thyself,
Cut off this arm that murderèd my love,

61   *simplest extracts* in alchemy, the pure elements
63   *metaphysical* supernatural, the science that went beyond physical knowledge
70   *rebated* blunted
71–2   lineation ed. (O1 prints as prose)

In whom the learnèd rabbis of this age
Might find as many wondrous miracles   85
As in the theoria of the world.
Now hell is fairer than Elysium,
A greater lamp than that bright eye of heaven,
From whence the stars do borrow all their light,
Wanders about the black circumference,   90
And now the damnèd souls are free from pain
For every Fury gazeth on her looks:
Infernal Dis is courting of my love,
Inventing masks and stately shows for her,
Opening the doors of his rich treasury   95
To entertain this queen of chastity,
Whose body shall be tombed with all the pomp
The treasure of my kingdom may afford.

                              Exit, taking her away

---

84   *rabbis* scholarly authorities
86   *theoria* observation, survey
87   *Elysium* ed. (Elisian O1) paradise or heaven in Greek mythology
93   *Dis* Hades, Pluto, god of the underworld
94   *masks* lavish entertainment

ACT IV, SCENE iii

[Enter] TAMBURLAINE *drawn in his chariot by* TREBIZON
and SORIA *with bits in their mouths, reins in his left hand,*
in his right hand a whip, with which he scourgeth them.
TECHELLES, THERIDAMAS, USUMCASANE, AMYRAS,
CELEBINUS; [ORCANES, *King of*] *Natolia, and* JERUSALEM,
led by five or six common SOLDIERS

TAMBURLAINE

Holla, ye pampered jades of Asia!
What, can ye draw but twenty miles a day,
And have so proud a chariot at your heels
And such a coachman as great Tamburlaine?
But from Asphaltis, where I conquered you,   5
To Byron here where thus I honour you?
The horse that guide the golden eye of heaven
And blow the morning from their nosterils,
Making their fiery gait above the clouds,
Are not so honoured in their governor   10
As you, ye slaves, in mighty Tamburlaine.
The headstrong jades of Thrace Alcides tamed,
That King Aegeus fed with human flesh
And made so wanton that they knew their strengths,
Were not subdued with valour more divine   15
Than you by this unconquered arm of mine.
To make you fierce and fit my appetite,
You shall be fed with flesh as raw as blood
And drink in pails the strongest muscadel –
If you can live with it, then live, and draw   20
My chariot swifter than the racking clouds;
If not, then die like beasts, and fit for naught

0.6   s.d. *led by* ed. (led by with O1)
  1   *jades* horses (a contemptuous term)
  5   *Asphaltis* a bituminous lake near Babylon
  6   *Byron* a city near Babylon
  7   *horse* a plural form
  8   *nosterils* O1's spelling retained for the sake of the metre
 12   *Alcides* Hercules. The passage refers to one of his twelve labours.
 19   *muscadel* strong sweet wine
 21   *racking* scudding before the wind

But perches for the black and fatal ravens.
Thus am I right the scourge of highest Jove,
And see the figure of my dignity   25
By which I hold my name and majesty.

AMYRAS

Let me have coach, my lord, that I may ride
And thus be drawn with these two idle kings.

TAMBURLAINE

Thy youth forbids such ease my kingly boy,
They shall tomorrow draw my chariot,   30
While these their fellow kings may be refreshed.

ORCANES

O thou that sway'st the region under earth
And art a king as absolute as Jove,
Come as thou didst in fruitful Sicily,
Surveying all the glories of the land,   35
And as thou took'st the fair Proserpina,
Joying the fruit of Ceres' garden plot,
For love, for honour, and to make her queen,
So for just hate, for shame, and to subdue
This proud contemner of thy dreadful power,   40
Come once in fury and survey his pride,
Haling him headlong to the lowest hell.

THERIDAMAS

Your majesty must get some bits for these
To bridle their contemptuous cursing tongues,
That like unruly never-broken jades   45
Break through the hedges of their hateful mouths
And pass their fixèd bounds exceedingly.

TECHELLES

Nay, we will break the hedges of their mouths
And pull their kicking colts out of their pastures.

USUMCASANE

Your majesty already hath devised   50
A mean as fit as may be to restrain

24   *right* indeed
25   *figure* image
32   *thou* Pluto, god of the underworld, who carried off Proserpina, the daughter of
      Ceres, goddess of the harvest
45–52 The simile compares the tongues of the captive kings to unruly horses leaping over
      hedges.
49   *pull . . . pastures* i.e. their over-active tongues will be cut out

These coltish coach-horse tongues from blasphemy.
CELEBINUS
How like you that, sir king? Why speak you not?
KING OF JERUSALEM
Ah cruel brat, sprung from a tyrant's loins,
How like his cursèd father he begins   55
To practise taunts and bitter tyrannies!
TAMBURLAINE
Ay Turk, I tell thee, this same boy is he
That must, advanced in higher pomp than this,
Rifle the kingdoms I shall leave unsacked
If Jove esteeming me too good for earth   60
Raise me to match the fair Aldebaran,
Above the threefold astracism of heaven,
Before I conquer all the triple world.
Now fetch me out the Turkish concubines,
I will prefer them for the funeral   65
They have bestowed on my abortive son.
                              The CONCUBINES *are brought in*
Where are my common soldiers now that fought
So lion-like upon Asphaltis' plains?
SOLDIERS
Here my lord.
TAMBURLAINE
Hold ye, tall soldiers, take ye queens apiece –   70
I mean such queens as were kings' concubines.
Take them, divide them and their jewels too,
And let them equally serve all your turns.
SOLDIERS
We thank your majesty.
TAMBURLAINE
Brawl not, I warn you, for your lechery,   75
For every man that so offends shall die.
ORCANES
Injurious tyrant, wilt thou so defame

---

61   *Aldebaran* a bright star in the constellation of Taurus, one of the fixed stars of heaven
     and associated with Mars by Ptolemy
62   *threefold astracism* an asterism, or cluster, of three stars in the constellation Taurus
63   *triple world* composed of Asia, Africa, and Europe
65   *prefer* promote, reward
70   *tall* brave
70–1 *queens . . . queens* Tamburlaine puns on 'queens' and 'queans' (whores).

174

The hateful fortunes of thy victory
To exercise upon such guiltless dames
The violence of thy common soldiers' lust?   80

TAMBURLAINE

Live continent then, ye slaves, and meet not me
With troops of harlots at your slothful heels.

CONCUBINES

O pity us my lord, and save our honours.

TAMBURLAINE

Are ye not gone, ye villains, with your spoils?

They [SOLDIERS] *run away with the* LADIES

KING OF JERUSALEM

O merciless infernal cruelty!   85

TAMBURLAINE

Save your honours? 'Twere but time indeed
Lost long before you knew what honour meant.

THERIDAMAS

It seems they meant to conquer us, my lord,
And make us jesting pageants for their trulls.

TAMBURLAINE

And now themselves shall make our pageant,   90
And common soldiers jest with all their trulls.
Let them take pleasure soundly in their spoils
Till we prepare our march to Babylon,
Whither we next make expedition.

TECHILLES

Let us not be idle then, my lord,   95
But presently be prest to conquer it.

TAMBURLAINE

We will Techelles. Forward then ye jades!
Now crouch, ye kings of greatest Asia,
And tremble when ye hear this scourge will come
That whips down cities and controlleth crowns,   100
Adding their wealth and treasure to my store.
The Euxine Sea, north to Natolia,
The Terrene, west, the Caspian, north-northeast,

---

81   *continent* ed. (content O1) chaste
89   *pageants* spectacles   *trulls* whores
94   *expedition* haste
96   *presently* quickly   *prest* ready
102 *Euxine Sea* the Black Sea

And on the south, Sinus Arabicus,
Shall all be loaden with the martial spoils   105
We will convey with us to Persia.
Then shall my native city Samarcanda
And crystal waves of fresh Jaertis' stream,
The pride and beauty of her princely seat,
Be famous through the furthest continents –   110
For there my palace royal shall be placed,
Whose shining turrets shall dismay the heavens
And cast the fame of Ilion's tower to hell.
Thorough the streets with troops of conquered kings
I'll ride in golden armour like the sun,   115
And in my helm a triple plume shall spring,
Spangled with diamonds dancing in the air,
To note me emperor of the three-fold world –
Like to an almond tree ymounted high
Upon the lofty and celestial mount   120
Of ever-green Selinus, quaintly decked
With blooms more white than Erycina's brows,
Whose tender blossoms tremble every one
At every little breath that thorough heaven is blown.
Then, in my coach, like Saturn's royal son   125
Mounted his shining chariot, gilt with fire,
And drawn with princely eagles through the path
Paved with bright crystal and enchased with stars,
When all the gods stand gazing at his pomp,
So will I ride through Samarcanda streets,   130
Until my soul dissevered from this flesh
Shall mount the milk-white way and meet him there.
To Babylon my lords, to Babylon!

Exeunt

104 *Sinus Arabicus* the Red Sea
108 *Jaertis' stream* See note to Part Two, IV.i.107 above.
113 *Ilion* Troy
119–24 *Like . . . blown* This passage has been adapted from Spenser's *Faerie Queene*, I, vii, 32, which Marlowe might have seen in manuscript.
121 *ever-green* ed. (every greene O1)   *Selinus* a town in Sicily
122 *Erycina* a name for Venus derived from her temple on Mt. Eryx in Sicily
125 *Saturn's royal son* Jove
126 *chariot* ed. (chariots O1)
127 *path* the Milky Way, mentioned again in l. 132
128 *enchased* set with
132 *him* i.e. Jove

[Enter] the GOVERNOR OF BABYLON *upon the walls
with [*MAXIMUS *and] others*

GOVERNOR

What saith Maximus?

MAXIMUS

My lord, the breach the enemy hath made
Gives such assurance of our overthrow
That little hope is left to save our lives
Or hold our city from the conqueror's hands.   5
Then hang out flags, my lord, of humble truce,
And satisfy the people's general prayers
That Tamburlaine's intolerable wrath
May be suppressed by our submission.

GOVERNOR

Villain, respects thou more thy slavish life   10
Than honour of thy country or thy name?
Is not my life and state as dear to me,
The city and my native country's weal,
As anything of price with thy conceit?
Have we not hope, for all our battered walls,   15
To live secure and keep his forces out,
When this our famous lake of Limnasphaltis
Makes walls afresh with every thing that falls
Into the liquid substance of his stream,
More strong than are the gates of death or hell?   20
What faintness should dismay our courages,
When we are thus defenced against our foe
And have no terror but his threat'ning looks?

*Enter another [*CITIZEN *above], kneeling to the* GOVERNOR

[FIRST CITIZEN]

My lord, if ever you did deed of ruth
And now will work a refuge to our lives,   25
Offer submission, hang up flags of truce,

14   *As . . . conceit* as anything which you may regard as valuable
17   *Limnasphaltis* the bituminous lake of Babylon

That Tamburlaine may pity our distress
And use us like a loving conqueror.
Though this be held his last day's dreadful siege,
Wherein he spareth neither man nor child,   30
Yet are there Christians of Georgia here
Whose state he ever pitied and relieved,
Will get his pardon if your grace would send.

GOVERNOR

How is my soul environèd,
And this eternized city Babylon   35
Filled with a pack of faint-heart fugitives
That thus entreat their shame and servitude!

[*Enter a second* CITIZEN]

[SECOND CITIZEN]

My lord, if ever you will win our hearts,
Yield up the town, save our wives and children,
For I will cast myself from off these walls   40
Or die some death of quickest violence,
Before I bide the wrath of Tamburlaine.

GOVERNOR

Villains, cowards, traitors to our state,
Fall to the earth and pierce the pit of hell
That legions of tormenting spirits may vex   45
Your slavish bosoms with continual pains.
I care not, nor the town will never yield
As long as any life is in my breast.

Enter [*below*] THERIDAMAS *and* TECHELLES,
with other SOLDIERS

[THERIDAMAS]

Thou desperate governor of Babylon,
To save thy life, and us a little labour,   50
Yield speedily the city to our hands,
Or else be sure thou shalt be forced with pains
More exquisite than ever traitor felt.

GOVERNOR

Tyrant, I turn the traitor in thy throat,
And will defend it in despite of thee.   55
Call up the soldiers to defend these walls.

35   *eternized* immortalized

TECHELLES

    Yield, foolish governor, we offer more
    Than ever yet we did to such proud slaves
    As durst resist us till our third day's siege:
    Thou seest us prest to give the last assault,   60
    And that shall bide no more regard of parley.

GOVERNOR

    Assault and spare not, we will never yield.

                  Alarm, and they scale the walls,
             *[*GOVERNOR *and* CITIZENS *exeunt, pursued*
                     by THERIDAMUS'*s army]*

    Enter TAMBURLAINE *[all in black drawn in his chariot*
       by the KINGS OF TREBIZON *and* SORIA*], with*
    USUMCASANE, AMYRAS, *and* CELEBINUS, *with others;*
    the two spare Kings [ORCANES *and* JERUSALEM]

TAMBURLAINE

    The stately buildings of fair Babylon
    Whose lofty pillars, higher than the clouds,
    Were wont to guide the seaman in the deep,   65
    Being carried thither by the cannon's force,
    Now fill the mouth of Limnasphaltis lake
    And make a bridge unto the battered walls.
    Where Belus, Ninus, and great Alexander
    Have rode in triumph, triumphs Tamburlaine,   70
    Whose chariot wheels have burst th'Assyrians' bones,
    Drawn with these kings on heaps of carcasses.
    Now in the place where fair Semiramis,
    Courted by kings and peers of Asia,
    Hath trod the measures, do my soldiers march,   75
    And in the streets where brave Assyrian dames
    Have rid in pomp like rich Saturnia,
    With furious words and frowning visages
    My horsemen brandish their unruly blades.

---

69   Belus was the son of Neptune and legendary founder of Babylon. Ninus, the founder
       of Nineveh, married Semiramis, who rebuilt Babylon. Alexander the Great con-
       quered Babylon in 331 BC.
71   *burst* broken
75   *measures* stately dances
76   *brave* finely arrayed, splendid
77   *Saturnia* Juno

Enter THERIDAMAS *and* TECHELLES [*below*],
bringing the GOVERNOR OF BABYLON

Who have ye there, my lords?   80
THERIDAMAS
The sturdy governor of Babylon,
That made us all the labour for the town,
And used such slender reckoning of your majesty.
TAMBURLAINE
Go bind the villain, he shall hang in chains
Upon the ruins of this conquered town.   85
Sirrah, the view of our vermilion tents,
Which threatened more than if the region
Next underneath the element of fire
Were full of comets and of blazing stars
Whose flaming trains should reach down to the earth,   90
Could not affright you; no, nor I myself,
The wrathful messenger of mighty Jove,
That with his sword hath quailed all earthly kings,
Could not persuade you to submission,
But still the ports were shut: villain I say,   95
Should I but touch the rusty gates of hell,
The triple-headed Cerberus would howl
And wake black Jove to crouch and kneel to me;
But I have sent volleys of shot to you,
Yet could not enter till the breach was made.   100
GOVERNOR
Nor if my body could have stopped the breach
Shouldst thou have entered, cruel Tamburlaine.
'Tis not thy bloody tents can make me yield,
Nor yet thyself, the anger of the Highest,
For though thy cannon shook the city walls,   105
My heart did never quake, or courage faint.
TAMBURLAINE
Well now I'll make it quake: go draw him up,
Hang him in chains upon the city walls
And let my soldiers shoot the slave to death.

87–8   *region . . . fire* the air
  93   *quailed* overpowered
  95   *ports* gates
  97   *Cerberus* the three-headed dog of hell
  98   *black Jove* Pluto, ruler of the underworld

GOVERNOR

Vile monster, born of some infernal hag,   110
And sent from hell to tyrannize on earth,
Do all thy worst: nor death nor Tamburlaine,
Torture or pain, can daunt my dreadless mind.

TAMBURLAINE

Up with him then, his body shall be scarred.

GOVERNOR

But Tamburlaine, in Limnasphaltis lake   115
There lies more gold than Babylon is worth,
Which when the city was besieged I hid –
Save but my life and I will give it thee.

TAMBURLAINE

Then, for all your valour, you would save your life.
Whereabout lies it?   120

GOVERNOR

Under a hollow bank, right opposite
Against the western gate of Babylon.

TAMBURLAINE

Go thither some of you and take his gold.
                           [*Exeunt some* ATTENDANTS]
The rest forward with execution.
Away with him hence, let him speak no more: 125
I think I make your courage something quail.
          [*Exeunt* ATTENDANTS *with* GOVERNOR OF BABYLON]
When this is done we'll march from Babylon
And make our greatest haste to Persia.
These jades are broken-winded and half tired,
Unharness them, and let me have fresh horse.   130
    [ATTENDANTS *unharness* KINGS OF TREBIZON *and* SORIA]
So, now their best is done to honour me,
Take them, and hang them both up presently.

KING OF TREBIZON

Vile tyrant, barbarous bloody Tamburlaine!

TAMBURLAINE

Take them away, Theridamas, see them dispatched.

THERIDAMAS

I will my lord.   135
    [*Exit* THERIDAMAS *with the* KINGS OF TREBIZON *and* SORIA]

132   *presently* immediately

TAMBURLAINE

    Come, Asian viceroys, to your tasks a while

    And take such fortune as your fellows felt.

ORCANES

    First let thy Scythian horse tear both our limbs

    Rather than we should draw thy chariot

    And like base slaves abject our princely minds   140

    To vile and ignominious servitude.

KING OF JERUSALEM

    Rather lend me thy weapon, Tamburlaine,

    That I may sheathe it in this breast of mine.

    A thousand deaths could not torment our hearts

    More than the thought of this doth vex our souls.   145

AMYRAS

    They will talk still, my lord, if you do not bridle them.

TAMBURLAINE

    Bridle them and let me to my coach.

                         They bridle them

[*The* GOVERNOR OF BABYLON *appears hanging in chains
on the walls. Enter* THERIDAMAS]

AMYRAS

    See now, my lord, how brave the captain hangs.

TAMBURLAINE

    'Tis brave indeed my boy, well done!

    Shoot first, my lord, and then the rest shall follow.   150

THERIDAMAS

    Then have at him to begin withal.

                     THERIDAMAS *shoots*

GOVERNOR

    Yet save my life and let this wound appease

137   *take . . . felt* share the fate of your fellow kings

140   *abject* abase

147   s.d. The soldiers who exited with the Governor at l. 126 re-appear above (having mounted an inner staircase to the second level), thrust their victim out of the window or over the edge of the balcony and fasten him with chains to the tiring-house wall. The shooting was presumably done with muskets (l. 158) and appropriate jets of pig's blood would no doubt have punctuated the grisly scene. On the modern stage, spectacular effects with arrows have also been managed. At the end of the scene, directed by the now sick Tamburlaine (l. 215), the soldiers return to remove the body. The staging invites us to link Tamburlaine's treachery to the Governor with his sudden distemper.

151   *have . . . withal* I'll have a go at him for a start.

The mortal fury of great Tamburlaine.

TAMBURLAINE

No, though Asphaltis lake were liquid gold
And offered me as ransom for thy life, 155
Yet shouldst thou die; shoot at him all at once.

They shoot

So, now he hangs like Bagdet's governor,
Having as many bullets in his flesh
As there be breaches in her battered wall.
Go now and bind the burghers hand and foot 160
And cast them headlong in the city's lake:
Tartars and Persians shall inhabit there,
And to command the city, I will build
A citadel that all Africa,
Which hath been subject to the Persian king, 165
Shall pay me tribute for in Babylon.

TECHELLES

What shall be done with their wives and children, my lord?

TAMBURLAINE

Techelles, drown them all, man, woman, and child,
Leave not a Babylonian in the town.

TECHELLES

I will about it straight; come soldiers. 170

Exit [with SOLDIERS]

TAMBURLAINE

Now Casane, where's the Turkish Alcoran
And all the heaps of superstitious books
Found in the temples of that Mahomet,
Whom I have thought a god? They shall be burnt.

USUMCASANE

Here they are, my lord. 175

TAMBURLAINE

Well said, let there be a fire presently.

[They light a fire]

In vain, I see, men worship Mahomet:

157   *Bagdet's* Baghdad's
171   *Alcoran* Koran
176   s.d. Again here, as with the burning of the bodies in III.iv, a trap might have been
used. But a simpler expedient would have been a brazier of some sort in which a
fire could be quickly kindled. The books, flung into the fire on Tamburlaine's orders
(l. 184), would then continue to burn onstage during his challenge to Mahomet and
the subsequent onset of his distemper – producing a telling ironic effect.

My sword hath sent millions of Turks to hell,
Slew all his priests, his kinsmen, and his friends,
And yet I live untouched by Mahomet.   180
There is a God full of revenging wrath,
From whom the thunder and the lightning breaks,
Whose scourge I am, and him will I obey.
So, Casane, fling them in the fire.

                           [They burn the books]

Now Mahomet, if thou have any power,   185
Come down thyself and work a miracle,
Thou art not worthy to be worshippèd
That suffers flames of fire to burn the writ
Wherein the sum of thy religion rests.
Why send'st thou not a furious whirlwind down   190
To blow thy Alcoran up to thy throne,
Where men report thou sitt'st by God himself,
Or vengeance on the head of Tamburlaine
That shakes his sword against thy majesty
And spurns the abstracts of thy foolish laws?   195
Well, soldiers, Mahomet remains in hell –
He cannot hear the voice of Tamburlaine.
Seek out another godhead to adore,
The God that sits in heaven, if any god,
For he is God alone, and none but he.   200

                    [Enter TECHELLES*]*

TECHELLES
I have fulfilled your highness' will, my lord:
Thousands of men drowned in Asphaltis lake
Have made the water swell above the banks,
And fishes fed by human carcasses,
Amazed, swim up and down upon the waves,   205
As when they swallow asafoetida,
Which makes them fleet aloft and gasp for air.
TAMBURLAINE
Well then, my friendly lords, what now remains
But that we leave sufficient garrison

195   *abstracts* written summaries
204   *fed* ed. (feed O1)
206   *asafoetida* a resinous gum with a strong odour, used in cooking and medicine
207   *fleet* float

And presently depart to Persia, 210
To triumph after all our victories.

THERIDAMAS

Ay, good my lord, let us in haste to Persia,
And let this captain be removed the walls
To some high hill about the city here.

TAMBURLAINE

Let it be so, about it soldiers. 215
But stay, I feel myself distempered suddenly.

TECHELLES

What is it dares distemper Tamburlaine?

TAMBURLAINE

Something, Techelles, but I know not what;
But forth ye vassals! Whatsoe'er it be,
Sickness or death can never conquer me. 220

Exeunt

216   *distempered* sick, disordered

ACT V, SCENE ii

[*Enter*] CALLAPINE, [KING OF] AMASIA,
[CAPTAIN, SOLDIERS,] *with drums and trumpets*

CALLAPINE

 King of Amasia, now our mighty host
 Marcheth in Asia Major, where the streams
 Of Euphrates and Tigris swiftly runs,
 And here may we behold great Babylon,
 Circled about with Limnasphaltis lake,   5
 Where Tamburlaine with all his army lies,
 Which being faint and weary with the siege,
 We may lie ready to encounter him
 Before his host be full from Babylon,
 And so revenge our latest grievous loss,   10
 If God or Mahomet send any aid.

KING OF AMASIA

 Doubt not, my lord, but we shall conquer him.
 The monster that hath drunk a sea of blood
 And yet gapes still for more to quench his thirst,
 Our Turkish swords shall headlong send to hell,   15
 And that vile carcass drawn by warlike kings
 The fowls shall eat, for never sepulchre
 Shall grace that base-born tyrant Tamburlaine.

CALLAPINE

 When I record my parents' slavish life,
 Their cruel death, mine own captivity,   20
 My viceroys' bondage under Tamburlaine,
 Methinks I could sustain a thousand deaths
 To be revenged of all his villainy.
 Ah sacred Mahomet, thou that hast seen
 Millions of Turks perish by Tamburlaine,   25
 Kingdoms made waste, brave cities sacked and burnt,
 And but one host is left to honour thee:
 Aid thy obedient servant Callapine
 And make him after all these overthrows

 9 *full from Babylon* i.e. fully recuperated from the siege
 19 *record* recall

186

To triumph over cursèd Tamburlaine.   30
KING OF AMASIA
　Fear not, my lord, I see great Mahomet
　Clothèd in purple clouds, and on his head
　A chaplet brighter than Apollo's crown,
　Marching about the air with armèd men
　To join with you against this Tamburlaine.   35
[CAPTAIN]
　Renowned general, mighty Callapine,
　Though God himself and holy Mahomet
　Should come in person to resist your power,
　Yet might your mighty host encounter all
　And pull proud Tamburlaine upon his knees   40
　To sue for mercy at your highness' feet.
CALLAPINE
　Captain, the force of Tamburlaine is great,
　His fortune greater, and the victories
　Wherewith he hath so sore dismayed the world
　Are greatest to discourage all our drifts;   45
　Yet when the pride of Cynthia is at full,
　She wanes again, and so shall his, I hope,
　For we have here the chief selected men
　Of twenty several kingdoms at the least.
　Nor plowman, priest, nor merchant stays at home: 50
　All Turkey is in arms with Callapine
　And never will we sunder camps and arms
　Before himself or his be conquerèd.
　This is the time that must eternize me
　For conquering the tyrant of the world.   55
　Come, soldiers, let us lie in wait for him,
　And if we find him absent from his camp
　Or that it be rejoined again at full,
　Assail it and be sure of victory.

　　　　　　　　　　　　　　　　　　　　　　　　Exeunt

33　*chaplet* wreath or garland
45　*drifts* purposes
49　*several* different
52　*sunder . . . arms* give up our campaign
58　*Or that* before

ACT V, SCENE iii

[*Enter*] THERIDAMAS, TECHELLES, USUMCASANE

[THERIDAMAS]
Weep heavens, and vanish into liquid tears!
Fall stars that govern his nativity
And summon all the shining lamps of heaven
To cast their bootless fires to the earth
And shed their feeble influence in the air; 5
Muffle your beauties with eternal clouds,
For hell and darkness pitch their pitchy tents,
And death with armies of Cimmerian spirits
Gives battle 'gainst the heart of Tamburlaine.
Now, in defiance of that wonted love 10
Your sacred virtues poured upon his throne,
And made his state an honour to the heavens,
These cowards invisibly assail his soul
And threaten conquest on our sovereign.
But if he die your glories are disgraced, 15
Earth droops and says that hell in heaven is placed.

TECHELLES
O then, ye powers that sway eternal seats
And guide this massy substance of the earth,
If you retain desert of holiness,
As your supreme estates instruct our thoughts, 20
Be not inconstant, careless of your fame,
Bear not the burden of your enemies' joys,
Triumphing in his fall whom you advanced,
But as his birth, life, health and majesty
Were strangely blest and governèd by heaven, 25
So honour heaven, till heaven dissolvèd be,
His birth, his life, his health and majesty.

USUMCASANE
Blush, heaven, to lose the honour of thy name,

4   *bootless* unavailing
8   *Cimmerian* dark, infernal. See note to Part One, III.ii.77 above.
19 *desert of holiness* that which deserves religious worship
20 *estates* ranks, authorities
22 *Bear . . . burden* do not join in the chorus

188

To see thy footstool set upon thy head,
And let no baseness in thy haughty breast   30
Sustain a shame of such inexcellence
To see the devils mount in angels' thrones,
And angels dive into the pools of hell.
And though they think their painful date is out,
And that their power is puissant as Jove's,   35
Which makes them manage arms against thy state,
Yet make them feel the strength of Tamburlaine,
Thy instrument and note of majesty,
Is greater far than they can thus subdue –
For if he die thy glory is disgraced,   40
Earth droops and says that hell in heaven is placed.

[*Enter* TAMBURLAINE, *drawn in his chariot by
the captive Kings,* ORCANES *and* JERUSALEM; AMYRAS,
CELEBINUS, *and* PHYSICIANS]

TAMBURLAINE

What daring god torments my body thus
And seeks to conquer mighty Tamburlaine?
Shall sickness prove me now to be a man
That have been termed the terror of the world?   45
Techelles and the rest, come take your swords
And threaten him whose hand afflicts my soul;
Come let us march against the powers of heaven
And set black streamers in the firmament
To signify the slaughter of the gods.   50
Ah friends, what shall I do? I cannot stand –
Come, carry me to war against the gods
That thus envy the health of Tamburlaine.

THERIDAMAS

Ah good my lord, leave these impatient words,
Which add much danger to your malady.   55

TAMBURLAINE

Why shall I sit and languish in this pain?
No, strike the drums, and in revenge of this,

---

31   *Sustain . . . inexcellence* bear so vile a shame
34   i.e though the powers of darkness think their time of submission is over
38   *note* distinguishing mark

Come let us charge our spears and pierce his breast
Whose shoulders bear the axis of the world,
That if I perish, heaven and earth may fade.   60
Theridamas, haste to the court of Jove,
Will him to send Apollo hither straight
To cure me, or I'll fetch him down myself.

TECHELLES

Sit still, my gracious lord, this grief will cease,
And cannot last, it is so violent.   65

TAMBURLAINE

Not last Techelles? No, for I shall die.
See where my slave, the ugly monster Death,
Shaking and quivering, pale and wan for fear,
Stands aiming at me with his murdering dart,
Who flies away at every glance I give,   70
And when I look away comes stealing on.
Villain away, and hie thee to the field!
I and mine army come to load thy bark
With souls of thousand mangled carcasses.
Look where he goes! But see, he comes again   75
Because I stay. Techelles, let us march
And weary Death with bearing souls to hell.

PHYSICIAN

Pleaseth your majesty to drink this potion,
Which will abate the fury of your fit
And cause some milder spirits govern you.   80

TAMBURLAINE

Tell me, what think you of my sickness now?

PHYSICIAN

I viewed your urine and the hypostasis,
Thick and obscure, doth make your danger great;
Your veins are full of accidental heat

58   *charge* level
      his Atlas's, with whom Tamburlaine is compared in Part One, II.i.10–11
62   *Apollo* the god of medicine
73   *bark* ship   76   *stay* delay
82   *hypostasis* sediment
84–97 The 'accidental [abnormal] heat' has parched Tamburlaine's arteries and 'dried up
      in his blood the radical moisture (*humidum*) which is necessary for the preser-
      vation of his natural heat (*calor*).' This depletion of moisture and heat prevents his
      soul's functions and slows his bodily activities by impeding the circulation of 'spirits',
      thus threatening his death. (See Johnstone Parr, *Tamburlaine's Malady*, University
      AL, 1953, p. 15)

Whereby the moisture of your blood is dried –   85
The humidum and calor, which some hold
Is not a parcel of the elements
But of a substance more divine and pure,
Is almost clean extinguishèd and spent,
Which being the cause of life imports your death.   90
Besides, my lord, this day is critical,
Dangerous to those whose crisis is as yours.
Your artiers which alongst the veins convey
The lively spirits which the heart engenders
Are parched and void of spirit, that the soul,   95
Wanting those organons by which it moves,
Cannot endure by argument of art.
Yet if your majesty may escape this day,
No doubt but you shall soon recover all.

TAMBURLAINE

Then will I comfort all my vital parts   100
And live in spite of death above a day.

Alarm within

[*Enter a* MESSENGER]

MESSENGER

My lord, young Callapine that lately fled from your majesty,
hath now gathered a fresh army, and hearing your absence in
the field, offers to set upon us presently.

TAMBURLAINE

See, my physicians, now, how Jove hath sent   105
A present medicine to recure my pain.
My looks shall make them fly and might I follow
There should not one of all the villain's power
Live to give offer of another fight.

USUMCASANE

I joy, my lord, your highness is so strong   110
That can endure so well your royal presence

87   *parcel* part
91   *day is critical* i.e. the stars are in an unfavourable conjunction for effecting a cure
93   *artiers* arteries
96   *organons* organs of the body which act as instruments of the soul (here, perhaps,
      in the sense of the fluid or 'spirits' that animate such organs)
97   *argument of art* i.e. the science of medicine
106   *recure* cure
111   *endure* make sturdy or robust

Which only will dismay the enemy.

TAMBURLAINE

I know it will Casane: draw you slaves!
In spite of death I will go show my face.

Alarm

TAMBURLAINE *goes in and comes out again*
with all the rest

Thus are the villains, cowards fled for fear,   115
Like summer's vapours vanished by the sun.
And could I but a while pursue the field,
That Callapine should be my slave again.
But I perceive my martial strength is spent;
In vain I strive and rail against those powers   120
That mean t'invest me in a higher throne,
As much too high for this disdainful earth.
Give me a map, then let me see how much
Is left for me to conquer all the world,
That these my boys may finish all my wants.   125

One brings a map

Here I began to march towards Persia,
Along Armenia and the Caspian Sea,
And thence unto Bithynia, where I took
The Turk and his great empress prisoners;
Then marched I into Egypt and Arabia,   130
And here not far from Alexandria,
Whereas the Terrene and the Red Sea meet,
Being distant less than full a hundred leagues,
I meant to cut a channel to them both
That men might quickly sail to India.   135
From thence to Nubia near Borno lake
And so along the Ethiopian sea,
Cutting the tropic line of Capricorn,
I conquered all as far as Zanzibar.
Then by the northern part of Africa   140
I came at last to Graecia, and from thence
To Asia, where I stay against my will,

112   *only* alone
132   *Whereas* where
134   *cut a channel* make a canal. The Suez Canal had been suggested before Marlowe's
      day.

Which is from Scythia, where I first began,
Backward and forwards near five thousand leagues.
Look here, my boys, see what a world of ground   145
Lies westward from the midst of Cancer's line,
Unto the rising of this earthly globe,
Whereas the sun declining from our sight
Begins the day with our antipodes:
And shall I die and this unconquerèd?   150
Lo here, my sons, are all the golden mines,
Inestimable drugs and precious stones,
More worth than Asia and the world beside;
And from th' Antarctic Pole eastward behold
As much more land, which never was descried,   155
Wherein are rocks of pearl that shine as bright
As all the lamps that beautify the sky:
And shall I die and this unconquerèd?
Here, lovely boys, what death forbids my life,
That let your lives command in spite of death.   160

AMYRAS

Alas my lord, how should our bleeding hearts,
Wounded and broken with your highness' grief,
Retain a thought of joy or spark of life?
Your soul gives essence to our wretched subjects,
Whose matter is incorporate in your flesh.   165

CELEBINUS

Your pains do pierce our souls, no hope survives.
For by your life we entertain our lives.

TAMBURLAINE

But sons, this subject, not of force enough
To hold the fiery spirit it contains,
Must part, imparting his impressions   170

---

162   *grief* suffering
164–5 *Your soul . . . flesh* Your soul has bequeathed an animating spirit ('essence') to our
        unhappy selves ('wretched subjects'), since our bodies are part of your flesh.
167   *entertain* maintain
168   *subject* material body
170   *his impressions* its spiritual power

By equal portions into both your breasts;
My flesh divided in your precious shapes
Shall still retain my spirit, though I die,
And live in all your seeds immortally.
Then now remove me, that I may resign   175
My place and proper title to my son:
[*To* AMYRAS] First take my scourge and my imperial crown,
And mount my royal chariot of estate,
That I may see thee crowned before I die.
Help me, my lords, to make my last remove.   180
                [*They help* TAMBURLAINE *out of his chariot*]

THERIDAMAS

A woeful change, my lord, that daunts our thoughts
More than the ruin of our proper souls.

TAMBURLAINE

Sit up, my son, let me see how well
Thou wilt become thy father's majesty.
                     They crown [AMYRAS]

AMYRAS

With what a flinty bosom should I joy   185
The breath of life and burden of my soul,
If, not resolved into resolvèd pains,
My body's mortifièd lineaments
Should exercise the motions of my heart,
Pierced with the joy of any dignity!   190
O father, if the unrelenting ears
Of death and hell be shut against my prayers
And that the spiteful influence of heaven
Deny my soul fruition of her joy,
How should I step or stir my hateful feet   195
Against the inward powers of my heart,
Leading a life that only strives to die,
And plead in vain unpleasing sovereignty?

---

176   *proper* own (also l. 182)
177   *scourge* whip
185–90   *With . . . dignity* How hard my heart would be if I could enjoy my life and the possession of my own soul [i.e. with Tamburlaine about to die], or if my body did not dissolve into extreme pain and its afflicted limbs ('mortified lineaments') were still able to carry out the promptings of a heart that could be touched to joy by earthly dignities (adapted from Ellis-Fermor).
195–8   *How . . . sovereignty* How could I act against the inner promptings of my heart, exercising unwanted sovereignty while my deepest desires pull me towards death?

TAMBURLAINE

    Let not thy love exceed thine honour, son,

    Nor bar thy mind that magnanimity   200

    That nobly must admit necessity:

    Sit up, my boy, and with those silken reins

    Bridle the steelèd stomachs of those jades.

THERIDAMAS

    My lord, you must obey his majesty

    Since fate commands and proud necessity.   205

AMYRAS [*mounting the chariot*]

    Heavens witness me with what a broken heart

    And damnèd spirit I ascend this seat,

    And send my soul, before my father die,

    His anguish and his burning agony!

TAMBURLAINE

    Now fetch the hearse of fair Zenocrate –   210

    Let it be placed by this my fatal chair

    And serve as parcel of my funeral.

USUMCASANE

    Then feels your majesty no sovereign ease

    Nor may our hearts, all drowned in tears of blood,

    Joy any hope of your recovery?   215

TAMBURLAINE

    Casane no, the monarch of the earth

    And eyeless monster that torments my soul,

    Cannot behold the tears ye shed for me,

    And therefore still augments his cruelty.

TECHELLES

    Then let some god oppose his holy power   220

    Against the wrath and tyranny of Death,

    That his tear-thirsty and unquenchèd hate

    May be upon himself reverberate.

                They bring in the hearse [of ZENOCRATE]

---

200   *magnanimity* fortitude

203   *steelèd stomachs* obdurately proud spirits

207   *damnèd* condemned to suffer

208   *send* may the heavens send. Amyras wants to share in his father's death-agony.

212   *parcel* part

216   *monarch of the earth* Death

222   *his* Death's

223   *be . . . reverberate* rebound

TAMBURLAINE

Now eyes, enjoy your latest benefit,
And when my soul hath virtue of your sight,   225
Pierce through the coffin and the sheet of gold
And glut your longings with a heaven of joy.
So, reign my son, scourge and control those slaves,
Guiding thy chariot with thy father's hand.
As precious is the charge thou undertak'st   230
As that which Clymen's brain-sick son did guide
When wand'ring Phoebe's ivory cheeks were scorched
And all the earth like Aetna breathing fire.
Be warned by him, then learn with awful eye
To sway a throne as dangerous as his.   235
For if thy body thrive not full of thoughts
As pure and fiery as Phyteus' beams,
The nature of these proud rebelling jades
Will take occasion by the slenderest hair,
And draw thee piecemeal like Hippolytus   240
Through rocks more steep and sharp than Caspian cliffs.
The nature of thy chariot will not bear
A guide of baser temper than myself,
More than heaven's coach the pride of Phaëton.
Farewell my boys, my dearest friends farewell,   245
My body feels, my soul doth weep to see
Your sweet desires deprived my company,
For Tamburlaine the scourge of God must die.

[*Dies*]

---

225   *when . . . sight* When (after death) Tamburlaine's soul, having been freed from the
body, will have the power of vision which in life belongs only to the eyes, he will be
able to see the spirit of Zenocrate.

231   *Clymen's* O2 (Clymeus O1)
       Clymen's . . . son Phaëton, son of Apollo and Clymene. See note to Part One, IV.ii.49
above.

232   *Phoebe* the moon

234   *awful* awe-inspiring

237   *Phyteus* Pythius, another name for Apollo, the sun god

238   *these . . . jades* the conquered kings

239   *take . . . hair* seize the slightest opportunity

240   *Hippolytus* killed when his horses bolted and dragged him to death

AMYRAS

    Meet heaven and earth, and here let all things end,
    For earth hath spent the pride of all her fruit   250
    And heaven consumed his choicest living fire.
    Let earth and heaven his timeless death deplore,
    For both their worths will equal him no more.

                            [*Exeunt*]

252   *timeless* untimely

The Famous

TRAGEDY

OF

THE RICH IEVV

OF *MALTA.*

AS IT WAS PLAYD

BEFORE THE KING AND
QVEENE, IN HIS MAJESTIES
Theatre at *White-Hall,* by her Majesties
Servants at the *Cock-pit.*

Written by CHRISTOPHER MARLO.

LONDON;
Printed by *I. B.* for *Nicholas Vavasour,* and are to be sold
at his Shop in the Inner-Temple, neere the
Church. 1633.

THE EPISTLE DEDICATORY

To my worthy friend, Mr. THOMAS HAMMON,
of Gray's Inn, &c.

This play, composed by so worthy an author as Mr. Marlo; and the
part of the Jew presented by so unimitable an actor as Mr. Allin,
being in this later age commended to the stage: as I ushered it unto
the Court, and presented it to the Cock-pit, with these Prologues
and Epilogues here inserted, so now being newly brought to the   5
press, I was loath it should be published without the ornament of
an Epistle; making choice of you unto whom to devote it; than
whom (of all those gentlemen and acquaintance, within the
compass of my long knowledge) there is none more able to tax
ignorance, or attribute right to merit. Sir, you have been pleased to   10
grace some of mine own works with your courteous patronage;
I hope this will not be the worse accepted, because commended by
me; over whom, none can claim more power or privilege than
yourself. I had no better a New-year's gift to present you with; receive
it therefore as a continuance of that inviolable obligement, by which,   15
he rests still engaged; who as he ever hath, shall always remain,

Tuissimus:

THO. HEYWOOD.

0.2   THOMAS HAMMON Heywood also dedicated two of his own plays to Hammon (Part II
      of *The Fair Maid of the West* (1631) and Part I of *The Iron Age* (1632)).
0.3   *Gray's Inn* one of the Inns of Court; a centre of legal training
  2   *Allin* Edward Alleyn (1566–1626), famous actor of the late sixteenth century; he first
      acted the roles of Tamburlaine, Faustus and Barabas.
  3   *ushered* introduced
  4   *Court* The title-page asserts that the play was performed 'before the King and Queen,
      in his Majesties Theatre at *White-Hall*'.
      Cock-pit located in Drury Lane, one of the two principal Caroline theatres (also
      known as The Phoenix)
  9   *tax* censure
 10   *right* just assessment
 15   *obligement* obligation
 17   *Tuissimus* (Latin) wholly yours

THE PROLOGUE

TO THE STAGE, AT THE COCK-PIT

We know not how our play may pass this stage,
But by the best of *poets in that age   *Marlo
The Malta Jew had being, and was made;
And he, then by the best of †actors played: †Allin
In *Hero and Leander*, one did gain   5
A lasting memory: in *Tamburlaine*,
This *Jew*, with others many: th' other wan
The attribute of peerless, being a man
Whom we may rank with (doing no one wrong)
Proteus for shapes, and Roscius for a tongue,   10
So could he speak, so vary; nor is't hate
To merit in ‡him who doth personate   ‡Perkins
Our Jew this day, nor is it his ambition
To exceed, or equal, being of condition
More modest; this is all that he intends,   15
(And that too, at the urgence of some friends)
To prove his best, and if none here gainsay it,
The part he hath studied, and intends to play it.

---

4   *Allin* Edward Alleyn. See note to Epistle Dedicatory.
5   *Hero and Leander* Marlowe's erotic narrative poem, based on Musaeus and published
     in 1598
6   *Tamburlaine* Alleyn also played the title role in Marlowe's *Tamburlaine*.
7   *wan* won
10   *Proteus* a sea god of Greek myth with the power of changing shape
     Roscius Quintus Roscius Gallus (d. 62 B.C.), the most famous Roman comic actor;
     later associated with great acting generally
11–12 *hate / To merit* i.e. an expression of jealousy to praise
12   *Perkins* Richard Perkins (d. 1650), a famous actor of the Jacobean and Caroline stage,
     acting c. 1602–37
14   *condition* temperament
16   *urgence* solicitation
17   *prove* try
     gainsay oppose

EPILOGUE

In graving, with Pygmalion to contend;
Or painting, with Apelles; doubtless the end
Must be disgrace: our actor did not so,
He only aimed to go, but not out-go.
Nor think that this day any prize was played,   5
Here were no bets at all, no wagers laid;
All the ambition that his mind doth swell,
Is but to hear from you, (by me) 'twas well.

1   *graving* sculpture
    Pygmalion the mythic king of Cyprus who fell in love with a beautiful statue he
    made (see Ovid, *Metamorphoses* X); the type of the great artist
2   *Apelles* a Greek painter (4th century B.C.) of legendary skill
4   *out-go* surpass
5   *prize was played* contest was engaged in (from fencing)
6   *no wagers laid* Apparently bets were sometimes made on the relative merits of actors.

203

THE PROLOGUE
SPOKEN AT COURT

Gracious and great, that we so boldly dare,
('Mongst other plays that now in fashion are)
To present this; writ many years agone,
And in that age, thought second unto none;
We humbly crave your pardon: we pursue   5
The story of a rich and famous Jew
Who lived in Malta: you shall find him still,
In all his projects, a sound Machevill;
And that's his character: he that hath past
So many censures, is now come at last   10
To have your princely ears, grace you him; then
You crown the action, and renown the pen.

EPILOGUE

It is our fear (dread Sovereign) we have been
Too tedious; neither can't be less than sin
To wrong your princely patience: if we have,
(Thus low dejected) we your pardon crave:
And if aught here offend your ear or sight,   5
We only act, and speak, what others write.

Prologue
    7   *still* always
    8   *sound* complete, thorough
         Machevill See note, Prologue 0.2.
   10   *censures* criticisms.

Epilogue
    1   *dread* revered
    2   *can't* can it
    4   *Thus low dejected* i.e. bowing

DRAMATIS PERSONAE

MACHEVILL, *the Prologue*
BARABAS, *the Jew of Malta*
FERNEZE, *the Governor of Malta*
ITHAMORE, *a Turkish slave to Barabas*
SELIM-CALYMATH, *the Turkish leader, son of the Turkish Emperor*
CALLAPINE, *a Bashaw*
ABIGAIL, *the daughter of Barabas*
DON LODOWICK, *the Governor's son*
DON MATHIAS, *his friend and lover of Abigail*
KATHERINE, *the mother of Don Mathias*
MARTIN DEL BOSCO, *Vice-Admiral of Spain*
FRIAR JACOMO
FRIAR BERNARDINE
BELLAMIRA, *a courtesan*
PILIA-BORZA, *a thief in league with her*
ABBESS
NUN
Two MERCHANTS; *three* JEWS; KNIGHTS; BASHAWS; OFFICERS;
SLAVES; CITIZENS; *Turkish* SOLDIERS; MESSENGER; CARPENTERS

No list of *Dramatis Personae* is given by Q.

205

PROLOGUE

[*Enter*] MACHEVILL

MACHEVILL

Albeit the world think Machevill is dead,
Yet was his soul but flown beyond the Alps,
And now the Guise is dead, is come from France
To view this land, and frolic with his friends.
To some perhaps my name is odious,   5
But such as love me, guard me from their tongues,
And let them know that I am Machevill,
And weigh not men, and therefore not men's words:
Admired I am of those that hate me most.
Though some speak openly against my books,   10
Yet will they read me, and thereby attain
To Peter's chair: and when they cast me off,
Are poisoned by my climbing followers.
I count religion but a childish toy,
And hold there is no sin but ignorance.   15

0.2 MACHEVILL ed. (Q *Macheuil*); rhyming with 'still' in Heywood's Court Prologue; here an embodiment of the spirit of Niccolò Machiavelli (1469–1527), understood as the essence of villainous self-interested calculation. The opinions of this stage figure diverge significantly from those to be found in Machiavelli's writings, and may be indebted to the anti-Machiavellian discourse of writers like Innocent Gentillet (see Minshull and Bawcutt).

 3 *the Guise* Henri de Lorraine, third Duke of Guise (1550–88), Roman Catholic opponent of the Huguenots and, in 1572, director of the St Bartholomew's Day massacre (see Marlowe's *Massace at Paris*).

 4 *this land* England (mocking the hope expressed in contemporary polemic (e.g. Gentillet) that political calculation would not contaminate England from the Continent)

5–6 Meaning unclear: either the devotees of Machiavellianism protect him from his critics or, more likely, the disciples follow Machiavelli's precepts while avoiding mention of his name.

 8 *weigh* esteem

 9 Even those who denounce Machiavelli admire him in secret.

12 *Peter's chair* the papacy
  cast me off i.e. abandon my precepts

14 *toy* trifle. Machiavelli actually took religion seriously as a factor of political life (see *Discourses* I.11–15), but his opponents often described his doctrine as atheism.

Birds of the air will tell of murders past?
I am ashamed to hear such fooleries:
Many will talk of title to a crown.
What right had Caesar to the empire?
Might first made kings, and laws were then most sure   20
When like the Draco's they were writ in blood.
Hence comes it, that a strong built citadel
Commands much more than letters can import:
Which maxima had Phalaris observed,
H'had never bellowed in a brazen bull   25
Of great ones' envy; o'th' poor petty wites,
Let me be envied and not pitied!
But whither am I bound, I come not, I,
To read a lecture here in Britaine,
But to present the tragedy of a Jew,   30
Who smiles to see how full his bags are crammed,
Which money was not got without my means.
I crave but this, grace him as he deserves,
And let him not be entertained the worse
Because he favours me.   [*Exit*]   35

16 *past?* ed. (Q past;) Such anecdotes, in which birds reveal an otherwise hidden crime, are taken by Machevill to exemplify the force of superstition rather than to evidence Providential order.
19 Here Machevill follows Machiavelli, who argues that Caesar was actually little different from the villainous Catiline, but won praise through wealth and power (*Discourses* I.10).
21 *Draco's* ed. (Q *Drancus*) referring to an Athenian legislator of proverbial severity
22 Citadels are traditionally used by tyrants to dominate their subjects (Bawcutt); the value of citadels is ambiguous in Machiavelli: in *The Prince* (XX) they are accorded limited value against internal enemies, but in *Discourses* (II.24) their usefulness is criticized.
23–5 According to legend the Sicilian tyrant Phalaris was killed in the brazen bull he had employed to roast his enemies. The opposition here implied is that between an interest in letters as a weakness and the use of force as a ruler's only true strength.
24 *maxima* ed. (Q maxime) maxim
26 *ones'* ed. (Q ones)
   wites either 'wights' (people) or 'wits'
27 *envied … not pitied* proverbial (Tilley, E 177)
29 *Britaine* Either 'Britain' or 'Britainy' – apparently the forms were equivalent in Elizabethan usage (compare *Edward II* 6.42).
31 *crammed,* ed. (Q cramb'd)
32 The suggestion that Machiavellian tactics have economic implications is odd, but, as Bawcutt points out, in keeping with Gentillet's polemical version of Machiavellianism.
33 *grace* honour
35 *favours* either 'resembles' or 'sides with'

[ACT I, SCENE i]

Enter BARABAS *in his counting-house,*
with heaps of gold before him

BARABAS

So that of thus much that return was made:
And of the third part of the Persian ships,
There was the venture summed and satisfied.
As for those Samnites, and the men of Uz,
That bought my Spanish oils, and wines of Greece,   5
Here have I pursed their paltry silverlings.
Fie; what a trouble 'tis to count this trash.
Well fare the Arabians, who so richly pay
The things they traffic for with wedge of gold,
Whereof a man may easily in a day   10
Tell that which may maintain him all his life.
The needy groom that never fingered groat,
Would make a miracle of thus much coin:
But he whose steel-barred coffers are crammed full,
And all his lifetime hath been tired,   15
Wearying his fingers' ends with telling it,
Would in his age be loath to labour so,
And for a pound to sweat himself to death:
Give me the merchants of the Indian mines,

1   BARABAS ed. (Q *Iew* throughout scene except in stage directions). The name Barabas is that of the criminal released in place of Jesus (Mark 15.7). This speech is remarkable for beginning a play in mid-sentence and for the resemblance of its catalogue of jewels to that found in the opening speech of the Jew Jonathas in the fifteenth-century Croxton *Play of the Sacrament.*

3   *summed and satisfied* reckoned up and paid off

4   *Samnites* ed. (Q *Samintes*) Central Italian people who fought Rome several times from 354 B.C. The reference to them combined with that to the biblical Uz (Job 1.1) and, subsequently, to Kirriah Jairim (after a city named in Joshua 15.9; Judges 18.12) suggests the extent of Barabas's trade, but also his polyglot associations of biblical and classical references and discourses.

6   *silverlings* (Q silverbings) silver coin equivalent to Jewish shekel

8   *Well fare* optative phrase: 'Good fortune to them' (compare V.i.61)
     pay ed. (Q pay,)

9   *traffic* trade

11 *Tell* Count

12 *groom* slave, servant
     groat coin of small value (compare IV.ii.107)

That trade in metal of the purest mould;   20
The wealthy Moor, that in the Eastern rocks
Without control can pick his riches up,
And in his house heap pearl like pebble-stones;
Receive them free, and sell them by the weight,
Bags of fiery opals, sapphires, amethysts,   25
Jacinths, hard topaz, grass-green emeralds,
Beauteous rubies, sparkling diamonds,
And seldseen costly stones of so great price,
As one of them indifferently rated,
And of a caract of this quantity,   30
May serve in peril of calamity
To ransom great kings from captivity.
This is the ware wherein consists my wealth:
And thus methinks should men of judgement frame
Their means of traffic from the vulgar trade,   35
And as their wealth increaseth, so inclose
Infinite riches in a little room.
But now how stands the wind?
Into what corner peers my halcyon's bill?
Ha, to the east? Yes: see how stands the vanes?   40
East and by south: why then I hope my ships
I sent for Egypt and the bordering isles
Are gotten up by Nilus' winding banks:
Mine argosy from Alexandria,
Loaden with spice and silks, now under sail,   45

20   *mould* constitution, character
22   *Without control* Without restraint
28   *seldseen* ed. (Q seildsene) seldom seen, rare
29   *rated* valued
30   *caract* ed. (Q Carrect) carat, measure of gem weight, or possibly sign of character
      (compare *Measure for Measure* V.i.59). This semantic ambiguity of quantity and
      quality is potentially significant in a work with such economic interests and such
      insistent punning.
34   *frame* define, distinguish
37   *Infinite riches in a little room* Hunter defines this as a parody of traditional Christian
      imagery concerning the Virgin Birth; however, the phrase is also proverbial for great
      worth in a humble package (Tilley, W 921).
39   *halcyon* kingfisher, when dead and hung up, supposed to act as a weather vane
40   *stands* As frequently in Marlowe, singulars and plurals are interchangeable; compare
      lines 46 and 109.
41   *East and by south* i.e. south-east
44   *argosy* large merchant ship

Are smoothly gliding down by Candy shore
To Malta, through our Mediterranean sea.
But who comes here? How now.

Enter a MERCHANT

MERCHANT
  Barabas, thy ships are safe,
  Riding in Malta road: and all the merchants   50
  With other merchandise are safe arrived,
  And have sent me to know whether yourself
  Will come and custom them.
BARABAS
  The ships are safe thou say'st, and richly fraught?
MERCHANT
  They are.
BARABAS   Why then go bid them come ashore,   55
  And bring with them their bills of entry:
  I hope our credit in the custom-house
  Will serve as well as I were present there.
  Go send 'em three score camels, thirty mules,
  And twenty waggons to bring up the ware.   60
  But art thou master in a ship of mine,
  And is thy credit not enough for that?
MERCHANT
  The very custom barely comes to more
  Than many merchants of the town are worth,
  And therefore far exceeds my credit, sir.   65
BARABAS
  Go tell 'em the Jew of Malta sent thee, man:
  Tush, who amongst 'em knows not Barabas?
MERCHANT
  I go.

---

46   *Candy* Crete
48   *But who comes here?* a formula for dramatic entry already archaic in Marlowe's day,
     but in keeping with some of the other stylistic qualities of the play
50   *road* ed. (Q Rhode) harbour
53   *custom* see them through customs procedures
54   *fraught* loaded with merchandise
63   *very custom barely* the duties alone

BARABAS

So then, there's somewhat come.

Sirrah, which of my ships art thou master of? 70

MERCHANT

Of the Speranza, sir.

BARABAS   And saw'st thou not

Mine argosy at Alexandria?

Thou couldst not come from Egypt, or by Caire

But at the entry there into the sea,

Where Nilus pays his tribute to the main. 75

Thou needs must sail by Alexandria.

MERCHANT

I neither saw them, nor inquired of them.

But this we heard some of our seamen say,

They wondered how you durst with so much wealth

Trust such a crazèd vessel, and so far. 80

BARABAS

Tush; they are wise, I know her and her strength:

But go, go thou thy ways, discharge thy ship,

And bid my factor bring his loading in.

                               [*Exit* MERCHANT]

And yet I wonder at this argosy.

Enter a SECOND MERCHANT

2 MERCHANT

Thine argosy from Alexandria, 85

Know Barabas doth ride in Malta road,

Laden with riches, and exceeding store

Of Persian silks, of gold, and orient pearl.

BARABAS

How chance you came not with those other ships

70   *Sirrah* a contemptuous form of address
      master of ed. (Q Master off)

71–2 ed. (Q And . . . Alexandria? / Thou)

73   *Caire* Cairo

80   *crazèd* unseaworthy

81   *they are wise* sarcastic

82   *But* ed. (Q By)
      go thou thy ways i.e. be off!

83   *factor* agent
      loading cargo

88   *orient* from the East, brilliant

That sailed by Egypt?

2 MERCHANT   Sir we saw 'em not.   90

BARABAS

Belike they coasted round by Candy shore
About their oils, or other businesses.
But 'twas ill done of you to come so far
Without the aid or conduct of their ships.

2 MERCHANT

Sir, we were wafted by a Spanish fleet   95
That never left us till within a league,
That had the galleys of the Turk in chase.

BARABAS

Oh they were going up to Sicily: well, go
And bid the merchants and my men dispatch
And come ashore, and see the fraught discharged.   100

2 MERCHANT

I go.   *Exit*

BARABAS

Thus trowls our fortune in by land and sea,
And thus are we on every side enriched:
These are the blessings promised to the Jews,
And herein was old Abram's happiness: 105
What more may heaven do for earthly man
Than thus to pour out plenty in their laps,
Ripping the bowels of the earth for them,
Making the sea their servant, and the winds
To drive their substance with successful blasts?   110

---

91   *Belike* Perhaps
94   *conduct* escort
95   *wafted* escorted
96   *within a league* i.e. within approximately 3 miles of our destination
97   *in chase* in pursuit
102   *trowls* rolls in
104–5   This refers to God's covenant with Abraham. This blessing from Genesis 15 is claimed by Christian theologians who, like Luther, assert that Jews misinterpret the divine blessing by 'applying it only to a carnal blessing, and do great injury to Scripture' (*Commentary on Galatians* (English ed. 1575)); see Hunter on Galatians 3.13–16; compare II.iii.47. The passage also echoes Ovid's description of the Age of Iron, as Bawcutt points out.
109   *servant* ed. (Q servants) Singulars and plurals are a source of difficulty from line 106 on.
109–10   *the winds . . . blasts* i.e. the winds propel the ships that carry their goods

Who hateth me but for my happiness?
Or who is honoured now but for his wealth?
Rather had I a Jew be hated thus,
Than pitied in a Christian poverty:
For I can see no fruits in all their faith,   115
But malice, falsehood, and excessive pride,
Which methinks fits not their profession.
Happily some hapless man hath conscience,
And for his conscience lives in beggary.
They say we are a scattered nation: 120
I cannot tell, but we have scambled up
More wealth by far than those that brag of faith.
There's Kirriah Jairim, the great Jew of Greece,
Obed in Bairseth, Nones in Portugal,
Myself in Malta, some in Italy,   125
Many in France, and wealthy every one:
Ay, wealthier far than any Christian.
I must confess we come not to be kings:
That's not our fault: alas, our number's few,
And crowns come either by succession,   130
Or urged by force; and nothing violent,
Oft have I heard tell, can be permanent.
Give us a peaceful rule, make Christians kings,
That thirst so much for principality.
I have no charge, nor many children,   135
But one sóle daughter, whom I hold as dear

111   *happiness* prosperity
115   *fruits . . . faith* common New Testament image (see John 15.1–6; compare Kocher,
       pp. 124–5)
117   *profession* religious faith
118   *Happily some hapless* haply, perhaps some unfortunate
120   *scattered nation* referring to belief that Jewish dispersal reflected God's anger
121   *scambled up* raked together, perhaps rapaciously
123   *Kirriah Jairim* personal name after a biblical city (see 4n.)
124   *Obed* the child of Ruth and Boaz, and ancestor of Jesus, 'notwithstanding', as the
       Geneva Bible gloss says, that Ruth was 'a Moabite of base condicion, and a stranger
       from the people of God' (Ruth 1, 'argument')
       Bairseth not identified
       Nones perhaps derived from the name of Dr Hector Nunez, a prominent member
       of the marrano community in London
128   *come not to be* do not become
131–2 *nothing . . . permanent* proverbial (see Gentillet, pp. 13, 200, 316)
134   *principality* rule
135   *charge* responsibility

214

As Agamemnon did his Iphigen:
And all I have is hers. But who comes here?

Enter THREE JEWS

1 JEW

Tush, tell not me 'twas done of policy.

2 JEW

Come therefore let us go to Barabas;   140
For he can counsel best in these affairs;
And here he comes.

BARABAS   Why how now countrymen?
Why flock you thus to me in multitudes?
What accident's betided to the Jews?

1 JEW

A fleet of warlike galleys, Barabas,   145
Are come from Turkey, and lie in our road:
And they this day sit in the council-house
To entertain them and their embassy.

BARABAS

Why let 'em come, so they come not to war;
Or let 'em war, so we be conquerors.   150
(Nay, let 'em combat, conquer, and kill all,
So they spare me, my daughter, and my wealth.)

1 JEW

Were it for confirmation of a league,
They would not come in warlike manner thus.

2 JEW

I fear their coming will afflict us all.   155

BARABAS

Fond men, what dream you of their multitudes?

137   Ironic, since Agamemnon was forced to sacrifice his daughter Iphigenia to obtain a
      favourable wind for the Greek military expedition against Troy.
139   *policy* cunning politics; often used pejoratively during the Renaissance to refer to
      Machiavellian deviousness
144   *betided to* happening to
147   *they* the rulers of Malta
151   ed. (Q has a marginal *'aside'*) This is the first of Barabas's many lines spoken only in
      part to his on-stage interlocutors. The precise limits of the aside portions of his lines
      are often ambiguous. However, it often appears that they are the final words or
      phrases which serve to modify or contradict what precedes them. Asides are marked
      in the present edition by parentheses.
156   *Fond* Foolish

What need they treat of peace that are in league?
The Turks and those of Malta are in league.
Tut, tut, there is some other matter in't.

1 JEW

Why, Barabas, they come for peace or war.   160

BARABAS

Happily for neither, but to pass along
Towards Venice by the Adriatic Sea;
With whom they have attempted many times,
But never could effect their stratagem.

3 JEW

And very wisely said, it may be so.   165

2 JEW

But there's a meeting in the senate-house,
And all the Jews in Malta must be there.

BARABAS

Umh; all the Jews in Malta must be there?
Ay, like enough, why then let every man
Provide him, and be there for fashion-sake.   170
If any thing shall there concern our state
Assure yourselves I'll look (unto myself).

1 JEW

I know you will; well brethren let us go.

2 JEW

Let's take our leaves; farewell good Barabas.

BARABAS

Do so; farewell Zaareth, farewell Temainte.   175

[*Exeunt* JEWS]

And Barabas now search this secret out.
Summon thy senses, call thy wits together:
These silly men mistake the matter clean

---

157   *in league* in agreement
163   *With whom* against whom
168   *Umh* a noise indicating reflectiveness
170   *Provide him . . . for fashion-sake* Get ready . . . according to form
171   *our state* the material conditions of Jews or their collective standing as a defined
       class or group
172   ed. (Q has a marginal *'aside'*)
175   *Temainte* perhaps a reminiscence of Eliphaz the Temanite, one of Job's comforters
       (Job 2)
178   *silly* simple, innocent
       clean completely

Long to the Turk did Malta contribute;
Which tribute all in policy, I fear,   180
The Turks have let increase to such a sum,
As all the wealth of Malta cannot pay;
And now by that advantage thinks, belike,
To seize upon the town: ay, that he seeks.
Howe'er the world go, I'll make sure for one,   185
And seek in time to intercept the worst,
Warily guarding that which I ha' got.
Ego mihimet sum semper proximus.
Why let 'em enter, let 'em take the town.   [*Exit*]

185   *make . . . one* look out for myself
186   *intercept* prevent
188   *Ego . . . proximus* adapted from Terence's *Andria*, 'Proximus sum egomet mihi,'
    (IV.i.12), 'I am always nearest to myself'

[ACT I, SCENE ii]

Enter [FERNEZE,] GOVERNOR *of Malta,* KNIGHTS
[*and* OFFICERS,] *met by* BASHAWS *of the Turk;* CALYMATH

FERNEZE

Now bashaws, what demand you at our hands?

BASHAW

Know knights of Malta, that we came from Rhodes,
From Cyprus, Candy, and those other isles
That lie betwixt the Mediterranean seas.

FERNEZE

What's Cyprus, Candy, and those other isles   5
To us, or Malta? What at our hands demand ye?

CALYMATH

The ten years' tribute that remains unpaid.

FERNEZE

Alas, my lord, the sum is over-great,
I hope your highness will consider us.

CALYMATH

I wish, grave Governor, 'twere in my power   10
To favour you, but 'tis my father's cause,
Wherein I may not, nay I dare not dally.

FERNEZE

Then give us leave, great Selim-Calymath.

CALYMATH

Stand all aside, and let the knights determine,

0.1   GOVERNOR Throughout this scene (e.g. lines 10, 17, 32) Q uses the plural, while the
       speech heading for the speaker who leads the Maltese Knights is 'Governor'. As in the
       case of 'Jew' in I.i, a general designation is subsequently replaced with a proper name;
       by II.ii the leader of Malta is 'Ferneze'.
       KNIGHTS members of the Order of St John of Jerusalem
0.2   BASHAWS ed. (Q BASSOES) pashas, Turkish military functionaries
4   seas The Adriatic, Aegean, etc. Many editors insert a dash here for Q's full stop to
       reinforce the idea that Ferneze interrupts the Bashaw's oratory.
9   consider grant consideration to
10   grave worthy of respect
       Governor, ed. (Q Governors)
13   give us leave allow us private conference
       Selim-Calymath Selim was the name of the son of Suleiman the Magnificent, Turkish
       ruler during the seige of Malta in 1565.

218

And send to keep our galleys under sail,   15
For happily we shall not tarry here:
Now Governor how are you resolved?

FERNEZE

Thus: since your hard conditions are such
That you will needs have ten years' tribute past,
We may have time to make collection   20
Amongst the inhabitants of Malta for't.

BASHAW

That's more than is in our commission.

CALYMATH

What Callapine a little courtesy.
Let's know their time, perhaps it is not long;
And 'tis more kingly to obtain by peace   25
Than to enforce conditions by constraint.
What respite ask you Governor?

FERNEZE   But a month.

CALYMATH

We grant a month, but see you keep your promise.
Now launch our galleys back again to sea,
Where we'll attend the respite you have ta'en,   30
And for the money send our messenger.
Farewell great Governor, and brave knights of Malta.
                    Exeunt [CALYMATH *and* BASHAWS]

FERNEZE

And all good fortune wait on Calymath.
Go one and call those Jews of Malta hither:
Were they not summoned to appear today?   35

OFFICER

They were, my lord, and here they come.

                Enter BARABAS *and* THREE JEWS

1 KNIGHT

Have you determined what to say to them?

FERNEZE

Yes, give me leave, and Hebrews now come near.
From the Emperor of Turkey is arrived

14   *Stand all aside* Give them room
17   *how . . . resolved?* What have you decided?
22   *than . . . commission* than we are authorized to do
35   *today?* ed. (Q to day.)

219

Great Selim-Calymath, his highness' son,   40
To levy of us ten years' tribute past,
Now then here know that it concerneth us:

BARABAS

Then good my lord, to keep your quiet still,
Your Lordship shall do well to let them have it.

FERNEZE

Soft Barabas, there's more longs to't than so.   45
To what this ten years' tribute will amount,
That we have cast, but cannot compass it
By reason of the wars, that robbed our store;
And therefore are we to request your aid.

BARABAS

Alas, my Lord, we are no soldiers: 50
And what's our aid against so great a prince?

1 KNIGHT

Tut, Jew, we know thou art no soldier;
Thou art a merchant, and a moneyed man,
And 'tis thy money, Barabas, we seek.

BARABAS

How, my lord, my money?

FERNEZE   Thine and the rest.   55
For to be short, amongst you't must be had.

1 JEW

Alas, my lord, the most of us are poor!

FERNEZE

Then let the rich increase your portions:

BARABAS

Are strangers with your tribute to be taxed?

2 KNIGHT

Have strangers leave with us to get their wealth?   60

---

42   Q's punctuation is a colon, which Ethel Seaton argues ('Marlowe's Map', *Essays and Studies* 10 (1924)) may signal 'rhetorical upward intonation' (p. 31); thus it may be suggested that Barabas interrupts Ferneze before he has completed his statement (compare line 58).

43   *keep . . . still* preserve your peace

45   *longs* belongs, pertains

46   *amount,* ed. (Q amount)

47   *cast . . . compass* calculated but cannot satisfy

48   *store* treasury

57   *1 JEW* ed. (Q Iew)

58   *increase your portions* contribute for you

59   *strangers* foreigners

Then let them with us contribute.

BARABAS

How, equally?

FERNEZE   No, Jew, like infidels.

For through our sufferance of your hateful lives,

Who stand accursèd in the sight of heaven,

These taxes and afflictions are befallen,   65

And therefore thus we are determinèd;

Read there the articles of our decrees.

OFFICER [*Reading*]

First, the tribute money of the Turks shall all be levied amongst the Jews, and each of them to pay one half of his estate.   70

BARABAS

How, half his estate? I hope you mean not mine.

FERNEZE

Read on.

OFFICER [*Reading*]

Secondly, he that denies to pay, shall straight become a Christian.

BARABAS

How, a Christian? Hum, what's here to do?   75

OFFICER [*Reading*]

Lastly, he that denies this, shall absolutely lose all he has.

ALL 3 JEWS

Oh my lord we will give half.

BARABAS

Oh earth-metalled villains, and no Hebrews born!

And will you basely thus submit yourselves   80

To leave your goods to their arbitrament?

FERNEZE

Why Barabas wilt thou be christened?

64   *accursèd* i.e. for a role in the Crucifixion of Christ (cf. Matthew 27.25, and line 108)
66   *determinèd* resolved
68   OFFICER [*Reading*] ed. (Q *Reader* as at lines 73, 76)
68–70 ed. (Q First . . . be / Leuyed . . . one / Halfe . . . estate.)
71   Many editors make all or part of this and line 75 asides.
73–4 ed. (Q Secondly . . . become / A Christian.)
76–7 ed. (Q *one line*)
79   *earth-metalled* base, dull in temperament
81   *arbitrament* disposal

BARABAS

No, Governor, I will be no convertite.

FERNEZE

Then pay thy half.

BARABAS

Why know you what you did by this device?   85
Half of my substance is a city's wealth.
Governor, it was not got so easily;
Nor will I part so slightly therewithal.

FERNEZE

Sir, half is the penalty of our decree,
Either pay that, or we will seize on all.   90

BARABAS

Corpo di Dio; stay, you shall have half,
Let me be used but as my brethren are.

FERNEZE

No, Jew, thou hast denied the articles,
And now it cannot be recalled.

                                   [*Exeunt* OFFICERS]

BARABAS

Will you then steal my goods?   95
Is theft the ground of your religion?

FERNEZE

No, Jew, we take particularly thine
To save the ruin of a multitude:
And better one want for a common good,
Than many perish for a private man: 100
Yet Barabas we will not banish thee,
But here in Malta, where thou got'st thy wealth,
Live still; and if thou canst, get more.

BARABAS

Christians, what or how can I multiply?
Of nought is nothing made.   105

85   Craik suggests an echo of Christ's 'They knowe not what they do' (Luke 23.34).
88   *slightly* easily, without resistance
91   *Corpo di Dio* (Italian) Body of God!
94   Many editors have the officers exit here to seize Barabas's wealth; they apparently re-enter at line 131.
96   *ground* basis
99–100   Hunter suggests an echo of John 11.50.
100   *private* individual
105   proverbial; but also potentially a point of contention between Aristotelian and biblical thinking concerning Creation

1 KNIGHT

    From nought at first thou cam'st to little wealth,
    From little unto more, from more to most:
    If your first curse fall heavy on thy head,
    And make thee poor and scorned of all the world,
    'Tis not our fault, but thy inherent sin.   110

BARABAS

    What? Bring you scripture to confirm your wrongs?
    Preach me not out of my possessions.
    Some Jews are wicked, as all Christians are:
    But say the tribe that I descended of
    Were all in general cast away for sin,   115
    Shall I be tried by their transgression?
    The man that dealeth righteously shall live:
    And which of you can charge me otherwise?

FERNEZE

    Out wretched Barabas,
    Sham'st thou not thus to justify thyself,   120
    As if we knew not thy profession?
    If thou rely upon thy righteousness,
    Be patient and thy riches will increase.
    Excess of wealth is cause of covetousness:
    And covetousness, oh 'tis a monstrous sin.   125

BARABAS

    Ay, but theft is worse: tush, take not from me then,
    For that is theft; and if you rob me thus,
    I must be forced to steal and compass more.

1 KNIGHT

    Grave Governor, list not to his exclaims:
    Convert his mansion to a nunnery,   130

108   *your first curse* i.e. that of the Jews (compare line 64)
      thy The shift in pronouns suggests a move from the racially general ('your') to the individual.
113   *as all Christians are* possibly an aside
115   *cast away* rejected by God
117   Compare Proverbs 10.2 ('The treasures of wickednes profite nothing: but righteousnes deliuereth from death') and 12.28.
119–22   ed. (Q Out . . . thus / To . . . not / Thy . . . righteousnesse,)
119   *Out* an expression of reproach
121   *profession* religious creed (compare line 146), personal code or occupation – i.e. as merchant or as usurer
128   *compass* contrive to attain
129   *exclaims* exclamations

Enter OFFICERS

His house will harbour many holy nuns.

FERNEZE

It shall be so: now officers, have you done?

OFFICER

Ay, my lord, we have seized upon the goods
And wares of Barabas, which being valued
Amount to more than all the wealth in Malta.   135
And of the other we have seizèd half.
Then we'll take order for the residue.

BARABAS

Well then my lord, say, are you satisfied?
You have my goods, my money, and my wealth,
My ships, my store, and all that I enjoyed;   140
And having all, you can request no more;
Unless your unrelenting flinty hearts
Suppress all pity in your stony breasts,
And now shall move you to bereave my life.

FERNEZE

No, Barabas, to stain our hands with blood   145
Is far from us and our profession.

BARABAS

Why, I esteem the injury far less,
To take the lives of miserable men,
Than be the causers of their misery.
You have my wealth, the labour of my life,   150
The comfort of mine age, my children's hope,
And therefore ne'er distinguish of the wrong.

FERNEZE

Content thee, Barabas, thou hast nought but right.

BARABAS

Your extreme right does me exceeding wrong:

---

136   *the other* the other Jews
137   *the residue* the balance of the tribute or the rest of the affair
146   *profession* Christian principles (compare line 121)
147   *Why,* ed. (Q Why)
150   *wealth,* ed. (Q wealth)
152   *distinguish of the wrong* draw false distinctions between murder and theft
153   *nought but right* nothing but justice
154   proverbial (Tilley, R 122), but also, of course, a potential nexus for one version of classical tragedy

But take it to you i' the devil's name. 155

FERNEZE

Come, let us in, and gather of these goods
The money for this tribute of the Turk.

1 KNIGHT

'Tis necessary that be looked unto:
For if we break our day, we break the league,
And that will prove but simple policy. 160

Exeunt [all except BARABAS *and* JEWS]

BARABAS

Ay, policy? that's their profession,
And not simplicity, as they suggest. [*Kneels*]
The plagues of Egypt, and the curse of heaven,
Earth's barrenness, and all men's hatred
Inflict upon them, thou great *Primus Motor*. 165
And here upon my knees, striking the earth,
I ban their souls to everlasting pains
And extreme tortures of the fiery deep,
That thus have dealt with me in my distress.

1 JEW

Oh yet be patient, gentle Barabas. 170

BARABAS

Oh silly brethren, born to see this day!
Why stand you thus unmoved with my laments?
Why weep you not to think upon my wrongs?
Why pine not I, and die in this distress?

155   *i'the* ed. (Q i'th')
159   *break our day* miss our deadline
160   *simple policy* foolish strategy
161–2   *Ay, policy? . . . simplicity* Picking up the phrase 'simple policy', Barabas offers an analysis of the hypocrisy of the Maltese Christians, who profess Christian honesty – 'the simplicitie that is in Christ' (II Corinthians 11.3) – but practice cunning strategy.
162   *Kneels* Barabas is clearly on his knees by line 166 and probably refers to his posture at line 172. His kneeling is one of this scene's many echoes of the dramaturgy of *The Spanish Tragedy*. The point at which he rises is not clear, but Bawcutt's suggestion of line 215 makes sense.
163   *plagues of Egypt* described in Exodus 7–12
165   *Primus Motor* (Latin) First Mover, 'The chiefest god' of *I Tamburlaine* IV.ii.8–9 and Aristotle's *Metaphysics*
167   *ban* curse
171   *silly* foolish
172–4   As Craik points out, the patterned repetition of these lines resembles stylistic devices of *The Spanish Tragedy*; see also III.iii.42–9 and III.v.35–6.

1 JEW

   Why, Barabas, as hardly can we brook   175
   The cruel handling of ourselves in this:
   Thou seest they have taken half our goods.

BARABAS

   Why did you yield to their extortion?
   You were a multitude, and I but one,
   And of me only have they taken all.   180

1 JEW

   Yet brother Barabas remember Job.

BARABAS

   What tell you me of Job? I wot his wealth
   Was written thus: he had seven thousand sheep,
   Three thousand camels, and two hundred yoke
   Of labouring oxen, and five hundred   185
   She-asses: but for every one of those,
   Had they been valued at indifferent rate,
   I had at home, and in mine argosy
   And other ships that came from Egypt last,
   As much as would have bought his beasts and him,   190
   And yet have kept enough to live upon;
   So that not he, but I may curse the day,
   Thy fatal birthday, forlorn Barabas;
   And henceforth wish for an eternal night,
   That clouds of darkness may enclose my flesh,   195
   And hide these extreme sorrows from mine eyes:
   For only I have toiled to inherit here
   The months of vanity and loss of time,
   And painful nights have been appointed me.

---

175   *brook* endure

182   *wot* know

182–208 These lines frequently echo chapters 1, 3 and 7 of the Book of Job. Lines 192–6 are very closely related to Job 3.1–10: 'Afterward Iob opened his mouthe, and cursed his day. And Iob cryed out, and said, Let the daye perish, wherein I was borne, and the night when it was said, There is a manchilde conceiued. Let that day be darkenes, let not God regarde it from above, nether let the light shine vpon it, But let darkenes, & the shadowe of death staine it: let the cloude remaine vpon it, & let them make it fearefull as a bitter day ... Because it shut not vp the dores of my mothers wombe: nor hid sorowe from mine eyes.' Similarly close relationships exist in lines 197–9 to Job 7.3 and in line 208 to Job 7.11.

187   *at indifferent rate* impartially evaluated

2 JEW

    Good Barabas be patient.   200

BARABAS

    Ay, I pray leave me in my patience.
    You that were ne'er possessed of wealth, are pleased with want.
    But give him liberty at least to mourn,
    That in a field amidst his enemies,
    Doth see his soldiers slain, himself disarmed,   205
    And knows no means of his recovery:
    Ay, let me sorrow for this sudden chance;
    'Tis in the trouble of my spirit I speak;
    Great injuries are not so soon forgot.

1 JEW

    Come, let us leave him in his ireful mood,   210
    Our words will but increase his ecstasy.

2 JEW

    On then: but trust me 'tis a misery
    To see a man in such affliction:
    Farewell Barabas.

                             Exeunt [JEWS]

BARABAS

    Ay, fare you well.   215
    See the simplicity of these base slaves,
    Who for the villains have no wit themselves,
    Think me to be a senseless lump of clay
    That will with every water wash to dirt:
    No, Barabas is born to better chance,   220
    And framed of finer mould than common men,
    That measure nought but by the present time.
    A reaching thought will search his deepest wits,
    And cast with cunning for the time to come:

---

201   *Ay, I* ed. (Q I, I)
210   *ireful* enraged
211   *ecstasy* passion
216–17   *simplicity ... base slaves ... villains* Barabas changes tone abruptly, condescending
        to the departed Jews as foolish, socially inferior and debased generally.
219   *with every water wash to dirt* fall into disarray at any sort of trouble
220   *chance* fortune
221   *mould* earth
223   *reaching thought* penetrating analyst
224   *cast with cunning* wisely anticipate

For evils are apt to happen every day.   225
But whither wends my beauteous Abigail?

Enter ABIGAIL *the Jew's daughter*

Oh what has made my lovely daughter sad?
What? Woman, moan not for a little loss:
Thy father has enough in store for thee.

ABIGAIL

Not for myself, but agèd Barabas: 230
Father, for thee lamenteth Abigail:
But I will learn to leave these fruitless tears,
And urged thereto with my afflictions,
With fierce exclaims run to the senate-house,
And in the senate reprehend them all,   235
And rent their hearts with tearing of my hair,
Till they reduce the wrongs done to my father.

BARABAS

No, Abigail, things past recovery
Are hardly cured with exclamations.
Be silent, daughter, sufferance breeds ease,   240
And time may yield us an occasion
Which on the sudden cannot serve the turn.
Besides, my girl, think me not all so fond
As negligently to forgo so much
Without provision for thyself and me.   245
Ten thousand portagues, besides great pearls,
Rich costly jewels, and stones infinite,
Fearing the worst of this before it fell,
I closely hid.

ABIGAIL   Where father?

BARABAS   In my house my girl.

---

226 *Abigail* On the association of the biblical Abigail (I Samuel 25) with conversion to
     Christianity, see Hunter, p. 225.
236 *rent* rend, tear
238–9 *things past . . . exclamations* proverbial (Tilley, C 921, 'past cure, past care')
240 *sufferance . . . ease* proverbial (Tilley, S 955)
     sufferance breeds 'patient endurance teaches'
241–2 *And time . . . turn* time may eventually present us with a better opportunity than
     now it offers
243 *fond* foolish
246 *portagues* Portuguese gold coins

ABIGAIL

    Then shall they ne'er be seen of Barabas: 250
    For they have seized upon thy house and wares.

BARABAS

    But they will give me leave once more, I trow,
    To go into my house.

ABIGAIL   That may they not:
    For there I left the Governor placing nuns,
    Displacing me; and of thy house they mean   255
    To make a nunnery, where none but their own sect
    Must enter in; men generally barred.

BARABAS

    My gold, my gold, and all my wealth is gone.
    You partial heavens, have I deserved this plague?
    What will you thus oppose me, luckless stars,   260
    To make me desperate in my poverty?
    And knowing me impatient in distress
    Think me so mad as I will hang myself,
    That I may vanish o'er the earth in air,
    And leave no memory that e'er I was?   265
    No, I will live; nor loathe I this my life:
    And since you leave me in the ocean thus
    To sink or swim, and put me to my shifts,
    I'll rouse my senses, and awake myself.
    Daughter, I have it: thou perceiv'st the plight   270
    Wherein these Christians have oppressèd me:
    Be ruled by me, for in extremity
    We ought to make bar of no policy.

ABIGAIL

    Father, whate'er it be to injure them
    That have so manifestly wrongèd us,   275
    What will not Abigail attempt?

BARABAS   Why so;

252 *trow* trust
256 *sect* sex, but perhaps resonant with the many references to sectarian division according to religion
259 *partial* biased
260 *luckless* malignant
268 *put me . . . shifts* force me to fend for myself. Both this and 'sink or swim' are proverbial (Tilley, S 485; S 337).
273 *make bar . . . policy* rule out no strategy

Then thus, thou told'st me they have turned my house
Into a nunnery, and some nuns are there.

ABIGAIL

I did.

BARABAS Then Abigail, there must my girl
Entreat the abbess to be entertained.   280

ABIGAIL

How, as a nun?

BARABAS   Ay, daughter, for religion
Hides many mischiefs from suspicion.

ABIGAIL

Ay, but father they will suspect me there.

BARABAS

Let 'em suspect, but be thou so precise
As they may think it done of holiness.   285
Entreat 'em fair, and give them friendly speech,
And seem to them as if thy sins were great,
Till thou hast gotten to be entertained.

ABIGAIL

Thus father shall I much dissemble.

BARABAS   Tush,
As good dissemble that thou never mean'st   290
As first mean truth and then dissemble it;
A counterfeit profession is better
Than unseen hypocrisy.

ABIGAIL

Well father, say I be entertained,
What then shall follow?

276–7   ed. (Q Why . . . house / Into . . .)
280   *entertained* received, admitted as a nun
281–2   *religion . . . suspicion* Compare the relevant portions of Machiavelli's *Prince* con-
        cerning the political uses of religion (esp. chapter XVIII) with the statement of
        Machevill in the Prologue and with Gentillet's attacks on the 'atheism' of Machia-
        vellians; compare Minshull's analysis.
284   *precise* scrupulous; often pejoratively applied to Puritans
286   *Entreat 'em fair* present yourself ingratiatingly
289–90 ed. (Q Thus . . . dissemble. / Tush . . . mean'st)
290–1   *As good . . . dissemble it* It's no worse to deceive deliberately than to begin with true
        intentions and subsequently turn to hypocrisy
292–3   *A counterfeit profession . . . unseen hypocrisy* This passage seems to say that self-
        conscious religious hypocrisy is preferable to an unwitting ideological blindness;
        see Hodge.
294   *say* suppose

BARABAS   This shall follow then;   295
·There have I hid close underneath the plank
That runs along the upper chamber floor,
The gold and jewels which I kept for thee.
But here they come; be cunning Abigail.

ABIGAIL
Then father go with me.

BARABAS   No, Abigail, in this   300
It is not necessary I be seen.
For I will seem offended with thee for't.
Be close, my girl, for this must fetch my gold.

        Enter three FRIARS [JACOMO *and* BERNARDINE
        among them] and two NUNS [*one the* ABBESS]

JACOMO
Sisters, we now are almost at the new-made nunnery.

1 NUN
The better; for we love not to be seen: 305
'Tis thirty winters long since some of us
Did stray so far amongst the multitude.

JACOMO
But, madam, this house
And waters of this new-made nunnery
Will much delight you.   310

1 NUN
It may be so: but who comes here?

ABIGAIL
Grave Abbess, and you happy virgins' guide,
Pity the state of a distressèd maid.

ABBESS
What art thou daughter?

ABIGAIL
The hopeless daughter of a hapless Jew,   315
The Jew of Malta, wretched Barabas;

296   *close* secretly
301   It is necessary I should not be seen
304   JACOMO ed. (Q 1 *Fry.*)
312   *you happy virgins' guide* This portion of the line may be addressed to the friar.
315   Compare Hieronimo's line from *The Spanish Tragedy:* 'The hopeless father of a
       hapless son' (IV.iv.84).
       hapless unfortunate

Sometimes the owner of a goodly house,
Which they have now turned to a nunnery.

ABBESS

Well, daughter, say, what is thy suit with us?

ABIGAIL

Fearing the afflictions which my father feels   320
Proceed from sin, or want of faith in us,
I'd pass away my life in penitence,
And be a novice in your nunnery,
To make atonement for my labouring soul.

JACOMO

No doubt, brother, but this proceedeth of the spirit.   325

BERNARDINE

Ay, and of a moving spirit too, brother; but come,
Let us entreat she may be entertained.

ABBESS

Well, daughter, we admit you for a nun.

ABIGAIL

First let me as a novice learn to frame
My solitary life to your strait laws,   330
And let me lodge where I was wont to lie;
I do not doubt by your divine precepts
And mine own industry, but to profit much.

BARABAS

(As much I hope as all I hid is worth.)

ABBESS

Come daughter, follow us.   335

BARABAS

Why how now Abigail, what mak'st thou
Amongst these hateful Christians?

JACOMO

Hinder her not, thou man of little faith,

317   *Sometimes* Sometime, formerly
320   *feels* ed. (Q *feels,*)
324   *labouring* struggling, troubled
325   *proceedeth of the spirit* comes of the Holy Spirit
326   BERNARDINE ed. (Q 2 *Fry.*)
        moving This and subsequent lines (see III.vi) permit interpretation in a sexual sense.
330   *strait* strict, confining
331   *wont* accustomed
334   ed. (Q has a marginal *'aside'*)
336   *what mak'st thou* what are you doing?
338   *thou man of little faith* biblical phrasing (e.g. Matthew 6.30, 8.26)

For she has mortified herself.

BARABAS   How, mortified!

JACOMO

And is admitted to the sisterhood.   340

BARABAS

Child of perdition, and thy father's shame,
What wilt thou do among these hateful fiends?
I charge thee on my blessing that thou leave
These devils, and their damnèd heresy.

ABIGAIL

Father give me –

BARABAS   Nay back, Abigail   345
(And think upon the jewels and the gold,
The board is marked thus that covers it).

                              [*Makes sign of the cross*]

Away, accursèd from thy father's sight.

JACOMO

Barabas, although thou art in misbelief,
And wilt not see thine own afflictions,   350
Yet let thy daughter be no longer blind.

BARABAS

Blind, friar? I reck not thy persuasions.
(The board is markèd thus † that covers it.)
For I had rather die, than see her thus.
Wilt thou forsake me too in my distress,   355
Seducèd daughter? (Go forget not.)
Becomes it Jews to be so credulous?

339   *has mortified herself* has died to worldly values
343   *charge* command
345–8 *Nay back . . . sight* Abigail apparently moves toward Barabas, allowing him to whisper
       to her between his two expressions of repulse. Q prints *'Whispers to her'* opposite line
       346.
347   *thus* A standard Elizabethan indication of stage business; the text prints a cross-like
       dagger at 'thus' in line 353.
350   *wilt not see* The Friar attributes Barabas's Jewish faith to his wilfully obstinate
       spiritual blindness.
352   *Blind, friar?* ed. (Q Blind, Fryer,)
       reck not pay no heed to
353–61 Q prints lines 353, 358, 361 and portions of line 356 in italics. Next to lines 356
       and 358 *'aside to her'* appears in the margin.
356   *Seducèd daughter?* ed. (Q Seduced Daughter,)
357   *credulous?* ed. (Q credulous,)

(Tomorrow early I'll be at the door.)
No come not at me, if thou wilt be damned,
Forget me, see me not, and so be gone.   360
(Farewell. Remember tomorrow morning.)
Out, out thou wretch.

> [*Exeunt:* BARABAS *on one side;*
> FRIARS, ABBESS, NUN, *and* ABIGAIL *on the other*]

Enter MATHIAS

MATHIAS

Who's this? Fair Abigail the rich Jew's daughter
Become a nun? Her father's sudden fall
Has humbled her and brought her down to this: 365
Tut, she were fitter for a tale of love
Than to be tirèd out with orisons:
And better would she far become a bed
Embracèd in a friendly lover's arms,
Than rise at midnight to a solemn mass.   370

Enter LODOWICK

LODOWICK

Why how now Don Mathias, in a dump?

MATHIAS

Believe me, noble Lodowick, I have seen
The strangest sight, in my opinion,
That ever I beheld.

LODOWICK   What was't, I prithee?

MATHIAS

A fair young maid scarce fourteen years of age,   375
The sweetest flower in Cytherea's field,
Cropped from the pleasures of the fruitful earth,
And strangely metamorphosed nun.

LODOWICK

But say, what was she?

MATHIAS   Why the rich Jew's daughter.

---

364   *Become a nun? Her* ed. (Q Become a Nun, her)
367   *orisons* prayers
371   *in a dump* in a state of gloom
374   *was't, I* ed. (Q wast I)
376   *Cytherea* Venus
378   *metamorphosed nun* transformed to a nun. Many editions add to this line to make
     it read: 'And strangely metamorphosed to a nun'.

LODOWICK

    What Barabas, whose goods were lately seized?   380

    Is she so fair?

MATHIAS   And matchless beautiful;

    As had you seen her 'twould have moved your heart,

    Though countermured with walls of brass, to love,

    Or at the least to pity.

LODOWICK

    And if she be so fair as you report,   385

    'Twere time well spent to go and visit her:

    How say you, shall we?

MATHIAS

    I must and will, sir, there's no remedy.

LODOWICK

    And so will I too, or it shall go hard.

    Farewell Mathias.

MATHIAS   Farewell Lodowick.   390

Exeunt

383   *countermured* ed. (Q countermin'd) fortified with a double wall

385   *And if* If

388   *remedy* alternative

389   *or it shall go hard* come what may

ACT II [SCENE i]

Enter BARABAS *with a light*

BARABAS

Thus like the sad presaging raven that tolls
The sick man's passport in her hollow beak,
And in the shadow of the silent night
Doth shake contagion from her sable wings,
Vexed and tormented runs poor Barabas   5
With fatal curses towards these Christians.
The incertain pleasures of swift-footed time
Have ta'en their flight, and left me in despair;
And of my former riches rests no more
But bare remembrance; like a soldier's scar,   10
That has no further comfort for his maim.
Oh thou that with a fiery pillar led'st
The sons of Israel through the dismal shades,
Light Abraham's offspring; and direct the hand
Of Abigail this night; or let the day   15
Turn to eternal darkness after this:
No sleep can fasten on my watchful eyes,
Nor quiet enter my distempered thoughts,
Till I have answer of my Abigail.

Enter ABIGAIL *above*

ABIGAIL

Now have I happily espied a time   20
To search the plank my father did appoint;

---

1   *presaging ... tolls* foreboding ... announces
2   *passport* i.e. allowing entry to death's kingdom
4   *wings,* ed. (Q wings;)
9   *rests* remains
11   *maim* wound
12–13 See Exodus 13.21–2.
18   *distempered* agitated
20–2   *Now ... here, behold, unseen,* ed. (Q (unseen)) Abigail, like her father in being unaware
       that anyone else is on-stage, is represented as discovering the treasure as she speaks.
       appoint designate

And here behold, unseen, where I have found
The gold, the pearls, and jewels which he hid.

BARABAS

Now I remember those old women's words,
Who in my wealth would tell me winter's tales,　　　　　25
And speak of spirits and ghosts that glide by night
About the place where treasure hath been hid:
And now methinks that I am one of those:
For whilst I live, here lives my soul's sole hope,
And when I die, here shall my spirit walk.　　　　　30

ABIGAIL

Now that my father's fortune were so good
As but to be about this happy place;
'Tis not so happy: yet when we parted last,
He said he would attend me in the morn.
Then, gentle sleep, where'er his body rests,　　　　　35
Give charge to Morpheus that he may dream
A golden dream, and of the sudden walk,
Come and receive the treasure I have found.

BARABAS

Bien para todos mi ganada no es:
As good go on, as sit so sadly thus.　　　　　40
But stay, what star shines yonder in the east?
The loadstar of my life, if Abigail.
Who's there?

ABIGAIL　　　　　Who's that?

BARABAS　　　　　　　　　Peace, Abigail, 'tis I.

ABIGAIL

Then father here receive thy happiness.

BARABAS

Hast thou't?　　　　　　　　　[ABIGAIL] *Throws down bags*　　45

25　*wealth* time of prosperity
　　winter's tales fanciful stories
31　*Now that* Now if only
36　*Morpheus* son of sleep and god of dreams (compare Ovid, *Metamorphoses* XI.623ff)
37　*walk* often amended to 'wake,' but possibly meaning 'arise' or 'sleepwalk'
39　*Bien para todos mi ganada no es:* ed. (Q *Birn para todos, my ganada no er:*) (Spanish)
　　My gain is not good for everybody
42　*loadstar* guiding star

ABIGAIL

    Here,

    Hast thou't?

    There's more, and more, and more.

BARABAS   Oh my girl,

    My gold, my fortune, my felicity;

    Strength to my soul, death to mine enemy;   50

    Welcome the first beginner of my bliss:

    Oh Abigail, Abigail, that I had thee here too,

    Then my desires were fully satisfied.

    But I will practise thy enlargement thence:

    Oh girl, oh gold, oh beauty, oh my bliss!   *Hugs his bags* 55

ABIGAIL

    Father, it draweth towards midnight now,

    And 'bout this time the nuns begin to wake;

    To shun suspicion, therefore, let us part.

BARABAS

    Farewell my joy, and by my fingers take

    A kiss from him that sends it from his soul.   60

    Now Phoebus ope the eye-lids of the day,

    And for the raven wake the morning lark,

    That I may hover with her in the air,

    Singing o'er these, as she does o'er her young.

    Hermoso placer de los dineros.   65

                                         Exeunt

46–8   *Here . . . more, and more, and more* The short lines and repetitions may suggest repeated action of throwing down the bags.

54   *practise thy enlargement* contrive your release

61   *Phoebus* Apollo, god of light and the sun

62   *for* in place of

65   *Hermoso placer de los dineros* ed. (Q *Hermoso piarer, de les Denirch*) (Spanish) beautiful pleasure of money

[ACT II, SCENE ii]

Enter GOVERNOR [FERNEZE], MARTIN DEL BOSCO,
the KNIGHTS [*and* OFFICERS]

FERNEZE

    Now Captain tell us whither thou art bound?
    Whence is thy ship that anchors in our road?
    And why thou cam'st ashore without our leave?

BOSCO

    Governor of Malta, hither am I bound;
    My ship, the Flying Dragon, is of Spain,   5
    And so am I, Del Bosco is my name;
    Vice-admiral unto the Catholic king.

1 KNIGHT

    'Tis true, my lord, therefore entreat him well.

BOSCO

    Our fraught is Grecians, Turks, and Afric Moors,
    For late upon the coast of Corsica,   10
    Because we vailed not to the Turkish fleet,
    Their creeping galleys had us in the chase:
    But suddenly the wind began to rise,
    And then we luffed and tacked, and fought at ease:
    Some have we fired, and many have we sunk;   15
    But one amongst the rest became our prize:
    The captain's slaine, the rest remain our slaves,
    Of whom we would make sale in Malta here.

FERNEZE

    Martin del Bosco, I have heard of thee;
    Welcome to Malta, and to all of us;   20

    1   *FERNEZE* Q calls Ferneze 'Governor' throughout the scene.
    2   *Whence* From where
    7   *Catholic king* according to Bawcutt a traditional title of the king of Spain
    8   *entreat* treat
    9   *fraught* cargo
   11   *vailed* lowered sails in token of respect
         Turkish ed. (Q Spanish)
   12   *creeping* slow
   14   *luffed and tacked* ed. (Q left, and tooke) turned our ship into the wind and sailed
         obliquely against it
   15   *fired* burned

But to admit a sale of these thy Turks
We may not, nay we dare not give consent
By reason of a tributary league.

1 KNIGHT

Del Bosco, as thou lovest and honour'st us,
Persuade our Governor against the Turk;   25
This truce we have is but in hope of gold,
And with that sum he craves might we wage war.

BOSCO

Will Knights of Malta be in league with Turks,
And buy it basely too for sums of gold?
My lord, remember that to Europe's shame,   30
The Christian isle of Rhodes, from whence you came,
Was lately lost, and you were stated here
To be at deadly enmity with Turks.

FERNEZE

Captain we know it, but our force is small.

BOSCO

What is the sum that Calymath requires?   35

FERNEZE

A hundred thousand crowns.

BOSCO

My lord and king hath title to this isle,
And he means quickly to expel them hence;
Therefore be ruled by me, and keep the gold:
I'll write unto his Majesty for aid,   40
And not depart until I see you free.

FERNEZE

On this condition shall thy Turks be sold.
Go officers and set them straight in show.

[*Exeunt* OFFICERS]

23   *tributary league* an alliance involving monetary payment
27   *he* the Turk
32   *lately lost* Rhodes fell to the Turks in 1522; in 1530 Malta was granted to the Knights
     by Charles V.
     stated installed in office
38   *them* ed. (Q you) Editors have assumed a confusion of pronouns here like the
     confusion of enemies in line 11; however, as Bawcutt argues, it is possible that the
     uncertainty is authorial. A multiple and evolving sense of who is the enemy of whom
     would fit with Emily Bartels's account of the play in terms of imperialism ('Malta,
     the Jew, and the Fictions of Difference: Colonialist Discourse in Marlowe's *Jew of
     Malta*', *ELR* 20 (1990), 3–16).

Bosco, thou shalt be Malta's general;
We and our warlike knights will follow thee   45
Against these barbarous misbelieving Turks.

BOSCO

So shall you imitate those you succeed:
For when their hideous force environed Rhodes,
Small though the number was that kept the town,
They fought it out, and not a man survived   50
To bring the hapless news to Christendom.

FERNEZE

So will we fight it out; come let's away:
Proud-daring Calymath, instead of gold,
We'll send thee bullets wrapped in smoke and fire:
Claim tribute where thou wilt, we are resolved,   55
Honour is bought with blood and not with gold.

Exeunt

---

46 *misbelieving* non-Christian
47–51 *So . . . Christendom.* The siege of Rhodes in 1522 did not result in the total destruc-
       tion Del Bosco claims.
51 *hapless* unfortunate
54 *send thee* ed. (Q send the)

[ACT II, SCENE iii]

Enter OFFICERS *with* [ITHAMORE *and other*] SLAVES

1 OFFICER

    This is the market-place, here let 'em stand:

    Fear not their sale, for they'll be quickly bought.

2 OFFICER

    Every one's price is written on his back,

    And so much must they yield or not be sold.

Enter BARABAS

1 OFFICER

    Here comes the Jew, had not his goods been seized,   5

    He'd give us present money for them all.

BARABAS

    In spite of these swine-eating Christians,

    Unchosen nation, never circumcised;

    Such as, poor villains, were ne'er thought upon

    Till Titus and Vespasian conquered us,   10

    Am I become as wealthy as I was:

    They hoped my daughter would ha' been a nun;

    But she's at home, and I have bought a house

    As great and fair as is the Governor's;

    And there in spite of Malta will I dwell: 15

    Having Ferneze's hand, whose heart I'll have;

    Ay, and his son's too, or it shall go hard.

---

    4   s.d. Q has entry directions for Barabas here and at line 7.

    6   *present money* ready cash

    8   *Unchosen nation* Referring to the idea of the Jews as God's chosen people

8–10   ed. (Q (Vnchosen . . . circumciz'd; / Such . . . vpon / Till . . . vs.))

    9   *Such as, poor villains,* ed. (Q Such as poore villaines)

        villains low fellows

        ne'er thought upon disregarded

  10 *Titus and Vespasian* Vespasian and his son Titus, successive Roman Emperors, led the campaigns that resulted in the fall of Jerusalem in A.D. 70.

  16 *Ferneze's hand* either Ferneze's written assurance of safety or his handshake in friendship

  17 *go hard* be unfortunate

I am not of the tribe of Levi, I,
That can so soon forget an injury.
We Jews can fawn like spaniels when we please;   20
And when we grin we bite, yet are our looks
As innocent and harmless as a lamb's.
I learned in Florence how to kiss my hand,
Heave up my shoulders when they call me dog,
And duck as low as any bare-foot friar,   25
Hoping to see them starve upon a stall,
Or else be gathered for in our synagogue;
That when the offering-basin comes to me,
Even for charity I may spit into't.
Here comes Don Lodowick the Governor's son,   30
One that I love for his good father's sake.

Enter LODOWICK

LODOWICK

I hear the wealthy Jew walked this way;
I'll seek him out, and so insinuate,
That I may have a sight of Abigail;
For Don Mathias tells me she is fair.   35

BARABAS

(Now will I show myself to have more of the serpent than the
dove; that is, more knave than fool.)

LODOWICK

Yond walks the Jew, now for fair Abigail.

BARABAS

(Ay, ay, no doubt but she's at your command.)

---

18   *tribe of Levi* the tribe associated with priestliness and jurisdiction over the cities of
refuge (Joshua 20–1)
20   *fawn* affect a servile fondness
21   *grin* smile
24   *Heave up* Shrug
25   *duck* bow humbly (see III.iii.51)
26   *stall* a commercial display platform sometimes used for a bed by impoverished
vagrants
27   *be gathered for* have a collection taken for them
33   *insinuate* work myself into favour
36–7 ed. (Q Now … serpent / Then … foole.)
      more of the serpent than the dove more cunning than innocence (twisting the admo-
nition of Matthew 10.16: 'be ye therefore wise as serpentes, and innocent as doues')

LODOWICK

Barabas, thou know'st I am the Governor's son.   40

BARABAS

I would you were his father too, sir, that's all the harm I wish
you. (The slave looks like a hog's cheek new singed.)

[BARABAS *turns away*]

LODOWICK

Whither walk'st thou Barabas?

BARABAS

No further: 'tis a custom held with us,
That when we speak with Gentiles like to you,   45
We turn into the air to purge ourselves:
For unto us the promise doth belong.

LODOWICK

Well, Barabas, canst help me to a diamond?

BARABAS

Oh, sir, your father had my diamonds.
Yet I have one left that will serve your turn: 50
I mean my daughter. (But ere he shall have her
I'll sacrifice her on a pile of wood.
I ha' the poison of the city for him,
And the white leprosy.)

LODOWICK

What sparkle does it give without a foil?`   55

BARABAS

The diamond that I talk of, ne'er was foiled
(But when he touches it, it will be foiled).

41–2   ed. (Q 1 . . . harm / I wish you . . . new sindg'd.) Unclear in meaning.
  42   *hog's cheek new singed* i.e. Lodowick is recently shaven
  47   *the promise* See I.i.104–5n.
  51   ed. (Q 1 mean my daughter: – but . . .) Q prints '*aside*' opposite line 52, but the dash
        in the Q version of line 51 may indicate the beginning of the aside (as apparently in
        lines 60 and 67). However, as Craik points out, 'I mean my daughter' may be an aside,
        since Lodowick and Barabas 'continue talking of Abigail obliquely as a diamond'.
53–4   ed. (Q the / White)
  53   *poison of the city . . . white leprosy* not satisfactorily explained but apparently refer-
        ences to a virulent poison and a natural disease associated with cities, such as the
        plague
  55   *foil* thin metallic leaf set under a gem to add to its brilliance
  56   *foiled* set by a jeweller
  57   ed. (Q But . . . foiled:)
        foiled defiled, dishonoured

Lord Lodowick, it sparkles bright and fair.

LODOWICK

Is it square or pointed? Pray let me know.

BARABAS

Pointed it is, good sir (but not for you).   60

LODOWICK

I like it much the better.

BARABAS   So do I too.

LODOWICK

How shows it by night?

BARABAS   Outshines Cynthia's rays:

You'll like it better far a' nights than days.

LODOWICK

And what's the price?

BARABAS

(Your life and if you have it.) O my lord   65

We will not jar about the price; come to my house

And I will give't your honour (with a vengeance).

LODOWICK

No, Barabas, I will deserve it first.

BARABAS

Good sir,

Your father has deserved it at my hands,   70

Who of mere charity and Christian ruth,

To bring me to religious purity,

And as it were in catechizing sort,

To make me mindful of my mortal sins,

Against my will, and whether I would or no,   75

Seized all I had, and thrust me out-a-doors,

---

  59   ed. (Q pointed,)
59–60   *pointed* denoting the cut of a gem, but used by Barabas to mean 'appointed' or
         'promised'
  60   ed. (Q Pointed it is, good Sir, – but not for you.) Q has an '*aside*' in the margin.
  62   *Cynthia* the moon
  63   Q marks the line '*aside*'; Craik suggests this may refer to line 65.
  65   ed. (Q Your life and if you haue it. – Oh my Lord)
         and if if
  66   *jar* quarrel
  67   ed. (Q And I will giu't your honour – with a vengeance.) Line 67 is marked '*aside*' in Q.
69–70   ed. (Q *one line*)
  71   *ruth* pity
  73   *in catechizing sort* in the manner of religious instruction

245

And made my house a place for nuns most chaste.

LODOWICK

No doubt your soul shall reap the fruit of it.

BARABAS

Ay, but my lord, the harvest is far off:
And yet I know the prayers of those nuns 80
And holy friars, having money for their pains,
Are wondrous; (and indeed do no man good)
And seeing they are not idle, but still doing,
'Tis likely they in time may reap some fruit,
I mean in fullness of perfection. 85

LODOWICK

Good Barabas glance not at our holy nuns.

BARABAS

No, but I do it through a burning zeal
(Hoping ere long to set the house afire;
For though they do awhile increase and multiply,
I'll have a saying to that nunnery). 90
As for the diamond, sir, I told you of,
Come home and there's no price shall make us part,
Even for your honourable father's sake.
(It shall go hard but I will see your death.)
But now I must be gone to buy a slave. 95

LODOWICK

And, Barabas, I'll bear thee company.

BARABAS

Come then, here's the marketplace; what's the price of this slave,

---

82   ed. (Q Are wondrous; *and indeed doe no man good:*) This line is also marked with a
       marginal '*aside*' Line 86 suggests that Lodowick hears the remainder of Barabas's
       speech.

83–5 *still doing* always copulating
       still doing . . . perfection Barabas employs the terms of Lodowick's theological dis-
       course to suggest the hypocrisy of the nuns' and friars' claims to chastity.

86   *glance not* do not criticize by innuendo

88–90 italicized in Q with marginal '*aside*' opposite line 89

89   *increase and multiply* The nuns, while professing chastity, fulfil God's command to
       Noah (Genesis 9).

90   *have a saying to* have something to say about

94   italicized in Q with marginal '*aside*'
       It shall go hard but Unless prevented by the power of circumstances it will happen that

97–8 ed. (Q Come . . . price / Of . . . much?)

two hundred crowns? Do the Turks weigh so much?

1 OFFICER

Sir, that's his price.

BARABAS

What, can he steal that you demand so much?   100
Belike he has some new trick for a purse;
And if he has, he is worth three hundred plates,
So that, being bought, the town seal might be got
To keep him for his lifetime from the gallows.
The sessions day is critical to thieves,   105
And few or none 'scape but by being purged.

LODOWICK

Ratest thou this Moor but at two hundred plates?

1 OFFICER

No more, my lord.

BARABAS

Why should this Turk be dearer than that Moor?

1 OFFICER

Because he is young and has more qualities.   110

BARABAS

What, hast the philosopher's stone? And thou hast, break my
head with it, I'll forgive thee.

SLAVE

No sir, I can cut and shave.

BARABAS

Let me see, sirrah, are you not an old shaver?

SLAVE

Alas, sir, I am a very youth.   115

---

98   *Turks* ed. (Q *Turke*)
102   *plates,* ed. (Q plats.) silver coins
102–6 *And if . . . purged* He might be worth so much as a thief if one could get governmental
       assurance of pardon; trial days are fatal to thieves, few escaping the 'cure' of being
       hanged
110   *qualities* abilities
111–12 ed. (Q What . . . hast, / Breake . . . thee.)
111   *philosopher's stone* the much sought-after goal of alchemy, a stone that would turn
       other metals to gold
       And if
113–22 SLAVE ed. (Q *Itha.* or *Ith.*)
114   *old shaver* rogue, rascal
115   *very* genuine

BARABAS

A youth? I'll buy you, and marry you to Lady Vanity if you
do well.

SLAVE

I will serve you, sir.

BARABAS

Some wicked trick or other. It may be under colour of shaving,
thou'lt cut my throat for my goods. Tell me, hast thou thy   120
health well?

SLAVE

Ay, passing well.

BARABAS

So much the worse; I must have one that's sickly, and't be but
for sparing vittles: 'tis not a stone of beef a day will maintain
you in these chops; let me see one that's somewhat leaner.   125

1 OFFICER

Here's a leaner, how like you him?

BARABAS

Where wast thou born?

ITHAMORE

In Thrace; brought up in Arabia.

BARABAS

So much the better, thou art for my turn;
An hundred crowns, I'll have him; there's the coin.   130

[*Pays money*]

1 OFFICER

Then mark him, sir, and take him hence.

BARABAS

(Ay, mark him, you were best, for this is he
That by my help shall do much villainy.)

116–17   ed. (Q A . . . vanity / If . . . well.) *Youth* and *Vanity* are stock figures of the morality
         plays; as Craik observes, Barabas's promise to marry Youth to Vanity would encour-
         age vice rather than virtue.

119–21   ed. (Q Some . . . colour / Of . . . goods. / Tell . . . well?)

119   *colour* pretence

123–5   ed. (Q So . . . sickly, / And . . . day / Will . . . one / That's . . . leaner.)

123–4   *and't be but for* ed. (Q And be but for) if only for the sake of

124   *stone* fourteen pounds

125   *chops* jowls

127   *wast* ed. (Q was)

128   *Thrace* ed. (Q Trace)

129   *for my turn;* ed. (Q for my turn,) suited for my purposes

132   *mark* observe, pay attention to

My lord farewell: [*To* ITHAMORE] come sirrah you are mine.
[*To* LODOWICK] As for the diamond, it shall be yours;   135
I pray, sir, be no stranger at my house,
All that I have shall be at your command.

Enter MATHIAS [*and his*] MOTHER [KATHERINE]

MATHIAS
(What makes the Jew and Lodowick so private?
I fear me 'tis about fair Abigail.)

BARABAS
Yonder comes Don Mathias, let us stay;   140
He loves my daughter, and she holds him dear:
But I have sworn to frustrate both their hopes,
And be revenged upon the – (Governor).

[*Exit* LODOWICK]

KATHERINE
This Moor is comeliest, is he not? Speak, son.

MATHIAS
No, this is the better, mother, view this well.   145

BARABAS
(Seem not to know me here before your mother,
Lest she mistrust the match that is in hand:
When you have brought her home, come to my house;
Think of me as thy father; son farewell.

MATHIAS
But wherefore talked Don Lodowick with you?   150

BARABAS
Tush man, we talked of diamonds, not of Abigail.)

KATHERINE
Tell me, Mathias, is not that the Jew?

BARABAS
As for the comment on the Maccabees,

137   s.d. ed. (Q *Enter Mathias, Mater;* her speeches so headed throughout)
140   *let us stay* let us break off our talk
141–3 The addressee of these lines is difficult to determine. Q's punctuation of line 143
       (And be reveng'd upon the – Governor) is typical of its treatment of Barabas's asides
       at the end of lines, and this suggests that he addresses most of the speech to Lodo-
       wick; but, as Bawcutt points out, at line 284 Lodowick appears unaware of Abigail's
       love for Mathias, so perhaps he exits as Mathias enters.
147   *mistrust* suspect
153   *comment on the Maccabees* commentary on the two apocryphal biblical books of
       the Maccabees

I have it, sir, and 'tis at your command.

MATHIAS

Yes, madam, and my talk with him was   155
About the borrowing of a book or two.

KATHERINE

Converse not with him, he is cast off from heaven.
[*To* OFFICER] Thou hast thy crowns, fellow, [*To* MATHIAS]
    come let's away.

MATHIAS

Sirrah, Jew, remember the book.

BARABAS

Marry will I, sir.   160

               Exeunt [MATHIAS *and* MOTHER *with* SLAVE]

1 OFFICER

Come, I have made a reasonable market, let's away.

                [*Exeunt* OFFICERS *with* SLAVES]

BARABAS

Now let me know thy name, and therewithal
Thy birth, condition, and profession.

ITHAMORE

Faith, sir, my birth is but mean, my name's Ithamore, my profession what you please.   165

BARABAS

Hast thou no trade? Then listen to my words,
And I will teach that shall stick by thee:
First be thou void of these affections,
Compassion, love, vain hope, and heartless fear,
Be moved at nothing, see thou pity none,   170
But to thyself smile when the Christians moan.

ITHAMORE

Oh brave, master, I worship your nose for this.

BARABAS

As for myself, I walk abroad a-nights
And kill sick people groaning under walls:

160   s.d. (Q places after line 158)
163   *condition* social standing
164   *mean* low
167   *stick by thee* be worth remembering
168   *affections* feelings
169   *heartless* cowardly
172   *brave* wonderful
       your nose alluding to Barabas's huge nose (see III.iii.9–10)

Sometimes I go about and poison wells;   175
And now and then, to cherish Christian thieves,
I am content to lose some of my crowns;
That I may, walking in my gallery,
See 'em go pinioned along by my door.
Being young I studied physic, and began   180
To practise first upon the Italian;
There I enriched the priests with burials,
And always kept the sexton's arms in ure
With digging graves and ringing dead men's knells:
And after that was I an engineer,   185
And in the wars 'twixt France and Germany,
Under pretence of helping Charles the Fifth,
Slew friend and enemy with my stratagems.
Then after that was I an usurer,
And with extorting, cozening, forfeiting,   190
And tricks belonging unto brokery,
I filled the jails with bankrouts in a year,
And with young orphans planted hospitals,
And every moon made some or other mad,
And now and then one hang himself for grief,   195
Pinning upon his breast a long great scroll
How I with interest tormented him.
But mark how I am blest for plaguing them,
I have as much coin as will buy the town.
But tell me now, how hast thou spent thy time?   200

ITHAMORE
  Faith, master,
  In setting Christian villages on fire,

178   *gallery* balcony (see V.v.33)
179   *pinioned* with arms tied together
180   *physic* medicine
183   *ure* use
185   *engineer* builder of military engines
186–7 Struggles betwen the forces of the Holy Roman Emperor, Charles V (1500–58), and
       the French king, Francis I, continued between 1519 and 1558.
189   *usurer* money-lender; usually associated with high rates (compare IV.i.54)
190   *cozening* cheating
       forfeiting profiting from the failure of borrowers to repay their loans
191   *brokery* dishonest financial transactions
192   *bankrouts* bankrupts
193   *planted* furnished   *hospitals* charitable institutions, almshouses
201–2 ed. (Q *one line*)

Chaining of eunuchs, binding galley-slaves.
One time I was an hostler in an inn,
And in the night time secretly would I steal   205
To travellers' chambers, and there cut their throats:
Once at Jerusalem, where the pilgrims kneeled,
I strowèd powder on the marble stones,
And therewithal their knees would rankle, so
That I have laughed a-good to see the cripples   210
Go limping home to Christendom on stilts.

BARABAS

Why this is something: make account of me
As of thy fellow; we are villains both:
Both circumcisèd, we hate Christians both:
Be true and secret, thou shalt want no gold.   215
But stand aside, here comes Don Lodowick.

Enter LODOWICK

LODOWICK

Oh Barabas well met;
Where is the diamond you told me of?

BARABAS

I have it for you, sir; please you walk in with me:
What, ho, Abigail; open the door I say.   220

Enter ABIGAIL

ABIGAIL

In good time, father, here are letters come
From Ormus, and the post stays here within.

BARABAS

Give me the letters, daughter, do you hear?
Entertain Lodowick the Governor's son

204   *hostler* stable keeper
209   *rankle* fester
210   *a-good* heartily
211   *stilts* crutches
212   *make account of me* think of me
215   *want* lack
217–18   ed. (Q Oh ... Diamond / You ... of?)
221   *In good time* Just in time
222   *Ormus* town on the Persian Gulf, known in the Renaissance for trading in luxuries
      post messenger
223–9   This edition follows Q, which has '*aside*' opposite line 227 and prints the word
      'Philistine' and lines 228–9 in italics. As Craik points out, it is typical of Barabas to

With all the courtesy you can afford;   225
Provided, that you keep your maidenhead.
Use him as if he were a (Philistine.
Dissemble, swear, protest, vow to love him,
He is not of the seed of Abraham.)
I am a little busy, sir, pray pardon me.   230
Abigail, bid him welcome for my sake.

ABIGAIL
For your sake and his own he's welcome hither.

BARABAS
Daughter, a word more. (Kiss him, speak him fair,
And like a cunning Jew so cast about,
That ye be both made sure ere you come out.   235

ABIGAIL
Oh father, Don Mathias is my love.

BARABAS
I know it: yet I say make love to him;
Do, it is requisite it should be so.)
Nay on my life it is my factor's hand,
But go you in, I'll think upon the account: 240
                      [*Exeunt* LODOWICK *and* ABIGAIL]
The account is made, for Lodowick dies.
My factor sends me word a merchant's fled
That owes me for a hundred tun of wine:
I weigh it thus much; I have wealth enough.
For now by this has he kissed Abigail;   245
And she vows love to him, and he to her.
As sure as heaven rained manna for the Jews,

employ final words to reverse the sense of phrases; the advice to Abigail in line 226, as Bawcutt observes, may be a coarse joke intended for Lodowick's appreciation. Q's comma after 'Provided' may suggest a slightly retarded ponderous pace, potentially indicative of self-irony.

227   *Philistine* biblical enemies of the Jews
229   *seed* offspring
233   ed. (Q Daughter, a word more; kisse him, speake him faire,)
234   *cast about* devise
235   *made sure* betrothed
239   *factor's hand* agent's handwriting
240   *account* financial reckoning, with a play on the next line's meaning of 'settling scores'
243   *tun* barrel
244   *thus much* Barabas probably makes a dismissive gesture.
245   *by this* by this time
247   *manna* food given the Jews by heaven (see Exodus 16)

So sure shall he and Don Mathias die:
His father was my chiefest enemy.

Enter MATHIAS

Whither goes Don Mathias? Stay a while.   250
MATHIAS
Whither but to my fair love Abigail?
BARABAS
Thou know'st, and heaven can witness it is true,
That I intend my daughter shall be thine.
MATHIAS
Ay, Barabas, or else thou wrong'st me much.
BARABAS
Oh heaven forbid I should have such a thought.   255
Pardon me though I weep; the Governor's son
Will, whether I will or no, have Abigail:
He sends her letters, bracelets, jewels, rings.
MATHIAS
Does she receive them?
BARABAS
She? No, Mathias, no, but sends them back,   260
And when he comes, she locks herself up fast;
Yet through the keyhole will he talk to her,
While she runs to the window looking out
When you should come and hale him from the door.
MATHIAS
Oh treacherous Lodowick!   265
BARABAS
Even now as I came home, he slipped me in,
And I am sure he is with Abigail.
MATHIAS
I'll rouse him thence.   [*Draws a sword*]
BARABAS
Not for all Malta, therefore sheathe your sword;
If you love me, no quarrels in my house;   270

---

249   *was* i.e. in the seizure of his property
       s.d. follows 250 in Q
261   *fast* securely
264   *hale* pull violently
266   *slipped me in* slipped in
268   *rouse* drive from concealment (as a hunter's quarry)

But steal you in, and seem to see him not;
I'll give him such a warning ere he goes
As he shall have small hopes of Abigail.
Away, for here they come.

Enter LODOWICK, ABIGAIL

MATHIAS
What hand in hand, I cannot suffer this.   275

BARABAS
Mathias, as thou lov'st me, not a word.

MATHIAS
Well, let it pass, another time shall serve.   *Exit*

LODOWICK
Barabas, is not that the widow's son?

BARABAS
Ay, and take heed, for he hath sworn your death.

LODOWICK
My death? What is the base-born peasant mad?   280

BARABAS
No, no, but happily he stands in fear
Of that which you, I think, ne'er dream upon,
My daughter here, a paltry silly girl.

LODOWICK
Why, loves she Don Mathias?

BARABAS
Doth she not with her smiling answer you?   285

ABIGAIL
(He has my heart, I smile against my will.)

LODOWICK
Barabas, thou know'st I have loved thy daughter long.

BARABAS
And so has she done you, even from a child.

---

275 *suffer* endure
281 *happily* perhaps
281–3 Whatever the exact sense of these lines, it appears that Barabas means to elicit a
       declaration of love by insinuating that Mathias takes Abigail more seriously than
       does Lodowick.
283 *silly* unsophisticated
284 *Why, loves* ed. (Q Why loves)
288 *even from a child* ever since childhood

LODOWICK

And now I can no longer hold my mind.

BARABAS

Nor I the affection that I bear to you.   290

LODOWICK

This is thy diamond, tell me, shall I have it?

BARABAS

Win it and wear it, it is yet unsoiled.
Oh but I know your lordship would disdain
To marry with the daughter of a Jew:
And yet I'll give her many a golden cross   295
With Christian posies round about the ring.

LODOWICK

'Tis not thy wealth, but her that I esteem,
Yet crave I thy consent.

BARABAS

And mine you have, yet let me talk to her.
(This offspring of Cain, this Jebusite   300
That never tasted of the Passover,
Nor e'er shall see the land of Canaan,
Nor our Messias that is yet to come,
This gentle maggot Lodowick I mean,
Must be deluded: let him have thy hand,   305
But keep thy heart till Don Mathias comes.

ABIGAIL

What shall I be betrothed to Lodowick?

289   *hold my mind* conceal my feelings
292   *unsoiled* undefiled, virginal
295   *cross* coin stamped with a cross
296   *Christian posies* pious mottoes to be found both on coins of the period and on wedding rings
299   ed. (Q And . . . her;)
300–312   *aside* opposite line 303 in Q
300   *offspring of Cain* a degenerate race in Jewish and Christian traditions, descended from the first biblical murderer
       Jebusite member of the original Canaanite tribe driven from Jerusalem by King David (see II Samuel 5)
301   *Passover* the important Jewish ritual, commemorating the deliverance from Egypt described in Exodus 12
302   *Canaan* the land promised the Jews in Genesis 17
303   *Messias* Messiah
304   *gentle maggot* punning on 'gentle' as 'gentleman', as 'gentile', and as a synonym for 'maggot'

BARABAS

    It's no sin to deceive a Christian;
    For they themselves hold it a principle,
    Faith is not to be held with heretics;   310
    But all are heretics that are not Jews;
    This follows well, and therefore daughter fear not.)
    I have entreated her, and she will grant.

LODOWICK

    Then gentle Abigail plight thy faith to me.

ABIGAIL

    I cannot choose, seeing my father bids: 315
    Nothing but death shall part my love and me.

LODOWICK

    Now have I that for which my soul hath longed.

BARABAS

    (So have not I, but yet I hope I shall.)

ABIGAIL

    (Oh wretched Abigail, what hast thou done?)

LODOWICK

    Why on the sudden is your colour changed?   320

ABIGAIL

    I know not, but farewell, I must be gone.

BARABAS

    Stay her, but let her not speak one word more.

LODOWICK

    Mute o' the sudden; here's a sudden change.

BARABAS

    Oh muse not at it, 'tis the Hebrews' guise,
    That maidens new betrothed should weep a while: 325

308–10   This doctrine is a favourite object of Protestant polemic, which associated it with Catholic treachery as exemplified by the Council of Constance (1415) in its justification of action against Jan Hus despite an agreement of safe-conduct. See *2 Tamburlaine* II.i.

    312   *This follows well* this is good logic

    314   *plight thy faith* enter into a binding betrothal, promising to marry

315–16   Line 315 may be audible to Lodowick, since it could be understood to represent a traditional view of a daughter's obligation rather than mere constraint; Abigail equivocates in line 316, since 'my love' could be taken by Lodowick to refer to himself.

    318   Q prints '*aside*' in the margin.

    322   *Stay her* either an injunction to Mathias to support Abigail in her distressed state or an aside to Ithamore commanding him to keep her quiet (see line 361)

    324   *guise* customary manner

Trouble her not, sweet Lodowick depart:
She is thy wife, and thou shalt be mine heir.

LODOWICK

Oh, is't the custom, then I am resolved;
But rather let the brightsome heavens be dim,
And nature's beauty choke with stifling clouds,   330
Than my fair Abigail should frown on me.
There comes the villain, now I'll be revenged.

Enter MATHIAS

BARABAS

Be quiet Lodowick, it is enough
That I have made thee sure to Abigail.

LODOWICK

Well, let him go.   *Exit*   335

BARABAS

Well, but for me, as you went in at doors
You had been stabbed, but not a word on't now;
Here must no speeches pass, nor swords be drawn.

MATHIAS

Suffer me, Barabas, but to follow him.

BARABAS

No; so shall I, if any hurt be done,   340
Be made an accessary of your deeds;
Revenge it on him when you meet him next.

MATHIAS

For this I'll have his heart.

BARABAS

Do so; lo here I give thee Abigail.

MATHIAS

What greater gift can poor Mathias have?   345
Shall Lodowick rob me of so fair a love?
My life is not so dear as Abigail.

BARABAS

My heart misgives me, that to cross your love,
He's with your mother, therefore after him.

---

328   *resolved* satisfied
329   *rather* ed. (Q rathe)
339   *Suffer* Allow
348   *misgives me* makes me fear
       cross hinder, prevent

MATHIAS
   What, is he gone unto my mother?   350

BARABAS
   Nay, if you will, stay till she comes herself.

MATHIAS
   I cannot stay; for if my mother come,
   She'll die with grief.   *Exit*

ABIGAIL
   I cannot take my leave of him for tears:
   Father, why have you thus incensed them both?   355

BARABAS
   What's that to thee?
ABIGAIL   I'll make 'em friends again.

BARABAS
   You'll make 'em friends?
   Are there not Jews enow in Malta,
   But thou must dote upon a Christian?

ABIGAIL
   I will have Don Mathias, he is my love.   360

BARABAS
   Yes, you shall have him: go put her in.

ITHAMORE
   Ay, I'll put her in.

                        [*Puts* ABIGAIL *in*]

BARABAS
   Now tell me, Ithamore, how lik'st thou this?

ITHAMORE
   Faith master, I think by this
   You purchase both their lives; is it not so?   365

BARABAS
   True; and it shall be cunningly performed.

ITHAMORE
   Oh, master, that I might have a hand in this.

BARABAS
   Ay, so thou shalt, 'tis thou must do the deed:
   Take this and bear it to Mathias straight,
   And tell him that it comes from Lodowick.   370

357–8   *You'll . . . friends / Are* ed. (Q You'll . . . Iewes / Enow)
          enow enough
  361   *put her in* lock her up in the house
  365   *purchase* obtain

ITHAMORE

'Tis poisoned, is it not?

BARABAS

No, no, and yet it might be done that way:
It is a challenge feigned from Lodowick.

ITHAMORE

Fear not, I'll so set this heart afire, that he shall verily think it
comes from him.   375

BARABAS

I cannot choose but like thy readiness:
Yet be not rash, but do it cunningly.

ITHAMORE

As I behave myself in this, employ me hereafter.

BARABAS

Away then.

Exit [ITHAMORE]

So, now will I go in to Lodowick,   380
And like a cunning spirit feign some lie,
Till I have set 'em both at enmity.   *Exit*

374–5   ed. (Q Feare . . . he / Shall . . . him.)
  381   *spirit* devil

ACT III [SCENE i]

Enter [BELLAMIRA] *a* COURTESAN

BELLAMIRA

Since this town was besieged, my gain grows cold:
The time has been, that but for one bare night
A hundred ducats have been freely given:
But now against my will I must be chaste.
And yet I know my beauty doth not fail.   5
From Venice merchants, and from Padua
Were wont to come rare-witted gentlemen,
Scholars I mean, learnèd and liberal;
And now, save Pilia-Borza, comes there none,
And he is very seldom from my house;   10
And here he comes.

Enter PILIA-BORZA

PILIA-BORZA

Hold thee, wench, there's something for thee to spend.
                              [*Offers bag of money*]

BELLAMIRA

'Tis silver, I disdain it.

PILIA-BORZA

Ay, but the Jew has gold,
And I will have it or it shall go hard.   15

BELLAMIRA

Tell me, how cam'st thou by this?

---

  0   s.d. *COURTESAN* high class prostitute
  1   *besieged* As Bennett notes, the siege does not truly begin until the defiance of the
      Turks in III.v. There may have been a rearrangement of scenes; or, as Bawcutt
      suggests, the mere presence of the Turkish fleet has effectively blockaded Malta.
      my . . . cold my profits have diminished
  2   *bare* single and/or naked
  6   *Venice . . . Padua* respectively, centres of trade and learning
6–7   *Padua / Were* ed. (Q Padua, / Were)
  8   *liberal* free-spending (with double sense, like 'cold' and 'bare')
  9   *Pilia-Borza* from the Italian for cutpurse or pickpocket
 12   *Hold thee* Here, take this

PILIA-BORZA

Faith, walking the back lanes through the gardens I chanced to
cast mine eye up to the Jew's counting-house, where I saw
some bags of money, and in the night I clambered up with
my hooks, and as I was taking my choice, I heard a rumbling   20
in the house; so I took only this, and run my way: but here's
the Jew's man.

Enter ITHAMORE

BELLAMIRA

Hide the bag.

PILIA-BORZA

Look not towards him, let's away: zoons what a looking thou
keep'st, thou'lt betray's anon.   25

[*Exeunt* BELLAMIRA *and* PILIA-BORZA]

ITHAMORE

O the sweetest face that ever I beheld! I know she is a courtesan
by her attire: now would I give a hundred of the Jew's crowns
that I had such a concubine.

Well, I have delivered the challenge in such sort,
As meet they will, and fighting die; brave sport.   *Exit*   30

17–22   ed. (Q Faith ... Gardens / I ... house / Where ... I / Clamber'd ... taking / My ...
        tooke / Onely ... man.)
   18   *counting-house,* ed. (Q counting-house)
        counting-house business office
   20   *hooks* standard item of burglary equipment
24–5   ed. (Q Looke ... away: / Zoon's ... keep'st, / Thou'lt ... anon.)
   24   *zoons* zounds, a contraction of 'by God's wounds'
24–5   *looking ... keep'st* obvious staring you engage in
   25   *anon* immediately
26–8   ed. (Q O ... is / A ... hundred / Of ... Concubine.)
   27   *attire* apparently a distinctive form of dress, whether the red taffeta worn by some
        English prostitutes or the more elaborate gowns of their notorious Venetian counter-
        parts
   29   *in such sort* in such a form
   30   *brave sport* admirable jest

[ACT III, SCENE ii]

Enter MATHIAS

MATHIAS

    This is the place, now Abigail shall see
    Whether Mathias holds her dear or no.

Enter LODOWICK *reading*

[LODOWICK]

    What, dares the villain write in such base terms?

[MATHIAS]

    I did it, and revenge it if thou dar'st.

Fight. Enter BARABAS *above*

BARABAS

    Oh bravely fought, and yet they thrust not home.   5
    Now Lodowick, now Mathias, so;   [*Both fall*]
    So now they have showed themselves to be tall fellows.

[VOICES] *Within*

    Part 'em, part 'em.

BARABAS

    Ay, part 'em now they are dead: farewell, farewell.   *Exit*

Enter GOVERNOR [FERNEZE],
MOTHER [KATHERINE], [*with* CITIZENS]

FERNEZE

    What sight is this? My Lodowick slain!   10
    These arms of mine shall be thy sepulchre.

KATHERINE

    Who is this? My son Mathias slain!

3–4   The text is doubtful. Q gives line 3 to Mathias and line 4 to Lodowick. The entrance 'reading' and his use of the status terms 'villain' and 'base' argue that it is Lodowick who reacts to a communication – probably Mathias's reply to Barabas's forged challenge ('feigned from Lodowick' (II.iii.373), since Mathias here acknowledges 'I did it'; but later Ithamore claims to have also brought a forged challenge to Lodowick (III.iii. 18–19), so perhaps both Lodowick and Mathias mistake a forgery for Mathias's own letter.

  5   *home* deeply, mortally

  6   *Now . . . now . . . so* The lines suggest the sword strokes.

  7   *tall* brave (ironically)

FERNEZE

    Oh Lodowick! had'st thou perished by the Turk,

    Wretched Ferneze might have venged thy death.

KATHERINE

    Thy son slew mine, and I'll revenge his death.   15

FERNEZE

    Look, Katherine, look, thy son gave mine these wounds.

KATHERINE

    O leave to grieve me, I am grieved enough.

FERNEZE

    Oh that my sighs could turn to lively breath;

    And these my tears to blood, that he might live.

KATHERINE

    Who made them enemies?   20

FERNEZE

    I know not, and that grieves me most of all.

KATHERINE

    My son loved thine.

FERNEZE   And so did Lodowick him.

KATHERINE

    Lend me that weapon that did kill my son,

    And it shall murder me.

FERNEZE

    Nay Madam stay, that weapon was my son's,   25

    And on that rather should Ferneze die.

KATHERINE

    Hold, let's enquire the causers of their deaths,

    That we may venge their blood upon their heads.

FERNEZE

    Then take them up, and let them be interred

    Within one sacred monument of stone;   30

    Upon which altar I will offer up

    My daily sacrifice of sighs and tears,

    And with my prayers pierce impartial heavens,

    Till they [reveal] the causers of our smarts,

---

17   *leave* cease

18   *lively* life-giving

33   *impartial* indifferent

34   *reveal* Most editors follow Dyce in assuming some such word to be omitted here.
    smarts pains, injuries

Which forced their hands divide united hearts: 35
Come, Katherine, our losses equal are,
Then of true grief let us take equal share.

Exeunt [with the bodies]

[ACT III, SCENE iii]

Enter ITHAMORE

ITHAMORE

Why, was there ever seen such villainy,
So neatly plotted, and so well performed?
Both held in hand, and flatly both beguiled.

Enter ABIGAIL

ABIGAIL

Why how now Ithamore, why laugh'st thou so?

ITHAMORE

Oh, mistress, ha ha ha.   5

ABIGAIL

Why what ail'st thou?

ITHAMORE

Oh my master.

ABIGAIL

Ha.

ITHAMORE

Oh mistress! I have the bravest, gravest, secret, subtle, bottle-
nosed knave to my master, that ever gentleman had.   10

ABIGAIL

Say, knave, why rail'st upon my father thus?

ITHAMORE

Oh, my master has the bravest policy.

ABIGAIL

Wherein?

  1–3   ed. (Q neatly / Plotted . . . and / Flatly)
           Why, was ed. (Q Why was)
     3   *held in hand* falsely encouraged
          flatly completely, utterly
     6   *what ail'st thou* what is wrong with you?
     9   *bravest* finest, most impressive
  9–10   *bottle-nosed* swollen, bottle-shaped
   10   *to* for
         had. ed. (Q had)
   11   *rail'st upon* abuse, mock
   12   *bravest* most admirable

ITHAMORE

 Why, know you not?

ABIGAIL

 Why no.   15

ITHAMORE

 Know you not of Mathias' and Don Lodowick's disaster?

ABIGAIL

 No, what was it?

ITHAMORE

 Why the devil invented a challenge, my master writ it, and

 I carried it, first to Lodowick, and *imprimis* to Mathias.

 And then they met, and as the story says,   20

 In doleful wise they ended both their days.

ABIGAIL

 And was my father furtherer of their deaths?

ITHAMORE

 Am I Ithamore?

ABIGAIL

 Yes.

ITHAMORE

 So sure did your father write, and I carry the challenge. 25

ABIGAIL

 Well, Ithamore, let me request thee this,

 Go to the new-made nunnery, and inquire

 For any of the friars of St Jacques,

 And say, I pray them come and speak with me.

ITHAMORE

 I pray, mistress, will you answer me to one question? 30

ABIGAIL

 Well, sirrah, what is't?

---

16 *Mathias' . . . Lodowick's* ed. (Q Mathia & Don Lodowick)

19 *imprimis* (Latin) first (Ithamore's error). See his mistaken usage at IV.ii.92.

20 *met, and as* ed. (Q met, as)

21 *In . . . days* Ithamore's deliberately archaic, literary diction, like his obvious delight
  in 'such villainy . . . neatly plotted', his misused Latin and his laughter are reminders
  of his relation to the Vice figure of the earlier stage.
  doleful wise sorrowful manner

22 *furtherer* agent

28 *Jacques* ed. (Q Iaynes) Dominican friars, named after their church of St Jacques in
  Paris

ITHAMORE

    A very feeling one; have not the nuns fine sport with the friars
    now and then?

ABIGAIL

    Go to, sirrah sauce, is this your question? Get ye gone.

ITHAMORE

    I will forsooth, mistress.   *Exit*   35

ABIGAIL

    Hard-hearted father, unkind Barabas,
    Was this the pursuit of thy policy?
    To make me show them favour severally,
    That by my favour they should both be slain?
    Admit thou lovedst not Lodowick for his sin,   40
    Yet Don Mathias ne'er offended thee:
    But thou wert set upon extreme revenge,
    Because the Prior dispossessed thee once,
    And couldst not venge it, but upon his son,
    Nor on his son, but by Mathias' means;   45
    Nor on Mathias, but by murdering me.
    But I perceive there is no love on earth,
    Pity in Jews, nor piety in Turks.
    But here comes cursed Ithamore with the friar.

Enter ITHAMORE, FRIAR [JACOMO]

JACOMO

    Virgo, salve.   50

ITHAMORE

    When, duck you?

32–3 ed. (Q A ... sport / With ... then?)

  32 *a very feeling one* a deeply emotional one (with ironic play on 'feeling' in a physical
      sense)

  34 *Go to, sirrah sauce* Enough, impudent fellow
      gone ed. (Q gon)

  36 *unkind* unfeeling and/or unnatural

  37 *pursuit* direction, outcome

  38 *favour* affection
      severally separately

  40 Q's *sinne* is frequently amended to read 'sire', since Lodowick himself has not harmed
      Barabas, but the attention of the play to assumptions about morality and inherited
      guilt gives Q's wording some claim to interest.

  43 *Prior* governing official

  50 *Virgo, salve* (Latin) Greetings (God save you), maiden

  51 *When, duck you?* ed. (Q When ducke you?) Do you bow? 'When' expresses impatience.

ABIGAIL

    Welcome grave friar: Ithamore be gone.

                                  Exit [ITHAMORE]

    Know, holy sir, I am bold to solicit thee.

JACOMO

    Wherein?

ABIGAIL

    To get me be admitted for a nun.   55

JACOMO

    Why Abigail it is not yet long since

    That I did labour thy admission,

    And then thou didst not like that holy life.

ABIGAIL

    Then were my thoughts so frail and unconfirmed,

    And I was chained to follies of the world: 60

    But now experience, purchasèd with grief,

    Has made me see the difference of things.

    My sinful soul, alas, hath paced too long

    The fatal labyrinth of misbelief,

    Far from the Son that gives eternal life.   65

JACOMO

    Who taught thee this?

ABIGAIL   The abbess of the house,

    Whose zealous admonition I embrace:

    Oh therefore, Jacomo, let me be one,

    Although unworthy of that sisterhood.

JACOMO

    Abigail I will, but see thou change no more,   70

    For that will be most heavy to thy soul.

ABIGAIL

    That was my father's fault.

JACOMO   Thy father's, how?

---

55 *To get me be admitted for* To procure my admission as

57 *labour* labour for

59 *unconfirmed* unsettled, unsolidified

65 *Son* ed. (Q *Sonne*) possibly punning on 'sun' and 'son'

67 *admonition* teaching, counsel

68 *Jacomo* ed. (Q *Iacomi*)

71 *heavy* grievous

ABIGAIL

 Nay, you shall pardon me. (Oh Barabas,
 Though thou deservest hardly at my hands,
 Yet never shall these lips bewray thy life.)   75

JACOMO

 Come, shall we go?

ABIGAIL   My duty waits on you.

            Exeunt

---

73 *pardon me* excuse me from answering
  ed. (Q Nay, you shall pardon me: oh *Barabas,*)
74 *hardly* severely
75 *bewray* betray

[ACT III, SCENE iv]

Enter BARABAS *reading a letter*

BARABAS
  What, Abigail become a nun again?
  False, and unkind; what, hast thou lost thy father?
  And all unknown, and unconstrained of me,
  Art thou again got to the nunnery?
  Now here she writes, and wills me to repent.   5
  Repentance? *Spurca*: what pretendeth this?
  I fear she knows – 'tis so – of my device
  In Don Mathias' and Lodovico's deaths:
  If so, 'tis time that it be seen into:
  For she that varies from me in belief   10
  Gives great presumption that she loves me not;
  Or loving, doth dislike of something done.
  But who comes here?

[*Enter* ITHAMORE]

              Oh Ithamore come near;
  Come near my love, come near thy master's life,
  My trusty servant, nay, my second life;   15
  For I have now no hope but even in thee;
  And on that hope my happiness is built:
  When saw'st thou Abigail?
ITHAMORE
  Today.
BARABAS
  With whom?   20
ITHAMORE
  A friar.

    2   *unkind* unnatural (compare III.iii.36)
        what, hast ed. (Q what hast)
    6   *Spurca* (Italian) filthy
        pretendeth signifies
    7   ed. (Q I feare she knowes ('tis so) of my deuice)
    9   *seen into* looked to
  11   *presumption* grounds for presuming
  15   *life* Many editions change Q's reading to 'self'.

BARABAS

A friar? False villain, he hath done the deed.

ITHAMORE

How, sir?

BARABAS

Why made mine Abigail a nun.

ITHAMORE

That's no lie, for she sent me for him.   25

BARABAS

O unhappy day,
False, credulous, inconstant Abigail!
But let 'em go: and Ithamore, from hence
Ne'er shall she grieve me more with her disgrace;
Ne'er shall she live to inherit aught of mine,   30
Be blest of me, nor come within my gates,
But perish underneath my bitter curse
Like Cain by Adam, for his brother's death.

ITHAMORE

Oh master.

BARABAS

Ithamore, entreat not for her, I am moved,   35
And she is hateful to my soul and me:
And 'less thou yield to this that I entreat,
I cannot think but that thou hatest my life.

ITHAMORE

Who I, master? Why I'll run to some rock and throw myself
headlong into the sea; why I'll do anything for your sweet   40
sake.

BARABAS

Oh trusty Ithamore; no servant, but my friend;
I here adopt thee for mine only heir,
All that I have is thine when I am dead,
And whilst I live use half; spend as myself;   45

---

31   *come within my gates* another of the play's many biblical phrasings (see, e.g.,
       Deuteronomy 17.2)
33   *Like Cain by Adam* As elsewhere, Barabas's use of familiar biblical or classical sources
       is pointedly ironic or inaccurate. Cain was cursed by God, not by his father Adam,
       for killing his brother, and, despite the curse, lived under God's protection (Genesis 4).
35   *moved* emotionally upset
37   *'less* ed. (Q least) unless
39–41 ed. (Q Who . . . and / Throw . . . any / Thing . . . sake.)

Here take my keys, I'll give 'em thee anon:
Go buy thee garments: but thou shalt not want:
Only know this, that thus thou art to do:
But first go fetch me in the pot of rice
That for our supper stands upon the fire.   50

ITHAMORE

(I hold my head my master's hungry.) I go sir.   *Exit*

BARABAS

Thus every villain ambles after wealth
Although he ne'er be richer than in hope:
But husht.

Enter ITHAMORE *with the pot*

ITHAMORE

Here 'tis, master.   55

BARABAS

Well said, Ithamore; what, hast thou brought the ladle with
thee too?

ITHAMORE

Yes, sir, the proverb says, he that eats with the devil had need
of a long spoon, I have brought you a ladle.

BARABAS

Very well, Ithamore, then now be secret;   60
And for thy sake, whom I so dearly love,
Now shalt thou see the death of Abigail,
That thou mayst freely live to be my heir.

ITHAMORE

Why, master, will you poison her with a mess of rice porridge
that will preserve life, make her round and plump, and batten   65
more than you are aware?

46–7   Apparently Barabas offers, but does not actually give, Ithamore the keys and wealth
           he promises.
   48   *thus thou art to do* this is what you will be able to do
   51   (*I . . . hungry.*) *I* ed. (Q I . . . hungry: I)
           hold wager
   52   *ambles* paces
   54   *husht* ed. (Q hush't) be silent
56–7   ed. (Q Well . . . brought / The . . . too?)
   56   *what,* ed. (Q what)
58–9   ed. (Q Yes . . . deuil / Had . . . Ladle.)
   64   *mess* serving
64–6   ed. (Q Porredge . . . plump, / And . . . aware.)
   65   *batten* grow fat   66   *aware?* ed. (Q aware.)

BARABAS

Ay but Ithamore seest thou this?
It is a precious powder that I bought
Of an Italian in Ancona once,
Whose operation is to bind, infect,   70
And poison deeply: yet not appear
In forty hours after it is ta'en.

ITHAMORE

How master?

BARABAS

Thus Ithamore:
This even they use in Malta here – 'tis called   75
Saint Jacques' Even – and then I say they use
To send their alms unto the nunneries:
Among the rest bear this, and set it there;
There's a dark entry where they take it in,
Where they must neither see the messenger,   80
Nor make enquiry who hath sent it them.

ITHAMORE

How so?

BARABAS

Belike there is some ceremony in't.
There Ithamore must thou go place this pot:
Stay, let me spice it first.   85

ITHAMORE

Pray do, and let me help you master. Pray let me taste first.

BARABAS

Prithee do: what say'st thou now?

ITHAMORE

Troth master, I'm loath such a pot of pottage should be spoiled.

---

69   *Ancona* an Italian port with a history of tolerance towards Jews until their forced
      conversion or expulsion on Papal orders in 1556
70   *bind* constipate
75   *This even they use* This evening they are accustomed to
75–6 *here – 'tis called / Saint Jacques' Even – and* ed. (Q here (tis call'd / Saint *Iagues* Euen)
      and)
83   *Belike* Perhaps
      ceremony customary observance
84   *pot* ed.(Q plot)
88   *Troth* In truth, by my faith
      pottage soup

BARABAS

    Peace, Ithamore, 'tis better so than spared.

                                [BARABAS *puts in poison*]

    Assure thyself thou shalt have broth by the eye.   90

    My purse, my coffer, and my self is thine.

ITHAMORE

    Well, master, I go.

BARABAS

    Stay, first let me stir it Ithamore.

    As fatal be it to her as the draught

    Of which great Alexander drunk, and died: 95

    And with her let it work like Borgia's wine,

    Whereof his sire, the Pope, was poisonèd.

    In few, the blood of Hydra, Lerna's bane;

    The juice of hebon, and Cocytus' breath,

    And all the poisons of the Stygian pool   100

    Break from the fiery kingdom; and in this

    Vomit your venom, and envenom her

    That like a fiend hath left her father thus.

ITHAMORE

    What a blessing has he given't! Was ever pot of rice porridge

    so sauced? What shall I do with it?   105

BARABAS

    Oh my sweet Ithamore go set it down

    And come again so soon as thou hast done,

    For I have other business for thee.

88–9   *spoiled . . . spared* perhaps playing on the biblical notion of sparing the rod and
          spoiling the child (Proverbs 13:24)

90   *by the eye* abundantly

95   *great Alexander* One story of Alexander the Great's death (told by Plutarch, among
          others) held that he was poisoned.

96   *Borgia's wine* Cesare Borgia was reputed to have poisoned his father, Pope Alexander
          VI, in 1503.

98   *In few* In short
          Hydra, Lerna's bane the nine-headed monster slain by Hercules that was troubling
          to Lerna, near Argos, and whose blood was poisonous

99   *hebon* a poisonous plant, perhaps the yew
          Cocytus one of the rivers of Hades

100   *Stygian* referring to the Styx, the principal river of Hades

104–5   ed. (Q What . . . of / Rice . . . it?)

105   *sauced* seasoned

ITHAMORE

Here's a drench to poison a whole stable of Flanders mares:

I'll carry't to the nuns with a powder.   110

BARABAS

And the horse pestilence to boot; away.

ITHAMORE

I am gone.

Pay me my wages for my work is done.   *Exit*

BARABAS

I'll pay thee with a vengeance Ithamore.   *Exit*

109–10   ed. (Q Here's . . . of / Flanders . . . powder.)

109   *drench* medicinal dose
       Flanders mares Belgian horses or lascivious women
110   *with a powder* quickly and/or with the powdered poison
111   *horse pestilence* unclear: apparently some horse disease
       to boot besides
114   *with a vengeance* to an extreme degree and/or with a curse

Enter GOVERNOR [FERNEZE], [MARTIN DEL] BOSCO,
KNIGHTS, BASHAW

FERNEZE

Welcome great Bashaw, how fares Calymath,
What wind drives you thus into Malta road?

BASHAW

The wind that bloweth all the world besides,
Desire of gold.

FERNEZE   Desire of gold, great sir?
That's to be gotten in the Western Ind: 5
In Malta are no golden minerals.

BASHAW

To you of Malta thus saith Calymath:
The time you took for respite is at hand,
For the performance of your promise past;
And for the tribute-money I am sent.   10

FERNEZE

Bashaw, in brief, shalt have no tribute here,
Nor shall the heathens live upon our spoil:
First will we race the city walls ourselves,
Lay waste the island, hew the temples down,
And shipping of our goods to Sicily,   15
Open an entrance for the wasteful sea,
Whose billows beating the resistless banks,
Shall overflow it with their refluence.

BASHAW

Well, Governor, since thou hast broke the league
By flat denial of the promised tribute,   20

---

1   *Bashaw* ed. (Q *Bashaws*)
2   As Craik points out, the stress on 'you' here helps to create a sense of Ferneze's surprise as feigned; he well knows why the Bashaw has come.
5   *Western Ind* the Western Hemisphere
8   *respite is* ed. (Q respite, is)
12   *spoil* goods, taken in war
13   *race* raze
15   *of* Many editors amend to 'off'.
18   *refluence* flowing back

Talk not of racing down your city walls,
You shall not need trouble yourselves so far,
For Selim-Calymath shall come himself,
And with brass bullets batter down your towers,
And turn proud Malta to a wilderness   25
For these intolerable wrongs of yours;
And so farewell.   [*Exit*]

FERNEZE

Farewell:
And now you men of Malta look about,
And let's provide to welcome Calymath: 30
Close your portcullis, charge your basilisks,
And as you profitably take up arms,
So now courageously encounter them;
For by this answer, broken is the league,
And nought is to be looked for now but wars,   35
And nought to us more welcome is than wars.

                                        Exeunt

26–7   ed. (Q *one line*)
  30   *provide* prepare
  31   *portcullis* a grid-like structure which could be lowered to block a gateway
       basilisks large cannon
  32   *profitably* beneficially. The sense of more financial sorts of 'profit' is also possible.
  33   *encounter* confront in battle

[ACT III, SCENE vi]

Enter two FRIARS [JACOMO *and* BERNARDINE]

JACOMO

    Oh brother, brother, all the nuns are sick,
    And physic will not help them; they must die.

BERNARDINE

    The abbess sent for me to be confessed:
    Oh what a sad confession will there be!

JACOMO

    And so did fair Maria send for me: 5
    I'll to her lodging; hereabouts she lies.   *Exit*

Enter ABIGAIL

BERNARDINE

    What, all dead save only Abigail?

ABIGAIL

    And I shall die too, for I feel death coming.
    Where is the friar that conversed with me?

BERNARDINE

    Oh he is gone to see the other nuns.   10

ABIGAIL

    I sent for him, but seeing you are come
    Be you my ghostly father; and first know,
    That in this house I lived religiously,
    Chaste and devout, much sorrowing for my sins,
    But ere I came –   15

BERNARDINE

    What then?

ABIGAIL

    I did offend high heaven so grievously,
    As I am almost desperate for my sins:

  0.1   ed. (Q *Enter two Fryars and Abigall.*)
 1–3   JACOMO . . . BERNARDINE ed. (Q *1 Fry ... 2 Fry*)
    2   *physic* medicine
    4   *be!* ed. (Q *be?*) The question mark in Elizabethan texts often simply registers
        emphasis, not interrogation.
  12   *ghostly father* spiritual confessor
  18   *desperate* despairing of salvation

And one offence torments me more than all.
You knew Mathias and Don Lodowick?   20

BERNARDINE
Yes, what of them?

ABIGAIL
My father did contract me to 'em both:
First to Don Lodowick, him I never loved;
Mathias was the man that I held dear,
And for his sake did I become a nun.   25

BERNARDINE
So, say how was their end?

ABIGAIL
Both jealous of my love, envied each other:
And by my father's practice, which is there
Set down at large, the gallants were both slain.

[*Gives a paper*]

BERNARDINE
Oh monstrous villainy!   30

ABIGAIL
To work my peace, this I confess to thee;
Reveal it not, for then my father dies.

BERNARDINE
Know that confession must not be revealed,
The canon law forbids it, and the priest
That makes it known, being degraded first,   35
Shall be condemned, and then sent to the fire.

ABIGAIL
So I have heard; pray therefore keep it close,
Death seizeth on my heart, ah gentle friar
Convert my father that he may be saved,
And witness that I die a Christian.   [*Dies*]   40

---

22   *contract* promise, betroth
28   *practice* contrivance, treachery
29   *Set down at large* Written out at length
     gallants fine gentlemen, ladies' men
30   *villainy!* ed. (Q villany:)
31   *work my peace* win my absolution
34   *canon law* ecclesiastical law, laid down by the pope and councils
36   *sent to the fire* Bawcutt points out that penalty and possible excommunication might
     follow such violation of canon law, but the death penalty twice mentioned here for
     violating confessional confidentiality is apparently Marlowe's exaggeration.
37   *close* secret

BERNARDINE

> Ay, and a virgin too, that grieves me most:
> But I must to the Jew and exclaim on him,
> And make him stand in fear of me.

Enter FRIAR [JACOMO]

JACOMO

> Oh brother, all the nuns are dead, let's bury them.

BERNARDINE

> First help to bury this, then go with me   45
> And help me to exclaim against the Jew.

JACOMO

> Why? What has he done?

BERNARDINE

> A thing that makes me tremble to unfold.

JACOMO

> What, has he crucified a child?

BERNARDINE

> No, but a worse thing: 'twas told me in shrift,   50
> Thou know'st 'tis death and if it be revealed.
> Come let's away.

Exeunt [with the body]

---

42   *exclaim on* denounce
48   *unfold* explain
49   *What,* ed. (Q What)
      crucified a child One traditional legend of anti-Semitism held that Jews crucified
      Christian children.
50   *shrift* confession
51   *and if* if

281

ACT IV [SCENE i]

Enter BARABAS, ITHAMORE. *Bells within*

BARABAS

    There is no music to a Christian's knell:

    How sweet the bells ring now the nuns are dead

    That sound at other times like tinkers' pans!

    I was afraid the poison had not wrought;

    Or though it wrought, it would have done no good,   5

    For every year they swell, and yet they live;

    Now all are dead, not one remains alive.

ITHAMORE

    That's brave, master, but think you it will not be known?

BARABAS

    How can it if we two be secret?

ITHAMORE

    For my part fear you not.   10

BARABAS

    I'd cut thy throat if I did.

ITHAMORE

    And reason too;

    But here's a royal monastery hard by,

    Good master let me poison all the monks.

BARABAS

    Thou shalt not need, for now the nuns are dead,   15

    They'll die with grief.

ITHAMORE

    Do you not sorrow for your daughter's death?

---

   1   *to* comparable to

        knell sound of a bell rung at a funeral

   3   *pans!* ed. (Q pans?)

   4   *wrought* worked

   6   *swell* i.e. from pregnancy

   8   *brave* fine

        known? ed. (Q has no end punctuation)

   9   *secret?* ed. (Q secret.)

  12   *And reason too* And with reason too

12–14   ed. (Q And . . . Hard / By . . . Monks.)

  13   *royal* fine, splendid

        hard by very near

BARABAS

No, but I grieve because she lived so long
An Hebrew born, and would become a Christian.
Cazzo, diavola.   20

Enter the TWO FRIARS [JACOMO *and* BERNARDINE]

ITHAMORE

Look, look, master, here come two religious caterpillars.

BARABAS

I smelt 'em ere they came.

ITHAMORE

(God-a-mercy nose.) Come let's be gone.

BERNARDINE

Stay wicked Jew, repent, I say, and stay.

JACOMO

Thou hast offended, therefore must be damned.   25

BARABAS

I fear they know we sent the poisoned broth.

ITHAMORE

And so do I, master, therefore speak 'em fair.

BERNARDINE

Barabas, thou hast –

JACOMO

Ay, that thou hast –

BARABAS

True, I have money, what though I have?   30

BERNARDINE

Thou art a –

JACOMO

Ay, that thou art, a –

BARABAS

What needs all this? I know I am a Jew.

18–19   ed. (Q No ... *Hebrew* / Borne ... *diabola*.) Many editors add punctuation after 'long'.
   20   *Cazzo, diavola* ed. (Q (marginally) *Catho diabola*); probably an oath derived from
           Italian 'cazzo' for 'penis' and 'diavola' for female devil
   21   *caterpillars* parasites upon the social order
   23   ed. (Q God-a-mercy nose; come let's begone.)
           God-a-mercy nose thanks to your big nose
28–40   For a useful consideration of Barabas's adoption of anti-Semitic discourse, see
           Hodge.

BERNARDINE
Thy daughter –
JACOMO
Ay, thy daughter –   35
BARABAS
Oh speak not of her, then I die with grief.
BERNARDINE
Remember that –
JACOMO
Ay, remember that –
BARABAS
I must needs say that I have been a great usurer.
BERNARDINE
Thou hast committed –
BARABAS   Fornication?   40
But that was in another country:
And besides, the wench is dead.
BERNARDINE
Ay, but Barabas remember Mathias and Don Lodowick.
BARABAS
Why, what of them?
BERNARDINE
I will not say that by a forged challenge they met.   45
BARABAS
(She has confessed, and we are both undone;)
My bosom inmates (but I must dissemble).
Oh holy friars, the burden of my sins
Lie heavy on my soul; then pray you tell me,
Is't not too late now to turn Christian?   50
I have been zealous in the Jewish faith,
Hard-hearted to the poor, a covetous wretch,
That would for lucre's sake have sold my soul.
A hundred for a hundred I have ta'en;
And now for store of wealth may I compare   55

39   *must needs* have to
40–2   ed. (Q Fornication . . . Country: / And . . . dead.)
46–7   Q marks 47 '*aside*' and uses italics for 'but I must dissemble' perhaps to signal Barabas's progress from conspiratorial aside ('we are both undone') to an address to the friars ('My bosom inmates'), to an aside possibly unheard by anyone onstage ('*but I must dissemble*').
53   *lucre's* wealth's
54   *A hundred for a hundred* one hundred per cent interest

With all the Jews in Malta; but what is wealth?
I am a Jew, and therefore am I lost.
Would penance serve for this my sin,
I could afford to whip myself to death.

ITHAMORE

And so could I; but penance will not serve.   60

BARABAS

To fast, to pray, and wear a shirt of hair,
And on my knees creep to Jerusalem.
Cellars of wine, and sollars full of wheat,
Warehouses stuffed with spices and with drugs,
Whole chests of gold, in bullion, and in coin,   65
Besides I know not how much weight in pearl
Orient and round, have I within my house;
At Alexandria, merchandise unsold:
But yesterday two ships went from this town,
Their voyage will be worth ten thousand crowns.   70
In Florence, Venice, Antwerp, London, Seville,
Frankfurt, Lubeck, Moscow, and where not,
Have I debts owing; and in most of these,
Great sums of money lying in the banco;
All this I'll give to some religious house   75
So I may be baptized and live therein.

JACOMO

Oh good Barabas come to our house.

BERNARDINE

Oh no, good Barabas come to our house.
And Barabas, you know –

BARABAS

I know that I have highly sinned,   80
You shall convert me, you shall have all my wealth.

---

58   *serve for* serve to atone for
60   Whether or not Ithamore understands Barabas's strategic hypocrisy here, he is
      characteristically uninterested in suffering.
62   *Jerusalem.* ed. (Q *Ierusalem,*)
63   *sollars* lofts
64   *drugs* medicines
65   *bullion* ed. (Q *Bulloine* i.e. Boulogne)
67   *Orient* precious, lustrous
70   *crowns.* ed. (Q crowns)
72   *where not* everywhere
74   *banco* bank

JACOMO

Oh Barabas, their laws are strict.

BARABAS

I know they are, and I will be with you.

BERNARDINE

They wear no shirts, and they go barefoot too.

BARABAS

Then 'tis not for me; and I am resolved   85

You shall confess me, and have all my goods.

JACOMO

Good Barabas come to me.

BARABAS

You see I answer him, and yet he stays;

Rid him away, and go you home with me.

BERNARDINE

I'll be with you tonight.   90

BARABAS

Come to my house at one o'clock this night.

JACOMO

You hear your answer, and you may be gone.

BERNARDINE

Why go get you away.

JACOMO

I will not go for thee.

BERNARDINE

Not, then I'll make thee go.   95

JACOMO

How, dost call me rogue?   *Fight*

ITHAMORE

Part 'em, master, part 'em.

BARABAS

This is mere frailty, brethren, be content.

Friar Bernardine go you with Ithamore.

You know my mind, let me alone with him.   100

84–96   The assignment of the friars' speeches has long been a problem; most modern
editors award line 84 to Bernardine rather than to Q's '1 [Friar]', i.e. Jacomo. On the
basis of lines 103–5 Craik argues compellingly that Bernardine must have made
critical remarks about the Dominicans in this passage. In any case the thrust of the
passage is that each friar naively believes himself in favour with Barabas and, hence,
in line for his wealth.

98   *frailty* weakness

100–1   Q gives both lines to Ithamore. Recent editors assume line 100 is intended to

286

JACOMO

Why does he go to thy house, let him be gone.

BARABAS

I'll give him something and so stop his mouth.

        [*Exeunt* ITHAMORE *and* FRIAR BERNARDINE]

I never heard of any man but he

Maligned the order of the Jacobins:

But do you think that I believe his words? 105

Why brother you converted Abigail;

And I am bound in charity to requite it,

And so I will, oh Jacomo, fail not but come.

JACOMO

But Barabas who shall be your godfathers?

For presently you shall be shrived. 110

BARABAS

Marry the Turk shall be one of my godfathers,

But not a word to any of your covent.

JACOMO

I warrant thee, Barabas. *Exit*

BARABAS

So now the fear is past, and I am safe:

For he that shrived her is within my house. 115

What if I murdered him ere Jacomo comes?

Now I have such a plot for both their lives,

As never Jew nor Christian knew the like:

One turned my daughter, therefore he shall die;

The other knows enough to have my life, 120

Therefore 'tis not requisite he should live.

But are not both these wise men to suppose

reassure Bernardine, but Bawcutt points out it is possible that 'let me alone with him' could be Ithamore's response to Barabas's own prompting – 'You know my mind.'

102   s.d. ed. (Q *Exit*)
104   *Jacobins* Dominicans (see III.iii.28)
109   *godfathers?* ed. (Q godfathers,)
110   *shrived* confessed
111   *the Turk* Ithamore
112   *covent* community, convent
113   *I warrant thee* I give you my promise
115   *house.* ed. (Q house,)
119   *turned* converted
121   *'tis not requisite . . . live* ironic understatement: 'it is not necessary that he live'

That I will leave my house, my goods, and all,
To fast and be well whipped; I'll none of that.
Now Friar Bernardine I come to you,   125
I'll feast you, lodge you, give you fair words,
And after that, I and my trusty Turk –
No more but so: it must and shall be done.
Ithamore, tell me, is the friar asleep?

Enter ITHAMORE

ITHAMORE
Yes; and I know not what the reason is: 130
Do what I can he will not strip himself,
Nor go to bed, but sleeps in his own clothes;
I fear me he mistrusts what we intend.
BARABAS
No, 'tis an order which the friars use:
Yet if he knew our meanings, could he 'scape?   135
ITHAMORE
No, none can hear him, cry he ne'er so loud.
BARABAS
Why true, therefore did I place him there:
The other chambers open towards the street.
ITHAMORE
You loiter, master, wherefore stay we thus?
Oh how I long to see him shake his heels.   140
                    [*Discovers* FRIAR BERNARDINE *asleep*]
BARABAS
Come on, sirrah,
Off with your girdle, make a handsome noose;
Friar awake.
BERNARDINE
What do you mean to strangle me?

---

128   *No more but so* Just so, without further ado
133   *mistrusts* suspects
134   *order* customary observance
135   *meanings* intentions
139   *stay* delay
140   *shake his heels* i.e. when he is hanged
141–2 ed. (Q *one line*)
142   *girdle* belt

ITHAMORE

    Yes, 'cause you use to confess.   145

BARABAS

    Blame not us but the proverb, 'Confess and be hanged'.

    Pull hard.

BERNARDINE

    What, will you have my life?

BARABAS

    Pull hard, I say, you would have had my goods.

ITHAMORE

    Ay, and our lives too, therefore pull amain.   150

    'Tis neatly done, sir, here's no print at all.

BARABAS

    Then is it as it should be, take him up.

ITHAMORE

    Nay, master, be ruled by me a little; so, let him lean upon his

    staff; excellent, he stands as if he were begging of bacon.

BARABAS

    Who would not think but that this friar lived?   155

    What time o' night is't now, sweet Ithamore?

ITHAMORE

    Towards one.

Enter [FRIAR] JACOMO

BARABAS

    Then will not Jacomo be long from hence.

               [*Exeunt* BARABAS *and* ITHAMORE]

JACOMO

    This is the hour wherein I shall proceed;

    Oh happy hour, wherein I shall convert   160

    An infidel, and bring his gold into our treasury.

    But soft, is not this Bernardine? It is;

---

145 *use to confess* make a practice of hearing (and making) confessions; punning on
      religious and judicial meanings

148 *have* ed. (Q saue)

150 *amain* strongly

151 *print* mark on his neck left by the noose

152 *take him up* pick him up and remove him

153 *Nay . . . so* Ithamore stands the friar up as he speaks.

159 *proceed* prosper

162 *But soft* But wait a moment

And understanding I should come this way,
Stands here o' purpose, meaning me some wrong,
And intercept my going to the Jew;   165
Bernardine!
Wilt thou not speak? Thou think'st I see thee not;
Away, I'd wish thee, and let me go by:
No, wilt thou not? Nay then I'll force my way;
And see, a staff stands ready for the purpose: 170
As thou lik'st that, stop me another time.

Strike[s] him, he falls.
Enter BARABAS [*and* ITHAMORE]

BARABAS
Why how now Jacomo, what hast thou done?
JACOMO
Why stricken him that would have struck at me.
BARABAS
Who is it, Bernardine? Now out alas, he is slain.
ITHAMORE
Ay, master, he's slain; look how his brains drop out on's nose. 175
JACOMO
Good sirs I have done't, but nobody knows it but you two,
I may escape.
BARABAS
So might my man and I hang with you for company.
ITHAMORE
No, let us bear him to the magistrates.
JACOMO
Good Barabas let me go.   180
BARABAS
No, pardon me, the law must have his course.
I must be forced to give in evidence,

165   *intercept* to intercept
166–7 ed. (Q And . . . *Bernardine*; / Wilt . . . not;)
171   *that* i.e. a blow from the staff
174   *it, Bernardine?* ed. (Q it *Bernardine?*)
       out alas exclamation, expressing grief or abhorrence
175   *on's* of his
176–7 ed. (Q Good . . . but / You . . . escape.)
181   *his* its

That being importuned by this Bernardine
To be a Christian, I shut him out,
And there he sat: now I to keep my word,   185
And give my goods and substance to your house,
Was up thus early; with intent to go
Unto your friary, because you stayed.

ITHAMORE

Fie upon 'em, master, will you turn Christian, when holy friars
turn devils and murder one another?   190

BARABAS

No, for this example I'll remain a Jew:
Heaven bless me; what, a friar a murderer?
When shall you see a Jew commit the like?

ITHAMORE

Why a Turk could ha' done no more.

BARABAS

Tomorrow is the sessions; you shall to it.   195
Come Ithamore, let's help to take him hence.

JACOMO

Villains, I am a sacred person, touch me not.

BARABAS

The law shall touch you, we'll but lead you, we:
'Las I could weep at your calamity.
Take in the staff too, for that must be shown: 200
Law wills that each particular be known.

                                        Exeunt.

183   *importuned* solicited
188   *stayed* delayed coming
189–90 ed. (Q Fie . . . when / Holy . . . another.)
190   *another?* ed. (Q another.)
195   *sessions* when the court sits
199   *'Las* Alas
201   *wills* demands
        particular piece of evidence

[ACT IV, SCENE ii]

Enter COURTESAN [BELLAMIRA] *and* PILIA-BORZA

BELLAMIRA

Pilia-Borza, didst thou meet with Ithamore?

PILIA-BORZA

I did.

BELLAMIRA

And didst thou deliver my letter?

PILIA-BORZA

I did.

BELLAMIRA

And what think'st thou, will he come?   5

PILIA-BORZA

I think so, and yet I cannot tell, for at the reading of the letter, he
looked like a man of another world.

BELLAMIRA

Why so?

PILIA-BORZA

That such a base slave as he should be saluted by such a tall man
as I am, from such a beautiful dame as you.   10

BELLAMIRA

And what said he?

PILIA-BORZA

Not a wise word, only gave me a nod, as who should say, 'Is it
even so?' And so I left him, being driven to a non-plus at the
critical aspect of my terrible countenance.

BELLAMIRA

And where didst meet him?   15

 6–7 ed. (Q I . . . of / The . . . world.)
  7 *man of another world* spirit
 9–10 ed. (Q That . . . such / A . . . you.)
  9 *saluted* addressed
   tall brave, splendid
  10 *dame* fine lady
  12 *as . . . say* as if he would say
  13 *even so?' And* ed. (Q euen so; and)
   non-plus state of perplexity
  14 *critical aspect* judgemental expression

PILIA-BORZA

Upon mine own freehold within forty foot of the gallows, conning his neck verse I take it, looking of a friar's execution, whom
I saluted with an old hempen proverb, *Hodie tibi, cras mihi,* and
so I left him to the mercy of the hangman: but the exercise being
done, see where he comes.   20

Enter ITHAMORE

ITHAMORE

I never knew a man take his death so patiently as this friar; he
was ready to leap off ere the halter was about his neck; and when
the hangman had put on his hempen tippet, he made such haste
to his prayers, as if he had had another cure to serve; well, go
whither he will, I'll be none of his followers in haste: and now   25
I think on't, going to the execution, a fellow met me with a
muschatoes like a raven's wing, and a dagger with a hilt like a
warming-pan, and he gave me a letter from one Madam Bellamira, saluting me in such sort as if he had meant to make clean
my boots with his lips; the effect was, that I should come to her   30
house, I wonder what the reason is; it may be she sees more in
me than I can find in myself: for she writes further, that she
loves me ever since she saw me, and who would not requite such
love? Here's her house, and here she comes, and now would
I were gone, I am not worthy to look upon her.   35

16–20   ed. (Q Vpon ... the / Gallowes ... a / Fryars ... hempen / prouerb ... mercy / Of ...
        where / He comes.)

16   *freehold* literally, land held as private estate; here perhaps the location of Pilia-Borza's
        career as pickpocket

16–17   *conning* studying

17   *neck verse* the Latin verse (generally Psalm 51) that the criminal must be able to read
        in order to claim 'benefit of clergy' and thereby escape punishment
        looking of looking at

18   *hempen* referring to the hangman's rope
        Hodie ... mihi ed. (Q *Hidie ... mihi*); (Latin) today you; tomorrow me

19–20   *exercise being done* religious service being over

21–35   ed. (Q I ... as / This ... was / About ... his / Hempen ... if / Hee ... whither / He ...
        haste: / And ... fellow / Met ... and / A ... he / Gaue ... *Belamira,* / Saluting ... make /
        Cleane ... that / I ... is; / It ... in / My ... me / Euer ... such / Loue ... now / Would ...
        her.)

23   *tippet* the scarf worn around a priest's neck

24   *cure to serve* parish to minister to

27   *muschatoes* moustache

28   *warming-pan* long-handled pan used for warming beds

30   *effect* upshot

PILIA-BORZA

This is the gentleman you writ to.

ITHAMORE

('Gentleman', he flouts me, what gentry can be in a poor Turk
of ten pence? I'll be gone.)

BELLAMIRA

Is't not a sweet-faced youth, Pilia?

ITHAMORE

(Again, 'sweet youth'.) Did not you, sir, bring the sweet youth   40
a letter?

PILIA-BORZA

I did sir, and from this gentlewoman, who as myself, and the
rest of the family, stand or fall at your service.

BELLAMIRA

Though woman's modesty should hale me back, I can withhold
no longer; welcome sweet love.   45

ITHAMORE

(Now am I clean, or rather foully out of the way.)

BELLAMIRA

Whither so soon?

ITHAMORE

(I'll go steal some money from my master to make me handsome.) Pray pardon me, I must go see a ship discharged.

BELLAMIRA

Canst thou be so unkind to leave me thus?   50

PILIA-BORZA

And ye did but know how she loves you, sir.

37–8   ed. (Q Gentleman . . . a / Poore . . . gone.)
  37   *flouts* mocks
37–8   *Turk of ten pence* i.e. worthless person
40–1   ed. (Q Agen sweet youth; did not you, Sir, bring the sweet / Youth a letter?)
42–3   ed. (Q I . . . my / Selfe . . . seruice.)
  43   *family* household
       fall with sexual connotation
  44   *hale* pull
  46   *clean* completely (with a pun contrasting 'foully')
       out of the way out of my depth; bewildered
48–9   ed. (Q I'le . . . to / Make . . . hansome: / Pray . . . discharg'd.)
  49   *discharged* unloaded
  51   *And* If

ITHAMORE

Nay, I care not how much she loves me; sweet Allamira, would I
had my master's wealth for thy sake.

PILIA-BORZA

And you can have it, sir, and if you please.

ITHAMORE

If 'twere above ground I could, and would have it; but he hides   55
and buries it up as partridges do their eggs, under the earth.

PILIA-BORZA

And is't not possible to find it out?

ITHAMORE

By no means possible.

BELLAMIRA

(What shall we do with this base villain then?

PILIA-BORZA

Let me alone, do but you speak him fair.)   60

But you know some secrets of the Jew, which if they were revealed,
would do him harm.

ITHAMORE

Ay, and such as – Go to, no more, I'll make him send me half he
has, and glad he scapes so too. Pen and ink: I'll write unto him,
we'll have money straight.   65

PILIA-BORZA

Send for a hundred crowns at least.

ITHAMORE

Ten hundred thousand crowns, – (*He writes*) 'Master Barabas'.

PILIA-BORZA

Write not so submissively, but threatening him.

52–3   ed. (Q Nay . . . me; / Sweet . . . sake.)
  52   *Allamira* Although Q frequently employs variant forms of characters' names, this
       variation suggests misspeaking.
  54   *and if* if
55–6   ed. (Q If . . . it; / But . . . doe / Their . . . earth.)
  60   ed. (Q Let . . . fair:)
       Let me alone Leave it to me
       speak him fair talk sweetly to him
63–5   ed. (Q I . . . more / I'le . . . too. / Pen and Inke: / I'le . . . strait.)
  63   *Go to* (exclamation) Go on; Come, come
  64   *scapes* escapes
  65   *straight* right away
  67   *He writes* (marginally after line 66 in Q)

ITHAMORE

'Sirrah Barabas, send me a hundred crowns.'

PILIA-BORZA

Put in two hundred at least.   70

ITHAMORE

'I charge thee send me three hundred by this bearer, and this
   shall be your warrant; if you do not, no more but so.'

PILIA-BORZA

Tell him you will confess.

ITHAMORE

'Otherwise I'll confess all.' Vanish and return in a twinkle.

PILIA-BORZA

Let me alone, I'll use him in his kind.   [*Exit*]   75

ITHAMORE

Hang him Jew.

BELLAMIRA

Now, gentle Ithamore, lie in my lap.
Where are my maids? Provide a running banquet;
Send to the merchant, bid him bring me silks,
Shall Ithamore my love go in such rags?   80

ITHAMORE

And bid the jeweller come hither too.

BELLAMIRA

I have no husband, sweet, I'll marry thee.

ITHAMORE

Content, but we will leave this paltry land,
And sail from hence to Greece, to lovely Greece,
I'll be thy Jason, thou my golden fleece;   85

69   *Sirrah* a disrespectful form of address (see I.i.70)
71–2 ed. (Q I . . . this / Shall . . . so.)
72   *no more but so* As Craik points out, this vague threat – something like 'you know
      what I mean' – is given a more precise form by Pilia-Borza's subsequent suggestions.
74   *all.' Vanish* ed. (Q all, vanish)
      in a twinkle instantly
75   *use* treat
      in his kind according to his nature. Bawcutt (citing Tilley, J 52) observes that to 'use
      someone like a Jew' later became proverbial for ill-treatment.
77   *lie in my lap* used with sexual implication
78   *running banquet* hastily prepared banquet
83   *Content* Agreed
85   *Jason . . . fleece* According to the Greek myth, Jason and the Argonauts recovered the
      magical golden fleece from Colchis.

296

Where painted carpets o'er the meads are hurled,
And Bacchus' vineyards o'er-spread the world:
Where woods and forests go in goodly green,
I'll be Adonis, thou shalt be Love's Queen.
The meads, the orchards, and the primrose lanes,   90
Instead of sedge and reed, bear sugar canes:
Thou in those groves, by Dis above,
Shalt live with me and be my love.

BELLAMIRA

Whither will I not go with gentle Ithamore?

Enter PILIA-BORZA

ITHAMORE

How now? Hast thou the gold?   95

PILIA-BORZA

Yes.

ITHAMORE

But came it freely, did the cow give down her milk freely?

PILIA-BORZA

At reading of the letter, he stared and stamped and turned
aside, I took him by the beard, and looked upon him thus; told
him he were best to send it, then he hugged and embraced me.   100

ITHAMORE

Rather for fear than love.

PILIA-BORZA

Then like a Jew he laughed and jeered, and told me he loved me
for your sake, and said what a faithful servant you had been.

---

86   *painted carpets* used metaphorically for bright flowers
     meads meadows
87   *Bacchus* Roman name for Dionysus, god of wine
88   *go* are dressed in
89   *Adonis . . . Love's Queen* In classical myth and verse, Adonis was a beautiful youth
     beloved by Venus, goddess of love.
91   *sedge* coarse grass
92   *Dis* Roman god (Greek Hades, Pluto) of the underworld; i.e. by no means 'above'
93   This alludes (probably parodically) to Marlowe's own lyric 'The Passionate Shepherd
     to his Love', which begins 'Come live with me and be my love'.
97   *give down her milk* let flow her milk
98–100 ed. (Q At . . . turnd / Aside . . . thus; / Told . . . me.)
98   *stared* ed. (Q sterd)
99   *took him by the beard* a serious insult
     thus an indication of staged action (see I.ii.347)

ITHAMORE

The more villain he to keep me thus: here's goodly 'parel, is there
not? 105

PILIA-BORZA

To conclude, he gave me ten crowns.

ITHAMORE

But ten? I'll not leave him worth a grey groat, give me a ream
of paper, we'll have a kingdom of gold for't.

PILIA-BORZA

Write for five hundred crowns.

ITHAMORE

[*Writes*] 'Sirrah Jew, as you love your life send me five hundred 110
crowns, and give the bearer one hundred.' Tell him I must have't.

PILIA-BORZA

I warrant your worship shall have't.

ITHAMORE

And if he ask why I demand so much, tell him,
I scorn to write a line under a hundred crowns.

PILIA-BORZA

You'd make a rich poet, sir. I am gone. *Exit* 115

ITHAMORE

Take thou the money, spend it for my sake.

BELLAMIRA

'Tis not thy money, but thy self I weigh:
Thus Bellamira esteems of gold; [*Throws it aside*]
But thus of thee. *Kiss[es] him*

ITHAMORE

That kiss again; she runs division of my lips. 120
What an eye she casts on me! It twinkles like a star.

BELLAMIRA

Come my dear love, let's in and sleep together.

104–5   ed. (Q The ... thus: / Here's ... not?)
104   '*parel* clothing
106   *ten crowns* as a tip
107–8   ed. (Q But. .. giue / Me ... for't.)
107   *grey groat* i.e. an insignificant amount
   ream a large amount of paper (480 sheets or more); with an apparent pun on 'realm'
110–11   ed. (Q Sirra ... crowns, / And ... hau't.)
111   *one hundred* ed. (Q 100)
117   *weigh* value
120   *runs division of* plays musically upon
121   *me!* ed. (Q What ... me? / It ... Starre.)

298

ITHAMORE

    Oh that ten thousand nights were put in one,

    that we might sleep seven years together afore we wake.

BELLAMIRA

    Come amorous wag, first banquet and then sleep.   125

                              [*Exeunt*]

123–4   Craik accurately sums up this speech as 'Marlowesque verse, tailing off into bathetic
         prose'.

   124   ed. (Q That . . . afore / We wake.)

   125   *wag* a term of endearment, impudent youth

[ACT IV, SCENE iii]

Enter BARABAS *reading a letter*

BARABAS

'Barabas send me three hundred crowns.'
Plain Barabas: Oh that wicked courtesan!
He was not wont to call me Barabas.
'Or else I will confess': ay, there it goes:
But if I get him *coupe de gorge*, for that.   5
He sent a shaggy tottered staring slave,
That when he speaks, draws out his grisly beard,
And winds it twice or thrice about his ear;
Whose face has been a grindstone for men's swords,
His hands are hacked, some fingers cut quite off;   10
Who when he speaks, grunts like a hog, and looks
Like one that is employed in catzerie,
And crossbiting, such a rogue
As is the husband to a hundred whores:
And I by him must send three hundred crowns.   15
Well, my hope is, he will not stay there still;
And when he comes: Oh that he were but here!

Enter PILIA-BORZA

PILIA-BORZA

Jew, I must ha' more gold.

---

3   *wont* accustomed
4   *there it goes* i.e. this shows his intentions
5   *coupe de gorge* (French) [I'll] cut [his] throat
     that. ed. (Q that)
6   *tottered* tattered
     staring looking fixedly, with wide-open eyes
7   *grisly* grim, ghastly
12   *in catzerie* i.e. in pimping; from Italian 'cazzo' (compare IV.i.20)
13   *crossbiting,* ed. (Q crossbiting)
     crossbiting cheating (probably implying reciprocity, as in wronging a wrongdoer)
14   *husband . . . whores* i.e. either a pimp who 'husbands' the resources of a hundred
     prostitutes, or a swindler who claims to be the husband of prostitutes in order to
     blackmail their clients
16   *still* forever

BARABAS

Why want'st thou any of thy tale?

PILIA-BORZA

No; but three hundred will not serve his turn. 20

BARABAS

Not serve his turn, sir?

PILIA-BORZA

No sir; and therefore I must have five hundred more.

BARABAS

I'll rather –

PILIA-BORZA

Oh good words, sir, and send it you were best; see, there's his
letter. 25

BARABAS

Might he not as well come as send? Pray bid him come and
fetch it; what he writes for you, ye shall have straight.

PILIA-BORZA

Ay, and the rest too, or else –

BARABAS

(I must make this villain away.) Please you dine with me, sir,
and you shall be most heartily (poisoned). 30

PILIA-BORZA

No god-a-mercy, shall I have these crowns?

BARABAS

I cannot do it, I have lost my keys.

PILIA-BORZA

Oh, if that be all, I can pick ope your locks.

BARABAS

Or climb up to my counting-house window: you know my
meaning. 35

---

19   *want'st . . . tale?* are you missing any of your desired amount?
20   *serve his turn* be sufficient for his purposes
24–5   ed. (Q Oh . . . see, / There's . . . letter.)
24   *good words* do not speak so aggressively (compare V.ii.61)
26–7   ed. (Q Might . . . him / Come . . . streight.)
27   *what . . . for you* the bearer's hundred crowns (compare IV.ii.111)
29   ed. (Q away: please)
29–30   ed. (Q I . . . dine / With . . . poyson'd.) Q's marginal '*aside*' does not indicate how
much of this speech is aside; compare Barabas's unexpected final words (e.g.
II.iii.67).
34–5   ed. (Q Or . . . window: / You . . . meaning.) Barabas implies knowledge of the
burglary attempt in III.i.

PILIA-BORZA

    I know enough, and therefore talk not to me of your counting-
    house; the gold, or know Jew it is in my power to hang thee.

BARABAS

    (I am betrayed.)
    'Tis not five hundred crowns that I esteem,
    I am not moved at that: this angers me,   40
    That he who knows I love him as myself
    Should write in this imperious vein! Why sir,
    You know I have no child, and unto whom
    Should I leave all but unto Ithamore?

PILIA-BORZA

    Here's many words but no crowns; the crowns.   45

BARABAS

    Commend me to him, sir, most humbly,
    And unto your good mistress as unknown.

PILIA-BORZA

    Speak, shall I have 'em, sir?

BARABAS

    Sir here they are.   [*Gives gold*]
    (Oh that I should part with so much gold!)   50
    Here take 'em, fellow, with as good a will –
    (As I would see thee hanged.) Oh, love stops my breath:
    Never loved man servant as I do Ithamore.

PILIA-BORZA

    I know it, sir.

BARABAS

    Pray when, sir, shall I see you at my house?   55

PILIA-BORZA

    Soon enough to your cost, sir: fare you well.   *Exit*

BARABAS

    Nay to thine own cost, villain, if thou com'st.
    Was ever Jew tormented as I am?
    To have a shag-rag knave to come –

36–7   *counting-house;* ed. (Q Counting-house,)
42   *vein!* ed. (Q vaine?)   *vein* manner, style
47   *as unknown* a polite locution: unknown to Barabas
52   ed. (Q – *As I wud see thee hang'd* oh, loue stops my breath:)
56   ed. (Q Soone . . . Sir: / Fare . . . well.)
59   *shag-rag* ragged
      come – ed. (Q come) Many editors conjecture a missing word such as 'demand' or
      'convey' after 'come'.

Three hundred crowns, and then five hundred crowns?   60
Well, I must seek a means to rid 'em all,
And presently: for in his villainy
He will tell all he knows and I shall die for't.
I have it.
I will in some disguise go see the slave,   65
And how the villain revels with my gold.   *Exit*

61   *rid* remove by violence, kill
62   *presently* immediately
63–4 ed. (Q *one line*)

303

[ACT IV, SCENE iv]

Enter COURTESAN [BELLAMIRA], ITHAMORE, PILIA-BORZA

BELLAMIRA

I'll pledge thee, love, and therefore drink it off.

ITHAMORE

Say'st thou me so? Have at it; and do you hear?

[Whispers to her]

BELLAMIRA

Go to, it shall be so.

ITHAMORE

Of that condition, I will drink it up; here's to thee.

BELLAMIRA

Nay, I'll have all or none.   5

ITHAMORE

There, if thou lov'st me do not leave a drop.

BELLAMIRA

Love thee, fill me three glasses.

ITHAMORE

Three and fifty dozen, I'll pledge thee.

PILIA-BORZA

Knavely spoke, and like a knight at arms.

ITHAMORE

Hey *Rivo Castiliano*, a man's a man.   10

---

2 *me* to me

4 *Of* On

5 *BELLAMIRA* ed. (Q Pil.) As Bawcutt argues, attribution of this line to Bellamira makes sense, both because she is engaged in a ritual of drinking toasts with Ithamore and because she has reasons to encourage him to get drunk.

8 *thee.* ed. (Q thee,)

9 *Knavely spoke.* Craik's argument that this phrase plays on 'bravely spoke' (as in 'bravely done' in line 18) with a clever antithesis between 'knave' and 'knight' is attractive, since this figure would compactly render Pilia-Borza's contempt for Ithamore and his drunken version of romantic exuberance.

10 *Rivo Castiliano* 'Rivo' is perhaps derived from Spanish *arriba* (up, upwards) and appears by itself as a drinker's cry (compare *I Henry IV* II.iv.108–9). 'Rivo Castiliano' could also be Italian for 'River of Castile', and thus might suggest a wish for Spanish wine.

   a man's a man a proverbial assertion of human equality despite social distinction (compare Tilley, M 243 and Iago's drinking song with 'A soldier's a man' in *Othello* II.iii.66)

BELLAMIRA

  Now to the Jew.

ITHAMORE

  Ha to the Jew, and send me money you were best.

PILIA-BORZA

  What would'st thou do if he should send thee none?

ITHAMORE

  Do nothing; but I know what I know, he's a murderer.

BELLAMIRA

  I had not thought he had been so brave a man.   15

ITHAMORE

  You knew Mathias and the Governor's son, he and I killed 'em
  both, and yet never touched 'em.

PILIA-BORZA

  Oh bravely done.

ITHAMORE

  I carried the broth that poisoned the nuns, and he and I,
  snickle hand too fast, strangled a friar.   20

BELLAMIRA

  You two alone.

ITHAMORE

  We two, and 'twas never known, nor never shall be for me.

PILIA-BORZA

  (This shall with me unto the Governor.

BELLAMIRA

  And fit it should: but first let's ha' more gold!)
  Come gentle Ithamore, lie in my lap.   25

---

12 *Ha to the Jew* Craik argues that Ithamore responds to the offer of an ironic toast to
      Barabas in the previous line; but it appears more likely that Bellamira proposes
      Ithamore turn his attention to extorting money from Barabas and that he here
      begins dictating his letter to that effect.
      you i.e. Barabas

14 ed. (Q Doe ... know / He's a murderer.)

16–17 ed. (Q You ... and / I ... 'em.)

19–20 ed. (Q I ... he / And ... Fryar.)
       I, snickle hand too fast, ed. (Q I snicle hand too fast,) Unclear; 'snickle' may mean
       'snare', so the phrase could mean 'I, with my snaring hand too fast to be escaped'.
       'Hand to fist' – a stock phrase for hand to hand combat – has been suggested; while
       Craik follows Kittredge in punctuating as reiterated dialogue 'snicle! hand to! fast!'

22 ed. (Q We ... shall / Be for me.)
      for me so far as I am concerned

25 *lie* suggesting sexual intercourse

ITHAMORE

> Love me little, love me long, let music rumble,
> Whilst I in thy incony lap do tumble.

Enter BARABAS *with a lute, disguised*

BELLAMIRA

> A French musician, come let's hear your skill?

BARABAS

> Must tuna my lute for sound, twang twang first.

ITHAMORE

> Wilt drink Frenchman, here's to thee with a – Pox on this   30
> drunken hiccup.

BARABAS

> Gramercy monsieur.

BELLAMIRA

> Prithee, Pilia-Borza, bid the fiddler give me the posy in his hat
> there.

PILIA-BORZA

> Sirrah, you must give my mistress your posy.   35

BARABAS

> *A vôtre commandement madame.*

BELLAMIRA

> How sweet, my Ithamore, the flowers smell.

ITHAMORE

> Like thy breath, sweetheart, no violet like 'em.

PILIA-BORZA

> Foh, methinks they stink like a hollyhock.

BARABAS

> (So, now I am revenged upon 'em all.   40
> The scent thereof was death, I poisoned it.)

---

26   *Love me little, love me long* proverbial (Tilley, L 559)
27   *incony* ed. (Q incoomy) attractive, with an obscene pun, as Craik notes, on 'coney'
       as used in Marlowe's translation of Ovid's *Elegies* (I.x): 'The whore stands to be
       bought for each man's money, / And seeks vile wealth by selling of her coney'.
30   ed. (Q Wilt . . . a – / Pox . . . hick-vp.)
       Pox an oath; literally, venereal disease
32   *Gramercy* Thank you
33–4   ed. (Q Prethe . . . me / The . . . there.)
       posy bouquet
36   *A vôtre commandement* (French) At your command

ITHAMORE

Play, fiddler, or I'll cut your cats' guts into chitterlings.

BARABAS

Pardonnez-moi, be no in tune yet; so now, now all be in.

ITHAMORE

Give him a crown, and fill me out more wine.

PILIA-BORZA

There's two crowns for thee, play.   45

BARABAS

(How liberally the villain gives me mine own gold.)

PILIA-BORZA

Methinks he fingers very well.

BARABAS

(So did you when you stole my gold.)

PILIA-BORZA

How swift he runs.

BARABAS

(You run swifter when you threw my gold out of my window.)   50

BELLAMIRA

Musician, hast been in Malta long?

BARABAS

Two, three, four month madame.

ITHAMORE

Dost not know a Jew, one Barabas?

BARABAS

Very mush, monsieur, you no be his man.

PILIA-BORZA

His man?   55

ITHAMORE

I scorn the peasant, tell him so.

BARABAS

(He knows it already.)

---

42   *cats' guts . . . chitterlings* lute strings . . . pork sausages
43   *Pardonnez-moi* ed. (Q Pardona moy) (French) Pardon me. It is not clear whether
     Barabas's French is intended to be as corrupt as his accented English in this scene.
44   *fill me out* pour for me
46   Q has a marginal '*aside*' here and at lines 48, 50, 60, 62 and 65.
47   *fingers* plays (with a pun on 'pilfering' that is picked up in Barabas's next line)
49   *runs* executes a rapid sequence of notes
50   ed. (Q You . . . of / My Window.)
54   *man* servant (this line is often made a question)

ITHAMORE

'Tis a strange thing of that Jew, he lives upon pickled grass-
hoppers, and sauced mushrumbs.

BARABAS

(What a slave's this? The Governor feeds not as I do.)   60

ITHAMORE

He never put on clean shirt since he was circumcised.

BARABAS

(Oh rascal! I change myself twice a day.)

ITHAMORE

The hat he wears, Judas left under the elder when he hanged
himself.

BARABAS

('Twas sent me for a present from the great Cham.)   65

PILIA-BORZA

A masty slave he is; whither now, fiddler?

BARABAS

Pardonnez moi, monsieur, we be no well.   *Exit*

PILIA-BORZA

Farewell fiddler: one letter more to the Jew.

BELLAMIRA

Prithee sweet love, one more, and write it sharp.

ITHAMORE

No, I'll send by word of mouth now; bid him deliver thee a   70
thousand crowns, by the same token, that the nuns loved rice,
that Friar Bernardine slept in his own clothes, any of 'em
will do it.

58–9   ed. (Q 'Tis . . . vpon / Pickled . . . Mushrumbs.)
   59   *sauced mushrumbs* seasoned mushrooms
   60   ed. (Q What . . . this? / The . . . doe.)
   61   *circumcised.* ed. (Q circumcis'd)
63–4   ed. (Q The . . . Elder / When . . . himselfe.)
       Judas . . . himself See Matthew 27; the elder tree is traditional, but the hat is
       apparently Marlowe's invention.
   65   *great Cham* emperor (Khan) of the Mongols, Tartars and Chinese
   66   ed. (Q A . . . is; / Whether . . . Fidler?)
       masty fattened, as a swine; or big-bodied. Craik amends to 'nasty', and Bawcutt sug-
       gests 'musty', but the metaphor of swinishness and the repulsive sense of physicality
       are appropriate to the prejudices of the speakers.
       whither ed. (Q whether)
   69   *sharp* sharply worded
70–3   ed. (Q No . . . now; / Bid . . . same / Token . . . *Bernardine* / Slept . . . clothes, / Any . . . it.)

PILIA-BORZA

Let me alone to urge it now I know the meaning.

ITHAMORE

The meaning has a meaning; come let's in: 75
To undo a Jew is charity, and not sin.

Exeunt

---

75   *The meaning has a meaning* Unclear; perhaps Ithamore pretends sagacity and deep
policy – such pretension would maintain his general parallelism with Barabas.

ACT V [SCENE i]

Enter GOVERNOR [FERNEZE], KNIGHTS, MARTIN DEL BOSCO
[*and* OFFICERS]

FERNEZE

Now, gentlemen, betake you to your arms,
And see that Malta be well fortified;
And it behoves you to be resolute;
For Calymath having hovered here so long,
Will win the town, or die before the walls.   5

KNIGHT

And die he shall, for we will never yield.

Enter COURTESAN [BELLAMIRA] *and* PILIA-BORZA

BELLAMIRA

Oh bring us to the Governor.

FERNEZE

Away with her, she is a courtesan.

BELLAMIRA

Whate'er I am, yet Governor hear me speak;
I bring thee news by whom thy son was slain: 10
Mathias did it not, it was the Jew.

PILIA-BORZA

Who, besides the slaughter of these gentlemen,
Poisoned his own daughter and the nuns,
Strangled a friar, and I know not what
Mischief beside.

FERNEZE   Had we but proof of this.   15

BELLAMIRA

Strong proof, my lord, his man's now at my lodging
That was his agent, he'll confess it all.

FERNEZE

Go fetch him straight,

                                        [*Exeunt* OFFICERS]
I always feared that Jew.

---

   6   *KNIGHT* Many editors designate as 1 Knight.
16–17   ed. (Q Strong . . . my / Lodging . . . all.)
  18   *straight* immediately

Enter [OFFICERS *with*] JEW [BARABAS], ITHAMORE

BARABAS
  I'll go alone, dogs do not hale me thus.
ITHAMORE
  Nor me neither, I cannot outrun you constable, oh my belly.   20
BARABAS
  (One dram of powder more had made all sure,
  What a damned slave was I!)
FERNEZE
  Make fires, heat irons, let the rack be fetched.
KNIGHT
  Nay stay, my lord, 't may be he will confess.
BARABAS
  Confess; what mean you, lords, who should confess?   25
FERNEZE
  Thou and thy Turk; 'twas you that slew my son.
ITHAMORE
  Guilty, my lord, I confess; your son and Mathias
  Were both contracted unto Abigail,
  Forged a counterfeit challenge.
BARABAS
  Who carried that challenge?   30
ITHAMORE
  I carried it, I confess, but who writ it? Marry even he that
  strangled Bernardine, poisoned the nuns, and his own daughter.
FERNEZE
  Away with him, his sight is death to me.
BARABAS
  For what? You men of Malta, hear me speak;
  She is a courtesan and he a thief,   35
  And he my bondman, let me have law,

19   *hale* drag
20   To 'outrun the constable' is proverbial (Tilley, C 615).
22   *damned slave* fool
     I! ed. (Q I?)
29   Many editors insert an initial 'he', although in the light of questions about agency in
     this scene, it may be worthwhile to keep the ambiguity of Ithamore's phrasing.
31–2 ed. (Q I . . . it? / Marry . . . the / Nuns . . . daughter.)
31   *Marry* interjection, 'Why, to be sure'
33   Compare in *The Spanish Tragedy* the Viceroy's irate dismissal of the man he believes
     to have murdered his son – 'Away with him, his sight is second hell' (I.iii.89).
36   *bondman* slave, serf

For none of this can prejudice my life.
FERNEZE

Once more away with him; you shall have law.
BARABAS

Devils do your worst, I live in spite of you.
As these have spoke so be it to their souls.   40
(I hope the poisoned flowers will work anon.)

[Exeunt OFFICERS *with* BARABAS, ITHAMORE,
BELLAMIRA, *and* PILIA-BORZA]

Enter [MATHIAS'S] MOTHER [KATHERINE]

KATHERINE

Was my Mathias murdered by the Jew?
Ferneze, 'twas thy son that murdered him.
FERNEZE

Be patient, gentle madam, it was he,
He forged the daring challenge made them fight.   45
KATHERINE

Where is the Jew, where is that murderer?
FERNEZE

In prison till the law has passed on him.

Enter OFFICER

OFFICER

My lord, the courtesan and her man are dead;
So is the Turk, and Barabas the Jew.
FERNEZE

Dead?   50

36–40   *let me have law . . . you shall have law* Echoes of this phrasing in Shakespeare's
        Merchant of Venice are pronounced: Shylock's demand 'I crave the law' (IV.i.204)
        and Portia's ironic acquiescence 'The Jew shall have all justice' (319) accentuate the
        play's representation of values and communities in confrontation. The charge of
        legalism has been a traditional feature of Christian responses to Judaism.
37   *life.* ed. (Q life:)
39   *Devils . . . you* These lines are frequently considered to be an aside, and many editors
        amend Q's 'I live' to 'I'll live', but the defiance in Barabas's voice is elsewhere evident
        in this scene, and 'I live in spite of you' is a notable instance of that heroic discourse
        which frequently comes in for ironic treatment in the play (e.g. II.ii.56).
40–1   ed. (Q As . . . soules: / I . . . anon.)
40   *so be it to* so let it be charged against
41   *anon* immediately
47   *passed* passed judgement

OFFICER

    Dead, my lord, and here they bring his body.

[Enter OFFICERS, carrying BARABAS as dead]

BOSCO

    This sudden death of his is very strange.

FERNEZE

    Wonder not at it, sir, the heavens are just.

    Their deaths were like their lives, then think not of 'em.

    Since they are dead, let them be buried.   55

    For the Jew's body, throw that o'er the walls,

    To be a prey for vultures and wild beasts.

[BARABAS thrown down]

    So, now away and fortify the town.

Exeunt [all except BARABAS]

BARABAS

    What, all alone? Well fare sleepy drink.

    I'll be revenged on this accursèd town;   60

    For by my means Calymath shall enter in.

    I'll help to slay their children and their wives,

    To fire the churches, pull their houses down,

    Take my goods too, and seize upon my lands:

    I hope to see the Governor a slave,   65

    And, rowing in a galley, whipped to death.

Enter CALYMATH, BASHAWS, TURKS

CALYMATH

    Whom have we there, a spy?

BARABAS

    Yes, my good lord, one that can spy a place

    Where you may enter, and surprise the town:

    My name is Barabas; I am a Jew.   70

CALYMATH

    Art thou that Jew whose goods we heard were sold

    For tribute money?

---

58   *So* A typical indication of the accomplishment of stage action; presumably Barabas's
        body is here thrown 'o'er the walls'. Subsequent lines are delivered from outside the
        city walls.

59   *Well fare* Blessings on
        sleepy sleep-inducing

62–3   This is a typically Marlovian invocation of destruction (see *Edward II* 4.100–2;
        Massacre at Paris V.v.61–4).

BARABAS   The very same, my lord:
   And since that time they have hired a slave my man
   To accuse me of a thousand villainies:
   I was imprisoned, but 'scaped their hands.   75
CALYMATH
   Didst break prison?
BARABAS
   No, no:
   I drank of poppy and cold mandrake juice;
   And being asleep, belike they thought me dead,
   And threw me o'er the walls: so, or how else,   80
   The Jew is here, and rests at your command.
CALYMATH
   'Twas bravely done: but tell me, Barabas,
   Canst thou, as thou reportest, make Malta ours?
BARABAS
   Fear not, my lord, for here against the sluice,
   The rock is hollow, and of purpose digged,   85
   To make a passage for the running streams
   And common channels of the city.
   Now whilst you give assault unto the walls,
   I'll lead five hundred soldiers through the vault,
   And rise with them i' th' middle of the town,   90
   Open the gates for you to enter in,
   And by this means the city is your own.
CALYMATH
   If this be true, I'll make thee Governor.
BARABAS
   And if it be not true, then let me die.
CALYMATH
   Thou'st doomed thyself, assault it presently.   95

Exeunt

---

78   *poppy . . . mandrake* sleep-inducing potions
79   *belike* probably
80   *how else* somehow
81   *rests* waits
84   *against* near
      sluice ed. (Q truce)
87   *common channels* public sewers
95   *doomed* sentenced
      presently at once

[ACT V, SCENE ii]

Alarms. Enter TURKS, BARABAS, [*with*] GOVERNOR [FERNEZE]
and KNIGHTS *prisoners*

CALYMATH

Now vail your pride you captive Christians,
And kneel for mercy to your conquering foe:
Now where's the hope you had of haughty Spain?
Ferneze, speak, had it not been much better
To keep thy promise than be thus surprised?   5

FERNEZE

What should I say, we are captives and must yield.

CALYMATH

Ay, villains, you must yield, and under Turkish yokes
Shall groaning bear the burden of our ire;
And Barabas, as erst we promised thee,
For thy desert we make thee Governor;   10
Use them at thy discretion.

BARABAS   Thanks, my lord.

FERNEZE

Oh fatal day to fall into the hands
Of such a traitor and unhallowed Jew!
What greater misery could heaven inflict?

CALYMATH

'Tis our command: and Barabas, we give   15
To guard thy person, these our Janizaries:
Entreat them well, as we have usèd thee.
And now, brave Bashaws, come, we'll walk about
The ruined town, and see the wrack we made:
Farewell brave Jew, farewell great Barabas.   20

1   *vail* abase (see II.ii.11)
5   *To keep* ed. (Q To kept)
8   *ire* rage
9   *erst* formerly
10 *thee Governor;* ed. (Q the Governor,)
11 *them* the captives
16 *Janizaries* Turkish infantry. On the dangers of relying upon Janizaries, see Machia-velli, *The Prince* XVIII.
17 *Entreat* Treat
19 *wrack* destruction

Exeunt [CALYMATH *and* BASHAWS]

BARABAS

May all good fortune follow Calymath.
And now, as entrance to our safety,
To prison with the Governor and these
Captains, his consorts and confederates.

FERNEZE

Oh villain, heaven will be revenged on thee.   25

Exeunt [TURKS *with* FERNEZE *and* KNIGHTS]

BARABAS

Away, no more, let him not trouble me.
Thus hast thou gotten, by thy policy,
No simple place, no small authority,
I now am Governor of Malta; true,
But Malta hates me, and in hating me   30
My life's in danger, and what boots it thee
Poor Barabas, to be the Governor,
Whenas thy life shall be at their command?
No, Barabas, this must be looked into;
And since by wrong thou got'st authority,   35
Maintain it bravely by firm policy,
At least unprofitably lose it not:
For he that liveth in authority,
And neither gets him friends, nor fills his bags,
Lives like the ass that Aesop speaketh of,   40
That labours with a load of bread and wine,
And leaves it off to snap on thistle tops:
But Barabas will be more circumspect.
Begin betimes, Occasion's bald behind,

22   *entrance to our safety* first step in our security
31   *boots* avails
33   *Whenas* seeing that
     at their command subject to their disposition
34   *looked into* considered carefully
39   *bags* purse
40–2 The fable may not be from Aesop, but the proverbial point is clear enough: the
     donkey does not profit from his labours but eats common thistles (compare *Julius
     Caesar* IV.i.21–8).
44   *betimes* quickly
     Occasion's bald behind As traditionally depicted, Occasion or Opportunity is a figure
     who must be grabbed by her long forelock before she passes because the rest of her
     head is bald.

Slip not thine opportunity, for fear too late   45
Thou seek'st for much, but canst not compass it.
Within here.

Enter GOVERNOR [FERNEZE] *with a* GUARD

FERNEZE
My lord?
BARABAS
Ay, 'lord', thus slaves will learn.
Now Governor stand by there – wait within –   50

[*Exit* GUARD]

This is the reason that I sent for thee;
Thou seest thy life, and Malta's happiness,
Are at my arbitrament; and Barabas
At his discretion may dispose of both:
Now tell me, Governor, and plainly too,   55
What think'st thou shall become of it and thee?
FERNEZE
This; Barabas, since things are in thy power,
I see no reason but of Malta's wrack,
Nor hope of thee but extreme cruelty,
Nor fear I death, nor will I flatter thee.   60
BARABAS
Governor, good words, be not so furious;
'Tis not thy life which can avail me aught,
Yet you do live, and live for me you shall:
And as for Malta's ruin, think you not
'Twere slender policy for Barabas   65
To dispossess himself of such a place?
For sith, as once you said, within this isle

45   *Slip not* Do not let slip away
46   *compass* achieve   *it.* ed. (Q it)
47   *Within here* a summons
50   *there – wait within* – ed. (Q there, wait within,). Barabas appears to want Ferneze to
      stay and the guard to depart.
53   *arbitrament* disposal
58   *no reason but of* no alternative but
61   *good words* i.e. do not speak so fiercely
62   *avail me aught* do me any good
63   *Yet* still
      for me i.e. as far as I am concerned
65   *slender* slightly grounded, ill-considered
67   *sith* since

317

In Malta here, that I have got my goods,
And in this city still have had success,
And now at length am grown your Governor, 70
Yourselves shall see it shall not be forgot:
For as a friend not known, but in distress,
I'll rear up Malta now remediless.

FERNEZE

Will Barabas recover Malta's loss?
Will Barabas be good to Christians? 75

BARABAS

What wilt thou give me, Governor, to procure
A dissolution of the slavish bands
Wherein the Turk hath yoked your land and you?
What will you give me if I render you
The life of Calymath, surprise his men, 80
And in an out-house of the city shut
His soldiers, till I have consumed 'em all with fire?
What will you give him that procureth this?

FERNEZE

Do but bring this to pass which thou pretendest,
Deal truly with us as thou intimatest, 85
And I will send amongst the citizens
And by my letters privately procure
Great sums of money for thy recompense:
Nay more, do this, and live thou Governor still.

BARABAS

Nay, do thou this, Ferneze, and be free;
Governor, I enlarge thee, live with me, 90
Go walk about the city, see thy friends:
Tush, send not letters to 'em, go thyself,
And let me see what money thou canst make;
Here is my hand that I'll set Malta free: 95
And thus we cast it: to a solemn feast
I will invite young Selim-Calymath,

69 *still* continually
72 *as a friend not known, but in distress* as a friend who is unrecognized until the moment of need
79 *render* grant
81 *out-house* outlying building
84 *pretendest* put forward for consideration
91 *enlarge* free
96 *cast* plot

Where be thou present only to perform
One stratagem that I'll impart to thee,
Wherein no danger shall betide thy life, 100
And I will warrant Malta free for ever.

FERNEZE

Here is my hand, believe me, Barabas,
I will be there, and do as thou desirest;
When is the time?

BARABAS   Governor, presently.
For Calymath, when he hath viewed the town, 105
Will take his leave and sail toward Ottoman.

FERNEZE

Then will I, Barabas, about this coin,
And bring it with me to thee in the evening.

BARABAS

Do so, but fail not; now farewell Ferneze:

                                        [*Exit* FERNEZE]

And thus far roundly goes the business: 110
Thus loving neither, will I live with both,
Making a profit of my policy;
And he from whom my most advantage comes,
Shall be my friend.
This is the life we Jews are used to lead; 115
And reason too, for Christians do the like:
Well, now about effecting this device:
First to surprise great Selim's soldiers,
And then to make provision for the feast,
That at one instant all things may be done, 120
My policy detests prevention:
To what event my secret purpose drives,
I know; and they shall witness with their lives.   *Exit*

100   *betide* happen to
101   *warrant* promise
106   *toward Ottoman.* ed. (Q toward, Ottoman,) i.e. Turkey
107   *about this coin* go about getting this money
110   *roundly* fairly, successfully
115   *used to* accustomed to
116   *And reason too* And with good reason
121   *prevention* being forestalled
122–3   The phrasing recalls that of Hieronimo's antagonist, Lorenzo, in *The Spanish Tragedy*
         III.iv.82–8.

[ACT V, SCENE iii]

Enter CALYMATH, BASHAWS

CALYMATH

Thus have we viewed the city, seen the sack,
And caused the ruins to be new repaired,
Which with our bombards' shot and basilisks',
We rent in sunder at our entry:
And now I see the situation,   5
And how secure this conquered island stands
Environed with the Mediterranean Sea,
Strong countermured with other petty isles;
And toward Calabria backed by Sicily,
Two lofty turrets that command the town.   10
When Syracusian Dionysius reigned;
I wonder how it could be conquered thus?

Enter a MESSENGER

MESSENGER

From Barabas, Malta's Governor, I bring
A message unto mighty Calymath;
Hearing his sovereign was bound for sea,   15
To sail to Turkey, to great Ottoman,

---

1   *sack* plundering
3   *bombards* cannons of an early type, throwing large shot or stone
     basilisks' ed. (Q Basiliske) brass cannon
4–12 The order here printed preserves that of Q; the lineation of this speech has been
     much debated, with some editors arguing line 10 is misplaced and belongs between
     lines 4 and 5, with a substitution of 'where' for 'when' in line 11.
8   *countermured* ed. (Q contermin'd) defended
9   *toward Calabria backed by Sicily* in the direction of Calabria (in Italy) defended by
     Sicily
10   *lofty turrets* perhaps the forts of Saint Angelo and Saint Elmo
11   *Syracusian Dionysius* probably Dionysius I (c. 430–367 B.C.), tyrant of Syracuse and
     aggressive military leader; from Plato to the end of the sixteenth century, a figure
     standing for oppressive tyranny
11–12 'When' Dionysius reigned, Calymath reasons, the military-political advantages of
     imperial tyranny would have compounded Malta's natural impregnability, so could
     it really have been conquered this easily? The question mark may indicate a tone
     mixing wonder with something like a rhetorical question.
16   *great Ottoman* the sultan of Turkey

320

He humbly would entreat your majesty
To come and see his homely citadel,
And banquet with him ere thou leav'st the isle.

CALYMATH

To banquet with him in his citadel;   20
I fear me, messenger, to feast my train
Within a town of war so lately pillaged,
Will be too costly and too troublesome:
Yet would I gladly visit Barabas.
For well has Barabas deserved of us.   25

MESSENGER

Selim, for that, thus saith the Governor,
That he hath in store a pearl so big,
So precious, and withal so orient,
As be it valued but indifferently,
The price thereof will serve to entertain   30
Selim and all his soldiers for a month;
Therefore he humbly would entreat your highness
Not to depart till he has feasted you.

CALYMATH

I cannot feast my men in Malta walls,
Except he place his tables in the streets.   35

MESSENGER

Know, Selim, that there is a monastery
Which standeth as an out-house to the town;
There will he banquet them, but thee at home,
With all thy Bashaws and brave followers.

CALYMATH

Well, tell the Governor we grant his suit,   40
We'll in this summer evening feast with him.

---

18   *homely* simple, plain
20   *citadel;* ed. (Q Citadell,)
21   *train* retinue
22   *of* by
     lately recently
26   *for that* concerning that objection
27   *in store* in reserve
28   *withal* in addition
     so orient so lustrous
35   *Except* Unless

MESSENGER

I shall, my lord. *Exit*

CALYMATH

And now bold Bashaws, let us to our tents,
And meditate how we may grace us best
To solemnize our Governor's great feast. 45

Exeunt

44   *meditate how we may grace* consider how we may equip

[ACT V, SCENE iv]

Enter GOVERNOR [FERNEZE], KNIGHTS, [MARTIN] DEL BOSCO

FERNEZE

    In this, my countrymen, be ruled by me,
    Have special care that no man sally forth
    Till you shall hear a culverin discharged
    By him that bears the linstock, kindled thus;
    Then issue out and come to rescue me,   5
    For happily I shall be in distress,
    Or you releasèd of this servitude.

1 KNIGHT

    Rather than thus to live as Turkish thralls,
    What will we not adventure?

FERNEZE

    On then, begone.

KNIGHTS   Farewell grave Governor.   10

                           [*Exeunt*]

---

  2   *sally forth* venture out
  3   *culverin* an elongated cannon
  4   *linstock* a staff holding the flame for igniting the charge
  6   *happily* perchance
  8   *thralls* slaves
  9   *adventure* risk
 10   KNIGHTS ed. (Q *Kni:*)
       grave respected

[ACT V, SCENE v]

Enter [BARABAS] *with a hammer above, very busy;*
[*and* CARPENTERS]

BARABAS

How stand the cords? How hang these hinges, fast?
Are all the cranes and pulleys sure?

CARPENTER   All fast.

BARABAS

Leave nothing loose, all levelled to my mind.
Why now I see that you have art indeed.
There, carpenters, divide that gold amongst you: 5
Go swill in bowls of sack and muscadine:
Down to the cellar, taste of all my wines.

CARPENTERS

We shall, my lord, and thank you.

Exeunt [CARPENTERS]

BARABAS

And if you like them, drink your fill and die:
For so I live, perish may all the world.   10
Now Selim-Calymath return me word
That thou wilt come, and I am satisfied.

Enter MESSENGER

Now sirrah, what, will he come?

MESSENGER

He will; and has commanded all his men
To come ashore, and march through Malta streets,   15
That thou mayst feast them in thy citadel.

---

1   *How stand* i.e. in what condition are
    fast secure
2   CARPENTER ed. (Q *Serv.*)
3   *levelled to my mind* in keeping with my plan
6   *swill* drink (as an animal) greedily
    bowls drinking vessels
    sack and muscadine wines (Spanish and muscatel)
9   *And if* If
    die Barabas has poisoned the wine.
10 *so* provided that
12 s.d. located after line 13 in Q

BARABAS

    Then now are all things as my wish would have 'em,
    There wanteth nothing but the Governor's pelf,

                Enter GOVERNOR [FERNEZE]

    And see he brings it: now, Governor, the sum.

FERNEZE

    With free consent a hundred thousand pounds.   20

BARABAS

    Pounds say'st thou, Governor? Well since it is no more
    I'll satisfy myself with that; nay, keep it still,
    For if I keep not promise, trust not me.
    And Governor, now partake my policy:
    First for his army they are sent before,   25
    Entered the monastery, and underneath
    In several places are field-pieces pitched,
    Bombards, whole barrels full of gunpowder,
    That on the sudden shall dissever it,
    And batter all the stones about their ears,   30
    Whence none can possibly escape alive:
    Now as for Calymath and his consorts,
    Here have I made a dainty gallery,
    The floor whereof, this cable being cut,
    Doth fall asunder; so that it doth sink   35
    Into a deep pit past recovery.
    Here, hold that knife, and when thou seest he comes,
    And with his Bashaws shall be blithely set,
    A warning-piece shall be shot off from the tower,
    To give thee knowledge when to cut the cord,   40

18   *pelf* money, with possible depreciatory sense
18   s.d. located after line 19 in Q
21   *Governor? Well* ed. (Q Gouernor, well)
24   *partake* be acquainted with
27   *field-pieces pitched* light cannon readied
28   *Bombards* large cannon
29   *dissever it* blow up the monastery
32   *consorts* associates
33   *dainty* delightful
36   *past recovery* without escape
37   Barabas gives (throws?) the knife to Ferneze.
38   *blithely set* merrily seated at table
39   *warning-piece* signal gun

And fire the house; say, will not this be brave?

FERNEZE

Oh excellent! Here, hold thee, Barabas,

I trust thy word, take what I promised thee.

BARABAS

No, Governor, I'll satisfy thee first,

Thou shalt not live in doubt of any thing.   45

Stand close, for here they come:

[FERNEZE *retires*]

why, is not this

A kingly kind of trade to purchase towns

By treachery, and sell 'em by deceit?

Now tell me, worldlings, underneath the sun,

If greater falsehood ever has been done.   50

Enter CALYMATH *and* BASHAWS

CALYMATH

Come, my companion Bashaws, see I pray

How busy Barabas is there above

To entertain us in his gallery;

Let us salute him. Save thee, Barabas.

BARABAS

Welcome great Calymath.   55

FERNEZE

(How the slave jeers at him?)

BARABAS

Will't please thee, mighty Selim-Calymath,

To ascend our homely stairs?

CALYMATH

Ay, Barabas, come Bashaws, attend.

FERNEZE [*Coming forward*]   Stay, Calymath;

For I will show thee greater courtesy   60

Than Barabas would have afforded thee.

---

41   *the house* the monastery
42   *hold thee* Ferneze offers Barabas money
46   *Stand close* Step aside into concealment
49–50 This boasting address to the audience under the name of 'worldlings' is strongly reminiscent of medieval drama.
49   *worldlings* those devoted to worldly pleasures or pursuits
      sun ed. (Q summe)
54   *salute him. Save* ed. (Q salute him, Saue)
      Save thee God save thee
58   *homely* simple, rude

KNIGHT

    [*Within*] Sound a charge there.

        A charge [sounded], the cable cut, a cauldron
        discovered [into which BARABAS *falls]*

      [*Enter* MARTIN DEL BOSCO *and* KNIGHTS]

CALYMATH

    How now, what means this?

BARABAS

    Help, help me, Christians, help.

FERNEZE

    See Calymath, this was devised for thee.   65

CALYMATH

    Treason, treason Bashaws, fly.

FERNEZE

    No, Selim, do not fly;

    See his end first, and fly then if thou canst.

BARABAS

    Oh help me, Selim, help me Christians.

    Governor, why stand you all so pitiless?   70

GOVERNOR

    Should I in pity of thy plaints or thee,

    Accursèd Barabas, base Jew, relent?

    No, thus I'll see thy treachery repaid,

    But wish thou hadst behaved thee otherwise.

BARABAS

    You will not help me then?

FERNEZE   No, villain, no.   75

BARABAS

    And villains, know you cannot help me now.

    Then Barabas breathe forth thy latest fate,

    And in the fury of thy torments, strive

---

    62   *charge* trumpet signal for attack
         s.d. *discovered* revealed. Ferneze cuts the rope, opening the trapdoor which Barabas
         has constructed over the cauldron. As Hunter has suggested, the fall into the cauld-
         ron strongly recalls representations of sinners' punishment in hell. It is appropriate
         that Barabas suffer the punishment for avarice.
    63. *this?* ed. (Q this)
    71   *plaints* expressions of sorrow and injury
    72   *Accursèd Barabas, base Jew, relent?* ed. (Q Accursed *Barabas;* base Jew relent:)
    77   *latest* last

To end thy life with resolution:
Know, Governor, 'twas I that slew thy son;   80
I framed the challenge that did make them meet:
Know, Calymath, I aimed thy overthrow,
And had I but escaped this stratagem,
I would have brought confusion on you all,
Damned Christians, dogs, and Turkish infidels;   85
But now begins the extremity of heat
To pinch me with intolerable pangs:
Die life, fly soul, tongue curse thy fill and die!   [*Dies*]

CALYMATH

Tell me, you Christians, what doth this portend?

GOVERNOR

This train he laid to have entrapped thy life;   90
Now Selim note the unhallowed deeds of Jews:
Thus he determined to have handled thee,
But I have rather chose to save thy life.

CALYMATH

Was this the banquet he prepared for us?
Let's hence, lest further mischief be pretended.   95

FERNEZE

Nay, Selim, stay, for since we have thee here,
We will not let thee part so suddenly:
Besides, if we should let thee go, all's one,
For with thy galleys could'st thou not get hence,
Without fresh men to rig and furnish them.   100

CALYMATH

Tush, Governor, take thou no care for that,
My men are all aboard,
And do attend my coming there by this.

FERNEZE

Why heard'st thou not the trumpet sound a charge?

79   *resolution* fortitude
82   *aimed* intended
84   *confusion* destruction
87   *pinch* torment, torture
89   *portend* mean
90   *train* plot
92   *determined* planned
95   *pretended* intended
98   *all's one* it would not make any difference
103   *attend . . . this* anticipate my return at this time

CALYMATH
    Yes, what of that?
FERNEZE   Why then the house was fired,   105
    Blown up and all thy soldiers massacred.
CALYMATH
    Oh monstrous treason!
FERNEZE   A Jew's courtesy:
    For he that did by treason work our fall,
    By treason hath delivered thee to us:
    Know therefore, till thy father hath made good   110
    The ruins done to Malta and to us,
    Thou canst not part: for Malta shall be freed,
    Or Selim ne'er return to Ottoman.
CALYMATH
    Nay rather, Christians, let me go to Turkey,
    In person there to meditate your peace;   115
    To keep me here will nought advantage you.
FERNEZE
    Content thee, Calymath, here thou must stay,
    And live in Malta prisoner; for come call the world
    To rescue thee, so will we guard us now,
    As sooner shall they drink the ocean dry,   120
    Than conquer Malta, or endanger us.
    So march away, and let due praise be given
    Neither to fate nor fortune, but to heaven.

                              [Exeunt]

FINIS

---

108   *work our fall* achieve our downfall
109   *treason* treachery
115   *meditate* plan
116   *nought advantage* do you no good
118   *come call the world* were all the world to come
123   *fate ... fortune ... heaven* Ferneze rejects alternative causalities in favour of Christian
        Providence. Whatever other ironies this may carry in the context of the play, it is
        potentially significant that he rejects the notion of fortune's sway, since Machiavelli's
        emphasis on fortune is such a focus in anti-Machiavellian polemic.

The troublesome

raigne and lamentable death of
Edward *the second*, *King of*
England: with the tragicall
fall of proud Mortimer:

As it was sundrie times publiquely acted
in the honourable citie of London, *by the*
right honourable the Earle of Pem-
brooke *his seruants.*

Written by Chri. Marlow *Gent.*

Imprinted at London for *William* Iones,
dwelling neere Holbourne conduit at the
signe of the Gunne · 1594

DRAMATIS PERSONAE

EDWARD II, *King of England*
ISABELLA, *Queen of England, the King of France's sister*
PRINCE EDWARD, *their son, later King Edward III*
EDMUND, EARL OF KENT, *the King's brother*

The King's Favourites
PIERS GAVESTON, *later Earl of Cornwall*
SPENCER JUNIOR, *Lady Margaret's servant, later Earl of Gloucester*
SPENCER SENIOR, *his father, later Earl of Wiltshire and Marquess of Winchester*
BALDOCK, *a scholar, Lady Margaret's tutor*

The Barons
MORTIMER JUNIOR, *of Wigmore*
MORTIMER SENIOR, *of Chirke, his uncle*
THE EARL OF LANCASTER
GUY, EARL OF WARWICK
THE EARL OF PEMBROKE
LORD BEAUMONT
LADY MARGARET DE CLARE, *Gaveston's fiancée*
LORD MALTRAVERS, EARL OF ARUNDEL, *the King's ally, later his keeper*
THE EARL OF LEICESTER
LORD BERKELEY

The Church
THE BISHOP OF COVENTRY
THE BISHOP OF CANTERBURY
THE ABBOT OF NEATH
MONKS
THE BISHOP OF WINCHESTER

THREE POOR MEN
THE CLERK OF THE CROWN
PEMBROKE'S MEN
JAMES, *Pembroke's servant*
A HORSE-BOY, *Pembroke's servant*
LEVUNE, *a Frenchman*
A HERALD
SIR JOHN OF HAINAULT, *the Queen's ally*
RHYS AP HOWELL
THE MAYOR OF BRISTOL
A MOWER
TRUSSEL, *a representative of Parliament*
GOURNEY, *the King's keeper*
LIGHTBORNE, *an assassin*
THE KING'S CHAMPION

Lords, Attendants, Guards, Posts, Ladies-in-Waiting, Soldiers

[Scene 1]

Enter GAVESTON *reading on a letter that was brought him
from the King*

GAVESTON

'My father is deceased; come, Gaveston,
And share the kingdom with thy dearest friend.'
Ah, words that make me surfeit with delight!
What greater bliss can hap to Gaveston,
Than live and be the favourite of a king?   5
Sweet prince, I come; these, these thy amorous lines
Might have enforced me to have swum from France,
And, like Leander, gasped upon the sand,
So thou wouldst smile and take me in thy arms.
The sight of London to my exiled eyes   10
Is as Elysium to a new-come soul;
Not that I love the city or the men,
But that it harbours him I hold so dear,
The King, upon whose bosom let me die,
And with the world be still at enmity.   15
What need the arctic people love starlight,
To whom the sun shines both by day and night?
Farewell, base stooping to the lordly peers;
My knee shall bow to none but to the King.
As for the multitude, that are but sparks   20
Raked up in embers of their poverty,

The traditional act-divisions are not adopted in this edition.
Head-title: ed. (The troublesome raigne and la- / *mentable death of* Edward *the /*
second, king of England: with the / *tragicall fall of proud* Mortimer. Q)
3   *surfeit* indulge, gorge
4   *hap to* happen to, befall
7   *France* Gaveston had been exiled by order of Edward I to his home in Gascony.
8   *Leander* Tragic lover in the classical story retold in Marlowe's narrative poem *Hero
      and Leander* (c. 1593). Leander fell in love with Hero and swam the Hellespont to
      Sestos every night in order to be with her. One night the light in the tower which
      guided Leander to the Sestos shore was blown out by a storm and he drowned. Hero
      committed suicide when Leander's body was washed up on the shore.
11   *Elysium* the islands of the blessed in classical mythology; equivalent to heaven
14   *die* (i) swoon (ii) experience sexual orgasm
20-1 *multitude . . . poverty* Gaveston, for whom the King is like the sun, disdains the
      common people as mere dull embers – they have to be raked even to show sparks
      of life. Merchant sees this metaphor as 'an extended play on the relationship between
      the sun as the principal light of the heavens and kingship and degree among men'.

Tanti! I'll fan first on the wind
That glanceth at my lips and flieth away.

Enter three POOR MEN

But how now, what are these?
POOR MEN
Such as desire your worship's service.   25
GAVESTON
What canst thou do?
FIRST POOR MAN
I can ride.
GAVESTON
But I have no horses. What art thou?
SECOND POOR MAN
A traveller.
GAVESTON
Let me see, thou wouldst do well to wait at my trencher and   30
tell me lies at dinner-time; and, as I like your discoursing, I'll
have you. And what art thou?
THIRD POOR MAN
A soldier, that hath served against the Scot.
GAVESTON
Why, there are hospitals for such as you;
I have no war, and therefore, sir, be gone.   35
THIRD POOR MAN
Farewell, and perish by a soldier's hand,
That wouldst reward them with an hospital.

22   *Tanti!* 'So much for them!' (spoken with contempt)
22–3 *fan . . . flieth away* This image of blowing air to keep a fire's embers burning builds
      upon the imagery of lines 20–1; it also depicts Gaveston's impudent assumption
      that he can control the common people.
23   s.d. ed.; after line 24 in Q
27   s.p. FIRST POOR MAN ed. (*1. poore.* Q)
29   s.p. SECOND POOR MAN ed. (*2. poore.* Q)
30   ed. (*Let . . . well / To . . . time, / And . . . you. / And . . . thou?* Q)
      trencher wooden plate
31   *lies* travellers' tales. Cf. proverb, 'A traveller may lie with authority' (Tilley T 476)
      as if
33   s.p. THIRD POOR MAN ed. (*3. poore.* Q)
      served . . . Scot England was troubled in the later years of Edward I's reign by a long
      war with Scotland, led by Robert Bruce.
34   *hospitals* charitable hospices for the needy
36   s.p. THIRD POOR MAN ed. (*Sold.* Q)

GAVESTON

    [*Aside*] Ay, ay. These words of his move me as much
    As if a goose should play the porcupine,
    And dart her plumes, thinking to pierce my breast.   40
    But yet it is no pain to speak men fair;
    I'll flatter these, and make them live in hope.
    [*To them*] You know that I came lately out of France,
    And yet I have not viewed my lord the King;
    If I speed well, I'll entertain you all.   45

POOR MEN

    We thank your worship.

GAVESTON

    I have some business; leave me to myself.

POOR MEN

    We will wait here about the court.

                                          Exeunt

GAVESTON

    Do. These are not men for me;
    I must have wanton poets, pleasant wits,   50
    Musicians, that with touching of a string
    May draw the pliant King which way I please.
    Music and poetry is his delight;
    Therefore I'll have Italian masques by night,
    Sweet speeches, comedies, and pleasing shows;   55
    And in the day when he shall walk abroad,
    Like sylvan nymphs my pages shall be clad,
    My men like satyrs grazing on the lawns

---

40   *dart . . . plumes* The Elizabethans believed that porcupines would shoot their quills
      in self-defence.
45   *speed well* am   *entertain* take into service
46, 48   s.p. POOR MEN ed. (*Omnes.* Q)
50   *wanton* lascivious
        pleasant wits jocular, intelligent, and pleasing orators
52   *pliant* malleable, readily influenced
54   *masques* Courtly dramatic entertainments which originated in Italy and became
      popular in the English court during the late sixteenth and early seventeenth
      centuries. The earlier form of masque involved singing and dancing, in which the
      performers would be partially disguised by masks. The later development involved
      great costliness of scenes and costumes.
56   *abroad* outside, out of doors
57   *sylvan nymphs* female wood spirits
58   *satyrs* woodland demons which are part-human, part-goat, and are usually asso-
      ciated with Bacchus, the classical god of wine and revelry

Shall with their goat-feet dance an antic hay;
Sometime a lovely boy in Dian's shape,   60
With hair that gilds the water as it glides,
Crownets of pearl about his naked arms,
And in his sportful hands an olive tree
To hide those parts which men delight to see,
Shall bathe him in a spring; and there hard by,   65
One like Actaeon peeping through the grove,
Shall by the angry goddess be transformed,
And running in the likeness of an hart,
By yelping hounds pulled down, and seem to die.
Such things as these best please his majesty.   70

Enter [EDWARD] *the King,* LANCASTER, MORTIMER SENIOR,
    MORTIMER JUNIOR, EDMUND EARL OF KENT,
    GUY EARL OF WARWICK[, *and attendants*]

My lord! Here comes the King and the nobles
From the parliament; I'll stand aside.

EDWARD

Lancaster.

LANCASTER

My lord.

GAVESTON

[*Aside*] That Earl of Lancaster do I abhor.   75

EDWARD

Will you not grant me this? [*Aside*] In spite of them
I'll have my will, and these two Mortimers
That cross me thus shall know I am displeased.

---

59   *antic* grotesque   *hay* a country dance with a serpentine movement
60   *Dian's shape* i.e. the appearance of Diana; in classical mythology, the moon goddess
     who was also associated with female chastity
61   *gilds . . . glides* i.e. covers the water with a golden colour. This image could also imply
     artifice: cf. Holland's trans. Pliny's *Naturalis Historia* (1601), 'I see that now adaies
     siluer only . . . is guilded by the means of this artificiall Quicksiluer.'
62   *Crownets* Coronets
63   *sportful* playful, sportive
65   *hard by* close by, near
66   *Actaeon* In classical mythology, the hunter who offended the goddess Diana by seeing
     her bathe naked. In her anger, she turned him into a stag, and he was later chased
     and killed by his own hounds. Cf. Ovid's *Metamorphoses,* III. 138ff.
70   s.d. ed.: after line 72 in Q
72   *stand aside* Gaveston withdraws to the side of the stage until line 138.
78   *cross* obstruct

MORTIMER SENIOR

    If you love us, my lord, hate Gaveston.

GAVESTON

    [*Aside*] That villain Mortimer, I'll be his death.   80

MORTIMER JUNIOR

    Mine uncle here, this earl, and I myself

    Were sworn to your father at his death,

    That he should ne'er return into the realm;

    And know, my lord, ere I will break my oath,

    This sword of mine that should offend your foes,   85

    Shall sleep within the scabbard at thy need,

    And underneath thy banners march who will,

    For Mortimer will hang his armour up.

GAVESTON

    [*Aside*] *Mort Dieu!*

EDWARD

    Well Mortimer, I'll make thee rue these words.   90

    Beseems it thee to contradict thy King?

    Frownst thou thereat, aspiring Lancaster?

    The sword shall plane the furrows of thy brows

    And hew these knees that now are grown so stiff.

    I will have Gaveston; and you shall know   95

    What danger 'tis to stand against your King.

GAVESTON

    [*Aside*] Well done, Ned.

LANCASTER

    My lord, why do you thus incense your peers

    That naturally would love and honour you,

    But for that base and obscure Gaveston?   100

    Four earldoms have I besides Lancaster:

    Derby, Salisbury, Lincoln, Leicester.

    These will I sell to give my soldiers pay,

---

87   *banners* fringed flags which were carried as standards before an army

89   *Mort Dieu!* A French oath meaning 'by God's death', reminding us of Gaveston's
      Continental origins.

90   *rue* regret

91   *Beseems it thee* i.e. is it fitting for you

92   *thereat* at that

97   *Ned* This diminutive emphasizes Gaveston's familiar relationship with the King.

99   *naturally* by nature, by birth (according to their social status)

100 *base* of low birth, poor stock
      obscure lowly

Ere Gaveston shall stay within the realm.
Therefore if he be come, expel him straight.   105
KENT
Barons and earls, your pride hath made me mute.
But now I'll speak, and to the proof I hope:
I do remember in my father's days,
Lord Percy of the North, being highly moved,
Braved Mowbery in presence of the King.   110
For which, had not his highness loved him well,
He should have lost his head, but with his look
The undaunted spirit of Percy was appeased,
And Mowbery and he were reconciled.
Yet dare you brave the King unto his face?   115
Brother, revenge it; and let these their heads
Preach upon poles for trespass of their tongues.
WARWICK
O, our heads!
EDWARD
Ay, yours; and therefore I would wish you grant.
WARWICK
Bridle thy anger, gentle Mortimer.   120
MORTIMER JUNIOR
I cannot, nor I will not; I must speak.
Cousin, our hands I hope shall fence our heads,
And strike off his that makes you threaten us.
Come uncle, let us leave the brainsick King,
And henceforth parley with our naked swords.   125
MORTIMER SENIOR
Welshry hath men enough to save our heads.

106   s.p. *KENT* ed. (*Edm.* Q; and throughout the text whenever '*Edm.*' is used)
107   *to the proof* irrefutably
109   *moved* angry
110   *Braved* challenged
     Mowbery Mowbray (*Mozeberie* Q; also at line 114)
117   *Preach . . . poles* After execution, traitors' severed heads were publicly displayed on poles as a warning to others.
119   *grant* assent
122   *Cousin* A term used by a sovereign when formally addressing a nobleman. In this instance Mortimer Junior, being Edward's subject, uses the term presumptuously.
     fence shield
126   *Welshry* ed. (Wilshire Q) the Welsh populace. Roma Gill has pointed out that the policy of most editors to adopt the reading 'Wiltshire' is historically incorrect and may well have been a compositorial misreading for 'Welshrye'. Mortimer Senior was

WARWICK

    All Warwickshire will love him for my sake.

LANCASTER

    And northward Gaveston hath many friends.

    Adieu my lord; and either change your mind,

    Or look to see the throne where you should sit   130

    To float in blood, and at thy wanton head

    The glozing head of thy base minion thrown.

                          Exeunt NOBLES [*except* KENT]

EDWARD

    I cannot brook these haughty menaces:

    Am I a king and must be overruled?

    Brother, display my ensigns in the field;   135

    I'll bandy with the barons and the earls,

    And either die or live with Gaveston.

GAVESTON

    I can no longer keep me from my lord.   [*He steps forward*]

EDWARD

    What, Gaveston! Welcome! Kiss not my hand;

    Embrace me, Gaveston, as I do thee!   140

    Why shouldst thou kneel; knowest thou not who I am?

    Thy friend, thy self, another Gaveston!

    Not Hylas was more mourned of Hercules

    Than thou hast been of me since thy exile.

GAVESTON

    And since I went from hence, no soul in hell   145

    Hath felt more torment than poor Gaveston.

        in fact Edward's Lieutenant and Justice of Wales, governing Wales from 1307 to 1321. See 'Mortimer's Men', *N&Q*, n.s. 27 (1980), 159.

128 spoken ironically, like the previous line: Lancaster means Gaveston has no friends at all in the north

132 *glozing* flattering

      minion A powerful man's favourite or homosexual lover; derived from the French *mignon* (= sweet), applied to the favourites of Henry III of France.

133 *brook* endure   *menaces* threats

135 *ensigns* military banners

      in the field in battle

136 *bandy* give and take blows, as in a game of tennis

141   ed. (Why . . . kneele, / Knowest . . . I am? Q)

143 *Hylas . . . Hercules* Hylas accompanied Hercules on the journey of the Argonauts. When they anchored at Mysia, Hylas was carried away by water-nymphs. In his grief, Hercules remained behind, searching for the lost boy while the Argonauts continued their journey.

EDWARD

> I know it. [*To* KENT] Brother, welcome home my friend.
> [*To* GAVESTON] Now let the treacherous Mortimers conspire,
> And that high-minded Earl of Lancaster.
> I have my wish, in that I joy thy sight,   150
> And sooner shall the sea o'erwhelm my land
> Than bear the ship that shall transport thee hence.
> I here create thee Lord High Chamberlain,
> Chief Secretary to the state and me,
> Earl of Cornwall, King and Lord of Man.   155

GAVESTON

> My lord, these titles far exceed my worth.

KENT

> Brother, the least of these may well suffice
> For one of greater birth than Gaveston.

EDWARD

> Cease, brother, for I cannot brook these words.
> [*To* GAVESTON] Thy worth, sweet friend, is far above my gifts,   160
> Therefore to equal it, receive my heart.
> If for these dignities thou be envied,
> I'll give thee more, for but to honour thee
> Is Edward pleased with kingly regiment.
> Fear'st thou thy person? Thou shalt have a guard.   165
> Wants thou gold? Go to my treasury.
> Wouldst thou be loved and feared? Receive my seal,
> Save or condemn, and in our name command
> What so thy mind affects or fancy likes.

GAVESTON

> It shall suffice me to enjoy your love,   170
> Which whiles I have, I think myself as great
> As Caesar riding in the Roman street,
> With captive kings at his triumphant car.

149   *high-minded* arrogant
150   *joy* enjoy
155   *King . . . Man* Until 1829, the rulers of the Isle of Man were known as kings, possessing certain sovereign rights (Gill).
164   *regiment* rule
167   *seal* A token of royal authority; in performance the seal is often in the form of a ring.
169   *affects* desires   *fancy* (i) caprice (ii) amorous inclination
172–3   *Caesar. . . kings* A popular image of conquest. Cf. George Peele's *Edward I*, 'Not Caesar leading through the streetes of Rome, / The captive kings of conquered nations, / Was in his princely triumphes honoured more' (i. 91–3).
173   *car* chariot

Enter the BISHOP OF COVENTRY

Whither goes my lord of Coventry so fast?

BISHOP OF COVENTRY

To celebrate your father's exequies.   175

But is that wicked Gaveston returned?

EDWARD

Ay, priest, and lives to be revenged on thee

That wert the only cause of his exile.

GAVESTON

'Tis true, and but for reverence of these robes

Thou shouldst not plod one foot beyond this place.   180

BISHOP OF COVENTRY

I did no more than I was bound to do;

And Gaveston, unless thou be reclaimed,

As then I did incense the parliament,

So will I now, and thou shalt back to France.

GAVESTON

Saving your reverence, you must pardon me.   185

EDWARD

Throw off his golden mitre, rend his stole,

And in the channel christen him anew.

                              [*Assaults* COVENTRY]

KENT

Ah brother, lay not violent hands on him,

For he'll complain unto the See of Rome.

GAVESTON

Let him complain unto the See of Hell;   190

I'll be revenged on him for my exile.

EDWARD

No, spare his life, but seize upon his goods.

---

175   s.p. BISHOP OF COVENTRY ed. (*Bish.* Q; also at ll. 181, 198, and 200)
       exequies funeral rites
182   *reclaimed* reformed, subdued
183   *incense* incite
185   *Saving your reverence* a sarcastic rendering of a proverbial expression which was
       usually said apologetically (Tilley R 93)
186   *golden mitre* head-dress which was a symbol of episcopal office; rarely worn in the
       Anglican Church after the Reformation
       rend tear   *stole* ecclesiastical vestment
187   *channel* gutter. For the exact nature of the violence done to the Bishop, cf. 2.35–6.
189   *See of Rome i.e.* the Pope
192   *goods* property, possessions

Be thou lord bishop, and receive his rents,
And make him serve thee as thy chaplain.
I give him thee; here, use him as thou wilt.   195

GAVESTON

He shall to prison, and there die in bolts.

EDWARD

Ay, to the Tower, the Fleet, or where thou wilt.

BISHOP OF COVENTRY

For this offence be thou accurst of God.

EDWARD

Who's there?

[Enter guards]

Convey this priest to the Tower.

BISHOP OF COVENTRY

True, true!   200

[Exit BISHOP *and guards]*

EDWARD

But in the meantime Gaveston, away,
And take possession of his house and goods.
Come, follow me, and thou shalt have my guard
To see it done and bring thee safe again.

GAVESTON

What should a priest do with so fair a house?   205
A prison may beseem his holiness.

[Exeunt]

---

193   *rents* (i) revenues, income (ii) taxes levied by the Church
196   *bolts* fetters
197   *the Fleet* in Marlowe's time, a prison which stood between the River Thames and Ludgate Hill
198   *accurst* doomed to damnation
199   *Convey* Conduct, escort
203   *guard* (i) body of soldiers (ii) guardianship, safe conduct
205   *fair* fine, beautiful
206   *beseem* be fitting, more appropriate (because of the meagre conditions which are commonly associated with a priest's cell)

[Scene 2]

Enter both the MORTIMERS *[on one side]*, WARWICK,
and LANCASTER *[on the other]*

WARWICK

'Tis true, the Bishop is in the Tower,

And goods and body given to Gaveston.

LANCASTER

What, will they tyrannize upon the Church?

Ah, wicked King! Accursèd Gaveston!

This ground which is corrupted with their steps   5

Shall be their timeless sepulchre, or mine.

MORTIMER JUNIOR

Well, let that peevish Frenchman guard him sure;

Unless his breast be sword-proof he shall die.

MORTIMER SENIOR

How now, why droops the Earl of Lancaster?

MORTIMER JUNIOR

Wherefore is Guy of Warwick discontent?   10

LANCASTER

That villain Gaveston is made an earl.

MORTIMER SENIOR

An earl!

WARWICK

Ay, and besides, Lord Chamberlain of the realm,

And Secretary too, and Lord of Man.

MORTIMER SENIOR

We may not, nor we will not suffer this.   15

---

  0 s.d. Characters usually entered the Elizabethan stage through two or more doors set
into the rear wall. Entry through different doors (as editorially indicated here)
signified that they had come from different directions.

  3 *tyrannize* Edward is acting tyrannically in that, by imprisoning the Bishop, he is
usurping the spiritual power of the Church.

  6 *timeless* (i) eternal (ii) untimely
     sepulchre tomb, grave

  7 *peevish* foolish
     him himself
     sure securely

  11 *villain* (i) rascal, scoundrel (ii) serf, bondman (deriving from 'villein', one of low
birth)

  15 *suffer* tolerate

MORTIMER JUNIOR

Why post we not from hence to levy men?

LANCASTER

'My Lord of Cornwall' now at every word;
And happy is the man whom he vouchsafes
For vailing of his bonnet one good look.
Thus, arm in arm, the King and he doth march –   20
Nay more, the guard upon his lordship waits,
And all the court begins to natter him.

WARWICK

Thus leaning on the shoulder of the King,
He nods, and scorns, and smiles at those that pass.

MORTIMER SENIOR

Doth no man take exceptions at the slave?   25

LANCASTER

All stomach him, but none dare speak a word.

MORTIMER JUNIOR

Ah, that bewrays their baseness, Lancaster.
Were all the earls and barons of my mind,
We'll hale him from the bosom of the King,
And at the court gate hang the peasant up,   30
Who, swoll'n with venom of ambitious pride,
Will be the ruin of the realm and us.

> *Enter the* BISHOP OF CANTERBURY [, *talking to
> an* ATTENDANT]

WARWICK

Here comes my lord of Canterbury's grace.

LANCASTER

His countenance bewrays he is displeased.

---

16 *post* i.e. travel with speed
    levy men assemble soldiers
19 *vailing* doffing
24 *scorns* mocks
26 *stomach* resent
27 *bewrays* reveals
29 *hale* draw, drag
31 *Who . . . pride* Cf. *Dr Faustus*, 'Till swollen with cunning of a self-conceit' (A-Text,
    Chorus 1, 20).
33 *grace* i.e. his grace (formal term of address)
34 *countenance* face, demeanour
    bewrays betrays

BISHOP OF CANTERBURY [*To* ATTENDANT]

    First were his sacred garments rent and torn,   35

    Then laid they violent hands upon him next,

    Himself imprisoned and his goods asseized;

    This certify the Pope. Away, take horse.

                             [*Exit* ATTENDANT]

LANCASTER

    My lord, will you take arms against the King?

BISHOP OF CANTERBURY

    What need I? God himself is up in arms   40

    When violence is offered to the Church.

MORTIMER JUNIOR

    Then will you join with us that be his peers

    To banish or behead that Gaveston?

BISHOP OF CANTERBURY

    What else, my lords? For it concerns me near;

    The bishopric of Coventry is his.   45

Enter [ISABELLA] *the Queen*

MORTIMER JUNIOR

    Madam, whither walks your majesty so fast?

ISABELLA

    Unto the forest, gentle Mortimer,

    To live in grief and baleful discontent;

    For now my lord the King regards me not,

    But dotes upon the love of Gaveston.   50

    He claps his cheeks and hangs about his neck,

    Smiles in his face and whispers in his ears;

    And when I come he frowns, as who should say,

    'Go whither thou wilt, seeing I have Gaveston.'

---

35 s.p. *BISHOP OF CANTERBURY* ed. (*Bish.* Q; also at ll. 40, 44, 61, 68 and 75)

37 *asseized* seized

38 *certify* inform (with certainty)

44 *near* (i) deeply (ii) personally (in that, by becoming a bishop, Gaveston becomes a matter of direct concern to Canterbury)

45 *bishopric* diocese

47 s.p. *ISABELLA* ed. (*Que.* Q; and throughout the play text)
    forest wastelands; a metaphorical expression which describes Isabella's feelings of isolation
    gentle kind

48 *baleful* wretched

49 *regards* considers

51 *claps* slaps affectionately

MORTIMER SENIOR

Is it not strange that he is thus bewitched?   55

MORTIMER JUNIOR

Madam, return unto the court again.

That sly inveigling Frenchman we'll exile,

Or lose our lives; and yet, ere that day come,

The King shall lose his crown, for we have power

And courage too, to be revenged at full.   60

BISHOP OF CANTERBURY

But yet lift not your swords against the King.

LANCASTER

No, but we'll lift Gaveston from hence.

WARWICK

And war must be the means, or he'll stay still.

ISABELLA

Then let him stay; for rather than my lord

Shall be oppressed by civil mutinies,   65

I will endure a melancholy life,

And let him frolic with his minion.

BISHOP OF CANTERBURY

My lords, to ease all this but hear me speak.

We and the rest that are his councillors

Will meet and with a general consent   70

Confirm his banishment with our hands and seals.

LANCASTER

What we confirm the King will frustrate.

MORTIMER JUNIOR

Then may we lawfully revolt from him.

WARWICK

But say, my lord, where shall this meeting be?

BISHOP OF CANTERBURY

At the New Temple.   75

---

57   *inveigling* deceiving
58   *ere* before
62   *lift* (i) steal (ii) raise (by hanging)
63   *still* always
67   *frolic* make merry (with overtones of sexual promiscuity)
68   *but* only
72   *frustrate* annul, defeat
75   *New Temple* A building established and used by the Knights Templar until their suppression in 1308.

MORTIMER JUNIOR
  Content.
BISHOP OF CANTERBURY
  And in the meantime I'll entreat you all
  To cross to Lambeth, and there stay with me.
LANCASTER
  Come then, let's away.
MORTIMER JUNIOR
  Madam, farewell.   80
ISABELLA
  Farewell, sweet Mortimer; and for my sake,
  Forbear to levy arms against the King.
MORTIMER JUNIOR
  Ay, if words will serve; if not, I must.

                                              [*Exeunt*]

[Scene 3]

Enter GAVESTON *and the* EARL OF KENT

GAVESTON
  Edmund, the mighty prince of Lancaster,
  That hath more earldoms than an ass can bear,
  And both the Mortimers, two goodly men,
  With Guy of Warwick, that redoubted knight,
  Are gone towards Lambeth; there let them remain.   5

                                              Exeunt

77   s.p. BISHOP OF CANTERBURY ed. (not in Q): (*Mor. iu.* Content. And . . . all, / To
     crosse . . . me. Q)
78   *Lambeth* Lambeth Palace, the official residence of the Archbishop of Canterbury

  1 Gaveston addresses Kent familiarly by his personal name
  4 *redoubted* feared

[Scene 4]

Enter NOBLES [LANCASTER, WARWICK, PEMBROKE,
MORTIMER SENIOR, MORTIMER JUNIOR, *and the*
BISHOP OF CANTERBURY, *with attendants*]

LANCASTER

Here is the form of Gaveston's exile;

May it please your lordship to subscribe your name.

BISHOP OF CANTERBURY

Give me the paper.

LANCASTER

Quick, quick, my lord; I long to write my name.

WARWICK

But I long more to see him banished hence.   5

MORTIMER JUNIOR

The name of Mortimer shall fright the King,

Unless he be declined from that base peasant.

Enter [EDWARD] *the King and* GAVESTON[, *with* KENT]
[EDWARD *assumes the throne, with* GAVESTON *at his side*]

EDWARD

What, are you moved that Gaveston sits here?

It is our pleasure; we will have it so.

LANCASTER

Your grace doth well to place him by your side,   10

For nowhere else the new Earl is so safe.

MORTIMER SENIOR

What man of noble birth can brook this sight?

Quam male conveniunt!

---

0 s.d. Q uses the terms 'nobles' and 'barons' indifferently to refer to the rebel lords.

1 *form* document

3 s.p. BISHOP OF CANTERBURY ed. (*Bish* Q; and throughout the scene)

7 *declined* turned aside

8 *sits here* 'Gaveston's seat beside the king (where the queen would normally sit) is both emblematic and shocking; it signifies that Edward has made his lover politically equal with himself' (Forker).

9 *pleasure* will

11 *new Earl* The emphasis on 'new' reiterates the nobles' annoyance that such an 'upstart' has acquired, not inherited, his aristocratic status.

13 *Quam male conveniunt!* How badly they go together (i.e. match, suit one another)! Derived from Ovid's *Metamorphoses*, II. 846–7.

See what a scornful look the peasant casts.

PEMBROKE

Can kingly lions fawn on creeping ants?   15

WARWICK

Ignoble vassal, that like Phaëthon

Aspir'st unto the guidance of the sun.

MORTIMER JUNIOR

Their downfall is at hand, their forces down;

We will not thus be faced and over-peered.

EDWARD

Lay hands on that traitor Mortimer!   20

MORTIMER SENIOR

Lay hands on that traitor Gaveston!

                    [*The* NOBLES *draw swords*]

KENT

Is this the duty that you owe your King?

WARWICK

We know our duties; let him know his peers.

                    [*The* NOBLES *seize* GAVESTON]

EDWARD

Whither will you bear him? Stay, or ye shall die.

MORTIMER SENIOR

We are no traitors, therefore threaten not.   25

GAVESTON

No, threaten not, my lord, but pay them home.

Were I a king –

MORTIMER JUNIOR

Thou villain, wherefore talks thou of a king,

That hardly art a gentleman by birth?

EDWARD

Were he a peasant, being my minion,   30

14   *scornful* derisive, contemptuous
16   *Ignoble* of low birth
     vassal slave
     Phaëthon In classical mythology, the son of Phoebus Apollo (the sun god), who ignored warnings not to drive his father's chariot, lost control, and caused devastation on earth before the chariot was destroyed by Jupiter. In the sixteenth century, the story was commonly used as an emblem of the fall of overweening ambition. Cf. Ovid's *Metamorphoses*, I. 755ff.
19   *faced* bullied
     over-peered looked down upon (with pun on 'peer' = nobleman)
24   *bear* conduct, take
26   *pay them home* chastise them

I'll make the proudest of you stoop to him.

LANCASTER

My lord, you may not thus disparage us.

Away, I say, with hateful Gaveston.

MORTIMER SENIOR

And with the Earl of Kent that favours him.

[Exeunt GAVESTON *and* KENT *guarded]*

EDWARD

Nay, then lay violent hands upon your King.   35

Here, Mortimer, sit thou in Edward's throne;

Warwick and Lancaster, wear you my crown.

Was ever king thus overruled as I?

LANCASTER

Learn then to rule us better and the realm.

MORTIMER JUNIOR

What we have done, our heart-blood shall maintain.   40

WARWICK

Think you that we can brook this upstart pride?

EDWARD

Anger and wrathful fury stops my speech.

BISHOP OF CANTERBURY

Why are you moved? Be patient, my lord.

And see what we your councillors have done.

[He presents the document of GAVESTON'*s exile to* EDWARD*]*

MORTIMER JUNIOR

My lords, now let us all be resolute,   45

And either have our wills or lose our lives.

EDWARD

Meet you for this, proud overdaring peers?

Ere my sweet Gaveston shall part from me,

This isle shall fleet upon the ocean

And wander to the unfrequented Inde.   50

BISHOP OF CANTERBURY

You know that I am legate to the Pope;

On your allegiance to the See of Rome,

32   *disparage* vilify; 'originally meant to degrade by marrying to one of inferior rank'
       (Charlton and Waller)
47   *overdaring* imprudent, foolhardy
49   *fleet* float
50   *Inde* East Indies
51   *legate* deputy, representative

Subscribe as we have done to his exile.

MORTIMER JUNIOR

Curse him if he refuse, and then may we
Depose him and elect another king.   55

EDWARD

Ay, there it goes, but yet I will not yield.
Curse me. Depose me. Do the worst you can.

LANCASTER

Then linger not, my lord, but do it straight.

BISHOP OF CANTERBURY

Remember how the Bishop was abused;
Either banish him that was the cause thereof,   60
Or I will presently discharge these lords
Of duty and allegiance due to thee.

EDWARD

It boots me not to threat; I must speak fair,
The legate of the Pope will be obeyed.
My lord, you shall be Chancellor of the realm;   65
Thou Lancaster, High Admiral of our fleet.
Young Mortimer and his uncle shall be earls,
And you, Lord Warwick, President of the North,
[*To* PEMBROKE] And thou of Wales. If this content you not,
Make several kingdoms of this monarchy,   70
And share it equally amongst you all,
So I may have some nook or corner left
To frolic with my dearest Gaveston.

BISHOP OF CANTERBURY

Nothing shall alter us; we are resolved.

LANCASTER

Come, come, subscribe.   75

MORTIMER JUNIOR

Why should you love him whom the world hates so?

EDWARD

Because he loves me more than all the world.

54   *Curse* excommunicate
59   *abused* insulted, ill-used (violently)
61–2   The subjects of an excommunicated monarch were absolved of their duty of
       obedience; Elizabeth I had been excommunicated by Pope Pius V in 1570.
63   *boots* avails
68   *President of the North* Gill cites John Cowell's *The Interpreter* (1607): 'President ...
       is used in Common law for the kings Lieutenant in any Province or function; as
       President of Wales, of York, of Barwick.'

Ah, none but rude and savage-minded men
Would seek the ruin of my Gaveston;
You that be noble born should pity him.   80

WARWICK

You that are princely born should shake him off.
For shame subscribe, and let the lown depart.

MORTIMER SENIOR

Urge him, my lord.

BISHOP OF CANTERBURY

Are you content to banish him the realm?

EDWARD

I see I must, and therefore am content;   85
Instead of ink, I'll write it with my tears.

                                    [*He signs the document*]

MORTIMER JUNIOR

The King is love-sick for his minion.

EDWARD

'Tis done, and now accursèd hand fall off.

LANCASTER

Give it me; I'll have it published in the streets.

MORTIMER JUNIOR

I'll see him presently dispatched away.   90

BISHOP OF CANTERBURY

Now is my heart at ease.

WARWICK   And so is mine.

PEMBROKE

This will be good news to the common sort.

MORTIMER SENIOR

Be it or no, he shall not linger here.

                    Exeunt NOBLES[, *the* BISHOP OF CANTERBURY,
                                              and attendants]

EDWARD

How fast they run to banish him I love;
They would not stir, were it to do me good.   95
Why should a king be subject to a priest?

78   *rude* uncivilized
82   *lown* peasant
89   *published* proclaimed
90   *presently* immediately
92   *common sort* i.e. the common people
95   *stir* act

Proud Rome, that hatchest such imperial grooms,
For these thy superstitious taper-lights,
Wherewith thy antichristian churches blaze,
I'll fire thy crazèd buildings and enforce   100
The papal towers to kiss the lowly ground,
With slaughtered priests make Tiber's channel swell,
And banks raised higher with their sepulchres.
As for the peers that back the clergy thus,
If I be King, not one of them shall live.   105

Enter GAVESTON

GAVESTON
My lord, I hear it whispered everywhere
That I am banished and must fly the land.
EDWARD
'Tis true, sweet Gaveston. O were it false!
The legate of the Pope will have it so,
And thou must hence, or I shall be deposed.   110
But I will reign to be revenged of them,
And therefore, sweet friend, take it patiently.
Live where thou wilt – I'll send thee gold enough.
And long thou shalt not stay, or if thou dost,
I'll come to thee; my love shall ne'er decline.   115
GAVESTON
Is all my hope turned to this hell of grief?
EDWARD
Rend not my heart with thy too-piercing words.
Thou from this land, I from my self am banished.
GAVESTON
To go from hence grieves not poor Gaveston,
But to forsake you, in whose gracious looks   120
The blessedness of Gaveston remains,
For nowhere else seeks he felicity.

97   *imperial* imperious
     grooms servants
98   *taper-lights* candles for devotional and penitential use
100 *crazèd* shattered, unsound. Cf. *Massacre at Paris*, 'I'll fire his crazèd buildings, and
     incense / The papal towers to kiss the holy earth' (xxiv. 62–3)
102 *make* ed. (may Q)
     Tiber's channel the River Tiber in Rome
121 *blessedness* superlative happiness

355

EDWARD

    And only this torments my wretched soul,

    That whether I will or no, thou must depart.

    Be Governor of Ireland in my stead,   125

    And there abide till fortune call thee home.

    Here, take my picture, and let me wear thine.

                       [*They exchange miniatures*]

    O might I keep thee here, as I do this,

    Happy were I, but now most miserable.

GAVESTON

    'Tis something to be pitied of a king.   130

EDWARD

    Thou shalt not hence; I'll hide thee, Gaveston.

GAVESTON

    I shall be found, and then 'twill grieve me more.

EDWARD

    Kind words and mutual talk makes our grief greater.

    Therefore, with dumb embracement, let us part –

    Stay, Gaveston, I cannot leave thee thus.   135

GAVESTON

    For every look my lord drops down a tear;

    Seeing I must go, do not renew my sorrow.

EDWARD

    The time is little that thou hast to stay,

    And therefore give me leave to look my fill.

    But come, sweet friend, I'll bear thee on thy way.   140

GAVESTON

    The peers will frown.

EDWARD

    I pass not for their anger; come, let's go.

    O that we might as well return as go.

      Enter EDMUND [EARL OF KENT] *and Queen* ISABELLA

131   *hence* i.e. go
134   *dumb* silent
140   *bear* accompany   142 *pass* care
143   s.d. ed. (*Enter Edmund and Queen Isabell.* Q) Kent has no lines, and there is a
        problem in finding a suitable point for him to exit. Other editors have reasoned that
        his presence is superfluous, detracting from the dramatic tension between the three
        lovers, and have deleted him from the stage direction. However, his presence as a
        silent witness to Edward's behaviour contributes a political dimension to an other-
        wise exclusively personal sequence, and helps to clarify the character's confused
        loyalties and subsequent changing allegiances,

ISABELLA

    Whither goes my lord?

EDWARD

    Fawn not on me, French strumpet; get thee gone.   145

ISABELLA

    On whom but on my husband should I fawn?

GAVESTON

    On Mortimer, with whom, ungentle Queen –

    I say no more; judge you the rest, my lord.

ISABELLA

    In saying this, thou wrongst me, Gaveston.

    Is't not enough that thou corrupts my lord,   150

    And art a bawd to his affections,

    But thou must call mine honour thus in question?

GAVESTON

    I mean not so; your grace must pardon me.

EDWARD

    Thou art too familiar with that Mortimer,

    And by thy means is Gaveston exiled;   155

    But I would wish thee reconcile the lords,

    Or thou shalt ne'er be reconciled to me.

ISABELLA

    Your highness knows it lies not in my power.

EDWARD

    Away then, touch me not; come Gaveston.

ISABELLA

    Villain, 'tis thou that robb'st me of my lord.   160

GAVESTON

    Madam, 'tis you that rob me of my lord.

EDWARD

    Speak not unto her; let her droop and pine.

ISABELLA

    Wherein, my lord, have I deserved these words?

145   *strumpet* sexually loose woman, prostitute
147   Gaveston makes the first insinuation of adultery between Isabella and Mortimer
       Junior.
149   To accuse a woman unjustly of sexual misconduct was a grave misdemeanour in
       Elizabethan England.
150   *my lord* implying 'husband' as well as 'sovereign'
151   *bawd* procurer, pander
       affections (i) desires, inclinations (ii) passions (with sexual overtones)
163   *Wherein* in what

Witness the tears that Isabella sheds,
Witness this heart, that sighing for thee breaks,   165
How dear my lord is to poor Isabel.

EDWARD

And witness heaven how dear thou art to me.
There weep; for till my Gaveston be repealed,
Assure thyself thou com'st not in my sight.

Exeunt EDWARD *and* GAVESTON
[*; exit* KENT *at the other door*]

ISABELLA

O miserable and distressèd Queen!   170
Would when I left sweet France and was embarked,
That charming Circe, walking on the waves,
Had changed my shape, or at the marriage-day
The cup of Hymen had been full of poison,
Or with those arms that twined about my neck   175
I had been stifled, and not lived to see
The King my lord thus to abandon me.
Like frantic Juno will I fill the earth
With ghastly murmur of my sighs and cries,
For never doted Jove on Ganymede   180
So much as he on cursèd Gaveston.
But that will more exasperate his wrath;
I must entreat him, I must speak him fair,
And be a means to call home Gaveston.
And yet he'll ever dote on Gaveston,   185
And so am I forever miserable.

---

167   *witness . . . to me* At this point many productions have Edward and Gaveston embrace or kiss as lovers.

168   *repealed* recalled from exile

169   s.d. *the other door* cf. 2. 0 s.d. n.

172   *Circe* witch who turned Odysseus' men into pigs. See Homer's *Odyssey*, X and Ovid's *Metamorphoses*, XIV. 48ff.

174   *Hymen* god of marriage

175   *those arms* i.e. Edward's arms (embracing Isabella)

178–80   *frantic Juno . . . Ganymede* In classical mythology, Juno became jealous when her husband Jove chose Ganymede to be his cup-bearer on account of his beauty. Marlowe dramatizes this homoerotic liaison in *Dido, Queen of Carthage*, I.i. See also Ovid's *Metamorphoses*, X. 155–61.

179   *murmur* (i) rumour (ii) expression of discontent

182   *exasperate* irritate, aggravate

183   *entreat* negotiate with   *fair* with kindness, courteously

185   *ever* always

Enter the NOBLES [LANCASTER, WARWICK, PEMBROKE,
MORTIMER SENIOR, *and* MORTIMER JUNIOR]
to [ISABELLA] *the Queen*

LANCASTER

Look where the sister of the King of France
Sits wringing of her hands and beats her breast.

WARWICK

The King, I fear, hath ill entreated her.

PEMBROKE

Hard is the heart that injures such a saint.   190

MORTIMER JUNIOR

I know 'tis long of Gaveston she weeps.

MORTIMER SENIOR

Why? He is gone.

MORTIMER JUNIOR   Madam, how fares your grace?

ISABELLA

Ah, Mortimer! Now breaks the King's hate forth,
And he confesseth that he loves me not.

MORTIMER JUNIOR

Cry quittance, madam, then; and love not him.   195

ISABELLA

No, rather will I die a thousand deaths.
And yet I love in vain; he'll ne'er love me.

LANCASTER

Fear ye not, madam; now his minion's gone,
His wanton humour will be quickly left.

ISABELLA

O never, Lancaster! I am enjoined   200
To sue unto you all for his repeal.
This wills my lord, and this must I perform
Or else be banished from his highness' presence.

LANCASTER

For his repeal! Madam, he comes not back

189   *entreated* treated
191   *long of* on account of
195   *Cry quittance* (i) retaliate (ii) renounce the marriage bond (legal terminology)
199   *humour* temperament, disposition. The Elizabethans believed that humours or
       bodily fluids (phlegm, blood, choler, melancholy) were responsible for the state of
       a person's mind and body.
200   *enjoined* obliged, bound by oath
201   *sue* beg

Unless the sea cast up his shipwrack body. 205

WARWICK
And to behold so sweet a sight as that
There's none here but would run his horse to death.

MORTIMER JUNIOR
But madam, would you have us call him home?

ISABELLA
Ay, Mortimer, for till he be restored,
The angry King hath banished me the court; 210
And therefore, as thou lovest and tend'rest me,
Be thou my advocate unto these peers.

MORTIMER JUNIOR
What, would ye have me plead for Gaveston?

MORTIMER SENIOR
Plead for him he that will, I am resolved.

LANCASTER
And so am I; my lord, dissuade the Queen. 215

ISABELLA
O Lancaster, let him dissuade the King,
For 'tis against my will he should return.

WARWICK
Then speak not for him; let the peasant go.

ISABELLA
'Tis for myself I speak, and not for him.

PEMBROKE
No speaking will prevail, and therefore cease. 220

MORTIMER JUNIOR
Fair Queen, forbear to angle for the fish
Which, being caught, strikes him that takes it dead –
I mean that vile torpedo, Gaveston,
That now, I hope, floats on the Irish seas.

ISABELLA
Sweet Mortimer, sit down by me a while, 225
And I will tell thee reasons of such weight
As thou wilt soon subscribe to his repeal.

---

205   *cast* throw up, vomit
      shipwrack shipwrecked
211   *tend'rest* care for
223   *torpedo* electric ray, cramp-fish
224   *floats* sails
226   *weight* importance

MORTIMER JUNIOR

It is impossible; but speak your mind.

ISABELLA

Then thus – but none shall hear it but ourselves.

> [ISABELLA *and* MORTIMER JUNIOR *talk apart*]

LANCASTER

My lords, albeit the Queen win Mortimer, 230
Will you be resolute and hold with me?

MORTIMER SENIOR

Not I, against my nephew.

PEMBROKE

Fear not, the Queen's words cannot alter him.

WARWICK

No? Do but mark how earnestly she pleads.

LANCASTER

And see how coldly his looks make denial. 235

WARWICK

She smiles! Now, for my life, his mind is changed.

LANCASTER

I'll rather lose his friendship, I, than grant.

MORTIMER JUNIOR

[*Returning to them*] Well, of necessity, it must be so.
My lords, that I abhor base Gaveston
I hope your honours make no question; 240
And therefore, though I plead for his repeal,
'Tis not for his sake, but for our avail –
Nay, for the realm's behoof and for the King's.

LANCASTER

Fie Mortimer, dishonour not thyself!
Can this be true, 'twas good to banish him? 245
And is this true, to call him home again?
Such reasons make white black and dark night day.

MORTIMER JUNIOR

My lord of Lancaster, mark the respect.

---

234   *mark* observe
235   *make denial* refuse (to be persuaded)
237   *grant* assent, agree (to Isabella's will)
242   *avail* advantage
243   *behoof* benefit
247   *Such reasons . . . day* proverbial (Tilley B 440)
248   *respect* consideration, special circumstances

LANCASTER
In no respect can contraries be true.
ISABELLA
Yet, good my lord, hear what he can allege. 250
WARWICK
All that he speaks is nothing; we are resolved.
MORTIMER JUNIOR
Do you not wish that Gaveston were dead?
PEMBROKE
I would he were.
MORTIMER JUNIOR
Why then, my lord, give me but leave to speak.
MORTIMER SENIOR
But nephew, do not play the sophister. 255
MORTIMER JUNIOR
This which I urge is of a burning zeal
To mend the King and do our country good.
Know you not Gaveston hath store of gold,
Which may in Ireland purchase him such friends
As he will front the mightiest of us all? 260
And whereas he shall live and be beloved,
'Tis hard for us to work his overthrow.
WARWICK
Mark you but that, my lord of Lancaster.
MORTIMER JUNIOR
But were he here, detested as he is,
How easily might some base slave be suborned 265
To greet his lordship with a poniard,
And none so much as blame the murderer,
But rather praise him for that brave attempt,
And in the chronicle, enrol his name
For purging of the realm of such a plague. 270

251   *nothing* i.e. irrelevant
254   *give me . . . leave* allow me
255   *sophister* philosopher who uses fallacious arguments
257   *mend* reform
260   *front* confront
261   *whereas* while
262   *work* effect, bring about
265   *suborned* bribed
266   *poniard* dagger
268   *brave* excellent, worthy   *attempt* attack, assault

PEMBROKE
He saith true.

LANCASTER
Ay, but how chance this was not done before?

MORTIMER JUNIOR
Because, my lords, it was not thought upon.
Nay more, when he shall know it lies in us
To banish him, and then to call him home,   275
'Twill make him vail the topflag of his pride
And fear to offend the meanest nobleman.

MORTIMER SENIOR
But how if he do not, nephew?

MORTIMER JUNIOR
Then may we with some colour rise in arms,
For howsoever we have borne it out,   280
'Tis treason to be up against the King.
So shall we have the people of our side,
Which, for his father's sake, lean to the King
But cannot brook a night-grown mushroom –
Such a one as my lord of Cornwall is –   285
Should bear us down of the nobility.
And when the commons and the nobles join,
'Tis not the King can buckler Gaveston;
We'll pull him from the strongest hold he hath.
My lords, if to perform this I be slack,   290
Think me as base a groom as Gaveston.

LANCASTER
On that condition Lancaster will grant.

PEMBROKE
And so will Pembroke.

276   *vail* lower
277   *meanest* i.e. of the lowest rank
279   *colour* pretext
280   *howsoever . . . borne it out* however much we have endured
282   *of* on
284   *mushroom* ed. (mushrump Q1–4) Mushrooms grow overnight; hence a metaphor
      for an upstart, someone who has suddenly acquired reputation and influence.
      Proverbial (Tilley M 1319)
286   i.e. should overwhelm us, members of the nobility
288   *buckler* shield
289   *hold* stronghold, castle
293   s.p. PEMBROKE ed. (*War.* Q); (*one line in* Q And so will *Penbrooke* and *I.*)

WARWICK

    And I.

MORTIMER SENIOR

    And I.   295

MORTIMER JUNIOR

    In this I count me highly gratified,

    And Mortimer will rest at your command.

ISABELLA

    And when this favour Isabel forgets,

    Then let her live abandoned and forlorn.

> *Enter* KING EDWARD *mourning*[, *with* BEAUMONT,
> *the* CLERK OF THE CROWN, *and attendants*]

    But see, in happy time, my lord the King,   300

    Having brought the Earl of Cornwall on his way,

    Is new returned. This news will glad him much,

    Yet not so much as me; I love him more

    Than he can Gaveston. Would he loved me

    But half so much, then were I treble blessed.   305

EDWARD

    He's gone, and for his absence thus I mourn.

    Did never sorrow go so near my heart

    As doth the want of my sweet Gaveston;

    And could my crown's revènue bring him back,

    I would freely give it to his enemies   310

    And think I gained, having bought so dear a friend.

ISABELLA

    Hark how he harps upon his minion.

EDWARD

    My heart is as an anvil unto sorrow,

    Which beats upon it like the Cyclops' hammers,

    And with the noise turns up my giddy brain   315

    And makes me frantic for my Gaveston.

    Ah, had some bloodless Fury rose from hell,

---

296   *gratified* pleased, content

299   s.d. ed.; after line 303 in Q

314   *Cyclops* In classical mythology, one-eyed giants employed to forge thunderbolts for
        Jupiter.

315   *up* i.e. upside down

317   *Fury* In classical mythology, the Furies punished wrongdoers, and lived in Tartarus
        (a part of the underworld).

And with kingly sceptre struck me dead,
When I was forced to leave my Gaveston.

LANCASTER

Diablo! What passions call you these?   320

ISABELLA

My gracious lord, I come to bring you news.

EDWARD

That you have parlied with your Mortimer.

ISABELLA

That Gaveston, my lord, shall be repealed.

EDWARD

Repealed? The news is too sweet to be true.

ISABELLA

But will you love me if you find it so?   325

EDWARD

If it be so, what will not Edward do?

ISABELLA

For Gaveston, but not for Isabel.

EDWARD

For thee, fair Queen, if thou lov'st Gaveston;
I'll hang a golden tongue about thy neck,
Seeing thou hast pleaded with so good success.   330

                                        [*He embraces her*]

ISABELLA

No other jewels hang about my neck
Than these, my lord; nor let me have more wealth
Than I may fetch from this rich treasury.
O how a kiss revives poor Isabel.

EDWARD

Once more receive my hand, and let this be   335
A second marriage 'twixt thyself and me.

ISABELLA

And may it prove more happy than the first.
My gentle lord, bespeak these nobles fair

320   *Diablo!* (Spanish) The devil!
       passions (i) lamentations, passionate speeches (ii) intense expressions of love
324   *The news ... true* proverbial (Tilley N 156)
329   *golden tongue* an item of jewellery. Charlton and Waller cite *The Account of the Lord
       High Treasurer of Scotland* (*1488–92*), 'A grete serpent toung set with gold, perle and
       precious stanes'.
332   *Than these* i.e. Edward's arms (embracing her)
338   *bespeak* speak to

That wait attendance for a gracious look,
And on their knees salute your majesty.   340

[*The* NOBLES *kneel*]

EDWARD

Courageous Lancaster, embrace thy King,
And as gross vapours perish by the sun,
Even so let hatred with thy sovereign's smile;
Live thou with me as my companion.

LANCASTER

This salutation overjoys my heart.   345

EDWARD

Warwick, shall be my chiefest counsellor:
These silver hairs will more adorn my court
Than gaudy silks or rich embroidery.
Chide me, sweet Warwick, if I go astray.

WARWICK

Slay me, my lord, when I offend your grace.   350

EDWARD

In solemn triumphs and in public shows
Pembroke shall bear the sword before the King.

PEMBROKE

And with this sword Pembroke will fight for you.

EDWARD

But wherefore walks young Mortimer aside?
Be thou commander of our royal fleet,   355
Or if that lofty office like thee not,
I make thee here Lord Marshal of the realm.

MORTIMER JUNIOR

My lord, I'll marshal so your enemies
As England shall be quiet and you safe.

EDWARD

And as for you, Lord Mortimer of Chirke,   360
Whose great achievements in our foreign war
Deserves no common place nor mean reward,

342   *gross vapours* thick mists, fog
348   *gaudy* ornate
351   *triumphs . . . public shows* pageants, processions, public entertainments
352   *bear the sword* The sword of state symbolized justice and was carried at the front of
      processions before the monarch.
354   *aside* (i) to one side (ii) apart, away from a group
356   *like* please
360   *Chirke* i.e. Mortimer Senior, whose estate bordered Shropshire and Wales

Be you the general of the levied troops
That now are ready to assail the Scots.
MORTIMER SENIOR
    In this your grace hath highly honoured me,   365
    For with my nature war doth best agree.
ISABELLA
    Now is the King of England rich and strong,
    Having the love of his renownèd peers.
EDWARD
    Ay, Isabel, ne'er was my heart so light.
    Clerk of the Crown, direct our warrant forth   370
    For Gaveston to Ireland; Beaumont, fly
    As fast as Iris or Jove's Mercury.
BEAUMONT
    It shall be done, my gracious lord.
        [*Exit* BEAUMONT, *with the* CLERK OF THE CROWN]
EDWARD
    Lord Mortimer, we leave you to your charge.
    Now let us in and feast it royally   375
    Against our friend the Earl of Cornwall comes.
    We'll have a general tilt and tournament,
    And then his marriage shall be solemnized;
    For wot you not that I have made him sure
    Unto our cousin, the Earl of Gloucester's heir?   380
LANCASTER
    Such news we hear, my lord.
EDWARD
    That day, if not for him, yet for my sake,
    Who in the triumph will be challenger,
    Spare for no cost; we will requite your love.
WARWICK
    In this, or aught, your highness shall command us.   385

---

370   *Clerk of the Crown* an officer of Chancery responsible for framing and issuing writs
      of various sorts in both the House of Lords and the House of Commons
372   *Iris . . . Mercury* In classical mythology, Iris was the rainbow and the messenger of
      the gods; Mercury also served the latter function.
376   *Against* until
377   *tilt* joust
379   *sure* betrothed
380   *Earl of Gloucester's heir* i.e. Lady Margaret de Clare

EDWARD

    Thanks, gentle Warwick; come, let's in and revel.

                Exeunt [*all, except the* MORTIMERS]

MORTIMER SENIOR

    Nephew, I must to Scotland; thou stayest here.

    Leave now to oppose thyself against the King;

    Thou seest by nature he is mild and calm,

    And seeing his mind so dotes on Gaveston, 390

    Let him without controlment have his will.

    The mightiest kings have had their minions:

    Great Alexander loved Hephaestion;

    The conquering Hercules for Hylas wept;

    And for Patroclus stern Achilles drooped. 395

    And not kings only, but the wisest men:

    The Roman Tully loved Octavius,

    Grave Socrates, wild Alcibiades.

    Then let his grace, whose youth is flexible

    And promiseth as much as we can wish, 400

    Freely enjoy that vain light-headed Earl,

    For riper years will wean him from such toys.

MORTIMER JUNIOR

    Uncle, his wanton humour grieves not me,

    But this I scorn, that one so basely born

    Should by his sovereign's favour grow so pert, 405

    And riot it with the treasure of the realm

---

386   s.d. ed. (*Manent* Mortimers. Q)

391   *controlment* restraint

393   *Great Alexander . . . Hephaestion* Alexander III of Macedon (356–323 B.C.), the celebrated ruler, had an intimate friendship with the military commander Hephaestion (d. 325 B.C.).

394   *Hercules* ed. (*Hector* Q). See l. 143. It seems unlikely that Marlowe would here bungle a classical reference which he got right in an earlier scene; and the emended line is metrically superior if the word 'conquering' is disyllabic, as it usually is in Marlowe's verse.

395   *Achilles* In classical mythology, the Greek warrior who murdered Hector in the Trojan Wars following the death of Patroclus, his closest companion. This narrative is best known in Homer's *Iliad* and was later dramatized by Shakespeare in *Troilus and Cressida*, which intimates a homosexual relationship between the two warriors.

397   *Tully* Marcus Tullius Cicero (106–43 B.C.), the Roman statesman. Octavius Caesar (63 B.C.–A.D. 14), however, did not have any particular relationship with Cicero.

398   *Socrates* Greek philosopher (469–399 B.C.)

       Alcibiades Athenian politician (c. 450–404 B.C.) and pupil of Socrates, renowned for his beauty

402   *toys* trifles

While soldiers mutiny for want of pay.
He wears a lord's revènue on his back,
And Midas-like he jets it in the court
With base outlandish cullions at his heels,   410
Whose proud fantastic liveries make such show
As if that Proteus, god of shapes, appeared.
I have not seen a dapper jack so brisk;
He wears a short Italian hooded cloak,
Larded with pearl; and in his Tuscan cap   415
A jewel of more value than the crown.
Whiles other walk below, the King and he
From out a window laugh at such as we,
And flout our train and jest at our attire.
Uncle, 'tis this that makes me impatient.   420

MORTIMER SENIOR
But nephew, now you see the King is changed.

MORTIMER JUNIOR
Then so am I, and live to do him service;
But whiles I have a sword, a hand, a heart,
I will not yield to any such upstart.
You know my mind. Come, uncle, let's away.   425

Exeunt

408   *wears ... back* proverbial (Tilley L 452). Cf. *2 Henry VI*, 'She bears a duke's revenues
       on her back' (1.3.83).
409   *Midas* king of Phrygia who was granted the power to turn all that he touched to
       gold. Cf. Ovid's *Metamorphoses*, XI. 92ff
       jets it struts
410   *outlandish* foreign
       cullions low fellows
412   *Proteus* sea god who had the ability to change shape. Cf. Ovid's *Metamorphoses*, VIII.
       730–7.
413   *dapper jack* fashionable gentleman
       brisk smartly dressed
414–15 Gaveston's taste in clothes serves to emphasize his homosexuality, thought by the
       Elizabethans to be a particularly Italian vice.
415   *Larded* excessively decorated
       Tuscan cap a fashionable hat from Tuscany, made from finely woven straw
417   *other* others
419   *flout* mock
       train attendants

[Scene 5]

Enter SPENCER [JUNIOR] *and* BALDOCK

BALDOCK

Spencer,
Seeing that our lord th' Earl of Gloucester's dead,
Which of the nobles dost thou mean to serve?

SPENCER JUNIOR

Not Mortimer, nor any of his side,
Because the King and he are enemies.   5
Baldock, learn this of me: a factious lord
Shall hardly do himself good, much less us;
But he that hath the favour of a king
May with one word advance us while we live.
The liberal Earl of Cornwall is the man   10
On whose good fortune Spencer's hope depends.

BALDOCK

What, mean you then to be his follower?

SPENCER JUNIOR

No, his companion; for he loves me well
And would have once preferred me to the King.

BALDOCK

But he is banished; there's small hope of him.   15

SPENCER JUNIOR

Ay, for a while; but, Baldock, mark the end:
A friend of mine told me in secrecy
That he's repealed and sent for back again;
And even now, a post came from the court
With letters to our lady from the King,   20
And as she read, she smiled, which makes me think
It is about her lover, Gaveston.

BALDOCK

'Tis like enough, for since he was exiled,

1–2   ed. (*Spencer,* seeing . . . Glo- / sters dead, Q)
  6   *factious* seditious
 10   *liberal* (i) one who displays the qualities of a gentleman (ii) one who behaves licentiously
 12   *follower* retainer
 14   *preferred . . . to* (i) recommended to (ii) favoured more than (i.e. sexually)
 16   *end* conclusion
 20   *our lady* i.e. Margaret de Clare, daughter of the dead Earl of Gloucester

She neither walks abroad nor comes in sight.
But I had thought the match had been broke off   25
And that his banishment had changed her mind.

SPENCER JUNIOR

Our lady's first love is not wavering;
My life for thine, she will have Gaveston.

BALDOCK

Then hope I by her means to be preferred,
Having read unto her since she was a child.   30

SPENCER JUNIOR

Then, Baldock, you must cast the scholar off
And learn to court it like a gentleman.
'Tis not a black coat and a little band,
A velvet-caped cloak, faced before with serge,
And smelling to a nosegay all the day,   35
Or holding of a napkin in your hand,
Or saying a long grace at a table's end,
Or making low legs to a nobleman,
Or looking downward, with your eyelids close,
And saying, 'Truly, an't may please your honour',   40
Can get you any favour with great men.
You must be proud, bold, pleasant, resolute,
And now and then, stab, as occasion serves.

---

28   *My life . . . thine* proverbial (Dent L 260.1)
30   *Having read unto her* Baldock, an Oxford scholar, is portrayed as Margaret de Clare's
     tutor.
31   *cast the scholar off* i.e. cease to behave like an academic
32   *court it* behave like a courtier
33–4 Spencer Junior 'gives a thumbnail sketch of the typical poor scholar who failed to
     achieve academic preferment and was compelled to take up duties in a nobleman's
     household, tutoring the children and acting as domestic chaplain' (Gill). Many
     editors cite John Earle's 'A young raw Preacher' in his *Micro-cos-mographie* (1628),
     'His fashion and demure habit gets him in with some town-precisian, and makes
     him a guest on Friday nights. You shall know him by his narrow veluet cape, and
     serge facing, and his ruffe, next his haire, the shortest thing about him' (Sig. B4[V]).
33   *black coat . . . little band* subfusc or academic dress
34   *faced* trimmed, patched   *serge* cheap woollen material
35   *nosegay* posy, bunch of flowers
37   *table's end* the bottom end of the table (below the salt) which signified the lowest
     position of social status
38   *low legs* deferential, obeisant bowing
40   *an't* if it
42   *pleasant* jocular
43   *stab* with pun on sexual thrusting

371

BALDOCK

Spencer, thou knowest I hate such formal toys,
And use them but of mere hypocrisy.   45
Mine old lord, whiles he lived, was so precise
That he would take exceptions at my buttons,
And, being like pins' heads, blame me for the bigness,
Which made me curate-like in mine attire,
Though inwardly licentious enough   50
And apt for any kind of villainy.
I am none of these common pedants, I,
That cannot speak without '*propterea quod*'.

SPENCER JUNIOR

But one of those that saith '*quandoquidem*'
And hath a special gift to form a verb.   55

BALDOCK

Leave off this jesting – here my lady comes.

                                          [*They withdraw*]

   Enter the LADY [MARGARET DE CLARE, *with letters*]

LADY MARGARET

The grief for his exile was not so much
As is the joy of his returning home.
This letter came from my sweet Gaveston.

                                    [*She reads the letter*]

What needst thou love, thus to excuse thyself?   60
I know thou couldst not come and visit me.

---

44   *formal toys* trivial formalities, conventions
46   *old* former
     whiles while
     precise punctilious, puritanical
47   *take exceptions at* find fault with
50   *licentious* (i) unrestrained, indecorous (ii) given to sexual licence
51   *apt* ready, prepared
52   *common* ordinary
     pedants ed. (pendants Q; pedants Q2–4) schoolmasters, tutors
53, 54   *propterea quod, quandoquidem* Even though both expressions mean 'because', the former phrase (as suggested by Briggs) is prosaic and less refined than the verse of 'quandoquidem'; perhaps varsity humour is implied. Arguably, their use of Latin ridicules the affected rhetoric of scholarship.
55   *to form* to conjugate
56   *off* ed. (of Q)
56   s.d. 1 *They withdraw* They move to the side of the stage, and Lady Margaret is apparently unaware of their presence, watching and overhearing her.

'I will not long be from thee, though I die':
This argues the entire love of my lord;
'When I forsake thee, death seize on my heart.'
But rest thee here where Gaveston shall sleep.   65

[She places the letter in her bosom]

Now to the letter of my lord the King.

[She reads another letter]

He wills me to repair unto the court
And meet my Gaveston. Why do I stay,
Seeing that he talks thus of my marriage-day?
Who's there? Baldock?   70

[BALDOCK *and* SPENCER JUNIOR *come forward*]

See that my coach be ready; I must hence.
BALDOCK
It shall be done, madam.
LADY MARGARET
And meet me at the park pale presently.

Exit [BALDOCK]

Spencer, stay you and bear me company,
For I have joyful news to tell thee of.   75
My lord of Cornwall is a-coming over
And will be at the court as soon as we.
SPENCER JUNIOR
I knew the King would have him home again.
LADY MARGARET
If all things sort out, as I hope they will,
Thy service, Spencer, shall be thought upon.   80
SPENCER JUNIOR
I humbly thank your ladyship.
LADY MARGARET
Come, lead the way; I long till I am there.

[Exeunt]

---

67   *repair* come
71   *coach* In fact, coaches were not ordinarily used in England until after 1564.
73   *park pale* the fencing of an estate or park
       presently directly
73   s.d. ed. (*Exit.* Q after 'madam', line 72)
74   *bear me company* i.e. keep me company
82   *long* am restless

[Scene 6]

Enter EDWARD, [ISABELLA] *the Queen,* LANCASTER, MORTIMER
    [JUNIOR], WARWICK, PEMBROKE, KENT, *attendants*

EDWARD

The wind is good, I wonder why he stays.
I fear me he is wrecked upon the sea.

ISABELLA

Look, Lancaster, how passionate he is,
And still his mind runs on his minion.

LANCASTER

My lord –   5

EDWARD

How now, what news? Is Gaveston arrived?

MORTIMER JUNIOR

Nothing but Gaveston! What means your grace?
You have matters of more weight to think upon;
The King of France sets foot in Normandy.

EDWARD

A trifle! We'll expel him when we please.   10
But tell me, Mortimer, what's thy device
Against the stately triumph we decreed?

MORTIMER JUNIOR

A homely one, my lord, not worth the telling.

EDWARD

Prithee let me know it.

MORTIMER JUNIOR

But seeing you are so desirous, thus it is: 15
A lofty cedar tree fair flourishing,
On whose top branches kingly eagles perch,
And by the bark a canker creeps me up

3   *passionate* grief-stricken, sorrowful
4   *runs on* is preoccupied with
9   Normandy was part of English crown territory; cf. 11. 64.
11 *device* an heraldic emblem (painted on a shield)
12 *Against* prepared for
    triumph public entertainment, pageant, festival
13 *homely* plain, not ostentatious
16 *lofty* A latent double meaning implies Gaveston's arrogance.
    cedar tree symbol of the structure of society with the King represented by the highest
    bough
18 *canker* worm which consumes plants   *creeps me up* creeps up

374

And gets unto the highest bough of all;
The motto: *Æque tandem.*   20

EDWARD

And what is yours, my lord of Lancaster?

LANCASTER

My lord, mine's more obscure than Mortimer's:
Pliny reports there is a flying fish
Which all the other fishes deadly hate,
And therefore, being pursued, it takes the air;   25
No sooner is it up, but there's a fowl
That seizeth it. This fish, my lord, I bear;
The motto this: *Undique mors est.*

EDWARD

Proud Mortimer! Ungentle Lancaster!
Is this the love you bear your sovereign?   30
Is this the fruit your reconcilement bears?
Can you in words make show of amity,
And in your shields display your rancorous minds?
What call you this but private libelling
Against the Earl of Cornwall and my brother?   35

ISABELLA

Sweet husband, be content; they all love you.

EDWARD

They love me not that hate my Gaveston.
I am that cedar; shake me not too much.
And you the eagles; soar ye ne'er so high,
I have the jesses that will pull you down,   40
And '*Æque tandem*' shall that canker cry
Unto the proudest peer of Britainy.

20 *Æque tandem* (Latin) Equal in height. Mortimer Junior is suggesting that Gaveston is the canker which is infecting the state, moving from the base (i.e. the commons) to the top (i.e. the nobility).
21 *yours* i.e. the device on Lancaster's shield
22 *obscure* hard to interpret
23 *Pliny* Gaius Plinius Secundus or Pliny the Elder (A.D. 23/4–79), Roman scholar and naturalist best known for his *Naturalis Historia* (A.D. 77)
28 *Undique mors est* (Latin) Death is on all sides.
31 *reconcilement* reconciliation
34 *libelling* Rowland points out that this is an anachronism: 'libel in the sense of a defamatory document or statement was a sixteenth-century development'.
35 *my brother* i.e. Gaveston
40 *jesses* (gresses Q) straps which were fastened to the legs of hawks
42 *Britainy* Britain (England and Scotland)

Though thou compar'st him to a flying fish,
And threatenest death whether he rise or fall,
'Tis not the hugest monster of the sea   45
Nor foulest harpy that shall swallow him.

MORTIMER JUNIOR

[*To the* NOBLES] If in his absence thus he favours him,
What will he do whenas he shall be present?

Enter GAVESTON

LANCASTER

That shall we see: look where his lordship comes.

EDWARD

My Gaveston!   50
Welcome to Tynemouth, welcome to thy friend.
Thy absence made me droop and pine away;
For as the lovers of fair Danaë,
When she was locked up in a brazen tower,
Desired her more and waxed outrageous,   55
So did it sure with me; and now thy sight
Is sweeter far than was thy parting hence
Bitter and irksome to my sobbing heart.

GAVESTON

Sweet lord and King, your speech preventeth mine,
Yet have I words left to express my joy: 60
The shepherd nipped with biting winter's rage
Frolics not more to see the painted spring
Than I do to behold your majesty.

43–6   Edward draws upon the images of the flying fish and the fowl (from Lancaster's
       description of his device) and exaggerates them in order to undermine the verbal
       assaults of the two nobles.
   46   *harpy* in classical mythology, bird-like creatures with female faces and breasts, which
       stole food and harassed Phineus, the blind King of Thrace, when he entertained the
       Argonauts
   48   *whenas* when
   48   s.d. ed.; after line 49 in Q
   53   *Danaë* In classical mythology, she was incarcerated by her father in a bronze tower
       after an oracle prophesied that her son would murder him; Jupiter then visited her
       in a shower of gold and she conceived the hero Perseus.
   55   *waxed* grew
       outrageous unrestrained (four syllables)
   59   *preventeth* anticipates
   62   *painted* colourful, decorated with flowers

EDWARD

    Will none of you salute my Gaveston?

LANCASTER

    Salute him? Yes! Welcome, Lord Chamberlain.   65

MORTIMER JUNIOR

    Welcome is the good Earl of Cornwall.

WARWICK

    Welcome, Lord Governor of the Isle of Man.

PEMBROKE

    Welcome, Master Secretary.

KENT

    Brother, do you hear them?

EDWARD

    Still will these earls and barons use me thus!   70

GAVESTON

    My lord, I cannot brook these injuries.

ISABELLA

    [*Aside*] Ay me, poor soul, when these begin to jar.

EDWARD

    Return it to their throats; I'll be thy warrant.

GAVESTON

    Base leaden earls that glory in your birth,

    Go sit at home and eat your tenants' beef,   75

    And come not here to scoff at Gaveston,

    Whose mounting thoughts did never creep so low

    As to bestow a look on such as you.

LANCASTER

    Yet I disdain not to do this for you.   [*Draws his sword*]

EDWARD

    Treason, treason! Where's the traitor?

PEMBROKE [*Indicating* GAVESTON]   Here, here!   80

---

70   *use* behave towards, treat

72   *jar* quarrel, wrangle

73   *Return . . . throats* i.e. reject their abuse, 'give them the lie' (a provocative act, normally a formal challenge to a duel); cf. Shakespeare, *Titus Andronicus*, 2.1.53–6 *warrant* document of authorization

74   *Base leaden* Gaveston likens the nobles to the dullness of cheap alloy coins, with a latent pun on the name of a gold coin, a 'noble'.

75   *eat . . . beef* an insult, implying that the nobles are 'beef-witted' (stupid, brainless). Forker suggests that Frenchmen such as Gaveston regarded the English as great eaters of beef.

79   s.d. It was an offence to brandish weapons in the King's presence.

EDWARD

Convey hence Gaveston; they'll murder him.

GAVESTON

The life of thee shall salve this foul disgrace.

MORTIMER JUNIOR

Villain, thy life, unless I miss mine aim.

[*He wounds* GAVESTON]

ISABELLA

Ah, furious Mortimer, what hast thou done?

MORTIMER JUNIOR

No more than I would answer were he slain.   85

[*Exit* GAVESTON, *attended*]

EDWARD

Yes, more than thou canst answer, though he live;

Dear shall you both aby this riotous deed.

Out of my presence! Come not near the court.

MORTIMER JUNIOR

I'll not be barred the court for Gaveston.

LANCASTER

We'll hale him by the ears unto the block.   90

EDWARD

Look to your own heads; his is sure enough.

WARWICK

Look to your own crown, if you back him thus.

KENT

Warwick, these words do ill beseem thy years.

EDWARD

Nay, all of them conspire to cross me thus;

But if I live, I'll tread upon their heads   95

That think with high looks thus to tread me down.

80–1   ed. Q erroneously prints Edward's line and speech prefix as part of
Pembroke's dialogue. (Heere here King: conuey ... thalle / murder him.)

82   *salve* atone, remedy (vindication is implied)

85   *answer* answer for

87   *both* i.e. Mortimer Junior and Lancaster
aby pay for, atone
riotous wanton, amoral

90   *hale* drag, pull (forcibly)

91   *sure* safe

93   *ill beseem ... years* i.e. you should display greater wisdom and prudence, considering
your age

94   *cross* obstruct, thwart

Come, Edmund, let's away and levy men;
'Tis war that must abate these barons' pride.

Exit [EDWARD] *the King*[, *with* ISABELLA *and* KENT]

WARWICK

Let's to our castles, for the King is moved.

MORTIMER JUNIOR

Moved may he be and perish in his wrath.   100

LANCASTER

Cousin, it is no dealing with him now.
He means to make us stoop by force of arms,
And therefore let us jointly here protest
To prosecute that Gaveston to the death.

MORTIMER JUNIOR

By heaven, the abject villain shall not live.   105

WARWICK

I'll have his blood or die in seeking it.

PEMBROKE

The like oath Pembroke takes.

LANCASTER   And so doth Lancaster.
Now send our heralds to defy the King
And make the people swear to put him down.

Enter a POST

MORTIMER JUNIOR

Letters? From whence?   110

POST

From Scotland, my lord.

LANCASTER

Why how now, cousin, how fares all our friends?

MORTIMER JUNIOR

[*Reading a letter*] My uncle's taken prisoner by the Scots.

LANCASTER

---

101   *Cousin* used more broadly than in modern English, to denote a variety of kinship
      and other associations
      it is there is
102   *stoop* submit
103   *protest* vow
104   *prosecute* pursue
105   *abject* most contemptible, servile
108   *heralds* messengers or officials used in time of war to carry messages to the enemy
109   s.d. POST messenger
111   s.p. POST ed. (*Messen.* Q)

We'll have him ransomed, man; be of good cheer.

MORTIMER JUNIOR

They rate his ransom at five thousand pound.   115
Who should defray the money but the King,
Seeing he is taken prisoner in his wars?
I'll to the King.

LANCASTER

Do cousin, and I'll bear thee company.

WARWICK

Meantime, my lord of Pembroke and myself   120
Will to Newcastle here and gather head.

MORTIMER JUNIOR

About it then, and we will follow you.

LANCASTER

Be resolute and full of secrecy.

WARWICK

I warrant you.

> [*Exeunt all but* MORTIMER JUNIOR *and* LANCASTER]

MORTIMER JUNIOR

Cousin, an if he will not ransom him,   125
I'll thunder such a peal into his ears
As never subject did unto his king.

LANCASTER

Content; I'll bear my part. Holla! Who's there?

> [*Enter a* GUARD]

MORTIMER JUNIOR

Ay, marry, such a guard as this doth well.

LANCASTER

Lead on the way.

GUARD   Whither will your lordships?   130

MORTIMER JUNIOR

Whither else but to the King?

GUARD

His highness is disposed to be alone.

---

116   *defray* pay for, settle the payment
121   *gather head* raise forces
123   *resolute* determined
124   *warrant* give assurance
128   *Content* agreed
129   *marry* to be sure (contracted form of the affirmation 'By Mary')

LANCASTER

Why, so he may, but we will speak to him.

GUARD

You may not in, my lord.

MORTIMER JUNIOR

May we not? 135

[*Enter* EDWARD *and* KENT]

EDWARD

How now, what noise is this?

Who have we there? Is't you?

[*He makes to exit, ignoring* MORTIMER JUNIOR
and LANCASTER]

MORTIMER JUNIOR

Nay, stay, my lord; I come to bring you news:

Mine uncle's taken prisoner by the Scots.

EDWARD

Then ransom him. 140

LANCASTER

'Twas in your wars: you should ransom him.

MORTIMER JUNIOR

And you shall ransom him, or else –

KENT

What, Mortimer, you will not threaten him?

EDWARD

Quiet yourself; you shall have the broad seal

To gather for him thoroughout the realm. 145

LANCASTER

Your minion Gaveston hath taught you this.

MORTIMER JUNIOR

My lord, the family of the Mortimers

Are not so poor but, would they sell their land,

Would levy men enough to anger you.

We never beg, but use such prayers as these. 150

[*He puts his hand on the hilt of his sword*]

---

134   *in* i.e. enter the King's chamber

144   *broad seal* letters patent giving the bearer the right to raise money for a specific purpose without being prosecuted for begging. Edward's offer insultingly implies that Mortimer Junior is impoverished.

145   *gather* collect money

     thoroughout throughout

EDWARD

Shall I still be haunted thus?

MORTIMER JUNIOR

Nay, now you are here alone, I'll speak my mind.

LANCASTER

And so will I; and then, my lord, farewell.

MORTIMER JUNIOR

The idle triumphs, masques, lascivious shows,

And prodigal gifts bestowed on Gaveston   155

Have drawn thy treasure dry and made thee weak;

The murmuring commons overstretchèd hath.

LANCASTER

Look for rebellion, look to be deposed:

Thy garrisons are beaten out of France,

And, lame and poor, lie groaning at the gates;   160

The wild O'Neill, with swarms of Irish kerns,

Lives uncontrolled within the English pale;

Unto the walls of York the Scots made road

And, unresisted, drave away rich spoils.

MORTIMER JUNIOR

The haughty Dane commands the narrow seas,   165

While in the harbour ride thy ships unrigged.

LANCASTER

What foreign prince sends thee ambassadors?

151   *haunted* persistently molested
154   *idle* vain, worthless
155   *prodigal* lavish, extravagant
156   *drawn* emptied, drained
      treasure treasury
157   *murmuring* discontented, disgruntled
      commons the common people
      overstretched i.e. created an intolerable strain
161   *The . . . O'Neill* prominent Ulster clan chieftain, not mentioned in the sources. In
      1592, the title was contested; it was conferred on Hugh O'Neill, 2nd Earl of Tyrone,
      in May 1593.
      Irish kerns footsoldiers, commonly recruited from the poorer class of the 'wild Irish'
162   *English pale* an area of land around Dublin established for the protection of English
      settlers
163   *made road* raided
164   *drave* drove
      spoils plunder, booty
165   *the narrow seas* the English Channel
166   *ride* lie at anchor
      unrigged without their rigging

MORTIMER JUNIOR

    Who loves thee but a sort of flatterers?

LANCASTER

    Thy gentle Queen, sole sister to Valois,

    Complains that thou hast left her all forlorn.   170

MORTIMER JUNIOR

    Thy court is naked, being bereft of those

    That makes a king seem glorious to the world –

    I mean the peers whom thou shouldst dearly love.

    Libels are cast again thee in the street,

    Ballads and rhymes made of thy overthrow.   175

LANCASTER

    The northern borderers, seeing their houses burnt,

    Their wives and children slain, run up and down

    Cursing the name of thee and Gaveston.

MORTIMER JUNIOR

    When wert thou in the field with banner spread?

    But once! And then thy soldiers marched like players,   180

    With garish robes, not armour; and thyself,

    Bedaubed with gold, rode laughing at the rest,

    Nodding and shaking of thy spangled crest

    Where women's favours hung like labels down.

LANCASTER

    And thereof came it that the fleering Scots,   185

    To England's high disgrace, have made this jig:

      'Maids of England, sore may you mourn.

---

168   *sort* group
169   *Valois* i.e. Philip, King of France (family name)
170   *forlorn* desolate, abandoned
171   *naked* destitute
172   *seem* appear
174   *Libels* subversive pamphlets
       again against
175   *Ballads and rhymes* In Elizabethan England, these were the cheapest and most demotic form of literature, costing one penny.
176   *their* ed. (the Q)
180   *players* actors
183   *crest* the plume or decoration on the top of a helmet
184   *favours* tokens of affection or keepsakes (gloves, scarves) given by ladies to knights and worn either in battle or in a tournament
       labels slips of paper or parchment for attaching seals to documents
185   *fleering* sneering, jeering
186   *jig* insulting song or ballad

For your lemans you have lost at Bannockburn.
   With a heave and a ho.
What weeneth the King of England,   190
   So soon to have won Scotland?
With a rumbelow.'

MORTIMER JUNIOR

Wigmore shall fly, to set my uncle free.

LANCASTER

And when 'tis gone, our swords shall purchase more.
If ye be moved, revenge it as you can;   195
Look next to see us with our ensigns spread.

      Exeunt NOBLES [LANCASTER *and* MORTIMER JUNIOR]

EDWARD

My swelling heart for very anger breaks!
How oft have I been baited by these peers
And dare not be revenged, for their power is great?
Yet, shall the crowing of these cockerels   200
Affright a lion? Edward, unfold thy paws
And let their lives' blood slake thy fury's hunger.
If I be cruel and grow tyrannous,
Now let them thank themselves and rue too late.

KENT

My lord, I see your love to Gaveston   205
Will be the ruin of the realm and you,
For now the wrathful nobles threaten wars;
And therefore, brother, banish him forever.

EDWARD

Art thou an enemy to my Gaveston?

KENT

Ay, and it grieves me that I favoured him.   210

---

188   *lemans* sweethearts
      Bannockburn The battle of Bannockburn (24 June 1314) ended in the defeat of
      Edward's forces following an attempt to secure Stirling Castle from the Scots. The
      Q spelling, 'Bannocksborne', emphasizes the rhyme.
190   *weeneth* hopes, expects
192   *rumbelow* meaningless refrain which maintains the rhyme of the song
193   *Wigmore* Wigmore Castle (Mortimer Junior's Herefordshire estate)
      shall fly i.e. shall be sold
194   *purchase* earn, acquire
196   *ensigns* banners (displayed by each side in battle)
200–1 *cockerels . . . lion* The lion was, in fact, proverbially afraid of the cock's crowing; see
      MLN 50 (1935), 352–4.

EDWARD

Traitor, be gone; whine thou with Mortimer.

KENT

So will I, rather than with Gaveston.

EDWARD

Out of my sight, and trouble me no more.

KENT

No marvel though thou scorn thy noble peers,
When I thy brother am rejected thus.   215

EDWARD

Away!

Exit [KENT]

Poor Gaveston, that hast no friend but me.
Do what they can, we'll live in Tynemouth here.
And, so I walk with him about the walls,
What care I though the earls begirt us round?   220

> *Enter* [ISABELLA] *the Queen, three ladies*
> [MARGARET DE CLARE *with two ladies in waiting,*
> GAVESTON], BALDOCK, *and* SPENCER [JUNIOR]

Here comes she that's cause of all these jars.

ISABELLA

My lord, 'tis thought the earls are up in arms.

EDWARD

Ay, and 'tis likewise thought you favour him.

ISABELLA

Thus do you still suspect me without cause.

LADY MARGARET

Sweet uncle, speak more kindly to the Queen.   225

GAVESTON [*Aside to* EDWARD]

My lord, dissemble with her, speak her fair.

EDWARD

Pardon me, sweet, I forgot myself.

ISABELLA

Your pardon is quickly got of Isabel.

216–17 ed. (one line in Q)
  220 *begirt* surround, enclose
  220 s.d. ed. (after 221 in Q: *Enter the Queene, Ladies 3, Baldock, / and Spencer.*)
  223 *him* Mortimer Junior; Edward is more preoccupied with personal than political betrayal
  226 *fair* courteously

EDWARD

> The younger Mortimer is grown so brave
> That to my face he threatens civil wars. 230

GAVESTON

> Why do you not commit him to the Tower?

EDWARD

> I dare not, for the people love him well.

GAVESTON

> Why then, we'll have him privily made away.

EDWARD

> Would Lancaster and he had both caroused
> A bowl of poison to each other's health. 235
> But let them go, and tell me what are these?

LADY MARGARET

> Two of my father's servants whilst he lived;
> May't please your grace to entertain them now.

EDWARD

> Tell me, where wast thou born? What is thine arms?

BALDOCK

> My name is Baldock, and my gentry 240
> I fetched from Oxford, not from heraldry.

EDWARD

> The fitter art thou, Baldock, for my turn;
> Wait on me, and I'll see thou shalt not want.

BALDOCK

> I humbly thank your majesty.

EDWARD

> Knowest thou him, Gaveston?

GAVESTON   Ay, my lord. 245

> His name is Spencer; he is well allied.

---

229   *brave* defiant, impertinent
233   *privily made away* secretly murdered
234   *caroused* quaffed
235   *health* well-being, prosperity (with ironic pun on physical health)
236   *let them go* i.e. enough talk of them (Forker)
238   *entertain* take into service, employ
239   ed. (Tell . . . borne? / What . . . armes? Q)   *arms* coat of arms
240   *gentry* rank (of a gentleman)
241   *fetched . . . Oxford* The status of a gentleman could be acquired through having been educated at Oxford.
       heraldry heraldic title, rank
245–6   ed. (*Edw.* Knowest . . . *Gaueston?* / *Gau.* I. . . alied, Q)
246   *well allied* well connected, of good birth

For my sake let him wait upon your grace;
Scarce shall you find a man of more desert.

EDWARD

Then, Spencer, wait upon me; for his sake
I'll grace thee with a higher style ere long.   250

SPENCER JUNIOR

No greater titles happen unto me
Than to be favoured of your majesty.

EDWARD [*To* LADY MARGARET]

Cousin, this day shall be your marriage feast.
And, Gaveston, think that I love thee well
To wed thee to our niece, the only heir   255
Unto the Earl of Gloucester late deceased.

GAVESTON

I know, my lord, many will stomach me,
But I respect neither their love nor hate.

EDWARD

The headstrong barons shall not limit me;
He that I list to favour shall be great.   260
Come, let's away; and when the marriage ends,
Have at the rebels and their complices.

Exeunt

[Scene 7]

Enter LANCASTER, MORTIMER [JUNIOR], WARWICK,
PEMBROKE, KENT

KENT

My lords, of love to this our native land
I come to join with you and leave the King;
And in your quarrel and the realm's behoof

---

250   *style* title, status
251   *happen unto me* i.e. could befall me
252   *of* by
253   *Cousin* Cf. 101 n. above.
257   *stomach* resent
260   *list* choose
262   *Have at* attack
        complices confederates

3   *behoof* benefit

Will be the first that shall adventure life.

LANCASTER

    I fear me you are sent of policy   5

    To undermine us with a show of love.

WARWICK

    He is your brother; therefore have we cause

    To cast the worst and doubt of your revolt.

KENT

    Mine honour shall be hostage of my truth;

    If that will not suffice, farewell, my lords.   10

MORTIMER JUNIOR

    Stay, Edmund; never was Plantagenet

    False of his word, and therefore trust we thee.

PEMBROKE

   But what's the reason you should leave him now?

KENT

    I have informed the Earl of Lancaster.

LANCASTER

    And it sufficeth. Now, my lords, know this,   15

    That Gaveston is secretly arrived,

    And here in Tynemouth frolics with the King.

    Let us with these our followers scale the walls,

    And suddenly surprise them unawares.

MORTIMER JUNIOR

    I'll give the onset.

WARWICK   And I'll follow thee.   20

MORTIMER JUNIOR

    This tattered ensign of my ancestors,

    Which swept the desert shore of that dead sea

    Whereof we got the name of Mortimer,

    Will I advance upon these castle walls.

    Drums strike alarum! Raise them from their sport,   25

    4   *adventure* risk

    5   *of policy* i.e. out of deceit, under false pretences

    8   *cast* reckon, fear

         doubt of suspect

   17   *frolics* makes merry (the verb also has sexual connotations)

 22–3   The Mortimers came from Mortemer in Normandy, and were not, as Marlowe

         suggests, connected with the Crusades and the Dead Sea (*Mortuum Mare* in Latin).

  24   *these* ed. (this Q) The Q reading could make sense if 'castle' is taken to be a genitive

        with silent final *-s*.

  25   *alarum* call to arms, battle-cry

       sport idle pastimes, amusements

And ring aloud the knell of Gaveston.   [*Alarums*]

LANCASTER

None be so hardy as to touch the King;

But neither spare you Gaveston nor his friends.

Exeunt

[Scene 8]

Enter [EDWARD] *the King and* SPENCER [JUNIOR;*
from another door enter] *to them* GAVESTON[*, unseen by*
EDWARD *and* SPENCER JUNIOR; *with* ISABELLA,
LADY MARGARET DE CLARE, *and attendants*]

EDWARD

O tell me, Spencer, where is Gaveston?

SPENCER JUNIOR

I fear me he is slain, my gracious lord.

EDWARD

No, here he comes! Now let them spoil and kill.

Fly, fly, my lords; the earls have got the hold.

Take shipping and away to Scarborough;   5

Spencer and I will post away by land.

GAVESTON

O stay, my lord; they will not injure you.

EDWARD

I will not trust them, Gaveston. Away!

GAVESTON

Farewell, my lord.

EDWARD

Lady, farewell.   10

LADY MARGARET

Farewell, sweet uncle, till we meet again.

EDWARD

Farewell, sweet Gaveston, and farewell, niece.

27   *hardy* bold, reckless

0   s.d. ed. (*Enter the king and Spencer, to them / Gaueston, &c.* Q)
3   *spoil* plunder, destroy
4   *hold* fortress
6   *post* go with speed (by horse)

ISABELLA

No farewell to poor Isabel, thy Queen?

EDWARD

Yes, yes – for Mortimer, your lover's sake.

Exeunt [all, except] ISABELLA

ISABELLA

Heavens can witness, I love none but you.   15
From my embracements thus he breaks away;
O that mine arms could close this isle about,
That I might pull him to me where I would,
Or that these tears that drizzle from mine eyes
Had power to mollify his stony heart   20
That when I had him we might never part.

Enter the Barons
[LANCASTER, WARWICK, MORTIMER JUNIOR]

Alarums

LANCASTER

I wonder how he 'scaped?

MORTIMER JUNIOR

Who's this, the Queen?

ISABELLA

Ay, Mortimer, the miserable Queen,
Whose pining heart, her inward sighs have blasted,   25
And body with continual mourning wasted.
These hands are tired with haling of my lord
From Gaveston, from wicked Gaveston,
And all in vain; for when I speak him fair,
He turns away and smiles upon his minion.   30

MORTIMER JUNIOR

Cease to lament, and tell us where's the King?

ISABELLA

What would you with the King? Is't him you seek?

LANCASTER

No, madam, but that cursèd Gaveston.
Far be it from the thought of Lancaster
To offer violence to his sovereign.   35

---

14   s.d. ed. (*Exeunt omnes, manet Isabella.* Q)
21   s.d. ed. (*Enter the Barons alarums.* Q)
27   *haling* dragging (forcibly)

We would but rid the realm of Gaveston;
Tell us where he remains, and he shall die.

ISABELLA

He's gone by water unto Scarborough.
Pursue him quickly and he cannot 'scape;
The King hath left him, and his train is small.   40

WARWICK

Forslow no time, sweet Lancaster; let's march.

MORTIMER JUNIOR

How comes it that the King and he is parted?

ISABELLA

That this your army, going several ways,
Might be of lesser force, and with the power
That he intendeth presently to raise   45
Be easily suppressed; and therefore be gone.

MORTIMER JUNIOR

Here in the river rides a Flemish hoy;
Let's all aboard and follow him amain.

LANCASTER

The wind that bears him hence will fill our sails.
Come, come aboard – 'tis but an hour's sailing.   50

MORTIMER JUNIOR

Madam, stay you within this castle here.

ISABELLA

No, Mortimer, I'll to my lord the King.

MORTIMER JUNIOR

Nay, rather sail with us to Scarborough.

ISABELLA

You know the King is so suspicious,
As if he hear I have but talked with you,   55
Mine honour will be called in question;
And therefore, gentle Mortimer, be gone.

MORTIMER JUNIOR

Madam, I cannot stay to answer you;
But think of Mortimer as he deserves.

[*Exeunt* LANCASTER, WARWICK, *and* MORTIMER JUNIOR]

40   *train* retinue
41   *Forslow* waste
47   *Flemish hoy* small fishing ship used by the Flemings in the North Sea
48   *amain* with all speed

ISABELLA

So well hast thou deserved, sweet Mortimer,   60
As Isabel could live with thee forever.
In vain I look for love at Edward's hand,
Whose eyes are fixed on none but Gaveston.
Yet once more I'll importune him with prayers;
If he be strange and not regard my words,   65
My son and I will over into France,
And to the King, my brother, there complain
How Gaveston hath robbed me of his love.
But yet I hope my sorrows will have end
And Gaveston this blessèd day be slain.   [*Exit*]   70

[Scene 9]

Enter GAVESTON *pursued*

GAVESTON

Yet, lusty lords, I have escaped your hands,
Your threats, your 'larums, and your hot pursuits;
And though divorcèd from King Edward's eyes,
Yet liveth Piers of Gaveston unsurprised,
Breathing, in hope (*malgrado* all your beards   5
That muster rebels thus against your King)
To see his royal sovereign once again.

Enter the NOBLES [LANCASTER, WARWICK, PEMBROKE,
MORTIMER JUNIOR, *with soldiers,* JAMES, HORSE-BOY,
and PEMBROKE'S MEN]

WARWICK

Upon him, soldiers! Take away his weapons.
MORTIMER JUNIOR

Thou proud disturber of thy country's peace,

---

65   *strange* estranged, unresponsive
70   s.d. (*Exeunt* Q)

1   *lusty* arrogant, insolent
2   *'larums* battle-cries
4   *unsurprised* unambushed (and therefore uncaptured)
5   *malgrado . . . beards* in defiance or direct opposition to your purposes; proverbial
    (Tilley S 764)

Corrupter of thy King, cause of these broils,   10
Base flatterer, yield! And were it not for shame –
Shame and dishonour to a soldier's name –
Upon my weapon's point here shouldst thou fall,
And welter in thy gore.

LANCASTER   Monster of men,
That, like the Greekish strumpet, trained to arms   15
And bloody wars so many valiant knights,
Look for no other fortune, wretch, than death;
King Edward is not here to buckler thee.

WARWICK

Lancaster, why talk'st thou to the slave?
Go, soldiers, take him hence; for by my sword,   20
His head shall off. Gaveston, short warning
Shall serve thy turn; it is our country's cause
That here severely we will execute
Upon thy person: hang him at a bough!

GAVESTON

My lord –   25

WARWICK

Soldiers, have him away.
But for thou wert the favourite of a king,
Thou shalt have so much honour at our hands.
                    [*He gestures to indicate beheading*]

GAVESTON

I thank you all, my lords; then I perceive
That heading is one, and hanging is the other,   30

---

10   *broils* battles
14–16   ed. (Monster ... strumpet / Traind ... warres, / So ... knights, Q)
   15   *Greekish strumpet* Helen of Troy in Homer's *Iliad*, the great beauty, wife of Menelaus,
        King of Sparta, who fell in love with Paris, son of Priam, King of Troy; she ran away
        with Paris to Troy, and this was the pretext for the Trojan War. Though scornfully
        alluded to here, Helen is elsewhere celebrated in some of Marlowe's most famous
        lines (*Dr Faustus*, A-Text, 5.1.90–1).
        trained lured, baited
   18   *buckler* shield, protect
20–2   ed. (Go ... hence, / For ... off: / *Gaueston* ... turne: / It ... cause, Q)
   21   *warning* notice – in this case, of execution, giving the condemned man time to
        prepare himself spiritually. The insinuation that Gaveston needs little time suggests
        the irredeemable state of his soul.
   28   *so much honour* Members of the nobility were, by privilege, exempt from hanging.
   30   *heading* beheading

And death is all.

Enter [LORD MALTRAVERS,] EARL OF ARUNDEL

LANCASTER
How now, my lord of Arundel?
MALTRAVERS
My lords, King Edward greets you all by me.
WARWICK
Arundel, say your message.
MALTRAVERS   His majesty,
Hearing that you had taken Gaveston,   35
Entreateth you by me, that but he may
See him before he dies; for why, he says,
And sends you word, he knows that die he shall;
And if you gratify his grace so far,
He will be mindful of the courtesy.   40
WARWICK
How now?
GAVESTON   Renownèd Edward, how thy name
Revives poor Gaveston.
WARWICK   No, it needeth not.
Arundel, we will gratify the King
In other matters; he must pardon us in this.
Soldiers, away with him.   45
GAVESTON
Why, my lord of Warwick,
Will not these delays beget my hopes?
I know it, lords, it is this life you aim at;
Yet grant King Edward this.

31   *death is all* i.e. death is still the same whether one is beheaded or hanged
       s.d. On the identification of Arundel with Maltravers, see the Note on the Text.
33   s.p. MALTRAVERS ed. (*Arun.* Q); also at ll. 34 (*Aru.*), 57, 65, 89
34–5 ed. (*one line in* Q)
36   *that* ed. (yet Q): the awkward Q reading probably arose from a compositorial
       misreading of copy 'y^t' (= that)
       but only. Edward is keeping his demands modest.
37   *for why* because
40   *be mindful* call to mind, take into consideration
47   *Will . . . hopes?* Gaveston is perturbed that the delay in his execution will not, after
       all, lead to a final meeting with Edward.
48   *aim at* intend (to take)

MORTIMER JUNIOR   Shalt thou appoint
   What we shall grant? Soldiers, away with him!   50
   [*To* MALTRAVERS] Thus we'll gratify the King:
   We'll send his head by thee; let him bestow
   His tears on that, for that is all he gets
   Of Gaveston, or else his senseless trunk.

LANCASTER
   Not so, my lord, lest he bestow more cost   55
   In burying him than he hath ever earned.

MALTRAVERS
   My lords, it is his majesty's request,
   And in the honour of a king he swears
   He will but talk with him and send him back.

WARWICK
   When, can you tell? Arundel, no; we wot   60
   He that the care of realm remits,
   And drives his nobles to these exigents
   For Gaveston, will, if he seize him once,
   Violate any promise to possess him.

MALTRAVERS
   Then if you will not trust his grace in keep,   65
   My lords, I will be pledge for his return.

MORTIMER JUNIOR
   It is honourable in thee to offer this,
   But for we know thou art a noble gentleman,
   We will not wrong thee so,
   To make away a true man for a thief.   70

GAVESTON
   How meanst thou, Mortimer? That is over-base.

MORTIMER JUNIOR
   Away, base groom, robber of kings' renown;
   Question with thy companions and thy mates.

49–50   ed. (*Mor. iu.* Shalt . . . graunt? / Souldiers . . . him: Q)
60   *wot* know
61   *remits* surrenders, resigns
62   *exigents* exigencies, extreme measures
63   *seize* (zease Q; seaze Q3–4) take possession of
65   *in keep* with the loan (i.e. of Gaveston)
66   *pledge* security
70   *make away* murder (If Gaveston is not returned, Maltravers will be executed in his place.)
73   *Question* argue   *companions* often used as a term of contempt

PEMBROKE

   My lord Mortimer, and you my lords each one,

   To gratify the King's request therein,   75

   Touching the sending of this Gaveston,

   Because his majesty so earnestly

   Desires to see the man before his death,

   I will upon mine honour undertake

   To carry him and bring him back again,   80

   Provided this, that you, my lord of Arundel

   Will join with me.

WARWICK   Pembroke, what wilt thou do?

   Cause yet more bloodshed? Is it not enough

   That we have taken him, but must we now

   Leave him on 'had I wist' and let him go?   85

PEMBROKE

   My lords, I will not over-woo your honours,

   But if you dare trust Pembroke with the prisoner,

   Upon mine oath I will return him back.

MALTRAVERS

   My lord of Lancaster, what say you in this?

LANCASTER

   Why, I say, let him go on Pembroke's word.   90

PEMBROKE

   And you, lord Mortimer?

MORTIMER JUNIOR

   How say you, my lord of Warwick?

WARWICK

   Nay, do your pleasures; I know how 'twill prove.

PEMBROKE

   Then give him me.

GAVESTON   Sweet sovereign, yet I come

   To see thee ere I die.

WARWICK [*Aside*]   Yet not perhaps,   95

   If Warwick's wit and policy prevail.

MORTIMER JUNIOR

   My lord of Pembroke, we deliver him you;

---

    85   '*had I wist*' had I known. Proverbial (Tilley H 8)

    93   ed. (Nay ... pleasures, / I... prooue. Q)

         do your pleasures i.e. do as you will

    96   *wit* cunning

         policy contrivance, stratagem

Return him on your honour. Sound away!

[Trumpets sound]

Exeunt [all but] PEMBROKE, MALTRAVERS, GAVESTON
and PEMBROKE'S MEN, *four soldiers [, with* JAMES,
and HORSE-BOY]

PEMBROKE

[*To* MALTRAVERS] My lord, you shall go with me;
My house is not far hence – out of the way   100
A little – but our men shall go along.
We that have pretty wenches to our wives,
Sir, must not come so near and balk their lips.

MALTRAVERS

'Tis very kindly spoke, my lord of Pembroke;
Your honour hath an adamant of power   105
To draw a prince.

PEMBROKE   So, my lord. Come hither, James.
I do commit this Gaveston to thee;
Be thou this night his keeper. In the morning
We will discharge thee of thy charge; be gone.

GAVESTON

Unhappy Gaveston, whither goest thou now?   110

Exit [GAVESTON, *with* PEMBROKE'S MEN *and* JAMES]

HORSE-BOY

My lord, we'll quickly be at Cobham.

Exeunt [PEMBROKE *and* MALTRAVERS,
with the HORSE-BOY *and soldiers*]

---

98   *Sound away!* He orders a trumpet call signalling a departure.
     s.d. ed. (*Exeunt. / Manent Penbrooke, Mat. Gauest. & Pen- / brookes men, foure
     souldiers.* Q)
103 *balk* neglect
104 *kindly* as befits *either* a nobleman *or* a husband
105 *adamant* magnet, lodestone
109 *discharge* relieve   *charge* responsibility
110 *Unhappy* unfortunate, unlucky
110 s.d. ed. (*Exit cum seruis Pen.* Q)
111 *Cobham* small town in Kent, near Gravesend
111 s.d. ed. (*Exeunt ambo.* Q)

[Scene 10]

Enter GAVESTON *mourning,* [*with* JAMES]
and the EARL OF PEMBROKE'S MEN

GAVESTON

O treacherous Warwick, thus to wrong thy friend!

JAMES

I see it is your life these arms pursue.

GAVESTON

Weaponless must I fall and die in bands.

O, must this day be period of my life,

Centre of all my bliss? An ye be men,   5

Speed to the King.

Enter WARWICK *and his company*

WARWICK   My lord of Pembroke's men.

Strive you no longer; I will have that Gaveston.

JAMES

Your lordship doth dishonour to yourself

And wrong our lord, your honourable friend.

WARWICK

No, James, it is my country's cause I follow.   10

Go, take the villain; soldiers, come away,

We'll make quick work. Commend me to your master,

My friend, and tell him that I watched it well.

[*To* GAVESTON] Come, let thy shadow parley with King Edward.

GAVESTON

Treacherous Earl, shall I not see the King?   15

WARWICK

The king of heaven perhaps, no other king. Away!

Exeunt WARWICK *and his men, with* GAVESTON.

---

1   *wrong thy friend* i.e. betray Pembroke
2   *arms* i.e. soldiers
3   *bands* bonds, fetters
4   *period* the end
5   *Centre* nadir, the greatest depth (possibly implying the centre of the earth)
6   *Speed* hasten, hurry
7   *Strive* struggle
13 *watched it well* i.e. guarded Gaveston efficiently
14 *shadow* ghost
17 s.d. ed. (*Exeunt Warwike and his men, with Gauest. / Manet Iames cum cæteris.* Q)

JAMES *remains with the others*

JAMES

Come fellows, it booted not for us to strive.
We will in haste go certify our lord.

Exeunt

[Scene 11]

Enter King EDWARD *and* SPENCER [JUNIOR, *and* BALDOCK],
with drums and fifes

EDWARD

I long to hear an answer from the barons
Touching my friend, my dearest Gaveston.
Ah, Spencer, not the riches of my realm
Can ransom him; ah, he is marked to die.
I know the malice of the younger Mortimer;   5
Warwick, I know, is rough, and Lancaster
Inexorable; and I shall never see
My lovely Piers, my Gaveston, again.
The barons overbear me with their pride.

SPENCER JUNIOR

Were I King Edward, England's sovereign,   10
Son to the lovely Eleanor of Spain,
Great Edward Longshanks' issue, would I bear
These braves, this rage, and suffer uncontrolled
These barons thus to beard me in my land,
In mine own realm? My lord, pardon my speech.   15
Did you retain your father's magnanimity,
Did you regard the honour of your name,
You would not suffer thus your majesty
Be counterbuffed of your nobility.

18   *booted not* was useless

11   *Eleanor of Spain* Eleanor of Castile, first wife of Edward I
12   *Longshanks* the nickname ascribed to Edward I because of his long legs
12   *braves* defiant insults
      suffer tolerate
14   *beard* defy with effrontery
16   *magnanimity* courage, fortitude
19   *counterbuffed of* opposed by

Strike off their heads, and let them preach on poles;　　　　20
No doubt such lessons they will teach the rest,
As by their preachments they will profit much
And learn obedience to their lawful King.

EDWARD

Yea, gentle Spencer, we have been too mild.
Too kind to them, but now have drawn our sword,　　　　25
And if they send me not my Gaveston,
We'll steel it on their crest and poll their tops.

BALDOCK

This haught resolve becomes your majesty,
Not to be tied to their affection
As though your highness were a schoolboy still,　　　　30
And must be awed and governed like a child.

Enter HUGH SPENCER [SENIOR] *an old man, father to
the young* SPENCER [JUNIOR], *with his truncheon, and soldiers*

SPENCER SENIOR

Long live my sovereign, the noble Edward,
In peace triumphant, fortunate in wars.

EDWARD

Welcome, old man. Com'st thou in Edward's aid?
Then tell thy prince of whence and what thou art.　　　　35

SPENCER SENIOR

Lo, with a band of bowmen and of pikes,
Brown bills and targeteers, four hundred strong,
Sworn to defend King Edward's royal right,
I come in person to your majesty:
Spencer, the father of Hugh Spencer there,　　　　40

20　*preach on poles* See 1.117 n.
22　*preachments* sermons
27　*steel it* i.e. sharpen his sword
　　poll their tops i.e. cut off their heads, punning on (i) the pollarding or cutting of
　　tree-tops (ii) Spencer Junior's 'poles' (line 20 above)
28　*haught* haughty, lofty
29　*affection* desire, will　　31 *awed* feared
31　s.d. 2 *truncheon* staff which symbolized authority
35　*of whence* from what place
　　what thou art i.e. what is your name
36　*bowmen . . . pikes* Lances with sharp metal tips at both ends were driven into the
　　ground just in front of the archers to protect them in battle.
37　*Brown bills* bronzed halberds (metonymic for the footsoldiers carrying them)
　　targeteers shield-carrying infantrymen

400

Bound to your highness everlastingly
For favours done in him unto us all.

EDWARD

Thy father, Spencer?

SPENCER JUNIOR   True, an it like your grace,
That pours in lieu of all your goodness shown,
His life, my lord, before your princely feet.   45

EDWARD

Welcome ten thousand times, old man, again.
Spencer, this love, this kindness to thy King
Argues thy noble mind and disposition.
Spencer, I here create thee Earl of Wiltshire,
And daily will enrich thee with our favour   50
That, as the sunshine, shall reflect o'er thee.
Beside, the more to manifest our love,
Because we hear Lord Bruce doth sell his land
And that the Mortimers are in hand withal,
Thou shalt have crowns of us, t'outbid the barons;   55
And Spencer, spare them not, but lay it on.
Soldiers, a largess, and thrice welcome all.

Enter [ISABELLA] *the Queen and* [PRINCE EDWARD]
her son, and LEVUNE, *a Frenchman*

SPENCER JUNIOR

My lord, here comes the Queen.

EDWARD   Madam, what news?

ISABELLA

News of dishonour, lord, and discontent:
Our friend Levune, faithful and full of trust,   60
Informeth us by letters and by words
That Lord Valois our brother, King of France,

43   *an it like* if it please
47   For the first time, Edward addresses Spencer Senior by name; their relationship is
      now personal.
48   *Argues* proves. Ironically, this statement emphasizes the fact that Spencer Senior
      is not, by birth, a nobleman.
54   *in hand withal* i.e. engaged with this business
56   *spare them not* i.e. do not be frugal (with the money)
      lay it on be extravagant, flamboyant
57   *largess* liberal bestowal of money, bounty
57   s.d. ed.; after line 58a in Q   57 s.d. 2 ed. LEVUNE (*Lewne* Q; and throughout the text)
61   *words* oral report

401

Because your highness hath been slack in homage,
Hath seizèd Normandy into his hands.
These be the letters, this the messenger. 65

EDWARD

Welcome Levune. [*To* ISABELLA] Tush, Sib, if this be all,
Valois and I will soon be friends again.
But to my Gaveston – shall I never see,
Never behold thee now? Madam, in this matter
We will employ you and your little son; 70
You shall go parley with the King of France.
Boy, see you bear you bravely to the King
And do your message with a majesty.

PRINCE EDWARD

Commit not to my youth things of more weight
Than fits a prince so young as I to bear. 75
And fear not, lord and father; heaven's great beams
On Atlas' shoulder shall not lie more safe
Than shall your charge committed to my trust.

ISABELLA

Ah, boy, this towardness makes thy mother fear
Thou art not marked to many days on earth. 80

EDWARD

Madam, we will that you with speed be shipped,
And this our son. Levune shall follow you
With all the haste we can dispatch him hence.
Choose of our lords to bear you company,
And go in peace; leave us in wars at home. 85

ISABELLA

Unnatural wars, where subjects brave their King:
God end them once. My lord, I take my leave
To make my preparation for France.

[*Exeunt* ISABELLA, PRINCE EDWARD *and* LEVUNE]

Enter LORD MALTRAVERS

EDWARD

What, Lord Maltravers, dost thou come alone?

66 *Sib* 'affectionate diminutive of Isabella' (Gill)
77 *Atlas* In classical mythology, the Titan who carried the burden of the sky on his shoulders.
79 *towardness* boldness
80 Ironically, King Edward III reigned for fifty years (1327–77).
87 *once* i.e. once and for all

MALTRAVERS

    Yea, my good lord, for Gaveston is dead.   90

EDWARD

    Ah, traitors, have they put my friend to death?

    Tell me, Maltravers, died he ere thou cam'st,

    Or didst thou see my friend to take his death?

MALTRAVERS

    Neither, my lord, for as he was surprised,

    Begirt with weapons and with enemies round,   95

    I did your highness' message to them all,

    Demanding him of them – entreating rather –

    And said, upon the honour of my name,

    That I would undertake to carry him

    Unto your highness, and to bring him back.   100

EDWARD

    And tell me, would the rebels deny me that?

SPENCER JUNIOR

    Proud recreants!

EDWARD   Yea, Spencer, traitors all.

MALTRAVERS

    I found them at the first inexorable;

    The Earl of Warwick would not bide the hearing,

    Mortimer hardly; Pembroke and Lancaster   105

    Spake least. And when they flatly had denied,

    Refusing to receive me pledge for him,

    The Earl of Pembroke mildly thus bespake:

    'My lords, because our sovereign sends for him

    And promiseth he shall be safe returned,   110

    I will this undertake: to have him hence

    And see him re-delivered to your hands.'

EDWARD

    Well, and how fortunes that he came not?

SPENCER JUNIOR

    Some treason or some villainy was cause.

MALTRAVERS

    The Earl of Warwick seized him on his way,   115

---

94   *surprised* ambushed

95   *Begirt* encompassed, enclosed   *round* i.e. encircling, surrounding

102   *recreants* breakers of allegiance

104   *bide* endure, abide

113   *fortunes* chances

For, being delivered unto Pembroke's men,
Their lord rode home, thinking his prisoner safe;
But ere he came, Warwick in ambush lay,
And bare him to his death, and in a trench
Struck off his head, and marched unto the camp.   120

SPENCER JUNIOR

A bloody part, flatly against law of arms.

EDWARD

O, shall I speak, or shall I sigh and die?

SPENCER JUNIOR

My lord, refer your vengeance to the sword
Upon these barons; hearten up your men.
Let them not unrevenged murder your friends.   125
Advance your standard, Edward, in the field,
And march to fire them from their starting holes.

EDWARD

[*Kneeling*] By earth, the common mother of us all,
By heaven and all the moving orbs thereof,
By this right hand and by my father's sword,   130
And all the honours 'longing to my crown,
I will have heads and lives for him as many
As I have manors, castles, towns, and towers.
Treacherous Warwick! Traitorous Mortimer!
If I be England's king, in lakes of gore   135
Your headless trunks, your bodies will I trail,
That you may drink your fill and quaff in blood,
And stain my royal standard with the same,
That so my bloody colours may suggest
Remembrance of revenge immortally   140

121   *part* action, deed
      flatly absolutely
123   *refer* assign
126   *Advance your standard* raise your ensign
      in the field in battle
127   *fire* smoke out
      starting holes place of refuge for animals
128   s.d. ed. (*Edward kneeles, and saith.* Q)
129   *moving orbs* in Ptolemaic cosmology, the moving concentric spheres surrounding
      the Earth; alternatively, the sun, moon, and planets, all of which were thought to
      orbit the Earth
130   *father's sword* The sword was wielded by monarchs as a symbol of divine justice on
      Earth; cf. Romans 13:1–4.
131   *'longing* belonging

On your accursèd traitorous progeny –
You villains that have slain my Gaveston.
And in this place of honour and of trust,
Spencer, sweet Spencer, I adopt thee here;
And merely of our love we do create thee   145
Earl of Gloucester and Lord Chamberlain,
Despite of times, despite of enemies.

SPENCER JUNIOR
My lord, here is a messenger from the barons
Desires access unto your majesty.

EDWARD
Admit him near.   150

Enter the HERALD *from the Barons, with his coat of arms*

HERALD
Long live King Edward, England's lawful lord.

EDWARD
So wish not they, iwis, that sent thee hither.
Thou com'st from Mortimer and his complices –
A ranker rout of rebels never was.
Well, say thy message.   155

HERALD
The barons up in arms, by me salute
Your highness with long life and happiness,
And bid me say as plainer to your grace,
That if without effusion of blood
You will this grief have ease and remedy,   160
That from your princely person you remove
This Spencer, as a putrefying branch
That deads the royal vine whose golden leaves

141   *progeny* lineage
145   *merely . . . love* i.e. rather than by right of succession; Spencer Junior was only a
      retainer of the previous Earl of Gloucester
148   *here is* ed. (heres is Q1–2; heers Q3; heer's Q4)
151, 156 s.p. ed. HERALD (Q *Messen.*)
152   *iwis* assuredly
153   *complices* confederates, conspirators
154   *rout* (route Q; roote Q2–3; rout Q4); unruly crowd
158   *plainer* complainant, one who brings an accusation
159   *effusion* shedding (four syllables)
163   *deads* deadens
      royal vine Edward's crown was, in fact, decorated with four large and four small straw-
      berry leaves. See *Boutell's Heraldry* (revised by J. P. Brooke-Little, London, 1970, p. 184).

405

Impale your princely head, your diadem,
Whose brightness such pernicious upstarts dim,   165
Say they; and lovingly advise your grace
To cherish virtue and nobility,
And have old servitors in high esteem,
And shake off smooth dissembling flatterers.
This granted, they, their honours, and their lives   170
Are to your highness vowed and consecrate.
SPENCER JUNIOR
   Ah, traitors, will they still display their pride?
EDWARD
   Away! Tarry no answer, but be gone.
   Rebels! Will they appoint their sovereign
   His sports, his pleasures, and his company?   175
   Yet ere thou go, see how I do divorce
   Spencer from me.   *Embrace[s* SPENCER JUNIOR]
                    Now get thee to thy lords,
   And tell them I will come to chastise them
   For murdering Gaveston. Hie thee, get thee gone;
   Edward with fire and sword follows at thy heels.   180
                                        [*Exit* HERALD]
   My lords, perceive you how these rebels swell?
   Soldiers, good hearts, defend your sovereign's right,
   For now, even now, we march to make them stoop.
   Away!

                                        Exeunt

164   *Impale* encircle
      diadem crown
168   *old servitors* retainers of long standing (Forker)
169   *smooth* (i) plausible (ii) obsequious
171   *consecrate* made sacred
173   *Tarry* wait for
174   *appoint* order, grant
175   *sports* pastimes
177   s.d. ed. (after 'deuorce' and 'lords,' respectively Q *Embrace / Spencer.*)
179   *Hie* hasten, hurry
181   *lords* ed. (lord Q)
      swell grow proud
183   *make them stoop* i.e. humiliate them

[Scene 12]

Alarums, excursions, a great fight, and a retreat

Enter [EDWARD] *the King,* SPENCER [SENIOR],
SPENCER JUNIOR, *and the noblemen of the King's side*

EDWARD

Why do we sound retreat? Upon them, lords!
This day I shall pour vengeance with my sword
On those proud rebels that are up in arms,
And do confront and countermand their King.

SPENCER JUNIOR

I doubt it not, my lord; right will prevail.   5

SPENCER SENIOR

'Tis not amiss, my liege, for either part
To breathe a while; our men with sweat and dust
All choked well near, begin to faint for heat,
And this retire refresheth horse and man.

Enter the Barons, MORTIMER [JUNIOR], LANCASTER,
[KENT,] WARWICK, PEMBROKE, *with the others*

SPENCER JUNIOR

Here come the rebels.   10

MORTIMER JUNIOR

Look, Lancaster,
Yonder is Edward among his flatterers.

LANCASTER

And there let him be,
Till he pay dearly for their company.

WARWICK

And shall, or Warwick's sword shall smite in vain.   15

EDWARD

What, rebels, do you shrink and sound retreat?

---

    0 s.d. 1 *Alarums* battle-cries, trumpet signals
       excursions rush of soldiers across the stage
    4 *countermand* oppose
    9 *retire* (i) respite (ii) retreat
    9 s.d. ed.; after line 10 in Q
11–12 ed. (Looke ... his / flatterers. Q)
13–14 ed. (*And* ... for / their companie. Q)

407

MORTIMER JUNIOR

No, Edward, no; thy flatterers faint and fly.

LANCASTER

Thou'd best betimes forsake thee and their trains,

For they'll betray thee, traitors as they are.

SPENCER JUNIOR

Traitor on thy face, rebellious Lancaster.   20

PEMBROKE

Away, base upstart; brav'st thou nobles thus?

SPENCER SENIOR

A noble attempt and honourable deed

Is it not, trow ye, to assemble aid

And levy arms against your lawful King?

EDWARD

For which ere long their heads shall satisfy   25

T'appease the wrath of their offended King.

MORTIMER JUNIOR

Then, Edward, thou wilt fight it to the last,

And rather bathe thy sword in subjects' blood

Than banish that pernicious company?

EDWARD

Ay, traitors all! Rather than thus be braved,   30

Make England's civil towns huge heaps of stones

And ploughs to go about our palace gates.

WARWICK

A desperate and unnatural resolution.

Alarum to the fight!

Saint George for England and the barons' right!   35

EDWARD

Saint George for England and King Edward's right!

> [*Exeunt* WARWICK *with his men at one door
> and* EDWARD *with his men at the other*]

---

18   *Thou'd* ed. (Th'ad Q) thou had
       betimes in good time
       trains tricks, political stratagems
23   *trow* know, think
25   *satisfy* atone, make amends
34–5 ed. (Alarum ... England, / And ... right. Q)
35   *Saint George* Patron Saint of England (not adopted until Edward III's reign)

[Scene 13]

[Alarums.] Enter EDWARD, [SPENCER SENIOR,
SPENCER JUNIOR, BALDOCK, LEVUNE, *and soldiers*]
with the Barons [KENT, WARWICK, LANCASTER, *and*
MORTIMER JUNIOR *and others*] *captives*

EDWARD

Now, lusty lords, now not by chance of war
But justice of the quarrel and the cause,
Vailed is your pride. Methinks you hang the heads,
But we'll advance them, traitors! Now 'tis time
To be avenged on you for all your braves
And for the murder of my dearest friend,
To whom right well you knew our soul was knit:
Good Piers of Gaveston, my sweet favourite –
Ah rebels, recreants, you made him away!

KENT

Brother, in regard of thee and of thy land,   10
Did they remove that flatterer from thy throne.

EDWARD

So, sir, you have spoke; away, avoid our presence.

                                        [Exit KENT]

Accursèd wretches, was't in regard of us,
When we had sent our messenger to request
He might be spared to come to speak with us,   15
And Pembroke undertook for his return,
That thou, proud Warwick, watched the prisoner,
Poor Piers, and headed him against law of arms?
For which thy head shall overlook the rest
As much as thou in rage outwent'st the rest.   20

WARWICK

Tyrant, I scorn thy threats and menaces;

---

0   s.d. 4 *and others* i.e. 'the rest' who are ordered to be executed at ll. 33–4
3   *Vailed* lowered
4   *advance* i.e. raise their severed heads on pikes
5   *braves* See 11.13 n.
10 *in regard* out of consideration
12 *avoid* depart from
17 *watched* kept watch over
18 *headed* beheaded
19 *head . . . the rest* i.e. his severed head will be mounted higher than the others'

'Tis but temporal that thou canst inflict.

LANCASTER

The worst is death, and better die to live,
Than live in infamy under such a king.

EDWARD

Away with them, my lord of Winchester,   25
These lusty leaders, Warwick and Lancaster.
I charge you roundly off with both their heads.
Away!

WARWICK

Farewell, vain world.

LANCASTER   Sweet Mortimer, farewell.

[*Exeunt* WARWICK *and* LANCASTER, *guarded by*
SPENCER SENIOR]

MORTIMER JUNIOR

England, unkind to thy nobility,   30
Groan for this grief; behold how thou art maimed.

EDWARD

Go take that haughty Mortimer to the Tower;
There see him safe bestowed. And for the rest,
Do speedy execution on them all.
Begone!   35

MORTIMER JUNIOR

What, Mortimer! Can ragged stony walls
Immure thy virtue that aspires to heaven?
No, Edward, England's scourge, it may not be;
Mortimer's hope surmounts his fortune far.

---

22   *but temporal* Edward can only inflict physical, not spiritual, suffering.
23   *The worst is death* Cf. *Richard II*, 'The worst is death, and death will have his day'
      (3.2.99).
23–4 *better . . . infamy* proverbial (Tilley H 576)
25   *Winchester* Spencer Senior was created Earl of Wiltshire at 11. 49, but is here ad-
      dressed as Marquess of Winchester. In Marlowe's time, the two titles were held by the
      same person, William Paulet (c. 1532–98).
27   *roundly* without hesitation
27–8 ed. (*one line in* Q)
29   *vain* worthless, futile
34–5 ed. (*one line in* Q)
36   *ragged* rugged
37   *Immure* enclose (within walls)   *virtue* power
38   *scourge* often used by Marlowe to describe a ruler who lays waste a nation. Cf.
      2 Tamburlaine, 'Be all a scourge and terror to the world' (1.3.63).
39   *surmounts* surpasses, rises above

[Exit MORTIMER JUNIOR *guarded]*

EDWARD

    Sound drums and trumpets! March with me my friends;   40
    Edward this day hath crowned him King anew.

                                Exit[, attended].

        SPENCER [JUNIOR], LEVUNE *and* BALDOCK *remain*

SPENCER JUNIOR

    Levune, the trust that we repose in thee
    Begets the quiet of King Edward's land.
    Therefore be gone in haste, and with advice
    Bestow that treasure on the lords of France;   45
    That therewithal enchanted, like the guard
    That suffered Jove to pass in showers of gold
    To Danaë, all aid may be denied
    To Isabel the Queen, that now in France
    Makes friends, to cross the seas with her young son,   50
    And step into his father's regiment.

LEVUNE

    That's it these barons and the subtle Queen
    Long levelled at.

BALDOCK   Yea, but Levune, thou seest
    These barons lay their heads on blocks together;
    What they intend, the hangman frustrates clean.   55

LEVUNE

    Have you no doubts, my lords; I'll clap 's close
    Among the lords of France with England's gold
    That Isabel shall make her plaints in vain,
    And France shall be obdurate with her tears.

---

  41   s.d. ed. (*Manent Spencer filius, Lewne & Baldock.* Q)
  42   *repose* place
  43   *Begets* will produce, obtain
  46   *therewithal* ed. (therewith all Q)
46–8   *like . . . Danaë* See 6. 53 n.
  51   *regiment* rule, authority
  52   *subtle* cunning, insidious
  53   *levelled at* ed. (leuied at Q) aimed at
  55   *clean* completely, absolutely
  56   *clap 's* ed. (claps Q); 'clap us'; strike a bargain; clap usually referred to the clapping
       of hands when securing a transaction
       close secretly
  59   *obdurate* unyielding

SPENCER JUNIOR

    Then make for France amain; Levune, away! 60
    Proclaim King Edward's wars and victories. *Exeunt*

[Scene 14]

Enter EDMUND [THE EARL OF KENT]

KENT

    Fair blows the wind for France; blow, gentle gale,
    Till Edmund be arrived for England's good.
    Nature, yield to my country's cause in this:
    A brother – no, a butcher of thy friends –
    Proud Edward, dost thou banish me thy presence? 5
    But I'll to France, and cheer the wrongèd Queen,
    And certify what Edward's looseness is.
    Unnatural King, to slaughter noblemen
    And cherish flatterers. Mortimer, I stay
    Thy sweet escape; stand gracious, gloomy night 10
    To his device.

Enter MORTIMER [JUNIOR] *disguised*

MORTIMER JUNIOR

    Holla! Who walketh there? Is't you my lord?

KENT

    Mortimer, 'tis I;
    But hath thy potion wrought so happily?

MORTIMER JUNIOR

    It hath, my lord; the warders all asleep, 15
    I thank them, gave me leave to pass in peace.
    But hath your grace got shipping unto France?

KENT

    Fear it not. *Exeunt*

  60 *amain* at once

   1 *gentle* not stormy, but also implying courtesy or generosity
   7 *looseness* (i) carelessness, incompetence (ii) sexual misconduct
   9 *stay* await
10–11 Kent invokes the darkness of night to aid Mortimer Junior's escape.
  11 *device* stratagem, intent
13–14 ed. (Mortimer … so I happilie? Q)
  14 *thy potion … happily*; i.e. have the guards been successfully drugged?
  16 *gave me leave* allowed me

[Scene 15]

Enter [ISABELLA] *the Queen and her son*
[PRINCE EDWARD]

ISABELLA

    Ah boy, our friends do fail us all in France;
    The lords are cruel and the King unkind.
    What shall we do?

PRINCE EDWARD   Madam, return to England
    And please my father well, and then a fig
    For all my uncle's friendship here in France.   5
    I warrant you, I'll win his highness quickly;
    A loves me better than a thousand Spencers.

ISABELLA

    Ah boy, thou art deceived at least in this,
    To think that we can yet be tuned together.
    No, no, we jar too far. Unkind Valois!   10
    Unhappy Isabel! When France rejects,
    Whither, O whither dost thou bend thy steps?

Enter SIR JOHN OF HAINAULT

SIR JOHN

    Madam, what cheer?

ISABELLA   Ah, good Sir John of Hainault,
    Never so cheerless, nor so far distressed.

SIR JOHN

    I hear, sweet lady, of the King's unkindness.   15
    But droop not, madam; noble minds contemn
    Despair. Will your grace with me to Hainault

---

  4   *a fig* obscene expression of contempt; usually accompanied by a phallic gesture
      in which the thumb was thrust into the mouth or between two closed fingers.
      Proverbial (Tilley F 210)

  6   *warrant* assure

  7   *A* unstressed form of 'he'

  9   *yet* still

10   *jar* (i) become discordant, playing upon the metaphor of the previous line
      (ii) quarrel

11   *Unhappy* unfortunate, unlucky

12   *bend . . . steps* i.e. what course of action should I next take?

13   *what cheer* i.e. what is your mood, disposition?

16   *contemn* despise, disregard

17   *Hainault* Flemish county in the Low Countries, bordering France

And there stay time's advantage with your son?
How say you, my lord, will you go with your friends,
And shake off all our fortunes equally?   20

PRINCE EDWARD

So pleaseth the Queen, my mother, me it likes.
The King of England nor the court of France
Shall have me from my gracious mother's side,
Till I be strong enough to break a staff,
And then have at the proudest Spencer's head.   25

SIR JOHN

Well said, my lord.

ISABELLA

Oh, my sweet heart, how do I moan thy wrongs,
Yet triumph in the hope of thee, my joy.
Ah, sweet Sir John, even to the utmost verge
Of Europe, or the shore of Tanaïs,   30
Will we with thee to Hainault, so we will.
The Marquis is a noble gentleman;
His grace, I dare presume, will welcome me.

Enter EDMUND [THE EARL OF KENT]
and MORTIMER [JUNIOR]

But who are these?
KENT   Madam, long may you live
Much happier than your friends in England do.   35

ISABELLA

Lord Edmund and Lord Mortimer alive!
Welcome to France. The news was here, my lord,
That you were dead, or very near your death.

MORTIMER JUNIOR

Lady, the last was truest of the twain;

20 *shake off* cast off
21 *So* as it
24 *staff* a lance or quarter-staff, used (and broken) in combat
25 *have at* attack, strike at (imperative)
27 *moan* lament (aloud)
29 *utmost verge* i.e. the furthest limit
30 *Tanaïs* the Latin name for the River Don which the Elizabethans regarded as the
    boundary between Europe and Asia
32 *Marquis* i.e. Sir John's brother, William, Count of Hainault
33 s.d. ed.; after line 34a in Q

But Mortimer, reserved for better hap,   40
Hath shaken off the thraldom of the Tower,
[*To* PRINCE EDWARD] And lives t'advance your standard,
    good my lord.

PRINCE EDWARD

How mean you, an the King my father lives?
No, my lord Mortimer, not I, I trow.

ISABELLA

Not, son? Why not? I would it were no worse;   45
But gentle lords, friendless we are in France.

MORTIMER JUNIOR

Monsieur le Grand, a noble friend of yours,
Told us at our arrival all the news:
How hard the nobles, how unkind the King
Hath showed himself. But madam, right makes room   50
Where weapons want; and though a many friends
Are made away – as Warwick, Lancaster,
And others of our party and faction –
Yet have we friends, assure your grace, in England
Would cast up caps and clap their hands for joy,   55
To see us there appointed for our foes.

KENT

Would all were well and Edward well reclaimed,
For England's honour, peace, and quietness.

MORTIMER JUNIOR

But by the sword, my lord, it must be deserved.
The King will ne'er forsake his flatterers.   60

40   *hap* fortune
41   *thraldom* servitude, bondage
42   *t'advance your standard* i.e. raise the banner or ensign of battle
44   *trow* think, reckon
47   *Monsieur le Grand* an invented character with no historical original
49   *hard* difficult, obdurate
      unkind unnatural (to his sister, Isabella)
      the King i.e. the King of France
50   *makes room* makes way
51   *want* i.e. are required
      a many many
52   *made away* i.e. dead (implicitly by murder and treachery)
55   *cast up caps* i.e. throw caps into the air as a sign of joy
56   *appointed* armed, prepared for battle
57   *reclaimed* subdued
59   *deserved* earned

SIR JOHN

My lords of England, sith the ungentle King
Of France refuseth to give aid of arms
To this distressèd queen his sister here,
Go you with her to Hainault. Doubt ye not,
We will find comfort, money, men, and friends   65
Ere long, to bid the English King a base.
How say, young prince, what think you of the match?

PRINCE EDWARD

I think King Edward will outrun us all.

ISABELLA

Nay son, not so; and you must not discourage
Your friends that are so forward in your aid.   70

KENT

Sir John of Hainault, pardon us, I pray;
These comforts that you give our woeful Queen
Bind us in kindness all at your command.

ISABELLA

Yea, gentle brother; and the God of heaven
Prosper your happy motion, good Sir John.   75

MORTIMER JUNIOR

This noble gentleman, forward in arms,
Was born, I see, to be our anchor-hold.
Sir John of Hainault, be it thy renown
That England's Queen and nobles in distress
Have been by thee restored and comforted.   80

SIR JOHN

Madam, along, and you, my lord, with me,
That England's peers may Hainault's welcome see.

[*Exeunt*]

61   *sith* since
66   *bid . . . a base* challenge to risk capture (from 'prisoner's base', a children's game
       involving running between two 'bases', between which the players might be caught
       by their opponents)
67   *match game*
74   *brother* i.e. brother-in-law
75   *motion* proposal
76   *forward* ardent

[Scene 16]

Enter [EDWARD] *the King,* MALTRAVERS, *the two* SPENCERS,
[SENIOR *and* JUNIOR,] *with others*

EDWARD

    Thus after many threats of wrathful war,

    Triumpheth England's Edward with his friends;

    And triumph Edward with his friends uncontrolled.

    [*To* SPENCER JUNIOR] My lord of Gloucester, do you hear

       the news?

SPENCER JUNIOR

    What news, my lord?   5

EDWARD

    Why man, they say there is great execution

    Done through the realm. My lord of Arundel,

    You have the note, have you not?

MALTRAVERS

    From the Lieutenant of the Tower, my lord.

EDWARD

    I pray let us see it. What have we there?   10

    Read it Spencer.

           SPENCER [JUNIOR] *reads their names* †

    Why so, they 'barked apace a month ago;

    Now, on my life, they'll neither bark nor bite.

    Now, sirs, the news from France; Gloucester, I trow

    The lords of France love England's gold so well   15

    As Isabella gets no aid from thence.

    What now remains? Have you proclaimed, my lord,

    Reward for them can bring in Mortimer?

---

3   *uncontrolled* without censure

8   *note* official list

11 s.d. SPENCER [JUNIOR] *reads . . . names* The details of those who have been executed
     are not included in the control text, thus creating some staging difficulties.
     Holinshed supplies the list reproduced overleaf; if required, this might be inter-
     polated in performance.

12 *'barked* embarked on committing treason (Forker)
     apace swiftly

13 *neither bark nor bite* Edward puns on the previous line, introducing a proverbial
     meaning (Tilley B 85, B 86).

15 *love England's gold* i.e. Edward's bribe has worked

16 *Isabella* ed. (*Isabell* Q)

SPENCER JUNIOR

My lord, we have; and if he be in England,
A will be had ere long, I doubt it not.   20

EDWARD

If, dost thou say? Spencer, as true as death,
He is in England's ground; our port masters
Are not so careless of their King's command.

Enter a POST [*with letters*]

How now, what news with thee? From whence come these?

POST

Letters, my lord, and tidings forth of France   25
To you, my lord of Gloucester, from Levune.

EDWARD

Read.

SPENCER JUNIOR *(Reads the letter)*

'My duty to your honour premised, *etcetera,* I have according
to instructions in that behalf, dealt with the King of France's
lords, and effected, that the Queen, all discontented and discom-   30
forted, is gone. Whither? If you ask, with Sir John of Hainault,

---

20 *A* he, i.e. Mortimer Junior   *had* captured (Forker)
21 *as true as death* proverbial (Tilley D 136)
27–8 ed. (Reade. / *Spencer reades the letter.* Q)
28 *premised* ed. (promised Q; premised Q2); that which serves as a formal prefix or
    introduction to a report   *etcetera* ed. (&c. Q)
28–9 *according . . . in that behalf* i.e. with respect to Edward's instructions
29 *France's* ed. (Fraunce his Q)
30 *effected* i.e. have caused, brought about
30–1 *discomforted* discouraged

---

† Extract from Holinshed, *Chronicles of England, Scotland, and Ireland*
(1587 ed., vol. 3, p. 331)

. . . the Lord William Tuchet, the Lord William Fitzwilliam, the Lord Warren de Lisle, the Lord
Henry Bradborne, and the Lord William Chenie, barons, with John Page, an esquire, were
drawn and hanged at Pomfret [Pontefract] . . . and then shortly after, Roger Lord Clifford, John
Lord Mowbray, and Sir Gosein D'Eivill, barons, were drawn and hanged at York. At Bristol in
like manner were executed Sir Henry de Willington and Sir Henry Montfort, baronets; and
at Gloucester, the Lord John Gifford and Sir William Elmebridge, knight; and at London, the
Lord Henry Tyes, baron; at Winchelsea, Sir Thomas Culpepper, knight; at Windsor, the Lord
Francis de Aldham, baron; and at Canterbury, the Lord Bartholomew de Badlesmere and the
Lord Bartholomew de Ashburnham, barons. Also, at Cardiff in Wales, Sir William Fleming,
knight, was executed. Divers were executed in their counties [*Holinshed reads* 'countries'], as
Sir Thomas Mandit and others.

brother to the Marquis, into Flanders. With them are gone Lord
Edmund and the Lord Mortimer, having in their company divers
of your nation, and others; and, as constant report goeth, they
intend to give King Edward battle in England sooner than he can   35
look for them. This is all the news of import.

                              Your honour's in all service, Levune.'

EDWARD

Ah, villains, hath that Mortimer escaped?
With him is Edmund gone associate?
And will Sir John of Hainault lead the round?   40
Welcome, i' God's name, madam, and your son;
England shall welcome you and all your rout.
Gallop apace bright Phoebus through the sky,
And dusky night, in rusty iron car,
Between you both shorten the time, I pray,   45
That I may see that most desirèd day
When we may meet these traitors in the field.
Ah, nothing grieves me but my little boy,
Is thus misled to countenance their ills.
Come, friends, to Bristol, there to make us strong;   50
And, winds, as equal be to bring them in
As you injurious were to bear them forth.

                                                      [*Exeunt*]

[Scene 17]

Enter [ISABELLA] *the Queen, her son* [PRINCE EDWARD],
EDMUND [THE EARL OF KENT], MORTIMER [JUNIOR],
and SIR JOHN [OF HAINAULT, *with soldiers*]

34   *constant* consistent, reliable
34–6   *they intend . . . for them* i.e. they will take the initiative in challenging Edward to
       fight before he is ready
36   *import* importance
40   *round* dance
42   *rout* unruly followers
43   *Phoebus* Phoebus Apollo, the sun god of classical mythology, who drove the sun
       across the sky in a chariot
44   *dusky night . . . car* Cf. *1 Tamburlaine*, 'ugly Darkness with her rusty coach' (V.ii.230).
49   *countenance* favour, support   *ills* sins, wickedness
50   *strong* resolute, determined
51   *equal* just

419

ISABELLA

Now lords, our loving friends and countrymen,
Welcome to England all. With prosperous winds
Our kindest friends in Belgia have we left,
To cope with friends at home. A heavy case,
When force to force is knit, and sword and glaive   5
In civil broils makes kin and countrymen
Slaughter themselves in others, and their sides
With their own weapons gored. But what's the help?
Misgoverned kings are cause of all this wrack;
And Edward, thou art one among them all,   10
Whose looseness hath betrayed thy land to spoil
And made the channels overflow with blood.
Of thine own people patron shouldst thou be,
But thou –

MORTIMER JUNIOR   Nay madam, if you be a warrior,
Ye must not grow so passionate in speeches.   15
Lords, sith that we are by sufferance of heaven
Arrived and armèd in this prince's right,
Here for our country's cause swear we to him
All homage, fealty, and forwardness.
And for the open wrongs and injuries   20
Edward hath done to us, his Queen, and land,
We come in arms to wreak it with the sword,
That England's Queen in peace may repossess
Her dignities and honours, and withal
We may remove these flatterers from the King,   25

---

2   *prosperous* favourable
3   *Belgia* the Low Countries
4   *cope* engage in battle
      friends kinsfolk, relatives
      heavy case sad predicament
5   *glaive* variously used of the spear, halberd, and broadsword
6   *civil broils* i.e. civil wars
8   *help* remedy
9   *Misgoverned* unruly   *wrack* destruction
11   *looseness* (i) frivolous, careless behaviour (ii) lasciviousness
13–14a ed. (*one line in* Q)
13   *patron* father-figure (and hence an example)
16   *sufferance* permission
19   *fealty* loyalty, fidelity   *forwardness* eagerness
22   *wreak* ed. (wrecke Q: a variant form of wreak) avenge
      sword ed. (swords Q; sworde Q2–3; sword Q4)

That havocs England's wealth and treasury.

SIR JOHN

Sound trumpets, my lord, and forward let us march;
Edward will think we come to flatter him.

KENT

I would he never had been flattered more.

[Sound trumpets. Exeunt]

[Scene 18]

Enter [EDWARD] *the King,* BALDOCK,
and SPENCER [JUNIOR], *flying about the stage*

SPENCER JUNIOR

Fly, fly, my lord! The Queen is over-strong;
Her friends do multiply and yours do fail.
Shape we our course to Ireland, there to breathe.

EDWARD

What, was I born to fly and run away,
And leave the Mortimers conquerors behind?   5
Give me my horse, and let's r'enforce our troops,
And in this bed of honour die with fame.

BALDOCK

O no, my lord; this princely resolution
Fits not the time. Away! We are pursued.

[Exeunt]

[Enter] EDMUND [THE EARL OF KENT] *alone*
with a sword and target

KENT

This way he fled, but I am come too late.   10

26   *havocs . . . treasury* i.e. misuses (literally lays waste) public money by indiscriminate
      spending

1   *Fly* run
2   *multiply* increase
      fail (i) become exhausted (ii) fall, die (iii) decline in number
3   *Shape* steer
5   *the Mortimers* Gill notes that the historical Mortimer Senior was, at this point,
      already dead.
6   *r'enforce* urge, encourage (once more)
7   *bed of honour* i.e. England
9   s.d. 3 *target* lightweight shield

421

Edward, alas, my heart relents for thee.
Proud traitor Mortimer, why dost thou chase
Thy lawful King, thy sovereign, with thy sword?
Vile wretch, and why hast thou of all unkind,
Borne arms against thy brother and thy King? 15
Rain showers of vengeance on my cursèd head,
Thou God, to whom in justice it belongs
To punish this unnatural revolt.
Edward, this Mortimer aims at thy life;
O fly him then! But Edmund, calm this rage; 20
Dissemble or thou diest, for Mortimer
And Isabel do kiss while they conspire;
And yet she bears a face of love, forsooth.
Fie on that love that hatcheth death and hate!
Edmund, away; Bristol to Longshanks' blood 25
Is false. Be not found single for suspect;
Proud Mortimer pries near into thy walks.

    Enter [ISABELLA] *the Queen,* MORTIMER [JUNIOR],
    the young PRINCE [EDWARD], *and* SIR JOHN OF HAINAULT

ISABELLA

Successful battles gives the God of kings
To them that fight in right and fear his wrath.
Since then successfully we have prevailed, 30
Thanks be heaven's great architect and you.
Ere farther we proceed, my noble lords,
We here create our well-beloved son,
Of love and care unto his royal person,
Lord Warden of the realm; and sith the fates 35

---

14   *Vile wretch* Kent addresses himself
      unkind unnatural (because he has acted against his own brother)
19   *aims . . . life* i.e. intends to kill Edward
21   *Dissemble* i.e. be a hypocrite, be deceptive
23   *forsooth* certainly, in truth (said with irony and contempt)
25–6 *Bristol . . . false* i.e. the Mayor of Bristol has betrayed the son of King Edward I
      (cf. 11. 12 n.)
26   *single* alone, by oneself
      for suspect i.e. for this causes suspicion
27   *walks* movements
31   *you* i.e. Isabella's allies
34   *Of* Out of
35   *Lord Warden* viceroy, usually appointed during a king's minority or absence
      fates goddesses of destiny

Have made his father so infortunate,
Deal you, my lords, in this, my loving lords,
As to your wisdoms fittest seems in all.

KENT
Madam, without offence, if I may ask,
How will you deal with Edward in his fall?   40

PRINCE EDWARD
Tell me, good uncle, what Edward do you mean?

KENT
Nephew, your father; I dare not call him King.

MORTIMER JUNIOR
My lord of Kent, what needs these questions?
'Tis not in her controlment, nor in ours,
But as the realm and Parliament shall please,   45
So shall your brother be disposèd of.
[*Aside to* ISABELLA] I like not this relenting mood in Edmund;
Madam, 'tis good to look to him betimes.

ISABELLA [*Aside to* MORTIMER JUNIOR]
My lord, the Mayor of Bristol knows our mind?

MORTIMER JUNIOR
[*Aside*] Yea, madam, and they 'scape not easily   50
That fled the field.

ISABELLA   Baldock is with the King;
A goodly chancellor, is he not, my lord?

SIR JOHN
So are the Spencers, the father and the son.

KENT
[*To himself*] This Edward is the ruin of the realm.

Enter RHYS AP HOWELL, *and the* MAYOR OF BRISTOL,
with SPENCER [SENIOR, *guarded by soldiers*]

36   *infortunate* unfortunate
37   *Deal* act, proceed
38   *fittest* most suitable, agreeable
41   'Kent is ungently reproved for lack of respect (by not referring to Edward by his
       title)' (Gill).
44   *controlment* (i) power (ii) ability to restrain
47   *relenting* pitying
48   *look to him* i.e. in anticipation of a change of loyalties
       betimes in good time
49   *knows our mind* i.e. is acquainted with our intentions

RHYS AP HOWELL

    God save Queen Isabel and her princely son.   55
    Madam, the Mayor and citizens of Bristol,
    In sign of love and duty to this presence,
    Present by me this traitor to the state –
    Spencer, the father to that wanton Spencer,
    That, like the lawless Catiline of Rome,   60
    Revelled in England's wealth and treasury.

ISABELLA

    We thank you all.

MORTIMER JUNIOR   Your loving care in this

    Deserveth princely favours and rewards.
    But where's the King and the other Spencer fled?

RHYS AP HOWELL

    Spencer the son, created Earl of Gloucester,   65
    Is with that smooth-tongued scholar Baldock gone,
    And shipped but late for Ireland with the King.

MORTIMER JUNIOR

    Some whirlwind fetch them back, or sink them all!
    They shall be started thence, I doubt it not.

PRINCE EDWARD

    Shall I not see the King my father yet?   70

KENT

    [*Aside*] Unhappy Edward, chased from England's bounds.

SIR JOHN

    Madam, what resteth? Why stand ye in a muse?

ISABELLA

    I rue my lord's ill fortune, but, alas,
    Care of my country called me to this war.

MORTIMER JUNIOR

    Madam, have done with care and sad complaint;   75
    Your King hath wronged your country and himself,
    And we must seek to right it as we may.

57   *presence* i.e. royal presence
60   *Catiline* Lucius Sergius Catalina (d. 62 B.C.), a corrupt Roman nobleman who was a byword for treason in the 1590s
67   *but late* just lately
69   *started* forced out (as an animal driven from its hiding-place)
71   *Unhappy* ed. (Vnhappies Q)
    bounds territory
72   *resteth* remains to be done
    in a muse in thought, perplexed

Meanwhile, have hence this rebel to the block;
Your lordship cannot privilege your head.

SPENCER SENIOR

Rebel is he that fights against his prince;   80
So fought not they that fought in Edward's right.

MORTIMER JUNIOR

Take him away; he prates.

                              [*Exit* SPENCER SENIOR, *guarded*]
                              You, Rhys ap Howell,
Shall do good service to her majesty,
Being of countenance in your country here,
To follow these rebellious runagates.   85
We in meanwhile, madam, must take advice
How Baldock, Spencer, and their complices
May in their fall be followed to their end.

                              Exeunt

[Scene 19]

Enter the ABBOT, MONKS, [*King*] EDWARD, SPENCER [JUNIOR],
    and BALDOCK [, *the latter three disguised as clergy*]

ABBOT

Have you no doubt, my lord, have you no fear;
As silent and as careful will we be
To keep your royal person safe with us,
Free from suspect and fell invasion
Of such as have your majesty in chase –   5

---

78 *have hence* take away
79 Spencer Senior's newly acquired status saves him from hanging, but not decapitation.
80 *prince* ruler
84 *countenance* authority, influence
85 *runagates* (i) renegades (ii) traitors. In Elizabethan England the term was associated with voluntary Catholic exiles who were, it was thought, trained for sedition and assassination in the Continental seminaries.
86 *must take advice* i.e. consider, deliberate
87 *complices* accomplices
88 *followed to their end* i.e. pursued to their deaths

4 *suspect* suspicion
   fell cruel
5 *in chase* i.e. being pursued, hunted (like an animal in sport)

Yourself, and those your chosen company –
As danger of this stormy time requires.

EDWARD

Father, thy face should harbour no deceit;
O hadst thou ever been a king, thy heart,
Pierced deeply with sense of my distress,   10
Could not but take compassion of my state.
Stately and proud, in riches and in train,
Whilom I was powerful and full of pomp;
But what is he, whom rule and empery
Have not in life or death made miserable?   15
Come Spencer, come Baldock, come sit down by me;
Make trial now of that philosophy
That in our famous nurseries of arts
Thou sucked'st from Plato and from Aristotle.
Father, this life contemplative is heaven –   20
O that I might this life in quiet lead!
But we, alas, are chased; and you, my friends,
Your lives and my dishonour they pursue.
Yet, gentle monks, for treasure, gold nor fee,
Do you betray us and our company.   25

MONKS

Your grace may sit secure, if none but we
Do wot of your abode.

SPENCER JUNIOR

Not one alive; but shrewdly I suspect
A gloomy fellow in a mead below;
A gave a long look after us, my lord,   30

13   *Whilom* formerly
     pomp splendour, magnificence
14   *empery* dominion
18   *nurseries of arts* i.e. the universities of Oxford and Cambridge
20   *life contemplative* The 'contemplative life', as distinct from the 'active life' (both
     concepts derived from St Augustine's *City of God*), entailed religious devotion and
     solitude.
27   *wot* know
28   *shrewdly* intuitively
29   *gloomy fellow* the Mower, whom Spencer Junior supposes to be the figure of Death
     the Grim Reaper in the field, holding a scythe. While this 'vision' adds to the tragic
     sense of foreboding, it may also suggest that Spencer Junior's imagination is being
     affected by exhaustion or fear.
     mead meadow
     below i.e. down, outside the abbey

And all the land, I know, is up in arms –
Arms that pursue our lives with deadly hate.

BALDOCK

We were embarked for Ireland, wretched we,
With awkward winds and sore tempests driven
To fall on shore and here to pine in fear   35
Of Mortimer and his confederates.

EDWARD

Mortimer! Who talks of Mortimer?
Who wounds me with the name of Mortimer,
That bloody man? [*He kneels*] Good father, on thy lap
Lay I this head, laden with mickle care.   40
O might I never open these eyes again,
Never again lift up this drooping head,
O never more lift up this dying heart!

SPENCER JUNIOR

Look up, my lord. Baldock, this drowsiness
Betides no good. Here even we are betrayed.   45

> *Enter, with Welsh hooks,* RHYS AP HOWELL, *a* MOWER,
> *and the* EARL OF LEICESTER[, *with soldiers*]

MOWER

Upon my life, those be the men ye seek.

RHYS AP HOWELL

Fellow, enough. [*To* LEICESTER] My lord, I pray be short;
A fair commission warrants what we do.

LEICESTER [*Aside*]

The Queen's commission, urged by Mortimer.
What cannot gallant Mortimer with the Queen?   50
Alas, see where he sits and hopes unseen

34   *sore* harsh
35   *fall on shore* become grounded
39   *bloody* bloodthirsty, causing bloodshed
40   *mickle* much
44   *drowsiness* traditionally an ill omen
45   *Betides* bodes
45   s.d. 1 *Welsh hooks* scythe-like tools. Michael J. Warren convincingly argues that these
      are long-handled hedging-bills and not, as many editors have previously assumed,
      military weapons. This would make sense considering the presence of the Mower.
      See 'Welsh Hooks in *Edward II*', *N&Q*, n.s. 25 (1978), 109–10.
48   *fair commission* formal written authority
      warrants authorizes
50   *gallant* (i) bold (ii) lover

T'escape their hands that seek to reave his life.
Too true it is: *quem dies vidit veniens superbum,*
Hunc dies vidit fugiens iacentem.
But Leicester, leave to grow so passionate.   55
[*Aloud*] Spencer and Baldock, by no other names,
I arrest you of high treason here.
Stand not on tides, but obey th'arrest;
'Tis in the name of Isabel the Queen.
My lord, why droop you thus?   60

EDWARD

O day! The last of all my bliss on earth,
Centre of all misfortune. O my stars!
Why do you lour unkindly on a king?
Comes Leicester, then, in Isabella's name
To take my life, my company, from me?   65
Here, man, rip up this panting breast of mine
And take my heart in rescue of my friends.

RHYS AP HOWELL

Away with them.

SPENCER JUNIOR   It may become thee yet
To let us take our farewell of his grace.

ABBOT

My heart with pity earns to see this sight;   70
A king to bear these words and proud commands!

EDWARD

Spencer, ah sweet Spencer, thus then must we part?

SPENCER JUNIOR

We must, my lord; so will the angry heavens.

EDWARD

Nay, so will hell and cruel Mortimer;

52   *reave* take away by force
53–4   *quem dies ... iacentem* taken from Seneca's *Thyestes,* ll. 613–14. Translated by Jasper
        Heywood in 1560: 'Whom dawne of day hath seene in pryde to raygne, / Hym
        overthrowne hath seene the evening late.'
56   *no other names* Spencer Junior and Baldock are stripped of their recently acquired
        titles ('names').
58   *Stand* (i) assert (ii) rely on. The favourites are warned that they cannot expect the
        protection of noble privileges.
61–2   *O day ... stars* Cf. 10. 4–5.
63   *lour* frown, look angry
66   *panting* (of the heart) palpitating
67   *rescue* release from legal custody   70 *earns* grieves
73, 74 *will* command, determine

The gentle heavens have not to do in this. 75

BALDOCK

My lord, it is in vain to grieve or storm.

Here humbly of your grace we take our leaves;

Our lots are cast. I fear me, so is thine.

EDWARD

In heaven we may, in earth never shall we meet.

And Leicester, say, what shall become of us? 80

LEICESTER

Your majesty must go to Kenilworth.

EDWARD

'Must'! 'Tis somewhat hard when kings must go.

LEICESTER

Here is a litter ready for your grace

That waits your pleasure; and the day grows old.

RHYS AP HOWELL

As good be gone, as stay and be benighted. 85

EDWARD

A litter hast thou? Lay me in a hearse,

And to the gates of hell convey me hence;

Let Pluto's bells ring out my fatal knell,

And hags howl for my death at Charon's shore,

For friends hath Edward none but these, and these, 90

And these must die under a tyrant's sword.

RHYS AP HOWELL

My lord, be going; care not for these,

For we shall see them shorter by the heads.

EDWARD

Well, that shall be shall be; part we must:

---

76 *storm* make a commotion
81 *Kenilworth* Q's old-spelling form, 'Killingworth', has an ominous aptness; some
    productions may wish to retain it in preference to the modernized version. See the
    Note on the Text for a full discussion of the modernization.
83 *litter* coach for one person which was usually carried by two men
85 i.e. it would be best to leave for Kenilworth before nightfall
88 *Pluto's bells* In classical mythology, Pluto was the keeper of the underworld and ruler
    of the dead. The bells were not part of classical tradition but probably represent the
    death knell ringing out for those about to die.
89 *Charon* the ferryman of the classical underworld who transported the dead across
    the River Styx
90 *but these . . . these* This could be an implicit stage direction prompting Edward to
    gesticulate or point to Spencer Junior and Baldock.
93 i.e. they will be beheaded

Sweet Spencer, gentle Baldock, part we must. 95
Hence feignèd weeds, unfeignèd are my woes.
Father, farewell. Leicester, thou stay'st for me,
And go I must. Life, farewell with my friends.

Exeunt EDWARD *and* LEICESTER

SPENCER JUNIOR

O, is he gone? Is noble Edward gone,
Parted from hence, never to see us more? 100
Rend, sphere of heaven, and fire forsake thy orb!
Earth melt to air! Gone is my sovereign,
Gone, gone, alas, never to make return.

BALDOCK

Spencer, I see our souls are fleeted hence;
We are deprived the sunshine of our life. 105
Make for a new life, man; throw up thy eyes,
And heart and hand to heaven's immortal throne,
Pay nature's debt with cheerful countenance.
Reduce we all our lessons unto this:
To die, sweet Spencer, therefore live we all; 110
Spencer, all live to die, and rise to fall.

RHYS AP HOWELL

Come, come, keep these preachments till you come to the place
appointed. You, and such as you are, have made wise work in
England. Will your lordships away?

---

96   *feignèd* false
     weeds clothes. Cf. Peele's *Edward I*, 'Hence faigned weedes, unfaigned is my griefe'
     (2519)
101 *Rend* ed. (Rent Q) be torn apart
     sphere of heaven the Sun
104 *fleeted hence* i.e. have flown out of the body
105 *sunshine of our life* The King was frequently likened to the sun in Elizabethan drama.
     Cf. Shakespeare, *Richard II*, 3.3.61–2.
108 *Pay nature's debt* i.e. die; proverbial (Tilley D 168)
109 *Reduce* summarize
     lessons learning. Ironically, Baldock's last words recall his earlier scholastic
     pretensions.
110–11 Baldock resigns himself to death by reflecting that we are born to die; but his
     meditation also invokes the medieval 'de casibus' notion of tragedy in which an
     individual's rise to success is always followed by their fall.
112 *preachments* sermons
112–14 ed. (Come ... till / you ... appointed / You ... in / England. / Will ... away? Q)
112–13 *place appointed* i.e. the scaffold
113 *made ... work* created havoc, caused trouble

MOWER

    Your worship, I trust, will remember me?   115

RHYS AP HOWELL

    Remember thee, fellow? What else?

    Follow me to the town.

                                    [Exeunt]

[Scene 20]

Enter [EDWARD] *the King,* LEICESTER, *with the*
BISHOP [OF WINCHESTER, *and* TRUSSEL]
for the crown[, and attendants]

LEICESTER

    Be patient, good my lord, cease to lament.

    Imagine Kenilworth Castle were your court.

    And that you lay for pleasure here a space,

    Not of compulsion or necessity.

EDWARD

    Leicester, if gentle words might comfort me,   5

    Thy speeches long ago had eased my sorrows,

    For kind and loving hast thou always been.

    The griefs of private men are soon allayed,

    But not of kings: the forest deer, being struck,

    Runs to an herb that closeth up the wounds;   10

    But when the imperial lion's flesh is gored,

    He rends and tears it with his wrathful paw,

    And, highly scorning that the lowly earth

    Should drink his blood, mounts up into the air.

115   i.e. will you reward me?
116   *What else?* But of course!

  0   s.d. ed. (*Enter the king, Leicester, with a Bishop / for the crowne.* Q)
  3   *lay* stayed, resided
       a space an interval, period of time
  8   *private men* i.e. those not holding public office
       allayed diluted, abated
9–10   *forest deer... wounds* Cf. the belief that the stag, when wounded by an arrow, would
       eat the herb dittany; this would close the wound, forcing the arrow out (Pliny,
       Naturalis Historia VIII.xli.97).
 13   *And,* ed. not in Q
 14   *mounts up* rises

And so it fares with me, whose dauntless mind   15
The ambitious Mortimer would seek to curb,
And that unnatural Queen, false Isabel,
That thus hath pent and mewed me in a prison.
For such outrageous passions cloy my soul,
As with the wings of rancour and disdain   20
Full often am I soaring up to heaven
To plain me to the gods against them both.
But when I call to mind I am a king,
Methinks I should revenge me of the wrongs
That Mortimer and Isabel have done.   25
But what are kings, when regiment is gone,
But perfect shadows in a sunshine day?
My nobles rule; I bear the name of King.
I wear the crown, but am controlled by them –
By Mortimer and my unconstant Queen   30
Who spots my nuptial bed with infamy.
Whilst I am lodged within this cave of care,
Where sorrow at my elbow still attends
To company my heart with sad laments,
That bleeds within me for this strange exchange.   35
But tell me, must I now resign my crown
To make usurping Mortimer a king?

BISHOP OF WINCHESTER

Your grace mistakes; it is for England's good
And princely Edward's right we crave the crown.

EDWARD

No, 'tis for Mortimer, not Edward's head,   40
For he's a lamb encompassèd by wolves
Which in a moment will abridge his life.

18   *pent shut* up
       mewed caged. Commonly used as a metaphor for imprisonment, a 'mew' was a cage
       or coop in which animals and birds were kept when being fattened for slaughter,
19   *outrageous* excessive
22   *plain* complain
26   *regiment* rule, power
27   *perfect* mere (Rowland)
30   *unconstant* unfaithful
34   *company* accompany
35   *strange exchange* i.e. the change of circumstances not becoming to a king
41   *lamb . . . by wolves* Cf. *3 Henry VI*, 'Such safety finds / The trembling lamb
       environèd with wolves' (1.1.242–3).

But if proud Mortimer do wear this crown,
Heavens turn it to a blaze of quenchless fire,
Or, like the snaky wreath of Tisiphon,   45
Engirt the temples of his hateful head;
So shall not England's vines be perishèd,
But Edward's name survives, though Edward dies.

LEICESTER

My lord, why waste you thus the time away?
They stay your answer: will you yield your crown?   50

EDWARD

Ah Leicester, weigh how hardly I can brook
To lose my crown and kingdom without cause,
To give ambitious Mortimer my right,
That like a mountain overwhelms my bliss;
In which extreme my mind here murdered is.   55
But what the heavens appoint, I must obey.

[*He removes his crown*]

Here, take my crown – the life of Edward too.
Two kings in England cannot reign at once.
But stay awhile; let me be King till night,
That I may gaze upon this glittering crown;   60
So shall my eyes receive their last content,
My head, the latest honour due to it,
And jointly both yield up their wishèd right.
Continue ever, thou celestial sun;
Let never silent night possess this clime.   65
Stand still, you watches of the element;
All times and seasons rest you at a stay,
That Edward may be still fair England's King.

43–4   *crown . . . quenchless fire* Cf. Euripides' *Medea* (1186ff.) in which Jason deserts Medea
        for Creusa. Medea exacts her revenge by giving Creusa a golden crown which bursts
        into flames.

45   *Tisiphon* Tisiphone, one of the Furies (see 4.315 n.), whose hair was made of snakes

47   *vines* The vine was the emblem of regal lineage.

50   *stay* await

50–111 Shakespeare was substantially indebted to this passage in the deposition scene (4.1)
        of *Richard II*.

51   *weigh* ed. (way Q1–2; waigh Q3–4)

64–8   Cf. Faustus' last speech (*Dr Faustus*, 5.2) in which he desperately hopes to escape
        the mutable effects of time and forestall his imminent demise.

66   *watches . . . element* the stars and planets of the sky. The 'watches' are the four parts
        of the night, while the 'element' is the sky.

67   *rest . . . a stay* i.e. remain fixed

But day's bright beams doth vanish fast away,
And needs I must resign my wishèd crown.   70
Inhuman creatures, nursed with tiger's milk,
Why gape you for your sovereign's overthrow?
My diadem, I mean, and guiltless life.
See, monsters, see, I'll wear my crown again.

[He puts on the crown]

What, fear you not the fury of your King?   75
But hapless Edward, thou art fondly led.
They pass not for thy frowns as late they did,
But seek to make a new-elected king,
Which fills my mind with strange despairing thoughts,
Which thoughts are martyred with endless torments;   80
And in this torment, comfort find I none
But that I feel the crown upon my head.
And therefore let me wear it yet a while.

TRUSSEL

My lord, the parliament must have present news,
And therefore say, will you resign or no?   85

The King rageth

EDWARD

I'll not resign, but whilst I live –
Traitors, be gone, and join you with Mortimer.
Elect, conspire, install, do what you will;
Their blood and yours shall seal these treacheries.

BISHOP OF WINCHESTER

This answer we'll return, and so farewell.   90

[The BISHOP OF WINCHESTER *and* TRUSSEL *begin to leave]*

LEICESTER

Call them again, my lord, and speak them fair,
For if they go, the Prince shall lose his right.

---

71 *tiger's milk* It was commonly believed that human moral characteristics were
    acquired from the mother through weaning; the tiger was a byword for cruelty.
76 *fondly* foolishly
77 *pass* care
    late i.e. recently
78 *seek* ed. (seekes Q)
86 The line is metrically short. Some editors emend to supply the missing foot ('be
    King'), but the Q reading can be interpreted as portraying Edward's exasperated
    inarticulacy.
88 *install* invest, place (someone) in authority

EDWARD
Call thou them back; I have no power to speak.

LEICESTER
My lord, the King is willing to resign.

BISHOP OF WINCHESTER
If he be not, let him choose –   95

EDWARD
O would I might! But heavens and earth conspire
To make me miserable.   [*He removes the crown*]
           Here, receive my crown. Receive it?
No, these innocent hands of mine
Shall not be guilty of so foul a crime.
He of you all that most desires my blood   100
And will be called the murderer of a king,
Take it. What, are you moved? Pity you me?
Then send for unrelenting Mortimer
And Isabel, whose eyes, being turned to steel,
Will sooner sparkle fire than shed a tear.   105
Yet stay, for rather than I will look on them,
Here, here!   [*He gives the crown to the* BISHOP]
         Now, sweet God of heaven,
Make me despise this transitory pomp,
And sit for aye enthronizèd in heaven,
Come death, and with thy fingers close my eyes,   110
Or if I live, let me forget myself.

BISHOP OF WINCHESTER
My lord.

EDWARD
Call me not lord! Away, out of my sight!
Ah, pardon me; grief makes me lunatic.
Let not that Mortimer protect my son;   115
More safety is there in a tiger's jaws
Than his embracements.   [*He gives a handkerchief*]
      Bear this to the Queen,

---

105   *sparkle fire* flash with anger or rage, like sparks struck from steel by friction
109   *for aye* for ever
       enthronized enthroned
111   ed. (*Enter Bartley* Q; s.d. moved to line 127 in this ed.)
112   s.p. BISHOP OF WINCHESTER ed. (*Bartley* Q)
113–14   ed. (Call . . . lorde, / Away . . . me, / Greefe . . . lunatick, Q)
115   *protect* be Protector to
117   *Than* ed. (This Q)

Wet with my tears and dried again with sighs.
If with the sight thereof she be not moved,
Return it back and dip it in my blood. 120
Commend me to my son, and bid him rule
Better than I. Yet how have I transgressed,
Unless it be with too much clemency?

TRUSSEL
And thus, most humbly, do we take our leave.

EDWARD
Farewell. I know the next news that they bring 125
Will be my death, and welcome shall it be;
To wretched men death is felicity.

[*Enter* BERKELEY *with a letter*]

LEICESTER
Another post. What news brings he?

EDWARD
Such news as I expect. Come, Berkeley, come,
And tell thy message to my naked breast. 130

BERKELEY
My lord, think not a thought so villainous
Can harbour in a man of noble birth.
To do your highness service and devoir,
And save you from your foes, Berkeley would die.

LEICESTER [*Reading the letter*]
My lord, the council of the Queen commands 135
That I resign my charge.

EDWARD
And who must keep me now? Must you, my lord?

BERKELEY
Ay, my most gracious lord, so 'tis decreed.

EDWARD [*Taking the letter*]
By Mortimer, whose name is written here.
[*He tears up the letter*]
Well may I rend his name that rends my heart! 140
This poor revenge hath something eased my mind.
So may his limbs be torn, as is this paper!

---

130   *naked breast* Many editors argue that Edward is 'offering himself as to a murderer's
       dagger' (Gill).
131   s.p. BERKELEY ed. (*Bartley* Q; and throughout)
133   *devoir* duty

Hear me, immortal Jove, and grant it too.
BERKELEY
    Your grace must hence with me to Berkeley straight.
EDWARD
    Whither you will; all places are alike,   145
    And every earth is fit for burial.
LEICESTER
    Favour him, my lord, as much as lieth in you.
BERKELEY
    Even so betide my soul as I use him.
EDWARD
    Mine enemy hath pitied my estate,
    And that's the cause that I am now removed.   150
BERKELEY
    And thinks your grace that Berkeley will be cruel?
EDWARD
    I know not; but of this am I assured,
    That death ends all, and I can die but once.
    Leicester, farewell.
LEICESTER
    Not yet, my lord; I'll bear you on your way.

                                                          Exeunt   155

[Scene 21]

Enter MORTIMER [JUNIOR], *and Queen* ISABELLA

MORTIMER JUNIOR
    Fair Isabel, now have we our desire.
    The proud corrupters of the light-brained King
    Have done their homage to the lofty gallows,
    And he himself lies in captivity.
    Be ruled by me, and we will rule the realm.   5
    In any case, take heed of childish fear,
    For now we hold an old wolf by the ears,

    143   *Jove* or Jupiter, the supreme god in the Roman pantheon
    149   *estate* condition
    153   *I . . . once* proverbial (Tilley M 219)

      2   *light-brained* frivolous, wanton
      7   *hold . . . ears* proverbial (Tilley W 603)

                                    437

That if he slip will seize upon us both,
And gripe the sorer, being griped himself.
Think therefore, madam, that imports us much   10
To erect your son with all the speed we may,
And that I be Protector over him,
For our behoof will bear the greater sway
Whenas a king's name shall be underwrit.

ISABELLA
Sweet Mortimer, the life of Isabel,   15
Be thou persuaded that I love thee well,
And therefore, so the Prince my son be safe,
Whom I esteem as dear as these mine eyes,
Conclude against his father what thou wilt,
And I myself will willingly subscribe.   20

MORTIMER JUNIOR
First would I hear news that he were deposed,
And then let me alone to handle him.

Enter MESSENGER

MORTIMER JUNIOR
Letters, from whence?
MESSENGER   From Kenilworth, my lord.
ISABELLA
How fares my lord the King?
MESSENGER
In health, madam, but full of pensiveness.   25
ISABELLA
Alas, poor soul, would I could ease his grief.

[*Enter the* BISHOP OF WINCHESTER *with the crown*]

Thanks, gentle Winchester.
[*To the* MESSENGER]   Sirrah, be gone.
                                        [*Exit* MESSENGER]

---

 9   *gripe . . . sorer* i.e. will seize upon (us) more grievously   *griped* afflicted
10   *imports us much* i.e. it is most important for us (*us* ed.; as Q)
11   *erect* establish on the throne
13–14 i.e. Mortimer and the Queen will have greater authority when he can act in the
       King's name (literally, sign official documents as if he were the King)
18   *as dear . . . eyes* proverbial (Dent E 249)
19   *Conclude* i.e. make a final decision about the King's fate
22   *let me alone* trust me
25   *pensiveness* sadness, melancholy

BISHOP OF WINCHESTER
    The King hath willingly resigned his crown.
ISABELLA
    O happy news! Send for the Prince, my son.
BISHOP OF WINCHESTER
    Further, ere this letter was sealed, Lord Berkeley came,   30
    So that he now is gone from Kenilworth.
    And we have heard that Edmund laid a plot
    To set his brother free; no more but so.
    The lord of Berkeley is so pitiful
    As Leicester that had charge of him before.   35
ISABELLA
    Then let some other be his guardian.
                        [*Exit* BISHOP OF WINCHESTER]
MORTIMER JUNIOR
    Let me alone – here is the privy seal.
    [*Calls offstage*] Who's there? Call hither Gourney and Maltravers.
    To dash the heavy-headed Edmund's drift,
    Berkeley shall be discharged, the King removed,   40
    And none but we shall know where he lieth.
ISABELLA
    But Mortimer, as long as he survives
    What safety rests for us, or for my son?
MORTIMER JUNIOR
    Speak, shall he presently be dispatched and die?
ISABELLA
    I would he were, so it were not by my means.   45

                Enter MALTRAVERS *and* GOURNEY

MORTIMER JUNIOR
    Enough. Maltravers, write a letter presently
    Unto the Lord of Berkeley from ourself,
    That he resign the King to thee and Gourney;
    And when 'tis done, we will subscribe our name.

30 s.p. *BISHOP OF WINCHESTER* ed. (*Bish* Q; and throughout the scene)
    ere ed. (or Q)
39 *dash* frustrate
    heavy-headed stupid, dull
    drift plot, scheme
43 *rests* remains
44 *dispatched* killed
48 *resign* surrender

MALTRAVERS

   It shall be done, my lord.

MORTIMER JUNIOR   Gourney.

GOURNEY   My lord?   50

MORTIMER JUNIOR

   As thou intendest to rise by Mortimer,

   Who now makes Fortune's wheel turn as he please,

   Seek all the means thou canst to make him droop,

   And neither give him kind word nor good look.

GOURNEY

   I warrant you, my lord.   55

MORTIMER JUNIOR

   And this above the rest, because we hear

   That Edmund casts to work his liberty,

   Remove him still from place to place by night,

   And at the last he come to Kenilworth,

   And then from thence to Berkeley back again.   60

   And by the way to make him fret the more,

   Speak curstly to him; and in any case

   Let no man comfort him if he chance to weep,

   But amplify his grief with bitter words.

MALTRAVERS

   Fear not, my lord, we'll do as you command.   65

MORTIMER JUNIOR

   So now away; post thitherwards amain.

ISABELLA

   Whither goes this letter? To my lord the King?

   Commend me humbly to his majesty,

   And tell him that I labour all in vain

   To ease his grief and work his liberty.   70

   And bear him this, as witness of my love.

                  [*She gives* MALTRAVERS *a jewel*]

MALTRAVERS

   I will, madam.

---

52 *Fortune's wheel . . . please* In sixteenth-century iconography, Fortune was represented with a wheel whose turning determined human fate; here Mortimer Junior arrogates that power to himself. Cf. *1 Tambutiaine*, 'I hold the Fates bound fast in iron chains / And with my hand turn Fortune's wheel about' (1.2.174–5).

57 *casts* plans

62 *curstly* malevolently, uncivilly

66 *post thitherwards amain* go there speedily

Exeunt MALTRAVERS *and* GOURNEY.
ISABELLA *and* MORTIMER [JUNIOR] *remain*

Enter the young PRINCE [EDWARD], *and the* EARL OF KENT
talking with him

MORTIMER JUNIOR [*Aside to* ISABELLA]
  Finely dissembled; do so still, sweet Queen.
  Here comes the young Prince with the Earl of Kent.
ISABELLA [*Aside to* MORTIMER JUNIOR]
  Something he whispers in his childish ears.   75
MORTIMER JUNIOR
  [*Aside*] If he have such access unto the Prince,
  Our plots and stratagems will soon be dashed.
ISABELLA
  [*Aside*] Use Edmund friendly, as if all were well.
MORTIMER JUNIOR
  How fares my honourable lord of Kent?
KENT
  In health, sweet Mortimer. How fares your grace?   80
ISABELLA
  Well – if my lord your brother were enlarged.
KENT
  I hear of late he hath deposed himself.
ISABELLA
  The more my grief.
MORTIMER JUNIOR
  And mine.
KENT
  [*Aside*] Ah, they do dissemble.   85
ISABELLA
  Sweet son, come hither; I must talk with thee.
MORTIMER JUNIOR
  Thou, being his uncle and the next of blood.
  Do look to be Protector over the Prince.
KENT
  Not I, my lord; who should protect the son
  But she that gave him life –1 mean, the Queen?   90
PRINCE EDWARD
  Mother, persuade me not to wear the crown;

73   *dissembled* feigned
81   *enlarged* released

Let him be King. I am too young to reign.

ISABELLA

But be content, seeing it his highness' pleasure.

PRINCE EDWARD

Let me but see him first, and then I will.

KENT

Ay, do, sweet nephew.   95

ISABELLA

Brother, you know it is impossible.

PRINCE EDWARD

Why, is he dead?

ISABELLA

No, God forbid.

KENT

I would those words proceeded from your heart.

MORTIMER JUNIOR

Inconstant Edmund, dost thou favour him   100

That wast a cause of his imprisonment?

KENT

The more cause have I now to make amends.

MORTIMER JUNIOR

I tell thee 'tis not meet that one so false

Should come about the person of a prince.

My lord, he hath betrayed the King, his brother,   105

And therefore trust him not.

PRINCE EDWARD

But he repents and sorrows for it now.

ISABELLA

Come son, and go with this gentle lord and me.

PRINCE EDWARD

With you I will, but not with Mortimer.

MORTIMER JUNIOR

Why, youngling, 'sdain'st thou so of Mortimer?   110

Then I will carry thee by force away.

PRINCE EDWARD

Help, uncle Kent, Mortimer will wrong me.

[*Exit* MORTIMER JUNIOR *with* PRINCE EDWARD]

---

92   *him* i.e. the Prince's father, Edward II
103   *meet* proper, appropriate
110   *youngling* stripling, novice (often spoken in a condescending manner)
      'sdain'st contracted form of 'disdainest'

ISABELLA

    Brother Edmund, strive not; we are his friends.

    Isabel is nearer than the Earl of Kent.

KENT

    Sister, Edward is my charge; redeem him.   115

ISABELLA

    Edward is my son, and I will keep him.   [*Exit*]

KENT

    Mortimer shall know that he hath wronged me.

    Hence will I haste to Kenilworth Castle

    And rescue agèd Edward from his foes,

    To be revenged on Mortimer and thee.   [*Exit*]

[Scene 22]

Enter MALTRAVERS *and* GOURNEY [*carrying torches,*] *with*
[EDWARD] *the King*[*, and soldiers*]

MALTRAVERS

    My lord, be not pensive; we are your friends.

    Men are ordained to live in misery;

    Therefore come, dalliance dangereth our lives.

EDWARD

    Friends, whither must unhappy Edward go?

    Will hateful Mortimer appoint no rest?   5

    Must I be vexèd like the nightly bird

    Whose sight is loathsome to all wingèd fowls?

    When will the fury of his mind assuage?

    When will his heart be satisfied with blood?

    If mine will serve, unbowel straight this breast,   10

115   *charge* responsibility
      redeem him i.e. return him
119   *agèd Edward* Presumably the adjective serves to differentiate him from his son,
      Prince Edward; the historical Edward II was, at this point, only 43 years old.
120   s.d. ed. (*Exeunt omnes.* Q)

  1   *pensive* full of sorrow
  3   *dalliance* idle delay
  4   *unhappy* unfortunate
  6   *vexèd* tormented
      nightly bird i.e. the owl (a common portent of death)
10   *unbowel* open up   *straight* without delay

And give my heart to Isabel and him;
It is the chiefest mark they level at.

GOURNEY

Not so, my liege; the Queen hath given this charge
To keep your grace in safety.
Your passions make your dolours to increase.   15

EDWARD

This usage makes my misery increase.
But can my air of life continue long
When all my senses are annoyed with stench?
Within a dungeon England's King is kept,
Where I am starved for want of sustenance.   20
My daily diet is heart-breaking sobs,
That almost rends the closet of my heart.
Thus lives old Edward, not relieved by any,
And so must die, though pitièd by many.
O water, gentle friends, to cool my thirst   25
And clear my body from foul excrements.

MALTRAVERS

Here's channel water, as our charge is given;
Sit down, for we'll be barbers to your grace.

EDWARD

Traitors, away! What, will you murder me,
Or choke your sovereign with puddle water?   30

GOURNEY

No, but wash your face and shave away your beard,
Lest you be known and so be rescuèd.

MALTRAVERS

Why strive you thus? Your labour is in vain.

EDWARD

The wren may strive against the lion's strength,
But all in vain; so vainly do I strive   35
To seek for mercy at a tyrant's hand.

They wash him with puddle water,
and shave his beard away

12   *mark* target
      level aim
17   *air of life* breath
22   *closet* private chamber
26   *excrements* faeces. (The word also carried the archaic sense of 'hair', which Maltravers
      and Gourney take – by deliberate error – to be Edward's meaning.)
27   *channel* drain, sewer. Cf. 1. 187.

Immortal powers, that knows the painful cares
That waits upon my poor distressèd soul,
O level all your looks upon these daring men,
That wrongs their liege and sovereign, England's King.   40
O Gaveston, it is for thee that I am wronged;
For me, both thou and both the Spencers died,
And for your sakes a thousand wrongs I'll take.
The Spencers' ghosts, wherever they remain,
Wish well to mine; then tush, for them I'll die.   45

MALTRAVERS

'Twixt theirs and yours shall be no enmity.
Come, come away. Now put the torches out;
We'll enter in by darkness to Kenilworth.

Enter EDMUND [THE EARL OF KENT]

GOURNEY

How now, who comes there?

MALTRAVERS

Guard the King sure; it is the Earl of Kent.   50

EDWARD

O gentle brother, help to rescue me.

MALTRAVERS

Keep them asunder; thrust in the King.

KENT

Soldiers, let me but talk to him one word.

GOURNEY

Lay hands upon the Earl for this assault.

KENT

Lay down your weapons; traitors, yield the King!   55

MALTRAVERS

Edmund, yield thou thyself, or thou shalt die.

[*Soldiers seize* KENT]

KENT

Base villains, wherefore do you grip me thus?

GOURNEY

Bind him, and so convey him to the court.

37–9   Forker compares Thomas Lodge's *Wounds of Civil War* (1588), 'Immortal powers
       that know the painful cares / That weight upon my poor distressed heart, / O bend
       your brows and level all your looks / Of dreadful awe upon these daring men.'
       (IV.ii.87–90).

44   *remain* dwell

EDMUND

    Where is the court but here? Here is the King,

    And I will visit him. Why stay you me?   60

MALTRAVERS

    The court is where Lord Mortimer remains.

    Thither shall your honour go; and so, farewell.

    Exeunt MALTRAVERS *and* GOURNEY, *with* [EDWARD] *the King.*

        EDMUND [THE EARL OF KENT] *and the soldiers* [*remain*]

KENT

    O, miserable is that commonweal, where lords

    Keep courts and kings are locked in prison!

SOLDIER

    Wherefore stay we? On, sirs, to the court.   65

KENT

    Ay, lead me whither you will, even to my death,

    Seeing that my brother cannot be released.

                              Exeunt

[Scene 23]

Enter MORTIMER [JUNIOR] *alone*

MORTIMER JUNIOR

    The King must die, or Mortimer goes down;

    The commons now begin to pity him.

    Yet he that is the cause of Edward's death

    Is sure to pay for it when his son is of age,

    And therefore will I do it cunningly.   5

    This letter, written by a friend of ours,

    Contains his death, yet bids them save his life:

    [*He reads*] 'Edwardum occidere nolite timere, bonum est,

    Fear not to kill the King, 'tis good he die.'

    But read it thus, and that's another sense: 10

    'Edwardum occidere nolite, timere bonum est,

    Kill not the King, 'tis good to fear the worst.'

---

59   *Where . . . but here* In the sixteenth century the court was understood not only as a
      fixed location but as the establishment which accompanied the person of the King.

63   *commonweal* state

Unpointed as it is, thus shall it go,
That, being dead, if it chance to be found,
Maltravers and the rest may bear the blame,   15
And we be quit that caused it to be done.
Within this room is locked the messenger
That shall convey it and perform the rest.
And by a secret token that he bears,
Shall he be murdered when the deed is done.   20
Lightborne, come forth.

[Enter LIGHTBORNE]

                  Art thou as resolute as thou wast?

LIGHTBORNE

What else, my lord? And far more resolute.

MORTIMER JUNIOR

And hast thou cast how to accomplish it?

LIGHTBORNE

Ay, ay, and none shall know which way he died.

MORTIMER JUNIOR

But at his looks, Lightborne, thou wilt relent.   25

LIGHTBORNE

Relent? Ha, ha! I use much to relent.

MORTIMER JUNIOR

Well, do it bravely, and be secret.

LIGHTBORNE

You shall not need to give instructions;
'Tis not the first time I have killed a man.
I learned in Naples how to poison flowers,   30

13   *Unpointed* unpunctuated. The letter's meaning is made ambiguous through its lack of punctuation; this is intended to obscure Mortimer Junior's involvement in Edward's death.

14   *being dead* i.e. once Edward is murdered

16   *quit* acquitted, exonerated

21   *Lightborne* The assassin derives from theatrical and not historical sources; such characters were popular in tragedies of the late 1580s and early 1590s. It is significant that he shares his name (which Anglicizes Lucifer) with one of Satan's associates in the Chester cycle of mystery plays (c. 1467–88): according to a well-known saying of the time, 'An Englishman Italianate is the Devil incarnate.'

26   *use much* i.e. am accustomed to (spoken facetiously)

27   *bravely* (i) without fear (ii) excellently, finely

30–6 *I learned . . . these* Lightborne's account of his studies in Naples – reputedly the most dangerous of Italian cities – may recall a panic of late 1591 about a trained Italian assassin being sent to England to assassinate the Queen; see Introduction, p. xv. Cf.

To strangle with a lawn thrust through the throat,
To pierce the windpipe with a needle's point,
Or, whilst one is asleep, to take a quill
And blow a little powder in his ears,
Or open his mouth and pour quicksilver down.   35
But yet I have a braver way than these.

MORTIMER JUNIOR

What's that?

LIGHTBORNE

Nay, you shall pardon me; none shall know my tricks.

MORTIMER JUNIOR

I care not how it is, so it be not spied.
Deliver this to Gourney and Maltravers.   40

[He gives the letter to LIGHTBORNE]

At every ten miles' end thou hast a horse.

[Giving a token] Take this. Away, and never see me more.

LIGHTBORNE

No?

MORTIMER JUNIOR

No, unless thou bring me news of Edward's death.

LIGHTBORNE

That will I quickly do. Farewell, my lord.   *[Exit]*   45

MORTIMER JUNIOR

The Prince I rule, the Queen do I command,
And with a lowly congé to the ground
The proudest lords salute me as I pass;
I seal, I cancel, I do what I will.
Feared am I more than loved; let me be feared,   50

---

also *The Jew of Malta,* 'I learned in Florence how to kiss my hand' (2.3.23), 'I walk abroad a-nights / And kill sick people groaning under walls; / Sometimes I go about and poison wells . . .' (2.3.175–7).

31   *lawn . . . throat* a piece of fine linen cloth forced down the victim's throat to block the windpipe

34   *powder in his ears* Cf. the murder of Hamlet's father in Shakespeare's play (1.5.61–70).

35   *quicksilver* mercury (which is poisonous)

36   *braver* more skilful

38   *tricks* skills, methods

42   *Take this* i.e. the 'secret token' (19) which will seal Lightborne's fate

47   *congé* bow

49   *seal* authorize official documents

50   *Feared . . . feared* Mortimer Junior follows the advice of Machiavelli's *The Prince,* a forbidden book of the period which circulated surreptitiously in manuscript:

And when I frown, make all the court look pale.
I view the Prince with Aristarchus' eyes,
Whose looks were as a breeching to a boy.
They thrust upon me the protectorship
And sue to me for that that I desire.   55
While at the council table, grave enough,
And not unlike a bashful Puritan,
First I complain of imbecility,
Saying it is *onus quam gravissimum*,
Till being interrupted by my friends,   60
Suscepi that *provinciam*, as they term it,
And to conclude, I am Protector now.
Now is all sure: the Queen and Mortimer
Shall rule the realm, the King, and none rule us.
Mine enemies will I plague, my friends advance,   65
And what I list command, who dare control?
Maior sum quam cui possit fortuna nocere.
And that this be the coronation day,
It pleaseth me, and Isabel the Queen.

                     [*Trumpets sound within*]
The trumpets sound; I must go take my place.   70

        Enter the young King [EDWARD III],
     BISHOP [OF CANTERBURY], CHAMPION,
        NOBLES, [*and*] *Queen* [ISABELLA]

BISHOP OF CANTERBURY
Long live King Edward, by the grace of God,

> 'because hardly can [love and fear] subsist both together, it is much safer to be feared, than to be lov'd' (XVII, trans. Edward Dacres, London, 1640, p. 130).

52   *Aristarchus* notoriously harsh schoolmaster and grammarian who lived in Alexandria in the second century B.C.
53   *breeching* whipping
55   *sue to* petition
57   *Puritan* follower of an extreme Protestant movement which emerged in the sixteenth century and was theologically rooted in Calvinism. Puritans were known for their hypocritical advocacy of self-restraint.
58   *imbecility* weakness
59   *onus quam gravissimum* (Latin) a very heavy burden
61   *Suscepi . . . provinciam* (Latin) I have undertaken that office
66   *list* desire to
67   *Maior sum quam cui possit fortuna nocere* I am so great that Fortune cannot harm me; from Ovid's *Metamorphoses*, VI. 195
71   s.p. BISHOP OF CANTERBURY ed. (*Bish.* Q)

King of England and Lord of Ireland.

CHAMPION

If any Christian, Heathen, Turk, or Jew
Dares but affirm that Edward's not true King,
And will avouch his saying with the sword,   75
I am the Champion that will combat him.   [*Silence*]

MORTIMER JUNIOR

None comes. Sound trumpets.   [*Trumpets sound*]

KING EDWARD III   Champion, here's to thee.
                                        [*He raises his goblet*]

ISABELLA

Lord Mortimer, now take him to your charge.

Enter SOLDIERS *with the* EARL OF KENT *prisoner*

MORTIMER JUNIOR

What traitor have we there with blades and bills?

SOLDIER

Edmund, the Earl of Kent.

KING EDWARD III   What hath he done?   80

MORTIMER JUNIOR

A would have taken the King away perforce,
As we were bringing him to Kenilworth.

MORTIMER JUNIOR

Did you attempt his rescue, Edmund? Speak.

KENT

Mortimer, I did; he is our King,
And thou compell'st this prince to wear the crown.   85

MORTIMER JUNIOR

Strike off his head! He shall have martial law.

KENT

Strike off my head? Base traitor, I defy thee.

KING EDWARD III

My lord, he is my uncle and shall live.

MORTIMER JUNIOR

My lord, he is your enemy and shall die.

KENT

Stay, villains.   90

---

77   s.p. KING EDWARD III ed. (*King.* Q; and throughout)
79   *blades and bills* swords and halberds
81   *perforce* by force, violently
86   *martial law* (here) summary execution without trial

KING EDWARD III

    Sweet mother, if I cannot pardon him,

    Entreat my Lord Protector for his life.

ISABELLA

    Son, be content; I dare not speak a word.

KING EDWARD III

    Nor I, and yet methinks I should command;

    But seeing I cannot, I'll entreat for him.   95

    My lord, if you will let my uncle live,

    I will requite it when I come to age.

MORTIMER JUNIOR

    'Tis for your highness' good, and for the realm's.

    [*To soldiers*] How often shall I bid you bear him hence?

KENT

    Art thou King? Must I die at thy command?   100

MORTIMER JUNIOR

    At our command. Once more, away with him.

KENT

    Let me but stay and speak; I will not go.

    Either my brother or his son is King,

    And none of both them thirst for Edmund's blood.

    And therefore, soldiers, whither will you hale me?   105

            They hale EDMUND [THE EARL OF KENT] *away,*

                     and carry him to be beheaded

            [*Exit* MORTIMER JUNIOR *with attendants,*

        BISHOP OF CANTERBURY, NOBLES, CHAMPION.

             KING EDWARD III *and* ISABELLA *remain*]

KING EDWARD III

    What safety may I look for at his hands,

    If that my uncle shall be murdered thus?

ISABELLA

    Fear not, sweet boy, I'll guard thee from thy foes.

    Had Edmund lived, he would have sought thy death.

    Come son, we'll ride a-hunting in the park.   110

KING EDWARD III

    And shall my uncle Edmund ride with us?

---

101   *our command* The text is ambiguous: the emphasis on 'our' can suggest Mortimer's
      responsible action as Protector, jointly with the Queen; but it can also suggest his
      overweening ambition in adopting the royal plural.

104   *none of both them* ed. (none of both, then Q) i.e. neither of them

ISABELLA

He is a traitor; think not on him. Come.

Exeunt

[Scene 24]

Enter MALTRAVERS *and* GOURNEY

MALTRAVERS

Gourney, I wonder the King dies not.
Being in a vault up to the knees in water,
To which the channels of the castle run,
From whence a damp continually ariseth
That were enough to poison any man,   5
Much more a king, brought up so tenderly.

GOURNEY

And so do I, Maltravers. Yesternight
I opened but the door to throw him meat,
And I was almost stifled with the savour.

MALTRAVERS

He hath a body able to endure   10
More than we can inflict; and therefore now
Let us assail his mind another while.

GOURNEY

Send for him out thence, and I will anger him.

Enter LIGHTBORNE

MALTRAVERS

But stay, who's this?

LIGHTBORNE   My Lord Protector greets you.
                            [*He presents them with the letter*]

GOURNEY

What's here? I know not how to construe it.   15

MALTRAVERS

Gourney, it was left unpointed for the nonce:

4   *damp* fog, mist
8   *meat* food
9   *savour* smell, stench
13 s.d. ed.; after line 14 in Q
16 *unpointed* unpunctuated
    for the nonce for the purpose in hand

[*Reading*] '*Edwardum occidere nolite timere*' –
That's his meaning.

LIGHTBORNE [*Showing the token*]

Know you this token? I must have the King.

MALTRAVERS

Ay, stay a while; thou shalt have answer straight.   20

[*Aside to* GOURNEY] This villain's sent to make away the King.

GOURNEY

[*Aside to* MALTRAVERS] I thought as much.

MALTRAVERS [*Aside to* GOURNEY] And when the murder's done,
See how he must be handled for his labour.
Pereat iste! Let him have the King.
What else? [*To* LIGHTBORNE] Here is the keys; this is the lake.   25
Do as you are commanded by my lord.

LIGHTBORNE

I know what I must do; get you away –
Yet be not far off; I shall need your help.
See that in the next room I have a fire,
And get me a spit, and let it be red hot.   30

MALTRAVERS

Very well.

GOURNEY

Need you anything besides?

LIGHTBORNE

What else? A table and a featherbed.

GOURNEY

That's all?

LIGHTBORNE

Ay, ay; so when I call you, bring it in.   35

MALTRAVERS

Fear not you that.

GOURNEY

Here's a light to go into the dungeon.

                             [*Exit* MALTRAVERS *and* GOURNEY]

---

21   *make away* i.e. murder
24   *Pereat iste!* Let him die!
25   *lake* dungeon; also associated with hell. Cf. *2 Tamburlaine,* 'And travel headlong to
        the lake of hell' (III.v.24).
33   *featherbed* stuffed palliasse; see notes on ll. 71 and 112

LIGHTBORNE

So now must I about this gear; ne'er was there any
So finely handled as this king shall be.
Foh! Here's a place indeed with all my heart. 40

[Enter EDWARD]

EDWARD

Who's there? What light is that? Wherefore comes thou?

LIGHTBORNE

To comfort you and bring you joyful news.

EDWARD

Small comfort finds poor Edward in thy looks.
Villain, I know thou com'st to murder me.

LIGHTBORNE

To murder you, my most gracious lord? 45
Far is it from my heart to do you harm.
The Queen sent me to see how you were used,
For she relents at this your misery.
And what eyes can refrain from shedding tears
To see a king in this most piteous state? 50

EDWARD

Weep'st thou already? List awhile to me,
And then thy heart, were it as Gourney's is,
Or as Maltravers', hewn from the Caucasus,
Yet will it melt ere I have done my tale.
This dungeon where they keep me is the sink 55
Wherein the filth of all the castle falls.

38   *about* i.e. proceed with, get on with   *gear* business
40   *Foh!* Lightborne is affected by the stench of the dungeon.
     with all my heart i.e. I must say (Bevington and Rasmussen)
40   s.d. Q gives no stage direction for Edward to enter, which may indicate that the entry
     was unconventional and possibly not under the prompter's direct control. An attrac-
     tive possibility is that the dungeon is imagined to be located in the under-stage area
     (often referred to as 'hell'), and that Lightborne reveals Edward by opening a trap-
     door at line 40; he would then emerge through it at some point in the ensuing
     dialogue. (Line 58 suggests that he is no longer in his dungeon.) Alternatively, some
     editors have assumed that he is 'discovered', i.e. revealed when a traverse curtain is
     drawn back at the rear of the stage.
47   *used* i.e. being treated
51   *List* listen
53   *Caucasus* the mountain range between the Black and Caspian Seas known for its
     harsh terrain and bitterly cold climate
55   *sink* cess-pool
56   *filth* sewage

454

LIGHTBORNE
  O villains!
EDWARD
  And there in mire and puddle have I stood
  This ten days' space; and lest that I should sleep,
  One plays continually upon a drum.   60
  They give me bread and water, being a king,
  So that for want of sleep and sustenance
  My mind's distempered and my body's numbed,
  And whether I have limbs or no, I know not.
  O, would my blood dropped out from every vein,   65
  As doth this water from my tattered robes.
  Tell Isabel the Queen I looked not thus
  When for her sake I ran at tilt in France
  And there unhorsed the Duke of Cleremont.
LIGHTBORNE
  O speak no more, my lord; this breaks my heart.   70
  Lie on this bed and rest yourself awhile.
EDWARD
  These looks of thine can harbour nought but death.
  I see my tragedy written in thy brows.
  Yet stay awhile; forbear thy bloody hand,
  And let me see the stroke before it comes,   75
  That even then when I shall lose my life,
  My mind may be more steadfast on my God.
LIGHTBORNE
  What means your highness to mistrust me thus?
EDWARD
  What means thou to dissemble with me thus?
LIGHTBORNE
  These hands were never stained with innocent blood,   80
  Nor shall they now be tainted with a king's.
EDWARD
  Forgive my thought, for having such a thought.

63   *distempered* deranged, mentally disturbed
64   *no* not
68–9 an invented incident not recounted in the chronicles
68   *ran at tilt* jousted
71   *this bed* i.e. the 'featherbed' called for by Lightborne at line 33. The text gives no
     indication of how and when the prop should be brought on stage.
73   *tragedy* destruction
76   *That even* ed. (That and euen Q)

One jewel have I left; receive thou this.
Still fear I, and I know not what's the cause,
But every joint shakes as I give it thee. 85
O if thou harbour'st murder in thy heart,
Let this gift change thy mind and save thy soul.
Know that I am a king – O, at that name,
I feel a hell of grief. Where is my crown?
Gone, gone. And do I remain alive? 90

LIGHTBORNE

You're overwatched, my lord; lie down and rest.

EDWARD

But that grief keeps me waking, I should sleep;
For not these ten days have these eyes' lids closed.
Now as I speak they fall, and yet with fear
Open again. O wherefore sits thou here? 95

LIGHTBORNE

If you mistrust me, I'll be gone, my lord.

EDWARD

No, no, for if thou mean'st to murder me.
Thou wilt return again, and therefore stay.

[*He falls asleep*]

LIGHTBORNE

He sleeps.

EDWARD

[*Starting*] O let me not die! Yet stay, O stay awhile. 100

LIGHTBORNE

How now, my lord?

EDWARD

Something still buzzeth in mine ears
And tells me, if I sleep I never wake.
This fear is that which makes me tremble thus;
And therefore tell me, wherefore art thou come? 105

LIGHTBORNE

To rid thee of thy life. Maltravers, come!

[*Enter* MALTRAVERS]

83   *One jewel* possibly the jewel sent by the Queen at 21.71; if so, Edward's handing it
      over to another potential favourite would be his final act of betrayal
89–90 *Where . . . remain alive* A king without a crown is usually dead.
91   *overwatched* depleted through lack of sleep
92   *grief* anxiety
102   *buzzeth* whispers

EDWARD

    I am too weak and feeble to resist;

    Assist me, sweet God, and receive my soul.

LIGHTBORNE

    Run for the table.

[Exit MALTRAVERS]

[Enter MALTRAVERS with GOURNEY,
carrying a table and hot spit]

EDWARD

    O spare me, or dispatch me in a trice!   110

LIGHTBORNE

    So, lay the table down and stamp on it;

    But not too hard, lest that you bruise his body.

[They seize EDWARD and hold him down, laying the
table on him. LIGHTBORNE murders him with the spit.
He screams and dies]

MALTRAVERS

    I fear me that this cry will raise the town,

    And therefore let us take horse and away.

LIGHTBORNE

    Tell me, sirs, was it not bravely done?   115

GOURNEY

    Excellent well. Take this for thy reward.

Then GOURNEY stabs LIGHTBORNE

    Come, let us cast the body in the moat,

    And bear the King's to Mortimer, our lord.

    Away!

Exeunt[, carrying the bodies]

109   s.d. 2 The 'featherbed' asked for at line 33 is already on stage, mentioned at line 71. Some editors treat that 'bed' as a separate prop, and have the featherbed for the murder brought on here. However, the effect of giving the two actors another bulky object to carry is unreasonably to slow down the action at a climactic point, with no covering dialogue provided by the text.

112   s.d. The text gives no indication as to how Lightborne uses the featherbed he asked for. It probably serves as a buffer to prevent bruising by direct contact with the table; if Edward is lying on it immediately beforehand, the murderers must first pitch him onto the ground. Alternatively, Lightborne may want it not for the murder itself but to offer Edward comfort, and so a false sense of security, during their preceding conversation.

115   *bravely* skilfully

118–19   ed. (*one line in* Q)   119 s.d. ed. (*Exeunt omnes.* Q)

[Scene 25]

Enter MORTIMER [JUNIOR] *and* MALTRAVERS

MORTIMER JUNIOR
Is't done, Maltravers, and the murderer dead?
MALTRAVERS
Ay, my good lord; I would it were undone.
MORTIMER JUNIOR
Maltravers, if thou now growest penitent
I'll be thy ghostly father; therefore choose
Whether thou wilt be secret in this,   5
Or else die by the hand of Mortimer.
MALTRAVERS
Gourney, my lord, is fled, and will, I fear,
Betray us both; therefore let me fly.
MORTIMER JUNIOR
Fly to the savages!
MALTRAVERS
I humbly thank your honour.   [*Exit*]   10
MORTIMER JUNIOR
As for myself, I stand as Jove's huge tree,
And others are but shrubs compared to me.
All tremble at my name, and I fear none;
Let's see who dare impeach me for his death.

Enter [ISABELLA] *the Queen*

ISABELLA
Ah, Mortimer, the King my son hath news   15
His father's dead, and we have murdered him.
MORTIMER JUNIOR
What if he have? The King is yet a child.
ISABELLA
Ay, ay, but he tears his hair and wrings his hands,
And vows to be revenged upon us both.
Into the council chamber he is gone   20
To crave the aid and succour of his peers.

4   *ghostly father* priest (who hears the confessions of those about to die)
9   *to the savages* i.e. beyond civilization, to the wilderness
11 *Jove's huge tree* the oak, a byword for size and steadfastness
17 *yet* still
21 *succour* support

458

Enter the King [EDWARD III], *with the* LORDS
[*and attendants*]

Ay me, see where he comes, and they with him.
Now, Mortimer, begins our tragedy.

FIRST LORD
Fear not, my lord; know that you are a king.

KING EDWARD III
Villain!   25

MORTIMER JUNIOR
How now, my lord?

KING EDWARD III
Think not that I am frighted with thy words.
My father's murdered through thy treachery,
And thou shalt die; and on his mournful hearse
Thy hateful and accursèd head shall lie   30
To witness to the world that by thy means
His kingly body was too soon interred.

ISABELLA
Weep not, sweet son.

KING EDWARD III
Forbid not me to weep; he was my father.
And had you loved him half so well as I,   35
You could not bear his death thus patiently.
But you, I fear, conspired with Mortimer.

FIRST LORD
Why speak you not unto my lord the King?

MORTIMER JUNIOR
Because I think scorn to be accused.
Who is the man dare say I murdered him?   40

KING EDWARD III
Traitor, in me my loving father speaks
And plainly saith, 'twas thou that murd'redst him.

MORTIMER JUNIOR
But hath your grace no other proof than this?

21   s.d. ed.; after line 23 in Q
24   s.p. FIRST LORD ed. (*Lords.* Q; also at ll. 38 and 93)
36   *patiently* calmly
41   *in me . . . speaks* 'Marlowe carefully withholds this final show of authority in the
     young prince until, at this point, at the death of his father, he is king in legal fact'
     (Merchant).

459

KING EDWARD III

Yes, if this be the hand of Mortimer.

[He presents the letter]

MORTIMER JUNIOR [*Aside to* ISABELLA]

False Gourney hath betrayed me and himself.   45

ISABELLA [*Aside to* MORTIMER JUNIOR]

I feared as much; murder cannot be hid.

MORTIMER JUNIOR

'Tis my hand; what gather you by this?

KING EDWARD III

That thither thou didst send a murderer.

MORTIMER JUNIOR

What murderer? Bring forth the man I sent.

KING EDWARD III

Ah, Mortimer, thou knowest that he is slain;   50

And so shalt thou be too. Why stays he here?

Bring him unto a hurdle, drag him forth;

Hang him, I say, and set his quarters up!

But bring his head back presently to me.

ISABELLA

For my sake, sweet son, pity Mortimer.   55

MORTIMER JUNIOR

Madam, entreat not; I will rather die

Than sue for life unto a paltry boy.

KING EDWARD III

Hence with the traitor, with the murderer.

MORTIMER JUNIOR

Base Fortune, now I see that in thy wheel

There is a point to which, when men aspire,   60

They tumble headlong down; that point I touched,

And seeing there was no place to mount up higher,

Why should I grieve at my declining fall?

Farewell, fair Queen. Weep not for Mortimer,

That scorns the world, and as a traveller   65

Goes to discover countries yet unknown.

KING EDWARD III

---

46   *murder cannot be hid* proverbial (Tilley M 1315)

52   *hurdle* frame or sledge which restrained traitors whilst being dragged through the streets to the place of execution

53   Mortimer Junior is to be hanged, drawn, and quartered rather than merely beheaded, the normal privilege of aristocratic traitors granted even to Gaveston, Baldock, and the Spencers.

What! Suffer you the traitor to delay?

[*Exit* MORTIMER JUNIOR, *with the* FIRST LORD *and guard*]

ISABELLA

As thou received'st thy life from me,
Spill not the blood of gentle Mortimer.

KING EDWARD III

This argues that you spilt my father's blood,   70
Else would you not entreat for Mortimer.

ISABELLA

I spill his blood? No!

KING EDWARD III

Ay, madam, you; for so the rumour runs.

ISABELLA

That rumour is untrue; for loving thee
Is this report raised on poor Isabel.   75

KING EDWARD III

I do not think her so unnatural.

SECOND LORD

My lord, I fear me it will prove too true.

KING EDWARD III

Mother, you are suspected for his death,
And therefore we commit you to the Tower
Till further trial may be made thereof;   80
If you be guilty, though I be your son,
Think not to find me slack or pitiful.

ISABELLA

Nay, to my death, for too long have I lived
Whenas my son thinks to abridge my days.

KING EDWARD III

Away with her. Her words enforce these tears,   85
And I shall pity her if she speak again.

ISABELLA

Shall I not mourn for my beloved lord,
And with the rest accompany him to his grave?

SECOND LORD

Thus, madam, 'tis the King's will you shall hence.

75   *report* rumour
      raised i.e. fabricated against
77   s.p. SECOND LORD (*Lords.* Q; also at ll. 89 and 91)
80   *trial* investigation
84   *abridge* shorten, cut short
85   *enforce* produce, cause

ISABELLA

He hath forgotten me; stay, I am his mother.   90

SECOND LORD

That boots not; therefore, gentle madam, go.

ISABELLA

Then come, sweet death, and rid me of this grief.

[Exit ISABELLA, *guarded]*

[Enter FIRST LORD *with the head of* MORTIMER JUNIOR]

FIRST LORD

My lord, here is the head of Mortimer.

KING EDWARD III

Go fetch my father's hearse, where it shall lie,

And bring my funeral robes.   *[Exit attendants]*

Accursèd head!   95

Could I have ruled thee then, as I do now,

Thou hadst not hatched this monstrous treachery.

[Enter attendants with the hearse of King EDWARD II
and funeral robes]

Here comes the hearse; help me to mourn, my lords.

Sweet father, here unto thy murdered ghost

I offer up this wicked traitor's head.   100

And let these tears, distilling from mine eyes,

Be witness of my grief and innocency.

[Exeunt, with a funeral march]

---

91   *boots* avails, matters
101   *distilling* falling from (in small droplets)
102   Colophon omitted ed. (FINIS. / [Device] / Imprinted at London for *William* /
      Ihones, *and are to be solde at his* / shop, neere vnto Houlburne / *Conduit. 1594.* Q)

THE
TRAGICALL
History of D. Faustus.

As it hath bene Acted by the Right
Honorable the Earle of Nottingham his seruants.

Written by Ch. Marl.

LONDON
Printed by V. S. for Thomas Bushell. 1604.

DRAMATIS PERSONAE

CHORUS

DR JOHN FAUSTUS
WAGNER, *his servant, a student*
VALDES
CORNELIUS } *his friends, magicians*
THREE SCHOLARS

THE GOOD ANGEL
THE EVIL ANGEL
MEPHASTOPHILIS
LUCIFER
BELZEBUB
OLD MAN

THE CLOWN
ROBIN
RAFE } *ostlers at an inn*

VINTNER
HORSE-COURSER

THE POPE
THE CARDINAL OF LORRAINE

THE EMPEROR CHARLES V
A KNIGHT *at the emperor's court*
DUKE OF VANHOLT
DUCHESS OF VANHOLT

MEPHASTOPHILIS This version of the character's name is used consistently throughout the A-text; the B-text spelling, 'Mephostophilis', is used in the Appendix of scenes from that text. William Empson has a note on the various spellings in *Faustus and the Censor* (1987), pp. 45–6n

Spirits presenting
THE SEVEN DEADLY SINS
    PRIDE
    COVETOUSNESS
    WRATH
    ENVY
    GLUTTONY
    SLOTH
    LECHERY
ALEXANDER THE GREAT *and his* PARAMOUR
HELEN OF TROY

Attendants, Friars, and Devils

[Chorus 1]

Enter CHORUS

CHORUS

Not marching now in fields of Thrasimene,
Where Mars did mate the Carthaginians,
Nor sporting in the dalliance of love,
In courts of kings where state is overturned,
Nor in the pomp of proud audacious deeds,   5
Intends our Muse to daunt his heavenly verse:
Only this (Gentlemen) we must perform,
The form of Faustus' fortunes good or bad.
To patient judgements we appeal our plaud,
And speak for Faustus in his infancy: 10
Now is he born, his parents base of stock,
In Germany, within a town called Rhodes;

s.d.   CHORUS Following the example of classical drama, many Elizabethan plays began
       with a Chorus or Prologue to introduce the action, and sometimes comment on the
       author's skill and the nature of his writing. The Chorus takes the persona of an actor
       in the company presenting the play, possibly the actor playing Faustus's servant Wagner,
       see l. 28n and Chorus 2.0n (p. 48).

1–5   The Chorus speaks of plays already performed, but – whether these were written by
       Marlowe or merely part of the company's repertoire – the references are unclear.
       There is no trace of any play showing the victory of the Carthaginians under Hannibal
       at Lake Thrasymenus in 217 B.C.; and any number of plays (including Marlowe's
       own *Edward II*) could be said to show 'the dalliance of love' in royal courts.

   2   *Mars* the Roman god of war
       mate ally himself with

   3   *dalliance* frivolity

   6   *our Muse* our poet; the Chorus is speaking on behalf of the acting company
       daunt A (vaunt B) a) control, tame, subdue, b) dally, caress. This wordplay immediately
       introduces a note of irony. The Chorus denies that the play is about war or love but
       this pun suggests it will combine both heroics and sensuality, and outdo any previous
       play. The B-text's 'vaunt' simply means 'show off'

   9   *appeal our plaud* ask for applause

  12   *Rhodes* Roda, since 1922 Stadtroda (in Germany)

Of riper years to Wittenberg he went,
Whereas his kinsmen chiefly brought him up.
So soon he profits in divinity,   15
The fruitful plot of scholarism graced,
That shortly he was graced with doctor's name,
Excelling all, whose sweet delight disputes
In heavenly matters of theology,
Till swollen with cunning of a self-conceit,   20
His waxen wings did mount above his reach,
And melting heavens conspired his overthrow.
For falling to a devilish exercise,
And glutted more with learning's golden gifts,
He surfeits upon cursed necromancy: 25
Nothing so sweet as magic is to him,
Which he prefers before his chiefest bliss.
And this the man that in his study sits.   *Exit*

---

13 *Wittenberg* B Hamlet's university, and Luther's, was the home of scepticism; but this
    Wittenberg is, in all outward appearances, Marlowe's own Cambridge. The A-text
    has 'Wertenberg[e]' here (and throughout: 1.89; 1.114; 10.92; 12.97; 13.17), i.e. the
    Duchy of Württemburg, a territory rather than a university town. The two names were
    often confused, as once in Marlowe's English source.
14 *Whereas* where
16 'a credit to the rich discipline of academic studies'
17 *graced* At Cambridge, an official 'grace' permits a candidate to proceed to his degree;
    Marlowe's name is entered in the Grace Book for 1584 and 1587.
18 *whose sweet delight disputes* whose great pleasure is in academic debate
20 *cunning* a) skill, knowledge, b) specifically magical skill. The word had also begun
    to acquire its modern sense of craftiness or deceitfulness
    self-conceit a) pride in his own abilities, b) individual thinking, unregulated by religion
    or convention, c) thinking himself to be something other than he is (i.e. Icarus, ll.
    21–2), d) 'self-fashioned'
21 *waxen wings* In Greek mythology, Icarus flew too near the sun on wings of wax; they
    melted, and he fell into the sea. The fall of Icarus became a popular Renaissance
    emblem throughout Europe.
24 *more* A (now B)
27 *chiefest bliss* i.e. hope of life after death
28 *this the man* This seems to be the cue for the Chorus to draw aside a curtain and
    disclose Faustus in his study, thus perhaps falling into his role as Faustus's servant.

467

[Scene 1]

Enter FAUSTUS *in his study*

FAUSTUS

Settle thy studies, Faustus, and begin
To sound the depth of that thou wilt profess:
Having commenced, be a divine in show,
Yet level at the end of every art,
And live and die in Aristotle's works.   5
Sweet *Analytics*, 'tis thou hast ravished me:
Bene disserere est finis logices.
Is to dispute well logic's chiefest end?
Affords this art no greater miracle?
Then read no more, thou hast attained the end;   10
A greater subject fitteth Faustus' wit.
Bid *on kai me on* farewell; Galen come:

2   *sound* measure
     profess specialize in, study and teach
3   *commenced* graduated; a Cambridge term
     divine theologian
     in show in appearance
4   consider the purpose of every discipline
5–37 In his survey of human scholarship Faustus resembles the protagonist of Lyly's
      Euphues (1578) who determines to return to the university:
          Philosophic, Phisicke, Divinitie, shal be my studie. O yᵉ hidden secrets of Nature,
          the expresse image of morall venues, the equall ballaunce of Justice, the medicines
          to heale all diseases, how they beginne to delyght me. The *Axiomaes* of *Aristotle*,
          the *Maxims* of *Justinian*, the *Aphorismes* of *Galen*, have sodaynelye made such a
          breache into my minde, that I seem onely to desire them which did onely earst
          detest them.   *Euphues*, ed. Bond (1902), i.241
5–7   Aristotle had been the dominant figure in the university curriculum since the thirteenth
      century, but in Marlowe's day his supremacy was challenged by the intellectual reformer
      Petrus Ramus. *Analytics* is the name given to two of Aristotle's works on the nature of
      proof in argument, but the definition of logic in line 7 comes in fact from Ramus'
      Dialecticae. Ramus, his ideas, and his violent death are displayed in Marlowe's *Massacre
      at Paris*
10   *the* A (that B)
12   *on kai me on* being and not being. A1 prints a jumble of letters, 'Oncaymaeon', which
      later editions, trying to make some sense out of them, changed to 'Oeconomy'. Bullen
      recognized the A-text's apparent gibberish as a transliteration of the Greek phrase,
      from a work attributed to the philosopher Georgias of Leontini (*c.* 483–376 B.C.)
      Galen a second-century Greek physician who was accepted as an authority on medical
      science throughout the Middle Ages

Seeing, *ubi desinit philosophus, ibi incipit medicus.*
Be a physician, Faustus, heap up gold,
And be eternized for some wondrous cure.   15
Summum bonum medicinae sanitas:
The end of physic is our body's health.
Why Faustus, hast thou not attained that end?
Is not thy common talk sound aphorisms?
Are not thy bills hung up as monuments,   20
Whereby whole cities have escaped the plague,
And thousand desperate maladies been eased?
Yet art thou still but Faustus, and a man.
Wouldst thou make man to live eternally,
Or, being dead, raise them to life again,   25
Then this profession were to be esteemed.
Physic farewell! Where is Justinian?
Si una eademque res legatur duobus,
Alter rem alter valorem rei, etc.

13   *ubi . . . medicus* 'since the doctor starts where the philosopher leaves off'; Aristotle, *De Sensu et Sensibili*, ch 1, 436a

14   *heap up gold* The association of gold and the medical profession is an old one; Shakespeare mentions the use of gold for 'Preserving life in med'cine potable' (2 *Henry IV*, IV. v. 162). Faustus, however, is thinking of the profit to be gained – like Chaucer's Physician in *The Canterbury Tales*:
> For gold in phisik is a cordial,
> Therefore he lovede gold in special.   (Prologue, 444–5)

15   *eternized* immortalized

16   Aristotle, *Nicomachean Ethics*, 1094. a. 8; Faustus translates in line 17

19   Faustus ranks himself with Hippocrates, whose *Aphorismes* was the most famous of medical textbooks.
sound aphorisms well-founded maxims or concise expressions of scientific principles particularly of a medical nature (after the well-known *Aphorisms* of Hippocrates, a Greek physician of the 4th century B.C.). The B-text has 'found' i.e. considered to be 'aphorisms'.

20   *bills* writings, perhaps specifically prescriptions or advertisements
monuments a) memorials, commemorations, b) portents, warnings, c) legal documents

21   *Whereby . . . plague* It seems that his writings are considered to have prophylactic powers.

24–5   *Wouldst . . . man* A (Could'st . . . men B). Since Faustus is still only a man and not a god (see ll. 62–3), there would be no relative advantage for him in making mankind live for ever. By contrast, the B-text smoothes out the blasphemy of this line (since in Christian theology only Christ can raise the dead) by accepting that the goal is impossible.

27   Justinian was a Roman emperor of the sixth century A.D., who re-organized the whole of Roman Law.

28–9   'If one and the same thing is bequeathed to two persons, one should have the thing itself, the other the value of the thing': Justinian, *Institutes*, ii. 20.

A pretty case of paltry legacies: 30
Exhereditare filium non potest pater nisi . . .
Such is the subject of the Institute,
And universal body of the Church:
His study fits a mercenary drudge
Who aims at nothing but external trash! 35
Too servile and illiberal for me.
When all is done, divinity is best:
Jerome's Bible, Faustus, view it well:
Stipendium peccati mors est: ha! *Stipendium, etc.*
The reward of sin is death? That's hard. 40
Si peccasse negamus, fallimur, et nulla est in nobis veritas
If we say that we have no sin,
We deceive ourselves, and there's no truth in us.
Why then belike we must sin,
And so consequently die. 45
Ay, we must die an everlasting death.
What doctrine call you this? *Che serà, serà*:
What will be, shall be! Divinity, adieu!
These metaphysics of magicians,
And necromantic books are heavenly! 50

---

31 'A father cannot disinherit his son unless . . .': Justinian, ii. 13
32–3 *subject . . . Church* Faustus sneers that Justinian's book concerns merely inheritance
and property law (i.e. 'external trash', l. 35). Punning on the overall title of Justinian's
work (*Corpus Juris*, i.e. 'Body of the Law'), he suggests that this is a preoccupation
of Christians generally (the 'body of the Church'), since Christian canon law was
based on Justinian.
32 *Institute* element of instruction, or basic principles of a body of knowledge, hence
the title of the legal textbook, *Institutes*, which was one part of Justinian's project to
codify Roman Law
33 *Church* A (law B)
34 *His study* A (This study B)
mercenary drudge wage slave
36 *Too servile* B (The devil A)
illiberal Faustus compares the mercenary concerns of the lawyers with the culturally
enriching studies of the 'liberal arts'.
38 *Jerome's Bible* the Vulgate, prepared mainly by St Jerome; but the texts that Faustus
quotes are not in the Latin of the Vulgate
39 Romans vi, 23; Faustus reads only half the verse: the quotation should continue 'but
the gift of God is eternal life through Jesus Christ our Lord'.
41–3 *Si peccasse . . . us* 1 John 1, 8 'If we say that we have no sin, we deceive ourselves, and
the truth is not in us.' Verse 9 continues 'If we confess our sins, he is faithful and just
to forgive us our sins, and to cleanse us from all unrighteousness.' By again making
only a partial reading, Faustus fails to register the offered comfort.

Lines, circles, schemes, letters and characters!
Ay, these are those that Faustus most desires.
O what a world of profit and delight,
Of power, of honour, of omnipotence
Is promised to the studious artisan!   55
All things that move between the quiet poles
Shall be at my command: emperors and kings
Are but obeyed in their several provinces,
Nor can they raise the wind, or rend the clouds;
But his dominion that exceeds in this   60
Stretcheth as far as doth the mind of man:
A sound magician is a mighty god.
Here Faustus, try thy brains to gain a deity.
Wagner,

Enter WAGNER

          commend me to my dearest friends,
The German Valdes, and Cornelius,   65
Request them earnestly to visit me.
WAGNER
    I will sir.   *Exit*
FAUSTUS
    Their conference will be a greater help to me,
    Than all my labours, plod I ne'er so fast.

Enter the GOOD ANGEL *and the* EVIL ANGEL

51 *schemes* ed. (scenes A; *om*, B); rhetorical figures, astronomical diagrams (see John
    Harvey, *An Astrological Addition*, 1583, B5)
    characters symbols, astrological signs
55 *artisan* craftsman
56 *quiet poles* the poles of the universe, quiet because unmoving
58 *several* respective
59–62 Compare the description of God in Jeremiah x, 13: 'He giveth by his voice the
    multitude of waters in the heaven, and he causeth the clouds to ascend from the
    ends of the earth: he turneth lightnings to rain, and bringeth forth the wind out of
    his treasures.'
60 *exceeds* excels
    this i.e. this magic art
63 *try* A (tire B)
64 s.d. Although both A- and B-texts agree in placing this s.d. after line 63, sixteenth-
    century printers would find it more economical not to split the line. Wagner enters
    because he is called, not on his own accord.

GOOD ANGEL

O Faustus, lay that damned book aside,   70
And gaze not on it, lest it tempt thy soul,
And heap God's heavy wrath upon thy head:
Read, read the Scriptures; that is blasphemy.

EVIL ANGEL

Go forward, Faustus, in that famous art,
Wherein all nature's treasury is contained: 75
Be thou on earth as Jove is in the sky,
Lord and commander of these elements.

                             Exeunt

FAUSTUS

How am I glutted with conceit of this!
Shall I make spirits fetch me what I please,
Resolve me of all ambiguities,   80
Perform what desperate enterprise I will?
I'll have them fly to India for gold,
Ransack the ocean for orient pearl,
And search all corners of the new found world
For pleasant fruits and princely delicates.   85
I'll have them read me strange philosophy,
And tell the secrets of all foreign kings;
I'll have them wall all Germany with brass,
And make swift Rhine circle fair Wittenberg;

---

76   *Jove* The names of the pagan deities were frequently attributed to the Christian God; there is special force in this coming from the Evil Angel.

77   *these elements* the four elements – earth, air, fire, and water – of which the world was made

78   *glutted with conceit* drunk with the thought

80   *Resolve ... ambiguities* reduce my doubts to certainties; solve my problems

81   *desperate* a) dangerous, b) reckless, with the sense of despairing, which is a denial of Christian salvation

83   *orient pearl* The most precious pearls were from the Indian Ocean.

84   *new found* newly discovered

85   *delicates* delicacies

86   *read me* teach me

88   *wall ... brass* Friar Bacon, in Greene's *Friar Bacon and Friar Bungay* (before 1592) intended to 'circle England round with brass' (ii. 29) when his magic schemes reached fruition.

89   *Wittenberg* B (Wertenberge A). Wittenberg in fact stands on the Elbe; it is the Duchy of Württemberg that is bordered by the southern Rhine (see Chorus 1.13n).

I'll have them fill the public schools with silk, 90
Wherewith the students shall be bravely clad.
I'll levy soldiers with the coin they bring,
And chase the Prince of Parma from our land,
And reign sole king of all our provinces.
Yea, stranger engines for the brunt of war 95
Than was the fiery keel at Antwerp's bridge,
I'll make my servile spirits to invent.
Come German Valdes and Cornelius,
And make me blest with your sage conference.

Enter VALDES *and* CORNELIUS

Valdes, sweet Valdes, and Cornelius, 100
Know that your words have won me at the last
To practise magic and concealed arts;
Yet not your words only, but mine own fantasy,
That will receive no object for my head,
But ruminates on necromantic skill. 105
Philosophy is odious and obscure,
Both law and physic are for petty wits;

90 *public schools* university lecture rooms
silk Dyce (skill Qq (all quartos)); in Marlowe's day, undergraduates were ordered to dress in woollen cloth, not silk.
91 *bravely* smartly
92 *coin they bring* Spirits were deemed to know the whereabouts of hidden treasure.
93–6 The Prince of Parma was Spanish governor-general of the United Provinces of the Netherlands, 1579–92, and feared in Protestant England. The bridge he built across the Scheldt during his siege of Antwerp was destroyed by *fiery keel* (fireship) on 4 April 1585.
94 *our* A (the B)
95 *engines* machines
brunt assault
102 *concealed* occult
103 *fantasy* a) in scholastic philosophy, the faculty whereby objects are conceived, b) imagination
103–5 i.e. Faustus is becoming wrapped up in his own inner thoughts and is finding it difficult to think about the external, material, or objective world.
104 *object* a) in metaphysics, a material thing external to the mind or to the subjective self, b) with a pun on 'objection'
105 *ruminates* meditates deeply, often used at this period with a sense of dark or dangerous melancholy
necromantic skill magic that works through conjuring and controlling spirits

Divinity is basest of the three,
Unpleasant, harsh, contemptible and vile.
'Tis magic, magic that hath ravished me.   110
Then, gentle friends, aid me in this attempt,
And I, that have with concise syllogisms
Gravelled the pastors of the German church,
And made the flowering pride of Wittenberg
Swarm to my problems, as the infernal spirits   115
On sweet Musaeus when he came to hell,
Will be as cunning as Agrippa was,
Whose shadows made all Europe honour him.

VALDES

Faustus, these books, thy wit, and our experience
Shall make all nations to canonize us.   120
As Indian Moors obey their Spanish lords,
So shall the subjects of every element
Be always serviceable to us three.
Like lions shall they guard us when we please,
Like Almaine rutters with their horsemen's staves,   125
Or Lapland giants trotting by our sides;

108 *three* either the three learned professions of law, medicine, and the Church or, more likely, the three divisions of human existence: body (the material world, *law and physic*); mind (*philosophy*); and soul (*divinity*)

112 *concise* brief and direct, not diffuse
syllogisms in logic, an argument in which two propositions or premises that share a common term result in a third proposition or conclusion

113 *Gravelled* confounded

115 *problems* topics of academic debate

116 *Musaeus* Virgil (*Aeneid* vi, 667–8) describes this legendary, pre-Homeric poet surrounded by the spirits of priests and bards in the Elysian fields of the Greek underworld.

117 *Agrippa* The magician and necromancer Henry Cornelius Agrippa von Nettesheim (1486–1535), author of *De Occulta Philosophia* and *De Vanitate Scientiarum*, was famous for his reputed power of invoking shadows – spirits or spirit representations – of the dead.

120 *canonise* deify, with ironic echo of ecclesiastical canon law and of the enrolling or canonising of saints

121 *Indian Moors* American Indians

122 *subjects* A (spirits B) a) the substances of which material forms are made (*OED* 5), hence materialised spirits (see the shapes in Shakespeare's *Tempest*, III.ii.18), b) those subject to a lord; servants, retainers. As a necromancer, Faustus intends to rule all the elements through his power over their spirits.

125 'Like German cavalry with lances'

126 *Lapland giants* On another occasion Marlowe refers to the inhabitants of the polar regions in this way: 'tall and sturdy men, Giants as big as hugy Polypheme' (*2 Tamburlaine*, I.i.37–8).

Sometimes like women, or unwedded maids,
Shadowing more beauty in their airy brows
Than in the white breasts of the Queen of Love.
From Venice shall they drag huge argosies,   130
And from America the golden fleece
That yearly stuffs old Philip's treasury,
If learned Faustus will be resolute.

FAUSTUS

Valdes, as resolute am I in this
As thou to live, therefore object it not.   135

CORNELIUS

The miracles that magic will perform
Will make thee vow to study nothing else.
He that is grounded in astrology,
Enriched with tongues, well seen in minerals,
Hath all the principles magic doth require: 140
Then doubt not, Faustus, but to be renowned
And more frequented for this mystery,
Than heretofore the Delphian oracle.
The spirits tell me they can dry the sea,
And fetch the treasure of all foreign wrecks,   145
Ay, all the wealth that our forefathers hid

---

129   *in the* Greg (in their A; has the B)
130   *From* A2 (For A1)
       argosies rich merchant ships from Ragusa, near Venice, later poetically linked with
       the Argo, the mythical ship in which Jason sailed to search for the golden fleece
131   *golden fleece* a) 'treasure' – from the magical pelt sought by Jason and the Argonauts,
       b) a pun on 'fleece': strip, plunder. The enormous wealth plundered from America
       was also the object of English piratical attacks on Spanish ships. The other specifically
       Spanish and Catholic connotation of the phrase concerns the chivalric Order of the
       Golden Fleece, founded by Philip III, Duke of Burgundy, which had passed to the
       control of the Spanish Hapsburg monarchy.
132   *stuffs* A (stuff'd B) The change from present to past tense between texts suggests
       that the B-text manuscript post-dates the death of '*old Philip*', (Philip II of Spain
       1527–98).
135   *object it not* don't raise any objections
138   *grounded* well schooled
139   *tongues* Greek and Hebrew were desirable for those who would converse with spirits, but
       Latin was the recognized common language: 'Thou art a scholar: speak to it Horatio.'
       Hamlet, I.i.42.
       seen in minerals B (seen minerals A); knowledgeable about the properties of minerals
142   'more sought after for practising this art'
143   *Delphian oracle* the oracle of Apollo at Delphi

Within the massy entrails of the earth.
Then tell me, Faustus, what shall we three want?
FAUSTUS
Nothing Cornelius! O this cheers my soul!
Come, show me some demonstrations magical,   150
That I may conjure in some lusty grove,
And have these joys in full possession.
VALDES
Then haste thee to some solitary grove,
And bear wise Bacon's and Abanus' works,
The Hebrew Psalter, and New Testament;   155
And whatsoever else is requisite
We will inform thee ere our conference cease.
CORNELIUS
Valdes, first let him know the words of art,
And then, all other ceremonies learned,
Faustus may try his cunning by himself.   160
VALDES
First, I'll instruct thee in the rudiments,
And then wilt thou be perfecter than I.
FAUSTUS
Then come and dine with me, and after meat
We'll canvass every quiddity thereof:
For ere I sleep, I'll try what I can do.   165
This night I'll conjure, though I die therefore.

Exeunt

147   *massy* solid
151   *lusty* A1 (little A2, 3; bushy B); in the sixteenth century, the word could mean 'pleasant'
154   *wise Bacon's and Abanus' works* Roger Bacon (?1214–94), protagonist of Greene's
      Friar Bacon and Friar Bungay, was an Oxford philosopher popularly supposed to
      have dabbled in black magic. Abanus is perhaps Pietro d'Abano (?1250–1316), Italian
      humanist and physician, who was also believed to have been a conjuror. As well as
      the works of these two, which would supply formulae for incantation, Faustus would
      need certain Psalms (especially 22 and 51) and the opening words of St John's Gospel
      for his conjuring.
161   *rudiments* 'all that which is called vulgarly the vertue of worde, herbe, & stone: which
      is used by unlawful charmes, without natural causes . . . such kinde of charmes as
      commonlie daft wives use.' James I, *Daemonologie* (Edinburgh, 1597), p. 11
164   *canvass every quiddity* explore every detail; *quiddity* is a scholastic term denoting the
      essence of a thing, that which makes it what it is

476

[Scene 2]

Enter two SCHOLARS

1 SCHOLAR

I wonder what's become of Faustus, that was wont to make our
schools ring with *sic probo.*

2 SCHOLAR

That shall we know; for see, here comes his boy.

Enter WAGNER

1 SCHOLAR

How now sirra, where's thy master?

WAGNER

God in heaven knows.   5

2 SCHOLAR

Why, dost not thou know?

WAGNER

Yes I know, but that follows not.

1 SCHOLAR

Go to sirra, leave your jesting, and tell us where he is.

WAGNER

That follows not necessary by force of argument, that you, being
licentiate, should stand upon't; therefore acknowledge your error,   10
and be attentive.

2 SCHOLAR

Why, didst thou not say thou knew'st?

WAGNER

Have you any witness on't?

1 SCHOLAR

Yes sirra, I heard you.

WAGNER

Ask my fellow if I be a thief.   15

---

    2   *sic probo* thus I prove it: a term from scholastic disputation

    5   *God . . . knows* would normally imply that *only* God knows, but it does not logically
        follow that if God knows, Wagner does *not* know

  10   *licentiate* licensed, i.e. a graduate allowed to progress to a higher degree, but also a
        pun on 'licensed man' (professional fool)
        stand upon't base yourself on that, i.e. think that that makes you wise

  15   *Ask . . . thief* proverbial; *fellow* companion, friend

2 SCHOLAR

Well, you will not tell us.

WAGNER

Yes sir, I will tell you; yet if you were not dunces you would never ask me such a question. For is not he *corpus naturale*? And is not that *mobile*? Then wherefore should you ask me such a question? But that I am by nature phlegmatic, slow to wrath, and prone to 20 lechery – to love I would say – it were not for you to come within forty foot of the place of execution, although I do not doubt to see you both hanged the next sessions. Thus having triumphed over you, I will set my countenance like a precisian, and begin to speak thus: Truly my dear brethren, my master is within at dinner 25 with Valdes and Cornelius, as this wine, if it could speak, it would inform your worships. And so the Lord bless you, preserve you, and keep you, my dear brethren, my dear brethren.   *Exit*

1 SCHOLAR

Nay then, I fear he is fallen into that damned art, for which they two are infamous through the world.   30

2 SCHOLAR

Were he a stranger, and not allied to me, yet should I grieve for him. But come, let us go and inform the Rector, and see if he by his grave counsel can reclaim him.

1 SCHOLAR

O, but I fear me nothing can reclaim him.

2 SCHOLAR

Yet let us try what we can do.   35

                                                            Exeunt

17   *dunces* blockheads. The followers of Duns Scotus were commonly known as Dunses, but here it is Wagner himself who indulges in the academic cavilling characteristic of the Scotists.

18–19   *corpus naturale* a natural body

mobile capable of movement; changeable. According to Aristotelian physics, the definitive property of a natural body is that it is subject to change.

20   *phlegmatic* In old physiology, there were four 'humours' that governed the body: black bile (cold and dry, which caused 'melancholy'); yellow bile (hot and dry, which caused 'choler'); blood (hot and wet, which caused 'sanguinity'); and phlegm, cold and wet. A phlegmatic person is predisposed to indolence and sluggishness, but slow to anger.

22   *place of execution* i.e. place where a formal act, or act of skill is being performed; here, a gathering of necromancers at dinner, introducing the wordplay on *hanged* (l. 23)

24   *precisian* puritan; Wagner now apes the unctuous speech of this sect

32   *Rector* head of the university

[Scene 3]

Enter FAUSTUS *to conjure*

FAUSTUS

Now that the gloomy shadow of the earth,
Longing to view Orion's drizzling look,
Leaps from th'antarctic world unto the sky,
And dims the welkin with her pitchy breath:
Faustus, begin thine incantations,   5
And try if devils will obey thy hest,
Seeing thou hast prayed and sacrificed to them.
Within this circle is Jehovah's name,
Forward and backward anagrammatized;
The breviated names of holy saints,   10
Figures of every adjunct to the heavens,

1 *shadow of the earth* In *The French Academie*, La Primaudaye explains that 'the night, also, is no other thing than the shadow of the earth'. See also John Norton Smith, 'Marlowe's *Faustus*', *N & Q* NS 25 (1978), pp. 436–7.

2 *Orion's drizzling look* the rainy constellation of Orion

3 Marlowe seems to have thought that night advances from the southern hemisphere.

4 *welkin* sky
    pitchy Pitch is a sticky substance obtained as a residue from the distillation of wood tar and was used for protecting wood from moisture; hence 'pitchy' meant both black and stinking.

7 *prayed and sacrificed* A period of prayer and sacrifice, a kind of spiritual preparation, was a pre-requisite for conjuring.

8 *circle* Before he began his conjuring, the magician would draw a circle round himself, inscribing on the periphery certain signs. So long as the circle was unbroken and the magician stayed inside it, no evil spirit could harm him.
    Jehovah a late medieval Hebrew word for God, combining the four Hebraic letters representing the name Yahweh (meaning 'God', but never spoken aloud) with the Hebraic vowels of Adonai (meaning 'lord'), the word commonly used to refer to Him. Sixteenth-century magic was greatly influenced by the Jewish Cabbala (the oral and sometimes later regarded as mystical tradition handed down from Moses).

9 *anagrammatized* B (and agramathist A), made into an anagram

9–12 Faustus's conjuring is, ironically, a literary act, depending on the patterns and control of spelling, rhetoric and grammar.

10 *breviated* A (Th'abbreviated B); shortened

11 *Figures* a) diagrams, b) tropes, rhetorical patterns
    adjunct a) in grammar, anything added to expand on the subject, b) in logic, an accompanying quality or circumstance added to the essence of a thing, c) hence, here, any heavenly body joined to the firmament

And characters of signs and erring stars,
By which the spirits are enforced to rise.
Then fear not Faustus, but be resolute,
And try the uttermost magic can perform.   15
Sint mihi dei acherontis propitii. Valeat numen triplex Jehovae! Ignei,
aerii, aquatici, terreni spiritus salvete! Orientis princeps, Belzebub
inferni ardentis monarcha, et Demogorgon, propitiamus vos, ut
appareat et surgat Mephastophilis. Quid tu moraris? Per Jehovam,
Gehennam, et consecratam aquam quam nunc spargo; signumque   20
crucis quod nunc facio; et per vota nostra, ipse nunc surgat nobis
dicatus Mephastophilis.

Enter a DEVIL

I charge thee to return and change thy shape,
Thou art too ugly to attend on me;

12   *characters* symbols
      signs i.e. of the zodiac
      erring stars planets, because they appear to err (wander, from the Latin *errare*, 'to
      lead astray') across the sky
16–22 'May the gods of Acheron look favourably upon me. Away with the spirit of the three-
      fold Jehovah. Welcome, spirits of fire, air, water, and earth. We ask your favour, O
      Prince of the East, Belzebub (monarch of burning hell), and Demogorgon, that
      Mephastophilis may appear and rise. Why do you delay? By Jehovah, Gehenna, and
      the holy water which I now sprinkle, and the sign of the cross which I now form, and
      by our vows, may Mephastophilis himself now rise, compelled to obey us.'
      Rejecting the God of Heaven, the Christian God in Three Persons, Faustus turns
      to His infernal counterpart: *Acheron* is one of the rivers in the Greek underworld,
      Orientis princeps (the Prince of the East) is Lucifer (see Isaiah xiv, 12), and *Demogorgon*
      is, in classical mythology, one of the most terrible primeval gods. Faustus hails the
      spirits of the elements: 'they make them believe, that at the fall of Lucifer, some spirits
      fell in the aire, some in the fire, some in the water, some in the lande' (*Daemonologie*,
      p. 20). The name *Mephastophilis* was not, apparently, known before the Faust legend;
      this seems to have been Marlowe's preferred spelling – it is the one used most fre-
      quently in the A-text. The different spellings are discussed by William Empson in
      Faustus and the Censor, 1987.
      Many invocations to the devil express similar surprise and impatience at his delay,
      after which the conjuror redoubles his efforts. Gehenna, the valley of Hinnom, was
      a place of sacrifice. Dr Faustus seems now to be renouncing his Christian baptism,
      misusing the baptismal water and forswearing the vows made at his christening. In
      devil-worship, the sign of the cross had a double function: a powerful charm to
      overcome diabolic disobedience, it also protected the conjuror from injury by any
      spirit that might appear.
17   *terreni* Greg (*om* Qq); Faustus would invoke the spirits of all four elements
18   *Belzebub* Marlowe's form of the name has been retained because at certain points (e.g.
      5.12) this suits better with the metre than the more commonly used Hebraic Beelzebub.

Go and return an old Franciscan friar,	25

That holy shape becomes a devil best. *Exit* DEVIL
I see there's virtue in my heavenly words!
Who would not be proficient in this art?
How pliant is this Mephastophilis,
Full of obedience and humility, 30
Such is the force of magic and my spells.
Now Faustus, thou art conjuror laureate
That canst command great Mephastophilis.
Quin redis, Mephastophilis, fratris imagine!

Enter MEPHASTOPHILIS [*disguised as a friar*]

MEPHASTOPHILIS
Now Faustus, what would'st thou have me do? 35
FAUSTUS
I charge thee wait upon me whilst I live,
To do what ever Faustus shall command,
Be it to make the moon drop from her sphere,
Or the ocean to overwhelm the world.
MEPHASTOPHILIS
I am a servant to great Lucifer, 40
And may not follow thee without his leave;
No more than he commands must we perform.
FAUSTUS
Did not he charge thee to appear to me?
MEPHASTOPHILIS
No, I came now hither of mine own accord.

19 *Quid tu moraris* Ellis (*quod tumeraris* Qq)
23 *change thy shape EFB* describes a creature of fire, which appears at this point and eventually takes the shape of a man; the B-text asks for a 'Dragon' in what seems to be an anticipatory stage direction, the woodcut on the B-text titlepage shows an emergent dragon on the ground beside the conjuror's circle, and an inventory of props belonging to the Admiral's men, dated 10 March 1598 records a 'dragon in fostes'. A wary magician always stipulated from the beginning that a pleasing shape should be assumed.
32 *laureate* The laurel wreath of excellence was given to poets in ancient Greece; see note 9–12 above.
34 'Why do you not return, Mephastophilis, in the likeness of a friar'
   redis Boas (*regis* A; this line, and the two preceding ones, are omitted in B)
38–9 *moon . . . world* These powers are common amongst enchanters in classical literature; compare Prospero's speech in Shakespeare's *The Tempest,* V.i.41-50.
44 Kocher (p. 160) calls this the well-established 'doctrine of voluntary ascent'.

FAUSTUS

Did not my conjuring speeches raise thee? Speak!

MEPHASTOPHILIS   45

That was the cause, but yet *per accidens*,

For when we hear one rack the name of God,

Abjure the Scriptures, and his saviour Christ,

We fly in hope to get his glorious soul,

Nor will we come, unless he use such means

Whereby he is in danger to be damned: 50

Therefore the shortest cut for conjuring

Is stoutly to abjure the Trinity,

And pray devoutly to the prince of hell.

FAUSTUS

So Faustus hath already done, and holds this principle:

There is no chief but only Belzebub,   55

To whom Faustus doth dedicate himself.

This word damnation terrifies not him,

For he confounds hell in Elysium:

His ghost be with the old philosophers.

But leaving these vain trifles of men's souls,   60

Tell me, what is that Lucifer thy lord?

MEPHASTOPHILIS

Arch-regent and commander of all spirits.

FAUSTUS

Was not that Lucifer an angel once?

46   *per accidens* literally 'by accident'; in logic, not of the real essence of a thing, i.e. a
     surface reason, incidental to the real cause
47   *rack* torture, tear apart (i.e. by anagrammatising it), hence 'strain the meaning of
     words' (*OED* v 1.3)
49   *glorious* a) shining, b) boastful, vainglorious
53   *stoutly* arrogantly, stubbornly, uncompromisingly
59   *confounds hell in Elysium* makes no distinction between the Christian concept of hell
     and the pagan (Greek) notion of the after-life in Elysium. Marlowe has already coupled
     the two: 'Hell and Elysium swarm with ghosts of men' (*1 Tamburlaine,* V.ii.403).
     Nashe may be referring to either of these passages when he scorns the writers that 'thrust
     Elisium into hell' (Preface to Greene's *Menaphon* [1589], ed. McKerrow, iii, 316)
60   *old philosophers* those who shared his disbelief in an eternity of punishment; the line
     seems to come from a saying of Averroes, the Arab commentator on Aristotle: *sit
     anima mea cum philosophis* (cf. J. C. Maxwell, *N & Q,* cxiv [1949], pp. 334–5; J. M.
     Steadman, *N & Q,* ccvii [1962], pp. 327–9)
62–76 This question and answer dialogue on matters of belief is a parody of the Christian
     'catechism' (a treatise for instruction in the principles of the Christian religion, in
     the form of question and answer).
64   *that Lucifer* A simple account of the history of Lucifer is given in Isaiah xiv, 12–15

MEPHASTOPHILIS
Yes Faustus, and most dearly loved of God.

FAUSTUS   65
How comes it then that he is prince of devils?

MEPHASTOPHILIS
O, by aspiring pride and insolence,
For which God threw him from the face of heaven.

FAUSTUS
And what are you that live with Lucifer?

MEPHASTOPHILIS
Unhappy spirits that fell with Lucifer,
Conspired against our God with Lucifer,   70
And are for ever damned with Lucifer.

FAUSTUS
Where are you damned?

MEPHASTOPHILIS
In hell.

FAUSTUS
How comes it then that thou art out of hell?

MEPHASTOPHILIS   75
Why this is hell, nor am I out of it.
Think'st thou that I, who saw the face of God,
And tasted the eternal joys of heaven,
Am not tormented with ten thousand hells
In being deprived of everlasting bliss?
O Faustus, leave these frivolous demands,   80
Which strike a terror to my fainting soul.

76–80 Caxton, while locating hell 'in the most lowest place, most derke, and most vyle of
the erthe', stressed that it is a state as well as a place; the condemned sinner is like a
man 'that had a grete maladye, so moche that he sholde deye, and that he were brought
into a fair place and plesaunt for to have Joye and solace; of so moche shold he be
more hevy and sorowful' (*The Mirrour of the World* [1480], ii, 18). Marlowe's concept
of hell at this point may be compared with Milton's; like Mephastophilis, Satan
cannot escape:

> For within him Hell
> He brings, and round about him, nor from Hell
> One step, no more than from himself can fly
> By change of place.   *Paradise Lost,* iv, 20–23

Mephastophilis' account of the torment of deprivation is translated from St John
Chrysostom: *si decem mille gehennas quis dixerit, nihil tale est quale ab illa beata
visione excidere* (see John Searle, *T.L.S.,* 15 February 1936).

FAUSTUS

    What, is great Mephastophilis so passionate
    For being deprived of the joys of heaven?
    Learn thou of Faustus manly fortitude,
    And scorn those joys thou never shalt possess.   85
    Go bear these tidings to great Lucifer,
    Seeing Faustus hath incurred eternal death
    By desperate thoughts against Jove's deity:
    Say, he surrenders up to him his soul
    So he will spare him four and twenty years,   90
    Letting him live in all voluptuousness,
    Having thee ever to attend on me,
    To give me whatsoever I shall ask,
    To tell me whatsoever I demand,
    To slay mine enemies, and aid my friends,   95
    And always be obedient to my will.
    Go, and return to mighty Lucifer,
    And meet me in my study at midnight,
    And then resolve me of thy master's mind.

MEPHASTOPHILIS   100

    I will Faustus.   *Exit*

FAUSTUS

    Had I as many souls as there be stars
    I'd give them all for Mephastophilis.
    By him I'll be great emperor of the world,
    And make a bridge through the moving air
    To pass the ocean with a band of men,   105
    I'll join the hills that bind the Afric shore
    And make that land continent to Spain
    And both contributory to my crown –

---

  83 *passionate* impassioned, swayed by strong feelings
  87 *these* B (those A)
  91 *So* on condition that
104–9 Both A- and B-texts punctuate very lightly here. Some modern editors add a semi-colon after 'men' (l. 106), but this interrupts the tumultuous association of word and idea whereby he imagines that by joining landmasses together a very small army could make him an emperor. Persian King Xerxes built a pontoon bridge across the Dardanelles to invade Greece. Alexander the Great (a figure who appears at 10.45–60) famously captured the island fortress of Tyre by joining it to the mainland with a 1000 metre causeway.
107–8 The hills on either side of the Straits of Gibraltar would, if joined together, unite Africa and Europe into a single continent.

The emperor shall not live but by my leave,   110
Nor any potentate of Germany.
Now that I have obtained what I desire
I'll live in speculation of this art
Till Mephastophilis return again.   *Exit*

110–11 *emperor ... Germany* The Holy Roman Emperor was elected by German princes. In Faustus's time, the Emperor was Charles V, Duke of Burgundy, King of the Spanish Empire (see l. 108), and ruler of Hapsburg lands in Austria/Hungary. Faustus wishes to be Emperor of the entire world (l. 104).

[Scene 4]

Enter WAGNER *and the* CLOWN

WAGNER

Sirra boy, come hither.

CLOWN

How, boy? Zounds, boy! I hope you have seen many boys with
such pickadevants as I have. Boy, quotha!

WAGNER

Tell me sirra, hast thou any comings in?

CLOWN

Ay, and goings out too; you may see else.   5

WAGNER

Alas poor slave, see how poverty jesteth in his nakedness! The
villain is bare, and out of service, and so hungry, that I know he
would give his soul to the devil for a shoulder of mutton, though
it were blood raw.

CLOWN

How, my soul to the devil for a shoulder of mutton though 'twere   10
blood raw? Not so good friend; by'rlady, I had need have it well
roasted, and good sauce to it, if I pay so dear.

WAGNER

Well, wilt thou serve me, and I'll make thee go like *qui mihi
discipulus*?

CLOWN

How, in verse?   15

WAGNER

No sirra; in beaten silk and stavesacre.

Scene 4   The B-text version of this scene, which is greatly changed to accommodate different
comedians and an altered theatrical taste, is printed in the Appendix.

   3   *pickadevants* small, pointed beards (Fr. *piqué devant*, pointed in front).

   4   *comings in* earnings, income

   5   *goings out* a) outgoings, expenses, b) the phrase becomes a visual joke ('see') if the
Clown pokes a finger through a hole in his clothes, or covers up a hole in mock
embarrassment.

 6–9   *see . . . raw* The language here might encourage an actor mockingly to adopt the
tones of an evangelical preacher; compare 2.24–8.

   7   *out of service* out of a job

13–14   *qui mihi discipulus* you who are my pupil: the opening words of a didactic Latin poem
by the schoolmaster William Lily which would be familiar to every Elizabethan schoolboy

486

CLOWN

How, how, knavesacre? Ay, I thought that was all the land his
father left him! Do ye hear, I would be sorry to rob you of your
living.

WAGNER

Sirra, I say in stavesacre.   20

CLOWN

Oho, oho, stavesacre! Why then belike, if I were your man, I should
be full of vermin.

WAGNER

So thou shalt, whether thou be'st with me or no. But sirra, leave
your jesting, and bind your self presently unto me for seven years,
or I'll turn all the lice about thee into familiars, and they shall tear   25
thee in pieces.

CLOWN

Do you hear sir? You may save that labour: they are too familiar
with me already – zounds, they are as bold with my flesh as if they
had paid for my meat and drink.

WAGNER

Well, do you hear sirra? Hold, take these guilders.   30

CLOWN

Gridirons; what be they?

16 *beaten silk* silk embroidered or with a woven pattern in gold or silver thread, but
here signifying that, as Wagner's servant, he will be well beaten
stavesacre powder made from seeds of delphinium (*delphinium staphisagria*) used
to kill vermin

17–22 Deliberate mishearing is still a stock comedy routine, as is mixing an onstage
conversation with direct address to the audience. The clown has been insulted by
Wagner since his entrance. He turns the tables with the invented word 'knavesacre'
by observing, probably to the audience but in such a manner that Wagner clearly
hears the insult, that Wagner only inherited one acre from his father. (Compare
'wiseacre', a contemptuous term for someone who thinks himself wise). He turns
back to Wagner with the comment that the revenue ('living') from one acre would
not be enough to pay wages. Wagner corrects the word, and the clown's repeated
'oho' again allows him to draw in the audience before delivering the killer blow that
any servant of Wagner's will be flea-ridden.

24 *presently* immediately
seven years the standard period for indentured service or apprenticeship

25 *familiars* familiar spirits or devils, often taking the form of domestic animals

29 *paid ... drink* (my A; their B) i.e. paid for his board (in order to fatten him up)

30 *guilders* Dutch gold or silver coins. Foreign coins were legal tender in England as
long as they were of the correct weight, see Harrison's *Description of England* in
Holinshed's *Chronicles* (1577, ii, 25).

31 *Gridirons* grids made of metal bars, used for cooking or as instruments of torture

WAGNER

Why, French crowns.

CLOWN

'Mass, but for the name of French crowns a man were as good
have as many English counters! And what should I do with these?

WAGNER

Why, now, sirra, thou art at an hour's warning whensoever or   35
wheresoever the devil shall fetch thee.

CLOWN

No, no, here take your gridirons again.

WAGNER

Truly I'll none of them.

CLOWN

Truly but you shall.

WAGNER

Bear witness I gave them him.   40

CLOWN

Bear witness I give them you again.

WAGNER

Well, I will cause two devils presently to fetch thee away. [*Calls*]
Baliol and Belcher!

CLOWN

Let your Baliol and your Belcher come here, and I'll knock them,
they were never so knocked since they were devils! Say I should   45
kill one of them, what would folks say? Do ye see yonder tall fellow

33   '*Mass* by the holy mass

34   *counters* worthless tokens, with pun on 'the Counter' (debtor's prison)

37–41   The business with the coins must be similar to that in scene viii of *The Taming of A
Shrew* where the Clown starts a sequence with 'Here, here, take your two shillings
again'. The actors draw the audience into their comic play to 'Bear witness'.

43   *Baliol* probably a corruption of 'Belial'; *Belcher* is also perhaps a mispronunciation
of 'Belzebub'

44–8   The Clown perhaps jokes on 'belly-all' and 'belch'. His lines depend for their humour
on the extended stage business they invite. He might act out the pummelling he
intends to give the devils and the kudos he will gain by beating them. A similar
passage occurs in *A Looking Glass for London* which was written by Lodge and Greene,
acted by Strange's Men in 1592, and printed in 1594. Here the Clown attacks the
devil who has come to carry him to hell; when the devil pleads that he is mortally
wounded, the Clown triumphs:

> Then may I count my selfe I thinke a tall man, that am able to kill a diuell. Now
> who dare deale with me in the parish, or what wench in *Ninivie* will not loue me,
> when they say, there goes he that beate the diuell.   (G3ᵛ)

44   *knock* beat

46   *tall* fine

in the round slop, he has killed the devil! So I should be called
'Killdevil' all the parish over.

Enter two DEVILS, *and the* CLOWN *runs up
and down crying*

WAGNER

Baliol and Belcher, spirits, away!

Exeunt [DEVILS]

CLOWN

What, are they gone? A vengeance on them! They have vile long   50
nails. There was a he devil and a she devil. I'll tell you how you
shall know them: all he devils has horns, and all she devils has
clefts and cloven feet.

WAGNER

Well sirra, follow me.

CLOWN

But do you hear? If I should serve you, would you teach me to   55
raise up Banios and Belcheos?

WAGNER

I will teach thee to turn thy self to anything, to a dog, or a cat, or
a mouse, or a rat, or any thing.

CLOWN

How! A Christian fellow to a dog, or a cat, a mouse, or a rat? No,
no sir, if you turn me into anything, let it be in the likeness of a   60
little pretty frisking flea, that I may be here, and there, and everywhere. O I'll tickle the pretty wenches' plackets! I'll be amongst
them i'faith.

WAGNER

Well sirra, come.

CLOWN

But, do you hear Wagner . . . ?   65

WAGNER

Baliol and Belcher!

---

47 *round slop* baggy pants, stock garments for comic characters; compare *Damon and
   Pythias*, 1571, Scene 13.83–94
53 *clefts* slits, with sexual pun
61 *frisking flea* In the medieval 'Song of the Flea', the poet envies the flea because it has
   free access to all parts of his mistress's body
62 *plackets* openings at the top of skirts, which also allowed access to the separate pocket
   worn beneath (also sometimes termed a placket); with sexual connotations

CLOWN

O Lord I pray sir, let Banio and Belcher go sleep.

WAGNER

Villain, call me Master Wagner; and let thy left eye be diametarily
fixed upon my right heel, with *quasi vestigias nostras insistere.*

Exit

CLOWN

God forgive me, he speaks Dutch fustian! Well, I'll follow him, I'll   70
serve him; that's flat.   *Exit*

---

68 *diametarily* diametrically
69 *quasi vestigias nostras insistere* 'as it were tread in our footsteps'; the construction is
     false (for *vestigiis nostris),* but this may be intentional
70 *Dutch fustian* gibberish – double Dutch; *fustian* is a coarse cloth made of flax and
     cotton

[Scene 5]

Enter FAUSTUS *in his study*

FAUSTUS

    Now Faustus, must thou needs be damned,
    And canst thou not be saved.
    What boots it then to think of God or heaven?
    Away with such vain fancies and despair,
    Despair in God, and trust in Belzebub.   5
    Now go not backward: no, Faustus, be resolute;
    Why waverest thou? O, something soundeth in mine ears:
    'Abjure this magic, turn to God again'.
    Ay, and Faustus will turn to God again.
    To God? He loves thee not: 10
    The god thou servest is thine own appetite
    Wherein is fixed the love of Belzebub.
    To him I'll build an altar and a church,
    And offer luke-warm blood of new-born babes.

Enter GOOD ANGEL *and* EVIL [ANGEL]

GOOD ANGEL

    Sweet Faustus, leave that execrable art.   15

FAUSTUS

    Contrition, prayer, repentance: what of them?

GOOD ANGEL

    O they are means to bring thee unto heaven.

EVIL ANGEL

    Rather illusions, fruits of lunacy,
    That makes men foolish that do trust them most.

GOOD ANGEL

    Sweet Faustus, think of heaven, and heavenly things.   20

EVIL ANGEL

    No Faustus, think of honour and of wealth.

                                 Exeunt [ANGELS]

FAUSTUS

    Of wealth!

---

    3   *boots it* good is it
   21   *and of wealth* A2 (and wealth A1)

Why, the signory of Emden shall be mine
When Mephastophilis shall stand by me.
What god can hurt thee, Faustus? Thou art safe,   25
Cast no more doubts. Come Mephastophilis,
And bring glad tidings from great Lucifer.
Is't not midnight? Come Mephastophilis:
Veni veni Mephastophile.

Enter MEPHASTOPHILIS

Now tell, what says Lucifer thy lord?   30
MEPHASTOPHILIS
That I shall wait on Faustus whilst he lives,
So he will buy my service with his soul.
FAUSTUS
Already Faustus hath hazarded that for thee.
MEPHASTOPHILIS
But Faustus, thou must bequeath it solemnly,
And write a deed of gift with thine own blood,   35
For that security craves great Lucifer.
If thou deny it, I will back to hell.
FAUSTUS
Stay Mephastophilis, and tell me,
What good will my soul do thy lord?
MEPHASTOPHILIS
Enlarge his kingdom.   40
FAUSTUS
Is that the reason he tempts us thus?

23 *signory of Emden* governorship of Emden – a port on the mouth of the Ems, at this time
    trading extensively with England. This is a somewhat modest ambition for someone
    who has the devil's assistance.
27 *glad tidings* This is ironic: the angels announced 'glad tidings of great joy', to the
    shepherds at the birth of Christ (Luke ii, 10).
29 *Veni . . . Mephastophile* 'Come, O come Mephastophilis'; a blasphemous parody of
    'veni, veni Emmanuel (translated in the nineteenth century as the hymn 'O come,
    O come Emmanuel')
30 *tell, what* A (tell me what B), see 5.145 below.
31 *he lives* B (I live A)
32 *So* provided that
33 *hazarded* jeopardized
40 *Enlarge his kingdom* 'Satan's chiefest drift & main point that he aimeth at, is the
    inlargement of his own kingdom, by the eternall destruction of man in the life to
    come', James Mason, *The Anatomie of Sorcerie* (1612), p. 55.

MEPHASTOPHILIS

Solamen miseris socios habuisse doloris.

FAUSTUS

Have you any pain that torture others?

MEPHASTOPHILIS

As great as have the human souls of men.

But tell me Faustus, shall I have thy soul?   45

And I will be thy slave and wait on thee,

And give thee more than thou hast wit to ask.

FAUSTUS

Ay Mephastophilis, I give it thee.

MEPHASTOPHILIS

Then stab thine arm courageously,

And bind thy soul, that at some certain day   50

Great Lucifer may claim it as his own,

And then be thou as great as Lucifer.

FAUSTUS

Lo Mephastophilis, for love of thee,

I cut mine arm, and with my proper blood

Assure my soul to be great Lucifer's,   55

Chief lord and regent of perpetual night.

View here the blood that trickles from mine arm,

And let it be propitious for my wish.

MEPHASTOPHILIS

But Faustus, thou must write it

In manner of a deed of gift.   60

FAUSTUS

Ay, so I will; but Mephastophilis,

My blood congeals and I can write no more.

MEPHASTOPHILIS

I'll fetch thee fire to dissolve it straight.   *Exit*

FAUSTUS

What might the staying of my blood portend?

---

42   proverbial; 'it is a comfort to the wretched to have had companions in misery'

43   *torture* B (tortures A), i.e. Do you who torture others have any pain? The B-text modernises the grammar rather than making a correction, but also reads 'Why, have you any pain that torture other?'

50   *certain* specified, fixed

52   *great* a) powerful, b) proud, arrogant

54   *proper* own

58   *propitious* a) favourable, b) an acceptable and effective sacrifice, c) blasphemously recalling Christ's own propitiatory sacrifice for the salvation of mankind

Is it unwilling I should write this bill? 65
Why streams it not, that I may write afresh:
'Faustus gives to thee his soul': ah, there it stayed!
Why should'st thou not? Is not thy soul thine own?
Then write again: 'Faustus gives to thee his soul'.

Enter MEPHASTOPHILIS *with a chafer of coals*

MEPHASTOPHILIS
Here's fire, come Faustus, set it on. 70
FAUSTUS
So, now the blood begins to clear again.
Now will I make an end immediately.
MEPHASTOPHILIS
O what will not I do to obtain his soul!
FAUSTUS
Consummatum est, this bill is ended,
And Faustus hath bequeathed his soul to Lucifer. 75
But what is this inscription on mine arm?
Homo fuge. Whither should I fly?
If unto God, he'll throw thee down to hell;
My senses are deceived, here's nothing writ;
I see it plain, here in this place is writ, 80
Homo fuge! Yet shall not Faustus fly.
MEPHASTOPHILIS
I'll fetch him somewhat to delight his mind. *Exit*

Enter [*again*] *with* DEVILS, *giving crowns and rich
apparel to* FAUSTUS; *and dance, and then depart*

65 *bill* written document
66 *streams* This word anticipates 13.68.
69 s.d. *chafer* usually a warming dish containing hot water (the source has 'dish of
water'). A dish of burning coals is more redolent of hell.
70 *set it on* 'set his blood in a saucer on warm ashes' *EFB*, vi
71 Greg observes that no earthly fire will liquefy congealed blood
74 *Consummatum est* 'It is completed'; the last words of Christ on the cross: St John
xix, 30
77–8 Compare Psalms cxxxix, 7–8 'Whither shall I go from thy spirit? Or whither shall I
flee from thy presence? If I ascend into heaven, thou art there: if I lie down in hell,
thou art there.'
77 *Homo fuge* Fly, O man

FAUSTUS

    Speak Mephastophilis, what means this show?

MEPHASTOPHILIS

    Nothing Faustus, but to delight thy mind withal,

    And to show thee what magic can perform.   85

FAUSTUS

    But may I raise up spirits when I please?

MEPHASTOPHILIS

    Ay Faustus, and do greater things than these.

FAUSTUS

    Then there's enough for a thousand souls!

    Here Mephastophilis, receive this scroll,

    A deed of gift of body and of soul: 90

    But yet conditionally, that thou perform

    All articles prescribed between us both.

MEPHASTOPHILIS

    Faustus, I swear by hell and Lucifer

    To effect all promises between us made.

FAUSTUS

    Then hear me read them. On these conditions following: 95

    First, that Faustus may be a spirit in form and substance.

    Secondly, that Mephastophilis shall be his servant, and at his command.

    Thirdly, that Mephastophilis shall do for him, and bring him whatsoever.   100

    Fourthly, that he shall be in his chamber or house invisible.

    Lastly, that he shall appear to the said John Faustus at all times, in what form or shape soever he please.

    I, John Faustus of Wittenberg, doctor, by these presents, do give both body and soul to Lucifer, Prince of the East, and his minister   105 *Mephastophilis; and furthermore grant unto them that, four and twenty years being expired, the articles above written inviolate, full*

---

96 *may* This permissive verb (in contrast to the 'shall' governing Mephastophilis's part in this contract) suggests that Faustus sees his spirit status as something to be put on and put off again as he pleases.

     a spirit A spirit, to the Elizabethans, was usually an evil one – a devil (see Shakespeare, Sonnet CXLIV); according to some theologians, who followed Aquinas, God could have no mercy on a devil who was *ipso facto* incapable of repenting. Compare 7.11–17.

101 *he* i.e. Mephastophilis

104 *these presents* the legal articles

power to fetch or carry the said John Faustus, body and soul, flesh,
blood, or goods, into their habitation wheresoever.

By me John Faustus.   110

MEPHASTOPHILIS

Speak Faustus, do you deliver this as your deed?

FAUSTUS

Ay, take it; and the devil give thee good on't.

MEPHASTOPHILIS

Now Faustus, ask what thou wilt.

FAUSTUS

First will I question with thee about hell:

Tell me, where is the place that men call hell?   115

MEPHASTOPHILIS

Under the heavens.

FAUSTUS

Ay, but whereabout?

MEPHASTOPHILIS

Within the bowels of these elements,

Where we are tortured and remain for ever.

Hell hath no limits, nor is circumscribed   120

In one self place; for where we are is hell,

And where hell is, must we ever be.

And to conclude, when all the world dissolves,

And every creature shall be purified,

All places shall be hell that is not heaven.   125

FAUSTUS

Come, I think hell's a fable.

MEPHASTOPHILIS

Ay, think so still, till experience change thy mind.

FAUSTUS

Why? thinkst thou then that Faustus shall be damned?

MEPHASTOPHILIS

Ay, of necessity, for here's the scroll

Wherein thou hast given thy soul to Lucifer.   130

FAUSTUS

Ay, and body too; but what of that?

Think'st thou that Faustus is so fond to imagine

---

118   *these elements* the four elements (fire, air, earth, and water) below the sphere of the
moon

121   *one self place* one particular place

132   *fond* foolish

That after this life there is any pain?

. Tush, these are trifles and mere old wives' tales.

MEPHASTOPHILIS

But Faustus, I am an instance to prove the contrary;   135

For I am damned, and am now in hell.

FAUSTUS

How, now in hell? Nay, and this be hell, I'll willingly be damned
here! What, walking, disputing, etc ... But leaving off this, let me
have a wife, the fairest maid in Germany, for I am wanton and
lascivious, and cannot live without a wife.   140

MEPHASTOPHILIS

How, a wife? I prithee Faustus, talk not of a wife.

FAUSTUS

Nay sweet Mephastophilis, fetch me one, for I will have one.

MEPHASTOPHILIS

Well, thou wilt have one; sit there till I come.

I'll fetch thee a wife in the devil's name.   [*Exit*]

> *Enter* [*again*] *with a* DEVIL *dressed like a woman,*
> *with fireworks*

MEPHASTOPHILIS

Tell Faustus, how dost thou like thy wife?   145

FAUSTUS

A plague on her for a hot whore!

MEPHASTOPHILIS

Tut Faustus, marriage is but a ceremonial toy;

          [*Exit* DEVIL]

If thou lovest me, think no more of it.

I'll cull thee out the fairest courtesans,

And bring them every morning to thy bed: 150

She whom thine eye shall like, thy heart shall have,

Be she as chaste as was Penelope,

---

133 *after ... pain* Compare Lucretius's poem *De Rerum Natura,* a triumphant hymn on
the mortality of the soul, and hence the impossibility of punishment after death.

138 *disputing* According to Chorus 1.18, this is Faustus's 'sweet delight'.

141 Mephastophilis is alarmed at this talk of marriage – which, in Christian terms, is
considered a holy sacrament that saves sex between the partners from the sin of
lechery.

147 *ceremonial toy* trifling ceremony

148 *think no more* B (think more A)

149 *cull* pick

152 *Penelope* wife of Ulysses, renowned for her fidelity to an absent husband

As wise as Saba, or as beautiful
As was bright Lucifer before his fall.
Hold, take this book, peruse it thoroughly: 155
The iterating of these lines brings gold;
The framing of this circle on the ground
Brings whirlwinds, tempests, thunder and lightning.
Pronounce this thrice devoutly to thy self,
And men in armour shall appear to thee,   160
Ready to execute what thou desir'st.

FAUSTUS

Thanks Mephastophilis, yet fain would I have a book wherein I
might behold all spells and incantations, that I might raise up
spirits when I please.

MEPHASTOPHILIS

Here they are in this book.   *There turn to them*   165

FAUSTUS

Now would I have a book where I might see all characters and
planets of the heavens, that I might know their motions and
dispositions.

MEPHASTOPHILIS

Here they are too.   *Turn to them*

FAUSTUS

Nay, let me have one book more, and then I have done, wherein   170
I might see all plants, herbs and trees that grow upon the earth.

MEPHASTOPHILIS

Here they be.

FAUSTUS

O thou art deceived!

MEPHASTOPHILIS

Tut, I warrant thee.   *Turn to them*
                                                         [*Exeunt*]

---

153   *Saba* the Queen of Sheba, who confronted Solomon with 'hard questions', 1 Kings x
156   *iterating* repeating over and over
      lines a) verbal phrases, b) symbols
166   *characters* symbols
167   *motions* movements
168   *dispositions* a) positions relative to each other, b) nature of planets relative to their
      supposed effects
173   It seems that the sum total of the knowledge for which Faustus has sold his soul can
      be contained in one book. No wonder he is dismayed.
174   s.d. If Faustus is at his desk in the upstage 'discovery' space, Mephastophilis could
      draw the curtain to hide them both.

[Scene 6]

Enter ROBIN *the ostler with a book in his hand*

ROBIN

O this is admirable! Here I ha' stolen one of Doctor Faustus'
conjuring books, and i'faith I mean to search some circles for my
own use: now will I make all the maidens in our parish dance at
my pleasure stark naked before me, and so by that means I shall
see more than ere I felt, or saw yet.   5

Enter RAFE *calling* ROBIN

RAFE

Robin, prithee come away, there's a gentleman tarries to have his
horse, and he would have his things rubbed and made clean. He
keeps such a chafing with my mistress about it, and she has sent
me to look thee out. Prithee, come away.

ROBIN

Keep out, keep out; or else you are blown up, you are dismem-   10
bered, Rafe. Keep out, for I am about a roaring piece of work.

RAFE

Come, what dost thou with that same book? Thou canst not read!

ROBIN

Yes, my master and mistress shall find that I can read – he for his
forehead, she for her private study. She's born to bear with me, or
else my art fails.   15

RAFE

Why Robin, what book is that?

Scene 6 In the A-text the two episodes with Robin and Rafe are presented as a single scene.
   This revised edition follows Bevington and Rasmussen in inserting the first Rafe and
   Robin scene at this point; Appendix 6 prints the B-text.
   0 *ostler* stable lad, groom
   2 *search* examine, probe
     circles magicians' circles; but the sexual overtones are obvious
   5 *ere* either 'previously' (archaic in Marlowe's time, and therefore perhaps chosen as
     a characteristic of Robin's speech) or 'ever'.
   8 *chafing* a) scolding, b) rubbing
   11 *roaring* dangerous
   14 *forehead* referring to cuckold's horns
     private study punning on 'private parts'
     bear with me a) put up with me, b) support my weight during sexual intercourse, c)
     bear my children

499

ROBIN

What book? Why the most intolerable book for conjuring that
ere was invented by any brimstone devil.

RAFE

Canst thou conjure with it?

ROBIN

I can do all these things easily with it: first, I can make thee drunk   20
with 'ipocrase at any tavern in Europe for nothing, that's one of
my conjuring works.

RAFE

Our master parson says that's nothing.

ROBIN

True Rafe! And more, Rafe, if thou hast any mind to Nan Spit, our
kitchen-maid, then turn her and wind her to thy own use, as often   25
as thou wilt, and at midnight.

RAFE

O brave Robin! Shall I have Nan Spit, and to mine own use? On
that condition I'll feed thy devil with horsebread as long as he
lives, of free cost.

ROBIN

No more, sweet Rafe; let's go and make clean our boots which lie   30
foul upon our hands, and then to our conjuring in the devil's name.

Exeunt

---

17 *intolerable* unbearable, playing on 'bear with me', but Robin probably means 'incom-
parable'
18 *brimstone* common name for sulphur, often used medicinally and as a fumigant, but
its stinking odour is associated with the fumes of hell
21 *'ipocrase* hippocras – a spiced wine
28 *horsebread* fodder for horses
29 *of free cost* free of charge

[Scene 7]

[*Enter* FAUSTUS *and* MEPHASTOPHILIS]

FAUSTUS

    When I behold the heavens, then I repent,

    And curse thee, wicked Mephastophilis,

    Because thou hast deprived me of those joys.

MEPHASTOPHILIS

    Why Faustus,

    Think'st thou heaven is such a glorious thing?   5

    I tell thee 'tis not half so fair as thou,

    Or any man that breathes on earth.

FAUSTUS

    How provest thou that?

MEPHASTOPHILIS

    It was made for man, therefore is man more excellent.

FAUSTUS

    If it were made for man, 'twas made for me: 10

    I will renounce this magic, and repent.

Enter GOOD ANGEL *and* EVIL ANGEL

GOOD ANGEL

    Faustus, repent yet, God will pity thee.

EVIL ANGEL

    Thou art a spirit, God cannot pity thee.

FAUSTUS

    Who buzzeth in mine ears I am a spirit?

    Be I a devil, yet God may pity me.   15

    Ay, God will pity me if I repent.

EVIL ANGEL

    Ay, but Faustus never shall repent.

Exeunt [ANGELS]

FAUSTUS

    My heart's so hardened I cannot repent!

    0   s.d. This ed. See 5.174 s.d.

   12   *repent yet* A (repent, yet B) i.e. repent even now, while there is still time

   14   *buzzeth* whispers

   15   *Be I* This could mean either 'Even if I am', or else 'Even though I were'

   18   Hardness (also called blindness) of heart is recognized as a very complex spiritual condition; the Litany of the Book of Common Prayer offers a special supplication: 'From all blindness of heart . . . Good Lord, deliver us'.

Scarce can I name salvation, faith, or heaven,
But fearful echoes thunders in mine ears,   20
'Faustus, thou art damned'; then swords and knives,
Poison, guns, halters, and envenomed steel,
Are laid before me to dispatch myself:
And long ere this I should have slain myself,
Had not sweet pleasure conquered deep despair.   25
Have not I made blind Homer sing to me
Of Alexander's love, and Oenon's death?
And hath not he that built the walls of Thebes
With ravishing sound of his melodious harp,
Made music with my Mephastophilis?   30
Why should I die then, or basely despair?
I am resolved Faustus shall ne'er repent.
Come Mephastophilis, let us dispute again,
And argue of divine astrology.
Tell me, are there many heavens above the moon?   35

22   *halters* hangman's ropes
26   *blind Homer* The Greek poet was traditionally held to be blind
27   *Alexander ... death* Alexander (Homer's name for Paris, son of Priam) fell in love
     with Oenone before he encountered Helen. After he was wounded in the Trojan War,
     he was carried to Oenone and died at her feet, whereupon she stabbed herself.
28–9 At the sound of Amphion's harp the stones were so affected that they rose of their
     own accord to form the walls of Thebes.
33–63 Faustus is both locked into his scholastic approach to knowledge through rhetorical
     disputation (7.33) and simultaneously hoping that Mephastophilis will give him
     hard information inaccessible to that method. His most urgent concern is to establish
     the structure of the universe. He briefly wonders whether the entire universe is not
     a single entity (7.37), but Mephastophilis swiftly returns him to the old Ptolemaic
     system, which taught that the earth is surrounded by a series of concentric chrystalline
     spheres. Each of the first seven spheres holds the orbit round the earth of one of the
     heavenly bodies (Moon, Mercury, Venus, Sun, Mars, Jupiter, Saturn). Beyond these
     is the sphere of the fixed stars, sometimes considered to include the *primum mobile*,
     the first mover, which imparts movement to the rest. The early church fathers
     postulated a further immoveable sphere, the *empyreal heaven* (7.58), which was the
     abode of God, and which shone with a piercing stainless light. Milton describes
     a similar cosmology in *Paradise Lost* when he identifies 'the planets seven'; 'the
     fixed'; 'And that crystalline sphere ... that first moved' (III, 481-3). Unfortunately,
     Mephastophilis's replies to Faustus's questions comprise a miscellaneous jumble of
     commonly received knowledge, as Faustus himself points out (7.49; 53-4).
35–43 *Tell me ... erring stars* Faustus asks first for confirmation of the number of spheres
     beyond the Moon, and whether in fact these do form a single ball. Mephastophilis
     replies that just as the four elements enclose each other (earth is surrounded by
     water, water by air, and air by fire), so each sphere or heaven is circled round by the

Are all celestial bodies but one globe,
As is the substance of this centric earth?

MEPHASTOPHILIS

As are the elements, such are the spheres,
Mutually folded in each other's orb.
And, Faustus, all jointly move upon one axletree   40
Whose termine is termed the world's wide pole,
Nor are the names of Saturn, Mars, or Jupiter,
Feigned, but are erring stars.

FAUSTUS

But tell me, have they all one motion, both *situ et tempore*?

MEPHASTOPHILIS

All jointly move from east to west in four-and-twenty hours upon   45
the poles of the world, but differ in their motion upon the poles
of the zodiac.

FAUSTUS

Tush, these slender trifles Wagner can decide!
Hath Mephastophilis no greater skill?
Who knows not the double motion of the planets?   50
The first is finished in a natural day, the second thus: as Saturn in
thirty years; Jupiter in twelve; Mars in four; the Sun, Venus, and
Mercury in a year; the Moon in eight-and-twenty days. Tush, these
are freshmen's suppositions. But tell me, hath every sphere a
dominion or *intelligentia*?   55

ones beyond it, and all rotate upon a single axletree. Saturn, Mars, and the other
planets are individually recognizable: they are called *erring* or wandering stars to
distinguish them from the fixed stars which are joined to the firmament.

41 *termine* boundary (astronomical)

44 *situ et tempore* in direction and time

44–53 *all . . . days* When the movement of the planets is observed from earth, the planets
appear to move from east to west across the earth every night. But on successive nights
it seems as if they are moving from west to east relative to the positions of the zodiacal
constellations. This is the double motion (7.50) of the planets. Occasionally movement
relative to the constellations is reversed, a phenomenon known as the retrograde
motion of the planets. The complete revolution of each planet relative to the constellations is variable: Saturn 29½ years; Jupiter 11¾ years; Mars 1 year 11 months; Venus
7½ months and Mercury 3 months. Caxton (*Mirrour of the World* [1480], 1.13)
explains that each planet is like a fly crawling on a wheel: if the fly crawls in one
direction and the wheel turns in the opposite, the fly may be said to have two motions.

54 *freshmen's suppositions* elementary facts given to first-year undergraduates for them
to build an argument upon

54–5 *hath . . . intelligentia* The next question at issue relates to a theory first propounded
by Plato and developed in the Middle Ages, that each planet was guided by an angelic
spirit, commonly called the *intelligence*.

MEPHASTOPHILIS

Ay.

FAUSTUS

How many heavens or spheres are there?

MEPHASTOPHILIS

Nine: the seven planets, the firmament, and the empyreal heaven.

FAUSTUS

Well, resolve me in this question: why have we not conjunctions, oppositions, aspects, eclipses, all at one time, but in some years 60 we have more, in some less?

MEPHASTOPHILIS

Per inaequalem motum respectu totius.

FAUSTUS

Well, I am answered. Tell me who made the world?

MEPHASTOPHILIS

I will not.

FAUSTUS

Sweet Mephastophilis, tell me. 65

MEPHASTOPHILIS

Move me not, for I will not tell thee.

> Let mans Soule be a Spheare, and then, in this,
> The intelligence that moves, devotion is.
>> Donne, 'Good Friday, Riding Westwards'

Mephastophilis affirms the *intelligence,* but the theory was never really accepted by scientists.

59–62 *resolve me . . . totius* Mephastophilis' answer to the next question sounds like a quotation from some astronomical textbook. Faustus asks about the behaviour of the planets, using technical but well-known astronomical terms; *conjunctions* are the apparent joinings together of two planets, whilst *oppositions* describes their relationships when most remote:

> Therefore the love which us doth bind,
> But Fate so enviously debars,
> Is the Conjunction of the Mind,
> And Opposition of the Stars.
>> Marvell, 'The Definition of Love'

Any position between the two extremes of conjunction and opposition was termed an *aspect.* To astrologers the differing situations and relations of the planets all have some particular significance – hence the horoscope. Faustus is finally told what he already knows: that the heavenly bodies do not all move at the same speed, and that for this reason ('through an irregular motion so far as the whole is concerned', 1. 62) there are more eclipses etc. in some years than in others.

62 'Because of their unequal motion in respect of the whole'

66 *Move me not* Don't make me angry

FAUSTUS

    Villain, have I not bound thee to tell me anything?

MEPHASTOPHILIS

    Ay, that is not against our kingdom; but this is.

    Think thou on hell Faustus, for thou art damned.

FAUSTUS

    Think, Faustus, upon God, that made the world.   70

MEPHASTOPHILIS

    Remember this.   *Exit*

FAUSTUS

    Ay, go accursed spirit, to ugly hell,

    'Tis thou hast damned distressed Faustus' soul:

    Is't not too late?

Enter GOOD ANGEL *and* EVIL [ANGEL]

EVIL ANGEL

    Too late.   75

GOOD ANGEL

    Never too late, if Faustus can repent.

EVIL ANGEL

    If thou repent, devils shall tear thee in pieces.

GOOD ANGEL

    Repent, and they shall never rase thy skin.

Exeunt [ANGELS]

FAUSTUS

    Ah Christ my Saviour, seek to save

    Distressed Faustus' soul.   80

Enter LUCIFER, BELZEBUB *and* MEPHASTOPHILIS

LUCIFER

    Christ cannot save thy soul, for he is just.

    There's none but I have interest in the same.

FAUSTUS

    O who art thou that look'st so terrible?

LUCIFER

    I am Lucifer, and this is my companion prince in hell.

    78 *rase* graze
    82 *interest* a) legal claim, b) financial interest; sin is sometimes spoken of as a debt that
         is redeemed by Christ's sacrifice

FAUSTUS

O Faustus, they are come to fetch away thy soul! 85

LUCIFER

We come to tell thee thou dost injure us.
Thou talk'st of Christ, contrary to thy promise.
Thou should'st not think of God; think of the devil,
And of his dame too.

FAUSTUS

Nor will I henceforth: pardon me in this, 90
And Faustus vows never to look to heaven,
Never to name God, or to pray to him,
To burn his Scriptures, slay his ministers,
And make my spirits pull his churches down.

LUCIFER

Do so, and we will highly gratify thee. Faustus, we are come from 95
hell to show thee some pastime; sit down, and thou shalt see all
the Seven Deadly Sins appear in their proper shapes.

FAUSTUS

That sight will be as pleasing unto me, as Paradise was to Adam,
the first day of his creation.

LUCIFER

Talk not of Paradise, nor creation, but mark this show; talk of the 100
devil and nothing else. Come away.

Enter the SEVEN DEADLY SINS

Now Faustus, examine them of their several names and dispositions.

FAUSTUS

What art thou, the first?

PRIDE

I am Pride: I disdain to have any parents. I am like to Ovid's flea,
I can creep into every corner of a wench: sometimes like a periwig, 105
I sit upon her brow; or like a fan of feathers, I kiss her lips. Indeed
I do – what do I not! But fie, what a scent is here? I'll not speak
another word, except the ground were perfumed and covered with
cloth of arras.

89　*dame* old woman, wife, housewife, mother
97　*proper* own
102　*several* different, various
104　*Ovid's flea* The poet of 'Song of the Flea' (probably medieval but attributed to Ovid)
　　envies the flea for its freedom of movement over his mistress' body (see 4.61n).
108　*except* unless

FAUSTUS

What are thou, the second? 110

COVETOUSNESS

I am Covetousness, begotten of an old churl in an old leathern
bag: and might I have my wish, I would desire that this house, and
all the people in it, were turned to gold, that I might lock you up
in my good chest. O my sweet gold!

FAUSTUS

What art thou, the third? 115

· WRATH

I am Wrath. I had neither father nor mother: I leaped out of a lion's
mouth when I was scarce half an hour old, and ever since I have
run up and down the world, with this case of rapiers, wounding
myself when I had nobody to fight withal. I was born in hell – and
look to it, for some of you shall be my father. 120

FAUSTUS

What art thou, the fourth?

ENVY

I am Envy, begotten of a chimney-sweeper, and an oyster- wife. I
cannot read, and therefore wish all books were burnt; I am lean
with seeing others eat – O that there would come a famine through
all the world, that all might die, and I live alone; then thou should'st 125
see how fat I would be! But must thou sit and I stand? Come down,
with a vengeance.

FAUSTUS

Away, envious rascal! What art thou, the fifth?

GLUTTONY

Who, I sir? I am Gluttony. My parents are all dead, and the devil
a penny they have left me but a bare pension, and that is thirty 130
meals a day and ten bevers – a small trifle to suffice nature. O, I
come of a royal parentage: my grandfather was a gammon of
bacon, my grandmother a hogshead of claret wine; my godfathers

---

109   *cloth of arras* tapestry; expensive, woven, pictorial wall-hangings originally from
        Arras in northern France
111–12   *leathern bag* the miser's purse
118   *case* pair
120   *some of you* Wrath addresses the audience
122   *begotten . . . wife* Envy is filthy, and stinks
131   *bevers* a) drinks, b) snacks, light meals
133   *hogshead* a barrel containing sixty-three gallons

were these: Peter Pickle-Herring, and Martin Martlemas-Beef.
O, but my godmother! She was a jolly gentlewoman, and well-   135
beloved in every good town and city; her name was Mistress
Margery March-Beer. Now, Faustus, thou hast heard all my
progeny; wilt thou bid me to supper?

FAUSTUS

Ho, I'll see thee hanged; thou wilt eat up all my victuals.

GLUTTONY

Then the devil choke thee!   140

FAUSTUS

Choke thyself, Glutton. What art thou, the sixth?

SLOTH

I am Sloth; I was begotten on a sunny bank, where I have lain ever
since – and you have done me great injury to bring me from
thence. Let me be carried thither again by Gluttony and Lechery.
I'll not speak another word for a king's ransom.   145

FAUSTUS

What are you Mistress Minx, the seventh and last?

LECHERY

Who, I, sir? I am one that loves an inch of raw mutton better than
an ell of fried stockfish; and the first letter of my name begins with
Lechery.

LUCIFER

Away! To hell, to hell!   150

Exeunt the [SEVEN DEADLY] SINS

Now Faustus, how dost thou like this?

FAUSTUS

O this feeds my soul.

---

134   *Peter Pickle-Herring* a fat, buffoon figure, popular at the beginning of the seventeenth
century on the stage and in carnival celebrations in Holland and Germany, where
they regarded him as of English origin. Salty pickled herring, a food to be eaten
during Lent, was also provided in taverns (as are modern salted snacks) to promote
drinking.
Martlemas-Beef Meat, salted to preserve it for winter, was hung up around Martinmas
(11 November).
137   *March-Beer* a rich ale, made in March and left to mature for at least two years
138   *progeny* lineage (obsolete)
147–9   *I am one ... Lechery* The words are rather obscure, but their sense is clear. Lechery prefers
a small quantity of virility to a large extent of impotence: *stockfish,* a long strip of dried
cod, is a common term of abuse, indicating impotence: 'he was begot between two
stockfishes', *Measure for Measure,* III.ii.98. The 'Minx' ends with a common form of
jest: cf. 'Her name begins with Mistress Purge', Middleton, *The Family of Love,* II.iii.53.

LUCIFER

Tut Faustus, in hell is all manner of delight.

FAUSTUS

O might I see hell, and return again, how happy were I then!

LUCIFER

Thou shalt; I will send for thee at midnight. In meantime, take   155
this book, peruse it thoroughly, and thou shalt turn thyself into
what shape thou wilt.

FAUSTUS

Great thanks, mighty Lucifer; this will I keep as chary as my life.

LUCIFER

Farewell, Faustus; and think on the devil.

FAUSTUS

Farewell, great Lucifer; come Mephastophilis.   160

Exeunt omnes

158   *chary* carefully

[Chorus 2]

Enter WAGNER *solus*

WAGNER

Learned Faustus,
To know the secrets of astronomy
Graven in the book of Jove's high firmament,
Did mount himself to scale Olympus' top,
Being seated in a chariot burning bright,   5
Drawn by the strength of yoky dragons' necks.
He now is gone to prove cosmography,
And, as I guess, will first arrive at Rome,
To see the pope, and manner of his court,
And take some part of holy Peter's feast,   10
That to this day is highly solemnized.   *Exit* WAGNER

---

0 s.d. *Enter Wagner solus* This Chorus-like speech is given to Wagner in both the A-
    and B-texts, see Chorus 1 notes 0 and 28.
    solus alone
3 *Graven* carved, engraved
4 *Olympus* Mount Olympus was the home of the gods of Greek mythology.
6 *yoky dragons' necks* A (*yoaked* B) i.e. two dragons, the fiercest of mythical beasts, have
    taken on the attributes of a pair of domesticated animals, acting as one (as if joined
    with a yoke, or perhaps with their necks curved like yokes under the strain) and
    subjected to a man's will. This is the first recorded instance of the word in *OED*.
7 *prove* put to the test
    cosmography The art of describing and making maps of the universe, including the
    heavens and the earth, and combining astronomy, geography and history. The B-text
    adds a line explaining that this 'measures costs, and kingdomes of the earth'.
10 *holy Peter's feast* St Peter's feast day is 29 June

[Scene 8]

Enter FAUSTUS *and* MEPHASTOPHILIS

FAUSTUS

Having now, my good Mephastophilis,
Passed with delight the stately town of Trier,
Environed round with airy mountain tops,
With walls of flint, and deep entrenched lakes,
Not to be won by any conquering prince;   5
From Paris next, coasting the realm of France,
We saw the river Main fall into Rhine,
Whose banks are set with groves of fruitful vines;
Then up to Naples, rich Campania,
Whose buildings fair and gorgeous to the eye,   10
The streets straight forth, and paved with finest brick,
Quarters the town in four equivalents;
There saw we learned Maro's golden tomb,
The way he cut an English mile in length
Thorough a rock of stone in one night's space.   15
From thence to Venice, Padua – and the rest –
In midst of which a sumptuous temple stands,
That threats the stars with her aspiring top.
Thus hitherto hath Faustus spent his time.
But tell me now, what resting place is this?   20
Hast thou, as erst I did command,
Conducted me within the walls of Rome?

2   *Trier* Treves, in West Germany
6   *coasting* skirting
9   *Campania* Naples lies within the region of Campania
13   *learned Maro* The poet Virgil (Publius Virgilius Maro) was buried in Naples in 19
     B.C., and posthumously acquired some reputation as a magician. His tomb stands
     at the end of the promontory of Posilippo between Naples and Pozzuoli; legend
     ascribes the tunnel running through this promontory to his magic art.
16-18   *Venice . . . top EFB* lists very many more places and buildings on Faustus's tour of
     the world than are mentioned here, hence perhaps the vagueness of the A-text's *and
     the rest* (8.16). This is printed here within dashes since the *aspiring top* (8.18) must
     refer to the striking silhouette of the Basilica of St Anthony in Padua; *EFB* (p. 35)
     justifiably describes its 'pinnacles' as unique in Christendom. The B-text prints
     'Venice, Padua, and the East' and adds a quotation from the *EFB* description of St
     Mark's in Venice.
21   *erst* earlier

MEPHASTOPHILIS

Faustus, I have; and because we will not be unprovided, I have
taken up his holiness' privy chamber for our use.

FAUSTUS

I hope his holiness will bid us welcome.   25

MEPHASTOPHILIS

Tut, 'tis no matter man, we'll be bold with his good cheer.
And now, my Faustus, that thou may'st perceive
What Rome containeth to delight thee with,
Know that this city stands upon seven hills
That underprop the groundwork of the same;   30
Just through the midst runs flowing Tiber's stream,
With winding banks, that cut it in two parts;
Over the which four stately bridges lean,
That makes safe passage to each part of Rome.
Upon the bridge called Ponte Angelo   35
Erected is a castle passing strong,
Within whose walls such store of ordinance are,
And double cannons, framed of carved brass,
As match the days within one complete year;
Besides the gates, and high pyramides   40
Which Julius Caesar brought from Africa.

FAUSTUS

Now by the kingdoms of infernal rule,
Of Styx, Acheron, and the fiery lake

---

23   *Faustus, I have* From this point the A- and B-texts are only occasionally similar; B's
     version of the remainder of the scene is printed in the Appendix.

24   *privy chamber* a room for personal not public use

27–41   Mephastophilis may have illustrated his little talk with reference to a topographical
     drawing of the city in the form of a stage hanging or painted cut-out, since a 'sittie
     of Rome' is listed in the 1598 Admiral's Men's inventory of properties in the Henslowe
     papers (*Henslowe's Diary*, ed. Foakes and Rickert, 1961, p. 319).

30   *underprop* B (underprops A)

31–2   The lines are supplied in the B-text to supply an obvious deficiency in A (the 'stately
     bridges' must have something to lean over).

35–6   *Upon . . . strong* The Ponte Angelo was built in A.D 135 by Hadrian, whose mausoleum
     (directly facing the bridge but never standing on it) became the Castello di S. Angelo.

37   *ordinance* ordnance, military supplies, artillery

38   *double cannons* cannons of very high calibre

40–1   *pyramides . . . Africa* the obelisk that stands in front of St Peter's; the description
     follows *EFB*, but it was in fact brought from Egypt by the emperor Caligula. The
     plural form *pyramides* is often used for the singular: here the extra syllable is needed
     for the regular pentameter.

43–4   *Styx . . . Phlegethon* the rivers in Hades, the Greek underworld

Of ever-burning Phlegethon, I swear
That I do long to see the monuments   45
And situation of bright-splendent Rome.
Come therefore, let's away.

MEPHASTOPHILIS

Nay Faustus stay, I know you'd fain see the pope,
And take some part of holy Peter's feast,
Where thou shalt see a troup of bald-pate friars,   50
Whose *summum bonum* is in belly-cheer.

FAUSTUS

Well, I am content to compass then some sport,
And by their folly make us merriment.
Then charm me that I may be invisible, to do what I please unseen
of any whilst I stay in Rome.   55

MEPHASTOPHILIS [*casts a spell on him*]

So Faustus, now do what thou wilt, thou shall not be discerned.

Sound a sennet; enter the POPE *and the* CARDINAL OF LORRAINE
to the banquet, with FRIARS *attending*

POPE

My lord of Lorraine, will't please you draw near.

FAUSTUS

Fall to; and the devil choke you and you spare.

POPE

How now, who's that which spake? Friars, look about.

1 FRIAR

Here's nobody, if it like your holiness.   60

POPE

My lord, here is a dainty dish was sent me from the bishop of Milan.

FAUSTUS

I thank you, sir.   *Snatch it*

POPE

46 *situation* lay-out
    bright-splendent resplendent
51 *summum bonum* greatest good; in scholastic theology this is a term used to
    describe the Almighty
52 *compass* contrive, plot, perhaps playing on the rounded bellies of the friars.
58 *Fall to* Get on with it
    and you if you
    spare eat sparingly

How now, who's that which snatched the meat from me? Will no
man look? My lord, this dish was sent me from the cardinal of
Florence.   65

FAUSTUS

· You say true? I'll have't.   [*Snatch it*]

POPE

What, again! My lord, I'll drink to your grace.

FAUSTUS

I'll pledge your grace.   [*Snatch the cup*]

LORRAINE

My lord, it may be some ghost newly crept out of purgatory come
to beg a pardon of your holiness.   70

POPE

It may be so; friars, prepare a dirge to lay the fury of this ghost.
Once again my lord, fall to.   -   *The* POPE *crosseth himself*

FAUSTUS

What, are you crossing of your self? Well, use that trick no more,
I would advise you.   *Cross again*

FAUSTUS

Well, there's the second time; aware the third! I give you fair warning.   75

Cross again, and FAUSTUS *hits him a box of the ear,*
and they all run away

FAUSTUS

Come on Mephastophilis, what shall we do?

MEPHASTOPHILIS

Nay, I know not; we shall be cursed with bell, book, and candle.

FAUSTUS

How! Bell, book, and candle; candle, book, and bell,

68 *pledge* toast
70 *pardon* papal indulgence
70 *dirge* a corruption of *dirige*, which starts the antiphon at Matins in the Office for the
     Dead; hence any requiem mass. The word is used correctly here by the pope, but the
     ritual performed is not in fact a mass but a formal cursing.
72 s.d. *crosseth himself EFB* describes how the pope 'would ever be blessing and crossing
     over his mouth'. If making the sign of the cross were an effective guard against spirits,
     Faustus and Mephastophilis should be overcome by this—hence, comically perhaps,
     Faustus's alarm here.
75 *aware* beware
77 *bell, book, and candle* At the close of the Office of Excommunication the bell is tolled,
     the bible closed, and the candle extinguished.

Forward and backward, to curse Faustus to hell.
Anon you shall hear a hog grunt, a calf bleat, and an ass bray,   80
Because it is St Peter's holy day.

Enter all the FRIARS *to sing the Dirge*

1 FRIAR
 Come brethren, let's about our business with good devotion.
             Sing this
 Cursed be he that stole away his holiness' meat from the table.
   Maledicat Dominus.
 Cursed be he that struck his holiness a blow on the face.   85
   Maledicat Dominus.
 Cursed be he that took Friar Sandelo a blow on the pate.
   Maledicat Dominus.
 Cursed be he that disturbeth our holy dirge.
   Maledicat Dominus.   90
 Cursed be he that took away his holiness' wine.
   Maledicat dominus.
    Et omnes sancti. Amen.
Beat the Friars, and fling fireworks among them, and so Exeunt

---

79 *forward and backward* compare 3.9
84 *Maledicat Dominus* May the Lord curse him
87 *took* gave
   Sandelo the name probably suggested by the friar's sandals
93 *Et omnes sancti* and all the saints

[Scene 9]

Enter ROBIN [*with conjuring book*] *and* RAFE *with a silver goblet*

ROBIN

Come Rafe, did not I tell thee we were for ever made by this Doctor
Faustus' book? *Ecce signum*! [*Pointing to the goblet*] Here's a simple
purchase for horse-keepers: our horses shall eat no hay as long as
this lasts.

Enter the VINTNER

RAFE

But Robin, here comes the vintner.   5

ROBIN

Hush, I'll gull him supernaturally! Drawer, I hope all is paid; God
be with you. Come, Rafe.   [*They start to go*]

VINTNER

Soft sir, a word with you. I must yet have a goblet paid from you
ere you go.

ROBIN

I a goblet, Rafe! I a goblet? I scorn you: and you are but a &c ...   10
I a goblet? Search me.

VINTNER

I mean so, sir, with your favour.   [*Searches* ROBIN]

Scene 9 In the A-text, this scene runs directly on from the previous Robin and Rafe scene
(Scene 6) even though time has evidently passed. The B-text version of this scene is
printed in the Appendix.

1 *for ever made* permanently advantaged, granted success in life

2 *Ecce signum* behold the proof – a fairly common catchword amongst Elizabethan
comic actors: see *1 Henry IV*, where Falstaff shows his 'sword hack'd like a handsaw
– *ecce signum*' (II.iv.168). Here it satirises what to Protestants was the 'conjuring' of
the Roman Catholic mass in turning wine in the Eucharistic chalice or goblet into
the blood of Christ.
simple purchase clear profit

3 *eat no hay* i.e. eat well

5 *vintner* inn-keeper, wine merchant. Rafe has cause to be alarmed since throughout
the scene he is repeatedly made to hold the stolen goblet.

6 *gull* trick
Drawer one who draws beer. Robin insults the vintner's status.

10 *but a &c* This gives the actor permission to ad-lib abusively

ROBIN

How say you now?

VINTNER

I must say somewhat to your fellow; you sir!

RAFE

Me sir! Me sir? [ROBIN *takes goblet from him*] Search your fill.   15
[VINTNER *searches* RAFE] Now sir, you may be ashamed to burden
honest men with a matter of truth.

VINTNER

Well, t'one of you hath this goblet about you.

ROBIN

[*Aside*]You lie, drawer, 'tis afore me. [*To the* VINTNER] Sirra you,
I'll teach ye to impeach honest men: [*To* RAFE] stand by; [*To the*   20
VINTNER] I'll scour you for a goblet; stand aside, you had best; I
charge you in the name of Belzebub – look to the goblet, Rafe!

VINTNER

What mean you, sirra?

ROBIN

I'll tell you what I mean: [*He reads*] Sanctobulorum Peri-
phrasticon – nay, I'll tickle you, vintner – look to the goblet,   25
Rafe – Polypragmos Belseborams framanto pacostiphos tostis
Mephastophilis, &c ...

> *Enter* MEPHASTOPHILIS [*unseen by them*]:
> *sets squibs at their backs: they run about*

VINTNER

O *nomine Domine*! What mean'st thou Robin, thou hast no goblet?

19 *afore me* (playing on *about you*, l. 18). Robin is holding the goblet in front of him,
     hidden perhaps in a bag or under clothing.
21 *scour* beat, scourge, punish
22, 25 *look ... goblet* Robin appears to be trying to pass the goblet to Rafe
24–7 a mixture of Latin- and Greek-sounding gibberish; *periphrasis* is a rhetorical term
     for 'roundabout', wordy language; *polypragmon* is Greek for busybody
25 *tickle* beat
28–31 In the panic and chaos caused by the fireworks, the Vintner sees his goblet, Rafe
     gives it to him and Robin pleads to the devil for forgiveness. The Latin phrases recall
     parts of the liturgy but are all corrupt to a greater or lesser extent: *In nomine Domini*
     ('in the name of God'); *Peccatum peccatorum*, 'sin of sins', recalls the structure 'King
     of kings' but also seems to be a misquotation from St Augustine, *peccata pecca-
     torum*, 'of sins upon sins' in Sermon 83 (sometimes number 33) based on Matthew
     xviii, 21–23 concerning Christian redemption; *Misericordia nobis* i.e. *miserere
     nobis*, 'have mercy on us' (*misericordia* is the noun 'pity').

RAFE

Peccatum peccatorum! Here's thy goblet, good Vintner.

ROBIN

Misericordia pro nobis! What shall I do? Good devil, forgive me   30
now, and I'll never rob thy library more.

Enter to them MEPHASTOPHILIS

MEPHASTOPHILIS

Vanish villains, th'one like an ape, an other like a bear, the third
an ass, for doing this enterprise.

[*Exit* VINTNER]

Monarch of hell, under whose black survey
Great potentates do kneel with awful fear;   35
Upon whose altars thousand souls do lie;
How am I vexed with these villains' charms!
From Constantinople am I hither come,
Only for pleasure of these damned slaves.

ROBIN

How, from Constantinople? You have had a great journey! Will   40
you take sixpence in your purse to pay for your supper, and be
gone?

MEPHASTOPHILIS

Well villains, for your presumption, I transform thee into an ape,
and thee into a dog; and so be gone.   *Exit*

ROBIN

How, into an ape? That's brave: I'll have fine sport with the boys;   45
I'll get nuts and apples enow.

RAFE

And I must be a dog.

ROBIN

I'faith, thy head will never be out of the potage pot.

Exeunt

31   s.d. *Enter to them* This suggests that he is now visible to them, having been invisible
     when he brought the fireworks.
32–33   *ape . . . ass* Mephastophilis angrily dismisses Robin and Rafe as ape and bear, and
     the Vintner as ass. While the Vintner must be glad to exit, with or without his cup,
     Robin, who thinks he has conjured Mephastophilis and has power to dismiss him
     (compare 3.40–6), is only scared off a little and comes back with Rafe in tow.
48   *potage* porridge

[Chorus 3]

Enter CHORUS

CHORUS

When Faustus had with pleasure ta'en the view
Of rarest things, and royal courts of kings,
He stayed his course, and so returned home;
Where such as bare his absence but with grief –
I mean his friends and nearest companions –   5
Did gratulate his safety with kind words.
And in their conference of what befell,
Touching his journey through the world and air,
They put forth questions of astrology,
Which Faustus answered with such learned skill,   10
As they admired and wondered at his wit.
Now is his fame spread forth in every land:
Amongst the rest the emperor is one,
Carolus the fifth, at whose palace now
Faustus is feasted 'mongst his noblemen.   15
What there he did in trial of his art
I leave untold: your eyes shall see performed.   *Exit*

Chorus 3 This Chorus occurs immediately after the Rome scene in the A-text and is missing
    from the B-text where Mephastophilis ends Scene 9 by saying he goes to join Faustus
    at the great Turk's court—an episode which occurs in neither text, although it is a
    feature of the sequel to *EFB*.
  3 *stayed his course* ceased his journey
  6 *gratulate* express joy
 11 *As* that
 14 *Carolus* Charles V (1519–56), whose court was at Innsbruck

[Scene 10]

Enter EMPEROR, FAUSTUS, *and a* KNIGHT,
with Attendants [*and* MEPHASTOPHILIS, *invisible*]

EMPEROR

Master Doctor Faustus, I have heard strange report of thy knowledge in the black art, how that none in my empire, nor in the
whole world, can compare with thee for the rare effects of magic.
They say thou hast a familiar spirit, by whom thou canst
accomplish what thou list! This therefore is my request: that thou   5
let me see some proof of thy skill, that mine eyes may be witnesses
to confirm what mine ears have heard reported. And here I swear
to thee, by the honour of mine imperial crown, that whatever thou
dost, thou shalt be no ways prejudiced or endamaged.

KNIGHT *Aside*

I'faith, he looks much like a conjuror.   10

FAUSTUS

My gracious sovereign, though I must confess myself far inferior
to the report men have published, and nothing answerable to the
honour of your imperial majesty, yet for that love and duty binds
me thereunto, I am content to do whatsoever your majesty shall
command me.   15

EMPEROR

Then Doctor Faustus, mark what I shall say. As I was sometime
solitary set within my closet, sundry thoughts arose about the
honour of mine ancestors – how they had won by prowess such
exploits, got such riches, subdued so many kingdoms, as we that
do succeed, or they that shall hereafter possess our throne, shall   20
(I fear me) never attain to that degree of high renown and great
authority. Amongst which kings is Alexander the Great, chief spectacle of the world's pre-eminence:

Scene 10   B's much-expanded version of this scene is printed in the Appendix.
    16   *sometime* recently
    17   *set* sitting
        closet small private room for contemplation, prayer, study etc.
 18–22   The extraordinary rise of the Hapsburg family, and their prolonged influence and
        power over most of continental Europe, largely through strategic marriage alliances
        rather than military conquest, is still a source of wonder to historians.

The bright shining of whose glorious acts
Lightens the world with his reflecting beams;   25
As when I hear but motion made of him,
It grieves my soul I never saw the man.
If therefore thou, by cunning of thine art,
Canst raise this man from hollow vaults below,
Where lies entombed this famous conqueror,   30
And bring with him his beauteous paramour,
Both in their right shapes, gesture, and attire
They used to wear during their time of life,
Thou shalt both satisfy my just desire,
And give me cause to praise thee whilst I live.   35

FAUSTUS

My gracious lord, I am ready to accomplish your request, so far
forth as by art and power of my spirit I am able to perform.

KNIGHT *Aside*

I'faith, that's just nothing at all.

FAUSTUS

But, if it like your grace, it is not in my ability to present before
your eyes the true substantial bodies of those two deceased princes   40
which long since are consumed to dust.

KNIGHT *Aside*

Ay, marry, master doctor, now there's a sign of grace in you, when
you will confess the truth.

FAUSTUS

But such spirits as can lively resemble Alexander and his paramour
shall appear before your grace, in that manner that they best   45
lived in, in their most flourishing estate: which I doubt not shall
sufficiently content your imperial majesty.

22 *Alexander the Great* Alexander III of Macedon (356–323 B.C.), pupil of Aristotle,
    conqueror of the Persian Empire, Iran and Northern India, and a subject for numerous
    heroic romances in medieval Europe

26 *motion* mention

31 *paramour* mistress, lover, consort. This is often assumed to be Roxana, a beautiful
    captured Bactrian princess and one of Alexander's many wives. A more elaborate
    dumb-show in the B-text involves Alexander's defeat of the Persian king Darius, in
    which case she might be the whore Thais who at a drunken banquet is sometimes
    supposed to have persuaded Alexander to burn Darius's city of Persepolis (see
    Diodorus Siculus, Bk. 17, Ch. 7 Athenaeus xiii.576, 585). This would link thematically
    with the show of Helen and the burning of Troy (12.90; see Nigel Alexander, 1972,
    pp. 14–19).

42 *marry* a mild oath, 'by the virgin Mary'

44 *lively* 'to the life', vividly

EMPEROR

Go to, master doctor, let me see them presently.

KNIGHT

Do you hear, master doctor? You bring Alexander and his paramour before the emperor!   50

FAUSTUS

How then, sir?

KNIGHT

I'faith, that's as true as Diana turned me to a stag.

FAUSTUS

No sir; but when Actaeon died, he left the horns for you! [*Aside*]
Mephastophilis, begone!

                Exit MEPHASTOPHILIS [FAUSTUS *starts to conjure*]

KNIGHT

Nay, and you go to conjuring I'll be gone.   55

                         Exit KNIGHT

FAUSTUS

I'll meet with you anon for interrupting me so. Here they are, my
gracious lord.

            Enter MEPHASTOPHILIS
       with ALEXANDER *and his* PARAMOUR

EMPEROR

Master doctor, I heard this lady, while she lived, had a wart or mole
in her neck; how shall I know whether it be so or no?

FAUSTUS

Your highness may boldly go and see.   60

             Exit ALEXANDER [*and his* PARAMOUR]

---

48 *Go to* a mild rebuke, 'enough', 'get on with it'
     presently immediately
53 *Actaeon* As a punishment for coming upon the goddess Diana and her nymphs
     when they were bathing, Actaeon was turned into a stag, and his own hounds tore
     him to pieces.
56 *meet with you* a) meet you, b) be even with you
60 s.d. *Exit Alexander* A. Editors usually add a s.d. here instructing the Emperor to
     inspect the neck of Alexander's paramour as happens in the B-text, delaying
     Alexander's exit until after the Emperor's next speech. It is, however, rather more
     in Alexander's character, and his status as conqueror of such a vast Empire, if he
     prevents this Emperor's presumption, exiting immediately, as marked in the A-
     text. This would also prompt the Emperor's admiration at l. 61 and his conviction
     that these apparitions are genuine—as there can be few, if any, people in his
     experience who would be so bold as to deny him.

EMPEROR

Sure, these are no spirits, but the true substantial bodies of those
two deceased princes.

FAUSTUS

Will't please your highness now to send for the knight that was
so pleasant with me here of late?

EMPEROR

One of you call him forth.   65

Enter the KNIGHT *with a pair of horns on his head*

How now sir knight? Why, I had thought thou hadst been a
bachelor, but now I see thou hast a wife that not only gives thee
horns but makes thee wear them! Feel on thy head.

KNIGHT

Thou damned wretch and execrable dog,
Bred in the concave of some monstrous rock,   70
How dar'st thou thus abuse a gentleman?
Villain I say, undo what thou hast done.

FAUSTUS

O not so fast sir, there's no haste but good. Are you remembered
how you crossed me in my conference with the emperor? I think
I have met with you for it.   75

EMPEROR

Good master doctor, at my entreaty release him; he hath done
penance sufficient.

FAUSTUS

My gracious lord, not so much for the injury he offered me here
in your presence, as to delight you with some mirth, hath Faustus
worthily requited this injurious knight; which being all I desire,   80
I am content to release him of his horns. And, sir knight, hereafter
speak well of scholars: [*Aside*] Mephastophilis, transform him

---

64 *pleasant* facetious, jesting
67 *bachelor* a) i.e. knight bachelor, a member of the lowest order of knighthood, b)
     unmarried man
67–8 *wife . . . wear them* It was an old joke that the cuckolded husband would grow horns
     to publish his shame.
70 *Bred . . . rock.* See *2 Tamburlaine*, III.ii.89: 'Fenced with the concave of some monstrous
     rock'.
73 *Are you remembered* Have you forgotten
75 *met with you* am even with you
78 *injury* insult

straight. [*To* EMPEROR] Now my good lord, having done my duty,
I humbly take my leave.

EMPEROR

Farewell master doctor; yet ere you go, expect from me a bounteous   85
reward.

Exit EMPEROR [*and his Attendants*]

FAUSTUS

Now Mephastophilis, the restless course

That time doth run with calm and silent foot,

Shortening my days and thread of vital life,

Calls for the payment of my latest years;   90

Therefore, sweet Mephastophilis, let us make haste to Wittenberg.

MEPHASTOPHILIS

What, will you go on horseback, or on foot?

FAUSTUS

Nay, till I am past this fair and pleasant green, I'll walk on foot.

Enter a HORSE-COURSER

HORSE-COURSER

I have been all this day seeking one Master Fustian: 'mass, see where
he is! God save you, master doctor.   95

FAUSTUS

What, horse-courser: you are well met.

HORSE-COURSER

Do you hear, sir; I have brought you forty dollars for your horse.

87–93   Faustus and Mephastophilis walk back to Wittenberg, meeting the Horse-courser
on the way. Lines 87–93 occur only in the A-text. A different version of lines 94–163
occurs in the B-text as a separate scene. This is printed in the Appendix as Scene 10c,
and follows an extra scene (10b) in which Benvolio tries to get his revenge on Faustus.

89   *thread of vital life* The image of life as a single thread comes from Greek mythology.

90   *payment* The idea of death as a debt owed to nature is a commonplace (See *Macbeth*,
V.ix.5: 'Your son, my lord, has paid a soldier's debt'); but it is revitalized here by
Faustus' predicament.
latest last

93   s.d HORSE-COURSER Horse-dealer; a reputation for dishonesty has always attached
to such traders

94   *Fustian* The Horse-courser, in mispronouncing Faustus's name, using a word for the
kind of coarse cloth he himself would wear, unwittingly puns on 'bombastic or made-
up language'; compare the clown's use of the word at 4.70, which may suggest that
one actor played both parts.

97   *dollars* English name for certain foreign coins including the German silver thaler,
later in the scene punning on 'dolours', physical or mental suffering

FAUSTUS

I cannot sell him so: if thou lik'st him for fifty, take him.

HOURSE-COURSER

Alas sir, I have no more. [*To* MEPHASTOPHILIS] I pray you speak
for me. 100

MEPHASTOPHILIS

I pray you let him have him; he is an honest fellow, and he has a
great charge – neither wife nor child.

FAUSTUS

Well; come, give me your money; my boy will deliver him to you.
But I must tell you one thing before you have him: ride him not
into the water at any hand. 105

HORSE-COURSER

Why sir, will he not drink of all waters?

FAUSTUS

O yes, he will drink of all waters, but ride him not into the water.
Ride him over hedge or ditch, or where thou wilt, but not into the
water.

HORSE-COURSER

Well sir. Now am I made man for ever: I'll not leave my horse for 110
forty! If he had but the quality of hey ding ding, hey ding ding,
I'd make a brave living on him! He has a buttock as slick as an eel.
Well, God b'y sir; your boy will deliver him me? But hark ye sir,
if my horse be sick, or ill at ease, if I bring his water to you, you'll
tell me what it is? 115

FAUSTUS

Away, you villain! What, dost think I am a horse-doctor?

Exit HORSE-COURSER

102 *charge* expenses
 wife nor child playing on the proverb 'wife and children are bills of charge'
103 *boy* servant, in this case Mephastophilis
105 *at any hand* whatever happens
106 *drink of all waters* go anywhere
110 *made man* well set up
 leave part with
111 *forty* a common term for 'any large amount', but of course forty is exactly what he
 paid
 quality of hey ding ding The Horse-courser seems to be wishing that the horse were
 a stallion, not a gelding; compare Nashe, *Have With You to Saffron Walden* (1596):
 'Yea, Madam *Gabriele*, are you such an old ierker? then Hey ding a ding, vp with
 your perticoate, haue at your plum-tree' (McKerrow iii, p. 113).
114 *his water* his urine (for diagnosis)
116 s.d. *Exit* HORSE-COURSER This s.d. occurs after the previous line in the A-text for
 reasons of space.

What art thou, Faustus, but a man condemned to die?
Thy fatal time doth draw to final end.
Despair doth drive distrust unto my thoughts:
Confound these passions with a quiet sleep.   120
Tush, Christ did call the thief upon the cross;
Then rest thee, Faustus, quiet in conceit.

Sleep in his chair

Enter HORSE-COURSER *all wet, crying*

HORSE-COURSER

Alas, alas, Doctor Fustian, quoth 'a: 'mass, Doctor Lopus was never
such a doctor! H'as given me a purgation, h'as purged me of forty
dollars! I shall never see them more. But yet, like an ass as I was,   125
I would not be ruled by him; for he bade me I should ride him
into no water. Now I, thinking my horse had had some rare quality
that he would not have had me known of, I, like a vent'rous youth,
rid him into the deep pond at the town's end. I was no sooner in
the middle of the pond, but my horse vanished away, and I sat   130
upon a bottle of hay, never so near drowning in my life! But I'll
seek out my doctor, and have my forty dollars again, or I'll make
it the dearest horse. O, yonder is his snipper-snapper! Do you hear,
you hey-pass, where's your master?

MEPHASTOPHILIS

Why sir, what would you? You cannot speak with him.   135

HORSE-COURSER

But I will speak with him.

MEPHASTOPHILIS

Why, he's fast asleep; come some other time.

---

118   *fatal time* time of death, allotted by fate
121   *Christ . . . cross* St Luke's Gospel tells of Christ's words of comfort to the crucified
     thief: 'This day shall thou be with me in paradise' (xxiii, 43)
122   *in conceit* in this thought
     s.d. *in his chair* Presumably at some point during the previous speech he has opened
     a curtain at the back of the stage to reveal his study in Wittenberg (see line 91).
123   *Doctor Lopus* This joke must have found its way into the text after the execution, in
     February 1594, of Roderigo Lopez, Queen Elizabeth's personal physician, who was
     accused of plotting to poison her.
124–5   *purgation . . . dollars* with reference to the proverb 'give one's purse a purgation'
128   *known of* aware of
131   *bottle* bundle
134   *hey-pass* a conjuror's 'magic' catchphrase

HORSE-COURSER

I'll speak with him now, or I'll break his glass-windows about his
ears.

MEPHASTOPHILIS

I tell thee, he has not slept this eight nights.   140

HORSE-COURSER

And he have not slept this eight weeks I'll speak with him.

MEPHASTOPHILIS

See where he is, fast asleep.

HORSE-COURSER

Ay, this is he; God save ye master doctor, master doctor, master
Doctor Fustian, forty dollars, forty dollars for a bottle of hay.

MEPHASTOPHILIS

Why, thou seest he hears thee not.   145

HORSE-COURSER

So ho ho; so ho ho.   *Halloo in his ear*

No, will you not wake? I'll make you wake ere I go.
                         Pull him by the leg, and pull it away

Alas, I am undone! What shall I do?

FAUSTUS

O my leg, my leg! Help, Mephastophilis! Call the officers! My leg,
my leg!   150

MEPHASTOPHILIS

Come villain, to the constable.

HORSE-COURSER

O Lord, sir! Let me go, and I'll give you forty dollars more.

MEPHASTOPHILIS

Where be they?

HORSE-COURSER

I have none about me: come to my ostry and I'll give them you.

MEPHASTOPHILIS

Begone quickly!   155

                                   HORSE-COURSER *runs away*

FAUSTUS

What, is he gone? Farewell he: Faustus has his leg again, and the
horse-courser – I take it – a bottle of hay for his labour! Well, this
trick shall cost him forty dollars more.

138 *glass-windows* spectacles
146 *So ho ho* the huntsman's cry when he catches sight of the quarry
154 *ostry* hostelry, inn

527

Enter WAGNER

How now Wagner, what's the news with thee?

WAGNER

Sir, the Duke of Vanholt doth earnestly entreat your company.   160

FAUSTUS

The Duke of Vanholt! An honourable gentleman, to whom I must
be no niggard of my cunning. Come Mephastophilis, let's away
to him.

Exeunt

160   Vanholt i.e. Anhalt (as in the source) a Duchy in central Germany

[Scene 11]

[Enter FAUSTUS *with* MEPHASTOPHILIS, *invisible]*
Enter to them the DUKE *and the* DUCHESS; *the* DUKE *speaks*

DUKE

Believe me, master doctor, this merriment hath much pleased me.

FAUSTUS

My gracious Lord, I am glad it contents you so well: but it may
be, madam, you take no delight in this; I have heard that great-
bellied women do long for some dainties or other – what is it,
madam? Tell me, and you shall have it.   5

DUCHESS

Thanks, good master doctor; and for I see your courteous intent
to pleasure me, I will not hide from you the thing my heart desires.
And were it now summer, as it is January and the dead time of
the winter, I would desire no better meat than a dish of ripe grapes.

FAUSTUS

Alas madam, that's nothing! *[Aside]* Mephastophilis, begone!   10
Exit MEPHASTOPHILIS
Were it a greater thing than this, so it would content you, you
should have it.

Enter MEPHASTOPHILIS *with the grapes*

Here they be, madam; will't please you taste on them?

DUKE

Believe me, master doctor, this makes me wonder above the rest:
that being in the dead time of winter, and in the month of January,   15
how you should come by these grapes.

> 0.2 s.d. *Enter to them . . . speaks* The A-text's slightly unusual stage direction suggests
> that Faustus and Mephastophilis have either remained on stage from the previous
> scene, or re-entered before the Duke and Duchess. Either there is then some unscripted
> business with sound effects (see *this merriment* l. 1), indicating the staging of a magic
> show off stage, or perhaps an additional scene took place which was written on a
> separate leaf of the manuscript and has not survived. The B-text has a tavern scene
> in which a Carter recounts a story about Faustus swindling him out of a load of hay,
> and the Horse-courser responds by retelling the story we have just witnessed; these
> characters are then conjured back at the end of the scene for the further entertainment
> of the Duke and Duchess.
> 3–4 *great-bellied* pregnant
>   9 *meat* food

FAUSTUS

If it like your grace, the year is divided into two circles over the
whole world, that when it is here winter with us, in the contrary
circle it is summer with them, as in India, Saba, and farther countries in the east; and by means of a swift spirit that I have, I had   20
them brought hither, as ye see. How do you like them, madam;
be they good?

DUCHESS

Believe me, master doctor, they be the best grapes that e'er I tasted
in my life before.

FAUSTUS

I am glad they content you so, madam.   25

DUKE

Come madam, let us in, where you must well reward this learned
man for the great kindness he hath showed to you.

DUCHESS

And so I will my lord; and whilst I live, rest beholding for this
courtesy.

FAUSTUS

I humbly thank your grace.   30

DUKE

Come, master doctor, follow us, and receive your reward.

Exeunt

---

17 *two circles* The explanation is confusing. The relevant circles would be the northern
and southern hemispheres, but the author appears to be thinking in terms of east
and west; *EFB* evades the matter while providing the detail of the twice-yearly fruit.
19 *Saba* Sheba; in modern times, this is the Yemen
28 *rest beholding* remain indebted

[Scene 12]

Enter WAGNER *solus*

WAGNER

    I think my master means to die shortly,
    For he hath given to me all his goods!
    And yet methinks, if that death were near,
    He would not banquet, and carouse, and swill
    Amongst the students, as even now he doth,   5
    Who are at supper with such belly-cheer,
    As Wagner ne'er beheld in all his life.
    See where they come: belike the feast is ended.   [*Exit*]

Enter FAUSTUS [*and* MEPHASTOPHILIS],
with two or three SCHOLARS

1 SCHOLAR

    Master Doctor Faustus, since our conference about fair ladies,
    which was the beautifullest in all the world, we have determined   10
    with ourselves that Helen of Greece was the admirablest lady
    that ever lived. Therefore, master doctor, if you will do us that
    favour as to let us see that peerless dame of Greece, whom all the
    world admires for majesty, we should think ourselves much
    beholding unto you.   15

FAUSTUS

    Gentlemen for that I know your friendship is unfeigned,
    And Faustus' custom is not to deny
    The just requests of those that wish him well,
    You shall behold that peerless dame of Greece,
    No otherways for pomp and majesty   20

Scene 12   The A- and B-text versions of this scene are closely related.

    0.1   s.d. *Enter* WAGNER *solus* Again, Wagner performs the function of Chorus, but this
        time in his role as Faustus's servant.

      6   *belly-cheer* food and drink

  10–11   *beautifullest ... admirablest* The clumsy form of these superlatives will help an actor
        to appear drunk on too much *belly-cheer.*

    11   *Helen of Greece* The wife of Menelaus, king of Sparta, who was given to the Trojan
        prince Paris as a reward for judging which of the three goddesses Hera, Athena and
        Aphrodite was the most beautiful. Thus began the ten-year Trojan war.

  16–23   as prose in A

Than when Sir Paris crossed the seas with her,
And brought the spoils to rich Dardania.
Be silent then, for danger is in words.

Music sounds, and HELEN *passeth over the stage*

2 SCHOLAR

Too simple is my wit to tell her praise,
Whom all the world admires for majesty.   25

3 SCHOLAR

No marvel though the angry Greeks pursued
With ten years' war the rape of such a queen,
Whose heavenly beauty passeth all compare.

1 SCHOLAR

Since we have seen the pride of Nature's works,
And only paragon of excellence,   30

Enter an OLD MAN

Let us depart; and for this glorious deed
Happy and blest be Faustus evermore.

FAUSTUS

Gentlemen farewell; the same I wish to you.

Exeunt SCHOLARS

OLD MAN

Ah Doctor Faustus, that I might prevail
To guide thy steps unto the way of life –   35
By which sweet path thou may'st attain the goal –
That shall conduct thee to celestial rest.
Break heart, drop blood, and mingle it with tears,
Tears falling from repentant heaviness

21 *Sir* The title was often applied to classical heroes in medieval romance.
22 *Dardania* Troy; in fact the city built by Dardanus on the Hellespont, but the name
    is often transferred to Troy
23 s.d. *passeth over* crosses
26 *pursued* followed up; with the sense of attacked, besieged (*OED* 6b)
27 *rape* a) abduction, b) rape
30 *paragon of excellence* Helen was not herself accounted blameless in most versions of
    the story.
36–7 *By . . . rest* Either the Old Man repeats himself in his anxiety (or perhaps as a
      characterisation of old age), or the manuscript contained alternative lines, marked
      in this edition by dashes.

Of thy most vile and loathsome filthiness,   40
The stench whereof corrupts the inward soul
With such flagitious crimes of heinous sins,
As no commiseration may expel;
But mercy, Faustus, of thy saviour sweet,
Whose blood alone must wash away thy guilt.   45

FAUSTUS

Where art thou Faustus? Wretch, what hast thou done!
Damned art thou Faustus, damned; despair and die!
Hell calls for right, and with a roaring voice
Says, 'Faustus, come: thine hour is come'!

          MEPHASTOPHILIS *gives him a dagger*

And Faustus will come to do thee right.   50

OLD MAN

Ah stay, good Faustus, stay thy desperate steps!
I see an angel hovers o'er thy head,
And with a vial full of precious grace
Offers to pour the same into thy soul!
Then call for mercy, and avoid despair.   55

FAUSTUS

Ah my sweet friend, I feel thy words
To comfort my distressed soul;
Leave me awhile to ponder on my sins.

OLD MAN

I go, sweet Faustus; but with heavy cheer,
Fearing the ruin of thy hopeless soul.   [*Exit*]   60

FAUSTUS

Accursed Faustus, where is mercy now?
I do repent, and yet I do despair:
Hell strives with grace for conquest in my breast!
What shall I do to shun the snares of death?

MEPHASTOPHILIS

Thou traitor, Faustus: I arrest thy soul   65

---

42 *flagitious* extremely wicked

43 *commiseration* pity, compassion, perhaps 'miseration' (obs.) mercy

49 s.d. MEPHASTOPHILIS … *dagger* The s.d. is inserted in the margin at this point in the
    A-text. In this position, the appearance of the dagger is a terrible (and perhaps ironic)
    response to Faustus's sin of despair. Some editors, however, insert the s.d. after line
    47, as in the B-text, where it has the effect merely of prompting the words 'Hell calls'.

50 *do thee right* i.e. pay what is due

59 *heavy cheer* sorrowful frame of mind

For disobedience to my sovereign lord.
Revolt, or I'll in piecemeal tear thy flesh.

FAUSTUS

Sweet Mephastophilis, entreat thy lord
To pardon my unjust presumption;
And with my blood again I will confirm   70
My former vow I made to Lucifer.

MEPHASTOPHILIS

Do it then quickly, with unfeigned heart,
Lest greater danger do attend thy drift.

FAUSTUS

Torment, sweet friend, that base and crooked age
That durst dissuade me from thy Lucifer,   75
With greatest torments that our hell affords.

MEPHASTOPHILIS

His faith is great, I cannot touch his soul,
But what I may afflict his body with,
I will attempt – which is but little worth.

FAUSTUS

One thing, good servant, let me crave of thee,   80
To glut the longing of my heart's desire:
That I might have unto my paramour
That heavenly Helen which I saw of late,
Whose sweet embracings may extinguish clean
These thoughts that do dissuade me from my vow: 85
And keep mine oath I made to Lucifer.

MEPHASTOPHILIS

Faustus, this, or what else thou shalt desire,
Shall be performed in twinkling of an eye.

Enter HELEN

FAUSTUS

Was this the face that launched a thousand ships,
And burnt the topless towers of Ilium?   90

67 *Revolt* Turn again to your allegiance
73 *drift* drifting; also purpose
74 *base . . . age* i.e. the Old Man
84 *clean* completely
89 *Was . . . ships* Compare Lucian's *Dialogues of the Dead,* no.18, where Hermes shows
    Helen's skull to Menippus who responds 'And for this a thousand ships carried
    warriors from every part of Greece' (*The Works of Lucian,* vol.1, 1935, pp. 137–8).

Sweet Helen, make me immortal with a kiss:
Her lips sucks forth my soul, see where it flies!
Come Helen, come, give me my soul again.
Here will I dwell, for heaven be in these lips,
And all is dross that is not Helena!   95

Enter OLD MAN

I will be Paris, and for love of thee,
Instead of Troy shall Wittenberg be sacked;
And I will combat with weak Menelaus,
And wear thy colours on my plumed crest:
Yea, I will wound Achilles in the heel,   100
And then return to Helen for a kiss.
O thou art fairer than the evening air,
Clad in the beauty of a thousand stars,
Brighter art thou than flaming Jupiter
When he appeared to hapless Semele;   105
More lovely than the monarch of the sky
In wanton Arethusa's azured arms;
And none but thou shalt be my paramour.
                               Exeunt [FAUSTUS *and* HELEN]
OLD MAN
Accursed Faustus, miserable man,

89–100   In these lines Marlowe is repeating his own memorable phrases:
            Helen, whose beauty summoned Greece to arms,
            And drew a thousand ships to Tenedos.
                               2 Tamburlaine, II, iv, 87–8
            And he'll make me immortal with a kiss.
                               Dido, IV, iv, 123
            So thou wouldst prove as true as Paris did,
            Would, as fair Troy was, Carthage might be sacked,
            And I be called a second Helena.
                               Dido, V,1, 146–8 82

   90   *Ilium* Troy
   95   s.d. The Old Man's entrance here and final speech (109–17) are omitted in the B-text.
   98   *weak* i.e. cuckolded
  100   *wound . . . heel* Achilles was invulnerable apart from one of his heels – where he was
        shot by Paris.
104–5   *flaming . . . Semele* Jupiter's mortal lover Semele demanded that he come to her in
        his real form. He appeared as a shower of flaming gold, which consumed her.
106–7   *monarch . . . arms* Arethusa was a nymph who was changed into a fountain after
        bathing in the river Alpheus and exciting the river-god's passion; Alpheus is said to
        have been related to the sun.

That from thy soul exclud'st the grace of heaven,   110
And fliest the throne of His tribunal seat!

Enter the DEVILS

Satan begins to sift me with his pride,
As in this furnace God shall try my faith.
My faith, vile hell, shall triumph over thee!
Ambitious fiends, see how the heavens smiles   115
At your repulse, and laughs your state to scorn.
Hence hell, for hence I fly unto my God.

Exeunt [*by different doors*]

112   *sift* Compare St Luke's Gospel xxii, 3: 'Satan hath desired to have you, that he may
      sift you as wheat.'
115   *the heavens* the celestial beings who inhabit the extra-terrestial spheres of the geocentric
      universe.
      smiles A singular verb following a plural subject is not uncommon in sixteenth-
      century literature.

[Scene 13]

Enter FAUSTUS *with the* SCHOLARS

FAUSTUS

Ah gentlemen!

1 SCHOLAR

What ails Faustus?

FAUSTUS

Ah my sweet chamber-fellow, had I lived with thee, then had I
lived still; but now I die eternally. Look, comes he not, comes he
not?   5

2 SCHOLAR

What means Faustus?

3 SCHOLAR

Belike he is grown into some sickness, by being over-solitary.

1 SCHOLAR

If it be so, we'll have physicians to cure him; 'tis but a surfeit, never
fear, man.

FAUSTUS

A surfeit of deadly sin that hath damned both body and soul.   10

2 SCHOLAR

Yet Faustus, look up to heaven; remember God's mercies are
infinite.

FAUSTUS

But Faustus' offence can ne'er be pardoned! The serpent that
tempted Eve may be saved, but not Faustus. Ah gentlemen, hear
me with patience, and tremble not at my speeches, though my   15
heart pants and quivers to remember that I have been a student
here these thirty years – O would I had never seen Wittenberg,
never read book – and what wonders I have done, all Germany
can witness – yea, all the world, for which Faustus hath lost both
Germany and the world, yea, heaven itself – heaven, the seat of   20
God, the throne of the blessed, the kingdom of joy – and must
remain in hell for ever – hell, ah, hell for ever! Sweet friends, what
shall become of Faustus, being in hell for ever?

Scene 13 B opens this scene with the arrival of the devils – Lucifer, Belzebub, and Mephastophilis – who have come to witness Faustus's end; see Appendix 13.1–25.
16 *pants* races, throbs

537

3 SCHOLAR

Yet Faustus, call on God.

FAUSTUS

On God, whom Faustus hath abjured? On God, whom Faustus   25
hath blasphemed? Ah my God, I would weep, but the devil draws
in my tears! gush forth blood instead of tears – yea, life and soul!
O, he stays my tongue! I would lift up my hands, but see, they hold
them, they hold them!

ALL

Who, Faustus?   30

FAUSTUS

Lucifer and Mephastophilis! Ah gentlemen, I gave them my soul
for my cunning.

ALL

God forbid!

FAUSTUS

God forbade it indeed, but Faustus hath done it: for vain pleasure
of four-and-twenty years hath Faustus lost eternal joy and felicity!   35
I writ them a bill with mine own blood, the date is expired, the
time will come, and he will fetch me.

1 SCHOLAR

Why did not Faustus tell us of this before, that divines might have
prayed for thee?

FAUSTUS

Oft have I thought to have done so, but the devil threatened to   40
tear me in pieces if I named God, to fetch both body and soul, if
I once gave ear to divinity; and now 'tis too late! Gentlemen away,
lest you perish with me.

2 SCHOLAR

O what shall we do to save Faustus?

FAUSTUS

Talk not of me but save yourselves and depart.   45

26–7 *draws in my tears* 'No not so much as their eyes are able to shed tears (thretten and
torture them as ye please) while first they repent (God not permitting them to
dissemble their obstinacie in so horrible a crime)', *Daemonologie*, by James VI and
I (Edinburgh, 1597), p. 81.

28 *stays* holds back

34 *for vain* A (for the vain B)
vain worthless, fruitless

36 *bill* written document, here legal deed or contract

44 *to save Faustus* B (to Faustus A)

3 SCHOLAR

God will strengthen me. I will stay with Faustus.

1 SCHOLAR

Tempt not God, sweet friend, but let us into the next room, and there pray for him.

FAUSTUS

Ay, pray for me, pray for me; and what noise soever ye hear, come not unto me, for nothing can rescue me.   50

2 SCHOLAR

Pray thou, and we will pray that God may have mercy upon thee.

FAUSTUS

Gentlemen, farewell. If I live till morning, I'll visit you; if not, Faustus is gone to hell.

ALL

Faustus, farewell.   *Exeunt* SCHOLARS

The clock strikes eleven

FAUSTUS

Ah Faustus,   55
Now hast thou but one bare hour to live,
And then thou must be damned perpetually.
Stand still, you ever-moving spheres of heaven,
That time may cease, and midnight never come.
Fair Nature's eye, rise, rise again, and make   60
Perpetual day, or let this hour be but
A year, a month, a week, a natural day,
That Faustus may repent and save his soul.
O lente, lente currite noctis equi!
The stars move still, time runs, the clock will strike,   65
The devil will come, and Faustus must be damned.

52   *farewell* See Appendix 13.93–126 for the B-text's insertion at this point.
58–63 Cf. *Edward II*, 20.64–8:
          Continue ever, thou celestial sun;
          Let never silent night possess this clime:
          Stand still, you watches of the element;
          All times and seasons rest you at a stay,
          That Edward may be still fair England's king.
60   *Fair Nature's eye* the sun
64   'Go slowly, slowly, you horses of the night': the play's final irony; the line is from
      Ovid's *Amores*, I, xiii, 40, where the poet longs for never-ending night in his mistress'
      arms

O I'll leap up to my God! Who pulls me down?
See, see where Christ's blood streams in the firmament!
One drop would save my soul, half a drop: ah my Christ –
Ah, rend not my heart for naming of my Christ;   70
Yet will I call on him – O spare me, Lucifer!
Where is it now? 'Tis gone: and see where God
Stretcheth out his arm, and bends his ireful brows!
Mountains and hills, come, come and fall on me,
And hide me from the heavy wrath of God.   75
No, no?
Then will I headlong run into the earth:
Earth, gape! O no, it will not harbour me.
You stars that reigned at my nativity,
Whose influence hath allotted death and hell,   80
Now draw up Faustus like a foggy mist
Into the entrails of yon labouring cloud,
That when you vomit forth into the air
My limbs may issue from your smoky mouths,
So that my soul may but ascend to heaven.   85

The watch strikes

Ah, half the hour is past: 'twill all be past anon.
O God, if thou wilt not have mercy on my soul,
Yet for Christ's sake, whose blood hath ransomed me,
Impose some end to my incessant pain:

67   *leap up* This common Renaissance image is also shown in the woodblock print on the title page of the 1604 edition, but the icon's meaning is ambivalent and Faustus's aspirations were also the cause of his tragedy; see the reference to Icarus at Chorus 1.20–2.

72   *it* the vision of Christ's blood; the momentary yielding to terror and the devil banishes even this hope of salvation

74–5   'And they shall say to the mountains: Cover us; and to the hills, Fall on us', Hosea x, 8 (see also Revelations vi, 16; and St Luke xxiii, 3). The Usurer in *A Looking Glass for London* has the same idea:

>Hell gapes for me, heaven will not hold my soule,
>You mountaines shroude me from the God of truth . . .
>Cover me hills, and shroude me from the Lord.

ll. 2054–5, 9

79–85   *You . . . heaven* Faustus prays the stars, whose positions at his birth ordained this fate, to suck him up into a cloud, as a fog or mist is drawn up, and then in a storm expel his body in order that his soul may be saved. See Introduction, p. xvii.

Let Faustus live in hell a thousand years, 90
A hundred thousand, and at last be saved.
O, no end is limited to damned souls!
Why wert thou not a creature wanting soul?
Or why is this immortal that thou hast?
Ah, Pythagoras' *metempsychosis* – were that true, 95
This soul should fly from me, and I be changed
Unto some brutish beast:
All beasts are happy, for when they die,
Their souls are soon dissolved in elements;
But mine must live still to be plagued in hell. 100
Cursed be the parents that engendered me:
No Faustus, curse thy self, curse Lucifer,
That hath deprived thee of the joys of heaven!

The clock striketh twelve

O it strikes, it strikes! Now body, turn to air,
Or Lucifer will bear thee quick to hell. 105

Thunder and lightning

O soul, be changed into little water drops,
And fall into the ocean, ne'er be found.
My God, my God, look not so fierce on me!

Enter DEVILS

Adders and serpents, let me breathe awhile!
Ugly hell gape not! Come not, Lucifer! 110
I'll burn my books – ah, Mephastophilis!

Exeunt with him

---

95 *Pythagoras' metempsychosis* the theory of the transmigration of souls, attributed to
Pythagoras, whereby the human soul at the death of the body took on some other form
of life
105 *quick* living
111 *burn my books* All magicians who renounced their art made a solemn act of disposing
of their magic books; cf. *The Tempest*, V.i.56–7: 'deeper than did ever plummet sound
I'll drown my book'.
s.d. *Exeunt with him* The B-text adds a macabre scene where the Scholars discover
Faustus' mangled body (see Appendix 13b).

Enter CHORUS

Cut is the branch that might have grown full straight,
And burned is Apollo's laurel bough,
That sometime grew within this learned man.
Faustus is gone! Regard his hellish fall, 115
Whose fiendful fortune may exhort the wise
Only to wonder at unlawful things:
Whose deepness doth entice such forward wits,
To practise more than heavenly power permits. [*Exit*]

Terminat hora diem, terminat author opus.

---

113 *Apollo's laurel bough* the wreath of the poet (in this case, conjuror – see scene 3, line 33) laureate

Terminat . . . opus The hour ends the day, the author ends his works. The origin is unknown, and it seems likely that the motto, with the final emblem, was appended by the printer and not by Marlowe.

The Latin motto is followed by another printer's device – McKerrow 313: 'Framed device of Justice striking a bushel of corn; with SUCH AS I MAKE. SUCH WILL I TAKE'

The Tragicall Hiſtory
of the Life and Death
of Doctor FAVSTVS.

With new additions.

Written by *Ch. Marlo[e],*

Printed at London for *John Wright*, and are to be fold at his ſhop without Newgate. 1628.

The title page to the second edition of *Dr Faustus*, the B-text. First published in 1616, this version was reprinted in 1619, 1620, 1624, 1628 and 1631. An inventory of properties belonging to the Admiral's Men who first performed the play at the Rose Theatre in London records that they possessed a dragon for use in this play (see p. xix). The dragon/devil in this picture looks as if it might be appearing through a hole in the floor – or a trapdoor in a stage.

APPENDIX

Scenes from the B-text: sometimes these are straightforward additions to the play presented in the A-text; in other cases, the A scenes have been substantially re-worked. The scenes in the Appendix are identified by the numbers of the A-text scenes which they replace or augment.

[Scene 4]

Enter WAGNER *and the* CLOWN

WAGNER

Come hither, sirra boy.

CLOWN

Boy? O disgrace to my person: zounds, boy in your face, you have seen many boys with beards, I am sure.

WAGNER

Sirra, hast thou no comings in?

CLOWN

Yes, and goings out too, you may see sir.   5

WAGNER

Alas poor slave, see how poverty jests in his nakedness. I know the villain's out of service, and so hungry, that I know he would give his soul to the devil, for a shoulder of mutton, tho' it were blood raw.

CLOWN

Not so neither! I had need to have it well roasted, and good sauce   10
to it, if I pay so dear, I can tell you.

WAGNER

Sirra, wilt thou be my man and wait on me? And I will make thee go like *Qui mihi discipulus.*

CLOWN

What, in verse?

WAGNER

No slave, in beaten silk and stavesacre.   15

CLOWN

Stavesacre? That's good to kill vermin: then belike if I serve you, I shall be lousy.

WAGNER

Why, so thou shalt be, whether thou dost it or no: for sirra, if thou dost not presently bind thy self to me for seven years, I'll turn all

545

the lice about thee into familiars, and make them tear thee in   20
pieces.

CLOWN

Nay sir, you may save yourself a labour, for they are as familiar
with me, as if they paid for their meat and drink, I can tell you.

WAGNER

Well sirra, leave your jesting, and take these guilders.

CLOWN

Yes, marry sir; and I thank you too.   25

WAGNER

So; now thou art to be at an hour's warning, whensoever, and
wheresoever the devil shall fetch thee.

CLOWN

Here, take your guilders; I'll none of 'em.

WAGNER

Not I; thou art pressed! Prepare thyself, for I will presently raise
up two devils to carry thee away: Banio, Belcher!   30

CLOWN

Belcher? and Belcher come here, I'll belch him: I am not afraid of
a devil.

Enter TWO DEVILS

WAGNER

How now, sir; will you serve me now?

CLOWN

Ay, good Wagner; take away the devil, then.

WAGNER

Spirits, away! Now sirra, follow me.   35

CLOWN

I will, sir! But hark you, master – will you teach me this conjuring
occupation?

WAGNER

Ay sirra, I'll teach thee to turn thyself to a dog, or a cat, or a mouse,
or a rat, or anything.

CLOWN

A dog, or a cat, or a mouse, or a rat? O brave, Wagner!   40

WAGNER

Villain, call me Master Wagner; and see that you walk attentively,
and let your right eye be always diametrally fixed upon my left
heel, that thou may'st, 'Quasi vestigias nostras insistere'.

CLOWN

Well sir, I warrant you.

Exeunt

[Scene 6]

Enter the CLOWN [ROBIN]

ROBIN

What, Dick, look to the horses there till I come again. I have gotten
one of Doctor Faustus' conjuring books, and now we'll have such
knavery as 't passes.

Enter DICK

DICK

What, Robin, you must come away and walk the horses.

ROBIN

I walk the horses! I scorn 't, i'faith. I have other matters in hand.   5
Let the horses walk themselves and they will. [*Reads*] 'A *per se* a,
t. h. e. the; o *per se* o; deny orgon, gorgon'. Keep further from me,
O thou illiterate and unlearned ostler.

DICK

'Snails, what hast thou got there? A book! Why, thou canst not tell
ne'er a word on't.   10

ROBIN

That thou shalt see presently. Keep out of the circle, I say, lest I
send you into the ostry with a vengeance.

DICK

That's like, 'faith. You had best leave your foolery, for an my master
come, he'll conjure you i'faith.

ROBIN

My master conjure me? I'll tell thee what, an my master come here,   15
I'll clap as fair a pair of horns on's head as ere thou saw'st in thy life.

DICK

Thou needst not do that, for my mistress hath done it.

ROBIN

Ay, there be of us here that have waded as deep into matters as
other men, if they were disposed to talk.

DICK

A plague take you. I thought you did not sneak up and down after   20
her for nothing. But I prithee tell me, in good sadness Robin, is
that a conjuring book?

ROBIN

Do but speak what thou't have me to do, and I'll do't! If thou't
dance naked, put off thy clothes and I'll conjure thee about
presently. Or if thou't go but to the tavern with me, I'll give thee   25
white wine, red wine, claret wine, sack, muscadine, malmesy,
and whippincrust – hold belly hold – and we'll not pay one penny
for it.

DICK

O brave! Prithee let's to it presently, for I am as dry as a dog.

ROBIN

Come then, let's away.   30

Exeunt

[Scene 8]

[*From line 48*]

MEPHOSTOPHILIS

Nay stay my Faustus, I know you'd see the pope
And take some part of holy Peter's feast,
The which this day with high solemnity,   50
This day is held through Rome and Italy,
In honour of the pope's triumphant victory.

FAUSTUS

Sweet Mephostophilis, thou pleasest me.
Whilst I am here on earth, let me be cloyed
With all things that delight the heart of man.   55
My four and twenty years of liberty
I'll spend in pleasure and in dalliance,
That Faustus' name, whilst this bright frame doth stand,
May be admired through the furthest land.

MEPHOSTOPHILIS

'Tis well said Faustus; come then, stand by me,   60
And thou shalt see them come immediately.

FAUSTUS

Nay, stay, my gentle Mephostophilis,
And grant me my request, and then I go.
Thou know'st within the compass of eight days
We view'd the face of heaven, of earth and hell.   65
So high our dragons soar'd into the air,
That looking down the earth appeared to me,
No bigger than my hand in quantity.

There did we view the kingdoms of the world,
And what might please mine eye, I there beheld.   70
Then in this show let me an actor be,
That this proud pope may Faustus' coming see.
MEPHOSTOPHILIS
Let it be so, my Faustus, but first stay,
And view their triumphs, as they pass this way.
And then devise what best contents thy mind,   75
By cunning in thine art to cross the pope,
Or dash the pride of this solemnity;
To make his monks and abbots stand like apes,
And point like antics at his triple crown:
To beat the beads about the friars' pates,   80
Or clap huge horns upon the cardinals' heads:
Or any villainy thou canst devise,
And I'll perform it Faustus: hark, they come:
This day shall make thee be admired in Rome.

Enter the CARDINALS *and Bishops, some bearing croziers, some
the pillars; monks and friars singing their procession.
Then the* POPE *and* RAYMOND *King of Hungary,
with* BRUNO *led in chains*

POPE
Cast down our footstool.
RAYMOND   Saxon Bruno stoop,   85
Whilst on thy back his holiness ascends
Saint Peter's chair and state pontifical.
BRUNO
Proud Lucifer, that state belongs to me:
But thus I fall to Peter, not to thee.
POPE
To me and Peter, shalt thou grovelling lie,   90
And crouch before the papal dignity.
Sound trumpets then, for thus Saint Peter's heir,
From Bruno's back ascends Saint Peter's chair.

A flourish while he ascends

Thus, as the gods, creep on with feet of wool,
Long ere with iron hands they punish men,   95
So shall our sleeping vengeance now arise,

And smite with death thy hated enterprise.
Lord cardinals of France and Padua,
Go forthwith to our holy consistory,
And read amongst the statutes decretal,   100
What by the holy council held at Trent,
The sacred synod hath decreed for him,
That doth assume the papal government,
Without election, and a true consent:
Away and bring us word with speed.   105

1 CARDINAL

We go my Lord.   *Exeunt* CARDINALS

POPE

Lord Raymond.

FAUSTUS

Go haste thee, gentle Mephostophilis,
Follow the cardinals to the consistory;
And as they turn their superstitious books,   110
Strike them with sloth, and drowsy idleness;
And make them sleep so sound, that, in their shapes,
Thyself and I may parley with this pope,
This proud confronter of the emperor;
And in despite of all his holiness   115
Restore this Bruno to his liberty,
And bear him to the states of Germany.

MEPHOSTOPHILIS

Faustus, I go.

FAUSTUS

Dispatch it soon,
The pope shall curse that Faustus came to Rome.   120
                   Exeunt FAUSTUS *and* MEPHOSTOPHILIS

BRUNO

Pope Adrian let me have some right of law,
I was elected by the emperor.

POPE

We will depose the emperor for that deed,
And curse the people that submit to him;
Both he and thou shalt stand excommunicate,   125
And interdict from church's privilege,
And all society of holy men:
He grows too proud in his authority,
Lifting his lofty head above the clouds,

And like a steeple overpeers the church.   130
But we'll pull down his haughty insolence:
And as pope Alexander our progenitor,
Trod on the neck of German Frederick,
Adding this golden sentence to our praise:
That Peter's heirs should tread on emperors,   135
And walk upon the dreadful adder's back,
Treading the lion and the dragon down,
And fearless spurn the killing basilisk:
So will we quell that haughty schismatic,
And by authority apostolical   140
Depose him from his regal government.

BRUNO

Pope Julius swore to princely Sigismond,
For him, and the succeeding popes of Rome,
To hold the emperors their lawful lords.

POPE

Pope Julius did abuse the church's rites,   145
And therefore none of his decrees can stand.
Is not all power on earth bestowed on us?
And therefore tho' we would we cannot err.
Behold this silver belt whereto is fixed
Seven golden seals fast sealed with seven seals,   150
In token of our seven-fold power from heaven,
To bind or loose, lock fast, condemn, or judge,
Resign, or seal, or what so pleaseth us.
Then he and thou, and all the world shall stoop,
Or be assured of our dreadful curse,   155
To light as heavy as the pains of hell.

Enter FAUSTUS *and* MEPHOSTOPHILIS *like the Cardinals*

MEPHOSTOPHILIS

Now tell me Faustus, are we not fitted well?

FAUSTUS

Yes Mephostophilis, and two such cardinals
Ne'er served a holy pope, as we shall do.
But whilst they sleep within the consistory,   160
Let us salute his reverend fatherhood.

RAYMOND

Behold my lord, the cardinals are returned.

551

POPE

    Welcome grave fathers, answer presently,

    What have our holy council there decreed,

    Concerning Bruno and the emperor,   165

    In quittance of their late conspiracy

    Against our state and papal dignity?

FAUSTUS

    Most sacred patron of the church of Rome,

    By full consent of all the synod

    Of priests and prelates, it is thus decreed: 170

    That Bruno, and the German emperor

    Be held as lollards, and bold schismatics,

    And proud disturbers of the church's peace.

    And if that Bruno by his own assent,

    Without enforcement of the German peers,   175

    Did seek to wear the triple diadem,

    And by your death to climb Saint Peter's chair,

    The statutes decretal have thus decreed,

    He shall be straight condemned of heresy,

    And on a pile of faggots burned to death.   180

POPE

    It is enough. Here, take him to your charge,

    And bear him straight to Ponte Angelo,

    And in the strongest tower enclose him fast.

    Tomorrow, sitting in our consistory,

    With all our college of grave cardinals,   185

    We will determine of his life or death.

    Here, take his triple crown along with you,

    And leave it in the church's treasury.

    Make haste again, my good lord cardinals,

    And take our blessing apostolical.   190

MEPHOSTOPHILIS

    So, so, was never devil thus blest before!

FAUSTUS

    Away, sweet Mephostophilis, be gone!

    The cardinals will be plagued for this anon.

                Exeunt FAUSTUS *and* MEPHOSTOPHILIS

POPE

    Go presently, and bring a banquet forth,

    That we may solemnize Saint Peter's feast,   195

And with Lord Raymond, King of Hungary,
Drink to our late and happy victory.   *Exeunt*

A sennet while the banquet is brought in; and then enter
FAUSTUS *and* MEPHOSTOPHILIS *in their*
own shapes

MEPHOSTOPHILIS
  Now Faustus, come prepare thyself for mirth;
  The sleepy cardinals are hard at hand,
  To censure Bruno, that is posted hence,   200
  And on a proud paced steed, as swift as thought,
  Flies o'er the alps to fruitful Germany,
  There to salute the woeful emperor.
FAUSTUS
  The pope will curse them for their sloth today
  That slept both Bruno and his crown away.   205
  But now, that Faustus may delight his mind,
  And by their folly make some merriment,
  Sweet Mephostophilis, so charm me here,
  That I may walk invisible to all,
  And do whate'er I please, unseen of any.   210
MEPHOSTOPHILIS
  Faustus thou shalt; then kneel down presently,
  Whilst on thy head I lay my hand,
  And charm thee with this magic wand.
  First wear this girdle, then appear
  Invisible to all are here: 215
  The planets seven, the gloomy air,
  Hell, and the Fury's forked hair,
  Pluto's blue fire, and Hecate's tree,
  With magic spells so compass thee,
  That no eye may thy body see.   220
  So Faustus, now for all their holiness,
  Do what thou wilt, thou shalt not be discerned.
FAUSTUS
  Thanks Mephostophilis; now friars, take heed
  Lest Faustus make your shaven crowns to bleed.
MEPHOSTOPHILIS
  Faustus, no more: see where the cardinals come.   225

Enter POPE *and all the lords. Enter the* CARDINALS *with a book*

POPE

    Welcome lord cardinals: come sit down.

    Lord Raymond, take your seat; friars, attend,

    And see that all things be in readiness,

    As beseems this solemn festival.

1 CARDINAL

    First, may it please your sacred holiness   230

    To view the sentence of the reverend synod,

    Concerning Bruno and the emperor.

POPE

    What needs this question? Did I not tell you,

    Tomorrow we would sit i'th' consistory,

    And there determine of his punishment?   235

    You brought us word even now, it was decreed,

    That Bruno and the cursed emperor

    Were by the holy council both condemned

    For loathed lollards, and base schismatics.

    Then wherefore would you have me view that book?   240

1 CARDINAL

    Your grace mistakes, you gave us no such charge.

RAYMOND

    Deny it not, we all are witnesses

    That Bruno here was late delivered you,

    With his rich triple crown to be reserved

    And put into the church's treasury.   245

AMBO CARDINALS

    By holy Paul we saw them not.

POPE

    By Peter you shall die,

    Unless you bring them forth immediately:

    Hale them to prison, lade their limbs with gyves!

    False prelates, for this hateful treachery,   250

    Cursed be your souls to hellish misery.

FAUSTUS

    So, they are safe: now Faustus to the feast,

    The pope had never such a frolic guest.

POPE

    Lord archbishop of Rheims, sit down with us.

BISHOP

    I thank your holiness.   255

FAUSTUS

Fall to, the devil choke you an you spare.

POPE

Who's that spoke? Friars, look about.

Lord Raymond pray fall to; I am beholding

To the bishop of Milan for this so rare a present.

FAUSTUS

I thank you sir.   260

POPE

How now? Who snatched the meat from me?

Villains, why speak you not?

My good lord archbishop, here's a most dainty dish,

Was sent me from a cardinal in France.

FAUSTUS

I'll have that too.   265

POPE

What lollards do attend our holiness

That we receive such great indignity? Fetch me some wine.

FAUSTUS

Ay, pray do, for Faustus is a-dry.

POPE

Lord Raymond, I drink unto your grace.

FAUSTUS

I pledge your grace.   270

POPE

My wine gone too? Ye lubbers, look about

And find the man that doth this villainy,

Or by our sanctitude you all shall die.

I pray my lords, have patience at this

Troublesome banquet.   275

BISHOP

Please it your holiness, I think it be some ghost crept out of

purgatory, and now is come unto your holiness for his pardon.

POPE

It may be so:

Go then command our priests to sing a dirge,

To lay the fury of this same troublesome ghost.   280

FAUSTUS

How now? Must every bit be spiced with a cross?

Nay then, take that.

POPE

    O I am slain, help me my lords;

    O come and help to bear my body hence.

    Damned be this soul for ever, for this deed.   285

                  Exeunt the POPE *and his train*

MEPHOSTOPHILIS

    Now Faustus, what will you do now? for I can tell you

    You'll be cursed with bell, book and candle.

FAUSTUS

    Bell, book, and candle; candle, book, and bell:

    Forward and backward, to curse Faustus to hell.

        Enter the FRIARS *with bell, book, and candle,*
                 for the dirge

1 FRIAR

Come brethren, let's about our business with good devotion.   290

    Cursed be he that stole his holiness' meat from the table.

           Maledicat Dominus.

    Cursed be he that struck his holiness a blow [on] the face.

           Maledicat Dominus.

    Cursed be he that struck friar Sandelo a blow on the pate.   295

           Maledicat Dominus.

    Cursed be he that disturbeth our holy dirge.

           Maledicat Dominus.

    Cursed be he that took away his holiness' wine

           Maledicat Dominus.   300

        Beat the FRIARS, *fling fireworks among them,*
                 and exeunt

                     Exeunt

[Scene 9]

    Enter CLOWN [ROBIN] *and* DICK, *with a cup*

DICK

    Sirra Robin, we were best look that your devil can answer the
    stealing of this same cup, for the vintner's boy follows us at the
    hard heels.

ROBIN

    'Tis no matter, let him come; an he follow us, I'll so conjure him, as
    he was never conjured in his life, I warrant him. Let me see the cup.   5

Enter VINTNER

DICK

Here 'tis. Yonder he comes: now Robin, now or never show thy
cunning.

VINTNER

O, are you here? I am glad I have found you, you are a couple of
fine companions: pray where's the cup you stole from the tavern?

ROBIN

How, how? We steal a cup? Take heed what you say, we look not   10
like cup-stealers, I can tell you.

VINTNER

Never deny't, for I know you have it, and I'll search you.

ROBIN

Search me? Ay, and spare not: hold the cup Dick – come, come,
search me, search me.

VINTNER

Come on sirra, let me search you now.   15

DICK

Ay, ay; do, do. Hold the cup, Robin. I fear not your searching; we
scorn to steal your cups, I can tell you.

VINTNER

Never outface me for the matter, for sure the cup is between you
two.

ROBIN

Nay there you lie, 'tis beyond us both.   20

VINTNER

A plague take you, I thought 'twas your knavery to take it away.
Come, give it me again.

ROBIN

Ay, much, when can you tell? Dick, make me a circle and stand
close at my back, and stir not for thy life. Vintner, you shall have
your cup anon – say nothing, Dick. *O per se o, demogorgon, Belcher* 25
and *Mephostophilis.*

Enter MEPHOSTOPHILIS

MEPHOSTOPHILIS

You princely legions of infernal rule,
How am I vexed by these villains' charms?
From Constantinople have they brought me now,
Only for pleasure of these damned slaves.   30

ROBIN

By lady sir, you have had a shrewd journey of it! Will it please you
to take a shoulder of mutton to supper, and a tester in your purse,
and go back again?

DICK

Ay, I pray you heartily sir, for we called you but in jest, I promise
you.   35

MEPHOSTOPHILIS

To purge the rashness of this cursed deed,

First, be thou turned to this ugly shape,

For apish deeds transformed to an ape.

ROBIN

O brave, an ape? I pray sir, let me have the carrying of him about
to show some tricks.   40

MEPHOSTOPHILIS

And so thou shalt: be thou transformed to a dog, and carry him
upon thy back. Away, be gone.

ROBIN

A dog? That's excellent: let the maids look well to their porridge-
pots, for I'll into the kitchen presently. Come Dick, come.

Exeunt the two CLOWNS

MEPHOSTOPHILIS

Now with the flames of ever-burning fire,   45

I'll wing my self, and forthwith fly amain

Unto my Faustus, to the great Turk's court.   *Exit*

[Scene 10]

Enter MARTINO *and* FREDERICK *at several doors*

MARTINO

What ho, officers, gentlemen,

Hie to the presence to attend the emperor.

Good Frederick, see the rooms be voided straight;

His majesty is coming to the hall;

Go back, and see the state in readiness.   5

FREDERICK

But where is Bruno, our elected pope,

That on a Fury's back came post from Rome?

Will not his grace consort the emperor?

MARTINO

    O yes; and with him comes the German conjuror,

    The learned Faustus, fame of Wittenberg,   10

    The wonder of the world for magic art.

    And he intends to show great Carolus

    The race of all his stout progenitors;

    And bring in presence of his majesty

    The royal shapes and warlike semblances   15

    Of Alexander and his beauteous paramour.

FREDERICK

    Where is Benvolio?

MARTINO

    Fast asleep, I warrant you;

    He took his rouse with stoops of Rhenish wine

    So kindly yesternight to Bruno's health,   20

    That all this day the sluggard keeps his bed.

FREDERICK

    See, see – his window's ope; we'll call to him.

MARTINO

    What ho, Benvolio!

Enter BENVOLIO *above at a window,*
in his nightcap: buttoning

BENVOLIO

    What a devil ail you two?

MARTINO

    Speak softly sir, lest the devil hear you: 25

    For Faustus at the court is late arrived,

    And at his heels a thousand furies wait

    To accomplish whatsoever the doctor please.

BENVOLIO

    What of this?

MARTINO

    Come, leave thy chamber first, and thou shalt see   30

    This conjuror perform such rare exploits

    Before the pope and royal emperor,

    As never yet was seen in Germany.

BENVOLIO

    Has not the pope enough of conjuring yet?

                                      35

He was upon the devil's back late enough,
And if he be so far in love with him,
I would he would post with him to Rome again.

FREDERICK

Speak, wilt thou come and see this sport?

BENVOLIO

Not I.

MARTINO

Wilt thou stand in thy window and see it then?   40

BENVOLIO

Ay, and I fall not asleep i'th' meantime.

MARTINO

The emperor is at hand, who comes to see
What wonders by black spells may compassed be.

BENVOLIO

Well, go you attend the emperor. I am content for this once to
thrust my head out at a window – for they say, if a man be drunk   45
overnight, the devil cannot hurt him in the morning. If that be
true, I have a charm in my head, shall control him as well as the
conjuror, I warrant you.   [*Withdraws*]

A sennet. [*Enter*] CHARLES *the German emperor,* BRUNO,
SAXONY, FAUSTUS, MEPHOSTOPHILIS,
[*to*] FREDERICK, MARTINO, *and Attendants*

EMPEROR

Wonder of men, renowned magician,
Thrice learned Faustus, welcome to our court.   50
This deed of thine, in setting Bruno free
From his and our professed enemy,
Shall add more excellence unto thine art
Than if by powerful necromantic spells
Thou couldst command the world's obedience: 55
For ever be beloved of Carolus.
And if this Bruno thou hast late redeemed
In peace possess the triple diadem,
And sit in Peter's chair, despite of chance,
Thou shalt be famous through all Italy,   60
And honoured of the German emperor.

FAUSTUS

These gracious words, most royal Carolus,

Shall make poor Faustus to his utmost power
Both love and serve the German emperor,
And lay his life at holy Bruno's feet.   65
For proof whereof, if so your grace be pleased,
The doctor stands prepared, by power of art,
To cast his magic charms, that shall pierce through
The ebon gates of ever-burning hell,
And hale the stubborn Furies from their caves,   70
To compass whatso'er your grace commands.

BENVOLIO [*Above*]

    'Blood, he speaks terribly! But for all that, I do not greatly believe
him: he looks as like conjuror as the pope to a costermonger.

EMPEROR

Then Faustus, as thou late didst promise us,
We would behold that famous conqueror,   75
Great Alexander, and his paramour,
In their true shapes and state majestical,
That we may wonder at their excellence.

FAUSTUS

Your majesty shall see them presently.
Mephostophilis, away,   80
And with a solemn noise of trumpets' sound,
Present before this royal emperor,
Great Alexander and his beauteous paramour.

MEPHOSTOPHILIS

Faustus I will.

BENVOLIO

    Well master doctor, an your devils come not away quickly, you   85
shall have me asleep presently: zounds, I could eat myself for anger,
to think I have been such an ass all this while, to stand gaping after
the devil's governor, and can see nothing.

FAUSTUS

I'll make you feel something anon, if my art fail me not.
My lord, I must forewarn your majesty   90
That when my spirits present the royal shapes
Of Alexander and his paramour,
Your grace demand no questions of the king,
But in dumb silence let them come and go.

EMPEROR

Be it as Faustus please, we are content.   95

BENVOLIO

Ay, ay; and I am content too: and thou bring Alexander and his
paramour before the emperor, I'll be Actaeon, and turn myself
into a stag.

FAUSTUS

And I'll play Diana, and send you the horns presently.

Sennet. Enter at one [door] the emperor ALEXANDER,
at the other [door] DARIUS; *they meet,* DARIUS *is thrown
down,* ALEXANDER *kills him, takes off his crown, and
offering to go out, his paramour meets him. He embraceth
her, and sets Darius' crown upon her head; and coming
back, both salute the emperor who, leaving his state, offers to
embrace them, which* FAUSTUS *seeing, suddenly stays him.
Then trumpets cease, and music sounds*

My gracious lord, you do forget yourself: 100
These are but shadows, not substantial.

EMPEROR

O pardon me, my thoughts are so ravished
With sight of this renowned emperor,
That in mine arms I would have compassed him.
But Faustus, since I may not speak to them,   105
To satisfy my longing thoughts at full,
Let me this tell thee: I have heard it said,
That this fair lady, whilst she lived on earth,
Had on her neck a little wart or mole;
How may I prove that saying to be true?   110

FAUSTUS

Your majesty may boldly go and see.

EMPEROR

Faustus, I see it plain!
And in this sight thou better pleasest me,
Than if I gained another monarchy.

FAUSTUS

Away, be gone.   *Exit Show*   115
See, see, my gracious lord, what strange beast is yon, that thrusts
his head out at window.

EMPEROR

O wondrous sight: see, duke of Saxony,
Two spreading horns most strangely fastened
Upon the head of young Benvolio.   120

SAXONY

What, is he asleep – or dead?

FAUSTUS

He sleeps, my lord, but dreams not of his horns.

EMPEROR

This sport is excellent: we'll call and wake him.
What ho, Benvolio!

BENVOLIO

A plague upon you, let me sleep awhile.   125

EMPEROR

I blame thee not to sleep much, having such a head of thine
own.

SAXONY

Look up, Benvolio; 'tis the emperor calls.

BENVOLIO

The emperor! Where? O zounds, my head.

EMPEROR

Nay, and thy horns hold, 'tis no matter for thy head, for that's   130
armed sufficiently.

FAUSTUS

Why, how now sir knight, what hanged by the horns? This [is]
most horrible: fie, fie, pull in your head for shame, let not all the
world wonder at you.

BENVOLIO

Zounds, doctor, is this your villainy?   135

FAUSTUS

O say not so, sir: the doctor has no skill,
No art, no cunning, to present these lords,
Or bring before this royal emperor
The mighty monarch, warlike Alexander.
If Faustus do it, you are straight resolved   140
In bold Actaeon's shape to turn a stag.
And therefore, my lord – so please your majesty –
I'll raise a kennel of hounds shall hunt him so
As all his footmanship shall scarce prevail
To keep his carcass from their bloody fangs.   145
Ho, Belimoth, Argiron, Asteroth!

BENVOLIO

Hold, hold! Zounds, he'll raise up a kennel of devils, I think, anon.
Good my lord, entreat for me: 'sblood, I am never able to endure
these torments.

EMPEROR

    Then, good master doctor, 150

    Let me entreat you to remove his horns:

    He has done penance now sufficiently.

FAUSTUS

    My gracious lord, not so much for injury done to me, as to delight

    your majesty with some mirth, hath Faustus justly requited this

    injurious knight; which being all I desire, I am content to remove 155

    his horns. Mephostophilis, transform him; and hereafter sir, look

    you speak well of scholars.

BENVOLIO

    Speak well of you? 'Sblood, and scholars be such cuckold-makers

    to clap horns of honest men's heads o'this order. I'll ne'er trust

    smooth faces and small ruffs more. But an I be not revenged for 160

    this, would I might be turned to a gaping oyster and drink nothing

    but salt water.   [*Exit*]

EMPEROR

    Come Faustus; while the emperor lives,

    In recompence of this thy high desert,

    Thou shalt command the state of Germany, 165

    And live beloved of mighty Carolus.

                                  Exeunt omnes

[Scene 10b]

Enter BENVOLIO, MARTINO, FREDERICK, *and* SOLDIERS

MARTINO

    Nay, sweet Benvolio, let us sway thy thoughts

    From this attempt against the conjuror.

BENVOLIO

    Away, you love me not to urge me thus.

    Shall I let slip so great an injury, 170

    When every servile groom jests at my wrongs,

    And in their rustic gambols proudly say,

    'Benvolio's head was graced with horns today'!

    O may these eyelids never close again,

    Till with my sword I have that conjuror slain. 175

    If you will aid me in this enterprise,

    Then draw your weapons, and be resolute:

    If not, depart: here will Benvolio die –

But Faustus' death shall quit my infamy!
FREDERICK
    Nay, we will stay with thee, betide what may,   180
    And kill that doctor if he come this way.
BENVOLIO
    Then gentle Frederick, hie thee to the grove,
    And place our servants, and our followers
    Close in an ambush there behind the trees;
    By this (I know) the conjuror is near: 185
    I saw him kneel, and kiss the emperor's hand,
    And take his leave, laden with rich rewards.
    Then soldiers, boldly fight; if Faustus die,
    Take you the wealth, leave us the victory.
FREDERICK
    Come soldiers, follow me unto the grove;   190
    Who kills him shall have gold, and endless love.

                 Exit FREDERICK *with the* SOLDIERS

BENVOLIO
    My head is lighter than it was by th'horns,
    But yet my heart more ponderous than my head,
    And pants until I see that conjuror dead.
MARTINO
    Where shall we place ourselves Benvolio?   195
BENVOLIO
    Here will we stay to bide the first assault.
    O were that damned hellhound but in place,
    Thou soon shouldst see me quit my foul disgrace.

                 Enter FREDERICK

FREDERICK
    Close, close, the conjuror is at hand,
    And, all alone, comes walking in his gown.   200
    Be ready then, and strike the peasant down.
BENVOLIO
    Mine be that honour then: now sword strike home,
    For horns he gave, I'll have his head anon.

           Enter FAUSTUS *with the false head*

MARTINO
    See, see, he comes.

BENVOLIO
  No words: this blow ends all! 205
                                      [*They attack* FAUSTUS]
  Hell take his soul, his body thus must fall.

FAUSTUS
  Oh.

FREDERICK
  Groan you, master doctor?

BENVOLIO
  Break may his heart with groans! Dear Frederick, see
  Thus will I end his griefs immediately. 210

MARTINO
  Strike with a willing hand, his head is off.

BENVOLIO
  The devil's dead, the furies now may laugh.

FREDERICK
  Was this that stern aspect, that awful frown,
  Made the grim monarch of infernal spirits
  Tremble and quake at his commanding charms? 215

MARTINO
  Was this that damned head, whose heart conspired
  Benvolio's shame before the emperor?

BENVOLIO
  Ay that's the head, and here the body lies,
  Justly rewarded for his villainies.

FREDERICK
  Come, let's devise how we may add more shame 220
  To the black scandal of his hated name.

BENVOLIO
  First, on his head, in quittance of my wrongs,
  I'll nail huge forked horns, and let them hang
  Within the window where he yoked me first,
  That all the world may see my just revenge. 225

MARTINO
  What use shall we put his beard to?

BENVOLIO
  We'll sell it to a chimney-sweeper: it will wear out ten birchen
  brooms, I warrant you.

FREDERICK
  What shall eyes do?

BENVOLIO

    We'll put out his eyes, and they shall serve for buttons to his lips,   230
    to keep his tongue from catching cold.

MARTINO

    An excellent policy! And now sirs, having divided him, what shall
    the body do?

                                   [FAUSTUS *gets up*]

BENVOLIO

    Zounds, the devil's alive again.

FREDERICK

    Give him his head, for God's sake.   235

FAUSTUS

    Nay keep it: Faustus will have heads and hands,
    Ay, all your hearts to recompense this deed.
    Knew you not, traitors, I was limited
    For four-and-twenty years to breathe on earth?
    And had you cut my body with your swords,   240
    Or hew'd this flesh and bones as small as sand,
    Yet in a minute had my spirit returned,
    And I had breathed a man made free from harm.
    But wherefore do I dally my revenge?
    Asteroth, Belimoth, Mephostophilis.   245

Enter MEPHOSTOPHILIS *and other* DEVILS

    Go, horse these traitors on your fiery backs,
    And mount aloft with them as high as heaven,
    Thence pitch them headlong to the lowest hell:
    Yet stay, the world shall see their misery,
    And hell shall after plague their treachery.   250
    Go Belimoth, and take this caitiff hence,
    And hurl him in some lake of mud and dirt;
    Take thou this other, drag him through the woods,
    Amongst the pricking thorns and sharpest briars,
    Whilst with my gentle Mephostophilis,   255
    This traitor flies unto some steepy rock,
    That rolling down, may break the villain's bones,
    As he intended to dismember me.
    Fly hence, dispatch my charge immediately.

FREDERICK

    Pity us, gentle Faustus, save our lives.   260

FAUSTUS

    Away.

FREDERICK

    He must needs go that the devil drives.

                Exeunt SPIRITS *with the* KNIGHTS

Enter the ambushed SOLDIERS

1 SOLDIER

    Come sirs, prepare yourselves in readiness,

    Make haste to help these noble gentlemen.

    I heard them parley with the conjuror.   265

2 SOLDIER

    See where he comes! Dispatch, and kill the slave.

FAUSTUS

    What's here? An ambush to betray my life!

    Then Faustus, try thy skill: base peasants stand,

    For lo, these trees remove at my command,

    And stand as bulwarks 'twixt yourselves and me,   270

    To shield me from your hated treachery!

    Yet to encounter this your weak attempt,

    Behold an army comes incontinent.

        FAUSTUS *strikes the door, and enter a* DEVIL *playing*
        on a drum; after him another bearing an ensign; and
        divers with weapons; MEPHOSTOPHILIS *with fireworks.*
        They set upon the SOLDIERS, *and drive them out*

    Enter at several doors BENVOLIO, FREDERICK, *and* MARTINO,
        their heads and faces bloody, and besmeared with
        mud and dirt; all having horns on their heads

MARTINO

    What ho, Benvolio!

BENVOLIO

    Here, what Frederick, ho!   275

FREDERICK

    O help me, gentle friend; where is Martino?

MARTINO

    Dear Frederick, here –

    Half smothered in a lake of mud and dirt,

    Through which the Furies dragged me by the heels.

FREDERICK

    Martino, see   280

    Benvolio's horns again!

MARTINO

    O misery! How now Benvolio?

BENVOLIO

    Defend me heaven, shall I be haunted still?

MARTINO

    Nay fear not, man; we have no power to kill.

BENVOLIO

    My friends transformed thus: O hellish spite,   285

    Your heads are all set with horns.

FREDERICK   You hit it right,

    It is your own you mean: feel on your head.

BENVOLIO

    'Zounds, horns again!

MARTINO

    Nay chafe not, man: we all are sped.

BENVOLIO

    What devil attends this damned magician,   290

    That spite of spite our wrongs are doubled?

FREDERICK

    What may we do, that we may hide our shames?

BENVOLIO

    If we should follow him to work revenge,

    He'd join long asses' ears to these huge horns,

    And make us laughing-stocks to all the world.   295

MARTINO

    What shall we do then, dear Benvolio?

BENVOLIO

    I have a castle joining near these woods,

    And thither we'll repair, and live obscure

    Till time shall alter this our brutish shapes.

    Sith black disgrace hath thus eclipsed our fame,   300

    We'll rather die with grief, than live with shame.

Exeunt omnes

[Scene 10c]

[This is a new scene in the B-text, and not a continuation of Scene 10, as in the A-text]

Enter FAUSTUS *and the* HORSE-COURSER, *and* MEPHOSTOPHILIS

HORSE-COURSER

I beseech your worship accept of these forty dollars.

FAUSTUS

Friend, thou canst not buy so good a horse, for so small a price: I have no great need to sell him, but if thou likest him for ten dollars more, take him, because I see thou hast a good mind to him. 5

HORSE-COURSER

I beseech you sir, accept of this; I am a very poor man, and have lost very much of late by horseflesh, and this bargain will set me up again.

FAUSTUS

Well, I will not stand with thee; give me the money. Now sirra I must tell you, that you may ride him o'er hedge and ditch, and spare him 10 not; but, do you hear, in any case ride him not into the water.

HORSE-COURSER

How sir, not into the water? Why, will he not drink of all waters?

FAUSTUS

Yes, he will drink of all waters, but ride him not into the water: o'er hedge and ditch, or where thou wilt, but not into the water. Go bid the ostler deliver him unto you, and remember what I say. 15

HORSE-COURSER

I warrant you sir. O joyful day! Now am I a made man for ever.

Exit

FAUSTUS

What art thou, Faustus, but a man condemned to die?
Thy fatal time draws to a final end;
Despair doth drive distrust into my thoughts.
Confound these passions with a quiet sleep: 20
Tush, Christ did call the thief upon the cross,
Then rest thee, Faustus, quiet in conceit.

He sits to sleep

Enter the HORSE-COURSER *wet*

HORSE-COURSER

O what a cozening doctor was this! I riding my horse into the
water, thinking some hidden mystery had been in the horse, I had
nothing under me but a little straw, and had much ado to escape   25
drowning! Well, I'll go rouse him, and make him give me my forty
dollars again. Ho, sirra doctor, you cozening scab; master doctor
awake, and rise, and give me my money again, for your horse is
turned to a bottle of hay, – master doctor.

He pulls off his leg

Alas I am undone, what shall I do? I have pulled off his leg.   30

FAUSTUS

O help, help, the villain hath murdered me.

HORSE-COURSER

Murder or not murder, now he has but one leg, I'll out-run him,
and cast this leg into some ditch or other.   *Exit*

FAUSTUS

Stop him, stop him, stop him – ha, ha, ha, Faustus hath his leg
again, and the horse-courser a bundle of hay for his forty dollars.   35

Enter WAGNER

How now Wagner, what news with thee?

WAGNER

If it please you, the Duke of Vanholt doth earnestly entreat your
company, and hath sent some of his men to attend you with provision fit for your journey.

FAUSTUS

The Duke of Vanholt's an honourable gentleman, and one to   40
whom I must be no niggard of my cunning. Come away.

Exeunt

[Scene 10d]

[*This scene is found only the B-text, where it follows Scene 10c*]

Enter CLOWN [ROBIN], DICK, HORSE-COURSER
and a CARTER

CARTER

Come, my masters, I'll bring you to the best beer in Europe.
What ho, hostess, where be these whores?

Enter HOSTESS

HOSTESS

How now, what lack you? What, my old guests, welcome.

ROBIN

Sirra Dick, dost thou know why I stand so mute?

DICK

No Robin, why is't? 5

ROBIN

I am eighteen pence on the score, but say nothing, see if she have forgotten me.

HOSTESS

Who's this, that stands so solemnly by himself? What, my old guest?

ROBIN

O hostess, how do you? I hope my score stands still. 10

HOSTESS

Ay, there's no doubt of that, for methinks you make no haste to wipe it out.

DICK

Why hostess, I say, fetch us some beer.

HOSTESS

You shall presently: look up into th'hall there, ho! *Exit*

DICK

Come sirs, what shall we do now till mine hostess comes? 15

CARTER

Marry sir, I'll tell you the bravest tale how a conjuror served me; you know Doctor Fauster?

HORSE-COURSER

Ay, a plague take him! Here's some on's have cause to know him; did he conjure thee too?

CARTER

I'll tell you how he served me. As I was going to Wittenberg t'other 20
day, with a load of hay, he met me, and asked me what he should give me for as much hay as he could eat; now sir, I thinking that a little would serve his turn, bade him take as much as he would for three-farthings; so he presently gave me my money, and fell to eating; and as I am a christen man, he never left eating, till he 25
had ate up all my load of hay.

ALL

O monstrous, eat a whole load of hay!

ROBIN

Yes, yes, that may be; for I have heard of one, that ha's ate a load of logs.

HORSE-COURSER

Now sirs, you shall hear how villainously he served me: I went to 30
him yesterday to buy a horse of him, and he would by no means
sell him under forty dollars; so sir, because I knew him to be such
a horse, as would run over hedge and ditch, and never tire, I gave
him his money; so when I had my horse, Doctor Fauster bade me
ride him night and day, and spare him no time; but, quoth he, in 35
any case ride him not into the water. Now sir, I thinking the horse
had had some quality that he would not have me know of, what
did I but rid him into a great river, and when I came just in the
midst my horse vanished away, and I sat straddling upon a bottle
of hay. 40

ALL

O brave, doctor!

HORSE-COURSER

But you shall hear how bravely I served him for it. I went me
home to his house, and there I found him asleep. I kept a hallowing
and whooping in his ears, but all could not wake him: I, seeing
that, took him by the leg, and never rested pulling, till I had pulled 45
me his leg quite off, and now 'tis at home in mine hostry.

ROBIN

And has the doctor but one leg then? That's excellent, for one of
his devils turned me into the likeness of an ape's face.

CARTER

Some more drink, hostess.

ROBIN

Hark you, we'll into another room and drink awhile, and then 50
we'll go seek out the doctor.

Exeunt omnes

[Scene 11]

Enter the DUKE *of Vanholt; his* DUCHESS,
FAUSTUS, *and* MEPHOSTOPHILIS

DUKE

Thanks, master doctor, for these pleasant sights; nor know I how
sufficiently to recompense your great deserts in erecting that
enchanted castle in the air; the sight whereof so delighted me, as

573

nothing in the world could please me more.

FAUSTUS

I do think myself, my good lord, highly recompensed, in that it 5
pleaseth your grace to think but well of that which Faustus hath
performed. But, gracious lady, it may be, that you have taken no
pleasure in those sights; therefore I pray you tell me, what is the thing
you most desire to have: be it in the world, it shall be yours. I have
heard that great-bellied women do long for things are rare and dainty. 10

DUCHESS

True, master doctor; and since I find you so kind I will make known
unto you what my heart desires to have; and were it now summer,
as it is January, a dead time of the winter, I would request no better
meat, than a dish of ripe grapes.

FAUSTUS

This is but a small matter: go Mephostophilis; away! 15

Exit MEPHOSTOPHILIS

Madam, I will do more than this for your content.

Enter MEPHOSTOPHILIS *again with the grapes*

Here now taste ye these: they should be good
For they come from a far country, I can tell you.

DUKE

This makes me wonder more than all the rest, that at this time of
the year, when every tree is barren of his fruit, from whence you 20
had these ripe grapes.

FAUSTUS

Please it your grace, the year is divided into two circles over the
whole world, so that when it is winter with us, in the contrary
circle it is likewise summer with them, as in India, Saba, and such
countries that lie far east, where they have fruit twice a year. From 25
whence, by means of a swift spirit that I have, I had these grapes
brought as you see.

DUCHESS

And trust me, they are the sweetest grapes that e'er I tasted.

The CLOWNS [ROBIN, DICK, CARTER, HORSE-COURSER]
bounce at the gate, within

DUKE

What rude disturbers have we at the gate?

Go pacify their fury, set it ope,   30
And then demand of them, what they would have.

They knock again, and call out to talk with FAUSTUS [*within*]

A SERVANT
Why how now masters, what a coil is there?
What is the reason you disturb the duke?
DICK
We have no reason for it, therefore a fig for him.
SERVANT
Why saucy varlets, dare you be so bold?   35
HORSE-COURSER
I hope sir, we have wit enough to be more bold than welcome.
SERVANT
It appears so. Pray be bold elsewhere,
And trouble not the duke.
DUKE
What would they have?
SERVANT
They all cry out to speak with Doctor Faustus.   40
CARTER
Ay, and we will speak with him.
DUKE
Will you sir? Commit the rascals.
DICK
Commit with us! He were as good commit with his father, as
commit with us.
FAUSTUS
I do beseech your grace let them come in,   45
They are good subject for a merriment.
DUKE
Do as thou wilt Faustus, I give thee leave.
FAUSTUS
I thank your grace:

Enter the CLOWN [ROBIN], DICK, CARTER, *and* HORSE-COURSER

Why, how now, my good friends?
'Faith you are too outrageous, but come near,
I have procured your pardons: welcome all.   50

ROBIN

Nay sir, we will be welcome for our money, and we will pay for what we take. What ho, give's half a dozen of beer here, and be hanged.

FAUSTUS

Nay, hark you, can you tell me where you are?

CARTER

Ay, marry can I, we are under heaven. 55

SERVANT

Ay; but, sir sauce-box, know you in what place?

HORSE-COURSER

Ay, ay: the house is good enough to drink in. Zounds, fill us some beer, or we'll break all the barrels in the house, and dash out all your brains with your bottles.

FAUSTUS

Be not so furious: come, you shall have beer. 60

My Lord, beseech you give me leave awhile,

I'll gage my credit, 'twill content your grace.

DUKE

With all my heart, kind doctor; please thyself,

Our servants, and our court's at thy command.

FAUSTUS

I humbly thank your grace: then fetch some beer. 65

HORSE-COURSER

Ay, marry; there spake a doctor indeed – and 'faith I'll drink a health to thy wooden leg for that word.

FAUSTUS

My wooden leg? what dost thou mean by that?

CARTER

Ha, ha, ha, dost hear him Dick? He has forgot his leg.

HORSE-COURSER

Ay, ay, he does not stand much upon that. 70

FAUSTUS

No 'faith, not much upon a wooden leg.

CARTER

Good Lord, that flesh and blood should be so frail with your worship! Do not you remember a horse-courser you sold a horse to?

FAUSTUS

Yes, I remember I sold one a horse.

CARTER

And do you remember you bid he should not ride into the water? 75

FAUSTUS

Yes, I do very well remember that.

CARTER

And do you remember nothing of your leg?

FAUSTUS

No, in good sooth.

CARTER

Then I pray remember your courtesy.

FAUSTUS [*Bowing*]

I thank you sir.   80

CARTER

'Tis not so much worth; I pray you tell me one thing.

FAUSTUS

What's that?

CARTER

Be both your legs bedfellows every night together?

FAUSTUS

Wouldst thou make a colossus of me, that thou askest me such
questions?   85

CARTER

No, truly sir, I would make nothing of you, but I would fain know
that.

Enter HOSTESS *with drink*

FAUSTUS

Then I assure thee certainly they are.

CARTER

I thank you; I am fully satisfied.

FAUSTUS

But wherefore dost thou ask?   90

CARTER

For nothing sir: but methinks you should have a wooden bedfellow
of one of 'em.

HORSE-COURSER

Why, do you hear sir, did not I pull off one of your legs when you
were asleep?

FAUSTUS

But I have it again now I am awake: look you here, sir.   95

ALL

O horrible! Had the doctor three legs?

CARTER

Do you remember sir, how you cozened me and eat up my load
of –

FAUSTUS *charms him dumb*

DICK

Do you remember how you made me wear an ape's –

HORSE-COURSER

You whoreson conjuring scab, do you remember how you cozened 100
me with a ho –

ROBIN

Ha' you forgotten me? You think to carry it away with your hey-
pass and re-pass: do you remember the dog's fa –

Exeunt CLOWNS

HOSTESS

Who pays for the ale – hear you, master doctor, now you have sent
away my guests. I pray who shall pay me for my a – 105

Exit HOSTESS

DUCHESS

My lord,
We are much beholding to this learned man.

DUKE

So are we madam, which we will recompense
With all the love and kindness that we may:
His artful sport drives all sad thoughts away. 110

Exeunt

[Scene 12]

Thunder and lightning. Enter DEVILS *with covered dishes;*
MEPHOSTOPHILIS *leads them into* FAUSTUS' *study*
Then enter WAGNER

WAGNER

I think my master means to die shortly. He has made his will, and
given me his wealth, his house, his goods, and store of golden
plate, besides two thousand ducats ready coined: I wonder what he
means? If death were nigh, he would not frolic thus: he's now at
supper with the scholars, where there's such belly-cheer, as Wagner 5
in his life ne'er saw the like! And see where they come, belike the
feast is done. *Exit*

Enter FAUSTUS, MEPHOSTOPHILIS,
and two or three SCHOLARS

1 SCHOLAR

Master doctor Faustus, since our conference about fair ladies, which
was the beautifullest in all the world, we have determined
with ourselves, that Helen of Greece was the admirablest lady that   10
ever lived: therefore master doctor, if you will do us so much favour,
as to let us see that peerless dame of Greece, whom all the world
admires for majesty, we should think ourselves much beholding unto
you.

FAUSTUS

Gentlemen, for that I know your friendship is unfained,   15
It is not Faustus' custom to deny
The just request of those that wish him well:
You shall behold that peerless dame of Greece,
No otherwise for pomp or majesty,
Than when sir Paris crossed the seas with her,   20
And brought the spoils to rich Dardania.
Be silent then, for danger is in words.

> *Music sound.* MEPHOSTOPHILIS *brings in* HELEN;
> *she passeth over the stage*

2 SCHOLAR

Was this fair Helen, whose admired worth
Made Greece with ten years' war afflict poor Troy?

3 SCHOLAR

Too simple is my wit to tell her worth,   25
Whom all the world admires for majesty.

1 SCHOLAR

Now we have seen the pride of Nature's work,
We'll take our leaves, and for this blessed sight
Happy and blest be Faustus evermore.

Exeunt SCHOLARS

FAUSTUS

Gentlemen farewell: the same wish I to you.   30

> *Enter an* OLD MAN

OLD MAN

O gentle Faustus, leave this damned art,
This magic, that will charm thy soul to hell,
And quite bereave thee of salvation.

Though thou hast now offended like a man,
Do not persevere in it like a devil.   35
Yet, yet, thou hast an amiable soul,
If sin by custom grow not into nature.
Then Faustus, will repentance come too late,
Then thou art banished from the sight of heaven.
No mortal can express the pains of hell!   40
It may be this my exhortation
Seems harsh, and all unpleasant; let it not,
For, gentle son, I speak it not in wrath,
Or envy of thee, but in tender love,
And pity of thy future misery.   45
And so have hope, that this my kind rebuke,
Checking thy body, may amend thy soul.

FAUSTUS

Where art thou, Faustus? wretch, what hast thou done?
Hell claims his right, and with a roaring voice,

MEPHOSTOPHILIS *gives him a dagger*

Says 'Faustus, come: thine hour is almost come';   50
And Faustus now will come to do thee right.

OLD MAN

O stay, good Faustus, stay thy desperate steps.
I see an angel hover o'er thy head,
And with a vial full of precious grace,
Offers to pour the same into thy soul!   55
Then call for mercy, and avoid despair.

FAUSTUS

O friend, I feel thy words to comfort my distressed soul!
Leave me awhile, to ponder on my sins.

OLD MAN

Faustus I leave thee, but with grief of heart,
Fearing the enemy of thy hapless soul.   *Exit*   60

FAUSTUS

Accursed Faustus, wretch, what hast thou done?
I do repent, and yet I do despair,
Hell strives with grace for conquest in my breast:
What shall I do to shun the snares of death?

MEPHOSTOPHILIS

Thou traitor Faustus, I arrest thy soul   65

580

For disobedience to my sovereign lord.
Revolt, or I'll in piecemeal tear thy flesh . . .

[*The two texts coincide for the remainder of the scene, except that
B omits the final appearance (and speech) of the Old Man*]

[Scene 13]

Thunder. Enter LUCIFER, BELZEBUB, *and* MEPHOSTOPHILIS

LUCIFER
Thus from infernal Dis do we ascend
To view the subjects of our monarchy,
Those souls which sin seals the black sons of hell.
'Mong which as chief, Faustus, we come to thee,
Bringing with us lasting damnation   5
To wait upon thy soul; the time is come
Which makes it forfeit.
MEPHOSTOPHILIS   And this gloomy night,
Here in this room will wretched Faustus be.
BELZEBUB
And here we'll stay,
To mark him how he doth demean himself.   10
MEPHOSTOPHILIS
How should he, but in desperate lunacy.
Fond worldling, now his heart-blood dries with grief;
His conscience kills it, and his labouring brain
Begets a world of idle fantasies,
To overreach the devil. But all in vain: 15
His store of pleasures must be sauced with pain.
He and his servant Wagner are at hand,
Both come from drawing Faustus' latest will.
See where they come.

Enter FAUSTUS *and* WAGNER

FAUSTUS
Say, Wagner, thou hast perused my will,   20
How dost thou like it?
WAGNER   Sir, so wondrous well,
As in all humble duty, I do yield

My life and lasting service for your love.

Enter the SCHOLARS

FAUSTUS

Gramercies Wagner. Welcome gentlemen.

1 SCHOLAR

Now worthy Faustus, methinks your looks are changed.   25

FAUSTUS

O gentlemen!

2 SCHOLAR

What ails Faustus?

FAUSTUS

Ah my sweet chamber-fellow, had I lived with thee,

Then had I lived still, but now must die eternally.

Look sirs, comes he not, comes he not?   30

1 SCHOLAR

O my dear Faustus, what imports this fear?

2 SCHOLAR

Is all our pleasure turned to melancholy?

3 SCHOLAR

He is not well with being over-solitary.

2 SCHOLAR

If it be so, we'll have physicians, and Faustus shall be cured.

3 SCHOLAR

'Tis but a surfeit sir, fear nothing.   35

FAUSTUS

A surfeit of deadly sin, that hath damned both body and soul.

3 SCHOLAR

Yet Faustus, look up to heaven, and remember mercy is infinite.

FAUSTUS

But Faustus' offence can ne'er be pardoned!

The serpent that tempted Eve may be saved,

But not Faustus. O gentlemen, hear with patience, and tremble   40

not at my speeches, though my heart pant and quiver to remem-

ber that I have been a student here these thirty years – O would

I had never seen Wittenberg, never read book; and what wonders

I have done, all Germany can witness – yea, all the world – for

which Faustus hath lost both Germany and the world – yea,   45

heaven itself, heaven, the seat of God, the throne of the blessed,

the kingdom of joy; and must remain in hell for ever. Hell, O hell
for ever. Sweet friends, what shall become of Faustus being in
hell for ever?

2 SCHOLAR

Yet Faustus call on God.   50

FAUSTUS

On God, whom Faustus hath abjured? On God, whom Faustus
hath blasphemed! O my God, I would weep, but the devil draws
in my tears. Gush forth blood instead of tears, yea life and soul:
O, he stays my tongue: I would lift up my hands, but see they hold
'em, they hold 'em.   55

ALL

Who Faustus?

FAUSTUS

Why, Lucifer and Mephostophilis!
O gentlemen, I gave them my soul for my cunning.

ALL

O God forbid.

FAUSTUS

God forbade it indeed, but Faustus hath done it: for the vain   60
pleasure of four-and-twenty years hath Faustus lost eternal joy
and felicity. I writ them a bill with mine own blood, the date is
expired: this is the time, and he will fetch me.

1 SCHOLAR

Why did not Faustus tell us of this before, that divines might have
prayed for thee?   65

FAUSTUS

Oft have I thought to have done so: but the devil threatened to
tear me in pieces if I named God: to fetch me body and soul, if I
once gave ear to divinity: and now 'tis too late. Gentlemen away,
lest you perish with me.

2 SCHOLAR

O what may we do to save Faustus?   70

FAUSTUS

Talk not of me, but save yourselves and depart.

3 SCHOLAR

God will strengthen me; I will stay with Faustus.

1 SCHOLAR

Tempt not God, sweet friend, but let us into the next room, and
pray for him.

FAUSTUS

Ay, pray for me, pray for me: and what noise soever you hear, come   75
not unto me, for nothing can rescue me.

2 SCHOLAR

Pray thou, and we will pray, that God may have mercy upon thee.

FAUSTUS

Gentlemen farewell. If I live till morning, I'll visit you: if not,
Faustus is gone to hell.

ALL

Faustus, farewell.   80

Exeunt SCHOLARS

MEPHOSTOPHILIS

Ay, Faustus, now thou hast no hope of heaven,
Therefore despair, think only upon hell;
For that must be thy mansion, there to dwell.

FAUSTUS

O thou bewitching fiend, 'twas thy temptation
Hath robbed me of eternal happiness.   85

MEPHOSTOPHILIS

I do confess it Faustus, and rejoice!
'Twas I, that when thou wer't i'the way to heaven,
Dam'd up thy passage; when thou took'st the book
To view the Scriptures, then I turned the leaves
And led thine eye.   90
What weep'st thou? 'Tis too late; despair; farewell.
Fools that will laugh on earth, must weep in hell.   *Exit*

Enter the GOOD ANGEL *and the* BAD ANGEL
at several doors

GOOD ANGEL

O Faustus, if thou hadst given ear to me,
Innumerable joys had followed thee.
But thou didst love the world.

BAD ANGEL   Gave ear to me,   95
And now must taste hell's pains perpetually.

GOOD ANGEL

O what will all thy riches, pleasures, pomps,
Avail thee now?

BAD ANGEL   Nothing but vex thee more,
To want in hell, that had on earth such store.

Music while the throne descends

GOOD ANGEL

    O thou has lost celestial happiness,   100

    Pleasures unspeakable, bliss without end.

    Hadst thou affected sweet divinity,

    Hell, or the devil, had had no power on thee.

    Hadst thou kept on that way, Faustus behold,

    In what resplendent glory thou hadst sat   105

    In yonder throne, like those bright shining saints,

    And triumphed over hell: that hast thou lost,

    And now poor soul must thy good angel leave thee,

    The jaws of hell are open to receive thee.   *Exit*

Hell is discovered

BAD ANGEL

    Now Faustus, let thine eyes with horror stare   110

    Into that vast perpetual torture-house.

    There are the Furies tossing damned souls,

    On burning forks; there, bodies boil in lead.

    There are live quarters broiling on the coals,

    That ne'er can die! This ever-burning chair   115

    Is for o'er-tortured souls to rest them in.

    These, that are fed with sops of flaming fire,

    Were gluttons, and loved only delicates,

    And laughed to see the poor starve at their gates.

    But yet all these are nothing. Thou shalt see   120

    Ten thousand tortures that more horrid be.

FAUSTUS

    O, I have seen enough to torture me.

BAD ANGEL

    Nay, thou must feel them, taste the smart of all.

    He that loves pleasure, must for pleasure fall:

    And so I leave thee Faustus till anon,   125

    Then wilt thou tumble in confusion.

                               Exit

The clock strikes eleven

FAUSTUS

    O Faustus,

    Now hast thou but one bare hour to live,

And then thou must be damned perpetually.
Stand still, you ever moving spheres of heaven,   130
That time may cease, and midnight never come.
Fair Nature's eye, rise, rise again and make
Perpetual day: or let this hour be but a year,
A month, a week, a natural day,
That Faustus may repent, and save his soul.   135
O lente lente currite noctis equi!
The stars move still, time runs, the clock will strike.
The devil will come, and Faustus must be damned.
O I'll leap up to heaven: who pulls me down?
One drop of blood will save me; O my Christ,   140
Rend not my heart for naming of my Christ.
Yet will I call on him: O spare me Lucifer.
Where is it now? 'Tis gone.
And see a threatening arm, an angry brow.
Mountains and hills, come, come, and fall on me,   145
And hide me from the heavy wrath of heaven.
No? Then will I headlong run into the earth:
Gape earth! O no, it will not harbour me.
You stars that reigned at my nativity,
Whose influence hath allotted death and hell,   150
Now draw up Faustus like a foggy mist,
Into the entrails of yon labouring cloud,
That when you vomit forth into the air,
My limbs may issue from your smoky mouths,
But let my soul mount, and ascend to heaven.   155

The watch strikes

O half the hour is past: 'twill all be past anon!
O, if my soul must suffer for my sin.
Impose some end to my incessant pain!
Let Faustus live in hell a thousand years,
A hundred thousand, and at last be saved.   160
No end is limited to damned souls.
Why wert thou not a creature wanting soul?
Or why is this immortal that thou hast?
O Pythagoras' *metempsychosis* – were that true,
This soul should fly from me, and I be changed   165
Into some brutish beast.

All beasts are happy, for when they die,
Their souls are soon dissolved in elements,
But mine must live still to be plagued in hell.
Cursed be the parents that engendered me;   170
No Faustus, curse thyself, curse Lucifer,
That hath deprived thee of the joys of heaven.

The clock strikes twelve

It strikes, it strikes! Now body, turn to air,
Or Lucifer will bear thee quick to hell.
O soul be changed into small water drops,   175
And fall into the ocean, ne'er be found.

Thunder, and enter the DEVILS

O mercy heaven, look not so fierce on me;
Adders and serpents, let me breathe awhile!
Ugly hell, gape not! Come not Lucifer!
I'll burn my books! O Mephostophilis!   180

Exeunt

[Scene 13b]

*[An additional scene, inserted between Faustus's soliloquy
and the final Chorus]*

Enter the SCHOLARS

1 SCHOLAR

Come gentlemen, let us go visit Faustus,
For such a dreadful night was never seen
Since first the world's creation did begin.
Such fearful shrieks and cries were never heard!
Pray heaven the doctor have escaped the danger.   5

2 SCHOLAR

O help us heaven! See, here are Faustus' limbs,
All torn asunder by the hand of death.

3 SCHOLAR

The devils whom Faustus served have torn him thus!
For 'twixt the hours of twelve and one, methought
I heard hm shriek and call aloud for help: 10

587

At which self time the house seemed all on fire
With dreadful horror of these damned fiends.

2 SCHOLAR

Well gentlemen, tho' Faustus' end be such
As every Christian heart laments to think on,
Yet, for he was a scholar, once admired   15
For wondrous knowledge in our German schools,
We'll give his mangled limbs due burial.
And all the students, clothed in mourning black,
Shall wait upon his heavy funeral.

Exeunt

NOTES ON THE TEXTS

Tamburlaine

ed. Anthony B. Dawson

The first edition of *Tamburlaine,* a black letter octavo containing both parts of the play (O1), was published in 1590. Three more early editions followed, an octavo in 1593 (O2), another octavo in 1597 (O3), and a quarto (Q). There has been some disagreement among scholars as to whether this edition is actually an octavo or a quarto; both its size and its signatures suggest the latter, but the way the paper was originally folded suggests an octavo (see Una Ellis-Fermor, ed., *Tamburlaine the Great* [London, 1930] p. 3 n. 6). I here follow J.S. Cunningham and others in designating it a quarto. in 1605–6, the last being a two volume edition. O2 and O3 both derive (independently) from O1, while Q was based on O3. All the reprints correct some obvious errors in O1, but also introduce new errors of their own, but add nothing substantially new. It is clear, then, that only O1 possesses independent authority and it, accordingly, must be the copy text.

O1 appears to be printed from a scribal or authorial manuscript, rather than from a theatrical one. Stage directions, even exit and entrance directions, are often omitted or left incomplete, scene breaks are omitted where they should appear or added where they should not (making for inconsistent principles of scene division), names of characters are inconsistently treated, and speech prefixes omitted; all of these are matters that would often be cleared up in order to prepare the script for performance, and would therefore be reflected in a playhouse manuscript. Hence editors have traditionally concluded that O1 does not have a theatrical provenance. At the same time, its relative clarity and freedom from error suggest a clean manuscript rather than authorial 'foul papers'; probably, then, it was printed from some sort of intermediate transcript made either by Marlowe or a scribe.

In the preface to the first edition, the printer, Richard Jones, declares that 'some fond and frivolous gestures' have deliberately been omitted from the printed text, despite (or perhaps because of) the fact that they were popular in the theatre. Exactly what was omitted, if anything, is not clear, nor is there any indication as to whether what has been left out was part of Marlowe's original script or something added extempore by actors. Jones's words suggest that what he had in front of him contained the offensive material which he then 'purposely' left out, but even this is uncertain since, as stated above, his manuscript was not a theatre-based one. Even as it stands, there is considerable variety of tone and texture in *Tamburlaine,* a fact that Elizabethan actors seem to have exploited, assuming that what Jones says about the theatre reflects actual practice. So, perhaps Jones was merely advertising his edition as something to appeal to the higher tastes of 'gentlemen readers and others that take pleasure in reading histories', thus distinguishing prospective buyers from those who found their pleasure in the raucous, considerably less rarefied atmosphere of the public theatre.

In this edition, the spelling and punctuation have been modernized, the most obvious misprints have been silently corrected, abbreviations expanded and speech prefixes regularized. Stage directions have occasionally been supplemented, proper names added, indications of 'asides' provided etc. All such changes appear in square brackets and are not therefore recorded in the notes.

The punctuation of O1, though at times it provides an indication of patterns of rhetorical phrasing appropriate to theatrical speech, is confusing to a modern reader and frequently fails to take the measure of Marlowe's complex syntax. It regularly introduces full stops into the middle of Marlowe's elaborate compound sentences, or breaks sentences up without adequate consideration of meaning, hence interfering with what T.S. Eliot long ago noted as one of Marlowe's most important verse accomplishments in *Tamburlaine* – the 'driving power' he achieved 'by reinforcing the sentence period against the line period'. In modernizing the punctuation, I have tried to make the meaning as clear as possible to the reader, while at the same time seeking to keep in mind the voice of the actor. Wherever possible, therefore, I have reduced the punctuation, keeping it light in order to facilitate the flow of the verse. Certainly the best way to grasp the text is to speak it aloud as one reads, using the punctuation as a guide to the voice which, ultimately, must make the meaning.

Where a reading of one of the later octavos or Q has been adopted, that fact has been indicated in the notes, but no attempt has been made to record all the substantive variants between O1 and the other early texts. Where I have adopted a reading suggested by previous editors, or introduced a new reading, the change is recorded in the notes (with the notation 'ed.'), but usually without indicating its history. In preparing the edition, I have incurred debts to many previous scholars, most especially J.W. Harper, who edited the earlier New Mermaid, Una Ellis-Fermor, whose 1930 edition has influenced all subsequent editions and whose annotations have frequently proved indispensable, and J.S. Cunningham, whose edition for the Revels series is the most thorough and far-reaching of modern texts.

The Jew of Malta
ed. James M. Siemon

Although *The Jew of Malta* was entered in the Stationers' Register for 17 May 1594, the only early text for it is the 1633 quarto published by Nicholas Vavasour and printed in the shop of John Beale (I.B.). I have used the Bodleian Library copy (shelf mark Mal. 172 [2]), consulting as well copies from the British Library (shelf mark 82.c.22 [5]) and the Houghton Library (shelf mark 14416.35.15). I have compared modern editions of N.W. Bawcutt (The Revels Plays, 1978), H.S. Bennett (*The Jew of Malta and The Massacre at Paris*, 1931), Fredson Bowers (*The Complete Works of Christopher Marlowe*, 1981), T.W. Craik (New Mermaids, 1966), R.A. Fraser (*Drama of the English Renaissance*, 1976), J.B. Steane (*The*